34TH
EDITION

TWO-YEAR-OLDS
OF 2018

34TH EDITION

TWO-YEAR-OLDS OF 2018

STEVE TAPLIN

Foreword by Ralph Beckett

Raceform

FRONT COVER: Rajasinghe (third from left) on the way to winning the Coventry Stakes at the 2017 Royal Ascot meeting, trained by Richard Spencer and ridden by Stevie Donohoe. Copyright © Racing Post/Edward Whitaker.

BACK COVER: Ralph Beckett (left) and Steve Taplin (right).

Published in 2018 by Raceform
27 Kingfisher Court, Hambridge Road, Newbury, Berkshire, RG14 5SJ

Copyright © Steve Taplin 2018

The right of Steve Taplin to be identified as the author of this work has been asserted by him in accordance with the Copyright, Designs and Patents Act 1988.

A catalogue record for this book is available from the British Library.

ISBN: 978-1-910497-69-2

Designed by Fiona Pike

Printed in Great Britain by CPI Group (UK) Ltd, Croydon, CR0 4YY

CONTENTS

FOREWORD

Every April when this book's author arrives for the interview, I remind myself not to tell him too much. Somehow I find that I always end up giving away more than I thought, when the book is published. That in itself is a tribute to Steve and his quiet (but clearly effective) interviewing style.

Where I have found it useful is in ascertaining how accurate the competition is at assessing their two-year-olds as early as March/April. If one looks back, we have been accurate some years, and less than accurate in others – far too many for my liking.

Yet the master trainer that is Peter Chapple-Hyam informed us in the 2015 edition that £20k yearling, subsequent Racing Post Trophy winner Marcel, was his pick – despite not running until mid-July. Indicating there are some trainers who are far better judges than others; you just have to know where to look.

I look forward to this year's edition as much as any previous one, and I recommend careful study of trainers who have decent strike rates with two-year-olds matched up with those who also get off the fence with their comments. Not many tick both those boxes, including yours truly.

Ralph Beckett
April 2018

INTRODUCTION

Here we are in 2018 with edition number thirty-four of Two-Year-Olds which aims to highlight the best juvenile racehorses in training in England and Ireland. Many of them will win this year, others will be better as three-year-olds in 2019. So the book can be used as a work of reference next year too.

I'd like to say 'Thank You' to the many readers who have supported me over the years. I hope you still enjoy it and find it as useful as ever. I must also thank the scores of trainers for their help and good humour every time they hear my knock on the door in the spring when I call to pick their brains – they make this book worth doing. I enjoy writing it, so I'll try my best to be back again next year for edition thirty-five.

I come from an area of England more tuned in to football and rugby league than horse racing but in the early '90s I turned my back on the odd-shaped ball and concentrated on the sport of kings (these days the sport of sheikhs). I became fascinated by thoroughbred pedigrees and somehow had the temerity to ring trainers up to ask for comments on their horses for my fledgling book on two-year-olds. My first attempts involved trainers like Robert Armstrong, Ian Balding, Neville Callaghan, Henry Cecil, John Dunlop, Guy Harwood, Michael Jarvis, Alec Stewart and Harry Thomson Jones. So they got me started, albeit in a very small way.

This year, trainer Ralph Beckett has kindly written the foreword for me. Ralph's string has gradually improved each year in terms of both quality and quantity to the point where this year his yard houses even more beautifully bred racehorses than ever. Always very kind and helpful, it's a pleasure to visit him at his yard in Hampshire, but when it comes to finding him I often have problems because he seems to be tucked away out of sight of the satnav and I end up touring the highways and byways around Kimpton. The penny has eventually dropped though, because this year I tracked him down without a problem!

The Living Legend Racing Partnership (not named after me by the way!) had another winner last year in the shape of the two-year-old Magnus, trained by Tom Dascombe. I said in the introduction last year, "I'm not dusting my top hat off for Ascot just yet," but guess what – Magnus did actually get us there – for the Windsor Castle Stakes! What a great occasion for us 'little people' to be rubbing shoulders with Ballydoyle, Godolphin etc. He was a gutsy little colt who tried his best and you can't ask for more than that. As I write this introduction, we haven't got a horse in training yet, but hopefully that will have changed by the time the book goes to print.

Glancing at the trainers I've managed to interview in time for publication, I'm aware there are a few less this year. I put it down to three things. Firstly, the large number of breeze-up two-year-olds who have yet to find a trainer when I'm going to press. Their numbers seem to increase each year. Secondly, there are a number of trainers who are reluctant to let people know the identity and number of their horses, particularly two-year-olds, so they keep them a secret. Goodness knows why; it baffles me but there must be a method in it somewhere. Thirdly, the number of trainers who until quite recently we may have considered to have 'small to medium' yards are now decidedly in the 'small' category. The number of horses they have has dwindled and they often rely on a couple of loyal owners to keep the ship afloat. Contrast that with half a dozen trainers who have a couple of thousand horses between them. Very good trainers, it must be said, but surely some of the sport's richest owners could 'spread the love' a little bit more?

It's always interesting seeing the names owners choose for their horses, especially when there's a 'theme'. This year I've noticed that Chelsea Thoroughbreds have chosen the theme of musicians. So, dotted around various trainers, we have Johnny Kidd (remember him with the Pirates?), Sam Cooke, Dinah Washington, George Gershwin, Ritchie Valens,

Brian Epstein, Eddie Cochran and even good old George Formby!

We all like to see a horse that's well named and this year I have to give top marks to Des Thurlby who has horses with Newmarket trainer Chris Wall. For his Dark Angel colt out of Meet Me Halfway, Des was clever enough to choose the name 'Purgatory'!

There is another Newmarket trainer who has to put a cold compress on his head whenever I interview him. That's just to get over the fact he's talking to me about his horses two months before he talks to anyone else! Incidentally Sir Mark, thank you so much for the very kind message you recently sent me.

Regular readers will be aware that each year the book has a number of horses to follow lists, such as the 'Fifty to Follow' and the 'Bloodstock Experts Mark Your Card'. They are always useful for those who want to follow a select number of horses. The 'Bloodstock Experts' always do well and last year they tipped 39 individual winners of 49 races.

The big-priced winners amongst the 'Trainers' Bargain Buys' no doubt make it a particular favourite section for lots of punters and what an inspired selection Jessie Harrington made last year. The purchase price of her 'bargain buy' rocketed from €3,000 to €300,000 in only nine months. That's some profit!

As usual, the two-year-olds in the book are listed under their trainers and my aim is to choose those horses most likely to be winners. You'll notice a 'star rating' for each of the two-year-olds, so take note in particular of those with three stars or more. There are no star ratings for those two-year-olds without any comments from the trainer. I think to give them a rating based on the pedigree alone is too speculative.

The following is a rough guide to my description of the ability of family members mentioned in the pedigree assessment of every two-year-old, based upon professional handicap ratings. Please note that these descriptions are standard throughout the book in the vast majority of cases, but there

are instances where I rely upon my own judgement of each horse's rating.

Below 60 = moderate
60 – 69 = modest
70 – 79 = fair
80 – 89 = quite useful
90 – 99 = fairly useful
100 – 107 = useful
108 – 112 = very useful
113 – 117 = smart
118 – 122 = very smart
123 – 127 = high-class
128 – 134 = top-class
135 and above = outstanding

To make it easier to find a specific horse, the book is comprehensively indexed. So you'll find an index of the horses, their dams and their sires.

The book is divided into the following sections:

- Fifty to Follow.

- Twelve to Follow in Ireland.

- Star Two-Year-Olds. This system gives an instant appraisal of the regard in which a horse is held. Those horses awarded the maximum of five stars are listed here.

- The Bloodstock Experts Mark Your Card. Bloodstock agents and stud managers suggest potentially smart two-year-olds bought or raised by them.

- Bargain Buys. A list of relatively cheaply bought two-year-olds the trainers feel will turn out to be good deals.

- Two-Year-Olds of 2018. The main section of the book, with each two-year-old listed under the trainer. Trainers' comments (when given) are in italics after the pedigree assessments. Readers should bear in mind that all the trainers' comments come from my interviews which took part from late March to mid-April.

- Sires Reference, detailing the racing and stud careers of sires with two-year-old representatives in the book.

- Index of Sires.

- Racing Trends. An analysis of some juvenile events that regularly highlight the stars of the future. It includes a list of three-year-olds to follow this season.

- Index of Two-Year-Olds.

- Index of Dams.

Inevitably there are some unnamed horses in the book, but please access my website www. stevetaplin.co.uk throughout the season for updates on those horses named after the book was published.

Researched and compiled by
Steve Taplin BA (Hons).

FIFTY TO FOLLOW

ADVERTISE
b.c. Showcasing – Furbelow (Pivotal). *"We like this colt, he's a big, strong type, probably 16.2 hands and if all goes well he's a Royal Ascot type. A horse that's done very well, we managed to get on with him early in the year and he's certainly going the right way".* Martyn Meade.

AFTER JOHN
b.c. Dutch Art – Rosacara (Green Desert). *"A smashing colt, he will win at five furlongs, will get six and he does everything right. I think he's a nice, real sharp 2-y-o".* Mick Channon.

AMAZING FOX (IRE)
b.c. Alhebayeb – Gold Again (Touch Gold). *"A strong colt and pretty forward with a good temperament, he'll probably appear in the spring. He has a good way of going and of the forward ones we have he would be a standout amongst the colts. So he's a nice horse".* Ralph Beckett.

ANGEL'S HIDEAWAY
gr.f. Dark Angel – The Hermitage (Kheleyf). *"She's a neat, racy, very active filly and light on her feet. She won't be backward by any means and I can see her being out in May".* John Gosden.

ARTAIR (IRE)
b.c. Kodiac – Bonnie Lesley (Iffraaj). *"We like him a lot, he's a three-parts brother to Coulsty who was a decent sprinter and he'll be one of our early birds. Racy, stocky and exactly what you would expect from the pedigree".* Michael Bell.

BALLISTIC
b.c. Kodiac – Pale Orchid (Invincible Spirit). *"He cost a bit of money but quite rightly so because he's a good-looking horse. He's a really early sort and will be coming out at Newmarket's Craven meeting I should think. His pedigree suggests he's all about five furlongs and his shape would reflect that too".* Robert Cowell.

BAYROOT (IRE)
b.c. Exceed And Excel – Alwarga (Street Sense). *"He's a big horse, so not an early Exceed And Excel, but he carries himself extremely well for a big 2-y-o and I'm sure he'll be winning races later in the year".* Roger Varian.

BRANDON (FR)
b.c. Showcasing – Be Released (Three Valleys). *"He should be a precocious type because there's speed in the family. He looked quite strong at the sales and hasn't disappointed since because he's done really well. Built like a sprinter, he has a good attitude and we like him".* Marco Botti.

CHIL CHIL
b.f. Exceed And Excel – Tiana (Diktat). *"A lovely filly, she's a beautiful physical specimen with a lovely attitude. She has a better conformation and a better action than her good half-brother we train, Beat The Bank. One to start off in May/June over six furlongs. She has a lot of quality".* Andrew Balding.

CHUCK WILLIS (IRE)
b.c. Kodiac – Xinji (Xaar). *"A very attractive looking colt and a good mover, he'll be running by the end of April, has a nice action and I think he has some scope. He's a horse that I like".* Charlie Hills.

CULTURE (FR)
b.c. Dream Ahead – Talon Bleu (Anabaa Blue). *"He was an absolute standout at the sale and I'm absolutely convinced if he'd been at a more mainstream sale he'd have cost a lot more. A gorgeous, big, black horse, he's doing everything nicely".* George Baker.

DESERT WAR (USA)
gr.c. Oasis Dream – Gracie Square (Awesome Again). *"I adore this colt and I love to see speed being bred to speed. He looks fast, has lots of natural muscle and a lot of style and quality about him".* Hugo Palmer.

FANAAR (IRE)
b.c. Dark Angel – Inca Trail (Royal Academy). *"A strong, well-made colt, he goes well, I like him and he's one of the more natural ones. We'll have to see, but he could develop into a Royal Ascot 2-y-o. He's strong, his knees are mature and he'll take the work".* William Haggas.

FENJAL (IRE)
gr.c. Kodiac – Spinamix (Spinning World). *"He looks like a proper early season runner and the sire is arguably the most phenomenal sire of 2-y-o's we've seen in some time. This colt is strong with a good action and is forward going. He looks the part to me".* Hugo Palmer.

FOX SHINJI
b.c. Iffraaj – Keene Dancer (Danehill Dancer). *"He goes well; he's a lovely, big, strong horse with a great attitude. He was showing plenty in January and he should be a six furlong colt to start with in mid-May".* Andrew Balding.

FRENCH MONTANA
ch.c. Showcasing – Moving Sea (Rock Of Gibraltar). *"A belter – he's the one that stands out at the moment. He's one of those that catches your eye going up the hill. A July or early August type, he's a beautiful mover and I like him".* Charlie Fellowes.

GREAT BEAR
b.c. Dansili – Great Heavens (Galileo). *"A very attractive horse from a very good family. A lovely mover, he's nearer the top of the list than most and although he's bred to stay he's a nice-looking horse for later in the season".* Roger Charlton.

HEATWAVE
b.f. Leroidesanimaux – Here To Eternity (USA) (Stormy Atlantic). *"A half-sister to a horse who did us so well, Time Warp, who won five off the reel for us including two Listed. This is a nice, good-topped filly and like him she'll need seven furlongs and a mile to win".* Sir Mark Prescott.

HESSLEWOOD (IRE)
b.c. Slade Power – Rochitta (Arch). *"Hopefully he'll be racing in May, he's quite a strong, well put-together colt and looks a sprinter type to me. He's grown a lot since we've had him and he's a very nice colt".* James Bethell.

INTRICATE
b.f. Showcasing – Last Slipper (Tobougg). *"A racy, well-balanced, forward filly and a good mover. You would have to think about her as a possible for Royal Ascot if she showed up in her work because she's very clued up. She has a good mind on her, we like her and she'll probably start out at six furlongs".* John Gosden.

JACK'S POINT
b.c. Slade Power – Electra Star (Shamardal). *"I really like this horse, he's big, strong, shows ability already and shows speed. The dam's first three foals have all won and I guarantee he will too; he's one of those that makes you want to get out of bed in the morning".* Willie Muir.

JFOUL
b.c. Zebedee – Worthington (Kodiac). *"A very strong-looking colt with a great attitude, he's in the forward bunch and showing nice ability at this early stage. One to start in May or June".* Saeed bin Suroor.

KHAADEM (IRE)
br.c. Dark Angel – White Daffodil (Footstepsinthesand). *"A very athletic horse, he looks a natural to me and we'll get him out before Royal Ascot to see if he's good enough to go there. One to follow".* Charlie Hills.

LADY SCATTERLEY (FR)
ch.f. No Nay Never – Camdara (Hawk Wing). *"A very nice, strong filly that's built like a colt. There's plenty of strength about her, she goes very well and is one for six furlongs. We think a lot of her".* Richard Hannon.

LAHESSAR
b.c. Exceed And Excel – Burlesque Star (Thousand Words). *"A brute of a colt ... he'll come to hand relatively quickly. He'd be a horse I like, he's tough and I would imagine he'll be doing most of his racing throughout the middle part of the summer".* George Scott.

ORANGE BLOSSOM
ch.f. Showcasing – Satsuma (Compton Place). *"I think she's a very nice filly, five furlongs should suit her, the sire is doing well and she was an early foal. So all she needs is some decent weather because she's done some good bits of work, the penny's dropping and we like her very much".* James Given.

PORTABELLO ROAD
b.c. Iffraaj – Represent (Exceed And Excel). *"Definitely a good-looking horse and being by Iffraaj he should have some precocity, so it's quite possible he could be running over six furlongs by June or July. I'm very happy with him, he's a nice horse".* Luca Cumani.

PRETTY POLLYANNA
b.f. Oasis Dream – Unex Mona Lisa (Shamardal). *"I like her, she moves very well and we had the half-sister Roulette who won at Goodwood last year. This filly is sharper, very much a 2-y-o and we like her. I can see her coming to hand pretty quickly".* Michael Bell.

RAHEEB (IRE)
b.f. Kodiac – Dream Date (Oasis Dream). *"Over the next few weeks she might be one of those to move on with. She's a nice, strong, mature filly and very straightforward in her work. She's all there, a good size and looks as if she should be able to trap a bit. I like her".* Owen Burrows.

REQUITED
b.c. Requinto – Joyfullness (Dixieland Band). *"Quite forward and mature, he's got speed and he could be a May 2-y-o. He looks sharp, speedy and physically quite strong".* Hughie Morrison.

ROXY ART (IRE)
ch.f. Dutch Art – Chicago Girl (Azamour). *"A nice, strong, powerful, good-looking filly. She's racy and relatively precocious".* Ed Dunlop.

RUMBLE INTHEJUNGLE (IRE)
ch.c. Bungle Inthejungle – Guana (Dark Angel). *"A lovely horse, we haven't done any fast work with him yet but we'll probably run him in late April or early May. He goes nicely,* has a very good attitude and a lot of natural ability. Maybe one for Royal Ascot if he proves good enough".* Richard Spencer.

SASH
b.c. Oasis Dream – Surcingle (Empire Maker). *"He's quite forward, the dam won as a 2-y-o and this colt was an early foal. A really nice individual with a bit of size and scope, we haven't done any fast work with him but he's got a good attitude, a good outlook and has done everything right".* Amanda Perrett.

SHADY AFFAIR
gr.c. Dark Angel – Capulet Montague (Camacho). *"A big, imposing colt, he's one for the second half of the season. He's grown enormously in the time we've had him and he's very correct, big-boned and just a big, strong colt. One to look out for I'd say".* Ed Vaughan.

SIGNORA CABELLO
b.f. Camacho – Journalist (Night Shift). *"A filly that we like, she'll be an early five furlong 2-y-o. It's a fast pedigree and the mare has done really well with stallions you wouldn't necessarily think would throw 2-y-o winners".* John Quinn.

SMITH (IRE)
ch.c. Dawn Approach – Alazeya (Shirocco). *"A tough, hard-knocking sort, he's really nice and does what it says on the tin. The sire didn't do too well with his first crop last year but they started to improve at the back-end and I like this colt. One for six or seven furlongs".* Eve Johnson Houghton.

SWINGING JEAN
b.f. Sixties Icon—Shrimpton (Cadeaux Genereux). *"You must put her in the book because she's a smasher and I can go with her whenever I want to. A filly with a lot of quality, she's a bit more forward than some of the others".* Mick Channon.

SWIPER (IRE)
b.c. Clodovil – Hawk Dance (Hawk Wing). *"A lovely big colt, we'll not be going early with him and he's probably one to start at six and then move up to seven furlongs. He's got a*

good attitude and we're happy with him at the moment. We all like him a lot". Richard Hannon.

TATSIA
b.f. Showcasing – Ombre (Galileo). *"A half-sister to Gavota who did well last year, this filly is stronger-bodied, moves well and although she's out of a Galileo mare, one would hope she'd be a six furlong filly in July".* Roger Charlton.

USTATH
ch.c. Exceed And Excel – Adorn (Kyllachy). *"I'd just like to see him strengthen up a bit because when he does I think he'll be quite early. A good-moving colt with a good mind on him, he's a proper 2-y-o 5f type and I like him".* Owen Burrows.

WALLAA
b.f. Dawn Approach – Shuhra (Marju). *"A sharp, racy, forward filly and I think she'll come to hand pretty quickly. We've started doing a bit of work with her, she shows plenty of pace and you definitely want to give her a mention".* Simon Crisford.

UNNAMED
ch.f. Speightstown – Aerocat (Tale Of The Cat). *"Our most expensive 2-y-o, she goes really nicely and shows plenty of speed. A bit on the small side, but she looks a 2-y-o and she looks quick".* James Tate.

UNNAMED
b.c. New Approach – Ahla Wasahl (Dubai Destination). *"A tall, rangy New Approach colt and whilst not a sprinting type he's very nice and we like him a lot".* James Tate.

UNNAMED
b.f. Scat Daddy – Entwine (Empire Maker). *"I really like this filly. She could be a summer 2-y-o, has a nice way of going, strong and with a bit of class".* Roger Varian.

UNNAMED
b.f. Australia – Have Faith (Machiavellian). *"A smashing filly, she'll be at her best next year but she's as nice a filly as I've had for some time as far as a specimen is concerned. She does everything easily and if she comes out in July I'll be getting excited about her".* David Lanigan.

UNNAMED
b.c. Sea The Stars – Honor Bound (Authorized). *"A gorgeous horse, he'll need some time but he's very good-looking, athletic and one we like very much. He'll be a seven furlong plus 2-y-o and amongst the colts he's an obvious pick".* Ralph Beckett.

UNNAMED
b.c. Kodiac – La Chicana (Invincible Spirit). *"He has a great way of going and a good action. Far more precocious than his brother, he's one I'd love to see out in May or June over six furlongs. Looks the type to get on with".* David Simcock.

UNNAMED
b.f. Acclamation – Lovely Thought (Dubai Destination). *"Our most expensive filly, she was lovely as a yearling and she still is. I should think she's going to give her owner a lot of fun this year for sure. She'll be like her siblings and be a speedy 2-y-o".* William Jarvis.

UNNAMED
b.f. Kyllachy – Night Affair (Bold Edge). *"She's very strongly built and to look at her she looks very fast although we haven't done anything with her yet. We like her and she'll be a sharp five/six furlong 2-y-o".* Henry Candy.

UNNAMED
b.f. No Nay Never – Sparkling Rock (Rock Of Gibraltar). *"A filly with an awful lot of quality, I'd say she could be ready whenever I want her to be. She does everything so easy and nothing fazes her. Probably the pick of the fillies at this stage and if she's good she'll be an Ascot filly".* Richard Hughes.

TWELVE TO FOLLOW IN IRELAND

BOSTON BRUIN
b.c. Kodiac – Sovana (Desert King).
"A nice horse, not as big as his half-sister Bocca Baciata but he goes well and I can see him being out in late May over six furlongs. He's a typical Kodiac as far as his size is concerned and he's a 2-y-o type". Jessie Harrington.

CARTESIENNE
ch.f. Pivotal – Modern Ideals (New Approach).
"A lovely filly that'll take a bit of time but we've liked her from the beginning and she's one of our nicer fillies. She'll make a 2-y-o from July onwards, probably over seven furlongs". Michael Halford.

INDIGO BALANCE
b.c. Invincible Spirit – Rose De France (Diktat).
"A very nice colt, he's forward-going, a good mover and light on his feet. A six furlong type 2-y-o, at least to begin with". Jessie Harrington.

KINCH
b.c. Dark Angel – Lapis Blue (Invincible Blue).
"A lovely horse, he has a lot of quality about him and is up there in our top half a dozen. He's smart". Ger Lyons.

MORAVIA
b.f. Siyouni – Demeanour (Giant's Causeway).
"A beautiful filly, she's ready to run. I have a lovely bunch of fillies and she'd be up there with the best. One for five/six furlongs". Ger Lyons.

MOTAWAAZY
b.c. Kingman – Shimah (Storm Cat).
"We've trained most of the family and this is a big, strong 2-y-o that'll want six furlongs with some ease in the ground. The sire was big and strong, I think he needed the ground to be on the easy side and this colt seems to take after him in that respect". Kevin Prendergast.

SCARLET SKIS
b.f. Kodiac – Red Lady (Dutch Art).
"She'll start her career in mid-April and might need her first run but we like her a lot and she'll improve with better ground; not a big filly but very active". Kevin Prendergast.

SHELIR
b.c. Dark Angel – Shelina (Dalakhani).
"A nice colt, he'll be out in midsummer over six/ seven furlongs and I'd keep an eye out for him". Dermot Weld.

TAKE SILK
b.f. Shamardal – Raw Silk (Malibu Moon).
"She was a late foal but she's a filly we really like. She's forward-going, has a good attitude and she's been showing us a nice bit despite her immaturity. A filly to start off in mid-season, she goes well and might be quick enough to start over six furlongs". Michael Halford.

TRANCHEE
b.c. War Front – Terrific (Galileo).
"Very much a quality colt, he's strong and I would like to have him out over seven furlongs in July". Dermot Weld.

WARGRAVE
b.c. Galileo – Scream Blue Murder (Oratorio).
"He goes nicely, looks sharp and we trained her mother who won over five furlongs. This colt will probably set off over six furlongs in May, he's not over-big, he's mature and one we can crack on with". Fozzy Stack.

UNNAMED
gr.f. Dark Angel – Elshamms (Zafonic).
"She certainly looks like a 2-y-o like most Dark Angel's; built like a 2-y-o, she's good-looking, nice tempered and one of the earlier ones". John Oxx.

STAR TWO-YEAR-OLDS

The stars placed along the side of each two-year-old in the main section of the book give the reader an instant appraisal of the regard in which they are held. The highest rating a horse can attain is five stars.

Bear in mind that some of the 'Five Star' horses will be at their peak as three-year-olds, so you should definitely keep an eye on them next year as well.

The five-star two-year-olds of 2018 are listed below for quick reference.

FOX PREMIER	**Andrew Balding**
KING POWER	**Andrew Balding**
QUEEN POWER (IRE)	**Ralph Beckett**
MANIC MONDAY	**Michael Bell**
BURJ	**Saeed bin Suroor**
b.br.c. War Front – Lerici (Woodman)	**John Gosden**
gr.c. Kitten's Joy – Cozzy Street (Street Cry)	**John Gosden**
MOFTRIS	**William Haggas**
GLORIOUS DANE	**Richard Hannon**
TRETHIAS	**Jessie Harrington**
KHAADEM	**Charlie Hills**
CALIFORNIA DADDY (USA)	**Ger Lyons**
HELEN OF ALBANY (IRE)	**Ger Lyons**
EAGLE HUNTER	**Hugo Palmer**
ZMHAR (IRE)	**James Tate**
AUTUMN SPLENDOUR (IRE)	**James Tate**
SAN DONATO (IRE)	**Roger Varian**

THE BLOODSTOCK EXPERTS MARK YOUR CARD

Last year the Experts tipped 36 winners of 49 races in this section, so make sure you take careful note of these selections!

The Experts who selected two individual winners apiece last year were Malcolm Bastard, Tom Goff, Charlie Gordon-Watson, Bruce Raymond, David Redvers and Larry Stratton.

Only two experts picked out three winners – Alastair Donald and Harry Herbert, but for once we have a runaway winner of the Top Tipster award because all four of Trevor Harris' selections won, including the dual winner Yafta and 20-1 shot Lethal Lunch. Well done sir!

I must also give a special mention to Paul & Sara Thorman for selecting the Coventry Stakes winner Rajasinghe.

Let's hope all the experts this year have been inspired to pick a similarly successful group of two-year-olds. Remember, most of the two-year-olds selected here can be found in the main section of the book listed under their trainers and highlighted by the symbol ♠

A few of these selections were yet to enter training when the book went to press, so you may not find them listed under their trainer.

MALCOLM BASTARD

AMBLING
b.f. Lope De Vega – Royale Danehill (Danehill). A big filly with a very good action, she travels up the hill very well and just needs time to get a lot stronger. John Gosden.

ARABIST
b.c. Invincible Spirit – Highest (Dynaformer). A big, strong colt, he's very green at the moment but I'd say he could be very nice. John Gosden.

EVER CHANGING (USA)
ch.c. Tapit – Rainbow View (Dynaformer). He only arrived in pre-training with us here at Christmas time. He has size, scope and strength and has a good action. John Gosden.

FRANKELLINA
ch.f. Frankel – Our Obsession (Shamardal). A medium-sized, very strong filly with a very good action when cantering. She needs time to mature but could be a very nice filly in the making. William Haggas.

GREAT BEAR
b.c. Dansili – Great Heavens (Galileo). To look at him he's very easy on the eye, he has a good temperament and looked like an autumn type 2-y-o while he was here; did everything easily. Roger Charlton.

INFUSE (IRE)
b.f. Lope De Vega – Fusion (Cape Cross). A tall filly, she's very good-looking, has a good temperament and travels nicely up the gallop. A back-end 2-y-o, she could be nice next year". Roger Charlton.

KING OF COMEDY (IRE)
b.c. Kingman – Stage Presence (Selkirk). A colt with a very good temperament, he's nice, strong and did his work very easily whilst with us. John Gosden.

NAHEMA
b.f. Dubawi – Sariska (Pivotal). An extremely good-looking, strong filly with a nice action, she's not showing a lot at present but her dam was here as a yearling/2-y-o and she was just the same until the autumn. Michael Bell.

NANTUCKET (IRE)
b.f. Sea The Stars – Lucy Cavendish (Elusive Quality). A 3-y-o type, she did her work very easily in the time she was here. She could be a very good filly in time. Sir Michael Stoute.

SEA WINGS
b.c. Sea The Stars – Infallible (Pivotal).
A quality horse that moves very well, he's
possibly a back-end of the season 2-y-o; a
really nice colt. William Haggas.

UNNAMED
b.c. Distorted Humor – Midnight Thoughts
(Henrythenavigator). A 190,000 Guineas
purchase from Tattersalls October Book 1.
This is a big, strong-topped colt with a very
good temperament. Like most of the horses
we have he needs time to get stronger but he
could be nice at the back-end of the season.
William Haggas.

UNNAMED
b.c. Slade Power – Musical Bar (Barathea).
A tall horse, quite attractive and with an
extremely good action. He's an autumn type
2-y-o for seven furlongs to start with. Travels
extremely well. He's in the Craven breeze-up
sale.

MATT COLEMAN

EXCELLED (IRE)
b.f. Exceed And Excel – Elle Woods (Lawman).
The dam is a half-sister to the Group winners
Brown Sugar and Burnt Sugar from a lucky
family for us. The trainer has been pleased
with her progress this spring. J Fanshawe.

ORANGE BLOSSOM
ch.f. Showcasing – Satsuma (Compton Place).
A sharp, strong filly whose dam finished
second in the Weatherbys Super Sprint; looks
a precocious type. James Given.

UNNAMED
c. Showcasing – Sunrise Star. Purchased from
the breeze-up sales where he breezed in a fast
time and was an excellent physical specimen.
Richard Fahey.

ALASTAIR DONALD

AIM POWER
gr.f. Zebedee – Montefino (Shamardal).
A very well-balanced, speedy filly, her full-
sister was black-type and she has more scope.
She'll be ready in May. Richard Hannon.

FOX PREMIER
b.c. Frankel – Fann (Diesis). Looks just like his
dad, is quite forward, could be out late May
and is hopefully a Chesham type. Andrew
Balding.

GLOBAL FALCON
ch.c. Siyouni – Maggi Fong (Dr Fong).
A lovely type, he has loads of quality and is a
mid-season, seven furlong type. Charlie Hills.

GLORY FIGHTER
b.c. Kyllachy – Isola Verde (Oasis Dream).
A very well-balanced type, moves well, looks
sharp and should be out in May. Charlie Hills.

HERO HERO
b.c. No Nay Never – Fancy (Galileo).
A very striking individual, he floats along,
should be out in May and the sire could be
good. Andrew Balding.

HUA HIN
ch.c. Dandy Man – Midnight Oasis (Oasis
Dream). A real, compact tank of a 2-y-o, he's
a good mover, looks very sharp and will be
ready in April/May. Richard Hannon.

QUEEN POWER
ch.f. Shamardal – Princess Serena (Unbridled's
Song). She's developed really well, has an
excellent pedigree that improves all the time
and is one for seven furlongs later in the
summer. Ralph Beckett.

QUICKSILVER
b.f. Coach House – Poulaine Bleue (Bertolini).
A bargain buy, she comes from a good, fast
family, has a great stride and the sire could be
a sleeper. Ed Walker.

ROSS DOYLE

DIXIELAND
b.c. Red Jazz – Signora Lina (High Chaparral).
Purchased at the Goffs UK Premier Yearling
sale for £60,000. He is a real early two-year-
old type that you always find at this sale over
the years. Hopefully he will be good enough
to make into a Royal Ascot horse if he goes
the right way. Richard Hannon.

ENTERTAINING
b.c. Dandy Man – Letizia Sophia (Shamardal).
Purchased at the Tattersalls Book One Yearling
sale for 92,000gns. He is a big, strong colt,

looks pretty hardy and mature. The fact that he is out of a Shamardal mare was a big bonus and he looks like a mid-season type. Richard Hannon.

GINGER NUT
ch.f. Sir Prancealot – Applauding (Royal Applause). We purchased her at the Goffs UK Silver Yearling sale for £23,000. She is a lovely, sweet filly, medium-sized with a great temperament by our old friend Sir Prancealot. She looks like she might be ready to go quite early in the season all being well. Richard Hannon.

THE PADDOCKS
b.c. Charm Spirit – Miss Plimsoll (Arch). We purchased him at the Arqana August sale for €120,000. He's a very well-made colt with great strength and a nice mover. He looks like he could be an early enough type and is in training with Richard Hannon.

WILL EDMEADES
FLOATING ARTIST
b.c. Nathaniel – Miss Kenton (Pivotal). A tough-looking, correct colt and a great pinhook for Willy Twiston-Davies. He is from a good female line and Pivotal mares work well with Galileo (Nathaniel is the son of Galileo). He doesn't look that backward and Richard Hannon is very happy with him.

MOT JUSTE
b.f. Distorted Humor – Time On (Sadler's Wells). A retained Barnett homebred that is a full sister in blood to Moyglare winner Cursory Glance, whose dam we sold for 1.2 million gns as a yearling before she won a maiden at Chester – in the stewards' room! Time On won the Malleret and the Cheshire Oaks, but she has been disappointing at stud. This filly has gone to Roger Varian for obvious reasons – she really looks the part and should be out midsummer.

STAR TERMS
ch.c. Sea The Stars – Best Terms (Exceed And Excel). Another filly retained by Robert Barnett, out of his Champion two-year-old filly Best Terms. This is by far the best filly that she has thrown – a powerful, good-moving sort with a great attitude. She is with Richard Hannon, who helped train her mother!

WINTER GLEAM
b.f. Kodiac – Boo Boo Bear (Almutawakel). A racy-looking filly bought from a good farm in Corduff Stud. Her sire can do no wrong and she comes from a good family. She looked precocious at the sale and during the breaking process, but has gone a little on the leg of late. She was purchased for Bunny Roberts and has gone to William Knight, as a replacement for Robanne whom he did so well with.

ALEX ELLIOTT
DAVE DEXTER
b.c. Stimulation – Blue Crest (Verglas). A 32,000gns buy from Tattersalls October Book 3. Ralph left me with a 20,000gns order for a colt in Book 3 and I ended up buying this guy for 32,000gns. Luckily he took him and reports are that he is a sharp, forward two-year-old. Ralph Beckett.

MOON KING (FR)
br.c. Sea The Moon – Maraba (Danehill Dancer). Bought for €60,000 at Arqana August. I was very happy to buy this horse privately after he was led out unsold at €100,000. I'm very keen on this stallion and this horse has gone to a trainer who excels with this type of late maturing animal. I can imagine seeing him starting off in a seven furlong maiden midsummer but you won't see the best of him until next year. Ralph Beckett.

MY EXCELSA (IRE)
b.f. Exceed And Excel – Emirates Joy (Street Cry). Purchased for £70,000 at Goffs UK Premier Sale. A sharp filly that I loved from the moment I set eyes on her. I was underbidder on her dam when she was culled by Godolphin (carrying this filly), as I adore Street Cry mares; should make her debut in the early part of the season. George Scott.

TAMOCK (IRE)
b.f. Australia – Anklet (Acclamation). A 400,000gns Tattersalls Book 1 purchase, she was the most expensive Australia filly sold at public auction last year. She is a late maturing, classic type of filly that will not be seen until later in the year and whatever she does in 2018 will be a bonus; a very exciting filly whose brother, Tonkin, is reportedly targeting the classics this year. Michael Bell.

TOM GOFF

CONFAB (USA)

gr.c. Exchange Rate – Callmenancy (Political Force). A lovely, grey colt who cost 65,000gns from Mountain View Stud at Tattersalls October Book 2. He looks a really tough and hardy sort and very typical of the sire with plenty of substance. I'd be very hopeful. George Baker.

GLOBAL MYTH

b.c. Scat Daddy – Excelente (Exceed And Excel). A really lovely colt purchased from Haras d'Ommeel for €320,000 at Arqana last August. He's by the great Scat Daddy out of an Exceed And Excel mare from a good Cliveden Stud family that includes an EP Taylor winner as well as the likes of Helmet and National Defense. He has grown and looks great and we have high hopes for him. Ed Dunlop.

JULIUS LIMBANI (IRE)

b.c. Anodin – Kshanti (Diesis). This is a sweet and very attractive colt who cost €67,000 from Baden-Baden Yearling Sale which has been a happy hunting ground over the years. He is by first season sire Anodin and I just fell in love with him at Philipp Graf Stauffenberg's consignment. I don't often get that sort of vibe so let's hope for the best! Archie Watson.

UNNAMED

b.f. No Nay Never – Danehill's Dream (Danehill). A really lovely filly sold by Glenvale Stud at Tattersalls October Yearling Sale for 155,000gns. She has loads of class and quality so I'm very hopeful. She is owned by Andrew Black's Chasemore Farm and comes from a lovely family that includes Dr Devious and Dancing Rain. Fingers crossed she can run a bit. John Gosden.

UNNAMED

b.c. Australia – Dorothy B (Fastnet Rock). A thoroughly likeable and racy bay colt who cost 350,000gns from Clare Castle Stud at Tattersalls October Book 2. A smart sort and a first foal, he has settled in well and we like him. John Gosden.

ANGUS GOLD

HASSAAD

b.f. Kodiac – Samaah (Cape Cross). A homebred filly out of a half-sister to Kingsgate Native, she has more scope than Raheeb (also on this list) and looks a very nice filly. Owen Burrows.

JIRNAAS

ch.c. Showcasing – Stresa (Pivotal). This is a short, sharp horse that we bought as a foal and looks as if he should definitely make a two-year-old. William Haggas.

MOHAATHER

b.c. Showcasing – Roodeye (Inchinor). Although a very immature horse when we bought him, this colt is out of a tremendously tough mare who has bred seven winners already. He is a full-brother to Prize Exhibit and he was very athletic at the sales. Marcus Tregoning.

MOLAAHETH

b.c. Heeraat – All Fur Coat (Multiplex). This was a sharp-looking horse we bought at Doncaster by a very tough horse we raced and looks a likely sort. Richard Hannon.

MUTAWAFFER (IRE)

b.c. Kodiac – Golden Flower (Royal Applause). This horse is bred to be a two-year-old and certainly looks the part. The trainer feels he should be quite sharp. Charlie Hills.

NOOR DUBAI

b.f. Invincible Spirit – Beach Frolic (Nayef). Although this filly has had a minor setback which will hold her up for two months, I had to include her as she was the classiest yearling filly we bought last year and I hope she will be running in the better races in the autumn. Owen Burrows.

RAHEEB (IRE)

b.f. Kodiac – Dream Date (Oasis Dream). Another filly that we bought as a foal and a sister to Extortionist, she looks as if she should be sharp and early. Owen Burrows.

CHARLIE GORDON-WATSON

GLOBAL DESTINATION (IRE)

b.c. Slade Power – Silk Trail (Dubai Destination). This horse has done nothing but go the right way, he looked a very strong two-year-old type as a yearling. He was a top price for his sire and he is out of a Dubai Destination mare who can do no wrong at the moment. Ed Dunlop.

OUT OF THIS TIME
b.c. Frankel – This Time (Zafeen). He is a first foal out of a Group Three winning two-year-old mare. He was a very solid type who I hope will be out midsummer. Sir Michael Stoute.

SNAZZY
b.f. Kodiac – Tilthe End Of Time (Acclamation). Will Douglass who works with me bought her with Charlie Fellowes at Tattersalls Ireland. She has already in fact won but the trainer picked her out very early and we hope she will make into a Royal Ascot two-year-old with the Albany being the aim. Charlie Fellowes.

UNNAMED
f. Frankel – Sefroua (Kingmambo). She was a very nice filly who for a Frankel was quite neat, the trainer told me he likes her a lot which is a very promising sign. Andre Fabre.

UNNAMED
f. Dabirsim – Amour Eternel (Elusive City). She was a beautiful yearling who was incredibly strong and looked like she could be anything. She had a lot of scope so I don't expect her to be too early. Richard has liked her a lot from day one. Richard Hannon.

UNNAMED
b.c. Footstepsinthesand – Masseera (Alzao). By one of my favourite stallions, who is also underrated. He is a big horse who is showing all the right signs. Richard Hannon.

ED HARPER
DREAM HOUSE
b.c. Coach House – Kummel Excess (Exceed And Excel). Another we sold as a foal, for 11,000gns, who resold at Doncaster for £24,000. He turned into a very imposing yearling. Tim Easterby has already trained two good sprinters out of the mare. He's bred to be fast and early. Tim Easterby.

PUNJAB MAIL
c. Charm Spirit – Harryana (Efisio). We sold him for 90,000gns as a foal and he resold to Juddmonte at Book 1 for 130,000gns. He is not the biggest but very typical of his tough

and precocious family; a bull of a horse with a lovely attitude.

UNNAMED
c. Mukhadram – Suelita (Dutch Art). A lovely colt who found everything very easy in his prep. We sold his half-brother The Broghie Man for very little money and he has turned out to be good, but this colt is much easier on the eye. Gordon Elliott.

TREVOR HARRIS
APERITIF
b.f. Pivotal – Swiss Dream (Oasis Dream). A quality filly, this homebred has impressed since day one. Her dam Swiss Dream was a triple Listed winner and is a half-sister to the stallion Swiss Spirit and dual Group 3 winner Swiss Diva. This filly is therefore closely related to Swiss Diva. She is an attractive, balletic goer and is the pick of the bunch. Should be seen mid-season. Clive Cox.

LOVING GLANCE
b.f. Invincible Spirit – Kissable (Danehill Dancer). This homebred filly is the second produce of Listed winner and Group 1 placed 2-y-o Kissable (by Danehill Dancer) and she looks the part. A 200,000 Gns purchase by Dermot Farrington for Martyn Meade at Tattersalls Book 1, this filly is an attractive, athletic mover and has been pleasing in her early work. Martyn Meade.

ON THE STAGE
b.f. Swiss Spirit—Spotlight (Dr Fong). A homebred, this filly is out of Group 2 and Listed winner Spotlight, who is a half-sister to Tyranny – the dam of Zoffany so she comes from a classy family. A half-brother Projection was a Group placed sprinter for Roger Charlton last season and looks set for big things this year. This filly is an early type and has been showing positive signs on the gallops. Ed Walker.

SWISS AIR
b.f. Oasis Dream – Swiss Lake (Indian Ridge). This homebred filly is a full sister to triple Listed winner Swiss Dream and is also a half-sister to multiple Group Winners Swiss Spirit and Swiss Diva. Given her siblings she has a lot to live up to but is going well enough so far. Should be out mid-season. William Haggas.

SWISS PEAK
b.c. Swiss Spirit – Easy To Love (Diesis). This homebred colt was sold at Tattersalls Book 3 for 21,000 guineas to Alex Elliott for Mike Bell. He is a half-brother to the 2-y-o Listed placed Easy Lover. The dam's half-sister Love Excelling produced the champion miler in Hong Kong, Dan Excel (Dunboyne Express) and this colt looks to have good speed at this early stage. Reports are very encouraging, and he looks to be one of his trainer's more forward two-year-olds. Michael Bell.

HARRY HERBERT
CAMBER
b.c. Garswood – Topflightcoolracer (Lujain). This is a well-bred and fairly precocious son of first season sire Garswood. He really is a magnificent looking horse and Richard Fahey seems very pleased with his progress to date. I suspect he could be running in June/July.

INTRICATE
b.f. Showcasing – Last Slipper (Tobougg). This filly is looking very precocious on the home gallops and was the subject of positive reports from her trainer when we were all up in Newmarket this week. I suspect that she could be running in May and just could be a Royal Ascot candidate. John Gosden.

PESTO
br.c. New Approach – Pickle (Piccolo). This good-looking son of New Approach is a half-brother to a horse we used to own called Gusto who won four Listed races. Although he is by New Approach he does appear to be fairly precocious and is one for the summer notebook. Richard Hannon.

SCINTILATING
b.f. Siyouni – Photo Flash (Bahamian Bounty). I love this filly who is a half-sister to Prolific who won the Richmond (Gr 2) for Highclere. She is a very strong, precocious looking filly and is likely to be making her mark this summer and just could be a big May/June starter. Ralph Beckett.

SNAZZY
b.f. Kodiac – Tilthe End Of Time (Acclamation). This is a very precocious daughter of Kodiac who is likely to be Highclere's first two-year-old runner this year. She is finding it very easy and the trainer is looking to start her at Newcastle at the end of this week. Charlie Fellowes.

RICHARD KNIGHT
HARD FOREST (IRE)
b.f. Hard Spun – Moojha (Forest Wildcat). Purchased as a yearling, she ran third on her debut at Newcastle and will have likely run again by the time of publication. Fast and liked. Mark Johnston.

KAREENA KAPOOR (USA)
ch.f. More Than Ready – Tabreed (Sakhee). Purchased as a yearling and another who is sharp and early. Simon Crisford.

PABLO ESCOBARR
b.c. Galileo – Bewitched (Dansili). One for later in the season but doing everything right at the moment. Mark Johnston.

UNNAMED
b.f. Slade Power – Piccola Sissi (Footstepsinthesand). A recent breeze-up purchase and well regarded. John Quinn.

LUKE LILLINGSTON
CARPE NOCTEM (IRE)
c. Sea The Stars – Scarlet And Gold (Peintre Celebre). A really classy colt by a great dual classic winner and exceptional classic sire, his dam is a half-sister to classic sire Le Havre. Shawn Dugan kept her hand up longest when buying him from our consignment at Goffs (€380,000). One for 2019 but has apparently made all the right physical progress and moves beautifully. Rod Collet.

FANCY DRESS (IRE)
gr.f. Mastercraftsman – What Style (Teofilo). Her sire continues to solidify his record as a really decent stallion, her dam was Group-placed for John Oxx and deemed worthy of a place in the Irish 1,000 Guineas. She is being trained by Ralph Beckett who knows a good filly when he sees one and some positive noises have already been made. Ralph Beckett.

HEARTWARMING
b.f. Showcasing – Place In My Heart (Compton Place). She is Heartache's half-sister and

thanks to Whitsbury Manor Stud she will also run in the Hot To Trot silks and be trained by Clive Cox. She is a lovely filly and with both her sire and dam getting off to flying starts in their respective careers we can all dream again. Clive Cox.

LARA
f. Camelot – La Spezia (Danehill Dancer). A beautiful retained homebred and a half-sister to Thomas Hobson. She is currently with Brendan Holland at Grove Stud who has spoken well of her. From the classic Hollingsworth family that recently produced Oaks winner Talent she is more for 2019 but nonetheless looks to be worth following. Ralph Beckett.

UNNAMED
f. Mayson – Rosa Mundi. (Alhaarth). We bought this filly as a foal in Arqana as a foal for €52,000. She has always really looked the part, I have plenty of respect for her sire, her second dam won the Prix Saint-Alary and she is with a very capable trainer so will get every chance. Joseph G Murphy.

JOHNNY McKEEVER
BRANDON (FR)
b.c. Showcasing – Be Released (Three Valleys). A very sharp-looking son of Showcasing bought at Doncaster. Marco Botti.

KAHINA
b.f. Camelot – Close Regards (Danehill). Although by Camelot she's out of a Danehill mare and a half-sister to Magic Hurricane a G1 winner in Australia. She's showing plenty of ability. Bought at Goffs Orby. Hugo Palmer.

UNNAMED
c. Olympic Glory – Heaven's Sake (Cape Cross). A sharp-looking sort to be trained by David Evans. Bought at Tattersalls Book 1. David Evans.

KIRSTEN RAUSING
ALL POINTS WEST
b.c. Speightstown – Albamara (Galileo). By a good US sire, out of a useful winning and stakes-placed mare, herself a daughter of Triple Gr 1 winner Albanova; this colt is an autumn prospect for his connections. Sir Mark Prescott.

ALOE VERA
b.f. Invincible Spirit – Almiranta (Galileo). A lovely filly and an own sister to 2-y-o Group 3 (Prix Thomas-Bryon) winner Alea Iacta who beat the colts in her Group success. The filly is also a half-sister to 5-time winner Alyssa (Park Hill Stakes, Gr 2). Their dam, Almiranta, was injured in her only start but herself a half-sister to black type winners Alla Speranza and Altesse, as well as a granddaughter of World Champion 3-y-o filly, dual Champion Stakes winner Alborada. A promising individual. Ralph Beckett.

ARCHDEACON
b.c. Archipenko – Akdarena (Hernando). This colt, not over-big but with plenty of quality, is the penultimate foal of the very good racemare Akdarena, a Group and Listed winner who stayed 10f. Her now 3-y-o, Akvavera, won for Ralph Beckett in her third of three starts in 2017. We rated this colt highly as a yearling and feel he could come to the fore from August onwards. Dean Ivory.

FERRUM
ch.f. Sea The Moon – Claiomh Solais (Galileo). An interesting first-crop representative of his sire, the brilliant German Derby winner by 11 lengths. This colt's winning dam was more than useful herself, being Group and Listed placed for a (TF) rating of 111. Jim Bolger.

LE DON DE VIE
b.c. Leroidesanimaux – Leaderene (Selkirk). A charming colt, he has already successfully passed the winning post twice, when carried by his dam during the last two of her six winning performances. Tough and genuine, Leaderene gained a TF rating of 98; she is a half-sister to Gr 1 winner, Champion German 3-y-o filly Lady Marion and Gr 3 winner Lucidor. Well-balanced and a very good mover, this colt might well mature earlier than his dam did. Andrew Balding.

BRUCE RAYMOND
AUTUMN SPLENDOUR (IRE)
b.c. Dandy Man – Harvest Joy (Daggers Drawn). An early 2-y-o, the trainer seems very positive about him. James Tate.

ZMHAR (IRE)
ch.c. Shamardal – Guarantia (Selkirk). One to

look out for early on, he's really pleasing us. James Tate.

UNNAMED
b.c. Kodiac – Bailonguera (Southern Halo). A colt that will make a 2-y-o around July time, probably a six furlong type and the trainer likes him. Richard Hannon.

DAVID REDVERS
UNNAMED
b.f. Charm Spirit – Air Biscuit (Galileo). A 30,000gns foal purchase who has always looked a smart precocious sort. Charlie Hills.

UNNAMED
b.f. Kodiac – By Jupiter (Sea The Stars). Cost £45k and was my pick of the Ascot breeze-up. She produced a very fast time in pretty awful conditions and appears to have an excellent mind and plenty of natural speed. Owned by a syndicate of owners including several first-timers who play for Gloucester Rugby. No pressure there then! Amy Murphy.

UNNAMED
b.c. Frankel – Marine Bleue (Desert Prince). A homebred colt who looks like he should be out mid-season and oozes athleticism. John Gosden.

UNNAMED
b.f. Scat Daddy – Secret Charm (Green Desert). A $150k filly from Keeneland who has a smashing outlook and action and is in the right hands to thrive at two. William Haggas.

UNNAMED
b.c. Charm Spirit – Ysper (Orpen). A homebred out of a full-sister to champion French two-year-old Vorda. He has a great head and is a very athletic two-year-old. The trainer is holding on to him for 6f maidens. David Simcock.

CHRIS RICHARDSON
ANGEL'S HIDEAWAY
gr.f. Dark Angel – The Hermitage (Kheleyf). A full sister to the Group 2 placed Perfect Angel, who was bought at the Goffs Orby Sale for €390,000. John Gosden.

DAVYDENKO
ch.c. Intello – Safina (Pivotal). A half-brother to

the Group 3 winner, Group 2 placed, Marenko. Sir Michael Stoute.

RARE EMERALD
ch.f. Dutch Art – Bahia Emerald (Bahamian Bounty). A filly from the family of Pass The Peace and Embassy. Richard Fahey.

SEA WINGS
ch.c. Sea The Stars – Infallible (Pivotal). A full brother to the dual Group 2 winner Mutakayyef and Group 3 winner Intimation, from the family of Garswood. William Haggas.

ROBIN SHARP
JOURNEY OF LIFE (IRE)
c. New Approach – Arsaadi. A strong, good-moving colt looked a two-year-old. His brother was totally the opposite and very good. This colt looks fast.

UNNAMED
c. Pivotal – Carlanda (Lando). Bred on a cross that has worked very successfully. A big, strong good moving colt, he won't be early. Bought very well by John Ferguson.

UNNAMED
b.c. Dutch Art – Privacy Order (Azamour). A fine, big colt, I can't believe he didn't fetch more but he has been bought by the right man. Mark Johnston.

UNNAMED
ch.c. Farhh – She Wolf (Medicean). I loved his work ethic and desire to please. I really hope he is successful for Marco as I told him of my belief. Marco Botti.

AMANDA SKIFFINGTON
BE QUICK
b.c. Mukhadram – Skyrider (Dalakhani). This is a lovely colt I bought in Book 3 at Tattersalls and I don't think I would have got near him had he been in Book 2, as I'm sure Shadwell would have wanted him. He's not bred to be early, but a lovely horse when he does appear. Roger Charlton.

BLONDE WARRIOR (IRE)
b.c. Zoffany – Dame Blanche (Be My Guest). A very good moving colt I bought at Deauville who looks like he could be a nice two year-old and then go on from there. Hugo Palmer.

ECHELLE DU LEVANT
b.f. Dabirsim – Elnadwa (Daaher). I thought this filly was a queen – she also came from Arqana in October. The Dabirsims looked pretty precocious and I hope this one is as good as she looks. Fabrice Chappet.

MODEL GUEST
ch.f. Showcasing – Looks All Right (Danehill Dancer). We stretched the budget a bit to buy this filly, who I thought was really lovely. I will be horrified if she isn't pretty good! George Margarson.

POPINJAY
ch.c. Dawn Approach – Extreme Green (Motivator). A really nice colt, bought at Arqana in October, who I thought was an absolute ringer for his sire, a lovely big, strong horse. The trainer is very keen on him. Fabrice Chappet.

ST OUEN
b.c. Alhebayeb – Heat (King's Best). A big strong colt I bought at Fairyhouse, who was very like a horse called Mister Links, whom I bought for the same connections – I'm hoping he will be as good. Richard Hannon.

UNNAMED
ch.c. New Approach – Anayid (A P Indy). A lovely colt, whom I think we stole, for €30,000. I don't know why he was so cheap – it certainly has not been apparent, and apparently he really stands out in the string. Hugo Palmer.

PETER STANLEY
BLACK ENVY
f. Kingman – Making Eyes (Dansili). Doing very well after a growth spurt. Rod Collet.

GLOBAL EXPRESS
c. New Approach – All For Laura (Cadeaux Genereux). Having a break but always loved this colt. Ed Dunlop.

KAHALA QUEEN (IRE)
b.f. Shamardal – Whazzis (Desert Prince). A very powerful filly, always a queen at home and good early reports. Roger Varian.

LINE OF DUTY (IRE)
ch.c. Galileo – Jacqueline Quest (Rock Of Gibraltar). A Classically bred colt but showing surprising early speed. Charlie Appleby.

LARRY STRATTON
MAYKIR
b.c. Mayson – Kiruna (Northern Park). A half-brother to the very useful Senafe, he's a good-looking colt and very athletic with it. He was a late foal so don't expect him to be making waves early on, but he has class and pedigree (traces to Special) and could be smart from midsummer onwards. Amanda Perrett.

PERFECTLY
b.f. Gregorian – Reveille (Sakhee's Secret). Second foal of a mare I bred, sold and bought back, this filly was bred in partnership with my partner Louise Parry and her brother Peter Steele Mortimer. Bred to be a midsummer 2-y-o, and reportedly goes OK. Richard Hannon.

UNNAMED
b.f. Slade Power – Bedouin Dancer (Pivotal). A foal purchase, first produce of a full-sister to Group 3 winner Summer Fete tracing to Whatton Manor Stud taproot mare Upend. Wonderfully easy-moving and if the sire is any good she will be a racehorse. William Haggas

UNNAMED
b.c. Bated Breath – On Her Way (Medicean) A 120,000 guineas yearling half-brother to Headway, bred, like that smart colt, by Whatton Manor Stud, Global Equine and me. A late foal and nothing like his much sharper-looking sibling, so he won't be an early sort but I can't really leave him out, can I?

UNNAMED
b.c. Morpheus – Dafariyna (Nashwan). As easy a mover as you could hope to see, he is a three-quarter brother to Stargaze, who won twice at two and was third in the Richmond; his grandam Dafayna won the Cork and Orrery and was placed in the July Cup and was half-sister to Doyoun. A class individual with a class page, he's in the Craven breeze-up sale.

TRAINERS' BARGAIN BUYS

It's always interesting to find out the trainers' picks from those purchases bought with a relatively modest sum. Each spring I put the following to each trainer: "Name one of your two-year-olds, bought at the yearling sales for 30,000 Guineas or less, you think will prove to be a bargain." The horses listed below are their recommendations for this year.

In 2017 we got 15 winners of 20 races. The two with the most handsome starting prices were Richard Hannon's Regimented (a remarkable 25-1) and George Scott's Holy Tiber (20-1).

Eve Johnson Houghton actually tipped a loser last year, but that was after seven winners in the previous eight years and I know she's very annoyed at spoiling her losing run! Other trainers to note are Tom Dascombe with an excellent six winners from eight and James Given (six winners from the last seven).

I must mention Jessie Harrington's tip from last year, Whitefountainfairy, who cost only €3,000 as a yearling but was sold nine months later for a cool €300,000 ... wow!

ch.f. Kendargent – I Stand Corrected	€16,000	George Baker
LANDA BEACH	€32,000	Andrew Balding
SAM COOKE	£29,000	Ralph Beckett
FAST ENDEAVOUR	£6,500	Michael Bell
WELL FUNDED	€20,000	James Bethell
SO HI CLASS	£25,000	Marco Botti
SOLDIER'S SON	£5,500	Henry Candy
KARALINI (IRE)	£28,000	Mick Channon
GYPSY SPIRIT	6,000 Gns	Tom Clover
BLAME ROBERTA	$27,000	Robert Cowell
HOWZER BLACK	£30,000	Keith Dalgleish
LIGHT MY FIRE	23,000 Gns	Tom Dascombe
ARCTIC SPIRIT	15,000 Gns	Ed Dunlop
ch.f. Australia – Peace Palace	22,000 Gns	Harry Dunlop
CAVALRY PARK	20,000 Gns	Charlie Fellowes
DASHWOOD BEAU	£28,000	William Haggas
b.c. Poet's Voice – Talkative	€18,000	Michael Halford
TIME FOR BED (IRE)	7,500 Gns	Richard Hannon
BEECHWOOD JAMES	€9,000	Richard Hannon
DINGLE BAY	€9,000	Jessie Harrington
MOONGAZER	1,500 Gns	Charlie Hills
UNCLE JERRY	20,000 Gns	Richard Hughes
GINVINCIBLE	£26,000	James Given
FIRE AND FURY	16,000 Gns	William Jarvis
TIN HAT	30,000 Gns	Eve Johnson Houghton
ARISHKA	£24,000	Daniel Kubler
ACHIEVABLE (IRE)	€30,000	Martyn Meade
MAUDE	£8,000	Rod Millman
NAKAKANDE	€1,000	Stan Moore
INDIAN VICEROY	30,000 Gns	Hughie Morrison
SUNVISOR	€14,000	Willie Muir
b.c. Dream Ahead – Nurture	€22,000	Jamie Osborne
b.c. Gale Force Ten – Rosa Grace	€18,000	John Oxx

ch.c. New Approach – Anayid	€30,000	Hugo Palmer
b.g. Charm Spirit – Arch Of Colours	5,000 Gns	Jonathan Portman
SESTRIERE	€33,000	Kevin Prendergast
THE GREAT STORY	22,000 Gns	John Quinn
USAIN BOAT	€23,000	George Scott
b.f. Rip Van Winkle – Red Avis	€34,000	David Simcock
CALIFORNIA LOVE	£18,000	Richard Spencer
b.f. Holy Roman Emperor – Mango Groove	€36,000	Fozzy Stack
DISTANT MIRAGE	28,000 Gns	James Tate
QUANAH	28,000 Gns	Mark Tompkins
ALL BACK TO MINE	£23,000	Joe Tuite
THRIVING	30,000 Gns	Roger Varian
ch.c. Ruler Of The World–Independent Girl	25,000 Gns	Ed Vaughan
ON THE STAGE	£20,000	Ed Walker

TWO-YEAR-OLDS OF 2018

CHARLIE APPLEBY
(GODOLPHIN)

1. ASSEMBLY OF TRUTH (IRE)
b.f. Shamardal – Flame Of Gibraltar (Rock of Gibraltar). January 5. Fifth foal. The dam, useful 10f winner and second in the Group 2 12f Ribblesdale Stakes, is a half-sister to numerous winners including the high-class Group 2 1m and Group 3 1m and 9f winner Echo Of Light, the smart dual 12f Listed winner Akarem and the useful 1m winner and Group 1 Coronation Stakes third Irish History (by Dubawi). The second dam, Spirit Of Tara (by Sadler's Wells), a 12f winner and second in the Group 2 Blandford Stakes, is a sister to the 1,000 Guineas, Oaks, Irish Derby and Prix Vermeille winner Salsabil and a half-sister to the St James's Palace Stakes winner Marju.

2. BAGATINO
b.c. Poet's Voice – Harlequin Girl (Where Or When). March 3. Second foal. 80,000Y. Tattersalls October Book 1. A C Elliott. The dam is an unplaced half-sister to 3 winners including the 2-y-o Group 2 6f Gimcrack Stakes winner Blaine and the 2-y-o Listed 6f winner Bogart. The second dam, Lauren Louise (by Tagula), a moderate 6f winner at 4 yrs, is a half-sister to 6 winners.

3. BEYOND REASON (IRE)
b.f. Australia – No Explaining (Azamour). January 31. Second foal. 370,000Y. Tattersalls October Book 1. Rabbah Bloodstock. Half-sister to the 2017 1m placed 2-y-o Abandon Ship (by Mastercraftsman). The dam, a 2-y-o 6f winner here, subsequently won a Grade 3 8.5f stakes in the USA, was Grade 2 placed twice over 9f and is a half-sister to 5 winners. The second dam, Claustra (by Green Desert), an Irish 4-y-o 9f winner, is a half-sister to 7 winners including the US Grade 2 winner Bayamo and the German Group 3 7f winner Wessam Prince.

4. BOSCONERO (IRE)
ch.c. Teofilo – Midget (Invincible Spirit).
March 4. Second foal. £200,000Y. Goffs UK Premier (Doncaster). Godolphin. The dam, a modest 2-y-o 5f winner, is a half-sister to 4 winners including the Australian Group 2 winner Amralah. The second dam, Sharp Mode (by Diesis), is an unraced half-sister to 2 winners.

5. KINVER EDGE (USA)
b.br.c. Speightstown – Peace Preserver (War Front). January 25. Second foal. $350,000Y. Keeneland September. Godolphin. The dam won 5 races in the USA from 2 to 4 yrs including the Grade 3 Noble Damsel Stakes and is a half-sister to 7 winners including the Grade 1 Maker's 46 Mile winner Jack Milton. The second dam, Preserver (by Forty Niner), was placed at 2 and 3 yrs and is a sister to the Grade 2 placed Tourney.

6. LEADING SPIRIT (IRE)
b.c. Exceed And Excel – Inspiriter (Invincible Spirit). February 10. First foal. The dam, a French Listed 6f winner of 4 races, is a half-sister to 2 winners including the fairly useful 2-y-o 7f winner Efflorescence. The second dam, Floristry (Fasliyev), a useful Listed 6f winner of 3 races, is a half-sister to 6 winners including the Group 3 1m winner Zibelina.

7. LINE OF DUTY (IRE) ♠
ch.c. Galileo – Jacqueline Quest (Rock Of Gibraltar). February 17. Fourth foal. 400,000Y. Tattersalls October Book 1. Godolphin. Half-brother to the fairly useful Listed-placed 10f winner Hibiscus and to the fairly useful 9.5f winner World War. The dam, a smart 2-y-o 7f winner, Group 1 1,000 Guineas second and Group 1 Coronation Stakes third, is a half-sister to 4 winners. The second dam, Coquette Rouge (by Croco Rouge), a quite useful Irish 12f and 17f winner, is a half-sister to 5 winners including the Group 3 Classic Trial winner Regime and the 2-y-o 5f Listed winner and dual Group 2 second Salut d'Amour.

8. STRINGS OF LIFE
b.f. Slade Power – Nashama (Pivotal). March 22. Fifth foal. Half-sister to the fair

Irish 2-y-o winner Virtudes (by Invincible Spirit). The dam is an unraced half-sister to 3 winners including the Group 2 Great Voltigeur Stakes winner Centennial and the Irish Listed winner Siren's Song. The second dam, Lurina (by Lure), a smart 1m winner, was third in the Group 2 1m Prix de Sandringham and is a half-sister to 6 winners including the dual Group 1 winner Croco Rouge and the Listed winner Alidiva (herself dam of the Group 1 winners Sleepytime, Ali Royal and Taipan).

9. UNNAMED

b.c. Dubawi – Abhisheka (Sadler's Wells). January 19. Half-brother to the 6f (at 2 yrs) and Group 1 1m Prix Jean Prat winner Aesop's Fables and to the modest French 7.5f winner Sense Of Fun (both by Distorted Humor). The dam, a useful 1m and dual 10f winner, was Listed-placed over 9f in the UAE and is a half-sister to 5 winners including the Derby, King George VI and Prix de l'Arc de Triomphe winner Lammtarra and the 2-y-o Group 3 1m Prix d'Aumale winner Saytarra. The second dam, Snow Bride (by Blushing Groom), was awarded the Oaks on the disqualification of Aliysa and won the Group 3 Musidora Stakes and the Group 3 Princess Royal Stakes.

10. UNNAMED

br.f. Iffraaj – Constant Dream (Kheleyf). March 25. Second foal. 525,000Y. Tattersalls October Book 1. Godolphin. Half-sister to Global Art (by Dutch Art), unplaced on his only start at 2 yrs in 2017. The dam, a moderate 2-y-o 5f winner, is a half-sister to 7 winners including the 2-y-o Group 2 5f Flying Childers Stakes and Group 3 5f Molecomb Stakes winner Wunders Dream and the Group 3 1m Ridgewood Pearl Stakes winner Grecian Dancer. The second dam, Pizzicato (by Statoblest), a modest 5f and 5.3f winner at 3 yrs, is a half-sister to 5 winners including the high-class Hong Kong horses Mensa and Firebolt.

11. UNNAMED

b.c. Excelebration – It's True (Kheleyf). March 24. Fourth foal. £95,000Y. Goffs UK Premier (Doncaster). Stroud/Coleman. Brother to the quite useful 2017 2-y-o 5f and 5.5f winner Billy Dylan. The dam ran once unplaced and is a half-sister to 7 winners

including the Group 2 Challenge Stakes and Canadian Group 2 winner Kahal. The second dam, Just A Mirage (by Green Desert), a fair maiden, was placed at up to 1m, is a full or half-sister to 7 winners including Wiorno (Group 2 9.8f Prix Dollar) and Reprimand (dual Group 2 winner).

12. UNNAMED

b.c. New Approach – Mazuna (Cape Cross). April 5. Eighth living foal. 150,000Y. Tattersalls October Book 1. Rabbah Bloodstock. Brother to the 1m (at 2 yrs), Group 2 Middleton Stakes and Australian Group 2 winner Beautiful Romance and half-brother to the useful Listed-placed 2-y-o 6f winner Executive Force (by Sepoy) and a minor French 3-y-o winner by Raven's Pass. The dam, winner of the Group 3 12f Princess Royal Stakes and second in the Group 2 Park Hill Stakes, is a half-sister to 6 winners. The second dam, Keswa (by King's Lake), a fairly useful 1m (at 2 yrs) and 12f winner, is a half-sister to 5 winners including the Listed Zetland Stakes winner Matahif and the dams of the Group 1 winners Mastercraftsman and Pressing.

13. UNNAMED

b.f. Exchange Rate – New Girlfriend (Diesis). March 23. Third living foal. 250,000Y. Tattersalls October Book 1. Godolphin. Half-sister to Broken Force (by Broken Vow), unplaced in two starts at 2 yrs in 2017 and to the useful Listed-placed 2-y-o 7f winner Diaz (by Azamour). The dam, winner of the Group 2 Prix Robert Papin and the Group 3 Prix de Seine et Oise, is a half-sister to 3 winners including the French 1m and Australian Listed winner Wazn. The second dam, New Story (by Dynaformer), won over 5f (at 2 yrs) and 10f in France and was second in the Group 1 Prix Marcel Boussac and is a sister to the US stakes winner Dyna's Club and a half-sister to 7 winners.

14. UNNAMED

b.f. Invincible Spirit – Patroness (Dubawi). March 6. Third foal. Half-sister to the 2017 2-y-o 7f winner, on his only start, Key Victory (by Teofilo) and to the fairly useful 8.5f (at 2 yrs) and UAE Group 1 9f winner Blair House (by Pivotal). The dam is a placed sister to the Group 1 1m Queen Elizabeth II Stakes Poet's

Voice and a half-sister to the Japanese $3.5 million earner Gold Tiara. The second dam, Bright Tiara (by Chief's Crown), a minor 2-y-o winner in the USA, is a sister to the Grade 1 Brooklyn Handicap winner Chief Honcho and a half-sister to 10 winners.

15. UNNAMED
ch.c. Iffraaj – Strictly Silca (Danehill Dancer). March 27. Second foal. 85,000Y. Tattersalls October Book 1. Rabbah Bloodstock. Half-brother to the fair 2017 2-y-o 6f winner Silca Mistress (by Dutch Art). The dam, a quite useful Listed placed 2-y-o, won over 6f and 1m at 3 yrs and is a half-sister to one winner. The second dam, Silca Chiave (by Pivotal), a smart 2-y-o 6f winner, was placed in the Group 1 Moyglare Stud Stakes and the Group 1 Cheveley Park Stakes and is a half-sister to 8 winners including the Group 1 6f Prix Morny winner Silca's Sister and the Group 2 6f Mill Reef Stakes and German Group 2 winner Golden Silca.

16. UNNAMED
gr.c. Dark Angel – Sur Choix (Galileo). January 28. Third foal. 260,000Y. Tattersalls October Book 1. Godolphin. Half-brother to the German Listed 11f winner Parviz (by Lope De Vega). The dam is an unraced half-sister to 4 winners including the Scandinavian Group 3 winner Eye In The Sky. The second dam, Saudade (by Linamix), a French dual 10f winner, is a half-sister to 5 winners including the Group 1 Italian Derby winner Gentlewave.

GEORGE BAKER
17. CONFAB (USA) ★★★ ♠
gr.c. Exchange Rate – Callmenancy (Political Force). January 4. Third foal. 65,000Y. Tattersalls October Book 2. Blandford Bloodstock. Half-brother to the 2017 US 2-y-o 5.5f winner Texas Wedge (by Colonel John). The dam, a minor US 2-y-o winner, is a half-sister to 3 winners including the US Grade 2 Pocahontas Stakes winner Dancinginherdreams. The second dam, Mayan Milagra (by Menifee), is an unplaced half-sister to 7 winners including two US stakes winners. *"A lovely horse, he's been doing plenty of work and he'll have a racecourse gallop soon; he has a bit of an attitude but we don't mind that".*

18. CONFILS (FR) ★★
ch.f. Olympic Glory – Mambo Mistress (Kingmambo). March 27. Tenth foal. €64,000Y. Osarus. ITS Bloodstock. Half-sister to the French dual Listed winner, over 10f and 12f, Mambomiss (by Mastercraftsman), to the fairly useful 7f to 9f winner Kajima (by Oasis Dream), the quite useful French 8.5f winner Bestofthem (by Stormin Fever), the fair 6f winner Silver Turn (by Shamardal) and a minor winner in the USA by Peace Rules. The dam is an unraced half-sister to 5 winners. The second dam, Mistress S (by Kris S), a US Listed winner of 3 races, was Grade 2 placed and is a full or half-sister to 7 winners and to the unraced dam of the US Grade 1 winner Gozzip Girl. (Free French 2). *"We're in no rush with her and we won't be seeing her until the latter part of the year but she's beautifully put together. We buy horses from France mainly because of where our yard is situated. We can easily head across the Channel and take advantage of the French premiums".*

19. CULTURE (FR) ★★★★
b.c. Dream Ahead – Talon Bleu (Anabaa Blue). February 25. Fifth foal. €80,000Y. Arqana. ITS Bloodstock. Half-brother to the French 2-y-o 6.5f winner and Italian Listed-placed Princesse Leila (by Slickly). The dam, a minor 2-y-o winner, is a half-sister to 6 winners. The second dam, Talon d'Aiguille (by Big Spruce), won at 3 yrs and was third in the Group 3 Prix de Flore and is a half-sister to the Group winners Keos, Proskona and Korveya (the dam of three Group 1 winners). (Highclere Thoroughbreds). *"He was an absolute standout at the sale down at La Teste-de-Buch in south-west France. I'm absolutely convinced if he'd been at a more mainstream sale he'd have cost a lot more. A gorgeous, big, black horse, he's doing everything nicely and I guess he'll be one to start over six, or more likely seven furlongs".*

20. HIGH PROOF (IRE) ★★★
b.f. Lawman – Rosia Bay (Rock Of Gibraltar). January 30. Second foal. €20,000Y. Arqana. Private Sale. The dam is an unplaced half-sister to 3 winners including the very useful 2-y-o 7f winner and Group 3 1m Autumn Stakes second Prompter. The second dam, Penny Cross (by Efisio), a useful 7f to 8.5f winner of 3 races, was Listed-placed twice and is a

half-sister to 7 winners including the Group 2 Celebration Mile winner Priors Lodge. (The Pantechnicons). *"She's been away for a couple of racecourse gallops already and she's a nice, strong, well put-together filly. She'll start off at six furlongs and was a relatively cheap purchase because she doesn't have the best walk, but if she can run that won't matter".*

21. PRINCESSE BASSETT (FR) ★★
b.f. Wootton Bassett – Mariposa (Oasis Dream). May 15. €60,000Y. ITS Bloodstock. Half-sister to the French 9f (at 2 yrs) and 7f winner of 3 races Arpani (by Tin Horse). The dam is an unplaced half-sister to one winner. The second dam, Mary Stuart (by Nashwan), a smart 10f to 12f winner of 3 races, is a half-sister to numerous winners including the Group 2 12f Great Voltigeur Stakes winner Bonny Scot and the dam of the 2,000 Guineas and King George VI and Queen Elizabeth Stakes winner Golan. (Free French). *"She's a lovely, scopey filly and should be starting out over seven furlongs, so we'll give her plenty of time; she's certainly not precocious".*

22. UNNAMED ★★★
ch.f. Kendargent – I Stand Corrected (Exceed And Excel). March 14. Third foal. €16,000Y. Osarus. ITS Bloodstock. Half-sister to the 2017 French 5f laced 2-y-o Bonjour Baileys (by Kyllachy). The dam was unplaced in 3 starts and is a half-sister to 10 winners including the US stakes winner Stormy Forever. The second dam, Forever Fine (by Sunshine Forever), a US stakes-placed winner at 2 yrs, is a half-sister to 7 winners. (Mr P. Bowden). *"If this filly had been deeper into the sale instead of being the first lot she'd have attracted a lot more interest, so I hope we've got a bit of value as a result. A well put-together, compact filly".* Trainer's Bargain buy

23. UNNAMED ★★★
b.g. Sunday Break (JPN) – Miss Alabama (Anabaa). April 24. Seventh foal. €50,000Y. Arqana. ITS Bloodstock. Half-brother to 4 winners including the French Listed 9.5f winner Miss Melbourne (by Kentucky Wildcat). The dam, a French Listed-placed winner of 3 races, is a half-sister to 8 winners including the Group 3 Prix Exbury winner Matarun. The second dam, Miss Mat (by Matahawk), a

French Listed-placed winner, is a half-sister to 7 winners. (Matt Firth). *"He needs a bit of time to mature both physically and mentally. We like him and we should see him over seven furlongs in June/July time. He has lovely conformation, a lovely walk and he's a big, scopey horse with a bit of a swagger about him".*

24. UNNAMED ★★
b.f. Bated Breath – Self Centred (Medicean). February 27. Third foal. 52,000Y. Tattersalls October Book 2. Angie Loder. Half-sister to the fair 2017 6f and 7f placed 2-y-o Barig Al Thumama (by Kyllachy) and to the fair 2-y-o 6f winner Himself (by High Chaparral). The dam, a quite useful Listed-placed 2-y-o 7f winner, is a half-sister to 7 winners including the useful 7f (at 2 yrs) and 1m winner and Listed-placed Chef. The second dam, Ego (by Green Desert), a dual Listed-placed 2-y-o dual 6f winner, is a half-sister to 3 winners. (Julian Pittam). *"She's very straightforward, very light on her feet and feminine but she won't be running until mid-season at the earliest".*

ANDREW BALDING
25. AGENT BASTERFIELD ★★★
b.c. Raven's Pass – Maridiyna (Sinndar). February 14. Fifth foal. 35,000Y. Tattersalls October Book 2. Andrew Balding. Half-brother to the quite useful 2-y-o 7f winner Come On Come On (by Lord Shanakill) and to the Italian Listed-placed winner of 4 races at 2 and 4 yrs Saint Steven (by Art Connoisseur). The dam is an unraced half-sister to 6 winners including the US dual Grade 1 winner Manndar and the dam of the French triple Group 1 winner Mandesha. The second dam, Madiriya (by Diesis), won 4 races including the Listed Galtres Stakes and is a half-sister to 4 winners. (Mr P Fox). *"He goes nicely, he's done little bits upsides already and I would have thought he'd have enough about him to start at six furlongs. I'm very happy with him".*

26. BANGKOK (IRE) ★★★★
b.c. Australia – Tanaghum (Darshaan). April 27. Eleventh foal. 500,000Y. Tattersalls October Book 1. Sackville/Donald. Closely related to the French Listed 12f winner Yaazy (by Teofilo) and half-brother to 6 winners including the smart Group 3 14f winner Tactic (by Sadler's Wells), the fairly useful 1m (at 2

yrs) and 10f winner and Listed 10f second Zahoo, the quite useful 11.5f winner Rawoof (both by Nayef) and the quite useful 1m to 12f and hurdles winner Taaresh (by Sakhee). The dam, a useful Listed-placed 10f winner, is a half-sister to 7 winners including Najah (Group 2 10f Premio Lydia Tesio). The second dam, Mehthaaf (by Nureyev), won the Irish 1,000 Guineas, the Tripleprint Celebration Mile and the Nell Gwyn Stakes and is closely related to the Group 1 July Cup winner Elnadim and to the dam of the dual Group 1 winner Occupandiste. (King Power Racing Ltd). *"From the first crop of Australia out of a Darshaan mare, this is a lovely, athletic horse for middle distances but I'd be disappointed if he couldn't start at seven furlongs this season and go from there".*

27. BAROSSA RED (IRE) ★★★
ch.c. Tamayuz – I Hearyou Knocking (Danehill Dancer). March 2. Fifth foal. £36,000Y. Goffs UK Premier (Doncaster). Andrew Balding. Half-brother to 4 winners including the fair 2017 2-y-o 7f winner Melisandre (by Intense Focus), the quite useful 2-y-o 1m winner Restive (by Rip Van Winkle) and the moderate 1m to 9f winner of 3 races Let Me In (by Pivotal). The dam is an unplaced half-sister to 5 winners and to the unraced dam of the Group/Grad 1 winner Landseer. The second dam, Flood (by Riverman), a 6f winner in the USA, is a half-sister to 3 winners including the US Grade 1 winner Sabona. (Kingsclere Training Stables). *"He looks relatively early, goes all right and I'd be disappointed if he wasn't capable of winning something this year".*

28. BELLROCK ★★★
b.c. Kingman – Liberally (Statue Of Liberty). April 24. Fourth foal. €240,000Y. Goffs Orby. Hugo Merry. Half-brother to a minor 3-y-o winner in the USA by Oasis Dream. The dam, a quite useful 1m to 10f winner of 3 races here, was Grade 3 placed over 9f in the USA and is a half-sister to 9 winners including the 1,000 Guineas and Group 2 Rockfel Stakes winner Speciosa and the US Grade 3 stakes winner of 13 races Major Rhythm. The second dam, Specifically (by Sky Classic), won once at 2 yrs in the USA and is a half-sister to 11 winners including the Group 1 Champion Stakes, Grand Prix de Saint-Cloud and Hong Kong

Cup winner Pride. (Mrs F Hay). *"He's done bits upsides, looked like he was going well but just had a small issue which meant we backed off him. He's back in full training now but I wouldn't be hurrying him and I'd be hoping he'd be racing by late July/early August".*

29. BLOOD EAGLE (IRE) ★★★
b.c. Sea The Stars – Directa Princess (Dubai Destination). April 6. Second foal. 100,000Y. Tattersalls October Book 2. Hugo Merry. The dam won 2 minor races in Germany at 3 and 5 yrs and is a half-sister to 6 winners including the German dual Group 1 winner Dai Jin. The second dam, Dawlah (by Shirley Heights), a quite useful 10f winner, is a half-sister to 6 winners. (Mrs F Hay). *"A lovely horse, not an obviously early type but he's very athletic and has a bit of quality. A nice colt for the second half of the season".*

30. CALEDONIAN BELLE ★★★
ch.f. Mastercraftsman – Impressionist Art (Giant's Causeway). March 7. Sixth foal. Half-sister to the fairly useful Listed-placed 10f winner Jasmine Blue (by Galileo). The dam, a moderate 7f to 11f placed maiden, is a half-sister to 4 winners including the very useful Listed 7f winner Secret Garden and the useful Group 3 third Lady Acquitaine. The second dam, Chalamont (by Kris), a quite useful 2-y-o dual 6f winner, is a half-sister to 5 winners including the dual Ascot Gold Cup winner Gildoran. (Mrs F H Hay). *"She's going to take a bit of time because she's done a lot of growing, but she has a good action and is a perfectly nice filly".*

31. CHIL CHIL ★★★★
b.f. Exceed And Excel – Tiana (Diktat). February 5. Seventh foal. 500,000Y. Tattersalls October Book 2. Sackville/Donald. Sister to the useful Listed-placed dual 6f winner at 2 and 3 yrs Salt Island and half-sister to 4 winners including the very smart Group 2 1m Joel Stakes and Group 3 1m Thoroughbred Stakes winner Beat The Bank (by Paco Boy), the fair 5f (at 2 yrs) and 6f winner Royal Warrior (by Royal Applause) and the fair 7f winner Polly's Rose (by Bahamian Bounty). The dam, a fairly useful 2-y-o 6f winner, was Listed-placed over 7f and is a half-sister to 8 winners including the useful 2-y-o Group 3 Molecomb Stakes second

Mary Read. The second dam, Hill Welcome (by Most Welcome), was placed twice at 2 yrs and is a half-sister to 5 winners including the Group 1 6f Middle Park Stakes winner Stalker. (King Power Racing Ltd). *"A lovely filly, she's a beautiful physical specimen with a lovely attitude. She has a better conformation and as a result a better action than her good half-brother we train, Beat The Bank. I would hope she'd be up to starting off in May/June over six furlongs. She has a lot of quality".*

32. COMPASS ★★★
b.g. Henrythenavigator – Medley (Danehill Dancer). February 9. Half-brother to the useful 2-y-o 7f winner and 3-y-o Group 3 7f second Light Music, to the fairly useful winner of 5 races at around 1m Sea Shanty (both by Elusive Quality) and the quite useful 1m winner Patchwork (by Paco Boy). The dam, a fairly useful 6f (at 2 yrs) and Listed 7f winner, is a half-sister to 8 winners. The second dam, Marl (by Lycius), a fairly useful 2-y-o 5.2f winner, is a half-sister to 4 winners including the very useful 2-y-o Listed 5f National Stakes winner Rowaasi. (The Queen). *"Not an obviously early 2-y-o because he's still a bit backward in his coat. He's a big sort and very straightforward so we'll get on with him from midsummer onwards".*

33. DASHING WILLOUGHBY ★★★★
b.c. Nathaniel – Miss Dashwood (Dylan Thomas). April 28. Second foal. 70,000Y. Tattersalls October Book 1. Andrew Balding. The dam, a quite useful 9f and 12f winner of 4 races at 3 and 4 yrs, is a half-sister to 3 winners including the very smart dual Group 1 10f winner Speedy Boarding. The second dam, Dash To The Front (by Diktat), a useful Listed 10.8f winner, is a half-sister to 3 winners including Dash To The Top, a very useful 2-y-o Listed 1m winner and placed in the Group 1 Fillies' Mile and the Group 1 Yorkshire Oaks. (Mick & Janice Mariscotti). *"He goes nicely for a Nathaniel at this early stage, he's just going through a growing stage at the moment but he showed a bit earlier on and I like him a lot. It's a good family and Meon Valley are good breeders – you've got a chance with those families. He's a particularly nice-looking horse and I think he was reasonably good value for what he cost".*

34. DISCO DORIS ★★★
b.f. Poet's Voice – Discophilia (Teofilo). April 2. 26000Y. Third foal. Half-sister to the 2016 Irish 2-y-o 7f winner, from two starts, Escape Clause (by Lawman). The dam, placed once at 3 yrs in France, is a half-sister to 5 winners including the Listed winner Etesaal. The second dam, Electric Society (by Law Society), won 6 races including the Grade 2 10f New York Handicap and the Grade 2 9f Diana Handicap and is a half-sister to 6 winners including the Australian Group 3 winner Bourbon Boy. (Mrs P. Veenbaas). *"She looks like she'll be a 2-y-o type. The sire's dead now so the chances are he'll probably get a good horse now and we have about four of his. This is a good, medium-sized type and very straightforward".*

35. DOUNE CASTLE ★★★
b.c. Camelot – Ape Attack (Nayef). February 15. Second foal. 82,000Y. Tattersalls October Book 1. A Balding. Brother to Arendelle, unplaced in both her starts at 2 yrs in 2017. The dam is an unraced half-sister to 3 winners including the 2-y-o 7.5f winner and Group 2 Dante Stakes second Fremantle and the smart triple Listed 10f winner and multiple Group 3 placed Mashaahed (by In The Wings). The second dam, Patcake Patacake (by Bahri), a modest 6f and 1m placed 2-y-o, is a half-sister to 10 winners including the Group 2 Champagne Stakes winner Bog Trotter and the US stakes winner and 2,000 Guineas second Poteen. (Mick & Janice Mariscotti). *"A nice, big, strong horse with a big stride on him, I would have thought he'd want seven furlongs to start with in midsummer. A nice type".*

36. DUTCH TREAT ★★★
ch.f. Dutch Art – Syann (Daylami). January 26. Third foal. 40,000Y. Tattersalls October Book 1. Hillen & Hughes. Half-sister to the fair 12f winner Investigation (by Rip Van Winkle) and to a minor 4-y-o winner in Australia by Manduro. The dam, a fairly useful Irish Listed-placed 9f winner, is a half-sister to 8 winners. The second dam, Hedera (by Woodman), a quite useful Listed-placed 2-y-o 7f winner, is a half-sister to 6 winners. (Mildmay Racing & D. H. Caslon). *"She's a sweet filly that goes nicely, I had the half-brother who was a bit of a monkey but she's*

very straightforward at the moment and I like her. Goes nicely and has a bit of quality".

37. EAGLE QUEEN ★★
ch.f. Dubawi – Opera Gal (Galileo).
February 2. Sister to the fair 7f (at 2 yrs) and 12f winner Galactic Prince. The dam, a very useful Listed 10f and Listed 12f winner, is a half-sister to 2 winners. The second dam, Opera Glass (by Barathea), a quite useful 8.5f winner, is a sister to the very smart 2-y-o Group 3 7f Solario Stakes winner and Group 1 Dewhurst Stakes third Opera Cape and a half-sister to the high-class stayer Grey Shot and the smart sprint winner of 4 races Night Shot. (J C Smith). *"I trained the dam who wasn't very big but she was very good. Both this filly and her full-sister Galactic Prince are very small too. She's nice, neat, a good mover and very straightforward but it's just a question of how much her lack of size hinders her".*

38. EDINBURGH CASTLE ★★★★
b.c. Sea The Stars – Evensong (Waky Nao).
March 3. Seventh foal. €130,000Y. Goffs Orby. Merry-Hillen. Brother to the fairly useful 10f and subsequent Australian winner Lead Choreographer and half-brother to the quite useful 9f and 10f winner Night And Dance (by Danehill Dancer) and to a minor winner abroad by Holy Roman Emperor. The dam won 4 races in France and Germany including a French Listed event over 9f and is a half-sister to 7 winners including the German Group 2 winners Eye Of The Tiger and Eagle Rise and the French Listed winner Echoes Rock. The second dam, Evening Breeze (by Surumu), a German Listed winner of 6 races, is a half-sister to the Singapore Group 1 winner Epalo and the French Group 2 winner Elopa. (Mrs F Hay). *"A lovely horse, he's full of quality and is just a lovely middle distance type for next year, but he should have enough about him to be winning this year".*

39. FIRELIGHT (FR) ★★★
b.f. Oasis Dream – Freedom's Light (Galileo).
February 2. First foal. The dam, a Listed 12f winner, is a half-sister to the Listed winners Face The Facts and Oh Beautiful. The second dam, Aricia (by Nashwan), a fairly useful 3-y-o 7f winner, is a half-sister to 8 winners including the Group 2 5f Kings Stand Stakes

winner Cassandra Go (herself the dam of three Group winners including the Irish 1,000 Guineas winner Halfway To Heaven) and the smart Group 3 6f Coventry Stakes winner and Irish 2,000 Guineas second Verglas. (George Strawbridge). *"Very much a 2-y-o type and nicely bred, we have four more of the same owner's two-year-olds, although three are still in pre-training".*

40. FLASHCARD (IRE) ★★★
ch.c. Fast Company – Portico (Pivotal).
February 2. First foal. €36,000Y. Tattersalls Ireland September. Kern/Lillingston. The dam is an unraced half-sister to 2 minor winners. The second dam, Pediment (by Desert Prince), a quite useful 11f winner, is a half-sister to 7 winners including the Listed winners Portal and Ice Palace and the dam of the dual Group 2 winner Spacious. (Kennet Valley Thoroughbreds). *"He's only just come into us but he goes well and looks a 2-y-o type. Kennet Valley always buy well so I'm sure this colt will be useful in time".*

41. FORSETI ★★★
b.c. Charm Spirit – Ravensburg (Raven's Pass).
January 23. Second dam. 60,000Y. Tattersalls October Book 2. Andrew Balding. Half-brother to Black Lotus (by Declaration Of War), unplaced in two starts at 2 yrs in 2017. The dam, placed fourth once over 1m from two starts, is a half-sister to 7 winners including the Group 2 12f King Edward VII Stakes and dual Group 3 winner High Accolade. The second dam, Generous Lady (by Generous), a Listed-placed middle-distance winner of 4 races in Ireland, is a half-sister to 6 winners including the Italian Group 2 winner Jape. (Mick & Janice Mariscotti). *"A nice horse that goes well, he's a little bit backward in his coat so I haven't pushed him but he's doing everything easily enough. So I'd be reasonably optimistic about him".*

42. FOX CHAIRMAN (IRE) ★★★
b.c. Kingman – Starfish (Galileo).
February 17. Seventh foal. 450,000Y. Tattersalls October Book 1. Sackville/Donald. Half-brother to the 2-y-o Group 1 6f Phoenix Stakes winner and Group 1 1m Matron Stakes winner La Collina, to the fair 1m (at 2 yrs) to 12f winner Kuantan One (both by Strategic

Prince), the useful Listed 10f winner of 3 races Entsar (by Fastnet Rock), the quite useful 7f (at 2 yrs) and 9f winner Next Edition (by Antonius Pius) and the fair 12f winner Black Night (by Excellent Art). The dam is an unraced half-sister to 3 winners including the Group 3 Chester Vase second Icon Dream. The second dam, Silver Skates (by Slip Anchor), is a placed half-sister to 8 winners. (King Power Racing Ltd). *"A nice horse that needs a bit more time. I haven't really got after him, he's one of the bigger Kingman's and he's one for the late summer or early autumn".*

43. FOX LEICESTER (IRE) ★★
gr.c. Dark Angel – Pop Art (Excellent Art). April 12. Second foal. €310,000Y. Goffs Orby. Sackville/Donald. The dam, a fairly useful 2-y-o 6f winner, was Listed-placed three times and is a half-sister to 5 winners. The second dam, Doctrine (by Barathea), a fairly useful 2-y-o 7f and 1m winner, is a half-sister 8 winners. (King Power Racing Ltd). *"My two Dark Angel's don't go quite as well as I expected them to, but I haven't had many by that sire and apparently that's the way with a lot of them but they start picking up in May. So I'm not going to lose faith in them, this colt is from a good family and it's early days for him".*

44. FOX PREMIER (IRE) ★★★★★ ♠
b.c. Frankel – Fann (Diesis). March 17. Seventh foal. 700,000Y. Tattersalls October Book 1. Sackville/Donald. Half-brother to the useful 2-y-o 7f winner and triple Group 3 placed Future Empire (by New Approach), to the German Listed 1m winner and dual Group 3 second Black Arrow and the fair 1m (at 2 yrs), 10f and hurdles winner Muhtaris (both by Teofilo). The dam, a useful 9f winner, was Listed-placed and is a half-sister to 5 winners. The second dam, Forest Storm (by Woodman), is an unraced half-sister to 4 winners including the Group 1 Hollywood Turf Cup Handicap winner Storm Trooper and the dual Group 3 winner Marillette. (King Power Racing Ltd). *"A very nice horse – no question. Although he's got a bit of stamina on his dam's side I could have run him last week if I'd wanted to. We'll hold fire and maybe start him off at six furlongs in mid-May. He goes very well".*

45. FOX SHINJI ★★★★
b.c. Iffraaj – Keene Dancer (Danehill Dancer). February 3. Second foal. 210,000Y. Tattersalls October Book 1. Sackville/Donald. The dam, a quite useful dual 1m winner. is a half-sister to 3 winners including the Group 2 Royal Lodge Stakes winner Berkshire and the dam of the 2-y-o dual Group 2 winner Ivawood. The second dam, Kinnaird (by Dr Devious), won the Group 1 Prix de l'Opera and the Group 3 May Hill Stakes and is a half-sister to the Group 3 Chester Vase winner Mickdaam. (King Power Racing Ltd). *"He goes well; he's a lovely, big, strong horse with a great attitude. A bit backward in his coat at the moment so I've just backed off him for the time being. He was showing plenty in January and he should be a six furlong colt to start with in mid-May".*

46. FOX TAL ★★★★
b.c. Sea The Stars – Maskunah (Sadler's Wells). March 21. Thirteenth foal. 475,000Y. Tattersalls October Book 1. Sackville/Donald. Closely related to the Group 3 Cumberland Lodge and Group 3 September Stakes winner Laaheb and to the useful dual 7f winner and Group 3 second Ruwaiyan (both by Cape Cross) and half-brother to 6 winners including the fairly useful Listed-placed 7f winner Guarantia (by Selkirk, the fair 2-y-o 1m winner Natural Beauty and the fair 7f and 8.5f winner of 4 races Street Force (by Street Cry). The dam is an unraced half-sister to 6 winners including the multiple Group 1 winners Warrsan and Luso, and the Group winners Cloud Castle and Needle Gun. The second dam, Lucayan Princess (by High Line), won the Listed 6f Sweet Solera Stakes at 2 yrs and is a half-sister to 7 winners. (King Power Racing Ltd). *"He looks a really nice middle-distance horse in the making. Obviously I'd be hoping he can do something this year, he's got a lot of quality and class so I'm looking forward to him".*

47. FOX WIN WIN (IRE) ★★
ch.c. Lope De Vega – What A Picture (Peintre Celebre). March 3. Ninth foal. 320,000Y. Tattersalls October Book 2. Sackville/Donald. Half-brother to 6 winners including the French Listed 1m winner of 3 races Partner Shift (by Night Shift), the useful 7f (at 2 yrs), 1m and 10f winner and Group 2 second Mufarrh, the fairly useful Listed-placed 11f and 12f winner

Majenta (both by Marju) and the quite useful 9f to 12f winner Art History (by Dalakhani). The dam is an unplaced half-sister to 8 winners including the Group 1 Gran Criterium winner Night Style. The second dam, Style For Life (by Law Society), a Listed-placed middle-distance winner, is a half-sister to 8 winners including the Irish Derby winner Grey Swallow. (King Power Racing Ltd). *"A nice type but not in the yard yet, he's a big colt, he's had a cough and is going to take a bit of time".*

48. GOOD BIRTHDAY (IRE) ★★★
b.c. Dabirsim – Chica Loca (American Post). April 4. Third foal. €500,000Y. Goffs Orby. Sackville/Donald. Half-brother to the minor French 2-y-o 7.5f winner Fils de L'Air (by Areion). The dam, a German 2-y-o Listed 6f winner and second in the Group 3 6f Prix Eclipse, is a half-sister to one winner. The second dam, Comete (by Jeune Homme), won 7 races in France including the Group 3 Prix du Pin and is a half-sister to 3 winners. (King Power Racing Ltd). *"He was going nicely in January but he's had a few niggling issues and I've backed off him a little bit, but he looked very nice early on. He's a fine, strong, good-looking horse".*

49. GRACE AND DANGER ★★★
b.f. Teofilo – Opinionated (Dubai Destination). April 5. Fourth foal. €60,000Y. Goffs Orby. Andrew Balding. Half-sister to the 10f winner, on his only start, Strong Belief (by Cape Cross). The dam ran once unplaced and is a half-sister to the US Grade 3 12f winner Niagara Causeway and to the winner dam of the Group 2 Mill Reef Stakes winner Moohaajim. The second dam, Theoretically (by Theatrical), won 2 races including the Group 3 7f C L Weld Park Stakes, was Grade 1 placed twice in the USA and is a half-sister to 8 winners including the Group 1 Prix Lupin winner Cudas. (Mr N Watts & Mr D Powell). *"A lovely filly, she has plenty of quality, is very athletic and probably more of a 3-y-o type but I'd be disappointed if she didn't do something this year".*

50. HAPPY POWER (IRE) ★★
gr.c. Dark Angel – Tamarisk (Selkirk). January 19. Second foal. 625,000Y. Tattersalls October Book 1. Sackville/Donald. The dam is an unraced half-sister to 5 winners including

the smart 2-y-o Group 2 7f Rockfel Stakes winner Cairns. The second dam, Tanami (by Green Desert), a very useful 5f and 6f winner and second in the Group 1 Cheveley Park Stakes, is a half-sister to 3 winners including the dam of the Cheveley Park Stakes winner Wannabe Grand. (King Power Racing Ltd). *"In the same boat as my other Dark Angel in that we've taken a bit of a back step with him and we'll take another look at him in April".*

51. HAT YAI (IRE) ★★★
b.c. Garswood – Takizada (Sendawar). February 17. Third foal. €50,000Y. Goffs Orby. Andrew Balding. Half-brother to the fairly useful dual 7.5f winner Starlight Romance (by Excelebration) and to the quite useful dual 10f winner Ecureuil (by Lope De Vega). The dam, placed from 1m to 10.5f, is a half-sister to 7 winners including the Group/Graded stakes winners Takarian, Tanoura, Takali and Takar. The second dam, Takarouna (by Green Dancer), won the Group 2 12f Pretty Polly Stakes and is a sister to the smart Group 2 Dante Stakes winner Torjoun and a half-sister to 3 winners. (King Power Racing Ltd). *"He's doing very well after going through a bit of a growth spurt and he's getting his action back now. We like the look of him, I bought him slightly on spec last year and offered him to the King Power guys who were keen to have him. He's a grand type and should be capable of winning".*

52. HAVANA ROCKET (IRE) ★★★
b.c. Havana Gold – Mawaakeb (Diesis). April 5. Seventh foal. €40,000Y. Goffs Orby. Andrew Balding. Half-brother to the quite useful 2-y-o 6f winner (from two starts) Tanfeer (by Dansili) and to the quite useful 7.5f (at 2 yrs) to 12f winner of 5 races Daaree (by Teofilo). The dam is an unraced half-sister to 4 minor winners. The second dam, Muwakleh (by Machiavellian), winner of the UAE 1,000 Guineas and second in the Newmarket 1,000 Guineas, is a sister to 2 winners including the high-class Dubai World Cup and Prix Jean Prat winner Almutawakel and a half-sister to 11 winners. (Rocket Racing). *"A lovely horse, he's grown a lot and done well so we've backed off him recently. He's an athletic, midsummer type 2-y-o".*

53. HERO HERO (IRE) ★★★ ♠
b.c. No Nay Never – Fancy (Galileo).
February 29. First foal. €325,000Y. Goffs Orby.
Sackville/Donald. The dam is an unraced
sister to the very useful 1m to 10f winner
and Listed-placed Seussical. The second dam,
Danehill Music (by Danehill Dancer), winner of
the Group 3 1m Park Express Stakes and the
Listed 1m Celebration Stakes, is a half-sister to
8 minor winners. (King Power Racing Ltd). *"A
strong, proper 2-y-o type that we'll be pressing
on with in April, so he should be one of our
earlier runners and he looks a nice type".*

54. INCLYNE ★★★
ch.f. Intello – Lady Brora (Dashing Blade).
April 10. Half-sister to the high-class 2-y-o
Group 1 1m Racing Post Trophy and Group 2
1m Royal Lodge Stakes winner Elm Park (by
Phoenix Reach), to the fairly useful 9f and 10f
winner of 4 races Brorocco (by Shirocco) and
the fair 7.5f winner Highland Pass (by Passing
Glance). The dam, a fair 1m winner, is a half-
sister to 2 winners. The second dam, Tweed
Mill (by Selkirk), a quite useful 3-y-o 8.5f
winner, is a half-sister to 5 winners. (Kingsclere
Racing Club). *"She's a very nice filly, she's got
quality and we'll take our time with her but
she's more than capable of being a 2-y-o".*

55. INDOMITABLE ★★★
b.c. Invincible Spirit – Mousse Au Chocolat
(Hennessy). February 15. Fourth foal. 170,000
foal. Tattersalls December. Hursley Bloodstock.
The dam, a French 2-y-o 6f and Listed 1m
winner, was second in the Group 2 Prix de
Sandringham and third in the Group 3 Prix
d'Aumale and is a half-sister to 7 winners
including the dam of the US Grade 2 winner
Bay To Bay. The second dam, Muskoka Dawn
(by Miswaki), placed once at 3 yrs in the USA,
is a half-sister to 6 winners including the
multiple US Listed winner Sigrun. (J C Smith).
*"He looks every inch a 2-y-o type. The owner's
racing manager Dave Bowe bought him as a
foal and I think the last one they sent us that
they'd bought as a foal was Dream Eater who
was a top 2-y-o and a top horse. So hopefully
lightning will strike twice".*

56. JOHNNY KIDD ★★★
ch.c. Australia – Sabreon (Caerleon). April
17. Twelfth foal. 75,000Y. Tattersalls October

Book 2. Andrew Balding. Half-brother to 7
winners including the Listed 1m and Listed
10f winner and Group 1 Nassau Stakes second
Moneycantbuymelove, the fairly useful Listed-
placed 8.5f to 10f winner Flood Warning
(both by Pivotal), the quite useful 1m and
hurdles winner Pillar Of Hercules (by Rock
Of Gibraltar), the fair 9f and hurdles winner
Osgood (by Danehill Dancer) and the fair 1m
winner Moon Crystal (by Fasliyev). The dam,
a quite useful 10.2f winner, is a half-sister to
9 winners including the French 2,000 Guineas
and US Grade 1 winner Landseer and the
Listed winner and Group 1 placed Ikhtyar.
The second dam, Sabria (by Miswaki), is an
unraced half-sister to 5 winners. (Chelsea
Thoroughbreds). *"A son of Australia that I
loved at the sales, he's a middle-distance type
for next year but he's got a bit of quality and
hopefully he'll be good in time".*

57. KING POWER ★★★★★
ch.f. Frankel – Prowess (Peintre Celebre).
March 20. Sixth foal. 2,500,000Y. Tattersalls
October Book 1. Sackville/Donald. Half-sister
to the Group 1 Epsom Oaks winner Talent
(by New Approach), to the smart 7f and 1m
winner and Listed-placed Skilful (by Selkirk),
the fairly useful 2-y-o 1m winner Forte (by
New Approach) and the fair 2-y-o 6f winner
Much Promise (by Invincible Spirit). The dam,
a fairly useful 12f winner, was Listed-placed
and is a half-sister to 5 winners including the
Listed placed Genoa and Clipper. The second
dam, Yawl (by Rainbow Quest), winner of
the Group 3 7f Rockfel Stakes, was second
in the 10f Lupe Stakes and is a half-sister to
7 winners. (King Power Racing Ltd). *"One of
the standouts in Book One in terms of price,
pedigree and looks. She's a stunning individual,
knows she's a little bit special and is a big filly
so we wouldn't want to hurry her in any way.
A great mover, I'd very much hope she'd be
racing this year but with next year very much
in mind".*

58. LANDA BEACH ★★★
b.c. Teofilo – Jameela's Dream (Nayef).
March 8. Second foal. €32,000Y. Baden
Baden. Richard Venn. The dam is an unplaced
half-sister to the very smart UAE 6f and 7f
winner of four Group 2 events Safety Check.
The second dam, Doors To Manual (by Royal

Academy), is an unraced half-sister to 3 winners including the Group 1 10f Criterium de Saint-Cloud winner and multiple Group 2 placed Marchand de Sable. (Mr P Fox). *"A lovely, athletic horse, he'll be a midsummer onwards type. We've been quite successful in the past with ones we've picked up in the Baden Baden sale".* TRAINER'S BARGAIN BUY

59. LE DON DE VIE ★★★ ♠
b.c. Leroidesanimaux – Leaderene (Selkirk). April 5. First foal. 50,000Y. Tattersalls October Book 2. Andrew Balding. The dam, a quite useful 10f to 12f winner of 6 races, is a half-sister to 7 winners including the Group 1 10f Prix de l'Opera and Group 3 10f Prix de la Nonette winner Lady Marian and the German Group 3 1m winner Lucidor. The second dam, La Felicita (by Shareef Dancer), a Listed-placed winner in Germany, is a half-sister to 4 winners. (Mick & Janice Mariscotti). *"A nice horse, he's a good, strong, long-striding type that goes nicely. He'll want seven furlongs to start with".*

60. LOOK AROUND ★★★
b.f. Kingman – Magic America (High Yield). March 29. Sixth foal. Half-sister to the French dual 5f winner at 2 and 3 yrs and Group 3 second Sara Lucille (by Dansili). The dam, a 2-y-o Group 3 7f Prix Miesque winner and second in the Group 1 6f Prix Morny, is a half-sister to the US Grade 3 placed Psychic Income. The second dam, Shoofha (by Bluebird), is an unplaced sister to the Group 3 and US Grade 3 winner Delilah and a half-sister to 4 winners. (George Strawbridge). *"A well-bred filly, she goes well and is a 2-y-o type".*

61. POT LUCK ★★★
b.f. Phoenix Reach – Marajuana (Robellino). January 23. Half-sister to the quite useful 7f and 1m winner of 4 races Tartan Trip (by Selkirk), to the fair 1m and hurdles winner Lord Huntingdon (by Lord Of England) and the fair dual 7f winner Hidden Stash (by Sakhee's Secret). The dam, a quite useful 2-y-o 5f winner on her debut, is a half-sister to several winners including the useful 5f to 1m winner of 8 races (from 2-6 yrs) Border Music. The second dam, Mara River (Efisio), a quite useful 6f to 1m winner, is a half-sister

to several winners. (Kingsclere Racing Club). *"A filly that looks quite sharp, she's reasonably early and I would have thought she'd be a six/seven furlong 2-y-o. Our Kingsclere Racing Club horses are really pretty nice this year".*

62. OLOROSO ★★★★
ch.c. Fast Company – Convidada (Trans Island). April 30. Fourth foal. 27,000Y. Tattersalls October Book 3. BBA (Ire) / A Balding. Half-brother to the modest 6f winner Harlequin Storm (by Clodovil). The dam won 3 races at 3 yrs in Spain and is a half-sister to 9 winners in Germany, two of them Group placed. The second dam, Provacatrice (by Irish River), won at 3 yrs in France and is a half-sister to 7 winners including Gracioso (Group 1 Prix Lupin). (Mr R Hetherington & Mr J Carey). *"He looks every inch a 2-y-o; he's strong, sharp and a really nice type".*

63. PASS THE GIN ★★★
br.f. Passing Glance – Oasis Spirit (Oasis Dream). February 28. First foal. £900. Tattersalls Ireland Ascot. The dam was a fair 6f winner. The second dam, Fearless Spirit (by Spinning World), a fair 12f winner, is a half-sister to numerous winners including the top-class colt Rodrigo de Triano, winner of the Group 1 6f Middle Park Stakes (at 2 yrs), the 2,000 Guineas, the Irish 2,000 Guineas, the Juddmonte International Stakes and the Champion Stakes and the Group 3 7f Tetrarch Stakes winner Modigliani. *"She looks like a 2-y-o type. The dam didn't win at two but she was quite big, whereas this filly is much more 'together' and should be a 2-y-o. For the first time Passing Glance actually had some horses going through the sales ring and that will make a big difference to his stats because they'll be eligible for median auctions".*

64. PATTAYA ★★★
b.f. Poet's Voice – Talampaya (Elusive Quality). January 30. Fifth foal. 375,000Y. Tattersalls October Book 1. Sackville/Donald. Half-sister to the 2-y-o Group 3 Dick Poole Stakes winner La Rioja (by Hellvelyn), to the useful 2-y-o 6f winner and Group 3 6f Princess Margaret Stakes second Pastoral Girl, the fairly useful 2-y-o triple 5f winner and Listed-placed Lilbourne Lass (both by Pastoral Pursuits) and the fair 5f winner Flirtinaskirt (by Avonbridge).

The dam is an unraced half-sister to 6 minor winners here and in the USA. The second dam, Argentina (by Storm Cat), a minor US 2-y-o winner, is a full or half-sister to 8 winners. (King Power Racing Ltd). *"A big filly from a speedy family, I've done little bits with her and although she goes all right I hope she's going to start shaping up when the weather improves. I think there's more to come and I haven't been tough on her".*

65. PEMPIE (IRE) ★★★

ch.f. Lope De Vega – Penelope Star (Acatenango). March 10. Fifth foal. €60,000Y. Goffs Orby. Peter & Ross Doyle / Thurloe. Half-sister to the German Group 3 11f winner Papagena Star (by Amadeus Star) and to a minor 15f winner in France by Oratorio. The dam, a Listed-placed winner in France, is a half-sister to 5 winners. The second dam, Prairie Queen (by Konigsstuhl), won 4 minor races in Germany and is a half-sister to 3 winners. (Thurloe Thoroughbreds XLV). *"A nice big filly, she goes well and doesn't look unlike a Lope De Vega horse I had called South Seas and he was pretty good. She doesn't necessarily grab you as one to be cracking one with but it wouldn't surprise me if she was ready to run in June".*

66. RECTORY ROAD ★★

b.c. Paco Boy – Caerlonore (Traditionally). March 17. Fifth foal. €9,000Y. Tattersalls Ireland September. Andrew Balding. Half-brother to the fair 4-y-o 7f winner Glorious Star (by Soviet Star). The dam is an unraced half-sister to 9 winners including the Irish 1,000 Guineas third La Nuit Rose (dam of the US Grade 2 winner Tam Lin). The second dam, Caerlina (by Caerleon), won the Group 1 Prix de Diane and the Group 3 Prix de la Nonette and is a full or half-sister to 8 winners including the dam of the dual Group 2 winner Sri Putra. (Park House Partnership). *"He goes all right and is the type for six furlongs in mid-May I'd hope. A nice horse".*

67. RIVER FRONT ★★★★

gr.c. Reliable Man – Why Worry (Cadeaux Genereux). March 12. €26,000Y. Arqana Deauville October. Andrew Balding. Half-brother to the fairly useful French 1m winner and Listed-placed Pleine Forme (by Grand Slam) and a minor winner in Scandinavia by Langfuhr. The dam, a fair French 1m winner, is a half-sister to 4 winners including the French Listed winner Lover Man. The second dam, Seltitude (by Fairy King), won 3 races including the Group 3 6f Prix de Seine-et-Oise and is a half-sister to 7 winners. *"We let David Redvers loose occasionally to buy something for us in France and with this colt he's done us proud, in fairness. This was his absolute pick and the sire's done very well from limited options. River Front was the old name of the Cincinnati Bengals stadium".*

68. RUX POWER ★★★

b.f. Kingman – Cut Short (Diesis). February 5. Eighth foal. 550,000Y. Tattersalls October Book 1. Sackville/Donald. Half-sister to the useful 2-y-o Listed 6f winner Brevity (by Street Cry), to the 2-y-o 1m winner and US Grade 1 third Concise (by Lemon Drop Kid), the fairly useful Irish 10.5f and 12.5f winner Fog Of War (by Azamour), the quite useful 9f winner Fluctuate (by Exchange Rate) and the fair 5f winner Special Quality (by Elusive Quality). The dam, a quite useful 1m (here) and US winner, is a sister to the dual Group 2 2-y-o winner Daggers Drawn. The second dam, Sun And Shade (by Ajdal), a useful 2-y-o 6f winner here and a stakes-placed winner in the USA, is a half-sister to 4 winners including the dual Group 2 winner Madame Dubois (dam of the Group 1 winners Indian Haven and Count Dubois). (King Power Racing Ltd). *"A lovely Kingman filly from a family I know well, she's a bit backward in her coat and I haven't hurried her in any way. She'll make a 2-y-o in mid-season".*

69. SAWASDEE (IRE) ★★★★

br.c. Shamardal – Beneventa (Most Welcome). March 20. Eighth foal. €325,000Y. Goffs Orby. Sackville/Donald. Brother to the Group 2 Celebration Mile and Group 2 Solonaway Mile winner Bow Creek and half-brother to the useful 1m and 10f winner and subsequent Australian Group 3 placed Dare To Dance (by Danehill Dancer), the quite useful 2-y-o 7f winner Makkaar (by Raven's Pass) and the fair 12f winner Bint Nayef (by Nayef). The dam won 7 races including the Group 3 Dahlia Stakes and two Listed events and is a half-sister to 4 minor winners. The second dam,

Dara Dee (by Dara Monarch), a quite useful 7f and 1m winner, is a half-sister to 10 winners including Bay Empress (Group 3 Brownstown Stakes). (King Power Racing Ltd). *"A full brother to a good horse in Bow Creek, I'd hope he'd be a 2-y-o type from midsummer onwards. He certainly goes well in the bits we've done with him".*

70. SEAUSOON (IRE) ★★★

b.c. Sea The Moon – Village Fete (Singspiel). April 27. €60,000Y. Baden Baden. Richard Venn. Half-brother to the smart Group 3 Glorious Stakes and Group 3 St Simon Stakes winner Kings Fete, to the fairly useful 6f and 1m winner Gymkhana (by Equiano) and the French 14f winner County Fair (by Nayef). The dam, a French 10f and Listed 12f winner, is a half-sister to 4 winners including the dual Group 3 winner Trade Fair. The second dam, Danefair (by Danehill), a smart winner of the Group 3 12f Prix de Minerve and two 10f Listed events in France, is a sister to the Group 3 winners Prove and Vortex and a half-sister to 7 winners including the Listed 12f Prix Joubert winner Erudite. (Mr P H Betts). *"A grand horse, he's going through a growing phase at the moment and he was a fairly late foal, so we've left him alone and we'll have another look in another month".*

71. SPIRIT WARNING ★★★

b.c. Charm Spirit – Averami (Averti). February 12. Half-brother to the very smart Australian Group 1 10f, Sandown Group 3 1m and Epsom Group 3 8.5f winner Side Glance, to the quite useful 10f to 14.5f winner Spectator and the fair 7f (at 2 yrs) and 1m winner Advertise (all by Passing Glance), the useful Listed-placed 8.5f to 14f winner Rawaki (by Phoenix Reach) and the fair 12f, 15f and hurdles winner Taglietelle (by Tagula). The dam, a moderate 7f winner, is a sister to 2 winners. The second dam, Friend For Life (by Lahib), was unplaced. (Kingsclere Racing Club). *"He looks to be the best looking out of the dam so far. A nice type".*

72. STRICT TEMPO ★★★

ch.f. Norse Dancer – Strictly Dancing (Danehill Dancer). February 10. Fourth foal. Sister to the quite useful 1m, 8.5f (both at 2 yrs) and 10f winner Dance Of Fire and half-sister to the

quite useful 2017 2-y-o Listed 6f third Foxtrot Lady and the useful 6f winner of 5 races at 2 and 3 yrs (including the Steward's Cup) Dancing Star (by Aqlaam). The dam, a quite useful 6f winner, is a half-sister to 3 winners here and abroad. The second dam, Lochangel (by Night Shift), a very smart winner of the Group 1 5f Nunthorpe Stakes, is a half-sister to the champion sprinter Lochsong. (J C Smith). *"She looks like a goer and we've had a few of the family, for example Foxtrot Lady and Dancing Star last year. Funnily enough I've only had one other Norse Dancer prior to this and he was a full-brother to this filly, a horse called Dance Of Fire who broke the 2-y-o track record over a mile at Doncaster. That colt was talented at two and this filly looks talented enough".*

73. TIPPY TIPPY (FR) ★★★★

b.f. Sea The Stars – Peinture Rose (Storm Cat). May 1. Ninth foal. 725,000Y. Tattersalls October Book 1. Sackville/Donald. Sister to the French Listed-placed 2-y-o 1m winner Zvalinska and half-sister to 3 winners including the French 7.5f winner and triple Listed placed Peinted Song (by Unbridled's Song). The dam, a Listed 1m winner, is a half-sister to 6 winners including the Arc winner Peinture Celebre. The second dam, Peinture Bleue (by Alydar), a French Listed and US Grade 2 12f winner, is a half-sister to the Group/Grade 3 winners Parme and Provins. (King Power Racing Ltd). *"A lovely, big, rangy filly. She's a middle-distance type but she should be racing over a mile towards the back-end and she has a lot of quality".*

74. TOP FOX ★★

b.c. Frankel – Lady Linda (Torrential). March 8. Ninth foal. 550,000Y. Tattersalls October Book 1. Sackville/Donald. Half-brother to 7 winners including the German 2-y-o and Group 1 German Oaks winner Penelopa (by Giant's Causeway) and three minor winners in the USA by Maria's Mon, Tale Of The Cat and Cherokee Run. The dam, a US winner of 7 races at 3 to 6 yrs, was Grade 3 placed three times and is a half-sister to 10 winners including the US triple Grade 2 stakes winner and Grade 1 placed Miss Isella and the US Grade 2 winner Sir Cherokee. The second dam, La Cucina (by Last Tycoon), is an unraced half-sister to 7 winners including the Listed winner and Group 2 second Ocean Air. (King Power Racing Ltd). *"A big colt that doesn't quite grab me like the other two Frankel 2-y-o's I've got, but I'm sure he'll be fine"*.

75. TOP POWER (FR) ★★★
ch.c. Le Havre – Altamira (Peintre Celebre). February 11. Sixth foal. 325,000Y. Tattersalls October Book 1. Sackville/Donald. Half-brother to 4 winners in France including the Listed Prix Finlande winner and Group 1 Prix du Moulin second Akatea (by Shamardal). The dam, a French Listed-placed 9f winner, is a sister to the Listed winner Andromeda Galaxy and a half-sister to the Group 3 Prix Exbury winner Affaire Solitaire. The second dam, Arlesienne (by Alzao), a French Listed winner and Group 3 placed, is a sister to the US dual Grade 1 winner Angara and a half-sister to 6 winners. (King Power Racing Ltd). *"A lovely big horse with a long raking stride on him. Probably the type for seven furlongs to start with, I like him and he's one for midsummer"*.

76. TUK POWER ★★★
b.f. Dubawi – Soon (Galileo). January 30. Third foal. 1,300,000Y. Tattersalls October Book 1. Sackville/ Donald. Sister to the quite useful 2017 2-y-o 7f winner Jousi. The dam, a useful 7f (at 2 yrs) and Listed 8.5f winner, was Group 3 placed twice and is a half-sister to 5 winners including the Derby second Walk In The Park. The second dam, Classic Park (by Robellino), won 3 races including the Irish 1,000 Guineas and is a half-sister to 10 winners including the US Grade 2 winner Rumpipumpy. (King Power Racing Ltd). *"She was a gorgeous looking yearling and has just gone through a bit of a growing phase so I've slightly backed off her but I'm sure she'll be fine. One for six/seven furlongs from June onwards"*.

77. UNNAMED ★★
b.f. Havana Gold – Dark Reckoning (Equiano). January 27. First foal. The dam, a 2-y-o Group 3 6f Firth Of Clyde Stakes winner of 3 races, is a half-sister to one winner. The second dam, Impressible (by Oasis Dream), a quite useful 6f (at 2 yrs) and 5f winner of 5 races, is a half-sister to 9 winners including the Group 1 Haydock Park Sprint Cup and Nunthorpe Stakes winner Reverence and the 2-y-o Listed

7f Chesham Stakes winner Helm Bank. (Qatar Racing Ltd). *"She's all right but I haven't done a lot with her. She should be a 2-y-o and she's nice enough, but she's just been cantering so far"*.

78. UNNAMED ★★
b.c. Mastercraftsman – Madonna Dell'orto (Montjeu). March 11. Fourth foal. 95,000Y. Arqana. Private Sale. Half-brother to the 2017 2-y-o 7f winner and Group 3 Oh So Sharp Stakes third I Can Fly (by Fastnet Rock), to the useful Listed 7f winner of 5 races and Group 3 third Viscount Barfield (by Raven's Pass) and the fair 12f winner All Of Me (by Teofilo). The dam, a fair 1m and 10f placed maiden, is a half-sister to 9 winners including the French 2,000 Guineas and Grade 1 Keeneland Turf Mile Stakes winner Landseer and the Listed 10f winner and Group 1 Prince Of Wales's Stakes third Ikhtyar. The second dam, Sabria (by Miswaki), is an unraced half-sister to 5 winners. *"A fine, big horse; I trained the half-brother Viscount Barfield who was pretty good but this colt is twice his size already. He's a nice horse but he's going to take a bit of minding throughout the first few months of the season"*.

79. UNNAMED ★★★
b.f. Iffraaj – Pink Flames (Redback). March 27. Fourth Foal. 95,000 foal. Tattersalls December. MAB Agency. Half-sister to the Spanish Listed 12f winner Flanders Flame (by Dutch Art) and to the quite useful 2-y-o triple 6f winner at 2 and 3 yrs Scorching Heat (by Acclamation). The dam ran once unplaced and is a sister to the 2-y-o Group 2 6f Rockfel Stakes and 3-y-o Group 1 10f E P Taylor Stakes winner Lahaleeb and a half-sister to the fairly useful dual 6f (at 2 yrs) and Listed 1m Masaka Stakes winner Precocious Star. The second dam, Flames (by Blushing Flame), is an unraced half-sister to 8 winners including the Listed winner Dance Partner. (Qatar Racing Ltd). *"She's got a bit of quality. I trained her half-brother Scorching Heat who won as a 2-y-o and she should certainly be racing as a 2-y-o because she looks nice"*.

80. UNNAMED ★★★
b.c. Camelot – Saphira's Fire (Cape Cross). March 1. Fifth foal. 100,000Y. Tattersalls October Book 1. Rabbah Bloodstock. Half-

brother to the very useful 2-y-o Group 3 6f Grangecon Stud Stakes winner Most Beautiful (by Canford Cliffs) and to the modest dual 1m winner Pick Your Battle (by Makfi). The dam, a Listed 10f winner, was twice placed third in the Group 2 Pride Stakes and is a half-sister to one winner. The second dam, All Our Hope (by Gulch), a winner at 3 yrs and third in the Group 2 Sun Chariot Stakes, is a half-sister to 7 winners. (Sheikh Juma Dalmook Al Maktoum). *"A fine, big, strong horse and a good mover, he looks like a galloper so he's one for seven furlongs and beyond in the second half of the season. Sheikh Juma bought him at the Book One sale".*

81. UNNAMED ★★★
ch.f. Iffraaj – Vakiyla (Galileo). January 31. Third foal. The dam, placed in France at 3 and 4 yrs, is a half-sister to 8 winners including the Group 1 Prix Saint-Alary winners Vadawina and Vazira and the dual Group 3 winner Vadapolina. The second dam, Vadaza (by Zafonic), a Listed-placed 10f winner in France, is a half-sister to the Group 1 Queen Anne Stakes winner Valixir. (Mrs M E Wates). *"She's just come into us from pre-training. A lovely filly with plenty of quality, I'd be hopeful that she'll make up into a nice filly in time".*

82. UNNAMED ★★★
br.f. Kodiac – Ventura Mist (Pastoral Pursuits). January 28. First foal. 120,000Y. Tattersalls October Book 1. Rabbah Bloodstock. The dam, a fairly useful 2-y-o dual 5f winner, was third in the Group 3 Firth Of Clyde Stakes and is a half-sister to one winner. The second dam, Kerry's Dream (by Tobougg), a quite useful 2-y-o 5f winner, is a half-sister to 8 winners including the Group 3 12f Prix de Royaumont winner Lady's Purse. (Sheikh Juma Dalmook Al Maktoum). *"She looks a proper 2-y-o type. Bought by Sheikh Juma from Book One, she looks a bit backward in her coat and I wouldn't put pressure on her yet. The bits she's done have been fine and she looks a neat, 2-y-o type".*

83. UNNAMED ★★★
b.c. Lope De Vega – Victrix Ludorum (Invincible Spirit). April 14. Second foal. Half-brother to the unplaced 2017 2-y-o Imperial Act (by Frankel). The dam, a fairly useful 2-y-o

6f and 7f winner, was Listed-placed over 6f at 3 yrs and is a half-sister to 2 winners. The second dam, Matikanehamatidori (by Sunday Silence), placed once at 3 yrs in Japan, is a full or half-sister to 7 winners including two Listed winners in Japan. (Qatar Racing Ltd). *"A nice colt that goes well, he's done bits upsides and I like him. Very much a six furlong type 2-y-o".*

84. UNNAMED ★★★
b.c. War Command – Zeyran (Galileo). February 27. First foal. £32,000Y. Goffs UK Premier (Doncaster). Andrew Balding. The dam, a fair 1m winner, is a half-sister to 4 minor winners. The second dam, Chervil (by Dansili), a quite useful 2-y-o 6f winner, is closely related to the US Grade 1 winner Light Jig (herself dam of the US Grade 1 winner Seek Again) and a half-sister to 9 winners including the Listed 1m winners Battledore and Lynton. (Mr D Brownlow). *"A big colt we bought at Doncaster, he wasn't a typical yearling for that sale by any stretch. He looks like he'll be a grand horse this year from seven furlongs onwards. We bought him for David Brownlow who has been a very good supporter of ours, so hopefully he'll be lucky with this one".*

RALPH BECKETT
85. ALOE VERA ★★★ ♠
b.f. Invincible Spirit – Almiranta (Galileo). February 2. Sister to the 2-y-o Group 3 1m Prix Thomas Bryon winner Alea Iacta and half-sister to the useful 12f and 14f winner of 5 races Alyssa (by Sir Percy). The dam, placed third over 9f at 3 yrs on her only start, is a half-sister to 3 winners including the Irish Group 3 10f winner Alla Speranza. The second dam, Alvarita (by Selkirk), a French Listed 10.5f winner, is a full or half-sister to 3 winners out of the dual Champion Stakes winner Alborada (by Alzao). (Miss K Rausing). *"She's a lovely filly and very different to her sister Alyssa who wasn't a robust 2-y-o, whereas this filly is. She's strong, but not forward and I would expect her to run a couple of times over seven furlongs or a mile in the autumn".*

86. AMAZING FOX (IRE) ★★★★
b.c. Alhebayeb – Gold Again (Touch Gold). February 27. Fourth foal. 180,000Y. Tattersalls October Book 2. Sackville/Donald. Half-

brother to the fairly useful 2-y-o 5f and 6f and subsequent US Grade 3 9f winner Spirit Of Xian (by Exceed And Excel), to the minor French 9.5f (at 2 yrs) and 10.5f winner Tout Va Bien (by Verglas) and a minor winner abroad by Lilbourne Lad. The dam is an unplaced half-sister to 8 winners including two US stakes winners. The second dam, Miss Insync (by Miswaki), a minor US 3-y-o winner, is a half-sister to 4 winners. (King Power Racing Ltd). *"A strong colt and pretty forward with a good temperament, he'll probably appear in the spring. He has a good way of going and of the forward ones we have he would be a standout amongst the colts. So he's a nice horse".*

87. ANTONIA DE VEGA (IRE) ★★★

b.f. Lope De Vega – Witches Brew (Duke Of Marmalade). March 9. First foal. €130,000Y. Goffs Orby. Ralph Beckett. The dam, a fairly useful Irish dual Listed-placed 7f winner, is a half-sister to 2 winners including the Group 3 Prix Djebel winner and 2,000 Guineas third Al Wukair. The second dam, Macheera (by Machiavellian), a quite useful 2-y-o 1m winner in France, is a half-sister to 8 winners including French and Irish 1,000 Guineas placed La Nuit Rose. (Jasros Racing). *"She looks quite forward and I don't think she'll take that long to come to hand. Most of this sire's stock improve with age but I would think she'll be forward enough to start at six furlongs and she'll get seven this year. Although she'll have some sort of a 2-y-o campaign I'm not sure she's an out-and-out 2-y-o".*

88. BRASCA ★★★

ch.c. Nathaniel – Regalline (Green Desert). April 19. Sixth foal. 60,000Y. Tattersalls October Book 2. Johayro Investments. Brother to the 2017 2-y-o 1m winner, on her only start, Highgarden and half-brother to the fairly useful Listed-placed 2-y-o 7f winner Reglisse (by Verglas) and a winner in Qatar by Lord Shanakill. The dam, a fair Irish 1m winner, is closely related to the Group 3 Irish 2,000 Guineas Trial winner and Group 1 placed Recharge and a half-sister to 5 winners including the Listed winner I'm Yours. The second dam, Rebelline (by Robellino), won 6 races from 7f to 10.5f including the Group 1 10.5f Tattersalls Gold Cup and the Group 2

10f Pretty Polly Stakes and is a half-sister to 6 winners including the Group 2 Blandford Stakes winner Quws. (Frank Brady & Brian Scanlon). *"His sister Highgarden was impressive in a decent back-end maiden at Newbury last year. There seemed to be a slight bias against Nathaniel colts in the sales ring and we bought this one privately after the sale. I think we got a bit of value. I'd be hopeful that this is a nice horse, we like him but with that pedigree you wouldn't think he'd appear until the autumn and he'll be a middle-distance horse next year. He has a good way of going and he's a straightforward horse".*

89. BURIRAM (IRE) ★★★

b.c. Reliable Man – Wild Step (Footstepsinthesand). February 10. First foal. €65,000Y. Goffs Orby. Sackville/Donald. The dam, a German 2-y-o 6.5f winner, was Listed-placed over 1m at 3 yrs and is a half-sister to 5 winners. The second dam, Zaynaat (by Unfuwain), a fair 1m fourth placed maiden, is a sister to the Group 1 Nassau Stakes winner Zahrat Dubai and a half-sister to 4 winners. (King Power Racing Ltd). *"A lovely individual, I liked him very much when I saw him at Goffs and I was delighted the owner sent him to me. Although Reliable Man had a couple of 2-y-o winners from his first crop in Germany he's not a horse I think will be particularly forward, but he's an athlete. He's a horse that fills the eye".*

90. CITY MASTER ★★★

br.c. Mastercraftsman – City Girl (Elusive City). February 28. Second foal. Half-brother to the fair 2017 2-y-o 6f winner City Gent (by Holy Roman Emperor). The dam, a fairly useful Listed-placed 6f winner of 2 races at 2 and 3 yrs, is a half-sister to 2 winners. The second dam, Lochridge (by Indian Ridge), a smart Listed 6f winner of 5 races, is a half-sister to 3 winners including the useful Listed 5f winner Loch Verdi. (J C Smith). *"The mare was quite small and stocky but this is a big lad that takes after his sire – he's a rangy sort. He's been quite backward but that wouldn't worry me because he'll come when he's ready and I would think he'll get seven furlongs and maybe a mile".*

91. CRUCK RAILE ★★★★

b.f. Kodiac – Cruck Realta (Sixties Icon). March 15. First foal. 60,000Y. Tattersalls

October Book 2. Not sold. The dam, a fairly useful 6f (at 2 yrs) and Listed 10f winner, is a half-sister to 4 winners. The second dam, Wansdyke Lass (by Josr Algharoud), a modest 10f winner, is a half-sister to 2 minor winners. (Wansdyke Farms Ltd). *"A busy, strong filly that looks tough, she's already done one nice piece of work and I expect she'll appear before the end of April. We're looking to crack on with her because she's forward-going. Her dam did better with racing and I hope she does as well".*

92. DANCING VEGA (IRE) ★★

ch.f. Lope De Vega – We Can Say It Now (Starcraft). April 2. Fourth foal. €150,000Y. Goffs Orby. Ralph Beckett. Half-sister to the Group 3 Prix du Prince d'Orange winner Sky Kingdom (by Montjeu). The dam, a winner of two Group 1 stakes in New Zealand over 1m at 3 yrs, is a half-sister to one winner. The second dam, We Can't Say That (by Generous), won 8 races in Australia and is a half-sister to 3 winners. (Jasros Racing). *"A big filly, she's quite plain at the moment but that's typical of her sire. She won't be at all early but there's plenty of her and she looks like a filly that will progress from two to three. I don't think we'll be seeing her until the autumn".*

93. DAVE DEXTER ★★★ ♠

b.c. Stimulation – Blue Crest (Verglas). February 29. Third foal. 32,000Y. Tattersalls October Book 3. A C Elliott. Brother to the quite useful 6f (at 2 yrs) and 5.5f winner My Amigo and half-brother to the quite useful 7f winner Mimic's Memory (by Sayif). The dam, a minor dual winner at 3 and 4 yrs in France, is a half-sister to 5 winners. The second dam, Ideale Dancing (by Shining Steel), a minor winner at 2 and 3 yrs in France, is a half-sister to 3 winners. (Philip Snow & Partners I). *"He's closely related to two fast horses who were both decent 2-y-o's. He's had a small hold-up with a sore shin but he's a horse I'd be looking to get on with. He'll be one for five and six furlongs I should think and we'll be rattling along with him".*

94. FANCY DRESS (IRE) ★★★ ♠

gr.f. Mastercraftsman – What Style (Teofilo). April 12. Second foal. €56,000Y. Goffs Orby. Kern/Lillingston. The dam, a useful Irish 2-y-o

7f winner, was second in the Group 3 1,000 Guineas Trial and is a sister to one winner and a half-sister to another. The second dam, Out Of Time (by Anabaa), is an unraced half-sister to 4 winners including the Group 2 placed Drill Sergeant and Nobilis. (Kennet Valley Thoroughbreds). "I thought she was well-bought because the dam was pretty good and this filly has strengthened up significantly since she came in from being broken in. I would think she'll have some sort of autumn campaign and she has a good way of going".

95. FELICIANA DE VEGA ★★★

b.f. Lope De Vega – Along Came Casey (Oratorio). February 15. €85,000Y. Goffs. Private Sale. The dam, a smart Listed 1m and Listed 9.5f winner, is a half-sister to the fairly useful 6f (at 2 yrs) and 1m winner and Group 3 C L Weld Park Stakes third Hallie's Comet. The second dam, Secretariat's Tap (by Pleasant Tap), a minor US winner at 3 yrs, is a half-sister to 6 minor winners. (Jasros Racing). *"A big filly and one we won't see much of until the autumn, but she's a good-moving sort and light on her feet for a big filly. We'll see how we go on".*

96. FOX FEARLESS ★★★

b.c. Camelot – Silent Music (Peintre Celebre). February 3. Third foal. 160,000Y. Tattersalls October Book 1. Sackville/Donald. Half-brother to the fair 2017 7f placed maiden Grace's Secret (by Mastercraftsman). The dam won once at 3 yrs in France over 7.5f and is a half-sister to 4 winners including the useful Listed Cheshire Oaks winner Hammiya. The second dam, Albacora (by Fairy King), winner of the Listed 1m Prix Herod, is closely related to the Prix de Saint-Georges winner and French 1,000 Guineas second Pont-Aven (dam of the Gimcrack Stakes winner Josr Algharoud and the dual Group winner Saint Marine). (King Power Racing Ltd). *"He's a very attractive colt and wouldn't look out of place in the show ring. He carries himself very well and has a bit of Montjeu (his grandsire) about him in that he has quite a streak in him. He takes the eye and you'd spot him in the string all the time".*

97. FUME (IRE) ★★★

b.c. Frankel – Puff (Camacho). March 30. Second foal. The dam, a useful 6f (at 2 yrs) and Group 3 7f Fred Darling Stakes winner, is a half-sister to 4 winners including the Group 1 Lockinge Stakes second Sovereign Debt. The second dam, Kelsey Rose (by Most Welcome), a fairly useful 2-y-o 5f winner of 3 races, was Listed-placed three times and is a half-sister to 3 winners. (Mr & Mrs David Aykroyd). *"He's slightly in two halves at the moment because he's growing. His mother was hard on herself but he's not – so far he's pretty straightforward. We're likely to find out if he's going to be a 2-y-o and after all the dam was a fast 2-y-o that got better at three. He's not quite there yet but we'll get on with him at some point".*

98. GLANCE ★★★★
b.f. Dansili – Look So (Efisio). April 11. Closely related to the useful 1m (at 2 yrs) and Listed 10f winner Regardez (by Champs Elysees) and half-sister to the fairly useful 6f (at 2 yrs) and 7f winner of 4 races and Listed-placed Compton (by Compton Place) and the quite useful dual 10f winner Sightline (by Rock Of Gibraltar). The dam, a quite useful 7f and 1m winner of 4 races, is a half-sister to numerous winners including the Oaks winner Look Here. The second dam, Last Look (by Rainbow Quest), is an unraced half-sister to two minor winners. (Mr J. H. Richmond-Watson). *"The best type out of the mare so far, she's a strong filly if a little bit coarse at the moment but I can see her doing well. She'll be running by midsummer and she's a filly we like".*

99. HEREBY ★★★
b.c. Pivotal – Look Here (Hernando). March 20. Fourth foal. Half-brother to the quite useful 12f and 12.5f winner Here And Now (by Dansili) and to the quite useful 10f and 14.5f winner Hereawi (by Dubawi). The dam, a 7f (at 2 yrs) and Group 1 Epsom Oaks winner, is a half-sister to numerous winners. The second dam, Last Look (by Rainbow Quest), is an unraced half-sister to two minor winners. (Mr J. H. Richmond-Watson). *"Very like her dam in that there's not much of her because she's a light-framed filly, but that isn't a bad thing and she'll appear in the autumn and have just one or two runs this year. I've seen enough of her to say we like her".*

100. LOPE ATHENA ★★★
b.f. Lope De Vega – Elas Diamond (Danehill Dancer). February 3. Third foal. 280,000Y. Tattersalls October Book 1. Green Star Bloodstock. Half-sister to the useful 1m (at 2 yrs) and Listed 10f winner Elas Ruby (by Raven's Pass). The dam, a fairly useful 2-y-o 1m winner, was Listed-placed and is a half-sister to 4 winners including the Group 2 Doncaster Cup winner Pallasator. The second dam, Ela Athena (by Ezzoud), a winner of 3 races including the Group 3 Lancashire Oaks, was placed in seven Group/Grade 1 events and is a half-sister to 5 winners. (Jasros Racing). *"Her half-sister Elas Ruby was a decent 2-y-o and even better at three and I would think this filly would be much the same. She'll be better next year but she's shown enough to say she'll have some sort of campaign this year and will probably end up going a mile".*

101. LOPE SCHOLAR ★★★
b.f. Lope De Vega – Varsity (Lomitas). March 24. Sixth foal. €120,000Y. Arqana. R Beckett. Half-sister to the very useful Listed 1m winner of 5 races GM Hopkins (by Dubawi), to the US 1m winner Zvarkhova (by Makfi) and the French 10f winner Kadnikov (by Henrythenavigator). The dam, a useful 10f to 12f winner of 4 races in France and Ireland, was Listed-placed three times and is a half-sister to 4 winners including the Italian Listed 11f winner Renowing. The second dam, Renowned (by Darshaan), is an unraced sister to the top-class colt Mark of Esteem, winner of the 2,000 Guineas, Queen Elizabeth II Stakes and Tripleprint Celebration Mile. (Jasros Racing). *"A big, tall, strong filly, she has a good way about her with plenty of size and strength. A good moving filly, we're already seeing what we wanted to see from her. She'll be a late summer 2-y-o".*

102. MANUELA DE VEGA (IRE) ★★★
b.f. Lope De Vega – Roscoff (Daylami). March 21. Seventh foal. €100,000Y. Goffs Orby. Ralph Beckett. Sister to the Italian 2-y-o Group 2 7.5f Premio Gran Criterium and Group 3 Italian 2,000 Guineas winner Hero Look and to the 2-y-o 7f winner and dual Listed-placed Isabel De Urbina and half-sister to the minor Italian winner of 3 races at 2 and 3 yrs Mawred (by Tamayuz). The dam, a French Listed-placed 7.5f winner, is a half-sister to 4 minor winners. The second dam, Traou Mad (by Barathea),

a French 2-y-o Listed 5f winner, was Group 3 placed four times and is a half-sister to 7 winners including the Group 2 sprint winners Josr Algharoud and Saint Marine. (Jasros Racing). *"I train her full-sister Isabel De Urbina who now looks completely different physically at four than she did at two. This filly might have a spring break soon, she's very light and angular at the moment and she'll probably have one run at the back-end. We like her though".*

103. MISTY ★★

b.f. Oasis Dream – Ceilidh House (Selkirk). May 3. Sister to Ceilidhs Dream, placed third over 1m on her only start at 2 yrs in 2017 and half-sister to the modest 2-y-o 5f winner Pillar (by Rock Of Gibraltar). The dam, a useful 1m (at 2 yrs) and Listed 10f winner, is a sister to two quite useful 10f winners and a half-sister to 3 winners. The second dam, Villa Carlotta (by Rainbow Quest), a smart 12f Listed winner of four races, is a full or half-sister to 9 winners including the US dual Grade 2 stakes winner Battle Of Hastings. (Mr J H Richmond-Watson). *"Not a big filly, at this stage she hasn't really grown yet so we haven't done very much with her. Quite a strong, close-coupled filly, her dam won her only start at two and I would think this filly would only have one run in the autumn as well. I'm confident she'll be a better filly next year".*

104. MOON KING (FR) ★★★ ♠

br.c. Sea The Moon – Maraba (Danehill Dancer). February 7. First foal. €75,000Y. Arqana Deauville August. Private Sale. The dam is an unraced half-sister to one winner. The second dam, Maid To Believe (by Galileo), a fairly useful 1m (at 2 yrs) to 12f winner of 4 races, is a half-sister to 7 winners including the useful 7f (at 2 yrs) and 10f winner Maid To Perfection (herself the dam of two Listed winners). (What Asham Partnership). *"A strong colt, it's quite a light pedigree close up and he's got quite a round action but he has a good way of going. He'll make a 2-y-o at some point and he's certainly not a horse we'll be minding".*

105. MY DEAR FRIEND ★★★★

b.c. Kodiac – Time Honoured (Sadler's Wells). March 24. Ninth living foal. 100,000Y. Tattersalls October Book 2. Sackville/Donald.

Half-brother to 6 winners including the quite useful 2017 2-y-o 7f winner Time Change (by Dutch Art), the fairly useful dual 10f winner Huge Future (by Shamardal), the quite useful 12f winner Infinitum (by Dalakhani), the fair UAE 7f to 9.5f winner of 4 races Baroot (by Dubawi) and the fair 10f to 12f winner of 3 races Bona Fortuna (by Mark Of Esteem). The dam, a quite useful 2-y-o 1m winner, is a sister to the Group 3 12f Princess Royal Stakes winner Time Allowed and a half-sister to the Group 3 12f Jockey Club Stakes winner Zinaad and the dams of five Group winners. The second dam, Time Charter (by Saritamer), won the Oaks, the King George VI, the Champion Stakes and the Coronation Cup. (King Power Racing Ltd). *"A sharp sort of horse, mentally he's quite 'busy' and I train his sister so that isn't a surprise because she's the same. We'll throw plenty of work at him and see where we end up but I don't think he'll take long to come to hand despite being out of a Sadler's Wells mare. He'll get seven furlongs this year I should think but before that we'll certainly be looking to win a six furlong race with him. A hardy sort".*

106. OYDIS ★★★

b.f. Nathaniel – Opera Dancer (Norse Dancer). February 18. Third foal. Half-sister to the fairly useful 7f (at 2 yrs) to 8.5f winner of 4 races Opera Baron (by Equiano) and to the modest 2-y-o 1m winner Zamadance (by Zamindar). The dam, a fair 2-y-o 7f winner, is a half-sister to numerous winners including the very smart 2-y-o Group 3 7f Solario Stakes winner and Group 1 Dewhurst Stakes third Opera Cape, the high-class stayer Grey Shot and the smart sprint winner of 4 races Night Shot. The second dam, Optaria (by Song), a quite useful 2-y-o 5f winner, is out of the unplaced Electo (by Julio Mariner). (J C Smith). *"Quite a raw, angular filly that's going to need a bit of time, but that's OK because we wouldn't be expecting anything else at this stage. She could go back to the stud shortly for a break".*

107. PHILONIKIA ★★★

b.f. Kingman – Colima (Authorized). February 11. Second foal. Half-sister to the fairly useful 12f and 14f winner Brimham Rocks (by Fastnet Rock). The dam, the fairly useful Listed placed 2-y-o 1m winner, is a half-sister to 3 winners including the useful Listed 12f winner and Group 3 Prix Gontaut-Biron third Eradicate and the Group 3 Park Express Stakes winner and Irish 1,000 Guineas third Oh Goodness Me. The second dam, Coyote (by Indian Ridge), was a fairly useful Listed-placed 1m winner. (Mr & Mrs David Aykroyd). *"A good individual and a better one than the previous horse out of the mare Brimham Rocks who did very well. I doubt she'll figure much at two, but I'd be disappointed if she's not competitive somewhere at the back-end because she's not backward and she's athletic as well. She's a filly we like".*

108. QUEEN POWER (IRE) ★★★★★ ♠

ch.f. Shamardal – Princess Serena (Unbridled's Song). March 12. Eighth foal. 500,000Y. Tattersalls October Book 1. Sackville/Donald. Sister to 4winners including the Australian dual Group 2 winner Puissance de Lune, the fairly useful 7f winner Princess De Lune and the quite useful 7f winner Majesty, closely related to the Listed Doncaster Mile winner Zabeel Prince (by Lope De Vega) and half-sister to 4 winners including the quite useful 2-y-o 7f winner Serena's Storm (by Statue Of Liberty and herself dam of the dual Group 1 winner Rizeena), the fairly useful dual 7f winner Invincible Fresh (by Footstepsinthesand) and the fair 7f winner of 4 races (including at 2 yrs) Serene Oasis (by Oratorio). The dam, a minor US 4-y-o winner, is a half-sister to 6 winners including the US Grade 2 winner Doubles Partner. The second dam, Serena's Sister (Rahy), is an unplaced sister to the US winner of eleven Grade 1 events and smart broodmare Serena's Song. (King Power Racing Ltd). *"She's a big, rangy sort of filly that's done very well since the yearling sales so I would think she'll first see the racecourse in the autumn. Although she was expensive it might turn out to be money well spent. The pedigree has just had a significant update with Zabeel Prince winning the Doncaster Mile".*

109. ROVING MISSION (USA) ★★★

ch.f. Noble Mission – Preferential (Dansili). March 1. The dam won four races in France and the USA from 1m (at 2 yrs) to 12f including a Listed event over 12f and is a half-sister to one winner. The second dam, Jolie Etoile (by Diesis), is an unplaced half-sister to 3 winners including the Group 1 Prix de la Foret winner Etoile Montante and the dam of the French Group 3 winner Glaswegian. (Khalid Abdullah). *"It's a real staying pedigree but she doesn't look backward at all, so as an individual you'd say there was something in her at two. She's a good model and has a good way of going, so it'll be interesting to see how she goes on".*

110. SABAI SABAI (IRE) ★★★★

b.f. Shamardal – Semayyel (Green Desert). April 10. Second foal. 260,000Y. Tattersalls October Book 1. Sackville/Donald. Half-sister to the fair 2018 3-y-o dual 5f winner Nomorecalls (by Dawn Approach). The dam, a fairly useful 7f (at 2 yrs) and Listed 10f winner, is a half-sister to 4 minor winners. The second dam, Lil Najma (by Medicean), a modest 7f and 1m winner of 4 races, is a half-sister to 3 winners. (King Power Racing Ltd). *"Not a big filly, she's a strong 2-y-o type and we'll get on with her. She's one we'd hope to get out in the spring and we're looking to move forward with her already".*

111. SAM COOKE (IRE) ★★★

b.c. Pour Moi – Saturday Girl (Peintre Celebre). February 17. Fourth foal. €36,000Y. Tattersalls Ireland September. Ralph Beckett. Half-brother to the useful 6f (at 2 yrs) and 7f winner and Group 2 7f Vintage Stakes third Room Key (by Mount Nelson). The dam is an unraced half-sister to 5 winners including the 7f (at 2 yrs) and Listed 10f winner Splashdown, the Listed 10f winner Cosmodrome and the fairly useful stakes-placed Boogie Shoes and Tadreeb. The second dam, Space Time (by Bering), was placed over 7f at 2 yrs in France and is a half-sister to 6 minor winners in France and Australia. (Chelsea Thoroughbreds – Wonderful World). *"Going off the pedigree you'd think he's going to need time, but the mare bred a 2-y-o stakes performer by Mount Nelson. This colt was a strong yearling but he's a bit rangier now, he's lengthened and grown. He's a long-term prospect, but despite being by Pour Moi he should have a 2-y-o campaign as well and there's a big upside to the fact that he's out of a Peintre Celebre mare because he's a very good broodmare sire".* TRAINER'S BARGAIN BUY

112. SCINTILATING ★★★★ ♠
b.f. Siyouni – Photo Flash (Bahamian Bounty).
February 29. Twelfth living foal. 150,000Y.
Tattersalls October Book 2. John & Jake
Warren. Half-sister to the Group 2 6f
Richmond Stakes winner Prolific (by Compton
Place), to the fairly useful 2-y-o 5f winner and
subsequent US stakes winner Deal Breaker (by
Night Shift), the quite useful dual 5f winner
at 2 and 3 yrs Blitz (by Exceed And Excel) and
the fair 10.5f winner Monolight (by Iffraaj).
The dam, a fair 1m winner, is a half-sister to
8 winners including the 2-y-o Group 2 1m
Royal Lodge Stakes7 winner Atlantis Prince.
The second dam, Zoom Lens (by Caerleon),
placed once over 7f at 2 yrs, is a half-sister to
4 winners. (Highclere Thoroughbred Racing).
*"A lovely filly, she was gorgeous as a yearling
and she's developed into a really nice, strong
2-y-o. Well-developed, being a half-sister to a
good 2-y-o you'd think there's a good chance
she'll make a 2-y-o as well. Although she cost a
fair bit she was probably well-bought".*

113. TEODORA DE VEGA (IRE) ★★★
b.f. Lope De Vega – Applauded (Royal
Applause). March 22. Seventh foal. 250,000Y.
Tattersalls October Book 1. Green Star
Bloodstock. Half-sister to 5 winners including
the quite useful 2-y-o 7f and subsequent US
stakes winner Mirage (by Oasis Dream), to the
fairly useful 6f winner and Group 3 Ballyogan
Stakes third Alphabet (by Lawman), the quite
useful 2-y-o 6f winner (here) and subsequent
minor US stakes winner Amnesia (by Invincible
Spirit) and the French 10f and 12.5f winner
Arthur The King (by Medicean). The dam, a
quite useful 2-y-o 7f winner, is a half-sister to
5 winners including Power (Group 1 National
Stakes) and Curvy (Grade 1 E P Taylor Stakes).
The second dam, Frappe (by Inchinor), a
fairly useful 2-y-o 6f winner, is a half-sister to
Footstepsinthesand (2,000 Guineas) and Pedro
The Great (Phoenix Stakes). (Jasros Racing).
*"Quite a small, light-framed 2-y-o, she's just
had a small blip lately but I don't expect her to
be particularly forward anyway. I think we'll see
her sometime in late summer and she has a
good way of going which is typical of the sire".*

114. TIGERSKIN ★★
ch.c. Nathaniel – Jamboretta (Danehill).
February 29. Sixth foal. 9,000 foal. Tattersalls

December. A C Elliott. Half-brother to the
fairly useful dual 1m winner Bowerman (by
Dutch Art), to the quite useful 2-y-o 7f winner
Music And Dance (by Galileo) and the fair 7f
and 1m winner Messila Star (by Pivotal). The
dam, a quite useful 9f winner, is a half-sister to
the Listed winner and Group 3 second Excusez
Moi. The second dam, Jiving (by Generous),
a fair 6f placed 2-y-o, is a half-sister to the
outstanding broodmare Hasili (dam of the
Group 1 winners Banks Hill, Cacique, Champs
Elysees, Heat Haze and Intercontinental and
the Group 2 winner and leading sire Dansili)
and to the dams of the Grade/Group 1
winners Leroidesanimaux and Promising Lead.
(Mr A. D. G. Oldrey & Mr G. C. Hartigan). *"A
cheap, well-bought foal at a time when you
couldn't give Nathaniel's stock away, but that
was before Enable won five Group 1's. Now
they're very popular. This colt will be a slow
burner, he's struggled with the bad weather this
spring so we'll take it steady with him".*

115. TOP TOP (IRE) ★★★
b.c. Frankel – Jira (Medicean). February 7.
Fourth foal. 260,000Y. Tattersalls October
Book 1. Sackville/Donald. Half-brother to the
fair triple 6f winner at 2 and 3 yrs Jameerah
and to the modest 6f winner Jaiyana (both
by Dansili). The dam, a useful 2-y-o Listed
6f winner, is a full or half-sister to 6 winners
including the smart 7f (at 2 yrs) and Group
2 12f King Edward VII Stakes winner Plea
Bargain and the very useful Group 3 10f
Winter Hill Stakes winner Lay Time. The
second dam, Time Saved (by Green Desert), a
fairly useful 10f winner, is a full or half-sister to
6 winners including Zinaad and Time Allowed
(both winners of the Group 2 12f Jockey Club
Stakes). (King Power Racing Ltd). *"A big horse,
he's tall and quite lean actually and he's going
to fill his frame over the next six months or so.
Although the dam was a stakes winning 2-y-o
I can't see him appearing particularly soon,
although he is a very athletic horse and light
on his feet".*

116. WILD ABANDON ★★★
b.f. Kingman – Sant Elena (Efisio). April 20.
Seventh foal. Half-sister to the 2017 2-y-o
7f debut winner Family Tree (by Galileo), to
the 2-y-o Group 1 Prix Morny and Group 1
Middle Park Stakes winner Reckless Abandon

(by Exchange Rate), the fair 7f winner Free Rein (by Dansili) and the modest 8.5f winner of 6 races Jumbo Prado (by El Prado). The dam, a quite useful dual 6f winner (including at 2 yrs) and then Listed-placed in Canada, is a half-sister to the US dual Grade 1 winner Ticker Tape and the Group 3 sprint winner Brando. The second dam, Argent Du Bois (by Silver Hawk), placed at 2 and 3 yrs in France, stayed 1m and is a half-sister to 9 winners including the Group 1 Racing Post Trophy winner Crowded House. (The Eclipse Partnership). *"She's a half-sister to a very fast horse and carries plenty of condition which isn't a bad thing. A solid filly, hopefully when she gets over the tough spell of weather we're having we'll be able to move forward. I expect her to make a 2-y-o over six furlongs".*

117. UNNAMED ★★★★
b.f. Speightstown – Dansette (Dansili). April 1. Fourth foal. 240,000Y. Tattersalls October Book 2. J J Gordon. Half-sister to Mav (by Henrythenavigator), a minor winner of 3 races at 3 yrs in the USA. The dam is an unplaced half-sister to 5 winners including the Group 1 Fillies Mile, Falmouth Stakes, Sussex Stakes and Matron Stakes winner Soviet Song, the useful 5f (at 2 yrs) and triple 6f winner Baralinka and the dam of the Group 1 winner Ribbons. The second dam, Kalinka (by Soviet Star), a quite useful 2-y-o 7f winner, is a half-sister to 2 winners. (Mr Sutong Pan). *"A lovely filly. I loved her at the sales and was delighted they sent her here. She's not a particularly forward filly but strong all the same and I would say we'll end up somewhere in midsummer with her. She has a good way of going, we've had a bit of luck with the sire – they tend to be tough horses – and this filly looks the same".*

118. UNNAMED ★★★
b.c. Holy Roman Emperor – Empress Of France (Storm Cat). April 3. Fifth foal. The dam, a minor winner of 2 races at 4 yrs in the USA, is a sister to the Group 3 Irish 1,000 Guineas Trial winner Kamarinskaya and a half-sister to 4 winners including the champion 2-y-o colt Fasliyev and to the unraced top-class broodmare Butterfly Cove (dam of the Group 1 winners Ballydoyle and Misty For Me). The second dam, Mr P's Princess (by Mr Prospector), is an unraced half-sister to

the US Grade 1 winners Menifee and Desert Wine. (H.H. Sheikh Mohammed bin Khalifa Al Thani). *"He's not a big horse, so he's typical of the sire in that respect, but he's strong and we'll be rolling along with him although it's not a particularly precocious family. We'll be getting on with him".*

119. UNNAMED ★★★★
b.f. Delegator – Hobby (Robellino). March 28. Fifth foal. Half-sister to the fair 2-y-o 6f winner Cotinga (by Paco Boy). The dam, a useful 2-y-o 7f winner on her debut, was third in the Group 2 12f Ribblesdale Stakes and is a half-sister to one winner abroad. The second dam, Wydah (by Suave Dancer), is an unraced half-sister to 5 winners including the Irish Listed winner Golden Temple. (Larksborough Stud). *"This filly is the best one out of the mare so far as an individual, I like her. There are 2-y-o winners in the family, so I'll be getting on with her".*

120. UNNAMED ★★★★
b.c. Sea The Stars – Honor Bound (Authorized). February 14. The dam, a fairly useful Listed 11.5f winner, is a half-sister to 4 winners including the Group 1 12f Irish Derby and US Grade 1 Secretariat Stakes winner Treasure Beach. The second dam, Honorine (by Mark Of Esteem), a quite useful 1m and 10f winner, is a half-sister to the Group 2 Hardwicke Stakes winner and triple Group 1 placed Indian Creek. (H.H. Sheikh Mohammed bin Khalifa Al Thani). *"A gorgeous horse, obviously he'll need some time but he's very good-looking, athletic and one we like very much. He'll be a seven furlong plus 2-y-o and a mile and a half horse next year. Amongst the colts he's an obvious pick".*

121. UNNAMED ★★
ch.c. Intikhab – Indolente (Diesis). April 11. Eighth living foals. 57,000Y. Tattersalls October Book 2. David Redvers. Brother to the fairly useful Listed-placed 10f and 11f winner Expense Claim, to the fairly useful Listed-placed 7f winner Swift Campaign and the minor French winner Filatelia and half-brother to the minor French 10f winner of 3 races Issacar (by Traditionally). The dam is an unraced half-sister to 2 winners. The second dam, Tycoon's Dolce (by Rainbows For

Life), won the Listed Prix de Lieurey and was Group 3 placed three times and is a half-sister to three Listed winners in France and Italy. (Qatar Racing Ltd). *"He's a bit of a thug at the moment – as they can be by that stallion. But he's a horse I like and he just needs managing. A full brother to a good horse, his time will come but probably not this year".*

122. UNNAMED ★★★

ch.c. Sea The Stars – Mambo Light (Kingmambo). April 2. Sixth foal. 340,000Y. Tattersalls October Book 1. David Redvers & Meridian International. Half-brother to the quite useful 2-y-o 7f winner Via Serendipity (by Invincible Spirit), to the useful 2-y-o 7f winner Strong Chemistry (by Oasis Dream) and the French Listed-placed dual 9.5f winner Le Juge (by Dansili). The dam, a German Listed 1m winner and Group 3 second, is a half-sister to 3 winners including the dual Group 3 5f winner Dietrich (the dam of two stakes winners). The second dam, Piquetnol (by Private Account), a minor French 3-y-o winner and second in the Group 1 Prix Marcel Boussac, is a sister to the dual Group 1 winner Chimes of Freedom (dam of the Group 1 winners Good Journey and Spinning World). (Qatar Racing Ltd & Mr Kin Hung Kei). *"A very athletic horse and one that'll need some time, but he's not particularly backward, he's got short cannon bones and plenty of bone. I'm a big fan of the sire and I hope he'll be a horse for next year, after a run or two over a mile at the back-end this year".*

123. UNNAMED ★★

b.f. Charm Spirit – Millisecond (Royal Applause). April 18. Fourth foal. Half-sister to the modest 5f and 1m winner Dashing Poet (by Poet's Voice) and to the minor French winner of 3 races Soho Rocks (by Rock Of Gibraltar). The dam, a fair 5f and 6f winner, is a half-sister to 4 winners and to the unplaced dam of the Group 2 Sun Chariot Stakes winner Kissogram. The second dam, Milligram (by (by Mill Reef), won the Group 1 1m Queen Elizabeth II Stakes, the Group 2 1m Coronation Stakes and the Group 2 Waterford Crystal Mile and is a half-sister to the Coronation Stakes placed Someone Special – herself dam of the Group winners One So Wonderful, Alnasr Alwasheek and Relatively Special. (Qatar

Racing Ltd). *"Quite a strong sort of filly that's going through an ugly duckling stage at the moment. She's done plenty of work without going fast and we'll carry on in that vein until we think she's ready to step up. I don't have a strong opinion about her either way".*

124. UNNAMED ★★★★

b.f. Mastercraftsman – Nina Celebre (Peintre Celebre). April 20. Fifth foal. €235,000Y. Baden Baden. Bertrand Le Metayer. Half-sister to the Hong Kong dual 7f winner Pakistan Star (by Shamardal) and to the German 2-y-o winner and Listed-placed Ninas Terz (by Tertullian). The dam, a dual Listed 10f winner, is out of the Group 1 German Oaks winner Next Gina. (H.H. Sheikh Mohammed bin Khalifa Al Thani). *"She was a very backward, lanky yearling and she only arrived here a month ago. She's all legs at the moment but that wouldn't worry me, she's a half-sister to a very fast horse. We'll be looking towards next year with her but she's a filly I like very much".*

125. UNNAMED ★★★★

gr.f. Dark Angel – Parle Moi (USA) (Giant's Causeway). March 1. First foal. 95,000Y. Tattersalls October Book 1. Not sold. The dam, placed twice over 6.5f in France, is a half-sister to 7 winners including the French Listed winners Sunday Doubt, Sonnerie and Saying. The second dam, Pas de Reponse (by Danzig), won 5 races including the 2-y-o Group 1 6f Cheveley Park Stakes and is a half-sister to 6 winners including the French dual Group 1 winner and sire Green Tune. (Wansdyke Farms Ltd, Oghill House Stud). *"A strong filly, she wouldn't want too many days off because she carries plenty of condition but that's not a bad thing. We'll be looking towards stepping her up in a month or so and she'll make a 2-y-o. Very laid-back, six furlongs will suit her".*

126. UNNAMED ★★★★

b.f. Dark Angel – Soxy Doxy (Hawk Wing). March 29. Fourth foal. 400,000Y. Tattersalls October Book 1. JJ Gordon Bloodstock. Half-sister to the fair 6f (at 2 yrs) and 1m winner Il Piccolo Grande (by Iffraaj), to the modest 8.5f and 10f winner Mister Mayday (by Kheleyf) and a winner in Singapore by Verglas. The dam, a moderate 12f placed maiden, is a half-sister to 5 winners including the Listed King

Charles II Stakes and subsequent US Grade 3 winner and Grade 1 placed Millennium Dragon. The second dam, Feather Bride (by Groom Dancer), won once at 3 yrs in France and is a half-sister to 5 winners. (Mr Sutong Pan). *"She's a filly who requires plenty of work and although she hasn't done anything quickly yet, that day isn't far away. She looks like she'll make a 2-y-o but she's a filly with plenty of size and scope as well".*

127. UNNAMED ★★★★

ch.f. Sea The Stars – Topaze Blanche (Zamindar). March 28. Second foal. The dam, a 2-y-o 7f and 1m winner, was second in the Group 1 Prix Marcel Boussac and the Group 2 Prix de Sandringham. The second dam, Pearl Earrine (by Kaldounevees), a minor French winner, is a half-sister to 4 winners including Varxi (Group 3 Prix Thomas Bryon). (H.H. Sheikh Mohammed bin Khalifa Al Thani). *"Finds life very easy, she's a very athletic, good-moving filly and I know the dam was a good 2-y-o but nevertheless you wouldn't expect this filly to be coping as well as she is. I'd say there's a chance she's a very nice filly. One to appear after July I'd say".*

MICHAEL BELL

128. ALLMANKIND ★★★★

b.c. Sea The Moon – Wemyss Bay (Sadler's Wells). March 5. Half-brother to the fair 12f winner Beach Break (by Cacique) and to a hurdles winner by Champs Elysees. The dam is an unraced sister to the 1m (at 2 yrs) and Group 1 10f Grand Prix de Paris winner Beat Hollow and a half-sister to 3 winners including the US Grade 3 winner Yaralino. The second dam, Wemyss Bight (by Dancing Brave), a very smart filly, won 5 races including the Group 1 12f Irish Oaks and the Group 2 12f Prix de Malleret. (W. J. and T. C. O. Gredley). *"I really like him, the dam was unraced but it's a very good Juddmonte family and I think this is a nice colt. He'll be a mid-season 2-y-o".*

129. ANTHONY E (IRE) ★★★

b.c. No Nay Never – Lace (Sadler's Wells). April 23. Seventh foal. 100,000Y. Tattersalls October Book 2. W J Gredley. Half-brother to two minor winners in the USA by Danehill Dancer. The dam is an unraced half-sister to 4 winners including Zarani Sidi Anna (third in

both the Group 1 Coronation Stakes and the Grade 1 Milady Handicap). The second dam, Emmaline (by Affirmed), won twice at up to 9f in the USA including a stakes event and is a half-sister to 8 winners including the Grade 1 winners Bates Motel and Hatim. (W. J. and T. C. O. Gredley). *"He's shown a bit of promise and seems to have a good attitude but we won't rush him because he's out of a Sadler's Wells mare which will take a bit of zip out of him. It's so far so good and I'd say he'll be a 2-y-o for mid-to-late summer".*

130. ANTIGUAN DUCHESS ★★★

ch.f. Dutch Art – Totally Millie (Pivotal). February 25. Second foal. £39,000Y. Goffs UK Premier (Doncaster). Not sold. The dam is an unraced half-sister to 4 winners. The second dam, Millistar (by Galileo), a fair dual 10f winner, is a half-sister to 4 winners and to the unplaced dam of the Group 2 Sun Chariot Stakes winner Kissogram. (Mr & Mrs A Smith-Maxwell & Mr W E A Fox). *"She looks very sharp, she's from a speedy family and looks one of our earlier 2-y-o types. Not very big, but a determined little thing for five and six furlongs".*

131. ANY SMILE (IRE) ★★★

b.f. Zoffany – Bahja (Seeking The Gold). May 2. Ninth foal. €60,000Y. Goffs Orby. A C Elliott (private sale). Half-sister to the 2017 7f placed 2-y-o on his only start Jurz (by Exceed And Excel), to the fair dual 6f winner Ghazwah (by Shamardal) and the fair 2-y-o 6f winner Ferjaan (by Oasis Dream). The dam, a fair 7f placed 2-y-o (from only 2 starts), is a half-sister to 2 winners including the Listed Oaks Trial winner Dyna Waltz (subsequently placed in three US Grade 3 stakes). The second dam, Valentine Waltz (by Be My Guest) won the French 1,000 Guineas and the Group 3 Nell Gwyn Stakes, was third in the 1,000 Guineas and the Coronation Stakes and is a half-sister to 6 winners. (Thurloe Thoroughbreds XLVI & Partners). *"She has a great temperament and is a particularly good-looking filly. The mare hasn't set the world alight yet but this filly moves well, she's straightforward and we like what we see. We haven't tested her yet because she was a fairly late foal".*

132. ARTAIR (IRE) ★★★★

b.c. Kodiac – Bonnie Lesley (Iffraaj).

March 1. First foal. £55,000Y. Goffs UK Premier (Doncaster). A C Elliott. The dam, a fair 2-y-o 6f and 7f winner here, won once at 3 yrs in the USA and is a half-sister to 3 winners including the very useful 5f (at 2 yrs) and Group 3 6f Prix de Meautry winner Coulsty. The second dam, Hazium (by In The Wings), a modest Irish 10f and 11f winner of 3 races, is a half-sister to 3 winners. (Secular Stagnation & Partner). *"We like him a lot, he's a three-parts brother to Coulsty who was a decent sprinter and he'll be one of our early birds. Racy, stocky and exactly what you would expect from the pedigree. Given how well the Kodiacs sold I think we did quite well to get him for that price".*

133. AT PEACE (IRE) ★★★
b.f. Australia – Cherrington (Lope De Vega). February 7. First foal. 75,000Y. Tattersalls October Book 1. Rabbah Bloodstock. The dam is an unraced half-sister to the Group 1 1m Sussex Stakes, Group 1 1m Queen Anne Stakes and Group 2 7f Champagne Stakes winner Toronado. The second dam, Wana Doo (by Grand Slam), a French 2-y-o 1m winner, is a half-sister to 4 winners including the Group 1 1m Racing Post Trophy and Group 2 1m Beresford Stakes winner Casamento. (Saif Ali). *"We haven't done a lot with her but she's strong and well-made. We like her and she's the most forward of the Australia's I've got. It's 'so far so good' and with a pedigree like hers there's certainly a licence for her to be ok".*

134. DINAH WASHINGTON (IRE) ★★
ch.f. Australia – Gainful (Gone West). March 23. Sixth foal. €70,000Y. Goffs Orby. Not sold. Half-sister to the quite useful Listed-placed 6f (at 2 yrs) to 8.5f winner Dornoch and to the minor French 9f winner Re Employ (both by Mizzen Mast). The dam, the French 2-y-o 1m winner, was Listed-placed three times and is a half-sister to 4 winners including the Australian Group 3 winner Index Linked. The second dam, Fully Invested (by Irish River), a useful 2-y-o 7f winner, is a half-sister to 9 winners including the Group 3 winners Multiplex and Memorise. (Chelsea Thoroughbreds – Mad About The Boy). *"She hasn't come in yet but she was a lovely filly at the sales and the sire line crossed with Gone West has done well for me in the past. She's due to come in shortly".*

135. EAGLES BY DAY ★★
b.br.c. Sea The Stars – Missunited (Golan). April 28. First foal. 125,000 foal. Tattersalls December. Joe Foley. The dam won 12 races from 4 to 7 yrs including the Group 3 Lillie Langtry Stakes and two Listed events and was placed in the Group 1 Ascot Gold Cup and Group 1 Prix Royal-Oak. The second dam, Lets Clic Together (by Don't Forget Me), a quite useful 7f to 12f winner of 3 races, is a half-sister to 7 winners. (Clipper Logistics). *"He hasn't come in yet but I know they like him a lot at the pre-training yard in Ireland. I saw him at the stud and the owner very kindly said he'd send him to me. A lovely, quality horse but a staying type for next year".*

136. EIGHTSOME REEL ★★★★
b.c. Iffraaj – Set To Music (Danehill Dancer). March 1. First living foal. The dam, a dual Listed 13f winner and second in the Group 2 Park Hill Stakes, is a half-sister to 3 winners including the fairly useful Listed-placed 10f winner Zarafsha. The second dam, Zarabaya (by Doyoun), is an unraced sister to the Listed winner and Group 2 Blandford Stakes second Zafadola. (The Queen). *"We like him, the dam was lucky for us and although she took a long time to come to hand this horse seems pretty forward in the way he goes and in his attitude. Presumably that's the influence of Iffraaj".*

137. FAST ENDEAVOUR ★★★
b.f. Pastoral Pursuits—Scented Garden (Zamindar). February 15. Sixth foal. £6,500Y. Goffs UK Silver. F Barberini & MPR. Sister to the minor Italian 3-y-o winner Royal Black and half-sister to the fair 5f (including at 2 yrs) and 6f winner Waking Warrior (by Sleeping Indian). The dam is an unraced half-sister to 6 winners. The second dam, April Lee (by Lyphard), a modest 2-y-o 7f winner, is a half-sister to 2 winners. (Middleham Park Racing CII & Partner 2). *"She's a good-looking, good bodied filly and the agent who bought her says she's a dead ringer for one of the sire's best progeny Rose Blossom. She's done nothing but please and I think she could be pretty useful".* TRAINER'S BARGAIN BUY

138. HEARTBREAK HOTEL ★★★
b.f. Le Havre – Daliana (Verglas). February 17. Fourth foal. 110,000Y. Tattersalls October Book

2. John Ferguson. Half-sister to the fair 2-y-o 6f winner My Dear Baby (by Arcano). The dam, a moderate 7f fourth placed maiden, is a half-sister to 8 winners including the dams of the Group winners Up In Time and Summer Fete. The second dam, Up And About (by Barathea), a fair 14.8f winner, is a half-sister to 9 winners including the Listed Atalanta Stakes winner and dual Group 1 placed Musicanna and to the unplaced dam of the champion European 3-y-o sprinter Overdose. (The Hon Mrs J. M. Corbett & Mr Christopher Wright). *"She hasn't been in that long and while she won't be early she's quite forward-going and I can see her coming to hand sooner than her pedigree suggests. We've been lucky for the owners and I hope this is another one".*

139. HEATHERDOWN (IRE) ★★★
b.c. Morpheus – Hapipi (Bertolini). April 19. Fifth foal. 30,000Y. Tattersalls October Book 2. A C Elliott. Half-brother to the quite useful 6f and 7f winner of 3 races at 2 and 3 yrs Notalot (by Sir Prancealot) and to the fair 2-y-o 5f and 7f winner Danot (by Zebedee). The dam is an unraced sister to the smart Group 3 6f Duke Of York Stakes and Listed 6f and 7f winner of 8 races Prime Defender. The second dam, Arian Da (by Superlative), a fair 2-y-o 5f winner, is a full or half-sister to 7 winners. (The Heatherdonians). *"I hope this works out because he's named after my prep school! We had his half-brother Notalot who improved significantly as the season went on. He was given that name because he wasn't any good early on! This is a very good-looking horse – better looking than his brother – and we'll be happy if he's as good as him. He's robust, quite sharp and strong".*

140. L'UN DEUX TROIS (IRE) ★★
ch.c. Mastercraftsman – Moment Juste (Pivotal). April 24. Third foal. €50,000Y. Goffs Orby. Richard Frisby. The dam, a fair 12f to 14.5f placed maiden, is a half-sister to 6 winners including the Group 3 12f St Simon Stakes winner High Pitched, the Group 2 Scottish Derby winner Imperial Stride and the dual Listed winner Zero Tolerance. The second foal, Place de l'Opera (by Sadler's Wells), a fairly useful Listed-placed dual 12f winner, is a half-sister to 9 winners including the Irish 2,000 Guineas winner Indian Haven

and the Group 1 Gran Criterium winner Count Dubois. (Mrs G. Rowland-Clark & Mr Timmy Hyde). *"A nice, easy-moving colt that will take a bit of time but we like what we see. He's a particularly good mover, but it's a middle distance family and he's more about next year really".*

141. LADY AIRA ★★★
b.f. Kodiac – Dot Hill (Refuse To Bend). March 14. Fifth foal. 125,000Y. Tattersalls October Book 2. A C Elliott. Half-sister to the fairly useful Listed-placed 5f winner of 4 races at 2 to 5 yrs Union Rose (by Stimulation) and to the quite useful 2017 2-y-o triple 6f winner Amazing Alice (by Sayif). The dam is an unraced half-sister to 3 winners including the very useful 6f (at 2 yrs) and 5f winner of 4 races and Group 2 6f Gimcrack Stakes second Taajub. The second dam, Purple Tiger (by Rainbow Quest), is an unraced half-sister to 7 winners including the German Group 2 winner and Italian Group 1 second Notability and the Group 3 7f Prix La Force winner Simon De Montfort. (Amo Racing Limited). *"We like her and she's very speedy and a particularly good mover from a good, fast family. I think she'll be relatively early and she's all speed".*

142. LOGIE BAIRD ★★★
b.c. Mastercraftsman – Strategy (Machiavellian). March 26. Eighth foal. 75,000Y. Tattersalls October Book 2. R Frisby. Half-brother to the US Grade 3 winner and Grade 1 placed Justaroundmidnight, to the fairly useful 1m (at 2 yrs) and 11f winner Towerlands Park (both by Danehill Dancer), the useful Irish 2-y-o 5f winner and Group 3 6f Anglesey Stakes third Boris Grigoriev (by Excellent Air) and the fair 1m (at 2 yrs) and 10f winner Havelovewilltravel (by Holy Roman Emperor). The dam, a quite useful 10f and 11f winner, is a half-sister to 2 winners. The second dam, Island Story (by Shirley Heights), a quite useful 10f winner, is a half-sister to 6 winners. (Mr J. Barnett & Mrs P. Shanahan). *"He's a horse that won't be early but he's good-bodied with a good temperament. On the back burner at the moment, but he should have a future as the season unfolds".*

143. LORCAN ★★★★
gr.c. Dark Angel – Vallado (Clodovil).

March 31. First foal. £72,000Y. Goffs UK Premier (Doncaster). F Barberini /Alex Elliott (private sale). The dam, an Irish 2-y-o 6f and 6.5f winner, is a half-sister to 4 winners. The second dam, Knapton Hill (by Zamindar), a quite useful 7f winner at 3 yrs, is a half-sister to 2 winners. (Mr A Cohen Mr D Hanafin & Mr S Kaznowski). *"A sharp 2-y-o type, he's in our early brigade and he'll be racing in April. Quite a nice horse with plenty of speed, it's a fast family and he looks just as you would imagine from his pedigree".*

144. MANIC MONDAY ★★★★★
b.f. Declaration Of War – Bohemian Dance (Dansili). February 23. First foal. €52,000Y. Goffs Orby. A.C Elliott. The dam, a fair 12f winner here, won twice at 4 yrs in the USA and is a half-sister to four other minor winners. The second dam, Islington (by Sadler's Wells), was a high-class winner of 6 races including the Group 1 Yorkshire Oaks (twice), the Grade 1 Filly and Mare Turf and the Group 1 Nassau Stakes. She is a half-sister to the smart stayer Election Day, the German Group 1 winner Greek Dance and the Group 3 winner New Morning. (Mr C. Wright & Miss E. Asprey). *"I like this filly, she's very nice. The second dam is Islington and something's got to happen from this family one day, especially as Islington had twelve daughters. This filly looks quite sharp considering her middle-distance family and she could just be a good one. I really like her, I think we bought her very well and she'll be out in the second half of the season. It's a lovely page and she's a beauty too".*

145. MASTER BREWER (FR) ★★★★
b.c. Reliable Man – Quenching (Street Cry). February 29. Second foal. 85,000Y. Arqana Deauville October. Alex Elliott. The dam, a minor winner at 3 yrs in France, is a half-sister to 3 winners including Whitman (Listed Ripon Champion 2-y-o Trophy). The second dam, Sundrop (by Sunday Silence), won the Group 3 8.5f Princess Elizabeth Stakes and the US Grade 3 9f Cardinal Handicap and is a half-sister to 6 winners. (The Fitzrovians 2 & Fair Salinia Ltd). *"The sire has very good stats in Germany and France so I was persuaded to buy him and I'm glad we did. From a good family, the second dam was very useful and I think this is a nice colt. He's very strong, well-*made with good bone and on this evidence you can see why the sire has done so well".*

146. NAHEMA ★★ ♠
b.f. Dubawi – Sariska (Pivotal). March 27. Fourth foal. Half-sister to the fairly useful Listed-placed 8.5f winner Snow Moon (by Oasis Dream). The dam, a 7f (at 2 yrs), Epsom Oaks, Irish Oaks and Group 2 Middleton Stakes winner, is a half-sister to the 8.7f (at 2 yrs), 10f and Listed 14f winner Gull Wing. The second dam, Maycocks Bay (by Muhtarram), a useful 14f Listed winner, is a half-sister to several winners including the useful 7f and 1m winner (at 2 yrs) and Listed 10.3f placed 3-y-o Indian Light. (Lady Bamford). *"She's about to come into the yard soon and is supposed to be a big, strong filly, but we haven't met yet".*

147. NUREMBERG (IRE) ★★★★
b.c. War Command – Mackenzie's Friend (Selkirk). February 23. Tenth foal. £35,000Y. Goffs UK Premier (Doncaster). Alex Elliott (private sale). Half-brother to 6 winners including the French 2-y-o 10f winner and Listed-placed Sallen, the modest 7f winner Represent Yourself (both by Oratorio), the quite useful 2-y-o 1m winner Ballard Down (by Canford Cliffs), the fair 12f winner Juno The Muffinman (by Holy Roman Emperor) and the fair 12f and hurdles winner Know The Law (by Danehill Dancer). The dam is an unraced half-sister to 6 winners including the Group 2 winners Allied Powers and Dane Friendly. The second dam, Always Friendly (by High Line), winner of the Group 3 12f Princess Royal Stakes, was second in the Group 1 Prix Royal-Oak. (The Fitzrovians 2). *"I was really keen on him at the sale because he was a particularly striking individual. He has a very good temperament, great limbs, great mind, he moves well and the mare's got a good record. It's a family we've done well with and he's a straightforward, good-moving horse. He's also a well-named colt because if you go to court and defend yourself without a lawyer you're 'Mackenzie's Friend' and of course Nuremberg is synonymous with the war trials".*

148. PORCELAIN GIRL (IRE) ★★★
ch.f. Exceed And Excel – Dresden Doll (Elusive Quality). April 29. Sister to the fairly useful 5f

and 6f winner of 5 races Dubai One and to the quite useful 6f and 7f winner Role Player and half-sister to the smart 1m (at 2 yrs) and UAE Group 2 12f winner Prize Money (by Authorized). The dam, a fair 2-y-o 5f winner, is a half-sister to 9 winners including the Irish 1,000 Guineas, Coronation Stakes and Nassau Stakes winner Crimplene, the Group 3 12.3f Chester Vase winner Dutch Gold and the 10f winner Group 2 12f Lancashire Oaks second Loyal Spirit. The second dam, Crimson Conquest (by Diesis), a quite useful 2-y-o 6f winner, is a half-sister to the US stakes winner Sword Blade. (Sheikh Marwan Al Maktoum). *"She goes well, she's athletic and the mare has done well".*

149. PRETTY POLLYANNA ★★★★
b.f. Oasis Dream – Unex Mona Lisa (Shamardal). February 25. Third foal. 50,000Y. Tattersalls October Book 1. Not sold. Half-sister to the quite useful 2017 2-y-o 7f winner Roulette (by Poet's Voice) and to the fair 7f winner Preobrajenska (by Paco Boy). The dam is an unraced half-sister to 5 winners including the US Grade 3 winner Gender Agenda. The second dam, Friendlier (by Zafonic), is an unraced half-sister to the Oaks and St Leger winner User Friendly. (W. J. and T. C. O. Gredley). *"I like her, she moves very well and we had the half-sister Roulette who won at Goodwood last year. This filly is sharper, very much a 2-y-o and we like her. I can see her coming to hand pretty quickly".*

150. REGULAR ★★★★
ch.c. Exceed And Excel – Humdrum (Dr Fong). March 18. Brother to the fair 2-y-o 1m winner Elementary (by Exceed And Excel) and half-brother to the quite useful 2-y-o 6f winner Husbandry (by Paco Boy). The dam, a fairly useful 7f and 1m winner of 4 races (including at 2 yrs), is a half-sister to 6 winners including the useful Listed 6f winner of 4 races Musical Comedy. The second dam, Spinning Top (by Alzao), a useful 10f winner, is a half-sister to numerous winners including the fairly useful 3-y-o 7f and subsequent US dual 9f winner Daytime. (The Queen). *"He moves really well and he's a nice, strong, good-moving colt that'll come to hand early. We had the full brother Elementary and this colt seems the stronger of the two, so we like what we see so far. I can see him being a six/seven furlong 2-y-o".*

151. ROBERT FITZROY (IRE) ★★
b.g. Big Bad Bob – Semiquaver (Mark Of Esteem). February 28. Fifth foal. €34,000Y. Goffs Sportsmans. A C Elliott. Brother to the fair dual 12f winner Bolder Bob and half-brother to the quite useful 6f (including at 2 yrs) and 7f winner of 6 races Harwoods Volante and the fair 5f and 6f winner of 8 races Heartsong (both by Kheleyf). The dam is an unraced half-sister to 2 winners. The second dam, Dal Segno (by Sadler's Wells), won 2 minor races at 3 yrs in France and is a half-sister to 4 winners. (The Fitzrovians 2). *"A big, strong colt who is a two-year prospect because of the pedigree but he's a fine horse, not over-expensive and he's probably a similar type to his full brother Bolder Bob. We like him but he's one for much later in the season and especially next year".*

152. STARLIGHT ★★
b.f. Iffraaj – Ighraa (Tamayuz). March 23. Second foal. 160,000Y. Tattersalls October Book 1. A C Elliott. The dam, a useful French Listed 9f winner, is a half-sister to 6 winners including the multiple Listed winner (from 7f to 10f) Nashmiah and the useful 2-y-o 7f and Listed 1m winner Streets Ahead. The second dam, Frond (by Alzao), a quite useful 2-y-o 7f winner, is a half-sister to 8 winners. (Mr Edward J Ware). *"She's just gone a little bit backward on us but it's been a tough spring for some fillies. She's yet to thrive but it's very early days, she has a nice pedigree and she's by a good stallion. We're just taking our time".*

153. SWISS PEAK ★★★★ ♠
b.c. Swiss Spirit – Easy To Love (Diesis). March 25. Thirteenth foal. €21,000Y. Tattersalls October Book 3. A C Elliott. Half-brother to the fairly useful 2-y-o 7f and 1m winner and Listed-placed Easy Lover (by Pivotal), to the fair 2-y-o 7f winner Pezula Bay (by Oasis Dream), the fair 12f and 13f winner Right Of Appeal (by Dubawi) and the modest 13f winner Blinka Me (by Tiger Hill). The dam, a quite useful 4-y-o 11.5f winner, is a sister to the Oaks winner Love Divine (herself dam of the St Leger winner Sixties Icon) and a half-sister to 5 winners including the Listed winners Floreeda and Dark Promise. The second dam, La Sky (by Law Society), a useful 10f winner and second in the Group 3 Lancashire Oaks, is closely related to the Champion Stakes winner

Legal Case and a half-sister to 4 winners. (Wayne & Sarah Dale & Lordship Stud). *"We like him, he's in our early brigade and he looks well bought. The mare has basically been disappointing but they brought her out of retirement to go to Swiss Spirit and I really like this colt, he's done nothing but please. He hasn't got a chink at the moment and it's a question of whether he's good enough. A good mover, good bodied and with a good attitude".*

154. TAMOCK (IRE) ★★★ ♠

b.f. Australia – Anklet (Acclamation). January 25. Third foal. 400,000Y. Tattersalls October Book 1. A C Elliott. Closely related to the promising 2017 2-y-o 7f winner Tonkin (by Camelot). The dam ran twice unplaced and is a half-sister to 4 winners including the Grade 1 12f Canadian International and Group 2 12.5f Prix de Pomone winner Sarah Lynx and the Group 3 10f Classic Trial winner Sugar Boy. The second dam, Steel Princess (by Danehill), a winner of 3 races including the Group 3 10.5f Prix Cleopatre, is a full or half-sister to 7 winners including the US Grade 1 placed Falcon Rock. (Amo Racing Limited). *"A beautiful filly at the sales, she's just gone a bit backward on us but we're not forcing her at all, she has a good temperament, good limbs and a great physique. She's telling us she's not an early 2-y-o which we knew anyway so we're just training her in the second brigade for now".*

155. THOMAS CUBITT (FR) ★★★★

b.c. Youmzain – Helsinka (Pennekamp). April 7. Eighth foal. €60,000Y. Goffs Orby. A C Elliott. Half-brother to 4 winners including the French dual 12f winner Lorietta (by Literato) and a minor winner in the USA by Giant's Causeway. The dam, placed twice over 10f in France, is a half-sister to 6 winners notably Shamardal (Dewhurst Stakes, French 2,000 Guineas, French Derby and St James's Palace Stakes). The second dam, Helsinki (by Machiavellian), a winner and Listed placed over 10f at 3 yrs in France, is a sister to the Dubai World Cup and US Grade 1 winner Street Cry and a half-sister to 8 winners out of the Irish Oaks winner Helen Street. (Men Fae the Clyde). *"I think the sire Youmzain has punched above his weight considering the few runners he's had and this colt has a very interesting pedigree, particularly with Shamardal being in there. I think this is*

a nice colt, he's very much one that's going to be trained with next year in mind, but we like him".

156. TRIBAL COMMANDER ★★★★

gr.c. Intikhab – Jessica Ennis (English Channel). March 22. Fourth foal. £11,000Y. Tattersalls Ireland Ascot. A C Elliott. Half-brother to the French 2018 3-y-o 6.5f winner Heptathlete (by Mount Nelson), to the modest 7f (at 2 yrs) and 10f winner Bayston Hill (by Big Bad Bob) and the modest 2-y-o 7f and 1m winner Indigo (by Medican). The dam is an unraced sister to the US stakes winner Susie Bee. The second dam, Susie Cat (by Storm Cat), is an unraced sister to the US Grade 1 Hollywood Futurity winner Tactical Cat. (Highclere Thoroughbred Racing). *"Interestingly enough when the breeders of this colt sent the mare to Intikhab they did so with me in mind as a potential buyer. I had the dam but she was injured in the stalls on her debut and could never race which was sad because we thought she was a very smart filly. This colt looks nice and we like him".*

157. WELD ALDAR ★★★

ch.c. Universal – Crystal Wish (Exceed And Excel). February 20. First foal. 3,500Y. Tattersalls October Book 3. Not sold. The dam, a modest 5f placed 2-y-o, is a half-sister to a Listed-placed winner in Ireland. The second dam, Crystal Mountain (by Monashee Mountain), is an unraced half-sister to 9 winners including the US Grade 2 winner Dr Brendler. (Ahmad Abdulla Al Shaikh & Co). *"He was a buy-back at the sale for peanuts but I don't know why. He looks fine, I like him and I've even given him a Derby entry which cost more than he did! He's a fine horse and he'll have the boot to run this year for sure".*

158. YOUTHFUL ★★★★

b.c. Shamardal – Good Hope (Cape Cross). February 26. First foal. The dam, a fair 10f winner, is a half-sister to the Australian Group 1 10f winner of 7 races My Kingdom Of Fife and the useful 1m (including at 2 yrs) and 7f winner and Group 3 1m Autumn Stakes third Four Winds. The second dam, Fairy Godmother (by Fairy King), a Listed 10f winner, is a half-sister to several winners including the Group 2 12f Jockey Club Stakes winner Blueprint. (The Queen). *"I like him, he's out of a mare I trained and he gets up the hill very nicely at this early stage. We like what we see and he's one that should be up and running by mid-season because he's strong and doesn't look like a first foal".*

159. UNNAMED ★★
ch.f. Farhh – Bianca Nera (Salse). May 22. Half-sister to the fairly useful 2-y-o 7f winner and Listed placed Pietra Dura (dam of the US Grade 3 winner Turning Top), the fairly useful Listed-placed 13f winner Bite Of The Cherry (by Dalakhani), the 5f and 7f winner Glencairn Star (by Selkirk), the 9.5f winner Catalyst (by Makfi), the 6f (at 2 yrs) and 7f winner Biaraafa (by Araafa) and the winner Ever Rigg (by Dubai Destination and herself dam of the multiple Group 1 winner Postponed) – the last four only fair winners. The dam won the Group 1 7f Moyglare Stud Stakes and is half-sister to 4 winners including the dam of the dual Group 1 winner Simply Perfect. (Mr R L W Frisby). *"She only arrives here this week but I've seen her and she moves well. We've had a lot of horses for this owner of late and from this family and hopefully this will be another asset. We won't be in a rush because she was a late foal, but she's light on her feet and we'll see how we go".*

160. UNNAMED ★★★★
gr.f. Oasis Dream – Boastful (Clodovil). February 25. Second foal. The dam, a useful Listed 1m winner, is a half-sister to 4 winners including the Group 3 6f Ballyogan Stakes and dual Listed winner and Group 1 second Lesson In Humility and the Group 3 Oh So Sharp Stakes winner Poet's Vanity. The second dam, Vanity (by Thatching), a fair 5f and 6f placed maiden, is a half-sister to 6 winners including the Listed winner Ffestiniog (herself the dam of 3 stakes winners). (Clipper Logistics). *"She came in relatively recently having been very well-prepped. I think she'll come to hand early, she's not very big but she looks to have a good temperament and moves well".*

161. UNNAMED ★★★
b.c. Lope De Vega – Free Rein (Dansili). March 12. First foal. 70,000Y. Tattersalls October Book 1. Sheikh Abdullah Almalek Alsabah. The dam, a fair 7f winner, is a half-sister to 3 winners including the 2-y-o Group 1 Prix Morny and

Group 1 Middle Park Stakes winner Reckless Abandon. The second dam, Sant Elena (by Efisio), a quite useful dual 6f winner (including at 2 yrs) and then Listed-placed in Canada, is a half-sister to the US dual Grade 1 winner Ticker Tape and the Group 1 Prix Maurice de Gheest winner Brando. (Sheikh Abdullah Almalek Alsabah). *"I like him, he moves very well, he's done his first easy piece and there's speed in the pedigree. He'll be a summer 2-y-o for sure".*

JAMES BETHELL

162. CONAGLEN ★★★★
b.c. Toronado – Infamous Angel (Exceed And Excel). January 29. Fifth foal. 30,000Y. Tattersalls October Book 2. James Bethell. Half-brother to the fair 6f (at 2 yrs) and 7.5f winner of 3 races Alpine Dream (by Dream Ahead). The dam won two races at 2 yrs including the Group 2 6f Lowther Stakes and is a half-sister to 2 winners. The second dam, Evangeline (by Sadler's Wells), is an unraced half-sister to 4 winners. (Patrick Hibbert Foy). *"A very nice colt and I'd like to think he could be out in May over six furlongs. He's done everything right but we've had a tricky winter in Yorkshire and we haven't done as much with them as we would normally. This colt has a very nice temperament, goes about his work well and we're quite hopeful.*

163. HESSLEWOOD (IRE) ★★★★
b.c. Slade Power – Rochitta (Arch). April 29. Fourth foal. 35,000Y. Tattersalls October Book 1. James Bethell & Sackville/ Donald. Half-brother to the fair 10f winner Third Rock (by Hat Trick). The dam, a minor US 3-y-o winner, is a half-sister to 6 winners including the UAE Group 2 and Irish Group 3 Ballycorus Stakes winner Lord Admiral. The second dam, Lady Ilsley (by Trempolino), a winner in France and Listed-placed twice, is a sister to the winner and Grade 2 second Najecam (herself dam of the Grade 1 Breeders' Cup Juvenile winner Action This Day) and a half-sister to 5 winners. (Clarendon Thoroughbred Racing). *"He was quite a late foal but he's coming together well and we think he'll do all right. Hopefully he'll be racing in May and he's quite a strong, well put-together colt. We'll start him at five furlongs and I wouldn't think he'd get much further than six because he looks a sprinter*

type to me. He's grown a lot since we've had him and he's a very nice colt".

164. MOSS GILL (IRE) ★★★

b.c. No Nay Never – Sharaarah (Oasis Dream). February 29. Second foal. £30,000Y. Goffs UK Premier. Not sold. Half-brother to the quite useful 2017 2-y-o 6f winner Ulshaw Bridge (by High Chaparral). The dam, a quite useful 6f (at 2 yrs) and 5f winner of 4 races, is a half-sister to 3 winners including the useful 2-y-o 5f winner and dual Group 2 placed Burwaaz. The second dam, Nidhaal (by Observatory), a very useful 2-y-o Listed 6f winner and second in the Group 3 6f Princess Margaret Stakes, is a half-sister to 4 winners. *"He's quite small and although I'd like to get him out early we X-rayed his knees the other day and they weren't as closed as we'd have liked. Maybe he's got a bit of growing to do but he's never going to be that big. It's a speedy pedigree and all things considered I doubt him getting much further than five furlongs. He's quite sharp and goes nicely".*

165. RICH APPROACH (IRE) ★★★

b.c. Dawn Approach – Kiss Me Goodbye (Raven's Pass). February 3. Second foal. 42,000Y. Tattersalls October Book 2. James Bethell. The dam, a French 3-y-o 7f winner, is a half-sister to 5 winners including the French Listed 1m winner Madhya and to the Listed winner and triple Group 3 placed Wilki. The second dam, Khumba Mela (by Hero's Honor), won the Group 3 Prix Chloe and the Grade 3 Noble Damsel Handicap and is a half-sister to 3 winners. *"He had a little setback and I shouldn't think we'll see him out before June. He's very powerful, well put-together and he'll start at six furlongs".*

166. SOPHIA MARIA ★★

b.f. Swiss Spirit – Malelane (Prince Sabo). February 16. Sixth living foal. 13,000Y. Tattersalls October Book 3. James Bethell. Half-sister to the fair dual 7f winner at 2 and 3 yrs Novinophobia (by Showcasing), to the quite useful 5f and 6f winner of 6 races from 2 to 5 yrs Secret Missile (by Sakhee's Secret), the modest 5f and 6f winner of 9 races Compton Prince (by Compton Place), the moderate 6f winner Magdalene Fox (by Foxwedge) and the moderate 5f to 7f winner of 7 races

Novalist (by Avonbridge). The dam, a poor 5f placed maiden, is a half-sister to 6 winners including the Group 3 Prix du Petit Couvert winner Bishops Court and the Listed winning sprinter Astonished. The second dam, Indigo (by Primo Dominie), a quite useful 2-y-o 5f winner, is a half-sister to 5 winners. (Clarendon Thoroughbred Racing). *"She should be a 2-y-o but she's a good 'doer' so it'll take a bit of time to get her fit. I couldn't say much about her really, but she'll be a sprinter when her time comes".*

167. TIE A YELLOWRIBBON ★★★

gr.f. Poet's Voice – Silver Games (Vergas). February 14. Fourth foal. Half-sister to the quite useful 2-y-o Listed-placed 6f winner and subsequent US 7.5f winner Chiringuita (by Hard Spun). The dam, a quite useful 7f (at 2 yrs) and 1m winner, is a half-sister to the Group 1 1m Falmouth Stakes and Group 2 6f Lowther Stakes winner Nahoodh. The second dam, Mise (by Indian Ridge), is an unraced half-sister to 6 winners including the Group 3 Prix du Hedouville winner Not Just Swing. *"A half-sister to a winner we had called Chiringuita; she's a very nice filly that should be out in June/July. A pretty strong, quite well put-together 2-y-o".*

168. TUCSON ★★

b.c. Lawman – Bruxcalina (Linamix). April 9. Fifth foal. 25,000Y. Tattersalls October Book 2. James Bethell & Sackville/Donald. Half-brother to the very smart Group 1 6f British Champions Sprint winner of 6 races Librisa Breeze (by Mount Nelson) and to a minor French 13f winner by Dalakhani. The dam, a winner over 10f in France and Listed-placed over 11f, is a half-sister to 7 winners including the Group 3 Prix La Force winner and French Derby third Baraan. The second dam, Brusca (by Grindstone), won 3 minor races at 3 and 4 yrs in the USA and is a half-sister to 7 winners including the US Grade 1 Diana Stakes winner Somali Lemonade. (Mr D R Kilburn & Mr A N Horncastle). *"About three days after we'd bought him his half-brother Librisa Breeze won his Group 1 at Ascot, so naturally we were feeling quite pleased with ourselves. This colt is very backward, he's going to need a lot of time and I'd have thought he'd want seven furlongs to start with, probably in the autumn".*

169. WELL FUNDED (IRE) ★★★

b.f. Camelot – Malikayah (Fasliyev). March 17. Third foal. €20,000Y. Goffs Orby. Bethell & Sackville/Donald. Half-sister to the 2017 Italian 2-y-o Listed 7.5f winner Captain Cirdan (by Big Bad Bob). The dam, an Italian 2-y-o Listed 5f winner, was second in the Group 3 Premio Carlo Chiesa and is a half-sister to 6 minor winners. The second dam, Trombe (by Bering), a French winner of 3 races at 2 and 3 yrs including over a mile and Listed-placed three times from 7f to 9f, is a half-sister to 3 minor winners. (Clarendon Thoroughbred Racing). *"She's really nice, one for July/August and moves extremely well. Doing everything right at the moment, there's not an awful lot of her and considering her relatively speedy family she might be a bit earlier than we think. Looks very good value for what she cost".* TRAINER'S BARGAIN BUY

170. WINTON ★★★

b.c. Harbour Watch – Arctic Song (Charnwood Forest). April 16. Seventh foal. 20,000Y. Tattersalls October Book 2. J Bethell. Half-brother to the very useful 6f winner (at 2 yrs) and dual Listed-placed Hartley (by Lucky Story), to the useful 2-y-o 7f winner and dual Group 3 placed Robanne (by Paco Boy), the quite useful Irish dual 10f and hurdles winner Peacock's Pride (by Groom Dancer) and the fair 2-y-o 6f winner State Anthem (by Royal Applause). The dam is an unraced half-sister to 4 winners including the triple Listed winner and Group 2 6f Gimcrack Stakes second Andronikos. The second dam, Arctic Air (by Polar Falcon), a quite useful 2-y-o 7f winner, is a sister to the Listed 7f winner Arctic Char and a half-sister to the Group 2 winners Barrow Creek and Last Resort. (J. Carrick & Clarendon Thoroughbred Racing). *"He's very nice, but quite backward. We had his half-brother Hartley who broke his maiden at Catterick as a 2-y-o by seven lengths and we ended up selling him to Hong Kong. This is a very nice horse but he's grown quite a lot and I doubt him being out before August. I should think he's one for six/seven furlongs".*

171. UNNAMED ★★

b.f. Garswood – Gerash (Layman). February 13. Second foal. €23,000Y. Goffs UK Premier. Highfield Farm. The dam, a winner of 5 races at 2 yrs in France including over 7f and 1m, is a half-sister to 3 winners including the Group 3 Prix Andre Baboin winner Mobaco. The second dam, Lunaa (by Anabaa), won twice at 2 and 3 yrs in France and was Listed-placed twice and is a half-sister to 4 winners including the dam of the dual Group 1 winning stayer Gentoo. *"A quite backward but nice moving filly, she's picked up enormously since she came in; probably one for the second half of the season".*

172. UNNAMED ★★★

b.c. Garswood – Heskin (Acclamation). February 19. Second foal. The dam, a fair 2-y-o 7f winner, is a sister to 2 winners including the useful 2-y-o Listed 5f winner of 4 races and Group 3 Cornwallis Stakes third Cake and a half-sister to 4 winners. The second dam, Carpet Lady (by Night Shift), a fair dual 6f placed 2-y-o, is a half-sister to 5 winners. *"A very nice colt by first-season sire Garswood and from a sprinting family, he's much more forward than my Garswood filly and he's done really well since we've had him".*

SAEED BIN SUROOR
(GODOLPHIN)

I want to say a big "thank you" to Saeed and assistant trainer Chris Burns for picking out twenty of their best two-year-olds.

173. ALFURAT RIVER ★★★★

b.c. Dubawi – Suez (Green Desert). March 12. Half-brother to the Group 1 Fillies' Mile winner Lyric Of Light, to the quite useful 9.5f winner Andrassy Avenue (both by Street Cry), the quite useful 2-y-o 6f winner Bitter Lake (by Halling) and the moderate 7f winner De Lesseps (by Selkirk). The dam, a very useful 2-y-o Listed 6f winner, was second in the Group 1 6f Cheveley Park Stakes. The second dam, Repeat Warning (by Warning), a fair 8.3f placed 3-y-o, is a half-sister to 9 winners including the high-class winners Cezanne, Bella Colora (dam of the Prince Of Wales's Stakes winner Stagecraft) and Colorspin (dam of the Group 1 winners Zee Zee Top, Opera House and Kayf Tara). *"A typical son of Dubawi with a great attitude, he's forward-going, not over-big but strong looking".*

174. BURJ ★★★★★
b.c. Dansili – Dysphonia (AUS) (Lonhro). April 30. Half-brother to the 2017 2-y-o 1m Ascot winner, from two starts, winner Soliloquy (by Dubawi) and to the fair dual 1m winner Musical Terms (by Shamardal). The dam won 8 races including two Listed 1m events and was third in the Group 1 1m Myer Classic (all in Australia). The second dam is Stutter (by Night Shift). *"A lovely, athletic colt and a standout at this early stage, he looks to have natural ability and is very forward. A leggy colt that looks a natural athlete".*

175. CITY OF LOVE ★★★
b.f. Exceed And Excel – Heart's Content (Daylami). May 2. Half-sister to French Listed 11f winner Heartily (by Dubawi) and to the French 2-y-o dual Listed-placed 6f winner Harcourt Street (by Lonhro). The dam is an unplaced half-sister to the French Group 3 winner and Group 1 Grand Prix de Paris second Desideratum and the Listed winner Poet Laureate. The second dam, Desired (by Rainbow Quest), is an unraced half-sister to the Queen Anne Stakes and Challenge Stakes winner Charnwood Forest and to the Racing Post Trophy winner Medaaly. *"A leggy, racy, light-framed filly who is showing natural speed at present. We won't be rushed and she does appear to have natural ability".*

176. DISTANT IMAGE ★★★★
b.f. Exceed And Excel – Sander Camillo (Dixie Union). April 12. Half-sister to the quite useful 2-y-o 6f winner Porta Rosa and to the modest 1m winner Vociferous (both by Street Cry). The dam, winner of the Group 2 Cherry Hinton Stakes and the Group 3 Albany Stakes at 2 yrs, is a half-sister to 3 winners. The second dam, Staraway (by Star de Naskra), won 20 races in the USA including three Listed stakes and is a half-sister to 5 winners. *"A filly that's showing ability, she's very nice and has scope and potential. In the forward group at present despite being an April foal and she'll be the one to tell us when she's ready".*

177. DUBAI BEAUTY ★★★
b.f. Frankel – Minidress (Street Cry). February 25. Third foal. Half-sister to the fairly useful Listed-placed 1m winner Petticoat (by Cape Cross). The dam, a fairly useful 2-y-o 7f winner, was Listed-placed at 3 yrs and is a half-sister to one winner. The second dam, Short Skirt (by Diktat), a very useful winner of 4 races including the Group 3 10.4f Musidora Stakes and the Group 3 12f St Simon Stakes, was third in the Oaks and is a full or half-sister to numerous winners including Little Rock (Group 2 Princess Of Wales's Stakes) and Whitewater Affair (Group 2 Prix de Pomone). *"A lovely big filly, a bit quirky and weak at the moment. She's an absolutely beautiful mover and one to look forward to later on this season. A nice filly".*

178. DUBAI FALCON ★★★
b.c. Teofilo – Star Blossom (Good Reward). March 28. Third foal. Half-brother to the quite useful 2-y-o 6f winner White Tower (by Cape Cross). The dam is an unraced half-sister to the US Grade 1 11f winner Prince Arch and to the Group 1 National Stakes winner Kingsfort. The second dam, Princess Kris (by Kris), a quite useful 3-y-o 1m winner, is half-sister to 8 winners including the Group 3 May Hill Stakes winner Intimate Guest and to the placed dam of the US Grade 1 winner Luas Line. *"He hasn't been in the yard long because of a little injury when being broken in. A very tall, leggy, imposing colt who moves well, he's a lovely back-end of the season project and given the time to develop he'll grow into a nice horse".*

179. DUBAI LADY ★★★
b.f. Invincible Spirit – Lady Marian (Nayef). March 10. Sister to the fairly useful 7f (including at 2 yrs) and 1m winner of 4 races Forest Maiden and half-sister to the quite useful 2017 2-y-o 9f winner Loxley (by New Approach) and the minor French 8.5f winner Edwinstowe (by Shamardal). The dam won the Group 1 10f Prix de l'Opera, the Group 3 10f Prix de la Nonette and a German Group 3 11f event and is a half-sister to 4 winners including the German Group 3 winner Lucidor. The second dam, La Felicita (by Shareef Dancer), a Listed-placed winner in Germany, is a half-sister to 4 winners. *"A nice-looking filly who shows ability. Strong-looking with a nice attitude, we'll take our time with her and she could be a nice July/August type 2-y-o".*

180. DUBAI TRADITION ★★★
b.c. Medaglia d'Oro – Wavering (Refuse To

Bend). April 5. Fourth foal. Half-brother to the French 9f winner and Group 3 10.5f Prix de Flore second Switching and to the French 1m and 9.5f winner Rueing (both by Street Cry). The dam won the Group 1 10f Prix Saint-Alary and is a half-sister to 7 winners including the 2-y-o Group 1 10f Criterium de Saint-Cloud winner Mandaean and the 2-y-o 7f winner and Group 1 Fillies' Mile third Winters Moon. The second dam, Summertime Legacy (by Darshaan), winner of the 2-y-o Group 3 1m Prix des Reservoirs and third in the Group 1 Prix Saint-Alary, is a half-sister to 6 winners. *"A lovely looking colt and a good mover, but a backward type at present and one for August or September. Well put-together, he's a nice size and one to look forward to".*

181. DUBAI VIEW ★★★

b.f. Pivotal – Gonbarda (Lando). February 21. Sister to the high-class Group 1 1m Lockinge Stakes and Group 1 10f Champion Stakes winner Farhh, to the very smart Group 3 10f winner and Group 1 Champion Stakes fourth Racing History, the very useful 1m winner of 4 races and Group 3 third Basem and the fairly useful 2-y-o 1m winner Welcome Gift and half-sister to 2 winners. The dam, a German dual Group 1 12f winner, is a full or half-sister to numerous winners including Gonfilia, winner of the Group 3 8.5f Princess Elizabeth Stakes and four Listed events. The second dam, Gonfalon (by Slip Anchor), is a half-sister to several winners. *"A strong, medium-sized, well put-together filly who comes from a great family. She has a lovely temperament and will be one to appear towards the end of the season".*

182. GLOBAL HUNTER ★★★

b.c. Kodiac – Romie's Kastett (Halling). April 28. Fifth foal. 300,000Y. Tattersalls October Book 2. Godolphin. Half-brother to 3 winners including the quite useful Irish 2-y-o 1m winner Eagle Spirit (by Holy Roman Emperor) and the minor French 3-y-o winner Al Dweha (by Invincible Spirit). The dam, a quite useful Irish 9f winner, is a sister to the Group 3 Earl Of Sefton Stakes and Group 3 Sovereign Stakes winner and multiple Group 1 placed Norse Dancer and a half-sister to 8 winners. The second dam, River Patrol (by Rousillon), a fairly useful 10.2f winner, is a half-sister to 3 winners including the smart middle-

distance stayer Dry Dock and to the dams of the Group/Grade 1 winners Mail The Desert, Good Faith and Band Gipsy. *"A strong-looking, medium-sized individual, he has a nice attitude and he's a good mover with natural ability".*

183. GREAT EXAMPLE ★★★

b.c. Cape Cross – Gower Song (Singspiel). February 9. Fifth foal. 170,000 foal. Tattersalls December. John Ferguson. Brother to the useful 8.5f and 10f winner and Group 2 Park Hill Stakes second Melodious and half-brother to the moderate 14f winner Wassail (by Shamardal). The dam, a very useful Listed 10f winner here and subsequently a Group 3 12f winner in Dubai, is a half-sister to 7 winners including the Group 2 placed Prince Of Denial and the dam of the Listed winner and Oaks second Something Exciting. The second dam, Gleaming Water (by Kalaglow), a quite useful 2-y-o 6f winner, is a sister to the Group 3 Solario Stakes winner Shining Water (dam of the Group 1 Grand Criterium winner Tenby) and a half-sister to 8 winners. *"Not over-big, he's a well put-together colt and probably one for the middle of the season. Shows a good attitude at home".*

184. GREAT HUNTER ★★★

b.c. Farhh – Siyasa (Rahy). May 7. Sixth foal. 82,000Y. Tattersalls December. Godolphin. Half-brother the fairly useful 2017 2-y-o 6f winner and Group 3 Silver Flash Stakes third Dawn Delivers (by Dawn Approach) and to the fairly useful Listed-placed 7.5f and 8.5f winner Mu'Ajiza (by Pivotal). The dam, a fair dual 10f placed maiden, is a sister to 3 winners including Fantastic Light, a winner of six Group/Grade 1 events including the Breeders' Cup Turf, the Prince of Wales's Stakes and the Irish Champion Stakes and the Listed Pretty Polly Stakes winner Hi Dubai and a half-sister to 4 winners. The second dam, Jood (by Nijinsky), placed over 7f (at 2 yrs) and 10f, is a half-sister to the US Grade 1 winners Gorgeous and Seaside Attraction, and the Group/Grade 3 winners Hiaam and Key to the Moon. *"Weak at the moment, he's not over-big and is like his sire in at least one respect in that he was very difficult to break in. He's a beautiful, athletic colt and very much one for the second half of the season. Just needs to strengthen up".*

185. ISLAND JUNGLE ★★★
b.c. Teofilo – Loreto (Holy Roman Emperor).
March 9. Third foal. 200,000Y. Tattersalls
October Book 2. Godolphin. Half-brother to
the very useful Irish 2-y-o 1m winner Brutal
(by Pivotal). The dam, a quite useful dual 1m
winner, is a half-sister to 6 winners including
the Group 3 winners Cabaret and Drumfire
and, the Group 2 6f Gimcrack Stakes second
and subsequent Hong Kong stakes winner Ho
Choi. The second dam, Witch Of Fife (by Lear
Fan), a fairly useful 2-y-o 6f and 7f winner, was
Listed-placed and is a half-sister to 6 winners.
*"A good-sized colt who shows nice ability at
this stage and will be a 7f+ horse".*

186. JFOUL ★★★★
b.c. Zebedee – Worthington (Kodiac). March
7. Second foal. £70,000Y. Goffs UK Premier
(Doncaster). Stroud/Coleman. Half-brother
to the fair 2017 2-y-o 6f and 7f winner One
For June (by Arcano). The dam, a quite useful
2-y-o 5f winner, is a half-sister to 6 winners.
The second dam, Idle Fancy (by Mujtahid), a
fair Irish 3-y-o 1m winner, is a half-sister to 7
winners including the French Listed 1m winner
Danish Field and the dam of the Lancashire
Oaks winner Ela Athena. *"A very strong-looking
colt with a great attitude, he's in the forward
bunch and showing nice ability at this early
stage. One to start in May or June".*

187. LABIBA ★★★★
b.c. Dubawi – Scatina (Samum). March 21.
Fourth foal. Half-brother to the Irish 2-y-o
5f winner Saburo (by Cape Cross) and to the
modest 2m winner Blue Dune (by Invincible
Spirit). The dam, a German 7f (at 2 yrs) and
Group 2 11f winner, is a half-sister to the
Group 3 14f Lillie Langtry Stakes winner
Sevenna. The second dam, Silvassa (by
Darshaan), won over 7f in Germany and is out
of the German Oaks winner Slenderella. *"A
small, strong-looking colt, he's in the forward
group at this stage. He's showing ability and
could be running in May or June".*

188. LAND OF LEGENDS ★★★★
b.br.c. Iffraaj – Homily (Singspiel). February 19.
Third foal. Half-brother to the moderate 1m
winner Monologue (by Manduro). The dam is
an unraced half-sister to 5 winners including
the US Grade 2 7f and Grade 3 1m winner

Rebellion. The second dam, Last Resort (by
Lahib), winner of the Group 2 7f Challenge
Stakes, is a half-sister to numerous winners
including the Group 2 winner Barrow Creek,
the useful Listed winners Arctic Char and
Heard A Whisper and the dam of the Group
2 winner Trans Island. *"Not very big, he looks
a 2-y-o type although he's an extremely laid-
back individual. He's small and very level so he
doesn't look like he's going to grow any more.
Has a lovely way about him".*

189. MILITARY TACTIC ★★★
b.c. Iffraaj – Lunar Spirit (Invincible Spirit).
February 20. First foal. 140,000Y. Tattersalls
October Book 2. Godolphin. The dam, a
fair 10f winner, is a half-sister to 5 winners
including the smart Irish 2-y-o 7f winner and
Group 1 Moyglare Stud Stakes third Kissable.
The second dam, Kitty O'Shea (by Sadler's
Wells), won over 1m on both her starts
(including at 2 yrs and a Listed event at 3
yrs) and is a sister to the Group 1 Racing Post
Trophy and Group 1 St Leger winner Brian
Boru and a half-sister to the Group 2 winners
Sea Moon and Moon Search and to the dam
of the Derby winner Workforce. *"A backward
type but a nice individual and one for seven
furlongs in July/August. He's progressing nicely
at present".*

190. PROMISE OF SUCCESS ★★★
b.f. Dansili – Summer School (Street Cry).
February 23. First foal. The dam, a 12f winner
at 3 yrs on her only start, is a half-sister to the
useful French 9f winner (at 2 yrs) and Group 3
third Franz Schubert (by Dansili). The second
dam, Measured Tempo (by Sadler's Wells), a
fairly useful Listed 10f winner, is a half-sister
to the Group 1 12f Prix du Jockey Club winner
Anabaa Blue and to the very useful Listed 10f
winner Reunite. *"A lovely, big, scopey filly with
a nice attitude, she's a backward type and still
weak so she's more of an August/September
type, but she's one to look forward to".*

191. SILENT HUNTER ★★★
b.c. Dutch Art – Yellow Rosebud (Jeremy).
March 17. Second foal. The dam, a Group
3 7.5f Concorde Stakes and Group 3 Irish
1,000 Guineas Trial winner, is a half-sister to
5 winners including the fairly useful Listed 6f
(at 2 yrs) and 10f winner and Group 3 third

Seeharn. The second dam, Nebraas (by Green Desert), is an unraced half-sister to 6 winners including the Group 1 Golden Jubilee Stakes winner Malhub. *"A good-looking colt, he's tall and leggy so he won't be rushed. He's a nice prospect for August/September time and one to look forward to".*

192. SUMMER SOLSTICE ★★★

ch.f. Toronado – Maid To Dream (Oasis Dream). March 20. Fourth foal. 85,000Y. Tattersalls October Book 2. Stroud/Coleman. Half-sister to the Group 3 6f Renaissance Stakes winner of 4 races The Happy Prince (by Rip Van Winkle). The dam, a modest dual 7f placed maiden, is a sister to the 2-y-o 6f winner and Listed-placed Run For The Hills and a half-sister to 7 winners including Maid To Perfection (herself the dam of two Listed winners). The second dam, Maid For The Hills (by Indian Ridge), a useful 2-y-o dual 6f winner including the Listed Empress Stakes, is a half-sister to 5 winners including the dams of the Group winners Stroll, Grassy, Lady In Waiting and Savannah Bay. *"A very pretty, flashy filly with a white face and four white socks. A leggy individual, she's showing natural speed at present but she'll be given all the time she needs".*

JIM BOLGER
193. ALMOST DAWN (IRE)

ch.c. New Approach – Hymn Of The Dawn (Phone Trick). April 29. Tenth foal. Brother to the Group 1 National Stakes, Dewhurst Stakes, 2,000 Guineas and St James's Palace Stakes winner Dawn Approach and to the 2-y-o Group 2 7f Futurity Stakes winner and Group 1 National Stakes second Herald The Dawn and half-brother to the fair 5f (at 2 yrs) to 7f winner Comadoir (by Medicis). The dam, placed fourth once at 2 yrs, is a half-sister to 3 winners including the Grade 1 third Galantas. The second dam, Colonial Debut (by Pleasant Colony), was placed in the USA and is a half-sister to 6 winners. (Mrs J S Bolger).

194. AMBITIOUS APPROACH (IRE)

b.c. Dawn Approach – Estiqbaal (Oasis Dream). February 29. The dam, unplaced in one start, is a half-sister to 2 winners. The second dam, Manayer (by Sadler's Wells), is an unraced half-sister to 5 winners. (Mrs J S Bolger).

195. BANDIUC EILE (IRE)

b.f. New Approach – Dream On Buddy (Oasis Dream). March 6. Half-sister to the very useful 12f and Listed 2m winner and triple Group 3 placed Twilight Payment (by Teofilo). The dam, a fair dual 1m winner, is a half-sister to the Group 2 Ribblesdale Stakes and Group 2 Royal Whip Stakes winner of 7 races Banimpire (by Holy Roman Emperor). The second dam, My Renee (Kris S), a very useful dual Listed 12f winner, was second in the Group 3 Princess Royal Stakes and is a half-sister to 5 winners including the useful 2-y-o 6f to 7f winner of 3 races Sutter's Fort. (Mrs J S Bolger).

196. CEISTIU (IRE)

b.f. Vocalised – Ceist Eile (Noverre). April 6. Sister to the Group 3 Killavullan Stakes winner Steip Amach and half-sister to the US Grade 3 winner Ceisteach (by New Approach) and the fair 9.5f winner Fiuntach (by Intense Focus). The dam, a fair Irish 9.5f placed maiden, is a half-sister to 2 minor winners. The second dam, Sharafanya (by Zafonic), is an unraced half-sister to 4 winners including the German Group 2 winner Giant Sandman. (Mrs J S Bolger).

197. CERRO BAYO (IRE)

b.f. Dansili – Villarrica (Selkirk). January 20. Seventh foal. Sister to the Group 2 10f Prix Guillaume d'Ornano winner Vancouverite and half-sister to the very useful 1m (at 2 yrs) and subsequent UAE Group 2 9.5f and Group 3 9.5f winner Khawlah (by Cape Cross). The dam, a fair 10f and 11f winner, is a half-sister to 7 winners including Masterstroke (Group 2 12.5f Grand Prix de Deauville. The second dam, Melikah (by Lammtarra), won the Listed 10f Pretty Polly Stakes and was third in the Oaks. She is a half-sister to the outstanding colt Sea The Stars, to the outstanding sire Galileo (both Derby winners) and the dual Group 1 winner Black Sam Bellamy. (Godolphin).

198. DATHULACHT (IRE)

b.f. Teofilo – Napping (Danzig). March 2. Half-sister to the fairly useful Irish 2-y-o 6f winner and 5f Listed placed Purple Glow (by Orientate) and to the minor US 2-y-o winner Becalm (by Dixie Union). The dam, a minor US 2-y-o winner, is a sister to the Grade 1 Go For Wand Stakes and the Grade

2 Astarita Stakes winner Easy Now and a half-sister to 7 winners including Easy Goer (nine Grade 1 wins in the USA) and the US Grade 1 winner Cadillacing (herself dam of the Grade 1 winner Strolling Along). The second dam, Relaxing (by Buckpasser), won two Grade 1 events in the USA and was a champion older mare. (Mrs J S Bolger).

199. EXCESS FEES (IRE)
b.c. Lawman – Solas Na Greine (Galileo). May 8. Third foal. Half-brother to the very useful Group 3 1m Park Express Stakes winner Rehn's Nest (by Authorized). The dam, a fairly useful Irish 2-y-o 7f winner, is a half-sister to 2 winners including the fairly useful Irish 1m to 11f winner Coolcullen Times. The second dam, Key To Coolcullen (by Royal Academy), is an unraced half-sister to numerous winners including the Group 1 6f Phoenix Stakes winner Eva Luna and the Group 3 1m Futurity Stakes winner Cois Na Tine. (Mrs J S Bolger).

200. FERRUM ♠
ch.f. Sea The Moon – Claiomh Solais (Galileo). April 5. Third foal. €100,000Y. Goffs. BBA (Ire). Half-sister to the quite useful 7f and 9f winner Proud Sky (by Acclamation). The dam, a very useful Irish 1m winner and dual Group 3 placed, is a sister to the smart 2-y-o dual Group 3 6f winner and 1,000 Guineas second Cuis Ghaire, to the Group 3 9f winner Scintillula and the Irish 2-y-o 7f winner and Group 1 Coronation Stakes second Gile Na Greine. The second dam, Scribonia (by Danehill), is an unraced half-sister to 6 winners including the 2-y-o Listed 6f winner and dual Group 1 placed Luminata.

201. FLOW OF WORDS (IRE)
b.c. Vocalised – Danemarque (Danehill). February 21. Thirteenth foal. €36,000Y. Tattersalls Ireland September. Bobby O'Ryan. Half-brother to 6 winners including the useful Irish Listed-placed 2-y-o 5f winner Whip Rule, the Irish 2-y-o 1m winner Roches Cross, the fair Irish 6f winner Whip Mark (all by Whipper) and the quite useful Irish 7f winner Plamas (by Teofilo). The dam ran unplaced in Australia and is a half-sister to 7 winners including the Listed winners Lady Shipley and Ellie Ardensky and to the unraced dam of the Group 3 Solario Stakes and US dual Grade

2 winner Brave Act. The second dam, Circus Ring (by High Top), a joint-champion 2-y-o filly and winner of 3 races at 2 yrs including the Group 2 Lowther Stakes, was a half-sister to 7 winners. (Mrs J S Bolger).

202. GEOLAI (IRE)
ch.f. New Approach – Maria Lee (Rock Of Gibraltar). March 10. Fourth foal. €200,000Y. Goffs Orby. BBA (Ire). Sister to the useful dual Listed 10f winner at 2 and 3 yrs Glamorous Approach. The dam ran once unplaced and is a half-sister to 2 minor winners. The second dam, Flida (by Royal Academy), a winner, is a sister to a Listed winner and a half-sister to the dam of the Group 1 Dewhurst Stakes winner and sire Teofilo. (Mrs J S Bolger).

203. HARRIET TUBMAN (IRE)
ch.f. Dubawi – Saoirse Abu (Mr Greeley). March 8. Half-sister to the fairly useful 1m (at 2 yrs) to 12f and hurdles winner Ennistown (by Authorized) and to the quite useful 12f winner Above Normal (by Street Cry). The dam, winner of the Group 1 Moyglare Stud Stakes and Group 1 Phoenix Stakes at 2 yrs, was third in the 1,000 Guineas. The second dam, Out Too Late (by Future Storm), is an unraced half-sister to the dam of the Oaks and Irish Derby winner Balanchine. (Godolphin).

204. NATIONAL IDENTITY (IRE)
b.f. New Approach – Irish Question (Giant's Causeway). February 28. Half-sister to the 2-y-o Group 1 1m Criterium International winner Loch Garman (by Teofilo) and to the quite useful Irish 2-y-o 5f winner Eireannach (by Rock Of Gibraltar). The dam, a fair Irish 1m winner, is a half-sister to 2 winners. The second dam, Key To Coolcullen (Royal Academy), is an unraced half-sister to numerous winners including the Group 1 6f Phoenix Stakes winner Eva Luna and the Group 3 1m Futurity Stakes winner Cois Na Tine. (Mrs J S Bolger).

205. POISED FOR A CHANGE (IRE)
b.f. Pour Moi – Teo's Sister (Galileo). February 25. Half-sister to the modest 10.5f winner Teo's Music (by Intense Focus). The dam, a quite useful Irish 7f winner, is a sister to 2 winners including the champion 2-y-o colt and Group 1 Dewhurst Stakes and Group 1 National Stakes winner Teofilo. The second dam,

Speirbhean (by Danehill), an Irish Listed 1m winner, is a half-sister to numerous winners including the Irish Listed 9f winner Graduated. (Mrs J S Bolger).

206. PRIMA LUX (IRE)

b.c. Dawn Approach – Imeall Na Speire (Galileo). February 28. Half-sister to the 2-y-o 7f winner and Group 3 7f CL & MF Weld Park Stakes second Legitimus (by Lawman). The dam is an unraced sister to 2 winners including the Group 3 12f Blue Wind Stakes and 9.5f Listed winner Galatee. The second dam, Altana (by Mountain Cat), is an unplaced half-sister to the top-class Grade 1 10f Breeders Cup Classic, Group 1 9f Prix d'Ispahan and Group 2 10f Prix Eugene Adam winner Arcangues and the very useful Group 3 10f Prix de Psyche winner and French 1,000 Guineas and Prix de Diane placed Agathe. (Mrs J S Bolger).

207. SLANEY SAND (IRE)

ch.c. Dawn Approach – Scribonia (Danehill). February 14. Eleventh foal. Half-brother to 6 winners including the Irish 2-y-o 7f winner, Coronation Stakes second and 1,000 Guineas third Gile Na Greine, the 2-y-o dual Group 3 6f winner and 1,000 Guineas second Cuis Ghaire, the Group 3 9f Meld Stakes winner and Group 1 Moyglare Stud Stakes second Scintillula, the smart Listed 12f winner The Major General and the Irish 1m winner and dual Group 3 placed Claiomh Solais (all by Galileo). The dam is an unraced half-sister to 7 winners including the 2-y-o Listed 6f winner and dual Group 1 placed Luminata. The second dam, Smaoineamh (by Tap On Wood), a 2-y-o 6f winner, is a half-sister the champion sprinter Double Form.

208. SMART FLIES (IRE)

ch.f. Dawn Approach – Take Flight (Pivotal). February 14. Fourth foal. €55,000Y. Goffs Orby. Not sold. Half-sister to the 2017 Irish 6f placed 2-y-o Impactful (by Iffraaj) and to the 2-y-o Group 3 6f Round Tower Stakes winner and Group 2 Criterium de Maisons-Laffitte third Smash Williams (by Fracas). The dam, a fair 2-y-o 5f winner, is a half-sister to 6 winners including the Irish 1,000 Guineas winner Saoire. The second dam, Polish Descent (by Danehill), is an unraced half-sister to 4 winners. (Mrs J S Bolger).

209. THE HALL (IRE)

ch.c. Teofilo – Halla Siamsa (Montjeu). May 27. Brother to the very smart 2-y-o Group 1 7f Dewhurst Stakes winner Parish Hall, to the useful 2-y-o 1m winner and Group 2 Futurity Stakes third Hall Of Fame, the fairly useful Listed-placed 9f (at 2 yrs) and 10f winner Siamsaiocht and the quite sueful 10f winner Ringside Support. The dam, a quite useful Irish 10f winner, is a half-sister to the Group 2 Irish Derby Trial winner Light Heavy. The second dam, Siamsa (by Quest For Fame), a fair Irish 9f and 11f winner, is a half-sister to 4 winners. (Mrs J S Bolger).

210. TIDAL ACTION (IRE)

b.f. Cape Cross – Attasliyah (Marju). February 11. Ninth foal. Half-sister to the 2-y-o Group 3 6f Round Tower Stakes and subsequent US winner Rabatash, to the moderate 6f winner of 4 races Joe Le Taxi (both by Johannesburg) and the fair dual 6f winner Patternmaker (by Elnadim). The dam is an unraced half-sister to 8 winners including the Irish Group 3 winner Windsor Castle and the Irish Listed winner Anna Karenina (dam of the dual Group 2 winner Battle Of Marengo) and the Group 3 Queen Mary Stakes second Al Ihsas. The second dam, Simaat (by Mr Prospector), a fair 1m winner, is a half-sister to 2 winners. (Mrs J S Bolger).

211. VIATICUS (IRE)

b.c. Teofilo – Toirneach (Thunder Gulch). March 12. Fourth foal. Sister to the Group 1 Irish 1,000 Guineas and Yorkshire Oaks winner Pleascach and half-sister to the fair dual 10f winner Brontide (by Vocalised). The dam, a fairly useful Irish 7f (at 2 yrs) and 10f winner, is a half-sister to 2 minor winners in the USA. The second dam, Wandering Pine (by Country Pine), won at 3 yrs in the USA and is a half-sister to 4 winners including the Listed winner and high-class broodmare Drina (the dam of 3 Group winners including the dual US Grade 1 winner Spain). (Mrs J S Bolger).

212. WESTERN DAWN (IRE)

b.c. Dawn Approach – Yes Oh Yes (Gone West). March 13. Half-sister to the quite useful 7f winner of 4 races at 2 and 4 yrs Theodorico (by Teofilo). The dam is an unraced half-sister to 4 winners including the Group/Grade 3 placed Aaroness and Sumba Sunset. The second dam, Diamonds For Lil (by Summer Squall), a minor US 2-y-o winner, is a half-sister to 5 winners. (Mrs J S Bolger).

MARCO BOTTI

213. BRANDON (FR) ★★★★ ♠
b.c. Showcasing – Be Released (Three Valleys). January 24. First foal. £65,000Y. Goffs UK Premier (Doncaster). McKeever/ Ferguson. The dam is an unraced half-sister to the Group 1 Haydock Sprint Cup and Group 1 7f Prix de la Foret winner Gordon Lord Byron. The second dam, Boa Estrela (by Intikhab), is an unraced half-sister to 5 winners including the smart Irish Group 3 7f and 1m winner Cheyenne Star. (Mr Manfredini, Mr J Allison & Mr D Fass). *"On pedigree he should be a precocious type because there's speed in the family. He looked quite strong at the sales and hasn't disappointed since because he's done really well. He seems a straightforward horse and we'll push on with him with a view to running him by the beginning of May. Built like a sprinter, he has a good attitude and we like him".*

214. BREATH OF SPRING ★★★
br.c. Bated Breath – Welcome Spring (Lawman). January 26. First foal. €70,000Y. Tattersalls Ireland September. Bobby O'Ryan/ Marco Botti. The dam is an unraced half-sister to 4 winners including the Irish Group 3 winner Flowers Of Spring. The second dam, Albaiyda (by Brief Truce), is an unraced half-sister to 5 winners, notably the top-class Irish Derby and King George winner Alamshar. (Excel Racing & Partner). *"He cost a bit more than we normally spend at the sales but he's a strong colt. Not the biggest, but in my experience the Bated Breath's take a bit of time and this horse is not ready to be stepped up into fast work just yet. He won't run until the summer and as he's quite laid back at present I can't say what trip will suit him".*

215. CAPLA ROCK (IRE) ★★★
br.f. Society Rock – Rublevka Star (Elusive Quality). April 17. Fifth foal. £42,000Y. Goffs UK Premier (Doncaster). Jamie Lloyd. Half-sister to the fairly useful 7f (at 2 yrs) and dual 10f winner Novoman (by Sir Prancealot) and to a minor 3-y-o winner in Germany

by Zebedee. The dam, a moderate 2-y-o 5f winner, is a half-sister to 3 winners including the South African Listed stakes winner Distance Done. The second dam, Al Desima (by Emperor Jones), a fairly useful 2-y-o 7f winner, subsequently won in the USA, was third in the Grade 1 Yellow Ribbon Stakes and is a half-sister to 9 winners. *"I really liked her at the sales where I thought she was very athletic. She hasn't disappointed us at all and has done very well physically. Her half-brother Novoman was trained by Mr Haggas and he's a useful sort. The filly is showing speed and is one of the group of 2-y-o's that we've stepped up into fast work and she's taken it really well, so she could be one of our first runners, quite possibly over five furlongs in May. I haven't trained many by this sire but they seem to have good attitudes and are straightforward horses".*

216. DON JUPP (USA) ★★★★
b.c. More Than Ready – Dame Ellen (Elusive Quality). February 8. Fifth foal. $50,000Y. Keeneland September. Global Equine Group. The dam, a minor US stakes winner, is a half-sister to the Group 3 Winter Derby winner of 9 races Gentleman's Deal and the Irish 2-y-o 7f winner and Group 3 Gallinule Stakes second Spanish Harlem. The second dam, Sleepytime (by Royal Academy), won the 1,000 Guineas and is a sister to the Group 1 1m Sussex Stakes winner Ali Royal and a half-sister to the dual Group 1 winner Taipan. (Gute Freunde Partnership). *"He's quite a big, immature type and he'll take a bit of time. A lovely horse with a good pedigree, he moves nicely and I can see him being a 2-y-o from the midsummer onwards. He has a great temperament and we like him".*

217. IMPRESSIONABLE ★★★
b.f. Exceed And Excel – Appealing (Bertolini). April 29. Second foal. Half-sister to unplaced 2017 2-y-o Elusif (by Elusive Quality). The dam, a fairly useful dual 7f winner at 2 and 3 yrs, was third in the Group 3 Oak Tree Stakes and second in the Grade 2 Yellow Ribbon Handicap. She is a half-sister to the 2-y-o Group 3 5f Cornwallis Stakes winner Electric Waves. The second dam, Radiant Energy (by Spectrum), a 1m winner at 3 yrs, is a half-sister to 6 winners. (Miss Y. M. G. Jacques). *"The second foal of the dam*

who I trained and who unfortunately died after foaling this filly. Not a precocious type, she's still a bit weak and unfurnished so we won't see her on the track until the second part of the season. A good mover, she's a half-sister to Elusif who we also have here and although he hasn't won yet I think he's capable of doing so".

218. MONIE LOVE (USA) ★★★★
b.br.f. English Channel – Bella Bandita (Dynaformer). April 11. Third foal. $57,000Y. Keeneland September. Global Equine Group. The dam, a minor US placed 3-y-o, is a half-sister to a stakes-placed winner. The second dam, Gourmet Girl (by Cee's Tizzy), won the Apple Blossom Handicap, Vanity Handicap and Milady Breeders' Cup Handicap (all US Grade 1 events) and is a half-sister to 5 winners. *"A good-looking filly, I wasn't over-keen on the stallion at first but I have to say we're very pleased with this filly. Since she's been here she's kept on improving, she's very light on her feet and is very straightforward. Being out of a Dynaformer mare I don't think she'll be a sprinter, but at the same time she shows class so maybe she's just mature and will be ready for a step up in her work in the spring".* The sire won over $5 million including the Grade 1 Breeders' Cup Turf and has sired three Grade 1 winners.

219. MY MAHARANI ★★★
b.f. Rip Van Winkle – Electric Feel (Firebreak). April 23. Second foal. 26,000Y. Tattersalls October Book 3. Marco Botti. The dam, a useful Listed 7f winner and second in the Group 3 Oh So Sharp Stakes, is a half-sister to 5 winners. The second dam, Night Gypsy (by Mind Games), a fair 2-y-o 5f winner, is a sister to 2 winners including the Listed 2-y-o winner On The Brink and a half-sister to 4 winners including the Listed winner and dual Group 3 placed Eastern Romance. *"I used to train the dam who did so well for us and this filly reminds me of her. She's not the biggest but she's very athletic and although Rip Van Winkle's produce can be a bit tricky she's very straightforward. We're already stepping up her work and there's speed in the family so she could be out in May".*

220. SIENNA ★★★
ch.f. Toronado – Wakeup Little Suzy (Peintre

Celebre). February 21. First foal. 20,000Y. Tattersalls October Book 3. Marco Botti. The dam, a fair 7f and 1m winner, is a half-sister to 2 winners. The second dam, Maramba (USA) (by Hussonet), a fairly useful 2-y-o Listed-placed 6f winner, is a half-sister to 8 winners. (Book 3 Partnership). *"A nice filly, quite forward both mentally and physically. I like her, she's the only Toronado we have and I used to train the dam who had a good attitude which seems to have been passed onto her daughter. Very straightforward, she's taking everything in her stride and shows speed. One that could be quite early".*

221. SO HI CLASS (IRE) ★★★
b.c. Dark Angel – Top Trail (Exchange Rate). April 14. Second foal. £25,000Y. Goffs UK Premier. Jamie Lloyd & Nick Bradley. Half-brother to the moderate 2017 2-y-o 1m winner Sauchiehall Street (by Mastercraftsman). The dam, a modest 6f winner, is a half-sister to 2 winners. The second dam, Trekking (by Gone West), quite useful 10f winner, is a half-sister to 4 winners including the smart dual Listed 7f winner Tantina (herself dam of the Group winners Bated Breath and Cityscape). (Nick Bradley Racing 25 & Partner). *"I was a bit concerned when we bought him because for a Dark Angel he was very cheap, but he wasn't one of the biggest at the sale. He's grown and filled out though and has turned into a nice, compact, strong colt. Showing speed, he has a great attitude and we're really pleased with him, so at this stage I'd have to say he was well-bought".* TRAINER'S BARGAIN BUY

222. SWEET CELEBRATION (IRE) ★★★
b.f. Excelebration – Snow Dust (First Defence). April 22. Second foal. 10,000Y. Tattersalls October Book 3. Jamie Lloyd. The dam is an unraced half-sister to 2 winners including the US Grade 2 and dual Grade 3 winner Starformer. The second dam, Etoile Montante (by Miswaki), won the Group 1 7f Prix de la Foret and is a half-sister to 5 winners including the Listed-placed Starfan (dam of the French Group 3 winner Glaswegian). (Ventura Racing 5 & Partner). *"I thought she was cheap because she doesn't have a bad pedigree and although she was quite weak at the sale she's grown and has done really well since. I know the sire of*

course and he wasn't a precocious type so I see this filly being one for the midsummer or later in the season. We do like her and she's got a great temperament".

223. WITHOUTDESTINATION ★★★

b.c. Epaulette – Where I Be (Dubawi). April 17. Fourth foal. €48,000Y. Tattersalls Ireland September. Stroud/Coleman & Jamie Lloyd. Half-brother to the minor Italian winner at 3 and 4 yrs Rossese (by Sixties Icon). The dam is an unplaced half-sister to 4 winners including the Group 2 Royal Lodge Stakes third On Our Way. The second dam, Singed (by Zamindar), won once at around 1m in France and is a half-sister to the French Listed winner and Group 3 placed Inhabitant. *"A nice colt, he's done really well since we bought him because he looked really unfurnished at the sale and looked like two different horses in front and behind. He's grown now, filled out and is a good-looking horse that moves well. A pleasant horse in his exercise, he does everything we ask of him and seems to cope well. I don't think he's going to be an early type because from what we saw of the Epaulette's last year they mostly seemed to take a bit of time. One for the late summer onwards I would say".*

224. UNNAMED ★★★★

gr.c. Dark Angel – Daghashah (Authorized). January 26. Second foal. 150,000Y. Tattersalls October Book 2. Mubarak Al Naemi. The dam ran twice unplaced and is a half-sister to 8 winners including the triple Listed winner Parasol and the Listed winner and triple Group 1 placed Mot Juste. The second dam, Bunting (by Shaadi), a useful 1m and 10f winner, was third in the Group 1 11f Italian Oaks and is a half-sister to 3 winners. (Mr M. Al Naemi). *"Quite a good-looking horse, he's tall and a bit unfurnished so he looks to me like a seven furlong type 2-y-o. We like him, but he's quite active and we just need to keep the lid on him so we're going quietly with him. He moves nicely and could be nice in time".*

225. UNNAMED ★★★

b.f. Dark Angel – Jellwa (Iffraaj). February 6. The dam is an unplaced half-sister to 3 minor winners and to the unraced dam of the Italian Group 3 winner Salford Secret. The second dam, Chatifa (by Titus Livius), a quite useful 1m winner, is a half-sister to 6 winners including the Group 1 winners Homecoming Queen (1,000 Guineas), Queen's Logic (Cheveley Park Stakes) and the top-class Dylan Thomas. (Sheikh M. B. K. Al Maktoum). *"A strong, stocky filly, we like her and although she was a bit difficult to break in she improved a lot once she got into a routine. A nice mover but not as forward as some of the other fillies, she shows speed and will probably be a June/July type".*

226. UNNAMED ★★★

b.c. Medaglia d'Oro – Queen Of Denmark (Kingmambo). February 5. Second foal. $50,000Y. Fasig-Tipton Kentucky September. Rabbah Bloodstock. Half-brother to the Irish 4-y-o 1m winner Robe And Honor (by Shamardal). The dam, a quite useful 11f and 12f winner, is a half-sister to 5 winners including the Group 1 12f Dubai Sheema Classic and multiple Hong Kong Group 1 winner Vengeance Of Rain and the Australian Group 1 10f winner Dizelle. The second dam, Danelagh (by Danehill), won the Group 1 6f Blue Diamond Stakes at 2 yrs in Australia. (Rabbah Racing). *"Bought in America, he's not the biggest colt but he's very agile and athletic. Being by Medaglia d'Oro I think he'll take a bit of time and I don't see him being out before the summer. He moves well, has a good temperament and we like him".*

227. UNNAMED ★★★★

ch.f. Lope De Vega – Shalwa (Galileo). March 25. Second foal. Half-sister to Heeyaam (by Galileo), unplaced on her only start at 2 yrs in 2017. The dam, a fair maiden, was placed 6 times from 10f to 12f and is a sister to the Group 2 Prix Vicomtesse Vigier and triple Group 3 winner (including at 2 yrs) Kite Wood and to the useful 9f winner and Group 2 Great Voltigeur Stakes third Odeon and half-sister to 3 winners. The second dam, Kite Mark (by Mark Of Esteem), ran once unplaced and is a half-sister to the dual Group 2 winner Madame Dubois (dam of the Group 1 winners Indian Haven and Count Dubois) and the dam of the Richmond Stakes winner Daggers Drawn. (Sheikh M. B. K. Al Maktoum). *"We have the 3-y-o Heeyaam who we think will be a nice filly. It's a good family, there's some stamina in there and this is a very athletic, flashy filly with four white legs. A filly that moves really well, we won't rush her, she's probably one for the summer onwards and we do like her".*

228. UNNAMED ★★★ ♠

ch.c. Farhh – She Wolf (Medicean). April 6. Fourth foal. 40,000Y. Tattersalls October Book 3. Stroud/Coleman. The dam ran twice unplaced and is a half-sister to 5 winners including the 1m (at 2 yrs) and Group 3 Park Express Stakes winner and Irish 1,000 Guineas third Oh Goodness Me and the useful Listed 12f winner and Group 3 Prix Gontaut-Biron third Eradicate. The second dam, Coyote (by Indian Ridge), a fairly useful Listed-placed 1m winner, is a half-sister to one winner. *"Quite a strong type, he was well-recommended by the consignor at the sale and we like him. A nice mover, he doesn't appear to be an early type but we should see him out in the second half of the season. He has a very good temperament and he's straightforward".*

KARL BURKE

229. BARASTI DANCER

gr.c. Helmet – My Girl Lisa (With Approval). March 1. Tenth foal. £35,000Y. Goffs UK Premier (Doncaster). Karl Burke / Ontoawinner. Half-brother to 7 winners including the fairly useful 2-y-o 5f winner and Group 3 third Explosive Lady, the quite useful 6f (at 2 yrs) and 7f winner Explosive Power (both by Alfred Nobel), the fair 2-y-o 6f winner Emma Dora (by Medaglia d'Oro) and the fair Irish 1m winner Giving Orders (by Encosta de Lago). The dam, a US stakes winner of 6 races at 2 to 4 yrs, is a half-sister to 4 winners. The second dam, Amynteon (by Rahy), is an unraced half-sister to 5 winners including the Canadian Grade 2 winner Benburb. (Ontoawinner 9 & Mrs E Burke).

230. CONSTANT

ch.c. Dutch Art – West Of The Moon (Pivotal). February 17. Second foal. 70,000Y. Tattersalls October Book 2. Not sold. The dam ran twice unplaced and is a half-sister to 4 winners including the 2-y-o Group 3 7f winner Horris Hill Stakes winner Evasive and the Group 3 Brigadier Gerard Stakes winner Autocratic. The second dam, Canda (by Storm Cat), is a Listed-placed half-sister to 3 winners including

the 2-y-o Group 3 5.5f Prix d'Arenburg winner Moon Driver and the Grade 2 Californian Stakes second Mojave Moon.

231. DARK HAVANA

b.c. Havana Gold – Top Of The Art (Dark Angel). March 23. First foal. €52,000Y. Tattersalls Ireland September. K Burke. The dam ran twice unplaced and is a sister to the Group 3 6f Hackwood Stakes winner Heeraat and a half-sister to the useful 2-y-o Listed 5f winner and Group 3 5f Molecomb Stakes third Ambiance. The second dam, Thawrah (by Green Desert), is an unraced half-sister to 6 winners including Malhub (Group 1 Golden Jubilee Stakes) and the US Grade 3 winner Dhaamer. (Mr D J Mackay & Mrs E Burke).

232. EXALTED ANGEL (FR)

b.c. Dark Angel – Hurryupharriet (Camacho). February 9. First foal. €150,000Y. Arqana Deauville August. Sackville/Donald. The dam, a 2-y-o Listed 5f winner, is a half-sister to the 2-y-o 7f and Group 2 Ridgewood Pearl Stakes winner and Group 1 Irish 1,000 Guineas third Devonshire. The second dam, Nova Tor (by Trans Island), a fair 5f winner of 6 races at 2 and 3 yrs, is a half-sister to 7 winners. (Mr D J MacKay & Mrs E Burke).

233. HAREEM QUEEN (IRE)

gr.f. Dark Angel – Dulcian (Shamardal). February 22. Third foal. 75,000Y. Tattersalls October Book 1. Creighton Schwartz & Sackville/Donald. Closely related to the fairly useful 2-y-o 7f winner Chessman and to the fair 6f winner Handbell (both by Acclamation). The dam is an unraced half-sister to 8 winners including the smart 6f (at 2 yrs) and Listed 8.3f winner Army Of Angels, the Group 1 Lowther Stakes second Seraphina and the dam of the dual Group 1 winner Serious Attitude. The second dam, Angelic Sounds (by The Noble Player), a minor 2-y-o 5f winner, is a half-sister to 8 winners including the Group 1 Prix de la Foret winner Mount Abu. (Mr J E Dance).

234. HIGH CONTRAST

b.f. Kingman – Parisi (Rahy). March 5. Third foal. 60,000 foal. Tattersalls December. Salcey Forest Stud. Half-sister to the fair 2017 2-y-o 1m winner Champarisi (by Champs Elysees) and to the modest 1m winner Dreaming Of

Paris (by Oasis Dream). The dam is an unraced half-sister to 2 minor winners. The second dam, Her Own Kind (by Dubai Millennium), a fairly useful 2-y-o 1m winner from two starts, is a half-sister to 7 winners including the multiple Group 1 winner (including the St Leger and Coronation Cup) Mutafaweq and the dual US Grade 1 Flower Bowl Invitational winner Dimitrova. (Mr J E Dance).

235. KODI KING
b.c. Kodiac – Throne (Royal Applause). January 19. Second foal. £48,000Y. Goffs UK Premier (Doncaster). Burke / Dance /Creighton /Sackville. The dam ran twice unplaced and is a half-sister to 11 winners including the top-class Group 1 5f Nunthorpe Stakes winner and sire Kyllachy and the very useful triple 5f winner Borders. The second dam, Pretty Poppy (by Song), a modest 2-y-o 5f winner, is a half-sister to 4 winners including the Criterium de Maisons-Laffitte winner Corviglia. (Mr J E Dance).

236. KODURO
b.f. Kodiac – Affability (Dalakhani). March 19. Third foal. £40,000Y. Goffs UK Premier (Doncaster). Dance/ Creighton/ Sackville/ Donald. The dam is an unraced half-sister to 8 winners including the Group 3 Gallinule Stakes winner Grand Ducal. The second dam, Mood Swings (by Shirley Heights), a fair 2-y-o 6f winner, is a sister to the Listed 2-y-o Sweet Solera Stakes winner Catwalk and a half-sister to 5 winners. (Mr J E Dance).

237. LIFE OF RILEY
b.c. Showcasing – Swan Wings (Bahamian Bounty). March 10. Fifth foal. 60,000Y. Tattersalls October Book 2. Howson & Houldsworth. Half-brother to the fairly useful 6f (at 2 yrs) and 7f winner Battered (by Foxwedge), to the quite useful 2-y-o 6f winner Sunflower (by Dutch Art) and the fair dual 7f winner Dutch Garden (by Fastnet Rock). The dam, a fairly useful 2-y-o 5f winner, is a half-sister to 7 winners. The second dam, Star Tulip (by Night Shift), a useful winner of 3 races over 6f including the Listed Sandy Lane Stakes, is a half-sister to 4 minor winners. (Ontoawinner, Strecker & Mrs E Burke).

238. LIL KIM
b.f. Garswood – Primo Lady (Lucky Story). February 19. Second foal. 45,000Y. Tattersalls October Book 2. Karl Burke. Half-sister to the useful 2017 2-y-o 5f winner and Group 2 5f Queen Mary Stakes third Out Of The Flames (by Showcasing). The dam, a fairly useful 2-y-o Listed 5f winner, is a half-sister to 5 winners. The second dam, Lady Natilda (by First Trump), a modest 2-y-o 5f winner, is a half-sister to 3 winners. (Nick Bradley 35, Strecker & Mrs E Burke).

239. MARDLE
ch.c. Mukhadram – Hoh Chi Min (Efisio). March 22. £30,000Y. Goffs UK Premier (Doncaster). Karl Burke. Half-brother to 7 winners including the fairly useful 1m to 2m winner Saigon City (by Mount Nelson), the fair 1m winner Khe Sanh (by Mtoto) and to the modest 6f winner Belle Bellino (by Robellino). The dam won 5 races here and abroad including a Listed event in Italy and was Group 3 placed four times. She is a half-sister to 8 winners including the very useful 7f Listed winner Cragganmore and the 2-y-o 5f winner Special One (herself dam of the Molecomb Stakes winner Inya Lake). The second dam, Special Guest (by Be My Guest), a modest 2-y-o 7f winner, is a half-sister to 3 minor winners. (Ontoawinner 14 & Mrs E Burke).

240. POWER PLAYER
b.c. Slade Power – Varnish (Choisir). March 2. Second foal. 70,000Y. Tattersalls October Book 2. Mark Crossman. Half-brother to the modest 5f winner Secret Agent (by Equiano). The dam, a quite useful 10f and 12f winner, is a half-sister to one winner. The second dam, Bronze Star (by Mark Of Esteem), a modest dual 10f winner, is a half-sister to 4 winners including the Group 2 12f Ribblesdale Stakes second Eldalil. (K A Dasmal).

241. REQUIREMENT
b.f. Charm Spirit – Bijou A Moi (Rainbow Quest). February 4. Seventh foal. £105,000Y. Goffs UK Premier (Doncaster). Joe Foley. Half-sister to 5 winners including the Group 3 10f winner Robin Hoods Bay (by Motivator), the fair dual 1m winner Bipartisan and the fair 7f winner Binthere Dunthat (both by Bhaamian Bounty). The dam is an unraced half-sister to

6 winners including the Irish 2-y-o 7f winner and Listed placed Pietra Dura (dam of the US Grade 3 winner and Grade 1 second Turning Top) and the dam of the Group 1 Juddmonte International Stakes winner Postponed. The second dam, Bianca Nera (by Salse), winner of the Group 1 7f Moyglare Stud Stakes, is half-sister to 4 winners including the dam of the dual Group 1 winner Simply Perfect. (Mr J E Dance).

242. ROBOTIQUE DANCER

b.f. Siyouni – Dawn To Dance (Selkirk). March 7. Third foal. 120,000Y. Tattersalls October Book 1. Sackville/Donald, Creighton Schwartz. The dam, a winner, is a sister to the useful Irish 2-y-o 7f winner and dual Group placed Natalis and a half-sister to 7 winners including the Group 1 5f Prix de l'Abbaye winner and smart sire Namid and to the very useful Group 3 6f and Group 3 7.5f winner Noelani. The second dam, Dawnsio (by Tate Gallery), winner of the Listed Topaz Sprint Stakes in Ireland, is a half-sister to 3 winners. (Mr J E Dance).

243. SWISSTERIOUS

b.c. Swiss Spirit – Mysterious Girl (Teofilo). February 17. Third foal. £44,000Y. Goffs UK Premier (Doncaster). Creighton Schwartz BS. Half-brother to the fair 2-y-o triple 5f winner Four Dragons (by Dragon Pulse). The dam is an unraced half-sister to one winner. The second dam, Mazaaya (by Cozzene), a quite useful 7f (at 2 yrs) and 10f winner, is a sister to the useful 10f winner and dual Listed-placed Cozy Maria (herself dam of the Group 2 Flying Childers winner and sire Zebedee) and a half-sister to 9 winners abroad. (Titanium Racing Club).

244. TRUE MASON

b.c. Mayson – Marysienka (Primo Dominie). March 18. Seventh living foal. 120,000Y. Tattersalls October Book 2. Mark Crossman. Half-brother to the fair 5f (at 2 yrs) and 6f winner of 4 races Be Bold (by Assertive), to the fair 2-y-o 6f winner Arctic Mirage (by Iceman) and the modest 14f and hurdles winner Ivanhoe (by Haafhd). The dam, a fair 5f placed maiden, is a half-sister to 4 winners including the Listed winner and Group 3 placed Irresistible (herself dam of the Group 3 Nell Gwyn Stakes winner Infallible). The second

dam, Polish Romance (by Danzig), a minor 7f winner in the USA, is a full or half-sister to 6 winners. (K A Dasmal).

245. UNNAMED

ch.c. Havana Gold – Blanc De Chine (Dark Angel). February 11. Second foal. 140,000Y. Tattersalls October Book 2. Karl Burke. Brother to the 2017 2-y-o Group 3 5f Molecomb Stakes and dual Listed winner and Group 1 Prix Morny second Havana Grey. The dam, a quite useful 5f winner of 6 races at 2 to 4 yrs, is a half-sister to 7 winners including the Group 3 Molecomb Stakes second Fast Act. The second dam, Nullarbor (by Green Desert), a minor French 2-y-o winner, is a half-sister to 5 winners including Radevore (Group 2 10f Prix Eugene Adam).

246. UNNAMED

b.f. Kodiac – One Giant Leap (Pivotal). March 8. Sixth living foal. 80,000Y. Tattersalls October Book 2. Karl Burke. Half-sister to the quite useful dual 5f and subsequent US winner Morocco Moon (by Rock Of Gibraltar), to the modest 5f and 6f winner Lunarian (by Bahamian Bounty) and the modest 7f winner Slow To Hand (by Sepoy). The dam, a modest 7f winner, is a half-sister to 9 winners including the useful 2-y-o Group 3 7f C L Weld Park Stakes winner Rag Top and the dam of the 2-y-o Listed winner Elhamri. The second dam, Petite Epaulette (by Night Shift), a fair 5f winner at 2 yrs, is a full or half-sister to 3 winners. (Mr H J Strecker).

247. UNNAMED

b.f. Kodiac – Payphone (Anabaa). February 22. Eighth living foal. 67,000Y. Tattersalls October Book 1. Karl Burke. Half-sister to 4 winners including the useful 5f (at 2 yrs) and Listed 6f winner and Group 2 Queen Mary Stakes third Newsletter (by Sir Percy), the fair 7f winner Touch Tone (by Selkirk) and a winner in Spain by Beat Hollow. The dam, a 5.5f winner at 3 yrs in France, is a half-sister to 3 winners including the French 2-y-o 7f and 1m winner and Group 1 Prix Marcel Boussac second Conference Call. The second dam, Phone West (by Gone West), was placed over 1m at 3 yrs in France. (Mr H Strecker, A F O'Callaghan & Mrs E Burke).

248. UNNAMED
ch.f. Shamardal – Viola Da Braccio (Vettori).
April 7. Eighth foal. 105,000Y. Tattersalls
October Book 2. Stroud/Coleman. Half-sister
to the Hong Kong Listed 9f winner Pleasure
Gains, to the fair 7f to 12f winner Sham Sheer
(both by Cape Cross), the German Listed 10f
winner Sarinda, the quite useful 6f (at 2 yrs)
and 7f winner Bowmaker (both by Dubawi)
and the quite useful 7f to 8.5f winner of 8
races Skytrain (by Exceed And Excel). The dam,
placed once at 3 yrs in France, is a half-sister
to 5 winners including the dam of Rock Of
Gibraltar. The second dam, Push A Button (by
Bold Lad, Ire), won once at 2 yrs and is a half-
sister to 6 winners including the French 2,000
Guineas winner and top-class sire Riverman.
(Mr H J Strecker).

OWEN BURROWS

249. ALMOKHTAAR (USA) ★★★
b.c. War Front – Fascinating (Smart Strike).
February 28. First foal. $620,000 foal. Shadwell
Estate Co. The dam was Grade 1 placed twice
at 2 yrs over 7f and 8.5f in the USA and is
a half-sister to the US Grade 1 9f Arkansas
Derby winner Bodemeister. The second dam,
Untouched Talent (by Storm Cat), a US 2-y-o
Grade 3 6.5f winner, was second in a Grade
1 stakes. (Hamdan Al Maktoum). *"He's just
come in from Dubai and even just looking at
his purchase price you can tell he must be a
quality colt, but I don't know anything more
about him yet".*

250. ALSIMSAAM (IRE) ★★★
b.c. Dark Angel – La Reine De Pearls (Dubawi).
April 9. Third foal. £100,000Y. Goffs UK
Premier (Doncaster). Shadwell Estate Co. The
dam was a French 1m winner at 2 and 3 yrs.
The second dam, Ochre (by Diktat), a modest
1m and 9f winner, is a sister to the Listed
winner and 1,000 Guineas third Vista Bella
and a half-sister to 7 winners. (Hamdan Al
Maktoum). *"Not the biggest, he's a neat colt
and needs to be racing this year. He's cantering
away and in April we'll step up his work".*

251. AMJAADY (USA) ★★★
b.c. War Front – Prize Catch (A P Indy).
May 10. Third foal. $400,000Y. Keeneland
September. Shadwell Estate Co. The dam
won 3 races at 3 and 4 yrs including a minor

stakes event in the USA and is a half-sister
to 8 winners including the US triple Grade 2
winner Lead Story and the Grade 2 placed
Strike Midnight. The second dam, Gwenjinsky
(by Seattle Dancer), is a placed half-sister to
the Grade 1 Breeders' Cup Distaff winner
Unbridled Elaine. (Hamdan Al Maktoum).
*"He was expensive but I've also got the 3-y-o
full-brother Althaaqib who cost a lot more and
never ran at two. This is a similar model except
he's a lot smaller and that should help his
2-y-o career. A nice type".*

252. BAALBEK (USA) ★★★
b.c. Elusive Quality – Nasmatt (Danehill).
February 19. Half-brother to the useful 2-y-o
1m and subsequent UAE Listed 10f winner
Emmrooz (by Red Ransom), to the quite
useful UAE 6f and 7f winner of 4 races Latkhaf
(by Pivotal), the fair 7f winner Owaseyf (by
Medaglia d'Oro) and the fair 1m winners
Jaahiez (by More Than Ready) and Towbaat
(by Halling). The dam, a fairly useful Listed-
placed 2-y-o 6f winner, is closely related to
the Group 2 6f Lowther Stakes and Group
3 5f Queen Mary Stakes winner Bint Allayl
and to the Group 3 7f Jersey Stakes winner
Kheleyf. The second dam, Society Lady (by
Mr Prospector), a fair 6f and 7f placed 2-y-o,
is a full or half-sister to numerous winners
including the useful French 2-y-o 5.5f winner
Kentucky Slew. (Sheikh Ahmed Al Maktoum).
*"Very straightforward, he looks like he wants
a bit of time but he's got a good mind on him
and he moves nicely. Strengthening up all the
time, we're likely to see him out anytime from
the middle of the season onwards".*

253. BADAYEL (IRE) ★★★
ch.c. Havana Gold – Raggiante (Rock Of
Gibraltar). April 14. Fourth foal. 110,000Y.
Tattersalls October Book 2. Shadwell Estate Co.
Half-brother to a minor 3-y-o winner abroad
by Aqlaam. The dam, a Listed-placed winner
at 3 yrs in Italy, is a half-sister to 6 winners the
Group 2 Summer Mile winner and dual Group
1 placed Arod. The second dam, My Personal
Space (by Rahy), a fair 2-y-o 6f winner, is a
half-sister to 8 winners including the Group
3 7f Darley Stakes winner Far Lane and the
dam of the US Grade 2 winner Dark Islander.
(Hamdan Al Maktoum). *"He's had a little injury
recently but he'll be fine and he'll be back soon.*

An athletic type, I like the sire and this colt should make a 2-y-o by midsummer".

254. BARAAJEEL ★★★
b.c. Kodiac – Madany (Acclamation). May 3. Third foal. Half-brother to the 2017 2-y-o 6f winner, from two starts, Eqtidaar (by Invincible Spirit), to the very smart 2-y-o 7f winner and Group 1 Dewhurst Stakes second Massaat (by Teofilo) and the quite useful 2-y-o 6f winner Hathiq (by Exceed And Excel). The dam, a fairly useful 2-y-o dual 6f winner, is a half-sister to 6 winners including the 2-y-o Group 3 Prix du Bois winner and Group 2 Prix Robert Papin third Dolled Up and the 2-y-o Listed Prix Zeddaan and subsequent US stakes winner Zeiting. The second dam, Belle De Cadix (by Law Society), The dam, a minor 13f winner at 3 yrs in Ireland, is a half-sister to 5 winners here and abroad. (Hamdan Al Maktoum). *"He had a small setback about a month ago but he should be back training in midsummer. He's a nice colt and a good mover, I know the family can trap a bit and being by Kodiac he shouldn't have any trouble either. It's a 2-y-o family and he's an athletic type".*

255. DAWAAM (USA) ★★★
b.c. Kitten's Joy – Nereid (Rock Hard Ten). March 31. Third foal. $450,000Y. Keeneland September. Shadwell Estate Co. The dam won the Grade 1 American Oaks, was Grade 1 placed another three times and is a half-sister to the winner and Grade 1 second Sea Queen. The second dam, Dowry (by Belong To Me), won 4 minor races in the USA and is a half-sister to two stakes winners. (Hamdan Al Maktoum). *"A lovely-looking colt that's just arrived from Dubai. He's a nice size with a bit of scope about him but I haven't seen enough of him yet to comment further".*

256. EDRAAK (IRE) ★★★
b.c. Elzaam – So Blissful (Cape Cross). April 18. Fifth foal. £82,000Y. Goffs UK Premier (Doncaster). Shadwell Estate Co. Half-brother to the modest 2017 7f and 8.5f placed 2-y-o Dewan (by Elzaam) and to the modest 6f and 7f winner Medicean Bliss (by Medicean). The dam, a fair 3-y-o 7f winner, is a half-sister to 3 minor winners. The second dam, Royal Devotion (by Sadler's Wells), an Irish Listed 12f winner, is a closely related to the

2-y-o Listed 6f Silver Flash Stakes winner April Starlight and to the dual Listed winner Thady Quill and a half-sister to the US Grade 3 8.5f winner Humble Eight. (Hamdan Al Maktoum). *"He's cantering away and looks nice but he's not precocious and needs time. He'll be a midsummer 2-y-o and there's not a lot wrong with him, he moves nicely and he's got a good mind on him".*

257. EITHAAR ★★★
b.f. Kingman – Hathrah (Linamix). April 17. Eighth foal. Half-sister to the smart Listed 10f winner and Group 1 Prix de l'Opera third Hadaatha (by Sea The Stars), to the quite useful 10f to 2m winner of 8 races Itlaak (by Alhaarth), the quite useful 1m winner Aghaany (by Dubawi) and the fair 8.5f winner Raddeh (by Shamardal). The dam, winner of the Listed 1m Masaka Stakes and third in the 1,000 Guineas, is a half-sister to 5 winners including the smart Group 2 12f Premio Ellington winner Ivan Luis and the French/German Listed winners Amathia and Zero Problemo. The second dam, Zivania (by Shernazar), a useful Irish winner of 4 races from 1m to 9.5f, is a half-sister to the Group 3 Prix Gontaut Biron winner Muroto. (Hamdan Al Maktoum). *"She's strengthening up and cantering away now, I have her 3-y-o Frankel half-sister Anasheed who is a lovely filly but she's big, but this one is smaller so hopefully that will give her a better chance of making a 2-y-o".*

258. HADHWAH (IRE) ★★★
b.f. Shamardal – Umseyat (Arch). March 23. Fourth foal. Sister to the quite useful Irish 2-y-o 6f winner Wayside Flower and half-sister to the fair 1m winner Senses Of Dubai (by Royal Applause). The dam, a quite useful 2-y-o 1m winner, is a half-sister to 4 winners including the smart Listed 11f winner and Group 2 12f Princess Of Wales's Stakes second Alwaary. The second dam, Tabrir (by Unfuwain), is an unraced full or half-sister to 6 winners including the 1,000 Guineas and Group 2 7f Rockfel Stakes winner Lahan. (Hamdan Al Maktoum). *"She's a nice filly and she's one of the few that's starting to get her summer coat, but even so she doesn't look as though she'll be too sharp. One for the second half of the season".*

259. HASSAAD ★★★★ ♠
b.f. Kodiac – Samaah (Cape Cross).
March 1. Third foal. Half-sister to the fair
7f winner Mulzim (by Exceed And Excel),
unplaced in two starts at 2 yrs in 2016. The
dam is an unraced half-sister to 4 winners
including the Group 1 Golden Jubilee Stakes
and Group 1 Nunthorpe Stakes winner
Kingsgate Native. The second dam, Native
Force (by Indian Ridge), a quite useful 1m
winner, is a half-sister to 2 winners. (Hamdan
Al Maktoum). *"We'll take a close look at her in
April to see if she's mature enough for faster
work. I was at Sir Michael Stoute's when the
dam Samaah was there and this filly looks
similar to her. Samaah wasn't the soundest,
so I hope this filly is better in that respect.
She's nice, has a good temperament and looks
strong and mature".*

260. JOMROK ★★
b.f. Mukhadram – Shadow Dancing
(Unfuwain). February 10. Seventh foal.
75,000Y. Tattersalls October Book 2. Shadwell
Estate Co. Half-sister to the useful 2-y-o 1m
winner and Group 3 10.3f Dee Stakes third
Rasmy (by Red Ransom), to the useful Listed-
placed triple 12f winner Dance The Dream (by
Sir Percy), the fairly useful 11f winner Black
Shadow (by New Approach) and the fair 2-y-o
1m winner Hazy Dancer (by Oasis Dream). The
dam, winner of the Listed Cheshire Oaks, was
third in the Oaks and second in the Group 2
Ribblesdale Stakes and in the Group 2 Prix de
Pomone and is a half-sister to 6 winners. The
second dam, Salchow (by Niniski), won the
Listed Cheshire Oaks, was second in the Group
2 Park Hill Stakes and is a half-sister to 7
winners. (Hamdan Al Maktoum). *"A lovely, big
filly that'll want a lot of time but there's nothing
not to like about her. We're not in too much of
a rush with her".*

261. MAKHLOOQ ★★★
b.c. Dubawi – Zahoo (Nayef). April 20. Half-
brother to the fair 2017 7f placed 2-y-o
Zaajer (by Shamardal), to the Listed 7.5f (at 2
yrs) and Group 3 7f Ballycorus Stakes winner
Convergence (by Cape Cross) and the quite
useful 2-y-o 1m winner Zaakhir (by Raven's
Pass). The dam, a fairly useful 1m (at 2 yrs)
and 10f winner and Listed 10f second, is a full

or half-sister to 5 winners including the smart
Group 3 14f winner Tactic and the Listed 12f
winner Yaazy. The second dam, Tanaghum (by
Darshaan), a useful Listed-placed 10f winner,
is a half-sister to 7 winners including the smart
Group 2 10f Premio Lydia Tesio winner Najah.
(Hamdan Al Maktoum). *"He's only got one
eye and I think he was born that way, but he
was good to break in and he's an athletic colt.
He's a nice size and looks pretty natural at the
minute, he's pleased me with what he's done
so I can't knock him at all because he's been
very trusting; probably one for seven furlongs
to begin with".*

262. MOTFAEL (IRE) ★★★
b.c. Invincible Spirit – Fidelite (In The Wings).
April 12. Ninth foal. 240,000Y. Tattersalls
October Book 1. Shadwell Estate Co. Brother
to the French Listed 10f winner Extremis and
half-brother to two minor winners in France
by Awesome Again and Dalakhani. The dam,
winner of the Group 1 10f Prix Saint-Alary and
third in the Group 1 Prix Vermeille, is a half-
sister to 6 minor winners. The second dam,
Onereuse (by Sanglamore), placed over 1m
and 10f in France, is a half-sister to 7 winners
including the Irish Derby winner Winged Love.
(Sheikh Ahmed Al Maktoum). *"A lovely horse,
he's a good mover with a good mind, but his
knees are still immature so I'd say he'll be a
nice colt for the second half of the season".*

263. MUHAARAR'S NEPHEW ★★★
b.c. Mukhadram – Rufoof (Zamindar).
February 27. Second foal. The dam, a fair dual
7f winner, is a half-sister to the multiple Group
1 winning sprinter Muhaarar, the very useful
2-y-o 7f winner and subsequent UAE Group
3 1m second Tamaathul and the useful 2-y-o
Listed 6f winner Sajwah. The second dam,
Tahrir (by Linamix), a useful dual 7f winner, is
a sister to the Listed winners Mister Charm and
Green Channel and a half-sister to the Group
3 Prix de Guiche winner Mister Sacha. (Hadi
Al-Tajir). *"I've got a couple by the first season
sire Mukhadram and they've both pleased me.
This colt has a bit of quality and what we've
seen so far we like. He's not going to be too
early because there's a bit of size about him. He
doesn't look like a sprinter at the minute and is
probably one for seven furlongs to start with".*

264. MULTAMIS (IRE) ★★★

gr.c. Charm Spirit – Dabista (Highest Honor). February 1. Sixth foal. €100,000 foal. Goffs November. Shadwell Estate Co. Half-brother to the fairly useful 9.5f and 10f winner Dabulena (by Siyouni) and to the fair dual 12f winner Dabadiyan (by Zamindar). The dam, placed at 3 yrs, is a half-sister to 3 winners. The second dam, Dabaya (by In The Wings), a Listed-placed 10f winner, is a half-sister to 4 winners. (Hamdan Al Maktoum). *"A nice type, he's athletic, moves well and is cantering away. We'll press on with him soon. He's the only one by the first-season sire Charm Spirit we have, but I liked the look of quite a few of them at the sales".*

265. NOOR DUBAI ★★★ ♠

b.f. Invincible Spirit – Beach Frolic (Nayef). March 4. Second foal. 650,000Y. Tattersalls October Book 1. Shadwell Estate Co. Half-sister to Bin Daahir (by Exceed And Excel), placed fourth once over 6f from two starts at 2 yrs in 2017. The dam is an unraced half-sister to 4 winners including Bonfire (Group 2 Dante Stakes) and Joviality (Group 2 Windsor Forest Stakes). The second dam, Night Frolic (by Night Shift), a modest 1m winner, is a half-sister to 5 winners including the US Grade 3 Cardinal Handicap winner Miss Caerleona (herself dam of the Group winners Karen's Caper and Miss Coronado). (Hamdan Al Maktoum). *"A lovely filly, she a beautiful mover and has a good mind on her. Over the last few weeks she's grown quite a bit so we'll be patient with her and she's one for the second half of the season".*

266. OJOOBA ★★★

b.f. Dubawi – Rumoush (Rahy). May 5. Fifth foal. Sister to the useful 2-y-o 7f winner and Group 2 Royal Lodge Stakes third Muntazah and half-sister to Wadilsafa (by Frankel), placed second over 7f on his only start at 2 yrs in 2017 and the fairly useful 7f (at 2 yrs) and Group 3 7f City Of York Stakes winner Talaayeb (by Dansili). The dam, a very useful 1m (at 2 yrs) and Listed 9f winner, was third in the Oaks and is a half-sister to numerous winners including the 1,000 Guineas and Coronation Stakes winner Ghanaati and the Group 3 12f Cumberland Lodge Stakes winner and Group 1 Champion Stakes second

Mawatheeq. The second dam, Sarayir (by Mr Prospector), winner of a Listed 1m event, is closely related to the Champion Stakes winner Nayef and a half-sister to Nashwan and Unfuwain. (Hamdan Al Maktoum). *"From a family we know well, she's a nice filly that's just cantering away for now. She just needs to fill out a bit and get some sun on her back. She was a May foal and we won't see her out until a bit later on in the season".*

267. RAHEEB (IRE) ★★★★ ♠

b.f. Kodiac – Dream Date (Oasis Dream). March 1. Fourth foal. 180,000 foal. Tattersalls December. Shadwell Estate Co. Sister to the Group 3 5f winner and Group 1 Nunthorpe Stakes third Extortionist and half-sister to the 2017 2-y-o 5f winner from two starts Utterly Charming (both by Dandy Man). The dam, a quite useful dual 7f winner, is a half-sister to 6 winners. The second dam, Femme Fatale (by Fairy King), a useful dual 6f winner of 2 races (including a Listed event at 2 yrs), is a half-sister to 4 winners including the dual Listed 10f winner and smart broodmare Foodbroker Fancy (herself dam of the Group 3 winner Dalvina). (Hamdan Al Maktoum). *"Over the next few weeks she might be one of those to move on with. She's a nice, strong, mature filly and very straightforward in her work. She's all there, a good size and looks as if she should be able to trap a bit. I like her".*

268. RAJWAA ★★★★

gr.f. Dark Angel – The Thrill Is Gone (Bahamian Bounty). February 25. Third foal. £200,000Y. Goffs UK Premier (Doncaster). Shadwell Estate Co. The dam, a fairly useful 2-y-o 5f winner, was Listed-placed three times and is a half-sister to 8 winners including the UAE Group 1 Golden Shaheen winner Muarrab, the very useful 2-y-o dual Group 3 5f winner Bungleinthejungle, the Listed winner Waveband and the Group-placed Group Therapy and Classic Encounter. The second dam, Licence To Thrill (Wolfhound), a quite useful dual 5f winner, is a half-sister to 4 winners. (Hamdan Al Maktoum). *"A good-sized, athletic, mature filly, she's one we'll be moving ahead with sometime in April".*

269. SHARQEYYA (IRE) ★★★

b.f. Oasis Dream – Daymooma (Pivotal).

March 20. Second foal. Half-sister to Anaakeed (by Dubawi), unplaced on her only start at 2 yrs in 2017. The dam, a fairly useful Listed-placed 9f and 10f winner, is a half-sister to 5 winners including the useful 2-y-o 6f winner and Group 3 7f Killavullan Stakes third Aaraas and the useful Irish 2-y-o 6f winner and Group 3 7f Silver Flash Stakes third Alshahbaa. The second dam, Adaala (by Sahm), an Irish 7f (at 2 yrs) and Listed 9f winner, is a half-sister to 2 winners. (Hamdan Al Maktoum). *"She's a little bit backward and just cantering away for now. Over the last few weeks she's been strengthening up, but she just wants a bit of sun".*

270. TAJAWOZ (USA) ★★★
b.c. War Front – Stanwyck (Empire Maker). March 28. First foal. $750,000Y. Keeneland September. Shadwell Estate Co. The dam, a US Grade 3 winner and placed in three Grade 1's, is a half-sister to 7 winners including Tiago (Grade 1 Santa Anita Derby) and Giacomo (Grade 1 Kentucky Derby). The second dam, Set Me Free (by Stop The Music), was a US Listed stakes winner. (Hamdan Al Maktoum). *"Another that's just arrived from Dubai, he's what I call just a nice size, so he's got a bit of size and scope about him".*

271. TANQEEB ★★★★
b.c. Garswood – Oasis Mirage (Oasis Dream). January 26. First foal. 75,000 Gns. Tattersalls December. Shadwell Estate Co. The dam, a fair 5f winner, is a half-sister to several winners including the 2-y-o Group 3 7f winner Horris Hill Stakes winner Evasive. The second dam, Canda (by Storm Cat), is an unraced half-sister to 3 winners including the 2-y-o Group 3 5.5f Prix d'Arenburg winner Moon Driver and the Grade 2 Californian Stakes second Mojave Moon. (Hamdan Al Maktoum). *"A horse I like, he looks sharp and mature, so we'll move on with him in mid-April".*

272. USTATH ★★★★
ch.c. Exceed And Excel – Adorn (Kyllachy). February 5. Fifth foal. 260,000Y. Tattersalls October Book 1. Shadwell Estate Co. Brother to the useful 2-y-o dual 5f winner Fendale and half-brother to the 2-y-o Group 2 Richmond Stakes winner Saayerr (by Acclamation) and the 2-y-o winner and Group 2 Flying Childers

Stakes second Ornate (by Bahamian Bounty). The dam, a useful 2-y-o 6f winner, is closely related to the US 5f (Listed) to 8.5f winner Red Diadem and a half-sister to 5 winners. The second dam, Red Tiara (by Mr Prospector), a moderate 7.6f fourth-placed maiden, is closely related to the Japanese sprint stakes winner Meiner Love and a half-sister to 4 winners. (Hamdan Al Maktoum). *"I'd just like to see him strengthen up a bit because when he does I think he'll be quite early. A good-moving colt with a good mind on him, he's a proper 2-y-o 5f type and I like him".*

273. WAMATHAAT (USA) ★★★
ch.f. Speightstown – Special Me (Unbridled's Song). April 24. Seventh foal. $550,000Y. Keeneland September. Shadwell Estate Co. Half-sister to 3 winners including the US dual Grade 2 winner and Grade 1 placed Stonetastic (by Mizzen Mast) and the US Grade 2 placed Gift Box (by Twirling Candy). The dam is an unplaced half-sister to 11 winners including the UAE Group 1 Golden Shaheen winner Our New Recruit. The second dam, Delta Danielle (by Lord Avie), was a Canadian stakes-placed winner of 8 races. (Hamdan Al Maktoum). *"Just arrived from Dubai, I hope she acclimatises well because she looks mature and she's bred to be quick, so we might be able to move on a bit with her in May time, all being well".*

274. WATHEERAH (USA) ★★★
b.f. Dubawi – Atayeb (Rahy). February 26. Sister to the useful dual 7f (at 2 yrs) and dual 1m winner Algaith and half-sister to the French 7f winner Arsheef (by Hard Spun). The dam, a fair 12f winner, is a sister to the useful 1m (at 2 yrs) and Listed 9f winner Rumoush and a half-sister to the 1,000 Guineas and Coronation Stakes winner Ghanaati and the Group 3 12f Cumberland Lodge Stakes winner and Group 1 Champion Stakes second Mawatheeq. The second dam, Sarayir (by Mr Prospector), winner of a Listed 1m event, is closely related to the Champion Stakes winner Nayef and a half-sister to Nashwan and Unfuwain. (Hamdan Al Maktoum). *"She's a neat filly, looks strong and I think she should be out around June time but she's been in Dubai and needs to acclimatise first. A nice, quality filly".*

275. UNNAMED ★★★
b.f. Dark Angel – Surrey Storm (Montjeu). March 17. Third foal. 100,000Y. Tattersalls October Book 2. Shadwell Estate Co. Sister to the modest 2-y-o 1m winner Booshbash. The dam, a minor French 3-y-o winner, is a half-sister to 3 winners including the French Listed winner Andry Brusselles. The second dam, Dont Dili Dali (by Dansili), a very useful 7f (at 2 yrs) and Listed 1m Masaka Stakes winner, was third in the Group 3 Dahlia Stakes and is a half-sister to 6 winners. (Hamdan Al Maktoum). *"A nice filly, she's cantering away and just wants a bit of sun on her back. When that happens I expect her to change because she does need to fill out and strengthen up. I picked her at the sales where she had a nice walk to her".*

HENRY CANDY
276. ADONIJAH ★★
b.c. Sea The Stars – Meeznah (Dynaformer). March 24. Fourth foal. 325,000Y. Tattersalls October Book 1. H Candy. The dam, winner of the Group 2 Park Hill Stakes and the Group 3 Lillie Langtry Stakes, is a half-sister to 5 winners including the smart Group 2 12f Princess Of Wales's Stakes second Shahin. The second dam, String Quartet (by Sadler's Wells), a 12.5f Listed winner in France and third in the Group 3 Lancashire Oaks, is a sister to the Irish and US Listed stakes winner Casey Tibbs and a half-sister to 4 winners. (T Barr). *"He's a huge horse – never stops growing – and I'd be delighted if I could get him on the track before the end of the year. A very good-looking horse and worth what he cost but he's going to be a long-term proposition".*

277. ALFRED BOUCHER ★★★
gr.c. Aussie Rules – Policy Term (Authorized). February 29. First foal. The dam is an unraced half-sister to numerous winners including the dual Group 3 10f Ballysax Stakes and Group 3 12f Ballyroan Stakes winner and Group 1 placed Mores Wells, the fairly useful dual 12f and hurdles winner and Group 3 2m Queens Vase third Galient and the quite useful 2-y-o 7f winner Road Rage. The second dam, Endorsement (by Warning), won the Group 3 2m Queen's Vase and is a half-sister to 3 winners. (Mr R. Allcock). *"He's a lovely moving horse but not surprisingly being out of an*

Authorized mare he's going to take a bit of time. I like the way he goes and he'll make a 2-y-o in the second half of the season".

278. ALL RIGHT ★★
b.f. Intello – Alice Alleyne (Oasis Dream). April 25. Fifth foal. Half- sister to the quite useful 2-y-o 5f and 6f winner Looting (by Bahamian Bounty), to the quite useful Irish 1m winner Araqeel (by Dutch Art) and the fair 7f and 1m winner Alice Thornton (by Hurricane Run). The dam, a quite useful 7f (at 2 yrs) and 6f winner, is a half-sister to 2 winners including the Irish Listed winner and Group 2 third Avenue Gabriel. The second dam, Vas Y Carla (by Gone West), a quite useful 7f placed 2-y-o, is a half-sister to 5 winners including the Group 2 Great Voltigeur Stakes third Avalon. (Major M G Wyatt). *"A very nice, attractive, home-bred filly. Like nearly all Intello's she's going to need plenty of time and she's back on the stud resting at the moment. One for the back-end of the season".*

279. BORDER WARRIOR ★★★
b.c. Sir Percy – Cheviot Heights (Intikhab). April 16. Fourth foal. £17,000Y. Goffs UK Premier (Doncaster). Henry Candy. Half-brother to the modest 7f to 2m winner Eilean Mor (by Ishiguru), to the modest 4-y-o 1m winner Lotara (by Monsieur Bond) and the moderate 2-y-o 1m winner Bonnie Fairy (by Notnowcato). The dam, a fair 7f placed 2-y-o, is a half-sister to 2 winners. The second dam, Cheviot Hills (by Gulch), a French 10f winner, is a half-sister to 6 winners including the triple US Grade 3 winner Fantastic Fellow. (Simon Broke & Partners). *"A fairly late foal, he was a very immature horse when I bought him. He has open knees at the moment so he's just trotting but he looks a real athlete and I would think in a couple of months he'll look the part. So we like him, but I see him being suited by a mile later on this year and it's a question of being patient at the moment".*

280. CANAL ROCKS ★★★★
br.c. Aussie Rules – In Secret (Dalakhani). March 8. Second foal. Half-brother to the quite useful 2017 10f placed 2-y-o Mt Augustus (by Champs Elysees). The dam, a modest 7f to 12f placed maiden, is a half-sister to numerous winners including the Group 3 7f

Minstrel Stakes winner Jedburgh. The second dam, Conspiracy (by Rudimentary), a useful 2-y-o Listed 5f winner, is a half-sister to 7 winners including the Group 2 10f Sun Chariot Stakes winner Ristna and the dual Listed winner Gayane. (The Earl Cadogan). *"Much more forward than my other Aussie Rules colt, he does everything very easily and I would think he'd be one of the earlier ones. A strong and compact horse".*

281. FOUR FEET (IRE) ★★
b.c. Harbour Watch – Royal Connection (Bahamian Bounty). March 28. First foal. €9,000Y. Tattersalls Ireland September. Henry Candy. The dam, a fair 7f winner, is a half-sister to 2 other minor winners. The second dam, Fisadara (by Nayef), a modest 12f winner, is a half-sister to 5 winners including the useful 10f and 12f Listed winner Film Script (herself dam of the Listed winner Free Agent) and the Group 3 Chipchase Stakes winner Barney McGrew. (Mr H Candy). *"We're only just breaking him in because we turned him out after the sales. He had a minor foot problem at the sales but other than that I thought he looked very athletic and was worth a punt. He'll be nice and won't actually take that much time now. I think he'll catch up quickly, it's a speedy pedigree and I'd be hopeful he'd be running in May or June".*

282. IFTON ★★★
b.c. Iffraaj – Flambeau (Oasis Dream). May 4. Third foal. 42,000Y. Tattersalls October Book 3. Con Marnane. The dam, a very useful Listed 7f winner and second in the Group 3 Chartwell Stakes, is a half-sister to 5 winners. The second dam, Flavian (by Catrail), a fairly useful 6f (at 2 yrs) and 7f winner, is a half-sister to 7 winners. (Major M G Wyatt). *"A nice, big, classy horse with the emphasis on 'big', I'd hope to get him out in the second half of the season. He's a beautifully bred horse and very good-looking, so I'd have hopes for him but he's not your typical 2-y-o. One for the future, but he should have a couple of runs this year, starting at seven furlongs".*

283. KURIOUS ★★★★
b.f. Kuroshio (AUS) – Easy To Imagine (Cozzene). February 21. Seventh living foal. Half-sister to the Group 1 Prix de l'Abbaye winner of 15 races over 5f and 6f Tangerine Trees (by Mind Games), to the very useful Listed 5f winner of 7 races and Group 3 second Alpha Delphini (by Captain Gerrard), the fairly useful 6f and 7f winner of 8 races Masai Moon (by Lujain) and the fair 5f to 7f winner of 5 races Galatian (by Traditionally). The dam is an unraced half-sister to 5 winners. The second dam, Zarani Sidi Anna (by Danzig), a dual 6f winner here and third in the Group 1 1m Coronation Stakes and the Grade 1 Milady Handicap, won twice over 6f in the USA and is a half-sister to 3 winners. (Hot To Trot Racing). *"Most of the dam's produce are very quick but not necessarily early and we don't know much about the sire. This filly does look sharp and I would think she'd be one of our most forward 2-y-o's".* The sire, a son of Exceed And Excel, was a 2-y-o Group 3 5.5f and 3-y-o Group 2 5f winner in Australia.

284. LONICERA ★★★
br.f. Lethal Force – Puya (Kris). March 27. Half-sister to the smart Group 3 and triple Listed 10f winner Chain Of Daisies (by Rail Link), to the fair 2-y-o 7f winner Pandorea (by Diktat) and the modest dual 10f winner Herbalist (by Haafhd). The dam, a quite useful dual 7f winner, is a half-sister to several winners including the multiple Group 3 6f winner Gorse. The second dam, Pervenche (by Latest Model), is an unplaced half-sister to the smart 2-y-o Cut Throat. (Girsonfield Ltd). *"A nice, strong-bodied filly, she's a great mover but her knees are still immature. So she's back at the stud for now and I should think she'll be ready to roll again around late April. She looks like a 2-y-o and she's one for six furlongs in the second half of the season".*

285. MERAKI ★★★
b.c. Heeraat – Sound Of Life (Cape Cross). February 3. First foal. €24,000Y. Tattersalls Ireland September. Creighton Schwartz. The dam, a poor 12f placed maiden, is a half-sister to one winner. The second dam, Stylist (by Sadler's Wells), a fair 4-y-o 8.5f winner, is a sister to French Ballerina (winner of four Listed events in Ireland from 1m to 2m) and a half-sister to 4 winners including the Group 1 Fillies Mile winner and Irish Oaks second Sunspangled. (Mr A. Davis). *"He's probably the sharpest of them all. He's small but I strongly*

suspect that he might start growing. A very easy mover, he looks a proper 2-y-o and as long as he doesn't suddenly shoot up we'll get on with him and see what happens".

286. QUARRY BEACH ★★★
b.f. Dutch Art – Free Offer (Generous). March 29. Half-sister to the smart Listed 1m winner Cape Peron (by Beat Hollow), to the fair 8.5f winners Tunnel Creek (by Tobougg) and Faure Island (by Myboycharlie) and the modest 12f winners Murchison River and Free Passage (both by Medicean). The dam was a quite useful 7f (at 2 yrs) and dual 10f winner. The second dam, Proserpine (by Robellino), a fairly useful 2-y-o 1m winner, is a half-sister to the 1m and 10f winner and subsequent US Grade 1 14f placed Chelsea Barracks. (The Earl Cadogan). *"All the dam's offspring tend to take time which isn't surprising considering she's by Generous. This is a very nice, athletic filly but mentally very immature at the moment. I would say she could be OK in the second half of the season and she'll end up getting a mile next year".*

287. SALVE ETOILES (IRE) ★★★
b.f. Sea The Stars – Salve Diana (Dalakhani). April 5. First foal. The dam is an unplaced half-sister to several winners including the US Grade 2 9.5f winner Salve Germania. The second dam, the Group 1 11f German Oaks winner Salve Regina (by Monsun), is a sister to the Group 1 winners Samum and Schiaparelli. (Hunscote Stud). *"She's going home for a break tomorrow because she's growing and growing, but I hope to run her at the back-end of the season because she's got a lot of class. Looks a nice filly for the future".*

288. SOLDIER'S SON ★★★
b.c. Epaulette – Elsie's Orphan (Pastoral Pursuits). March 13. Second foal. £5,500Y. Tattersalls Ireland Ascot. H Candy. The dam, a fair 6f and 7f winner of 3 races at 3 and 4 yrs, is a half-sister to 2 winners. The second dam, Elsie Plunkett (by Mind Games), a fairly useful 2-y-o 5f winner of 3 races, was Listed-placed twice and is a half-sister to 3 winners. (Mr H. Candy). *"He came in at the same time as Four Feet so he's just being broken in at the moment. He looks a good, strong sort of horse and hopefully if we get a clear run with him*

he'll be racing in midsummer. Looks a good sort of individual". TRAINER'S BARGAIN BUY

289. UNNAMED ★★★
b.f. Assertive – Layla's Oasis (Oasis Dream). February 18. Second foal. The dam, a fair 5f winner, is a half-sister to 5 winners including the fairly useful dual 10f winner (including at 2 yrs) and Group 2 Lancashire Oaks third Natalie Jane. The second dam, Kirk (by Selkirk), a fair 1m winner, is closely related to the smart Group 2 placed Carmelite House and a half-sister to 6 other winners. (Lady Whent). *"A nice, big, rangy filly, because of her size she'll take a bit of time but she's a nice-looking filly and she'll make a 2-y-o".*

290. UNNAMED ★★★
b.f. Kyllachy – Night Affair (Bold Edge). April 30. Third foal. 40,000Y. Tattersalls October Book 2. H Candy. The dam, a fair 6f (including at 2 yrs) and 5f winner of 3 races, is a half-sister to 5 winners including the Group 1 Diamond Jubilee Stakes and Group 1 6f Haydock Park Sprint Cup winner Twilight Son, the Group 3 6f Hackwood Stakes winner Music Master and the Listed winner Spring Fling. The second dam, Twilight Mistress (by Bin Ajwaad), a quite useful 5f to 7f winner of 3 races, is a half-sister to 3 winners. (Six Too Many). *"An absolute midget when I bought her but she's growing very fast now and she's another one that's back at her stud having a break. She's very strongly built and to look at her she looks very fast although we haven't done anything with her yet. We like her and one of the reasons I was attracted to her is that she's out of a half-sister to one of the best I've trained, Twilight Son. There aren't any similarities though, as this filly will be purely a sharp five/six furlong 2-y-o".*

291. UNNAMED ★★★
ch.c. Camacho – Pashmina (Barathea). April 4. Fourth foal. 68,000Y. Tattersalls October Book 3. Stroud/Coleman & Thurloe. Half-brother to the quite useful 2017 2-y-o dual 5f winner Arcavallo (by Arcano). The dam is an unraced half-sister to 4 winners including the Group 3 5f Prix du Petit Couvert and Listed 5f Prix du Cercle winner of 8 races Monsieur Joe (by Choisir). The second dam, Pascali (by Compton Place), a modest 6f winner, is a half-sister to 3

winners. (Thurloe Thoroughbreds XLV). *"He's a lovely moving horse, very immature at the moment but he should be OK in the second half of the season".*

MICK CHANNON

292. ABENAKI ★★
b.gr.c. Gregorian – Blakeshall Rose (Tobougg). April 29. Ninth foal. Half-brother to the quite useful Listed-placed 5f and 6f winner of four races at 2 and 3 yrs Effie B, to the fair 6f (at 2 yrs) to 7f winner Willsy (by Sakhee's Secret) and the modest 2-y-o dual 6f winner Miss Muga (by Imperial Dancer). The dam, a modest 6f placed maiden, is a half-sister to 2 winners. The second dam, Giggleswick Girl (by Full Extent), was a modest 6f (at 2 yrs) and 5f winner of 4 races. (Bastian Family). *"He came in quite late and he's been a bit backward but he'll be all right a bit later on".*

293. AFTER JOHN ★★★★
b.c. Dutch Art – Rosacara (Green Desert). March 31. Ninth foal. 30,000Y. Tattersalls October Book 2. Gill Richardson. Half-brother to the useful 2-y-o 6f winner and Group 2 6f Cherry Hinton Stakes second Russelliana (by Medicean), to the fair 2-y-o 7f winners Kingarrick (by Selkirk) and Papa Meilland (by Dr Fong) and the fair 10f winner Nathan Mayer (by Nathaniel). The dam, a modest 7f and 1m placed maiden, is a half-sister to the triple Group 1 winner Notnowcato (Eclipse Sakes, Juddmonte International, etc). The second dam, Rambling Rose (by Cadeaux Genereux), won over 8.2f (at 2 yrs) and the Listed 12f Galtres Stakes and is a half-sister to 7 winners. (Mrs John Lee, Alf Heaney, Alec Tuckerman). *"A smashing colt, he will win at five furlongs, will get six and he does everything right. I think he's a nice, real sharp 2-y-o".*

294. ARCADIAN ROCKS (IRE) ★★★
b.c. Society Rock – Spirit Of Success (Invincible Spirit). April 11. Third foal. 22,000Y. Tattersalls October Book 3. Gill Richardson. Half-brother to the modest 2017 dual 7f placed 2-y-o Southpark (by Epaulette). The dam is an unplaced half-sister to 2 minor winners. The second dam, Isabella Glyn (by Sadler's Wells), placed over 7f at 2 yrs on her only start, is a closely related to the Group 3 10f Prix Corrida and Group 3 10.5f Prix de Flore winner Trumbaka and a half-sister to the Listed winners Arctic Hunt and Spirit Of Dubai. (John & Zoe Webster). *"He's got plenty of speed and he will be a 2-y-o. He had a little setback so he won't run until May but he's something we'll get on with".*

295. AZOR AHAI ★★★
b.c. Sixties Icon – Good Morning Lady (Compton Place). March 2. First foal. The dam is an unplaced half-sister to 4 winners including the very useful 7f winner of 4 races here and in the UAE Sirocco Breeze, the fairly useful 5f and 6f winner of 4 races Show Flower and the 5f and 6f winner of 15 races (including when useful at 2 yrs) Caustic Wit. The second dam, Baldemosa (by Lead On Time), won over 1m in France at 3 yrs and is a half-sister to 4 winners including the Group 1 5.5f Prix Robert Papin winner Balbonella (herself dam of the top-class sprinter and sire Anabaa, the French 1,000 Guineas winner Always Loyal and the sire Key Of Luck) and the French Listed 12f winner Bamwhite. *"A very nice colt, more of a six/seven furlong 2-y-o and all Sixties Icon horses are full of quality – all good-looking horses".*

296. BARBILL (IRE) ★★★
b.c. Zebedee – Fiuise (Montjeu). May 8. Second foal. €30,000Y. Tattersalls Ireland September. Gill Richardson. The dam is an unraced half-sister to 3 minor winners. The second dam, Winning Sequence (by Zafonic), a minor 2-y-o 7.5f winner at Deauville, is closely related to the Group 1 Prix Saint-Alary winner Coquerelle and a half-sister to 5 winners. (M R Channon). *"A very nice colt, he's just had a bit of ringworm that's set us back and he's a May foal so I haven't bothered him. He'll be a six/seven furlong 2-y-o going forward".*

297. BUNGLE BROWN SUGAR (IRE) ★★★
b.c. Bungle Inthejungle – Splashofchocolate (Intikhab). February 6. First foal. €8,000Y. Tattersalls Ireland Ascot. C de Moubray. The dam is an unraced half-sister to 6 winners including the fairly useful 2-y-o Group 3 Oh So Sharp Stakes third Hasty. The second dam, Saramacca (by Kahyasi), a 12f winner at 4 yrs, is a half-sister to 6 winners. (Mr Chris Wright).

"A very nice horse, she's a big filly but she's one we'll be looking at soon to see if she's a 2-y-o. She's a bit like her sire, has a fair bit of speed and I like her. Showing all the right signs".

298. CERTAIN LAD ★★

b.c. Clodovil – Chelsey Jayne (Galileo). April 29. Seventh foal. 13,000Y. Tattersalls October Book 3. Gill Richardson. Half-brother to the fairly useful 12f and 14f winner of 7 races Brandon Castle (by Dylan Thomas), to the fairly useful 10f and 2m winner The Statesman (by Zoffany) and the fair 2-y-o 7f winner Chelsea Mick (by Hawk Wing). The dam, placed fourth once over 10f, is a sister to the fairly useful 2-y-o Listed 1m winner Classic Legend, closely related to the useful 10f winner and Listed-placed Popmurphy and a half-sister to 4 winners including the Group 3 July Stakes third Jallota. The second dam, Lady Lahar (by Fraam), a useful 2-y-o Group 3 7f Futurity Stakes and 3-y-o 8.3f winner, was third in the Group 2 Falmouth Stakes and is a half-sister to 4 winners. (Mr C. R. Hirst). *"A lovely horse, he does everything like a professional and I think he'll be all right if we give him a bit of time".*

299. CHERRY COLA ★★★

ch.f. Sixties Icon – Rose Cheval (Johannesburg). May 3. Fifth foal. Sister to the quite useful 2-y-o dual 6f winner Sixties Sue, to the quite useful 5f (at 2 yrs) and 6f winner of 4 races Marquee Club and the fair 2-y-o dual 5f winner Scargill. The dam, a fair 7f (at 2 yrs) to 9f placed maiden, is a half-sister to 2 winners in North America. The second dam, La Samanna (by Trempolino), won 2 minor races at 3 and 4 yrs in the USA and is a half-sister to 5 winners. *"A nice filly that just needs to mature – she's just not there yet. She's got a bit of speed and shows that she'll be a 2-y-o but she's long and gangly at the moment".*

300. CHYNNA ★★★

br.f. Gregorian – Natalie Jay (Ballacashtal). May 6. Half-sister to the fairly useful 6f (at 2 yrs) and 10f winner and Group 3 7f Prix du Calvados third Fork Handles (by Doyen), to the modest dual 11f and hurdles winner Hoar Frost (by Fraam), the modest 12f winner Ingleby Mackenzie (by Sixties Icon) and the poor 8.5f winner Think (by Sulamani). The

dam, a fair winner of 5 races from 6f to 1m, is a half-sister to 3 winners including the Listed Sceptre Stakes winner You Know The Rules. The second dam, Falls Of Lora (by Scottish Rifle), won 6 races from 6f to 14f and from 2 to 4 yrs and is a half-sister to 10 winners. *"A smashing filly, she'll be a 2-y-o and she goes well. Quite a late foal but she'll be an April runner".*

301. CITY WANDERER (IRE) ★★★★

b.c. Kodiac – Viletta (Doyen). April 18. Second foal. 120,000Y. Tattersalls October Book 1. Gill Richardson. Half-brother to Soldiers Bay (by Acclamation), a fair 2017 1m fourth placed 2-y-o. The dam, a German Listed 2-y-o 7.5f winner, was Group 3 placed and is a half-sister to 8 winners – mainly in Germany. The second dam, Vallauris (by Surumu), is an unraced half-sister to 6 winners in Germany. (George Materna & Roger Badley). *"Yes, he's a very nice colt and is probably one to start off in late April. He'll most likely want six furlongs and he goes well".*

302. COTTONTAIL ★★

b.f. Champs Elysees – Effie B (Sixties Icon). February 10. Second foal. Half-sister to the fairly useful Listed-placed 2-y-o 5f and 6f winner Neola (by Foxwedge). The dam, a quite useful Listed-placed 5f and 6f winner of four races at 2 and 3 yrs, is a half-sister to 2 winners including the fair 6f (at 2 yrs) to 7f winner Willsy. The second dam, Blakeshall Rose (by Tobougg), a modest 6f placed maiden, is a half-sister to 2 winners. (Bastian Family). *"I think she'll be all right a bit later on, but she was late coming in and the poor weather we've had has set all the 2-y-o fillies back a bit. Being by Champs Elysees isn't likely to help to get her out any earlier either".*

303. COTUBANAMA ★★★

b.f. Heeraat – Saona Island (Bahamian Bounty). April 3. The dam is an unraced half-sister to 3 winners. The second dam, Perfect Partner (by Be My Chief), is an unraced half-sister to 6 winners including the Ayr Gold Cup winner Funfair Wane and the Italian Listed winner Cabcharge Striker. (Box 41). *"Quite a nice filly, she did a bit of work yesterday and pleased me. I think she'll be a 2-y-o and she goes all right".*

304. DEAR MIRIAM (IRE) ★★
b.f. Acclamation – Phillippa (Galileo). March 9. Seventh foal. €50,000Y. Goffs Orby. Gill Richardson. Half-sister to the fairly useful 10f and 12f winner and Group 3 13f second Naseem Alyasmeen (by Clodovil), to the fairly useful triple 10f winner Rockspirit (by Fastnet Rock), the fair 2-y-o 8.5f winner Aabir (by Invincible Spirit) and the fair 7f (at 2 yrs) and 1m winner Starlight Symphony (by Oratorio). The dam is an unraced half-sister to 4 winners including the 2-y-o Listed 10f Zetland Stakes winner Amir Zaman. The second dam, Kardashina (by Darshaan), won 3 races in France from 11f to 12.5f and is a full or half-sister to 5 winners including the Listed winners Kart Star and Karmifira. (Mr T P Radford). *"She's a lovely filly for later on, being out of a Galileo she's probably one for seven furlongs from the mid-season onwards".*

305. IZZER ★★★★
gr.c. Clodovil – Broadway Musical (Exceed And Excel). March 14. First foal. 11,000Y. Tattersalls Book 3. Gill Richardson. The dam, a moderate dual 10.5f fourth placed maiden, is a half-sister to 5 minor winners. The second dam, Broadway Hit (by Sadler's Wells), is an unraced half-sister to the Group 1 winners Dank, Eagle Mountain and Sulk. (David Hudd & Chris Wright). *"Winner of the Brocklesby, we think he's quite a nice little horse – not a superstar but he's a real Clodovil with a good brain. I think he'll go on because of his temperament – he's a real street fighter".*

306. JUNGLE INTHEBUNGLE (IRE) ★★★★
ch.c. Bungle Inthebungle – Princess Banu (Oasis Dream). March 10. Third foal. €8,000Y. Tattersalls Ireland September. Emerald Bloodstock. Half-brother to the fair 5f winner at 2 and 3 yrs The Nazca Lines (by Fast Company). The dam, a modest 2-y-o 5f winner, is a half-sister to 3 winners. The second dam, Paradise Isle (by Bahamian Bounty), a useful 5f (at 2 yrs) and 6f winner of 8 races including two Listed events, was third in the Group 3 6f Summer Stakes and is a full or half-sister to 9 winners including the useful broodmare Clincher Club. (Mrs T. Burns). *"A smashing colt, I want to start him on the all-weather because he's a top of the ground horse and he's not going to get that for a while*

on the turf. He goes really well, has a great cruising speed and he's a proper 2-y-o".

307. JUNGLE JUICE (IRE) ★★
b.f. Bungle Inthejungle – Riymaisa (Traditionally). April 24. Seventh foal. €32,000Y. Goffs Sportsmans. Gill Richardson. Half-sister to the quite useful 2-y-o dual 6f winner and Group 3 6f Dick Poole Stakes third Unilit (by Approve), to the fair 7f and 1m winner Ray's The Money (by Dragon Pulse) and a 2-y-o winner in Sweden by Majestic Missile. The dam, placed at 3 yrs in France, is a half-sister to 5 winners including the Listed 10f Pretty Polly Stakes winner Riyalma. The second dam, Riyafa (by Kahyasi), was a Listed 12f winner at Ascot. *"She's a nice filly but like a lot of them she's got a coat on her like a teddy bear because of the poor weather. She shows plenty of ability and I thought she'd have been one of the early ones. The fillies are definitely behind this year".*

308. KARALINI (IRE) ★★★★
b.f. Es Que Love – Lucky Leigh (Piccolo). March 4. Fifth foal. £28,000Y. Goffs UK Silver. Gill Richardson. Half-sister to the Listed-placed 5f to 6.5f winner of 7 races from 2 to 6 yrs Something Lucky (by Clodovil). The dam, a fairly useful dual 5f winner (including at 2 yrs), was fourth in the Group 2 Queen Mary Stakes and is a full or half-sister to 5 winners. The second dam, Solmorin (by Fraam), is an unplaced half-sister to 2 minor winners. (Mrs John Lee, Alf Heaney, Alec Tuckerman). *"A smashing filly, she's very hairy and backward at the moment but she's got bags of scope. I think she's very nice but she's still untapped. Does everything in a very professional manner and I'm very happy with her".* TRAINER'S BARGAIN BUY

309. KINKS ★★★★
b.c. Sixties Icon – Crazee Diamond (Rock Of Gibraltar). March 27. First foal. €14,000Y. Goffs Sportsmans. Gill Richardson. The dam, a modest 6f winner, is a half-sister to the fairly useful Listed-placed winning sprinter Thesme. The second dam, Final Dynasty (by Komaite), a useful 5f winner at 2 and 3 yrs, was Listed-placed twice and is a sister to the 2-y-o Group 3 5f Cornwallis Stakes winner Castelletto and a half-sister to 8 winners including the useful 6f winner (including at 2 yrs) Lake Garda. *"A*

smashing little horse, he's ready to go and I think he'll win early doors. A home-bred, I sold him as a foal and bought him back as a yearling! He's a definite 2-y-o and out of a fast mare".

310. KNOCKABOUT QUEEN ★★★
b.f. Sixties Icon – Rough Courte (Clodovil). February 12. First foal. The dam, a fair 1m winner of 3 races, is a half-sister to one winner. The second dam, Straight Sets (by Pivotal), a fair 4-y-o 7f winner, is a half-sister to 4 winners including the very smart Group 3 10.3f Huxley Stakes and 2-y-o Listed 7f winner Championship Point. *"She's quite a nice filly. A first foal, she goes well and I think she'll be ready to run in May".*

311. LETHAL GUEST ★★★★
b.c. Lethal Force – Holberg Suite (Azamour). February 6. Second foal. £72,000Y. Goffs UK Premier (Doncaster). Gill Richardson. The dam, a fair 11f winner, is a half-sister to 5 winners. The second dam, Humouresque (by Pivotal), a smart Group 3 10.5f Prix Penelope winner, is a sister to 2 winners including the Group 2 placed Mighty and a half-sister to 4 winners including the very smart sprinter and multiple Group 3 winner Danehurst. (John Guest Racing Ltd). *"A smasher, he's not likely to be really early when you look what his dam did, but he's definitely worth keeping an eye on".*

312. MODERN MILLIE ★★★
b.f. Sixties Icon – Hairspray (by Bahamian Bounty). April 26. Fourth foal. Sister to the useful Listed 7f (at 2 yrs) and Group 3 8.5f Princess Elizabeth Stakes winner Epsom Icon and half-sister to the fair 2017 5f placed 2-y-o Dusty (by Paco Boy). The dam, a fairly useful 6f winner of 4 races (including at 2 yrs), is a sister to 2 winners and a half-sister to 5 winners including the useful Listed-placed 2-y-o Medieval. The second dam, Quickstyx (by Night Shift), a fair 1m winner, is a half-sister to 5 winners including the smart 12f Listed winner and US dual Grade 1 placed Red Fort and the useful 12f Listed winner Red Carnation. *"She's very nice and one for a bit later on. She's got a lot of quality, her sister won a Listed over seven furlongs as a 2-y-o and this is a better individual. I've got a lot of top drawer Sixties Icon fillies that just need a bit more time to mature".*

313. QUIRKY GERTIE (IRE) ★★★
b.f. Fast Company – Acushladear (Tagula). March 22. Fourth foal. 19,000Y. Tattersalls October Book 3. Gill Richardson. Half-sister to the fairly useful Irish 2-y-o 5f winner Ready To Roc (by Roderic O'Connor). The dam, a quite useful 7.5f to 10.5f winner of 3 races, is a half-sister to 4 minor winners. The second dam, Darling Smile (by Darshaan), is an unraced half-sister to 4 winners. *"A lovely filly, doing everything right and very professional. She'll probably need six furlongs".*

314. RAKASTAVA (IRE) ★★★
gr.c. Clodovil – Shemissa (Fairy King). April 3. Twelfth foal. £36,000Y. Tattersalls Ireland Ascot. Gill Richardson. Half-brother to 6 winners including the US Listed stakes winner and Group 1 Prix Jean-Luc Lagardere winner Shediak (by Selkirk) and the fairly useful Irish 1m winner Shehira (by Sendawar). The dam is an unraced half-sister to 6 winners including the French dual Group 3 winner Shemima. The second dam, Shemaka (by Nishapour), won the Group 1 Prix de Diane and is a half-sister to 5 winners. (Box 41). *"He's a smasher and I thought he'd have been early but he had a bit of a setback. We'll have a look at him in May because he goes real well. Early on he was bowling along with all my early colts".*

315. RED FLOWER (IRE) ★★★
b.f. Bungle Inthejungle – Common Cause (Polish Patriot). March 28. 8,500Y. Tattersalls October Book 3. Gill Richardson. Half-sister to 6 winners including the Irish Listed 9f winner of 9 races Wovoka, the quite useful 2-y-o 7.5f winner Apple Anni (by Fast Company), the modest 7f winner Banjo Bandit (both by Mujadil), the fair 1m and hurdles winner Letham Island (by Trans Island) and to the placed dam of the Italian 2-y-o Group 2 second Singapore Lilly. The dam, a quite useful 11.5f and 11.8f winner, is a half-sister to 4 minor winners. The second dam, Alongside, (by Slip Anchor), an Irish 4-y-o 9f winner, is a half-sister to 3 winners including the Group 2 Prix Eugene Adam winner Kirkwall. (Mrs T. Burns). *"I haven't done a lot with her but she's a very nice filly. She's going to need a bit of time, so she's one for the middle of the season".*

316. SOCIETY GUEST ★★★★

b.f. Society Rock – Bronze Baby (Silver Charm). May 12. Sixth foal. £58,000Y. Goffs UK Premier (Doncaster). Gill Richardson. Half-sister to the fair 2017 2-y-o 6f and 7f winner Lexington Grace (by Sir Prancealot), to the fair 2-y-o 7f winner Scutum, the modest 7f winner Sunbaked (both by Kodiac) and the poor 10f winner Redlorryyellowlorry (by Bushranger). The dam is an unplaced half-sister 4 winners including the dual Group 3 winner and triple Group 1 placed Arch Swing. The second dam, Gold Pattern (by Slew O'Gold), a minor US winner of 4 races, is a half-sister to 7 winners. (John Guest Racing Ltd). *"A lovely filly, she'll be a 2-y-o but she was a late foal and like a lot of my fillies she needs some sun on her back. She's very nice".*

317. SOLESMES ★★★

b.f. Gregorian – Bridie ffrench (Bahamian Bounty). March 19. First foal. The dam, a fair 7f and 1m winner, is a half-sister to 4 winners including the fairly useful 6f (at 2 yrs) and Listed 10f winner Cruck Realta. The second dam, Wansdyke Lass (by Josr Algharoud), a modest 10f seller winner, is a half-sister to 2 minor winners. *"A smashing filly, she's forward enough to be a 2-y-o for five/six furlongs. I like her and in fact I like all the Gregorian 2-y-o's I've seen. They're all different shapes and sizes but they're all all right and I think he'll shake a few up because nobody's mentioning him amongst the first season sires".*

318. SWINGING JEAN ★★★★

b.f. Sixties Icon – Shrimpton (Cadeaux Genereux). March 28. First foal. The dam, a fair 2-y-o 5f winner, is a half-sister to 4 winners including the fairly useful 1m and 9f winner Just Hiss and the quite useful 2-y-o 5f winner Mazzanti. The second dam, Feather Boa (by Sri Pekan), a quite useful 2-y-o dual 6f winner, is a half-sister to 6 winners including the Listed winner Wagtail. *"You must put her in the book because she's a smasher and I can go with her whenever I want to. A filly with a lot of quality, she's a bit more forward than some of the others".*

319. TWO BLONDES (IRE) ★★★★

ch.c. Dragon Pulse – Itaya (Namid). March 22. Fourth foal. £25,000Y. Goffs UK Premier.

Gill Richardson. The dam is an unplaced half-sister to 5 winners including the very smart 7f (at 2yrs) and Group 1 12f Irish Oaks winner Winona and the Irish 6f (at 2 yrs) and Group 3 7f Killavullen Stakes third Carlisle Bay. The second dam, My Potters (by Irish River), an Irish 3-y-o 1m handicap winner, is a half-sister to numerous winners including the champion US sprinter My Juliet (herself the dam of two Grade 1 winners), the good middle-distance colt Lyphard's Special and the 2-y-o 6f Blue Seal Stakes winner New Trends. (Mr J Turner). *"A lovely horse, he goes really well and does everything like a professional. I think we'll wait for the six furlong races with him".*

320. VALENTINO SUNRISE ★★

b.c. Sixties Icon – Leleyf (Kheleyf). February 14. Second foal. The dam, a fair 2-y-o triple 5f winner, was Listed-placed at 3 yrs and is a half-sister to 3 winners. The second dam, Titchwell Lass (by Lead On Time), a moderate 10f winner, is a half-sister to numerous winners. (Peter Taplin). *"There's a bit of speed there because the dam was sharp. He shows a bit but I would think he'd need six or seven furlongs".*

321. UNNAMED ★★★★

b.c. Slade Power – Bound Copy (Street Cry). March 4. First foal. 27,000Y. Tattersalls October Book 2. Gill Richardson. The dam, placed once at 3 yrs, is a half-sister to 2 minor winners. The second dam, In A Bound (by Ashkalani), a Group 2 winner in Australia, is out of the multiple Australian Group 1 winner Bounding Away. *"A very nice colt, I think he could be anything; he's very professional but he's big and has plenty of scope, so he could be a proper horse".*

322. UNNAMED ★★

b.f. Mukhadram – Classical Dancer (Dr Fong). March 15. Ninth foal. 13,000Y. Tattersalls October Book 3. Gill Richardson. Half-sister to the fairly useful 1m (at 2 yrs) and 7f winner Brave Hero (by Poet's Voice), to the quite useful 7f, 1m (both at 2 yrs) and 12f winner Zaaqya, the quite useful 2-y-o 7f winner Double Touch (by Dutch Art) and the fair 9f winner Topanga Canyon (both by Nayef). The dam, a fairly useful 8.3f winner, was Listed-placed twice and is a half-sister to 6 winners including the Group 1 Premio Roma winner Imperial Dancer. The second dam, Gorgeous Dancer (by Nordico), an Irish 3-y-o 1m winner and third in the Listed Irish Oaks Trial, is a half-sister to 3 winners. *"One for later in the season, she's a nice filly and she goes quite nicely but she needs a bit of time".*

323. UNNAMED ★★★
ch.f. Sixties Icon – Madame Hoi (Hawk Wing). February 20. Sister to the fairly useful 1m and 10f winner here and US Grade 2 1m winner Nancy From Nairobi. The dam, a fair 6f winner, is a half-sister to the 2-y-o Group 1 Phoenix Stakes second Amadeus Mozart. The second dam, Lindesburg (by Doyoun), was placed 3 times over 6f including at 2 yrs and is a half-sister to 6 winners including the very smart triple Group 2 1m winner Gothenburg. (Norman Court Stud). *"She's a very nice filly and one I'm treating like she's a good one, but like a lot of the fillies she's a bit behind at the moment because of the weather".*

324. UNNAMED ★★
b.c. Rip Van Winkle – Miss Lahar (Clodovil). March 6. Second foal. The dam, a Listed 6f winner, was dual Group 3 placed and is a half-sister to 4 winners including the 2-y-o Group 3 7f Futurity Stakes winner and Group 2 1m Falmouth Stakes third Lady Lahar (herself the dam of two stakes winners). The second dam, Brigadiers Bird (by Mujadil), is an unraced half-sister to 3 winners. (Barry Walters Catering). *"A lovely big colt for later on, I haven't rushed him, he's out of a Listed winner and he'll want six or seven furlongs".*

325. UNNAMED ★★★
b.f. Society Rock – Liscoa (Foxhound). April 18. Seventh foal. €20,000Y. Tattersalls Ireland. Gill Richardson. Half-sister to the fairly useful 2-y-o 5.5f and 6f winner Dougal (by Zebedee), to the fair 5f (at 2 yrs) to 11f winner of 4 races Megamunch (by Camacho), the Italian dual 2-y-o winner Last Child (by Night Shift), the fair 7f and 10f winner Captain Pugwash (by Sir Prancealot) and the fair Irish 5f winner Red Army Blues (by Soviet Star). The dam, a fair Irish 1m and 10f winner, is a half-sister to 4 winners including the useful Irish Listed 6f winner Spencers Wood. The second dam, Ascoli (by Skyliner), an Irish, 10f, 12f and

hurdles winner, is a half-sister to 3 winners. (M R Channon). *"A lovely little filly, not the biggest but she goes really well. She had a little setback otherwise she'd have been one of the more forward ones, but she's all right".*

ROGER CHARLTON

326. ABATE ★★★
br.c. Bated Breath – Red Kyte (Hawk Wing). April 20. Sixth foal. 30,000Y. Tattersalls Book 3. Not sold. Half-brother to the quite useful 1m and 8.5f winner Auberge Du Lac (by Lope De Vega) and to the modest 6f (at 2 yrs) and 7f winner Scarlet Bounty (by Bahamian Bounty). The dam, a quite useful dual winner (including at 2 yrs), is a half-sister to 7 winners including the useful 2-y-o 6f and UAE Listed 5f winner Hammadi. The second dam, Ruby Affair (by Night Shift), a modest 7f placed 3-y-o, is a half-sister to 5 winners including the 2,000 Guineas winner Island Sands. (Malih Al Basti). *"He only came to me recently, Bated Breath seems to be doing well at stud and this colt went through the ring at Tattersalls Book 3 and there's quite a good race for those horses. He looks quite early and strong and I'm happy with him. This colt's dam won at two, so you'd hope he'd be a 2-y-o. This year we have to factor in the fact that because of the bad weather the horses haven't worked on the grass yet, they've just been on the polytrack".*

327. AUSSIE BREEZE ★★★
ch.f. Australia – Terre Du Vent (Kutub). February 21. Second foal. 50,000Y. Tattersalls October Book 1. Not sold. Half-sister to the quite useful 2017 6f placed 2-y-o Carouse (by Excelebration). The dam, a Listed 12f and Listed 15f winner in France, was second in the Group 2 Prix de Malleret and is a half-sister to 6 minor winners abroad. The second dam, Phlizz (by Kaldoun), was placed over 1m in France and is a half-sister to 10 winners including the French Group 3 winner Latona. (Simon Clarke). *"She's a nice filly, scopey and bred to stay but she's a nice mover and we like her. Promising".*

328. BASILISK (USA) ★★★
ch.c. Speightstown – Treat Gently (Cape Cross) April 22. Fifth foal. The dam won the Group 2 12f Prix de Malleret and the US Grade 2 11f Sheepshead Bay Stakes. The second dam, Kid

Gloves (by In The Wings), a minor French 11f winner, is a half-sister to several winners and to the outstanding broodmare Hasili. (Khalid Abdullah). *"From a very good Juddmonte family, he's a late foal and the dam has been slightly disappointing so far in terms of her progeny, but this colt is a nice-looking horse and he's done well".*

329. BE QUICK ★★★ ♣
b.c. Mukhadram – Skyrider (Dalakhani). April 16. Fifth foal. 90,000Y. Tattersalls October Book 3. Amanda Skiffington. Half-brother to a minor winner abroad by Dylan Thomas. The dam, a fair 6f (at 2 yrs) and 10f placed maiden, is a sister to the Italian Group 3 Premio Chiusura winner Gothic Dance and a half-sister to 2 winners. The second dam, Future Flight (by Polar Falcon), a 6f winner at 3 yrs, is a half-sister to 6 winners including the Group 1 Haydock Park Sprint Cup winner Tante Rose, the Sweet Solera Stakes winner Bay Tree and the 2-y-o winner Rosie's Posy (dam of the Group 1 winners Dubawi Heights and Make Believe). (Inglett & De Zoete). *"I trained his dam and he's from the family of Tante Rose. He was a very attractive horse from Book 3, he's not necessarily obvious on pedigree but he moves well and I guess he's bred to stay quite well. Nevertheless he looks a 2-y-o to run in the middle of the year. Shows promise".*

330. BLOWING DIXIE ★★
b.c. Dubawi – Time Control (Sadler's Wells). April 1. Seventh foal. Half-brother to the 2-y-o Group 1 7f Moyglare Stud Stakes and Group 3 6f Albany Stakes winner Cursory Glance (by Distorted Humor). The dam, a quite useful 10f winner, is a sister to the Group 2 Prix de Malleret and Listed Cheshire Oaks winner Time On. The second dam, Time Away (by Darshaan), won the Group 3 10.4f Musidora Stakes, was third in the Group 1 Prix de Diane and the Group 1 Nassau Stakes and is a half-sister to 6 winners including the Prix de Diane second Time Ahead. (Merry Fox Stud). *"A nice horse, he's very big, moves well and I guess on pedigree he'll be a middle-distance horse. So all being well we'll see him in the autumn. The Dubawi/Sadler's Wells is tending to produce horses that want twelve furlongs plus".*

331. CASUAL REPLY ★★★
b.f. Frankel – Passing Parade (Cape Cross). January 23. First foal. The dam is an unraced half-sister to 9 winners including the Group 1 6f Haydock Park Sprint Cup winner Regal Parade, the Group 3 Acomb Stakes winner Entifaadha and the useful triple Group 3 placed Hot Prospect. The dam was unraced. The second dam, Model Queen (by Kingmambo), a fair 3-y-o 7f winner, is a half-sister to 5 winners including the French Listed 1m winner Arabride. (Merry Fox Stud). *"Henry Cecil had the dam and I believe he gave her a Group One entry but she must have had a setback because she was unraced. This filly is attractive but still 'up behind' so she'll grow quite a lot. A nice filly".*

332. DOUBLY BEAUTIFUL (IRE) ★★★
ch.c. Born To Sea – Bella Bella (Sri Pekan). March 1. Seventh foal. 40,000Y. Tattersalls October Book 1. Amanda Skiffington. Half-brother to the fairly useful 7f (at 2 yrs) and 6f winner and Listed-placed Courageous (by Refuse To Bend) and to a bumpers winner by Kalanisi. The dam, a quite useful dual 7f winner, is a half-sister to 5 winners including the German Listed winner and Group 3 third Silk Petal (herself dam of the Listed winner Star Tulip) and the dam of the Group 2 winners Tashawak and Fairy Queen. The second dam, Salabella (by Sallust), is a placed half-sister to 7 winners including the Irish St Leger and the Grosser Preis von Baden winner M-Lolshan. (Paul Inglett). *"He was probably in the wrong catalogue being in Book One because he didn't really appeal enough on pedigree. He's an attractive colt but he's grown up behind quite a lot so he's not as reasonably forward as he once looked. A nice-looking horse that just needs a bit of time".*

333. EUCALYPTUS ★★
b.f. Nayef – Merayaat (Darshaan). March 16. Ninth foal. 90,000Y. Tattersalls October Book 1. John & Jake Warren. Sister to the smart 1m (at 2 yrs) and Group 3 12f Cumberland Lodge Stakes winner Hawaafez and half-sister to the quite useful 2-y-o 1m winner Midhmaar (by Iffraaj) and the fair 14f and 15f winner Nateeja (by Shamardal). The dam was a quite useful 14f winner. The second dam, Maddelina (by Sadler's Wells), is an unplaced half-sister to

2 winners including the dam of the multiple Group 1 winner Moonlight Cloud. (Highclere Thoroughbred Racing – Waddesdon). *"A strong filly, she's not bred to be early but she's physically strong and moves well. She shows a little bit of character but you'd hope she'd be running in the second half of the year".*

334. GREAT BEAR ★★★★ ♠

b.c. Dansili – Great Heavens (Galileo). March 14. Third foal. Half-brother to the fairly useful 2017 2-y-o 1m winner Dubhe (by Dubawi). The dam won the Group 1 Irish Oaks and the Group 2 Lancashire Oaks and is a sister to the King George VI and Queen Elizabeth Stakes and Eclipse winner Nathaniel and a half-sister to 8 winners including Playful Act (Group 1 Fillies' Mile), Percussionist (Group 3 11.5f Lingfield Derby Trial) and Echoes In Eternity (Group 2 1m Sun Chariot Stakes). The second dam, Magnificient Style (by Silver Hawk), won the Group 3 10.5f Musidora Stakes and is a half-sister to the US Grade 1 10f winner Siberian Summer. (Lady Rothschild). *"A very attractive horse from of a very good family. A lovely mover, he's nearer the top of the list than most and although he's bred to stay he's a nice-looking horse for later in the season".*

335. HEADMAN ★★★

b.c. Kingman – Deliberate (King's Best). March 21. Half-brother to the French triple Listed-placed 6.5f and 7f winner of four races at 2 and 3 yrs Projected (by Showcasing), to the French 10f winner and Group 3 9f Prix Chloe second Delivery (by Rail Link) and the fairly useful 7f winner at 2 and 3 yrs Hyde Park (by Oasis Dream). The dam, a French 10f winner, is a half-sister to the Group 1 12f Grand Prix de Paris winner Flintshire and to the French Listed 10f and Listed 12f winner Dance Moves. The second dam, Dance Routine (by Sadler's Wells), winner of the Group 2 12.5f Prix de Royallieu, is a sister to the French 11f winner and Group 3 placed Light Ballet and to the French Listed 10f winner Concentric and a half-sister to the dual Group 3 1m winner Apsis. (Khalid Abdullah). *"He's not here yet, he's in pre-training, but they say he's a very nice horse".*

336. IMPERIUM ★★

ch.c. Frankel – Ramruma (Diesis). June 14.

Thirteenth foal. €100,000Y. Goffs Orby. Badgers Bloodstock. Brother to the moderate 1m placed maiden Touch Of Paradise and half-brother to 2 winners including the smart 1m and 12f winner and Group 1 Irish St Leger third Flying Cross (by Sadler's Wells). The dam won the Oaks, the Irish Oaks and the Yorkshire Oaks and is a sister to the Lingfield Oaks Trial winner and good broodmare Ausherra and to the Listed winner Royal Scimitar and a half-sister to 7 winners. The second dam, Princess Of Man (by Green God), won three races including the Group 3 Musidora Stakes and is a half-sister to 6 winners. (Weston, Brook Farm and Bromfield). *"A very big, backward horse, he was here before Christmas but he's had a break and is due to come back in shortly. The mare has been disappointing but for a Frankel he wasn't expensive and he's a nice-looking individual".*

337. JUNIOR RIP ★★★

b.c. Rip Van Winkle – Sarawati (Haafhd). March 18. Fourth foal. €50,000Y. Goffs Orby. Nick Bradley / Roger Charlton. Half-brother to the Group 1 Italian Derby winner of 6 races Ventura Storm (by Zoffany) and to the modest 10f winner Bella Varenna (by Lawman). The dam, placed fourth once over 9f in Ireland from four starts, is a half-sister to 5 winners including the Listed winner and Group 2 Lancashire Oaks second Sahool and the dams of the dual Group 2 Hardwicke Stakes winner Maraahel and the Group 2 Flying Childers winner Gutaifan. The second dam, Mathaayl (by Shadeed), a quite useful 6f and 10f winner, is a half-sister to 3 winners including Muhbubh (Group 3 Princess Margaret Stakes). (Nick Bradley 19). *"Well-bought by Nick Bradley, he's a very good mover and reasonably forward. Quite a strong colt, I'd expect him to stay well but seven furlongs in mid-season might be possible to start with".*

338. LADY ADELAIDE (IRE) ★★★

b.f. Australia – Confusion (Anabaa). February 23. Second foal. The dam, a minor French 3-y-o winner, is a half-sister to 3 other minor winners. The second dam, Red Stella (by Nureyev), a French Listed 12f winner, is a half-sister to Special Quest (Group 1 Criterium de Saint-Cloud) and Moiava (Group 2 Criterium de Maisons-Laffitte). (Fishdance). *"We like her, she's quite strong and deep, moves well and looks OK".*

339. MIDPORT (IRE) ★★
b.c. Dabirsim – Monspa (Monsun). February 9. Second foal. 90,000Y. Tattersalls October Book 2. Amanda Skiffington. The dam, a minor French 3-y-o winner, is a half-sister to 9 winners including the smart 1m (at 2 yrs) and Listed 10f winner and Group 2 Hardwicke Stakes third Persian Majesty. The second dam, Spa (by Sadler's Wells), is an unraced half-sister to 5 winners including the Group 2 Hardwicke Stakes winner Sandmason and the Listed 10f winner Sardegna. (P Inglett & P Hearson). *"A very attractive horse by Dabirsim. He was a good 2-y-o, didn't train on, but is starting to do well at stud. The dam is from a good staying family and this colt is a big, good-looking horse so I'd expect him to stay well. I like him".*

340. MISTER MERLIN ★★
gr.c. Dark Angel – Rosehill Artist (Excellent Art). February 1. First foal. 80,000Y. Tattersalls October Book 2. Amanda Skiffington. The dam, a quite useful 7f (at 2 yrs) and 10f winner, is a half-sister to one minor winner in France. The second dam, Conference (by Montjeu), is an unraced half-sister to 7 winners including the minor US stakes winner and Group 3 Chester Vase third Distant Mirage. (Paul Inglett & Simon de Zoete). *"A big horse, he'll need a bit of time and is one for the autumn and next year".*

341. MOMKIN (IRE) ★★★★
b.c. Bated Breath – Contradict (Raven's Pass). February 20. Second foal. The dam, a fair 10f winner, is a half-sister to two minor winners. The second dam, Acts Of Grace (by Bahri), won the Group 3 12f Princess Royal Stakes and is a half-sister to 10 winners including the Group 1 Sprint Cup winner and good sire Invincible Spirit. (Prince A A Faisal). *"He's a nice horse, very attractive, moves well and we like him. He's apparently got an unraced 3-y-o half-brother with Andre Fabre who is going to debut in a Classic trial".*

342. NED MACKAY ★★★
b.c. Kodiac – Marywell (Selkirk). January 31. Fourth foal. Half-brother to the very useful

Listed 12f winner Martlet, to the 10f winner, from two starts, Keswick (both by Dansili) and the fair 1m and 8.5f winner Palmerston (by Oasis Dream). The dam, a quite useful 11f winner, is a sister to the fairly useful 10f and 12f winner Rosslyn Castle and a half-sister to 3 winners including the Australian Group 1 2m winner Grand Marshal (by Dansili). The second dam, Margarula (by Doyoun), a 1m (at 2 yrs) and Group 1 12f Irish Oaks winner, is a half-sister to 4 winners including the Irish 2-y-o Listed 9f winner Wild Heaven. (Lady Rothschild). *"He's only just arrived but he's a strong, forward-looking horse – as you'd hope a Kodiac might be. There is stamina on the dam's side which I'm not sure suits Kodiac but we'll see. He looks a strong colt and he's a cheeky horse so you'd hope that he'd be a seven furlong/mile horse later in the year".*

343. ORCHIDIA (IRE) ★★★
ch.f. Bated Breath – New Orchid (Quest For Fame). April 17. Ninth foal. €120,000Y. Goffs Orby. Badgers Bloodstock. Half-sister to 5 winners including the Group 1 6f Haydock Sprint Cup and French Listed 7f winner African Rose (dam of the 2-y-o Group 3 winner Fair Eva), the 2-y-o Group 3 1m Prix d'Aumale winner Helleborine (both by Observatory) and the quite useful dual 10f winner Cultivar (by Xaar). The dam, a useful 10f winner and third in the Group 3 Lancashire Oaks, is a half-sister to 3 winners including the champion 2-y-o and Group 1 Dewhurst Stakes winner Distant Music. The second dam, Musicanti (by Nijinsky), a French 14.5f winner, is a half-sister to Vanlandingham, winner of the Washington D.C. International, the Jockey Club Gold Cup and the Suburban Handicap. (Glentree Pastoral Pty. Ltd). *"She's from a family we know quite well and is a big, rangy filly. She's on a break at the moment but she moves well, will need time but what we've seen we like".*

344. RED IMPRESSION ★★★
gr.f. Dark Angel – Purissima (Fusaichi Pegasus). April 22. Half-sister to the quite useful 8.5f winner Perigee (by Cacique) and to the fair 7f winner Ramshackle (by Dansili). The dam, a fairly useful 2-y-o 6f winner, is a half-sister to numerous winners including the Group 1 7f Prix de la Foret winner Etoile Montante. The second dam, Willstar (by Nureyev), won over

1m in France and is a half-sister to the US Grade 2 winner Revasser. (Khalid Abdullah). *"A nice filly, she's strong and a typical Dark Angel. There's a bit of stamina on the dam's side but she ought to be a 2-y-o. She's one of those we'll push on with if we can".*

345. SAILING (GER) ★★
b.f. Lope De Vega – Sail (Sadler's Wells). April 13. Seventh foal. 230,000Y. Tattersalls October Book 2. Juddmonte Farms. Closely related to the 5.5f to 1m winner and Group 3 Prix de Meautry second Walec (by Shamardal) and half-sister to the modest 2-y-o 9.5f winner Sailor's Way (by Dubawi). The dam, a Listed Cheshire Oaks winner, is a sister to the Listed winners Rave Review and Fermion and a half-sister to 4 winners including the Group 3 winner Hearthstead Maison. The second dam, Pieds De Plume (by Seattle Slew), placed second once over 1m at 3 yrs in France, is closely related to the French Listed and US stakes winner Slew The Slewor and a half-sister to the Group 1 Prix Lupin winner and sire Groom Dancer, the French Group 3 winner Tagel and the dam of the French Group 1 winner Plumania. (Khalid Abdullah). *"Bought by Juddmonte Farms at the sales, she still at the stud and hasn't arrived yet".*

346. SHORE (USA) ★★★
b.c. First Defence – Romantica (Galileo). May 26. First foal. The dam won four races including the Group 1 Prix Jean Romanet and is a half-sister to the dual Listed winner Ideal World. The second dam, Banks Hill (by Danehill), won the Coronation Stakes, Prix Jacques Le Marois and Breeders Cup Filly & Mare Turf and is a full or half-sister to the Group/Grade 1 winners Heat Haze, Intercontinental, Cacique and Champs Elysees and to the Group 2 winner and high-class sire Dansili. (Khalid Abdullah). *"A nice horse but a very late foal, he's out of a Group 1 winning mare from one of the best families in the book. He's strong and is obviously going to grow a bit but you'd have to have him on the list".*

347. TATSIA ★★★★
b.f. Showcasing – Ombre (Galileo). March 24. Second foal. Half-sister to the useful 2017 2-y-o 6f and 7f winner, Group 2 Rockfel Stakes third and Group 3 Oh So Sharp Stakes

second Gavota (by Bated Breath). The dam is an unraced half-sister to 4 winners including the useful French 7f (at 2 yrs) and 1m winner and Listed placed World Ruler and the useful French 2-y-o dual 6f winner and Group 3 1m third Grand Vista. The second dam, Revealing (by Halling), a very useful 2-y-o 1m winner, is a half-sister to the useful 12f winner and dual Group 3 placed Singleton and the useful 6f winner Brevity. (Khalid Abdullah). *"A half-sister to Gavota who did well last year, this filly is stronger-bodied, moves well and although she's out of a Galileo mare one would hope she'd be a six furlong filly in July".*

348. TAVUS (IRE) ★★
b.c. Pour Moi – La Persiana (Daylami). April 30. Eighth living foal. 65,000Y. Tattersalls December. Amanda Skiffington /Tony Bloom. Half-brother to the quite useful 7f (at 2 yrs), 12f and subsequent US Listed 12f winner Qushchi (by Encosta De Lago), to the quite useful 1m winner Persepolis (by Dansili), the quite useful 10f winner Perrault (by Rip Van Winkle) and the fair 2-y-o 6f winner Djinni (by Invincible Spirit). The dam, a very useful dual Listed 10f winner, is a half-sister to 7 winners including the champion 2-y-o Grand Lodge (Group 1 7f Dewhurst Stakes and Group 1 1m St James's Palace Stakes etc,) and the useful Listed 1m winner Papabile. The second dam, La Papagena (by Habitat), is an unraced half-sister to 7 winners including the Listed winners Lost Chord and Eagling. (Tony Bloom). *"A good mover, he's on a break at the moment but he's quite a nice horse. I think he was reasonably good value because the sire isn't fashionable. I'd be happy with him, he was bought as a long-term prospect and I don't see any reason why he won't be that".*

349. TEMPUS ★★★
b.c. Kingman – Passage Of Time (Dansili). April 5. Half-brother to the Group 2 1m Joel Stakes, Group 2 10.5f York Stakes and dual Group 3 winner Time Test, to the fairly useful 1m and 10f winner Time Chaser (both by Dubawi) and the useful 11f and 12f winner Retirement Plan (by Monsun). The dam, winner of the Group 1 10f Criterium de Saint-Cloud (at 2 yrs) and the Group 3 10.3f Musidora Stakes, is a sister to the Group 2 12f King Edward VI Stakes winner Father Time and

a half-sister to the Group 1 Falmouth Stakes winner Timepiece. The second dam, Clepsydra (by Sadler's Wells), a quite useful 12f winner, is a half-sister to numerous winners including the useful Listed 10.5f winner Double Crossed. (Khalid Abdullah). *"He's a bit like Time Test and Time Chaser who are both trained here. He's a deep, strong horse, it's early days for him but he has a nice pedigree and he's a good physical individual".*

350. THORN ★★★★
b.c. Dansili – Thistle Bird (Selkirk). February 12. First foal. The dam, a smart Group 1 10f Pretty Polly Stakes and dual Group 3 9f winner of 8 races, is a half-sister to 3 winners including the fairly useful 7f (at 2 yrs) and 1m winner McCreery. The second dam, Dolma (by Marchand de Sable), won 6 races over 6f and 7f (including at 2 yrs), notably three Listed events at 3 yrs. (Lady Rothschild). *"The first foal out of Thistle Bird, a filly that did us a lot of favours and ended up winning a Group One. He's a bit immature looking and has a lot of growing to do, but what we've seen we like, he moves well and I think he'll end up being a strong horse. Could be anything really".*

351. YIMKIN (IRE) ★★
b.f. Kingman – Orpha (New Approach). March 10. Second foal. The dam, a fairly useful 2-y-o 6f winner, is a half-sister to 4 winners including the Group 1 9f Prix Jean Prat winner Olden Times and the useful 1m (at 2 yrs) and Listed 6f winner and Group 1 Cheveley Park Stakes third Festoso. The second dam, Garah (by Ajdal), a very useful winner of 4 races over 6f, was second in the Group 3 5f Duke Of York Stakes and is a half-sister to 6 winners. (Prince A A Faisal). *"A little bit small, she needs to strengthen up so she may have a break in a few weeks' time. So she's a bit of an unknown quantity but she's out of a filly that Mick Channon trained and thought a lot of".*

352. UNNAMED ★★★
ch.f. Frankel – Ascot Family (Desert Style). April 7. Seventh foal. Half-sister to the 2-y-o Group 2 5.5f Prix Robert Papin and Group 3 5f Prix du Bois winner Family One (by Dubai Destination) and to the French Listed-placed 2-y-o 5f winner Modern Family (by Excellent Art). The dam, a French 2-y-o Listed 5f winner,

is a half-sister to numerous winners including the very useful Listed Scarborough Stakes winner and Group 2 Kings Stand Stakes second Flanders (herself dam of the US Grade 3 winner Louvain). The second dam, Family At War (by Explodent), a fair 2-y-o 5f winner, is a half-sister to 4 minor winners in the USA. (Andrew Rosen). *"It's a fast family so she's bred to be a sprinter and we hope she'll make a 2-y-o".*

353. UNNAMED ★★
b.c. Dansili – Could It Be (Galileo). February 12. Second foal. The dam is an unraced sister to the Group 1 Moyglare Stud Stakes, Prix Marcel Boussac (both at 2 yrs), Irish 1,000 Guineas and Pretty Polly Stakes winner Misty For Me, to the 2-y-o Group 1 1m Prix Marcel Boussac winner Ballydoyle and the useful Listed 9f winner and dual Group 3 placed Twirl. The second dam, Butterfly Cove (by Storm Cat), is an unraced sister to the Irish 1,000 Guineas Trial winner Kamarinskaya and a half-sister to the champion 2-y-o colt Fasliyev. (Sheikh Mohammed bin Khalifa Al Thani). *"A rangy, back-end/3-y-o type horse, he has a nice pedigree and he's a nice individual".*

354. UNNAMED ★★★
b.c. Exceed And Excel – Crysdal (Dalakhani). February 14. First foal. 90,000Y. Tattersalls October Book 1. Badgers Bloodstock. The dam was unplaced on both her starts and is a half-sister to 5 winners and to the unraced dam of the Group 2 Prix Greffulhe winner Ocovango. The second dam, Crystal Music (by Nureyev), winner of the Group 1 Fillies' Mile at 2 yrs and second in the Irish 1,000 Guineas and the Coronation Stakes, is closely related to the Group 3 12f John Porter Stakes winner Dubai Success and a half-sister to the Group 3 winners Solar Crystal and State Crystal. (Brook Farm Bloodstock). *"A strong horse and probably more of a 2-y-o than some of the others, the sire does well with his 2-y-o's and this is quite a good family. I'd like to think that he'd be a six/seven furlong colt from mid-season onwards. Not an early 2-y-o then, but he's one we'll be pressing on with".*

355. UNNAMED ★★★
br.c. Oasis Dream – Ferevia (Motivator). January 29. First foal. The dam won the Group

3 Prix Penelope winner and was third in the Group 1 Prix Saint-Alary. The second dam, Frynia (by Cat Thief), a minor French winner of 2 races at 3 yrs, is a half-sister to 5 winners. (Sheikh Mohammed bin Khalifa Al Thani). *"A neat horse out of a very smart middle-distance mare, he should make a 2-y-o".*

356. UNNAMED ★★★
b.c. Iffraaj – Lady Nouf (Teofilo). February 13. Second foal. 100,000Y. Tattersalls October Book 1. Not sold. The dam, a fairly useful 2-y-o 7f placed three times and is a half-sister to 4 winners including the very useful dual Listed 10f winner Nouriya. The second dam, Majestic Sakeena (by King's Best), is an unraced half-sister to 7 winners including the German Listed sprint winner Shy Lady (the dam of four stakes winners including the St James's Palace Stakes winner Zafeen) and the French Listed winner Sweet Story. (Saleh Al Homaizi & Imad Al Sagar). *"He was bought back at the sales and hasn't been here that long but he's a rangy, quite strong horse that moves nicely. So far we're happy and we like him".*

357. UNNAMED ★★★★
b.f. Dansili – Nessina (Hennessy). April 30. Third foal. Half-sister to the 2017 2-y-o 1m debut winner Extra Elusive (by Mastercraftsman) and to the smart 2-y-o Group 2 6f Gimcrack Stakes winner Ajaya (by Invincible Spirit). The dam is an unraced half-sister to 6 winners including the dual Listed winner Tantina (herself dam of the UAE Group 1 winner Cityscape and the Group 2 winner Bated Breath). The second dam, Didina (by Nashwan), a 2-y-o 6f winner here, subsequently won the Grade 2 8.5f Dahlia Handicap in the USA and is a full or half-sister to 7 winners including the Listed winners Espionage and Star Cluster. (Saleh Al Homaizi & Imad Al Sagar). *"A very nice filly, she's very much a Dansili, a nice mover and looks quite 'together'. One for the second half of the year, but she looks like she should be doing OK as a 2-y-o".*

358. UNNAMED ★★★
b.f. Australia – Nouriya (Danehill Dancer). April 2. Fourth foal. Half-sister to the smart 7f (at 2 yrs) and Group 3 1m winner and Group 2

placed Aljazzi (by Shamardal). The dam, a very useful dual Listed 10f winner, is a half-sister to 4 winners including the fairly useful 2-y-o 7f winner and triple Listed 10f placed Lady Nouf. The second dam, Majestic Sakeena (by King's Best), is an unraced half-sister to the German Listed sprint winner Shy Lady (dam of the St James's Palace Stakes winner Zafeen) and to the French Listed winner Sweet Story. (Saleh Al Homaizi & Imad Al Sagar). *"She hasn't been here long but she's done well, seems good-natured and has a nice pedigree. She's an April foal, so there's plenty of improvement to come".*

359. UNNAMED ★★★
b.f. Giant's Causeway – Rebridled Dreams (Unbridled Song). May 5. Tenth foal. $700,000Y. Keeneland September. Tony Nerses. Sister to the US dual Grade 1 winner at 2 and 3 yrs Carpe Diem and half-sister to 6 winners including the US 2-y-o Grade 1 winner J.B's Thunder (by Thunder Gulch) and the dual Listed 6f winner Doncaster Rover. The dam, a US stakes winner, was Grade 2 placed and is a half-sister to 6 winners. The second dam, Key Cents (by Corridor Key), was a US stakes winner of 23 races. *"An attractive, well-made, quite forward filly, she's quite strong so hopefully she'll make a 2-y-o; the dam has certainly been a very successful broodmare".*

TOM CLOVER
360. AMOREENA ★★
b.f. Swiss Spirit – Harryana To (Compton Place). March 4. Fourth foal. £11,000Y. Tattersalls Ireland Ascot. Tom Clover. Half-sister to a minor winner abroad by Sakhee's Secret. The dam, a moderate 7f placed maiden, is a half-sister to 7 winners including the 2-y-o Group 2 Mill Reef Stakes winner Temple Meads. The second dam, Harryana (by Efisio), was a fair 2-y-o dual 5f winner. (C V Wentworth). *"She was relatively cheap because she was lame at the sale but the stud owner was prepared to stand over her and sure enough it turned out to be just a foot abscess. She's fine and the second dam has bred plenty of winners. She should be out in high summer and she's up to winning a race or two".*

361. CELSIUS ★★★★
ch.c. Dragon Pulse – Grecian Artisan (Mastercraftsman). February 16. Second foal.

€30,000Y. Goffs Open. Not sold. The dam is an unraced half-sister to 6 winners including the useful Listed 6f winner of 4 races at 2 and 3 yrs Shanghai Glory and the very useful Listed 7f winner of 4 races Choose Me (herself dam of the Group 1 1m Queen Elizabeth II Stakes winner of 6 races Persuasive and the useful Listed 1m winner of 5 races Tisbutadream). The second dam, Hecuba (by Hector Protector), a fairly useful 10f winner, is a half-sister to 7 winners including the German Group 2 winner Bad Bertrich Again and the Group 3 Scottish Classic winner Prolix. (C Fahy, J Collins & S Piper). *"Bred by John Tuthill who is a very good breeder, he was originally down as a lease but some existing owners decided to buy him. He has a lovely way of going and he's from a nice family. He'll start over six furlongs in May/June time I would have thought, he has a good action, covers a lot of ground and he's a strong colt".*

362. CHARACTERISTIC (IRE) ★★★★
ch.c. Casamento – Stunned Silence (Officer). February 9. Second foal. €45,000Y. Tattersalls Ireland September. Amanda Skiffington. The dam, a quite useful 2-y-o 7f winner, is a half-sister to 4 winners including the US Group 2 second Anita Partner. The second dam, Offbeat Fashion (by Rock Of Gibraltar), a fairly useful dual 7f winner (including at 2 yrs), is a half-sister to 5 winners. (H Moorhead, C Fahy & J Collins). *"A horse with a lovely way of going, he'll be out in May, has a lovely action and was reasonably expensive for us. It was great to have Amanda Skiffington help us buy one because her record speaks for itself. Six furlongs on goodish ground should be fine for him and he's in the Weatherbys race at Doncaster on St Leger day".*

363. CHENG GONG ★★★
b.c. Archipenko – Kinetica (Stormy Atlantic). February 25. Third foal. €25,000Y. Goffs Orby. Badgers Bloodstock. Half-brother to Kinaesthesia (by Sea The Stars), a winner over 8.5f on her only start at 2 yrs in 2017. The dam, a 2-y-o Listed 7f winner, was third in the Group 3 Sweet Solera Stakes and the Prix d'Aumale and is a half-sister to 3 winners. The second dam, Kiswahili (by Selkirk), won 4 races including a Listed 14f event in Germany and is a half-sister to 3 winners including the

dam of the Group 1 winner Madame Chiang. (R & S Marchant, D Fawdon & G Jarvis). *"We bought him from Miss Rausing at Goffs and since we bought him the half-sister has won for Ralph Beckett, which is nice. He'll take a bit of time and is probably one for the back-end but he has a nice stride to him and it's a decent pedigree. The name Cheng Gong is Chinese for success".*

364. DAWN AFFAIR ★★
b.f. Dawn Approach – Dubai Affair (Dubawi). January 24. Third foal. 10,000Y. Tattersalls October Book 3. Not sold. Half-sister to the modest 2-y-o 6f winner Compton Lane (by Compton Place). The dam, a modest 2-y-o 5f winner, is a half-sister to 6 winners including the useful 2-y-o Listed 6f winner Queen's Grace. The second dam, Palace Affair (by Pursuit Of Love), a multiple Listed winner from 5f to 7f, is a sister to one winner and a half-sister to 9 winners including Sakhee's Secret (Group 1 6f July Cup). (Bearstone Stud). *"She came in late but she has a nice page and is probably one for the back-end and especially as a 3-y-o. She's a very pretty filly with the look of her damsire Dubawi, which is always a good thing!*

365. FREE LOVE ★★
b.f. Equiano – Peace And Love (Fantastic Light). April 25. Fifth foal. 10,000Y. Tattersalls October Book 3. Tom Clover. Half-sister to the quite useful 5f winner of 5 races at 2 and 4 yrs Lydia's Place, to the fair 2-y-o dual 5f winner Lawless Louie (both by Equiano) and the modest 7f and 1m winner of 4 races Dimitar (by Mizzen Mast). The dam, a quite useful 2-y-o 7f winner, is a half-sister to 6 winners. The second dam, Muschana (by Deploy), a quite useful Listed-placed dual 10f winner, is a half-sister to 4 winners including the Melbourne Cup and Group 2 12f Hardwicke Stakes winner Jeune and the Group 2 12f King Edward VII Stakes winner Beneficial. (The North South Syndicate). *"This filly is very sharp, not very big and she'll be out in April over five furlongs. She shows a bit of speed at home and should be a bit of fun for her enthusiastic owners".*

366. GYPSY SPIRIT ★★★
b.f. Gregorian – Romany Gypsy (Indesatchel). March 22. Fourth foal. 6,000Y. Tattersalls

October Book 3. Tom Clover. Half-sister to the modest 6f and 7f winner Gypsy Major (by Major Cadeaux) and to a 2-y-o winner in Italy Firebreak. The dam is an unplaced half-sister to 2 winners. The second dam, River Song (by Siphon), a US stakes-placed winner, is a half-sister to 7 winners including the Group 2 Queen Anne Stakes and US dual Grade 2 winner Allied Forces. (The Gypsy Spirit Partnership). *"We bought her very cheaply, the first lot through on the afternoon of the sale so I think we did well to pick her up for only six grand. A fun syndicate horse, she was a bit light of bone but she has a good step and she's working grand. She'll be racing by the end of May if not sooner. She has a good way of going and she's a tough filly".* TRAINER'S BARGAIN BUY

367. HANBURY DREAMS ★★★

b.f. Heeraat – Lady O Malley (Oratorio). April 10. Second foal. Half-sister to the fair 2017 2-y-o 6f winner Hunni (by Captain Gerrard). The dam, a fair 9f winner, is a half-sister to the fairly useful 1m to 10f winner Nice Style. The second dam, Great Idea (by Lion Cavern), a quite useful 2-y-o 7f winner, is a half-sister to 5 winners including the Listed 14f March Stakes winner Jadalee. (B Keane & S Nugent). *"Her half-sister Hunni did well for us last year winning the 40 grand nursery here at Newmarket. She's very similar to Hunni and should be one for nurseries too. I've got a couple by this sire Heeraat and they both look good".*

368. RAJY ★★★

b.f. Society Rock – Cape Mystery (Cape Cross). April 6. First foal. 19,000Y. Tattersalls October Book 3. Tom Clover. The dam, a modest 10f placed maiden, is a sister to the Listed 10f winner Cape Amber and a half-sister to 3 winners including the 2-y-o 5f, 6f Listed and 6.5f Watership Down Stud Sales Race winner and Group 3 placed Nyramba. The second dam, Maramba (by Rainbow Quest), a fairly useful 3-y-o 1m winner, is a half-sister to 7 winners. (Raj Matharu & Nick Bradley Racing 39). *"Although out of a Cape Cross mare she's been showing plenty, she's growing a bit now but I like to think we'll have her out in May or June. She's been working well and has a nice way of going".*

369. SAMARITAINE ★★

ch.f. Archipenko – Samando (Hernando). April 29. Half-sister to the French 1m winner Samardal (by Shamardal) and to the minor French 11f winner Samuraj (by Zamindar). The dam, winner of the Group 2 12.5f Prix de Royallieu and the Group 3 10f Prix Exbury is out of the unraced Samshu (by Nashwan). (Miss K. Rausing). *"A nicely-bred filly and although not the biggest she goes nicely and she has a nice stride. She'll be out in high summer and it's nice to have another owned by Kirsten Rausing".*

370. TIGERINMYTANK ★★

b.f. Heeraat – Tiger Cub (Dr Fong). March 20. Third foal. €7,000Y. Goffs Open. M Wanless/D Evans. The dam, a fair 1m (at 2 yrs) and 6f winner, is a half-sister to 2 winners. The second dam, Clouded Leopard (by Danehill), placed once over 7f at 2 yrs, is a half-sister to 5 winners including the Breeders' Cup Juvenile Turf winner Pounced. (Shimplingthorne Syndicate). *"Owned by my mother's syndicate, this filly has a good, long stride to her and I would have thought June time over six furlongs would be right for her. Quite innocuous, she has a nice way of going and should be up to winning races".*

371. TULLOONA ★★

b.c. Coach House – Minnola (Royal Applause). April 12. Fifth living foal. £22,000Y. Goffs UK Silver. Anglia Bloodstock. Half-brother to the fair dual 1m winner Miniskirt (by Naaqoos). The dam, a moderate 5f and 6f placed maiden, is a half-sister to 3 minor winners. The second dam, Miss Anabaa (by Anabaa), won the Group 3 Ballyogan Stakes and the Listed Naas Sprint Stakes and is a half-sister to 7 winners. (Mr C. F. E. Hill). *"He's a lovely individual and has grown a lot since the sale. He'll be out around August I would have thought. Not a sharp sort then, but he looks nice and should be OK given a bit of time".*

372. UNNAMED ★★★

b.c. Gale Force Ten – City Vaults Girl (Oratorio). April 28. Fifth foal. 38,000Y. Tattersalls October Book 3. Tom Clover Racing. Half-brother to the fair 2-y-o 7f winner and Italian Listed-placed City Of Stars (by Lilbourne Lad). The dam, a fair 10f winner, is a half-sister to 3 winners including the Canadian Grade 3 winner Uchenna and the Hong Kong stakes winner Uramazin. The second dam, Uriah (by Acatenango), won 5 races from 10f to 12f in Germany and the USA including the Grade 2 Long Island Handicap and is a full or half-sister to 10 winners. (I Barratt, A Signy & B Spiers). *"A nice, fun, sharp 2-y-o who should be out in May and we'll go from there. He looked great at the sale and had a nice walk to him".*

PAUL COLE

373. CATHOLIC POETRY (IRE)

ch.f. Lope De Vega – Tinaheely (Intikhab). April 23. Third foal. 48,000Y. Tattersalls October Book 2. Not sold. Half-sister to the quite useful 2-y-o 7f to 10f winner of 3 races Count Calabash (by Big Bad Bob). The dam, placed, is a half-sister to 3 winners including the US Grade 1 second Tangle. The second dam, Tertia (by Polish Patriot), a Listed-placed Irish winner of 3 races at 3 yrs, is a half-sister to 8 minor winners. (Mr F. P. Stella).

374. CELTIC CLASSIC (IRE)

b.c. Cacique – Dabtiyra (Dr Devious). April 10. Seventh foal. 40,000Y. Tattersalls October Book 2. Paul Cole. Half-brother to the useful 2-y-o dual Listed winner (over 7f and 1m) and Group 3 third Washaar (by Kodiac). The dam, placed third over 10f on her only start at 3 yrs in Ireland, is a half-sister to 3 winners. The second dam, Dabtiya (by Shirley Heights), winner of the Listed Ballyroan Stakes and second in the Group 3 Meld Stakes, is a half-sister to 4 winners. (Evans, Wright, Asprey, PJL Racing, Wilcock).

375. HAZE

b.f. Oasis Dream – Dorelia (Efisio). March 10. Sister to the Group 3 Fred Darling Stakes winner and Group 1 Cheveley Park Stakes second Rimth (by Oasis Dream). The dam, a fair 1m winner, is a half-sister to 3 winners including the smart Group 2 5f Kings Stand Stakes and Group 3 5f Cornwallis Stakes winner Dominica. The second dam, Dominio (by Dominion), a useful 5f winner and second in the Group 2 5f Temple Stakes, is a half-sister to 6 winners including the very smart Group 1 5f Nunthorpe Stakes winner Ya Malak. (Denford Stud Ltd).

376. HIGH COMMISSIONER (IRE)

ch.c. Australia – Winesong (Giant's Causeway). April 18. Eighth foal. €270,000Y. Goffs Orby. Hugo Merry. Half-brother to the Group 2 Princess Of Wales's Stakes and Group 2 Jockey Club Stakes winner of 7 races Universal, to the fair Irish 9f and 10.5f winner Windward Passage (both by Dubawi) and the fair Irish 12f winner Madam Mo (by Motivator). The dam, placed third over 10f, is a half-sister to 6 winners including the 2-y-o Group 1 6f Cheveley Park Stakes winner Seazun. The second dam, Sunset Café (by Red Sunset), a minor Irish 12f winner, is a sister to the Group 3 Prix Foy winner Beeshi and a half-sister to 8 winners. (Mrs F. H. Hay).

377. LI KUI

br.c. Poet's Voice – Lily Again (American Post). March 14. Third foal. 36,000Y. Tattersalls October Book 3. Paul Cole. Half-brother to the fairly useful 2017 2-y-o 6f winner Ertiyad (by Dark Angel). The dam, a fairly useful 2-y-o Listed 7f winner, is a half-sister to 4 winners including the fairly useful Listed-placed 2-y-o winner Genari. The second dam, Sari (by Faustus), a quite useful 7f winner of 2 races (including at 2 yrs), is a half-sister to one winner. (P. F. I. Cole Ltd).

378. MAJESTIC DAWN (IRE)

ch.c. Dawn Approach – Jolie Chanson (Mount Nelson). February 15. First foal. £42,000Y. Goffs UK Premier (Doncaster). Ollie Cole. The dam is an unraced half-sister to 6 winners including the French Group 3 and Listed winner Slow Pace. The second dam, Slow Down (by Seattle Slew), a winner in France and a Listed winner in the USA, is a half-sister to 8 winners including the US dual Grade 3 winner Olmodavor. (Green & Norman).

379. MELYA

b.f. Equiano – Percolator (Kheleyf). April 13. Fifth foal. Half-sister to the 2017 2-y-o 5f winner from two starts Plunger (by Helmet) and to the fair 2-y-o 5f winner Cajmere (by Kyllachy). The dam, a 2-y-o winner of the Group 3 Prix du Bois and second in the Group 2 Prix Robert Papin, is a half-sister to 4 minor winners. The second dam, Coffee Cream (by Common Grounds), was a quite useful 7f (at 2 yrs) and 1m winner. (A H Robinson).

380. PHYSICS (IRE)

b.c. Acclamation – Precipitous (Indian Ridge). April 2. Ninth foal. €180,000Y. Goffs Orby. Stephen Hillen. Half-brother to 3 winners including the Group 3 7f Brownstown Stakes winner Tobann (by Teofilo), to the quite useful 2-y-o 6f winner Cardigan (by Barathea) and the fair Irish 5f winner Focus Of Attention (by Intense Focus). The dam, a quite useful Irish 7f and 1m winner, is a half-sister to 7 minor winners. The second dam, Dathuil (by Royal Academy), a fairly useful 1m winner, was subsequently Grade 3 placed in the USA and is a half-sister to 6 winners including the 2-y-o Listed 6f winner and Group 1 placed Luminata. (Mrs F. H. Hay).

381. RIVER DAWN

ch.c. Dawn Approach – Echo River (Irish River). April 18. Tenth foal. 42,000Y. Tattersalls October Book 2. Paul Cole. Half-brother to 4 winners including the quite useful 2-y-o 6f and smart hurdles winner Marsh Warbler (by Barathea), the fair 7f (including at 2 yrs) to 12f and hurdles winner of 8 races (including at 2 yrs) Ravi River and the modest 1m and hurdles winner My Manekineko (by Authorized). The dam, a useful 2-y-o 6f and Listed 7f winner, is a half-sister to 6 winners. The second dam, Monaassabaat (by Zilzal), a Listed 10f Virginia Stakes winner, is a half-sister to 8 winners including Bitooh (Group 2 Criterium de Maisons-Laffitte). (Mrs F. H. Hay).

382. SELOUS (IRE)

b.c. Showcasing – Miss Lacey (Diktat). March 30. Seventh foal. €130,000Y. Goffs Orby. Richard Knight. Half-brother to the fairly useful Listed 1m winner of 4 races Burke's Rock (by Cape Cross), to the fair 7f and subsequent Italian winner Winning Hunter (by Iffraaj) and the modest 9f winner Khelac (by Kheleyf). The dam is an unplaced half-sister to 9 winners including the Group 2 Superlative Stakes and Group 2 Bosphorus Cup winner Halicarnassus. The second dam, Launch Time (by Relaunch), is a US placed half-sister to 4 winners including the US Grade 2 winner Palace March and the Group/Grade 1 placed Executive Pride. (Mrs F. H. Hay).

383. SHIR KHAN

ch.c. Leroidesanimaux – Sterling Sound (Street Cry). February 28. Fifth foal. 50,000Y. Tattersalls October Book 2. Paul Cole. Half-brother to the fairly useful 2-y-o 7f winner Argenterie and to the minor dual Italian winner at 2 and 3 yrs Worgait (both by Archipenko). The dam, a quite useful 1m winner, was Listed-placed over 10f and is a sister to one winner and a half-sister to 5 winners including the unraced dam of the US Grade 2 winner Quintons Gold Rush. The second dam, Lady In Silver (by Silver Hawk), winner of the Group 1 Prix de Diane and second in the Grade 1 Arlington Million, is a half-sister to 8 winners. (Arbib, Robinson & Cole).

384. WALKMAN (IRE)

b.c. War Command – Mooching Along (Mujahid). April 5. Seventh foal. £95,000Y. Goffs UK Premier (Doncaster). Ollie Cole. Half-brother to 4 winners including the quite useful 2017 2-y-o 5f winner Falabelle (by Choisir), the 5f winner of 5 races Primo Uomo, the quite useful 5f and 6f winner Strategic Force (both by Strategic Prince) and the fair 7f (at 2 yrs) and 6f winner Great Spirit (by Tagula). The dam is an unraced half-sister to 5 winners. The second dam, Inching (by Inchinor), was placed 9 times over 5f and 6f from 2 to 4 yrs and is a half-sister to 8 winners including the triple Group 3 winning sprinter Majestic Missile. (Mr A. Altazi).

ROBERT COWELL

385. ADAM TILER (USA) ★★★★

b.c. Justin Phillip – Moneygrabber (Awesome Again). February 14. Second foal. $95,000Y. Keeneland September. A C Elliott. The dam, a minor US 3-y-o winner of 3 races, is a half-sister to 2 winners including the Grade 3 third Conquest Windycity. The second dam, Lasting Appeal (by A P Indy), a minor 2-y-o winner in the USA on her only start, is a sister to the Grade 2 winner and Grade 1 placed Jump Start. (Mr T. W. Morley). *"A good-looking horse I bought in America, he might need a little bit of time but he shows speed. He'll be one for the middle of the season and we'll have some fun with him, probably over six or seven furlongs. Some of these American sires are quite obscure to European eyes but I look at an awful lot of yearlings at Keeneland and pick out nice individuals that I really like".* The sire won the

Grade 1 6f Vanderbilt Handicap on dirt at 5 yrs in the USA.

386. AWARDED ★★★
b.f. Swiss Spirit – Royal Award (Cadeaux Genereux). February 22. Second foal. 9,000Y. Tattersalls October Book 3. Robert Cowell. The dam, a fair dual 5f winner, is a half-sister to 2 other minor winners. The second dam, Red Sovereign (by Danzig Connection), a fair 6f (including at 2 yrs) and 5f winner of 5 races, is a half-sister to 2 winners. (J Sargeant, B Rose & Partner). *"I like this filly, I bought her at the sale and got a few people involved in her. She's a little bit 'on the leg' but has loads of speed and looks like a runner to me. One of my earlier fillies and there's a little bit of something about her that gets me excited".*

387. BALLISTIC ★★★★
b.c. Kodiac – Pale Orchid (Invincible Spirit). April 1. Third foal. €180,000Y. Goffs Orby. Sackville/Donald. Half-brother to the quite useful 3-y-o 5.5f and 6f winner of 5 races Goodwood Crusader (by Sir Prancealot). The dam, a quite useful 5f and 6f winner of 5 races, is a half-sister to the smart Group 3 6f Prix de Ris-Orangis winner and Group 1 Prix Maurice de Gheest second Thawaany. The second dam, Chelsea Rose (by Desert King), won the Group 1 7f Moyglare Stud Stakes and three Listed events, was Group 1 placed twice and is a half-sister to 8 winners including the Irish Listed 1m winner and subsequent US Grade 2 placed European. (Mrs F. H. Hay). *"He cost a bit of money but quite rightly so because he's a good-looking horse. He's a really early sort and will be coming out at Newmarket's Craven meeting I should think. His pedigree suggests he's all about five furlongs and his shape would reflect that too".*

388. BLAME ROBERTA ★★★★
b.f. Blame – Royal Parisian (Royal Applause). April 19. First foal. $27,000Y. Keeneland September. Robert Cowell. The dam, unplaced in one start, is a half-sister to 6 winners including the useful 7f winner (at 2 yrs) and Listed 6f placed March On Beetroot and the fairly useful triple 1m winner Cosmopolitan. The second dam, Parisian Elegance (by Zilzal), a fairly useful dual 5f winner at 2 yrs and third in the Group 3 Princess Margaret Stakes, is

a half-sister to 7 winners including the triple Group 3 winning sprinter Majestic Missile. (K A Dasmal). *"I bought her in America, partly because I trained the second dam and I saw her walking around and thought she'd make a bit of money. As it happens she wasn't that popular and I was able to buy her reasonably well. She'll be running in early April because she knows her job and she's ready to fly the nest".* TRAINER'S BARGAIN BUY

389. HOOFLEPUFF (IRE) ★★★
b.c. Gale Force Ten – Hflah (Dubawi). March 1. Third foal. £60,000Y. Goffs UK Premier (Doncaster). Cool Silk Partnership. Half-brother to the French 7f (at 2 yrs) and Listed 1m winner of 4 races and Group 2 Prix Hocquart third Royal Julius (by Royal Applause). The dam is an unraced half-sister to 6 winners including the 2-y-o Group 1 Criterium de Saint-Cloud winner Goldamix. The second dam, Gold's Dance (by Nureyev), a minor French winner at 3 and 4 yrs, is a half-sister to 5 winners including the Group 3 Prix Fille de l'Air winner Solveig. (The Cool Silk Partnership). *"We liked him at the sales, he was a strong, stocky sort but he might need a bit of time because he's growing. He goes well but he's not in fast work yet and I'd say he'd be a seven furlong horse in time".*

390. JEWEL OF THE SEA (IRE) ★★★
b.f. Born To Sea – Madame Boulangere (Royal Applause). January 16. Eleventh foal. 25,000Y. Tattersalls October Book 3. Dan Tunmore/ GB Horseracing. Half-sister to the useful 5f (including at 2 yrs) and 6f winner of 7 races Barracuda Boy, to the fair 5f and 6f winner Madame Bounty (both by Bahamian Bounty), the fairly useful 2-y-o dual 7f winner Lamh Albasser (by Mr Greeley), the quite useful Irish 10f to 12f winner of 8 races Jazz Girl (by Johar) and the minor French 2-y-o winner Mrs Lovett (by Sir Percy). The dam, a useful dual 6f winner (including at 2 yrs), was Listed-placed and is a half-sister to one winner. The second dam, Jazz (by Sharrood), a fair 7f (at 2 yrs) and 10f placed maiden, is a half-sister to 12 winners including the US Grade 2 winner Sign Of Hope and the Group 2 placed Finian's Rainbow and Carmot. (D Tunmore & Partner). *"We quite liked her at the sales, the mare knows how to breed a winner and they're usually speedy. This*

filly looks the part, she just needs the penny to drop but we're getting there. She has the shape to make an out-and-out sprinter and just needs a bit more education".

391. MISS GRADENKO ★★★

b.f. Foxwedge – Instructress (Diktat). April 3. Fourth foal. Half-sister to the fairly useful 2017 2-y-o dual 5f winner and Group 2 Flying Childers Stakes third May Girl (by Mayson). The dam, a fair dual 5f winner (including at 2 yrs), is a half-sister to 5 winners including the quite useful 2-y-o Listed-placed dual 5f winner Smooch. The second dam, Two Step (by Mujtahid), a modest 5f and 7f winner at 4 and 5 yrs, is a half-sister to 3 winners. (Bottisham Heath Stud). *"She's very speedy, as you can imagine from the pedigree. Not very big, she'll make a 2-y-o and will do all her winning this year. She's working quite nicely and we'll move on with her fairly sharply".*

392. POCKET DYNAMO (USA) ★★★

b.c. Dialed In – Little Bit Tiny (Cuvee). March 29. Second foal. $35,000Y. Keeneland September. R Cowell. The dam, a minor US winner of 3 races at 3 and 4 yrs, is a half-sister to 5 winners including the US Grade 3 winner Blue Tone. The second dam, Princess Cart (by Cartwright), is a placed sister to a US stakes winner. (Mr T. W. Morley). *"He's not very big – hence the name – but he's quite quick and a typical 2-y-o. If he'd been bred here he'd look like he was a Kodiac. A nice looking horse, he's fast – in fact if anything he's too fast in that he's trying to do everything a bit too quickly at the moment so we've just stepped him back a notch. He'll certainly make his presence felt in the sprint nurseries".* The sire, a son of Mineshaft, won the Grade 1 Florida Derby and his first crop are now four-year-olds. His best winner to date is the US Grade 2 winner Gunnevera.

393. REEVES ★★★

b.c. Tamayuz – Mania (Danehill). February 5. Eleventh foal. 95,000Y. Tattersalls October Book 2. Hugo Merry. Half-brother to 8 winners including the fairly useful 2-y-o 6f winner Fanatical (by Mind Games), the quite useful 2-y-o 6f winners Koptoon (by Rip Van Winkle) and Gower Valentine (by Primo Valentino), the German Listed-placed 6f winner Domineer (by

Shamardal), the quite useful 2-y-o 6f winner Nautical Haven (by Harbour Watch) and the fair 2-y-o 6f winner Marrayah (by Fraam). The dam is an unraced half-sister to 7 winners including the dam of the Group 1 winners Youmzain and Creachadoir. The second dam, Anima (by Ajdal), was placed once at 3 yrs and is a half-sister to 8 winners (including 6 stakes winners), notably the multiple Group 1 winner Pilsudski. (Mrs F. H. Hay). *"A very good-looking colt that was showing up quite nicely in his work until he got a touch of a sore shin. He'll make a 2-y-o, he's strong and sturdy and he's got some scope. It's a good family and we like Tamayuz as a sire. He's one to follow".*

394. SIR OX ★★★

b.c. Oxbow – Lady Melesi (Colonial Affair). April 22. Thirteenth foal. $215,000Y. Keeneland September. Robert Cowell. Half-brother to 7 winners including the US stakes winner and dual Grade 2 placed Seruni (by Saint Liam), the US stakes winner Roman Emperor (by Empire Maker) and the US Grade 2 placed winners Doc Cheney (by Saint Ballado) and Liberated (by Curlin). The dam, a US stakes winner of 4 races at 3 and 4 yrs, was second in the Grade 1 Milady Breeders' Cup Handicap and is a half-sister to 5 winners. The second dam, Eye Catching (by Alydar), was a minor winner at 3 yrs in the USA. (K. A. Dasmal). *"This was the most expensive yearling by Oxbow last year and the underbidders were from a big stud farm in America, so they were looking for the same thing we were. He's a really good-looking horse, he's pretty early and will be running by late April. He's got scope but he has speed too and I'd say he'd be better over six furlongs than five. Quite a snazzy looking colt".* The sire, a son of Awesome Again, won the Grade 1 Preakness Stakes and was second in the Belmont Stakes. His first two-year-olds appear this season.

395. SO HI SPEED (USA) ★★★

b.c. Central Banker – Quietly Elegant (Quiet American). May 4. Tenth foal. $37,000Y. Keeneland September. Nick Bradley Racing. Half-brother to 4 winners in North America including the stakes-placed Why Take A Chance (by Hook And Ladder). The dam, a minor US 3-y-o winner, is a half-sister to 3 winners. The second dam, Beautiful Legend (by Lyphard), a US stakes-placed winner of 2 races at 4 yrs, is a half-sister to the US stakes winner and multiple Grade 1 placed Fast Account. (Nick Bradley Racing 21 & Partner). *"We bought him at Keeneland in partnership with Nick Bradley because we found ourselves looking at the same horses and rather than bid against each other we bought this colt together. He's a scopey horse but he's ready to run now and although he's quick enough for five furlongs to start with he'll stay six or seven later on".* The sire, a son of Speightstown, won a Grade 2 stakes at Churchill Downs and was Grade 1 placed twice. His first foals are now two-year-olds.

396. VIKIVAKI ★★★
ch.f. Congrats – Smart Dancer (Smart Strike). March 19. Second foal. $70,000Y. Keeneland September. Robert Cowell. The dam, placed in the USA at 3 and 4 yrs, is a half-sister to 7 winners including the US dual Grade 2 winner and Grade 1 second Suave and the US stakes winner and Grade 2 and 3 placed Worldly. The second dam, Urbane (by Citidancer), won the Grade 1 Ashland Stakes and the Grade 1 John A Morris Handicap in the USA. (Mr T W Morley). *"Another early filly, she's ticking all the right boxes at the moment and being very professional. Some of these American horses had a bit of tuition beforehand because they seem to know a bit more. She's quite a nice sort and has a bit of size to her as well. She'll probably be out before the Craven meeting, so she's precocious. She'll look better once she gets some sun on her back, so it's nice that she's getting us excited even though she doesn't look the part yet".*

397. UNNAMED ★★
b.f. Kodiac – Dance Bid (Authorized). February 27. First foal. 300,000Y. Tattersalls October Book 2. J J Gordon. The dam, a fair 2-y-o 7.5f winner, is a half-sister to 5 winners. The second dam, Dancing Fire (by Dayjur), is an unraced half-sister to 6 winners including Scintillo (Group 1 Gran Criterium) and the multiple Group 3 winner Jumbajukiba. (Mr S. Pan). *"She's quite a backward-looking filly and a bit leggy, so not a typical Kodiac. She was sent to us – we didn't buy her – and she's going to need plenty of time".*

398. UNNAMED ★★
b.f. Poet's Voice – Elhaam (Shamardal). March 17. First foal. The dam, a modest 6f winner, is a half-sister to numerous winners including the useful Listed winner of 5 races over 5f and 6f and Group 2 third Justineo . The second dam, Loulwa (by Montjeu)., a fairly useful 11f and Listed 13f winner, is a half-sister to 5 winners including the Group 2 6f Mill Reef Stakes winner and Group 1 placed Galeota and the fairly useful 2-y-o 5f Weatherbys Supersprint winner Lady Livius. (Saleh Al Homaizi & Imad Al Sagar). *"She's a strong sort, not obviously sharp or quick to look at but she'll certainly grow into her frame and will be a back-end type".*

399. UNNAMED ★★★
ch.f. Exceed And Excel – Epiphany (Zafonic). February 19. Half-sister to 6 winners including the 2017 Italian 2-y-o Listed 5.5f winner Vik The Billy (by Bated Breath), the quite useful 2-y-o 7f winner Idder (by Authorized), the quite useful dual 6f winner (including at 2 yrs) Agerzam (by Holy Roman Emperor) and the fair 1m winner Zakiy (by Selkirk). The dam, a fair 2-y-o 6f winner, is a half-sister to one winner abroad. The second dam, Galette (Caerleon), a fairly useful 12f winner, is a half-sister to 6 winners including the Irish 2,000 Guineas winner Indian Haven, the smart Group 1 Gran Criterium winner Count Dubois and the dam of the Group winners Imperial Stride and High Pitched. (Saleh Al Homaizi & Imad Al Sagar). *"She's only just come to us but she has a good shape to her, she's cantering away and looks a good, strong individual".*

400. UNNAMED ★★
b.c. Dawn Approach – Step Lightly (Danehill Dancer). April 15. Third foal. 28,000 foal. Tattersalls December. Not sold. The dam is an unplaced half-sister to 7 winners including the Irish 2-y-o winners and stakes-placed Juliet Capulet and Fly To The Moon. The second dam, Royal Ballerina (by Sadler's Wells), winner of the Group 2 12f Blandford Stakes and second in the Oaks, is a half-sister to 7 winners including the dual Group 2 10f Sun Chariot Stakes winner Free Guest (herself dam of the Group 1 Fillies Mile winner and Oaks second Shamshir). (Mr N. Al Habtoor). *"He's quite a big horse and is just cantering at*

the moment, so he wouldn't be early and he's certainly not a sprinter, but he's a good stamp. One for the second half of the season".

SIMON CRISFORD

401. AKWAAN (IRE) ★★★
b.c. Camacho – Saytara (Nayef). May 5. First living foal. 45,000Y. Tattersalls October Book 2. Shadwell Estate Co. The dam, a fairly useful 1m (at 2 yrs) and dual 12f winner, is a half-sister to 4 winners including the very useful 7f (at 2 yrs) and Group 3 1m Premio Dormello winner and Group 2 May Hill Stakes third Celtic Slipper. The second dam, Celtic Silhouette (by Celtic Swing), placed four times at 4 and 5 yrs in France, is a sister to the Listed winner and Group 2 Dante Stakes second Celtic Silence and a half-sister to the dual Group 3 winner Royal And Regal. *"Not an early sort but he's pleasing me and doing everything right at this time in his career. He's going to start around mid-season over seven furlongs and I can see him being a ten furlong horse next year".*

402. ANGEL OF FREEDOM ★★
b.f. Dark Angel – Angelic Air (Oasis Dream). January 15. First foal. 60,000Y. Tattersalls October Book 2. Stroud/Coleman. The dam, a quite useful 7f winner, is a half-sister to 2 winners. The second dam, Innocent Air (by Galileo), won two Listed events over 7f and 10f at 2 and 3 yrs and is a half-sister to 6 winners including the French Listed and US stakes winner and US Grade 1 placed Skipping. *"She's more backward than you'd think for a Dark Angel and she'll take plenty of time. She's been growing a lot and is a nice filly for next year".*

403. ARISTOCRATIC LADY (IRE) ★★★★
b.f. Invincible Spirit – Dubai Queen (Kingmambo). March 7. Fourth foal. Half-sister to the useful 7.5f (at 2 yrs) and dual 10f winner Sharja Queen (by Pivotal). The dam, a fairly useful Listed-placed 1m winner, is a half-sister to 5 winners, notably Dubawi. The second dam, Zomaradah (by Deploy), a winner of 6 races including the Group 1 Italian Oaks, the Group 2 Royal Whip Stakes and the Group 2 Premio Lydia Tesio, is a half-sister to several winners. *"She's got some toe and hopefully isn't going to take too long. A nice filly, I'm hoping*

she'll be ready for when the six furlong races start. She's forward-going and looks racy".

404. CAPE CAVALLI (IRE) ★★★
b.c. Cape Cross – Matauri Pearl (Hurricane Run). April 3. First foal. 475,000Y. Tattersalls October Book 1. Godolphin. The dam, a Listed-placed winner of 4 races in Scandinavia at 2 and 3 yrs, is a sister to the Group 3 Prix Chloe and US Grade 3 winner and triple Group 1 placed Wakeela and a half-sister to 3 winners. The second dam, Moonrise (by Grand Lodge), won 4 minor races in France and Switzerland at 2 and 3 yrs and is a half-sister to 5 other minor winners. *"A nice type of horse, I think he's going to stay well and we're taking our time with him because he'll be a second half of the season 2-y-o".*

405. IMPERIAL CHARM ★★★
b.f. Dubawi – Reem Three (Mark Of Esteem). April 3. Seventh foal. Half-sister to the 2017 dual 7f placed 2-y-o Ostilio (by New Approach), to the smart Group 1 10f Prix Jean Romanet and Listed 12f winner Ajman Princess (by Teofilo), the useful 7f (at 2 yrs) to 12f winner Naqshabban, the fairly useful 2-y-o 7f winner from two starts Cape Byron (by Shamardal) and a hurdles winner (both by Street Cry). The dam, a useful 8.5f to 10.5f winner of 3 races, was Listed placed and is a half-sister to 3 winners including the very smart Group 2 Celebration Mile winner Afsare. The second dam, Jumaireyah (by Fairy King), a fairly useful 8.3f (at 2 yrs) and 10.3f winner, is a half-sister to numerous winners including the useful 10f to 14f winner Lost Soldier Three and the useful 10.5f and 12f winner Altaweelah. *"A nice filly, she's straightforward and moving forward with her training. I think she'll start over six furlongs in early summer".*

406. ISOCRATES (USA) ★★
b.c. Dansili – I Am Beautiful (Rip Van Winkle). April 3. First foal. 340,000Y. Tattersalls October Book 1. Godolphin. The dam, a useful 2-y-o Group 3 6f Balanchine Stakes winner, is a half-sister to 7 winners including the Group 1 Prix Marcel Boussac and Group 1 Moyglare Stud Stakes winner Rumplestiltskin (herself dam of the Group 1 Yorkshire Oaks winner Tapestry) and the Group 2 Irish Derby Trial second Tower Rock. The second dam, Monevassia (by

Mr Prospector), is a placed sister to the triple Group 1 1m winner Kingmambo and to the smart Group 3 6f winner Miesque's Son and a half-sister to the high-class triple Group 1 winner East of the Moon. *"A very backward type of horse, he'll take time to come together so he's on the back burner at the moment. He'll be a middle distance horse next year".*

407. JASH (IRE) ★★★★
b.c. Kodiac – Miss Azeza (Dutch Art). March 18. Second foal. 185,000Y. Tattersalls October Book 2. Shadwell Estate Co. Half-brother to the quite useful 7f (at 2 yrs) and 8.5f winner Hansian Prince (by Arcano). The second dam, Miss Respect (by Mark Of Esteem), is an unraced half-sister to 2 winners including the Group 1 Fillies' Mile, Grade 1 Yellow Ribbon Stakes and Group 2 12f Ribblesdale Stakes winner Hibaayeb. *"A nice type of colt that's doing everything right and hopefully he'll be on the track by early summer; he's a nice, big, scopey colt with a very pleasing outlook and potentially a six furlong horse to start with".*

408. KAREENA KAPOOR (USA) ★★★ ♠
ch.f. More Than Ready – Tabreed (Sakhee). March 24. First foal. €80,000Y. Goffs Orby. Richard Knight. The dam, a French 1m and US 9f winner, was second in four Grade 3 events in the USA and is a half-sister to 5 winners including the Group 3 10f Ballysax Stakes winner Moiqen and the Group 2 1m Beresford Stakes second Rekaab. The second dam, Za Aamah (by Mr Prospector), is an unraced sister to the Listed winner Siyadah and a half-sister to the Listed winner and Group 1 Fillies Mile third Esloob. *"A sharp, early 2-y-o that has some speed and hopefully she'll be ready to start over five furlongs in late April".*

409. KUNG FU ★★★
b.c. Kingman – Cubanita (Selkirk). January 28. First foal. €50,000Y. Goffs Orby. Richard Knight. The dam, a Group 3 John Porter and Group 3 St Simon Stakes winner, was Group 1 placed in Germany and is a half-sister to one winner. The second dam, Caribana (by Hernando), a fair 9.5f winner, is a half-sister to 2 minor winners. *"Not a super early horse, but I think we'll be starting him over six furlongs and then next year he'll be a miler. Doing everything right at this stage, he certainly looks like being*

speedier than his dam and I see him being out around June/July time".

410. LISEO ★★★
ch.c. Lope De Vega – Harem Lady (Teofilo). February 29. Second foal. €220,000Y. Arqana Deauville October. Stroud/Coleman. The dam, a winner of 4 races at 3 and 4 yrs in France, was Group 3 placed twice and is a half-sister to 8 winners including the US Grade 2 and Grade 3 winner Little Treasure and to the dams of the Listed winners Rhythm Of Light and Elusive Beauty. The second dam, Luminosity (by Sillery), won once at 2 yrs in France and is a half-sister to 4 minor winners. *"A nice colt with a very nice profile and a good action, he covers the ground well and this season we'll be looking to start him off at seven furlongs and then building him up from there; he's a really nice type of horse".*

411. MAAMORA (IRE) ★★★
b.f. Dubawi – Zoowraa (Azamour). January 25. Half-sister to the useful 2-y-o 5f to 7f winner of 4 races Kananee (by Exceed And Excel). The dam, a useful 2-y-o Listed 7f winner, is a half-sister to 3 winners including the useful 6f to 1m UAE winner of 5 races Almaram. The second dam, Beraysim (by Lion Cavern), a very useful winner of the Listed 7f Oak Tree Stakes, is a half-sister to the useful 2-y-o 7f winner Velour. *"A nice filly and, touch wood, she'll make a 2-y-o from mid-season onwards. A seven furlong type to start with, but she's all about next year when she'll be a ten furlong filly".*

412. MANNAAL (IRE) ★★
b.f. Dubawi – Soraaya (Elnadim). March 1. The dam, a 2-y-o Group 3 6f Princess Margaret Stakes winner, is a half-sister to 5 winners including the smart 2-y-o Listed 6f winner and Group 1 Prix Jean-Luc Lagardere second Declaration Of War. The second dam, Date Mate (by Thorn Dance), is a placed half-sister to 4 winners including the dam of the Italian Group 1 winner Le Vie Dei Colori. *"I think she's just going to take a bit of time and is one for later on this season. She's nice but much more of a 3-y-o type".*

413. MANNGUY ★★★
b.c. Oasis Dream – Galaxy Highflyer (Galileo). February 17. Seventh foal. 280,000Y. Tattersalls

October Book 1. Shadwell Estate Co. Brother to the very useful 2-y-o 6f and 7f winner and Group 2 Beresford Stakes second Oklahoma City and half-brother to a 2-y-o winner in Russia by Dansili. The dam is an unraced half-sister to 7 winners including the Group 1 winners Opera House, Kayf Tara and Zee Zee Top (dam of the Group 1 winner Izzi Top) and to the dam of the Group 1 Moyglare Stud Stakes winner Necklace. The second dam, Colorspin (by High Top), won the Irish Oaks and is a half-sister to the Irish Champion Stakes winner Cezanne and the Group 2 Prix de l'Opera winner Bella Colora (the dam of four stakes winners). *"We're just taking our time with him but he'll be a nice midsummer seven furlong horse. I'm very happy with him and he'll be a ten furlong horse next season".*

414. MASAAQAAT (USA) ★★★
b.f. Quality Road (USA)—Mufajaah (Tapit). May 9. First foal. The dam, a US Grade 3 8.5f winner, was Grade 2 placed over the same trip. The second dam, Carolyn's Cat (by Forestry), won 4 races in the USA including the Grade 2 Vagrancy Handicap and the Grade 3 Cicada Stakes and is a half-sister to 2 winners. *"She's just arrived from Dubai and is settling into a new routine. She's a nice filly that goes well, but I can't say anything more than that as I don't know enough about her yet".*

415. MOFAAJI ★★
ch.c. Animal Kingdom – My Dubai (Dubai Millennium). April 4. Half-brother to the quite useful 6f to 1m winner of 4 races Mishaal (by Kheleyf), to the quite useful dual 7f winner Mizwaaj (by Invincible Spirit), the fair 7f and 9f winner Naddwah (by Pivotal) and the fair UAE 1m winner Naaeebb (by Lonhro). The dam, placed over 7f on her only start, is a half-sister to 7 winners including the very smart triple Group 2 7f winner Iffraaj, the useful 2-y-o Group 3 7f Prix du Calvados winner Kareymah and the useful dual 1m winner Jathaabeh. The second dam, Pastorale (by Nureyev), a fairly useful 3-y-o 7f winner, ran only twice more including in a walk-over. *"He's settled in well and will be a six/seven furlong 2-y-o in the middle of summer".*

416. NEESAAN ★★★
b.f. New Approach – Red Dune (Red Ransom).

March 30. Half-sister to the useful 2017 2-y-o Listed-placed 7f winner Red Mist (by Frankel) and to the fairly useful 2-y-o 7f and 1m winner and 3-y-o UAE Group 3 9.5f third Feedyah (by Street Cry). The dam, a useful 7f and 1m winner, was Listed-placed and is a full or half-sister to 4 winners. The second dam, Desert Beauty (Green Desert), a useful 7f and 1m winner, is a half-sister to the Yorkshire Oaks and Nassau Stakes winner Islington, to the smart stayer Election Day and the smart 10f performer Greek Dance. *"She's going to want a bit of a trip next year but she's a very nice filly, has plenty of quality and I'm bringing her along quietly".*

417. NOBLE ANCESTRY ★★★★
b.c. Dubawi – Joys of Spring (Invincible Spirit). February 27. First foal. The dam, a quite useful 1m winner, is a half-sister to 2 winners including the 2-y-o Group 3 Sweet Solera Stakes winner Albabilia. The second dam, Sonachan (by Darshaan), a minor Irish 14f winner, is a half-sister to the Listed 1m Brownstown Stud Stakes and US stakes winner Inchacooley. *"A nice type of colt, he's one for the midsummer and is doing everything right. He's moving forward, has a good attitude and is pleasing us".*

418. PERSIAN BEAUTY (IRE) ★★★★
b.f. Dubawi – Zeeba (Barathea). April 4. Seventh foal. Sister to the very smart Group 3 Huxley Stakes winner of 6 races at around 10f Danadana and to the fairly useful 10f to 14f winner of 6 races Semeen and the fair 12f winner Zeelander. The dam, a fair 12f winner, is a sister to the useful Listed 14f winner Lost Soldier Three and a half-sister to 5 winners including the useful 10.5f and 12f winner Altaweelah. The second dam, Donya (Mill Reef), was placed once over 10f from 2 outings and is a half-sister to the Rothmans International winner French Glory and the useful Irish winner at up to 12f Golden Isle. *"A very nice filly, she'll take a bit of time but should be racing in midsummer over seven furlongs. Hopefully she's a filly with a future".*

419. SIAM DAWN (IRE) ★★★
b.c. Dawn Approach – Tea Cup (Danehill Dancer). April 25. Second foal. 50,000Y. Tattersalls October Book 2. Stroud/Coleman.

Half-brother to the unplaced 2017 2-y-o Conversant (by Zebedee). The dam, a winner, is a half-sister to 5 winners including the useful Irish 2-y-o 7f winner Listed Flame Of Tara Stakes second Forest Storm (dam of the 2,000 Guineas and Lockinge Stakes winner Night Of Thunder). The second dam, Quiet Storm (by Desert Prince), a fairly useful 7f and 10f winner, was Listed-placed twice and is a half-sister to 4 winners. *"He could be reasonably early and as soon as the six furlong races start in May he'll be ready. He's just stepping into fast work now, goes nicely and has a good attitude, so he's very straightforward"*.

420. TROLIUS (IRE) ★★★

b.c. Cape Cross – Trikala (High Chaparral). February 21. First foal. 32,000Y. Tattersalls October Book 2. Stroud/Coleman. The dam, a fair dual 7f placed 2-y-o, is a half-sister to 2 winners including the very smart 2-y-o Group 2 6f Mill Reef Stakes winner and Group 1 Middle Park Stakes second Moohaajim (by Cape Cross). The second dam, Thiella (by Kingmambo), a fairly useful Irish 2-y-o 7f and subsequent US winner, is a half-sister to the US Grade 3 12f winner Niagara Causeway. *"A midsummer type 2-y-o, he has a very playful character and he's muscular, strong and neat; one to start off at six furlongs"*.

421. WALLAA ★★★★

b.f. Dawn Approach – Shuhra (Marju). April 22. Third foal. The dam, a fair 8.5f to 12f placed maiden, is a sister to 2 winners including the very useful 2-y-o 6f and 7f winner Oriental Fashion and a half-sister to 4 winners including the US Grade 2 10f winner Makderah. The second dam, Wijdan (by Riverman), a useful 1m and 10.4f winner, is a sister to the 7f (at 2 yrs) and Listed 1m winner Sarayir and a half-sister to Nashwan, Nayef and Unfuwain. *"A sharp, racy, forward filly and I think she'll come to hand pretty quickly. We've started doing a bit of work with her, she shows plenty of pace and you definitely want to give her a mention"*.

422. WISE RULER ★★★

ch.c. Dawn Approach – Bint Almukhtar (Halling). February 29. Third foal. Half-brother to the fair 2017 1m placed 2-y-o Revolutionary Man (by Exceed And Excel). The dam is an unraced half-sister to one winner.

The second dam, Dabawiyah (by Intikhab), placed once over 10f from two starts, is a half-sister to 7 winners including the very smart 7f (at 2 yrs) and Group 3 12f Gordon Stakes winner Rabah and the useful 2-y-o 6f winner and Group 1 Cheveley Park Stakes third Najiya and to the placed dam of the Irish Oaks second Ice Queen. *"A stronger version of his half-brother Revolutionary Man, he's going well at the moment, looks a nice type of horse and is one for the middle of the summer. I should imagine that in time he'll stay further than his half-brother"*.

423. UNNAMED ★★★

b.c. Pivotal – Masarah (Cape Cross). March 7. First foal. The dam, a fairly useful 6f (at 2 yrs) and 1m winner, is a half-sister to 3 winners including the useful Listed 1m winner and Group 3 placed Pelerin. The second dam, Fragrancy (by Singspiel), a useful 1m (including at 2 yrs) and 10f winner, was Listed-placed and is a half-sister to 5 winners. *"A nice type of horse, he has strength and depth to him and he's not over-big. A nice, straightforward Pivotal he won't be all speed and I think he'll stay a fair bit next year"*.

424. UNNAMED ★★★

ch.f. No Nay Never – Saturn Girl (Danehill Dancer). April 3. Fifth foal. The dam, a fair 1m winner, is a half-sister to 8 winners including the useful Listed 10f winner Livadiya. The second dam, Lilissa (by Doyoun), a French 9f and 10.5f winner, is a half-sister to 5 winners including the Group 3 12f Prix Minerve winner Linnga. *"She's a sharp, quick filly, pleasing us in every way and one that should be running in May"*.

425. UNNAMED ★★★

ch.f. Exceed And Excel – Shama's Crown (New Approach). February 12. First foal. The dam, a fair 1m winner, is a half-sister to 5 winners including the Derby second Walk In The Park and the Listed winner Soon. The second dam, Classic Park (by Robellino), won 3 races including the Irish 1,000 Guineas and is a half-sister to 10 winners including the US Grade 2 winner Rumpipumpy. *"A nice filly, she can be a little bit hot like her dam was, but she's a forward-going filly, very athletic and covers the ground very well"*.

426. UNNAMED ★★

ch.c. Poet's Voice – Umneyati (Iffraaj). February 1. First foal. 50,000Y. Tattersalls October Book 3. Crisford Racing. The dam, a fairly useful Listed-placed 2-y-o triple 5f winner, is a half-sister to 2 winners. The second dam, Honky Tonk Sally (by Dansili), a quite useful 2-y-o 7f winner, is a half-sister to 7 winners including the Group 3 1m Prix Saint-Roman winner Eco Friendly. *"A nice type of horse but he's not going to be early, he'll take a bit of time, is growing at the moment and very much one for the second half of the season".*

LUCA CUMANI
427. CARDANO ★★★★

b.c. Oasis Dream – Astorgs Galaxy (Galileo). February 4. Second foal. 47,000Y. Tattersalls October Book 2. Charlie Gordon-Watson. The dam, a fair 10f and 12f placed maiden, is a half-sister to 5 winners including the US stakes winner and Group 1 Prix Saint-Alary second Asti. The second dam, Astorg (by Lear Fan), won the Listed 1m Prix de la Calonne and is a half-sister to 8 winners including the Group 3 winners Android and Article Rare. *"He's quite mature and well-built. It's a bit difficult to say what his 2-y-o prospects are because being by Oasis Dream you'd think he'd be a 2-y-o but he's out of a Galileo mare which suggests a bit more distance. He's probably one for midsummer but he has all the credentials to be a nice horse".*

428. ERNEST ALDRICH ★★

b.c. Oasis Dream – Wallis (King's Best). April 22. Fourth foal. Half-brother to the quite useful 7.5f winner Atteq (by Invincible Spirit). The dam, a quite useful 6f and 1m winner here, subsequently won and was stakes-placed in the USA. She is a half-sister to 5 winners including the Grade 1 Northern Dancer Turf and dual Grade 2 Sky Classic winner Forte Dei Marmi (by Selkirk) and the very useful 12f and Listed 14f winner Savarain. The second dam, Frangy (by Sadler's Wells), a fair dual 12f winner, is a full or half-sister to 8 winners including the German 1m to 9.5f winner of 7 races and Listed-placed Flying Heights. (Fittocks Stud). *"He should run this year but he's pretty unfurnished and needs more time to develop, so it won't be until later on".*

429. FELIX ★★★★

ch.c. Lope De Vega – Luminance (Danehill Dancer). March 27. Fourth foal. 32,000Y. Tattersalls October Book 2. Not sold. The dam is an unraced half-sister to 4 winners including the Group 3 Irish 1,000 Guineas Trial second Devotion. The second dam, Bright Bank (by Sadler's Wells), is an unraced half-sister to 8 winners including the very useful Listed 6f and 7f winner and dual Group 1 placed My Branch (herself the dam of the Group 1 Sprint Cup winner Tante Rose). (Fittocks Stud). *"He's OK and should be a seven furlong horse in July or August. Doing well physically, he might well be able to do something as a 2-y-o".*

430. HONFLEUR (IRE) ★★★★

ch.f. Le Havre – Galistic (Galileo). May 15. Seventh foal. 72,000Y. Tattersalls October Book 1. Fittocks Stud. Half-sister to the quite useful 7f winner Aldayha (by Acclamation), to the fair 2-y-o 5f winner Trick Of The Light (by Dragon Pulse), the German Listed 7f winner Guinnevre (by Duke Of Marmalade) and the fair 2-y-o 7f and 1m winner Hala Hala (by Invincible Spirit). The dam, a useful 10f, 12f and Listed 14f winner in Ireland at 3 and 4 yrs, is a half-sister to one winner. The second dam, Mockery (by Nashwan), won 2 minor races at 3 yrs in France and is a half-sister to 3 other minor winners. (Fittocks Stud). *"She's quite nice and even though she's a late foal she's a very good mover and covers a lot of ground. Very straightforward and forward-going, she's one for the midsummer onwards and all things being equal she looks like being one of the nicer ones".*

431. LOVEHEART ★★★

br.f. Dubawi – Love Divine (Diesis). April 18. Half-sister to 7 winners including the Group 1 St Leger and Group 2 Jockey Club Cup winner and sire Sixties Icon (by Galileo), the useful 10f winner and Group 2 12f Jockey Club Stakes second Native Ruler, the fairly useful dual 12f winner Hamelin (both by Cape Cross) and the quite useful 12f and 14f winner Touch The Sky (by Sea The Stars). The dam won the Oaks and the Listed Lupe Stakes and is a half-sister to 6 winners including the Listed winners Floreeda and Dark Promise. The second dam, La Sky (by Law Society), a useful 10f winner and second in the Lancashire Oaks, is closely related to the Champion Stakes winner Legal Case and a half-sister to 4 winners. (Lordship Stud). *"A well-bred filly, she's a bit on the small side but she's doing well and improving all the time. It's very nice to have a filly with a pedigree like hers in the yard because she could be anything. It's more likely that she'll be at her peak next year though"*.

432. LOVINA ★★★

b.f. Alhebayeb – Mount Lavinia (Montjeu). April 20. Fifth foal. 48,000Y. Tattersalls October Book 2. Amanda Skiffington /Luca Cumani. Half-sister to the fair 12f winner Dr Drey (by Bahamian Bounty) and to two minor winners abroad by Born To Sea and Paco Boy. The dam, a quite useful 11.5f and 14f winner of 3 races, is a half-sister to 4 winners including the US Listed stakes winner and French Group 2 Prix Dollar second Lord Cromby. The second dam, Havinia (by Habitat), a French 3-y-o winner, is a half-sister to 3 other minor winners. *"She was bought entirely because of her looks rather than her pedigree. A good-looking filly that's going well, it's entirely possible that she'll be a nice six furlong 2-y-o come June/July"*.

433. MARLOWE ROSE ★★★

b.f. Camelot – Gameday (Zamindar). February 28. First foal. The dam is an unraced half-sister to numerous winners including the Group 2 14f Prix Maurice de Nieuil and Group 3 12f Prix d'Hedouville winner Bellamy Cay and the French Listed 1m winner Cinnamon Bay. The second dam, Trellis Bay (Sadler's Wells), a useful 12f winner, is a sister to the 12f winners Coraline, Spanish Wells and New Abbey and a half-sister to the very smart Group 1 Irish Oaks and Group 2 Prix de Malleret winner Wemyss Bight. (Mr P. Stokes & Partners). *"A nice filly, she's a bit small but very lively and she could well win as a 2-y-o. It's not a sprinting pedigree so she's more likely to want seven furlongs to a mile this year and middle-distances next year"*.

434. MYTHICAL TRIBE ★★★

b.c. Cape Cross – Allegheny Creek (Teofilo). April 27. Third foal. 47,000Y. Tattersalls October Book 2. Amanda Skiffington. The dam is an unraced half-sister to 8 winners including the Irish 2-y-o Listed 6f winner and Group 2 placed He's A Decoy and the high-class 6f Stewards Cup winner, dual Group 1 third and smart sire Danetime. The second dam, Allegheny River (by Lear Fan), won once over 7f at 3 yrs in Ireland and is a half-sister to one winner. *"He's small, compact, goes well and so as a type he looks quite precocious, but on pedigree you wouldn't think he'd be a 2-y-o. He's well put-together though, so he could start over six furlongs although on pedigree you'd say seven"*.

435. PREJUDICE ★★★★

ch.c. Dubawi – Ever Rigg (Dubai Destination). April 30. Sixth foal. 525,000Y. Tattersalls October Book 1. Not sold. Brother to the multiple Group 1 winner Postponed (King George VI and Queen Elizabeth Stakes, Juddmonte International, etc) and half-brother to the Group 3 Prix Minerve and Listed 12f winner God Given (by Nathaniel). The dam, a fair 12f winner, is a half-sister 5 winners including the Listed-placed Bite Of The Cherry and Pietra Dura (dam of the US Grade 3 winner and Grade 1 second Turning Top). The second dam, Bianca Nera (by Salse), winner of the Group 1 7f Moyglare Stud Stakes and the Group 2 6f Lowther Stakes, is half-sister to 4 winners including the Group 1 second Hotelgenie Dot Com (dam of the dual Group 1 winner Simply Perfect). (St Albans Bloodstock Limited). *"Seems to be going well, he's a bit on the small side so he's not in the same mould as his brother Postponed. He seems to have ability though, as you'd expect with his pedigree. Physically he looks more precocious than you might think and I wouldn't put it past him to win as a 2-y-o but his future is probably ahead of that"*.

436. PORTABELLO ROAD ★★★★

b.c. Iffraaj – Represent (Exceed And Excel). February 16. Third foal. 57,000Y. Tattersalls October Book 2. Charlie Gordon-Watson. Half-brother to the fair 2017 Irish 2-y-o 7.5f winner Ballot Box (by Big Bad Bob) and to the modest 6f winner Ghaseedah (by Kyllachy). The dam, a fair 6f and 7f winner, is a half-sister to 11 winners including the Group 2 Bosphorus Cup winner Connecticut, the smart 1m winner and Listed-placed Castleton and the German Listed winner and Group 3 placed Fleurie Domaine. The second dam, Craigmill (by Slip Anchor), a fair 2-y-o 7f winner, is a half-sister to 6 winners including the Group 3 Park Hill Stakes winner Coigach and the Park Hill Stakes second and smart broodmare Applecross. *"He's definitely a good-looking horse and being by Iffraaj he should have some precocity, so it's quite possible he could be running over six furlongs by June or July and he'll get seven or a mile later on. I'm very happy with him, he's a nice horse. The name should be Portobello of course, but that wasn't available".*

437. SWANSDOWN ★★★
ch.f. Dubawi – Pongee (Barathea). April 20. Ninth foal. 210,000Y. Tattersalls October Book 1. Not sold. Half-sister to 6 winners including the Listed 10f winner Pinzolo (by Monsun), the fairly useful Listed-placed 2-y-o 1m winner Poplin (by Medicean), the fairly useful 7f (at 2 yrs) and 8.5f winner Materialistic (by Oasis Dream) and the fair 10f winner Paisley (by Pivotal). The dam, a Group 2 12f Lancashire Oaks winner, is closely related to the Listed 12f and Listed 14f winner Lion Sands and to the Listed-placed 11f winner Pukka and a half-sister to 5 winners. The second dam, Puce (by Darshaan), a Listed 12f winner, is a half-sister to 10 winners including the dam of the dual Oaks winner Alexandrova and the Cheveley Park Stakes winner Magical Romance. (Fittocks Stud). *"It's a late-developing middle-distance family so her best will come next year, but of course she'll be given some racing as a 2-y-o. Come September we'll see what we do with her, but I'd say she's good enough to win as a 2-y-o".*

438. UNNAMED ★★
b.c. Intello – Angelic Note (Excellent Art). March 2. Third foal. 60,000Y. Tattersalls October Book 2. Allan Bloodlines. Half-brother to the quite useful 11f and 12f winner Koeman (by Dutch Art). The dam is an unplaced half-sister to 3 winners including the Group 2 Lowther Stakes winner Infamous Angel. The second dam, Evangeline (by Sadler's Wells), is an unraced half-sister to 4 winners including the Listed winner Sgt Pepper. (Dahab Racing). *"A very nice, big, middle-distance horse for next year but we'll be looking to get him out this year to try and win something".*

439. UNNAMED ★★
b.c. Dark Angel – Rougette (Red Ransom). May 4. Third foal. 50,000Y. Tattersalls October

Book 2. Not sold. The dam, a quite useful 1m winner, is a half-sister to 3 winners including the useful 5f (at 2 yrs) and Listed 7f winner and Group 2 7f Rockfel Stakes third Royal Confidence. The second dam, Never A Doubt (by Night Shift), a very useful 2-y-o winner of the Group 2 5.5f Prix Robert Papin, is a half-sister to 4 winners. (Dahab Racing). *"Still in pre-training, he was very backward at the sales, which is why he didn't sell. I haven't seen him since so I can't really comment any further".*

KEITH DALGLEISH
440. BEECHWOOD ELLA (IRE) ★★
b.f. No Nay Never – Tamazug (Machiavellian). April 8. Eighth foal. £38,000Y. Goffs UK Premier (Doncaster). Bobby O'Ryan / MPR. Half-sister to the quite useful Irish dual 1m winner Maskoon (by Aqlaam). The dam, a useful Irish 7f and 1m winner, was third in the Group 3 Derrinstown Stud 1,000 Guineas Trial and is a full or half-sister to 4 winners. The second dam, Nasheed (by Riverman), a useful 7f (at 2 yrs) and 10f winner, is a half-sister to 7 winners including the high-class Prix de l'Arc de Triomphe and Juddmonte International winner Sakhee. (Middleham Park Racing XVI). *"A nice filly, she's quite athletic-looking, needs to grow and is doing so. I haven't been too hard on her and she's probably at least a couple of months off a run".*

441. BEECHWOOD IZZY (IRE) ★★★
b.f. Dandy Man – Rugged Up (Marju). March 8. Fifth foal. £40,000Y. Goffs UK Premier (Doncaster). Bobby O'Ryan /MPR. Half-sister to the quite useful dual 6f winner Red Tycoon (by Acclamation). The dam is an unraced half-sister to the Japanese Group 3 winner Meiner Eternel and to the very useful Irish 2-y-o Listed 5f winner Warsaw. The second dam, For Evva Silca (by Piccolo), placed once at 2 yrs, is a half-sister to 9 winners including the 2-y-o Group 1 6f Prix Morny winner Silca's Sister and the dual Group 2 winner Golden Silca. (Middleham Park Racing LII). *"A strong filly with plenty of bone, she's got a bit of scope about her too. She's working well and she'll start her career soon over five furlongs and will stay at least six later on. She just gets her head down and gets on with it".*

442. CABALLERO (IRE) ★★★
ch.c. Camacho – Dame D'Honneur (Teofilo). February 19. Fourth foal. €55,000Y. Goffs Sportsmans. Bobby O'Ryan/K Dalgleish. Half-brother to the Group 3 Prix des Reservoirs second Turf Laurel (by Footstepsinthesand) and to the modest Irish 9.5f winner Mystery Gal (by Big Bad Bob). The dam is an unraced half-sister to 4 winners. The second dam, La Reine Mambo (by High Yield), a Listed-placed winner of 2 races over 1m at 2 and 3 yrs in France, is a half-sister to 6 winners including the triple Group/Grade 3 winner and US Grade 1 third Danzon. (Weldspec Glasgow Limited). *"He's a big, strong horse but everything's in the right place and he's actually working like a sharp horse. I'll probably wait for six furlongs with him and I do like him".*

443. CHAPMAN BILLY ★★
ch.c. Poet's Voice – Good Health (Magic Ring). March 1. Ninth foal. 33,000Y. Tattersalls October Book 3. Jill Lamb. Half-brother to the quite useful 6f (at 2 yrs) and 5f winner of 6 races Your Pal Tal (by Dark Angel), to the quite useful 2-y-o 5f and 6f winner of 4 races The Magic Of Rio (by Captain Rio), the modest 5f winners Kiringa (by Kyllachy) and Somedaysrdiamonds (by Equiano) and the poor 6f winner Amoureuse (by Needwood Blade). The dam was a fair 2-y-o 5f winner. The second dam, Fiddling (by Music Boy), won once at 3 yrs and is a half-sister to 4 winners including the Group 2 and Group 3 placed sprinter Clantime. (Mrs J. M. MacPherson). *"He's a compact horse but still has a bit of height about him. He's been in pre-training so I haven't had him long. From what I've seen so far he's working well enough and will start over a stiff six furlongs or seven later in the year".*

444. EPONA ★★★★
b.f. Epaulette – Jackline (Diktat). March 23. Fifth foal. £12,000Y. Goffs UK Silver. Bobby O'Ryan & Keith Dalgleish. Half-sister to 2 minor winners abroad by Excellent Art and Gladiatorus. The dam was placed in Italy and is a half-sister to 7 winners including the smart Group 3 6f Sirenia Stakes winner of 6 races Elnawin. The second dam, Acicula (by Night Shift), a useful 2-y-o 5f and 6f winner, is a half-sister to 5 winners. *"She's a long, scopey, very athletic filly and just needs a bit of time to*

strengthen up. She has a super attitude, moves great and does everything you ask. We'll start her over a stiff six furlongs".

445. EURO IMPLOSION (IRE) ★★
b.c. Battle Of Marengo – Mikes Baby (Key Of Luck). April 15. Eighth foal. €22,000Y. Goffs Sportsmans. Bobby O'Ryan / Keith Dalgleish. Half-brother to the US winner and stakes-placed Ace Of Aces (by Antonius Pius) and to the minor Italian winner of 8 races from 2 to 6 yrs Su Contadori (by Indian Haven). The dam, a modest 4-y-o 6f winner, is a half-sister to 5 winners including the Listed-placed Palace Royale. The second dam, Trojan Tale (by Critique), is an unplaced half-sister to 4 winners. (J. S. Morrison). *"A compact, very good-looking horse, he gets on with things but probably won't debut until August time over seven furlongs".*

446. GEOMETRA GINTY (IRE) ★★★
b.f. Morpheus – Silver Cache (Silver Hawk). February 10. Ninth foal. 7,000Y. Tattersalls October Book 3. K Dalgleish. Half-sister to the quite useful 2-y-o dual 5f winner Ko Cache (by Kodiac), to the Italian 2-y-o Listed 1m winner and Group 3 second Diva Cattiva (by Lujain), the modest 9f winner Grey Willow (by Zebedee) and to the modest 7f and 1m winner Barbary (by Rock Of Gibraltar). The dam is an unplaced half-sister to 4 winners including the Peruvian Grade 1 winner Maeto. The second dam, Nina Ashley (by Criminal Type), a dual winner in Peru and Grade 3 placed, is a half-sister to 6 winners. *"Still unsold, this is a big filly, she's quite plain-looking but moves well and has been working quite well. We'll get her out when the six furlong races start and she'll get seven furlongs at the back-end. She's very tough and I trained her half-sister by Kodiac who was just the same".*

447. HOWZER BLACK (IRE) ★★
b.c. Requinto – Mattinata (Tiger Hill). March 25. Seventh foal. £30,000Y. Goffs UK Premier. Bobby O'Ryan/MPR. Half-brother to the fair 6f and 8.5f winner Reaver (by Sabiango) and three minor winners abroad by Silvano, Lord Shanakill and Lomitas. The dam, a winner in the Netherlands at 3 yrs, is a half-sister to 8 winners including the Group 2 12.5f Prix de

Pomone winner Macleya and the Group 3 Prix de Barbeville winner Montclair. The second dam, Minaccia (by Platini), won a Listed event in Germany over 7f at 3 yrs and is a half-sister to 4 winners. *"He'll be racing before the book is out, he's a sharp five furlongs type and a medium-sized, rangy colt. He's working well and is very level-headed".* TRAINER'S BARGAIN BUY

448. IRON MIKE ★★
gr.c. Gregorian – Regal Velvet (Halling). March 5. Eighth foal. €60,000Y. Goffs Sportsmans. Bobby O'Ryan / K Dalgleish. Half-brother to the fair 2017 5f and 7f placed maiden Zalshah (by Mayson) and to 4 winners including the quite useful 10f winner Regal Silk, the modest 9f winner Rakematiz (both by Pivotal) and the quite useful 1m winner Robemaker (by Oasis Dream). The dam, a quite useful 10f winner, is a half-sister to 9 winners including the Group 1 6f Cheveley Park Stakes winner Regal Rose and the Japanese dual Listed winner Generalist. The second dam, Ruthless Rose (by Conquistador Cielo), ran twice unplaced and is a half-sister to 9 winners including the high-class miler Shaadi. (Weldspec Glasgow Limited). *"He's very big, has lots of bone about him and as a result I haven't been very hard on him. He'll need time and most probably I'll just get him out over seven furlongs or so at the back-end".*

449. RED BOND (IRE) ★★
b.c. Red Jazz – Faithfulbond (Elbio). April 12. Tenth foal. £10,000Y. Goffs UK Silver. Bobby O'Ryan & Keith Dalgleish. Half-brother to 3 minor winners, including over hurdles. The dam, a fair 7f winner, is a half-sister to 8 minor winners. The second dam, Inter Madera (by Toca Madera), is an unraced half-sister to 6 winners. (Middleham Park Racing XXVII). *"A strong, good-sized, good-looking horse, he moves well and he's been working OK. He should start off in May".*

450. THEATRE OF WAR (IRE) ★★★
b.c. War Command – Final Opinion (King's Theatre). February 13. Eighth foal. €14,000Y. Goffs Orby. Bobby O'Ryan/Keith Dalgleish. Half-brother to the French 2-y-o 1m winner and Group 3 1m second Footsteppy (by Footstepsinthesand), to the fair dual 1m

winner Juvenal (by Holy Roman Emperor), the fair Irish 10f and 12f winner Fammi Sognare (by Bertolini) and the modest 8.5f and 10f winner Big Time Dancer (by Zoffany). The dam, a quite useful Irish 10f and dual 13f winner, is a half-sister to 5 winners including the Group 3 6f Greenlands Stakes winner Final Exam and the 2-y-o Group 2 6f Lowther Stakes third Spirit Of Chester. The second dam, It Takes Two (by Alzao), is an unplaced half-sister to 2 minor winners. *"A very level-headed horse, he's a good size and a size to train on. He's athletic looking and is probably going to start over a stiff six furlongs, or I could wait for the seven furlong races because there's a bit of stamina on the dam's side".*

451. WOODSIDE WONDER ★★★★
br.c. Camacho – Cambridge Duchess (Singspiel). April 22. Second foal. £20,000Y. Goffs UK Premier. Bobby O'Ryan/MPR. Half-brother to the fair 5f and 6f winner Melonade (by Mayson). The dam is an unplaced half-sister to 6 winners including the Group 2 Mill Reef Stakes third Dubai Builder. The second dam, Roseum (by Lahib), a useful 5f and 6f winner of 5 races, is a half-sister to 4 winners. (Middleham Park Racing XIV). *"A medium-sized, strong colt, he's a 2-y-o type but with a bit of scope to train on. He should hopefully be ready to start in May over five furlongs".*

452. ZIMAZAMAZOOM (IRE) ★★★
ch.c. Tagula – Muffin (Halling). April 30. Fourth foal. £25,000Y. Goffs UK Premier (Doncaster). Bobby O'Ryan/Keith Dalgleish. Half-brother to 2 minor winners abroad by Strategic Prince and Elusive Pimpernel. The dam is an unraced half-sister to 8 minor winners here and abroad. The second dam, Gretel (by Hansel), a useful 2-y-o 7f winner and third in the Group 3 1m May Hill Stakes and is a half-sister to 5 winners. *"He's a 2-y-o to look at but he's not small and everything's in the right place. He's working well and ready to run, we'll start him over five furlongs and he'll end up over six".*

453. UNNAMED ★★★
b.f. Kyllachy – Al Joudha (Green Desert). February 14. Eighth foal. £26,000Y. Goffs UK Premier (Doncaster). Bobby O'Ryan / Keith Dalgleish. Half-sister to the fair 2-y-o 7f winner Gilbey's Mate, to the modest 7f winner All

Honesty, the modest dual 7f winner Medicean El Diablo (all by Medicean), the fair 6f winner Premier Lad (by Tobougg) and a minor winner at 2 and 3 yrs in Italy by Nayef. The dam is an unplaced half-sister to 5 winners and to the placed dam of the dual Group 1 winner and sire Dutch Art. The second dam, Palacegate Episode (by Drumalis), a sprint winner of 11 races including a Group 3 in Italy and six Listed events, is a full or half-sister to 5 winners including the triple Listed winning sprinter Palacegate Jack. (Weldspec Glasgow Limited). *"She's a handy sized, strong filly, looks like a 2-y-o and seems sharp at home. She should be racing in May over five furlongs, but probably has a bit of scope about her and so potentially will stay six".*

454. UNNAMED ★★★
ch.c. Havana Gold – Bounty Box (Bahamian Bounty). March 8. Fourth foal. £55,000Y. Goffs UK Premier (Doncaster). Half-brother to Pheidippides (by Sepoy), placed third over 6f from 2 starts at 2 yrs in 2017 and to the fair 6f winner Gabrielle (by Paco Boy). The dam, a useful dual Listed 6f winner of 6 races from 2 to 5 yrs, is a sister to the French 2-y-o winner and Listed-placed Bahamian Box and a half-sister to 3 winners. The second dam, Bible Box (by Bin Ajwaad), was a quite useful 7f to 9f winner of 3 races from 3 to 5 yrs. *"He's a flashy looking fella – a chestnut with plenty of white about him. A medium-sized, quite athletic looking colt, he's just starting to get on with things now, I'm happy with him and he'll hopefully start over six furlongs around June time".*

455. UNNAMED ★★
b.c. Battle Of Marengo – Misrepresent (Distorted Humor). March 24. Third foal. €85,000Y. Goffs Orby. Bobby O'Ryan/Keith Dalgleish. Half-brother to the quite useful 2017 2-y-o 5.5f and 6f winner Jedi Master (by Red Jazz) and to a minor winner in Italy by Frozen Power. The dam, a fair 7f winner, is a half-sister to 3 minor winners in the USA and Sweden. The second dam, Halory Leigh (by Halory Hunter), a US dual Grade 2 winner, is a half-sister to 9 winners. (Weldspec Glasgow Limited). *"A gorgeous, big horse with loads of scope, I've just been taking my time with him because he's one for seven furlongs or a mile at the back-end".*

TOM DASCOMBE

456. ANGEL ALEXANDER (IRE) ★★★★
b.c. Dark Angel – Majestic Alexander (Bushranger). February 20. Second foal. £92,000Y. Goffs UK Premier (Doncaster). Sackville/Donald. The dam, a fairly useful Listed-placed 2-y-o dual 5f winner, is a half-sister to 7 winners including the triple Group 3 winning sprinter Majestic Missile and the Irish Listed winner Santo Padre. The second dam, Tshusick (by Dancing Brave), a quite useful 7f winner at 3 yrs, is a half-sister to 3 winners here and abroad. (Birbeck, Mound, Trowbridge & Owen). *"I thought he was going to be our Chester May Festival 2-y-o, he was really "on it"; sharp, racy and athletic but he got a little niggling issue and we've had to back off him. He's definitely a decent 2-y-o and if we don't get to Chester we might aim for something like the National Stakes at Sandown. A proper 2-y-o type".*

457. ARTHUR KITT ★★★★
b.c. Camelot – Ceiling Kitty (Red Clubs). February 24. Third foal. Half-brother to the quite useful 2017 2-y-o 5f winner Formidable Kitt (by Invincible Spirit) and to the fairly useful Listed 6f winner of 3 races at 2 and 3 yrs and Group 3 Summer Stakes third Eartha Kitt (by Pivotal). The dam, winner of the Group 2 5f Queen Mary Stakes, is a half-sister to the fair 2-y-o triple 5f winner Van Go Go. The second dam, Baldovina (by Tale Of The Cat), is a placed half-sister to 4 winners including the Japanese dual Group 3 winner One Carat. (Chasemore Farm). *"He's a lovely horse and perhaps my favourite 2-y-o, but I'm bound to like him because I trained the dam and her first two foals. Camelot did really well with his first crop towards the end of last season but surprisingly this lad is working already. He's got a great attitude, he's tall (not a family trait), very athletic and shows more speed than you would have expected. All he wants to do is please you and I might be wrong but I would guess we'll aim him for a six furlong maiden in May and then the Chesham, because he's a proper 2-y-o".*

458. ARTISTIC STREAK ★★
b.f. New Approach – Artisti (Cape Cross). February 1. Sixth foal. Sister to the quite useful 12f winner Point Of View and half-sister to

3 winners including the Italian and German Group 3 10f winner Magic Artist and the fair 5-y-o dual 6f winner Artscape (both by Iffraaj). The dam is an unraced half-sister to 5 winners including the Group 1 winner Gran Criterium winner Kirklees and the Group 1 St Leger and Hong Kong Vase winner Mastery and to the dam of the Group 1 Eclipse Stakes winner Mukhadram. The second dam, Moyesii (by Diesis), won once at 3 yrs in France and is a half-sister to 3 winners including the Group 3 Prix de Fontainebleau winner Bowman. (Mr D. M. Shaw). *"She's tall, leggy and backward, so she'll need a bit of time. We'll take our time with her and see how we get on".*

459. AUSSIE NUGGET (IRE) ★★★
b.c. Dansili – Anticipation (Muhtathir). March 24. Second foal. €105,000Y. Goffs Orby. Sackville/Donald. The dam is an unplaced half-sister to 12 winners including the Champion Stakes, Grand Prix de Saint-Cloud and Hong Kong Cup winner (all Group 1 events), the Group 3 winner and Group 1 placed Fate and the dam of the 1,000 Guineas and Group 2 Rockfel Stakes winner Speciosa. The second dam, Specificity (by Alleged), winner of the Listed 12f George Stubbs Stakes, is a half-sister to the 10 winners including the St Leger and Irish St Leger winner Touching Wood. (Timothy Storey & Roofing Consultants Gp). *"A big, strong horse, he's going to take a bit of time, he's tall but not gangly and physically he's a nice horse but he's going to want at least seven furlongs".*

460. BARRISTAN THE BOLD ★★
b.c. Excelebration – Cradle Of Life (Notnowcato). March 10. First foal. 35,000Y. Tattersalls October Book 2. Howson & Houldsworth. The dam is an unplaced half-sister to 5 winners including the Italian Group 3 winner and Group 1 Gran Premio de Milano third Gimmy and the Group 3 Italian 1,000 Guineas winner Stay Alive. The second dam, Pursuit Of Life (by Pursuit Of Love), a winner of 4 races in Italy at 2 and 3 yrs and Listed-placed three times, is a half-sister to 5 winners including the French dual Group 3 winner Di Moi Oui. (Chasemore Farm & Mr Kevin Costello). *"He's going perfectly well, has just started working and I would guess he'll start in the middle of May. We've had so much rain*

the horses aren't as forward as I'd have liked them to be".

461. BLYTON ★★★
b.c. Kodiac – Minwah (Oasis Dream). February 28. Second foal. £85,000Y. Goffs UK Premier (Doncaster). Sackville/Donald. The dam is an unraced half-sister to 5 winners including the Listed winner and Group 3 Nell Gwyn Stakes third Festivale. The second dam, Cephalonie (by Kris S), a minor 3-y-o winner, is a half-sister to 3 winners. (The Famous Five Partnership). *"He's had a couple of little niggling issues which have stopped us from getting him going, but nothing too serious. I haven't really got stuck into him yet but he shows a good attitude, he's a trier and on his pedigree you'd say he'd be a sharp 2-y-o".*

462. DARK ENVOY ★★★★
gr.c. Dark Angel – Moonvoy (Cape Cross). April 7. First foal. €80,000Y. Tattersalls Ireland September. Sackville/Donald. The dam, a quite useful 7f winner, is a half-sister to 4 winners including the useful 2-y-o Group 3 7f Oh So Sharp Stakes winner Alsindi. The second dam, Needles And Pins (by Fasliyev), a useful 2-y-o Listed 5.2f winner and second in the Group 3 5.5f Prix d'Arenburg, is a half-sister to 3 winners. (Mr D. R. Passant). *"To look at him you'd say he's not ready yet, but when he gets going in his quicker paces he shows he is. Mentally he's not quite there, but it won't take long for the penny to drop. I love Dark Angel as a sire because I think we've had five and four of them have been rated over 100".*

463. DARK THUNDER (IRE) ★★★★
gr.c. Alhebayeb – Call This Cat (One Cool Cat). April 7. Fourth foal. £42,000Y. Goffs UK Premier (Doncaster). Sackville/Donald. Half-brother to the fair 10f and 11.5f winner Cat Royale (by Lilbourne Lad). The dam, a modest 5f placed maiden, is a half-sister to 7 winners including the US Grade 3 winner Pasar Silbano and the 2-y-o Listed sprint winners Come To Heel and Gerfalcon. The second dam, Give A Whistle (by Mujadil), a dual 5f winner at 3 and 4 yrs, is a half-sister to one winner. (Birbeck, Burke, Goss, Hyden, Jones). *"I like the sire, we've got two of them and they both go well. This colt is strong and he'll be ready by the middle of May and we might even try and*

push him to see if he can get to the Chester May meeting. He goes well, is very forward–thinking and sharp".

464. DONTHOLDYOURBREATH (IRE) ★★★
ch.f. Bated Breath – Don't Tell Mary (Starcraft). February 23. Half-sister to the fair 7f to 9f winner of 3 races Beverley Bullet (by Makfi). The dam, a fairly useful 2-y-o Listed 5f winner, is a half-sister to the very useful 2-y-o 5f and 6f winner and Group 2 July Stakes second Cape Fear and to the useful 6f (at 2 yrs) and Listed 5f winner Exceptional Art. The second dam, Only In Dreams (by Polar Falcon), a fair 2-y-o 7f winner, is a full or half-sister to 4 other minor winners. (Keith Trowbridge). *"A nice filly out of a mare that won the Hilary Needler for us. Sadly she's had no luck producing so far, but this is the first one with a bit of size and scope about her. She's quite a nice homebred filly that'll probably want six furlongs. I'm just going easy on her for the moment because she's had sore shins but we'll start building her up soon and see where we go".*

465. DROGON (IRE) ★★★
b.c. Zoffany – Flames To Dust (Oasis Dream). April 19. Sixth foal. 45,000Y. Tattersalls October Book 3. Sackville/Donald. Half-brother to the modest 2017 7f placed 2-y-o Flamin Audi (by Medicean). The dam is an unraced sister to one winner and a half-sister to 6 winners including the 2-y-o Group 2 Royal Lodge Stakes second and subsequent Hong Kong stakes winner Bahamian Dancer. The second dam, Fantastic Flame (by Generous), a fair 10f winner, is a sister to the Group 3 Gordon Richards Stakes winner Germano and a half-sister to 9 winners including the US Grade 2 winner Moon Solitaire. (APCC Limited). *"He's had one or two little niggles so I've been easy on him. He hasn't worked yet and I think Zoffany's often take a little bit of time, but he shows a good attitude, he's a good-looking horse and I'm sure he'll be fine, maybe over six or seven furlongs".*

466. FINOAH (IRE) ★★★
b.c. Kodiac – Burstingdalak (Dalakhani). April 7. Second foal. 52,000Y. Tattersalls October Book 2. Sackville/Donald. The dam won 2 minor races at 3 yrs in Italy and is

a half-sister to another minor winner in Germany. The second dam, Second Burst (by Sadler's Wells), was placed at 3 yrs in France and is a sister to the 2-y-o Group 1 Racing Post Trophy winner Commander Collins and a half-sister to the Grade 1 Breeders' Cup Sprint winner Lit de Justice, the 2,000 Guineas and Derby placed Colonel Collins and the Group 2 Royal Lodge Stakes winner City Leader. (Alan & Sue Cronshaw and Peter Birbeck). *"A nice, racy colt that galloped for the first time the other day. He might start over five furlongs but probably wants six and he's nearly ready to run".*

467. FIVE AMARONES (IRE) ★★★
b.c. Alhebayeb – Mokama (Motivator). March 4. Third foal. 35,000Y. Tattersalls October Book 2. Sackville/Donald. The dam, a moderate 12f placed maiden in Ireland, is a half-sister to 4 winners. The second dam, Carambola (by Danehill), a useful Listed Irish 1,000 Guineas Trial winner and second in the Group 3 1m Matron Stakes, is a sister to the useful 2-y-o 6f winner and South African Grade 1 second Toreador and a half-sister to 7 winners including the Irish 1,000 Guineas winner Matiya. (The Famous Five Partnership). *"He thinks that he's a racehorse because he's so full of himself. He was ready to run in January I should think and as a result we've just had to try to slow him down and relax him rather than wind him up. He looks a nice type, probably not as fast as he thinks he is and probably wants six furlongs, but he's aggressive".*

468. FIVE ANGELS (IRE) ★★
b.c. Dark Angel – Clear Impression (Danehill). February 7. Seventh foal. £80,000Y. Goffs UK Premier (Doncaster). Sackville/Donald. Half-brother to the quite useful 5f and 6f winner of 9 races Pettochside (by Refuse To Bend) and to two minor winners abroad by Dubawi and Dubai Destination. The dam, a fairly useful 3-y-o 6f winner, was Listed-placed three times and is a half-sister to 2 winners. The second dam, Shining Hour (by Red Ransom), won the Group 3 5f Queen Mary Stakes and is a full or half-sister to 7 winners. (The Famous Five Partnership). *"He's taking a little bit of time to understand the job and he's backward-thinking, not a sharp 2-y-o and just needs to*

do everything twice before he understands it. But that's fine, he'll be one for the middle of the season".

469. FIVE HELMETS (IRE) ★★★

b.c. Helmet – Sweet Home Alabama (Desert Prince). April 12. Eighth foal. 26,000Y. Tattersalls October Book 3. Sackville/Donald. Half-brother to the useful 2-y-o 1m winner and dual Group 3 third Havana Beat (by Teofilo), to the fair 5f and 10f winner Rahmah (by Vale Of York), the fair 2-y-o 6f winner Ediye (by Fast Company) and the modest 1m and hurdles winner King's Realm (by King's Best). The dam, placed fourth over 7f and 1m, is a half-sister to the Group 1 1m Sussex Stakes winner Proclamation and to the German dual Listed winner No Refuge. The second dam, Shamarra (by Zayyani), is an unraced half-sister to the smart middle-distance performer Shantaroun and to the dams of the Group winners Sardaniya and Shaiybara. (The Famous Five Partnership). *"He just had a couple of niggling issues early doors and so he's a bit behind some of the others, but he's cantering away and I really like the sire. A good-looking horse, he's grown a lot and I think that's part of the problem because he was small when he came in. He's ready for more work now and he's getting it. Six furlongs should be fine for him".*

470. FRANKADORE (IRE) ★★★

ch.c. Frankel – Adoration (Honor Grades). April 30. Tenth foal. 100,000Y. Tattersalls October Book 1. Sackville/Donald. Closely related to the quite useful dual 1m winner Vantage Point and to a winner in Japan (both by Galileo). The dam, a US dual Grade 1 winner, is a half-sister to 8 winners including the US Grade 3 placed Mo Mon. The second dam, Sewing Lady (Key To The Mint), is an unraced half-sister to 9 winners including the Irish Listed winner Astraeus. (Clyne, Dance, Mound & Partner). *"Relatively speaking for a Frankel he was cheap and you could see why, he was very weak. But not any more, he's a really good-looking, strong colt and I think we might have nicked one there. His pedigree is perfectly good enough, he's by the right sire and has improved and developed dramatically over the last three months, so we're happy with him".*

471. GREAT SCOT ★★

b.c. Requinto – La Rosiere (Mr Greeley). March 19. First foal. £2,500Y. Tattersalls Ireland Ascot. Not sold. The dam, a moderate 1m placed 3-y-o, is a half-sister to 3 minor winners. The second dam, Snowtime (by Galileo), is an unraced half-sister to 9 winners including the Group 1 winners Ali-Royal, Sleepytime and Taipan. (Empire State Racing Partnership). *"A home-bred colt, he's a bit weak-looking and leggy but he's improved an awful lot. I don't mind the sire and this colt is just going to need a bit of time; there's nothing wrong with him and we just have to be patient".*

472. GUANDI (USA) ★★★

ch.c. Declaration Of War – Hoh Buzzard (Alhaarth). April 5. Ninth foal. €90,000Y. Goffs Orby. Sackville/Donald. Half-brother to 6 winners including the US Grade 3 Railbird Stakes winner and Grade 1 placed Via Villagio (by Bernardini), the US Grade 3 placed Little Curlin (by Curlin) and the US stakes-placed Dr Smarty Jack (by Smarty Jones). The dam, winner of the Listed Upavon Stakes here and the Grade 2 Revere Stakes in the USA, is a half-sister to 6 winners including the Group 3 Bentinck Stakes winner Ashdown Express. The second dam, Indian Express (by Indian Ridge), a modest 8.5f and 10f winner, is a sister to the Listed 6f winner Cheyenne Spirit and a half-sister to 4 winners. (Empire State Racing Partnership). *"We like the sire and have a nice 3-y-o by him. This horse was small when he came in but he's not now. He's ready for more work but there's no real rush with him because on pedigree you'd think he'd want further than six furlongs".*

473. ICONIC CHOICE ★★★

ch.f. Sixties Icon – Adorable Choice (Choisir). January 31. First foal. £4,500Y. Tattersalls Ireland Ascot. Not sold. The dam, a fair 7f and 1m winner at 2 and 3 yrs, is a half-sister to 3 winners including the useful Irish 2-y-o 6f winner and Group 2 Railway Stakes second In Some Respect. The second dam, Burnin' Memories (by Lit de Justice), won 5 races at 2 to 5 yrs in the USA including a minor stakes event and is a half-sister to 7 winners. (Mr J. D. Brown). *"A home-bred filly out of a mare that won a few races for us. I quite like the sire, this filly is probably going to want at least six furlongs and she's tall so she wants a bit of time. Consequently we've gone easy on her and she'll be fine given another month or six weeks".*

474. JACKSTAR (IRE) ★★★★
gr.c. Dark Angel – Starbright (Duke Of Marmalade). February 3. Second foal. £120,000Y. Goffs UK Premier (Doncaster). Sackville/Donald. The dam, a fairly useful 2-y-o 1m winner and third in the Group 3 Park Express Stakes, is a half-sister to 2 winners. The second dam, Starry Messenger (by Galileo), a fair 12f winner, is a half-sister to the US Grade 1 Gamely Handicap winner Tuscan Evening and the dual Listed winner Barbican. (Mrs C. L. Ingram). *"We really love this horse. By our standards he was an expensive purchase and so far he's given us no reason to think we've wasted our money. Richard Kingscote gave him a canter in January and said he was ready to run! He hadn't even worked at that stage and is just one of those total professionals. He probably wants six furlongs but we'll start him at the Craven meeting".*

475. JENSUE ★★★
b.f. Red Jazz – Gold Tobougg (Tobougg). April 7. Third foal. £13,000Y. Tattersalls Ireland Ascot. Sackville/Donald. Half-sister to the quite useful 2-y-o 5.5f winner Fast Gold (by Fast Company). The dam, a modest 6f winner at 3 yrs, is a sister to the triple Listed winner 6 races and Group 3 Musidora Stakes second Sweet Lilly and a half-sister to 2 winners including the useful 9f and 10f winner of 7 races Ofaraby. The second dam, Maristax (by Reprimand), a fair 2-y-o 7f winner, is closely related to the useful 2-y-o Listed 5f winner Four-Legged-Friend and a half-sister to 6 winners including the dual US Grade 3 winner Superstrike and the dam of the Group 1 winning sprinters Goodricke and Pastoral Pursuits. (Alan & Sue Cronshaw). *"A sharp 2-y-o, she'll probably be running in April and we'll have one eye on the Chester May festival. A proper 2-y-o, I don't know how good she is but she's ready to rock and roll".*

476. JONAH JONES ★★
b.c. No Nay Never – Conniption (Danehill Dancer). April 13. Fourth foal. 60,000Y. Tattersalls October Book 2. Sackville/Donald. Closely related to the minor US 3-y-o winner Scattered Thought (by Scat Daddy). The dam, a fairly useful 2-y-o 6f winner, subsequently won a minor race in the USA and is a half-sister to 3 minor winners. The second dam, Showbiz (by Sadler's Wells), a quite useful Irish Listed-placed 2-y-o 7f winner, is a half-sister to two Listed-placed winners. (Mr D. Ward). *"A slightly backward horse, he was a mid-April foal and he's improved enormously because he was a big individual when he came in but now he just looks an average size. We've gone easy on him and he's only cantered so far, we'll take our time and he'll come when he's ready".*

477. KATIESHEIDINLISA ★★
b.f. Camelot – Spritza (Spectrum). April 8. Sixth foal. 75,000Y. Tattersalls October Book 1. Sackville/Donald. Closely related to 2 winners including the quite useful 2-y-o 7f and 10f winner and Group 3 Classic Trial third Rougemont (by Montjeu) and half-brother to a minor winner in Sweden by Pivotal. The dam, a modest 11f and 12f winner, is a half-sister to 4 winners including the fairly useful 12f winner of 4 races and Listed-placed Portrait Of A Lady and to the placed dam of the dual Group 1 winner Covert Love. The second dam, Starlight Smile (by Green Dancer), is an unraced half-sister to 4 winners including the dam of the Irish Derby winner Grey Swallow. (Mr D.R Passant & Hefin Williams). *"A lovely-looking filly, she's backward but I'm in no rush with her at all because she needs a bit of time and wants seven furlongs".*

478. LIBERATION DAY ★★★
b.c. Iffraaj – Welsh Cake (Fantastic Light). April 15. Sixth foal. £50,000Y. Goffs UK Premier (Doncaster). Sackville/Donald. Half-brother to the useful 2-y-o 5f winner Upward Spiral, to the fair 2-y-o 7f winner Chica de la Noche (both by Teofilo) and the quite useful 5f (at 2 yrs) and 6f winner Al Gomry (by Exceed And Excel). The dam, a fair 7f winner, is a half-sister to 9 winners including the Trans Island (Group 2 1m Prix du Rond-Point and Group 3 8.5f Diomed Stakes) and Welsh Diva (Group 3 Premio Sergio Cumani). The second dam, Khubza (by Green Desert), a quite useful 7f winner, is a half-sister to 7 winners including the Group 2 winners Barrow Creek and Last Resort (dam of the US Grade 2 winner Rebellion). (Allen, Lennon, Nolan, Rutherford).

"He's been galloping, shows plenty of speed and we had a nice filly out of this dam who was fourth in the Queen Mary. This colt looks like he's probably going to want six furlongs, he moves well, he's a tough, straightforward horse and wants to do it, so we like him".

479. LIGHT MY FIRE (IRE) ★★★
ch.f. Dragon Pulse – Shawaaty (Monsun). March 17. Fourth foal. 23,000Y. Tattersalls Ireland. Sackville/Donald. Sister to the quite useful 2017 2-y-o dual 5f winner Porchy Party and half-sister to a 2-y-o winner in the Czech Republic by Lilbourne Lad. The dam, placed once at 3 yrs in France, is a half-sister to 5 winners including the French Listed winner Mahaatheer. The second dam, Al Ihtithar (by Barathea), a very useful 10f and 10.3f Listed winner, is a full or half-sister to 9 winners including the Group 3 Prix Berteux winner and dual Group 2 second Samsaam. (The Light My Fire Partnership). *"We have the full-brother Porchy Party who won a couple last year. This filly worked the other day, goes nicely and she'll certainly be out in May if not before. She has a great attitude just like her brother and she's straightforward, honest and can go a bit".* TRAINER'S BARGAIN BUY

480. LOLA'S THEME ★★★
gr.f. Iffraaj – Lady's Art (Verglas). March 22. Third foal. 35,000Y. Tattersalls October Book 2. Sackville/Donald. Half-sister to the minor 2017 Italian 2-y-o winner Yakima (by Dutch Art). The dam, a moderate 1m winner, is a sister to the French Listed winner and Group 3 second Chill and a half-sister to the French Group 3 winner Remus De La Tour. The second dam, Calithea (by Marju), is an unplaced half-sister to 6 minor winners. (Dave Lowe & Russell Jones). *"She's 'gassy' and certainly thinks she's a racehorse but I'd say she's probably a six furlong 2-y-o, not five. But when the stalls open she'll be out and gone and good luck catching her!"*

481. MAGNETIC LOVE ★★
b.f. Exceed And Excel – Coral Mist (Bahamian Bounty). January 27. First foal. £140,000. Goffs UK Premier (Doncaster). Dance/ Creighton/ Sackville/ Donald. The dam won the Group 3 6f Firth Of Clyde Stakes at 2 yrs and is a half-sister to 7 winners including the

Group 1 7f Prix de la Foret winner of 16 races Toylsome. The second dam, Treasure Trove (by The Minstrel), a modest 5f to 7f placed 2-y-o, is a half-sister to 4 winners including the US Grade 3 winner Ocean Queen and the Queen Mary Stakes, Fred Darling Stakes and US Grade 2 winner Dance Parade (dam of the Ascot Gold Cup winner Leading Light). (Mr J E Dance). *"She's had a slight setback so I can't say too much except that she has a good pedigree".*

482. METATRON (IRE) ★★★
gr.c. Dark Angel – Orikawa (Gold Away). March 10. £120,000. Goffs UK Premier (Doncaster). Robin O'Ryan. The dam, a minor French placed 3-y-o, is a half-sister to 6 winners including the UAE Group3 winner Allybar. The second dam Irika (by Irish River), a Minor French 3-y-o w\ner, is a half-sister to 6 winners including the French dual Group 2 winner Athyka. (Burns, Smyth, Studholme). *"A lovely colt that's just had a couple of little problems and he's doing a lot of swimming and cantering just to get his weight down because he's quite a tubby type. I can't tell you how good he is but he's honest, relaxed and by a great sire, so he'll be fine from midsummer onwards".*

483. MOGSY (IRE) ★★★
br.c. Dandy Man – Dictatrice (Anabaa). May 17. Eighth foal. 30,000Y. Tattersalls October Book 3. Not sold. Half-brother to the fairly useful 10f to 12f winner of 5 races Cymro (by Dark Angel), to the Scandinavian triple Listed winner over 1m Tatoosh (by Xaar), to the quite useful (including at 2 yrs) and 1m winner Madam Macie (by Bertolini) and the fair 1m winner Dianella (by Gold Away). The dam, a minor winner at 3 yrs in France, is a half-sister to 5 winners including the French Listed 3-y-o 7f winner Danella. The second dam, Dixianella (by Bering), won twice at 3 yrs in France and is a half-sister to 8 minor winners. (Satchell Moran Solicitors). *"A very late foal, we had his half-brother Cymro who was a twelve furlong horse. You'd think this colt would be a bit sharper and he'll be suited by six/seven furlongs this year".*

484. NAVIGATE BY STARS (IRE) ★★
br.f. Sea The Stars – Bitooh (Diktat). May

9. Sixth foal. €35,000Y. Tattersalls Ireland September. Sackville/Donald. Sister to the fairly useful 8.5f and 10f winner Sealife, the fair 14f and 2m winner Be My Sea and the modest 12f winner (on her only start) Pechora and half-sister to the French winner of 6 races Speed Pack (by King's Best). The dam, a minor French 3-y-o winner, is a half-sister to 4 winners including the Group 2 Curragh Stakes winner Rekindling and the Group 3 12f Chester Vase winner and Irish Derby second Golden Sword. The second dam, Sitara (by Salse), a fair 12f winner, is a half-sister to 10 winners including the dam of the Oaks winner Alexandrova and the Cheveley Park Stakes winner Magical Retreat. (The Wilmshurst Partnership). *"A black filly, I expect she gets that from being out of a Diktat mare. She was a May foal and is just cantering away now, so she could just do with growing a bit. One for the midsummer onwards, she'll be trained with her 3-y-o career in mind".*

485. NOT SO SHY ★★
b.f. Heeraat – Littlemisstutti (Noverre). February 9. Fourth foal. £5,000Y. Goffs UK Autumn. Joe Murphy. Half-sister to the modest 2-y-o 6f winner Nidnod (by Myboycharlie) and to the modest 5f winner Tooty Fruitti (by Captain Gerrard). The dam is an unraced half-sister to 6 winners including the 2-y-o Group 3 Sirenia Stakes winner and Group 1 placed Dhanyata. The second dam, Preponderance (by Cyrano de Bergerac), a quite useful 2-y-o dual 5f winner, is a half-sister to 6 winners. (Jockey Club Haydock Park Racing Club). *"She's a feisty little thing! Small but sharp, she's racy, enthusiastic and galloped really well the other day loose across the fields; she seems to go on any ground! She's sharp but not very big, so I guess she won't want too much further than five furlongs".*

486. POLISHED (IRE) ★★★
b.f. Helmet – Bawaakeer (Kingmambo). March 31. Fourth foal. €41,000Y. Tattersalls Ireland September. Sackville/Donald. Half-sister to the fair 6f winner Dirchill (by Power). The dam is an unraced half-sister to 3 winners including the French winner and dual Group 3 third Ipswich. The second dam, Imperial Beauty (by Imperial Ballet), winner of the Group 1 5f Prix de l'Abbaye and second in the

Group 1 6f Cheveley Park Stakes, is a full or half-sister to 6 winners. (Mr J E Dance). *"She's sharp, racy and a good type; probably wants six but is going to start over five furlongs and she's virtually ready to go".*

487. RAJINSKY ★★★
b.c. Zoffany – Pink Moon (Namid). April 11. Second foal. €30,000Y. Tattersalls Ireland September. Sackville/Donald. Half-brother to the modest dual 10f winner Bahkit (by Intikhab). The dam, placed fourth once in Ireland over 5.5f at 2 yrs, is a half-sister to 3 winners including the useful French and German Listed winner and Group 2 Criterium des Maisons-Laffitte second Boomshackerlacker. The second dam, Allegrina (by Barathea), was a fair 7f winner. (Mr R S Matharu). *"A nice, big, tall horse, he looks a little bit gangly and he's just cantering at the moment. He's pretty straightforward and it'll be June before he runs".*

488. RED DRAGONESS ★★★
ch.f. Dragon Pulse – Salydora (Peintre Celebre). May 4. Eleventh foal. €22,000Y. Tattersalls Ireland September. Sackville/Donald. Sister to the quite useful 2017 2-y-o 1m winner Simpson and to the quite useful 7f and 10f winner of 3 races Komodo and half-sister to four minor winners abroad by Dubawi, Green Tune, Oasis Dream and Halling. The dam, a Listed 9f winner in France, is a half-sister to one winner. The second dam, Silwana (by Nashwan), a French 2-y-o 1m winner, is a half-sister to 7 winners including the French Group 2 Prix de Malleret winner Silver Fun. (T C & Sebastian Lennon). *"A sharp, early 2-y-o for five/six furlongs. It's a bit surprising that her full-brother won over a mile last year because she doesn't look anything like a miler, but the dam is by Peintre Celebre so she might be fooling me. She looks like a six furlong type to me though".*

489. SESAME (IRE) ★★★
b.f. Slade Power – Tiger Spice (Royal Applause). April 21. Seventh foal. €52,000Y. Goffs Orby. Sackville/Donald. Half-sister to 4 winners including the quite useful 7f winner of 5 races including at 2 yrs Azrur (by Sir Percy), the fair 6f (at 2 yrs) and 7.5f winner Spiceupyourlife (by Sakhee's Secret) and the

fair 5f and 6f winner Monteamiata (by Dream Ahead). The dam, a modest 2-y-o 9f winner, is a half-sister to 7 winners including the dam of the Group 3 Oak Tree Stakes winner Summer Fete and to the unplaced dam of the US Grade 2 and Grade 3 winner Up In Time. The second dam, Up And About (by Barathea), a fair 14.8f winner, is a half-sister to 9 winners including the Group 1 placed Musicanna and the dam of the champion European 3-y-o sprinter Overdose. (Laurence Bellman & Caroline Ingram). *"A sharp filly, she's racy and by a first season sire that could be anything. She shows up nicely, is going well and you'd think she'd be wanting five/six furlongs; could start at Nottingham in mid-April".*

490. SEVENHILLSOFROME (FR) ★★★
ch.c. Siyouni – Hill Of Grace (Desert Prince). May 5. Seventh foal. €80,000Y. Goffs Orby. Sackville/Donald. Half-brother to 4 winners including the French 2-y-o 9.5f winner and Listed-placed Grace Of Dubai (by Dubai Destination). The dam, a fair 2-y-o 6f winner, is a half-sister to one winner. The second dam, Tycoon's Dolce (by Rainbows For Life), won the Listed Prix de Lieurey and was Group 3 placed three times and is a half-sister to two Listed winners in France and Italy. (FDC Holdings, Rutherford, Witheridge). *"A nice colt, his knees are still a bit immature so we won't be going crazy, he's by a good sire, has a great attitude and he's a trier. He was a May foal and just wants a bit of time".*

491. SHE CAN BOOGIE ★★★
b.f. Dandy Man – Disko (Kodiac). February 2. Second foal. €28,000Y. Tattersalls Ireland September. Sackville/Donald. Half-sister to the unplaced 2017 2-y-o Disapproval (by Approve). The dam, a fairly useful 2-y-o 5f winner, is a half-sister to 2 winners. The second dam, Dissonance (by Rossini), is an unraced sister to the 2-y-o Group 3 Firth Of Clyde Stakes winner Golden Legacy and a half-sister to a winner in Italy. (Mike Nolan & Partner). *"She was going really nicely but then had a minor setback and she needs to recover from that. Beforehand she was showing loads, she's speedy, sharp and racy. I'm sure she'll be fine but she's going to miss April".*

492. SIR VICTOR (IRE) ★★★
b.c. Sir Prancealot – Victoria Lodge (Grand Lodge). February 3. Ninth foal. €40,000Y. Tattersalls Ireland September. Sackville/Donald. Half-brother to 6 winners including the useful 2017 2-y-o triple 5f winner and Group 3 Sirenia Stakes second Corinthia Knight (by Society Rock), the quite useful 5f (at 2 yrs) to 1m winner of 11 races Chiswick Bey (by Elusive City), the minor Italian Listed-placed winner of 7 races North Ireland (by Zebedee) and the fair 2-y-o 6f winner Lady Victory (by Kheleyf). The dam is an unraced half-sister to the French 2-y-o winner and Group 2 second Ascot Glory. The second dam, Lake Victoria (by Lake Coniston), was Listed-placed in Ireland and is a half-sister to 5 winners including the US Grade 1 winner Delighter and the Oaks third Oakmead. (Deva Racing Sir Prancealot P/ship). *"I thought he'd be running at Chester in May and he still might be, but we have a few weeks now in which to run him and see if he's sharp enough for five furlongs. He's had a couple of bits of work and is looking more like a six furlong colt, but he's a straightforward 2-y-o".*

493. SMOKI SMOKA (IRE) ★★★
ch.c. Dragon Pulse – Creating Speed (Lord Shanakill). February 23. First foal. £34,000Y. Goffs UK Premier (Doncaster). Sackville/Donald. The dam is an unraced half-sister to 2 minor winners abroad. The second dam, Collioure (by Gulch), was placed at 3 yrs and is a half-sister to 4 winners including Sarafan (US Grade 1 Eddie Read Handicap winner). (Duncan, Dunnington & Shaw). *"A big, strong colt, he's looking a bit weak just now but we'll give him a month off. He's done lots but he's not quite the finished article. That's fine because he's got plenty of size and we'll wait until he's ready for it".*

494. STARFIGHTER ★★
b.c. Sea The Stars – Starlit Sands (Oasis Dream). February 17. Fourth foal. €90,000Y. Goffs Orby. Sackville/Donald. Half-brother to the fairly useful 6f and 7f winner of 4 races Seychelloise (by Pivotal) and to the fair 1m winner Scottish Strand (by Oasis Dream). The dam, winner of the Group 3 6f Prix d'Arenburg and Group 2 placed twice, is a half-sister to 7 winners including Summer Night (the dam

of four stakes winners). The second dam, Shimmering Sea (by Slip Anchor), a fairly useful Irish 2-y-o 5f and 7f winner and third in the Group 3 Silken Glider Stakes, is a half-sister to 5 winners including the King George VI and Queen Elizabeth Stakes winner Petoski. (Mr L Bellman). *"A lovely colt with plenty of size and scope; he's one who'll be trained with his 3-y-o career in mind, but he's done nothing wrong, has only cantered and is very straightforward bearing in mind some of these Sea The Stars' colts can be quite colty".*

495. SWIFT JUSTICE ★★★

b.c. Sixties Icon – Wansdyke Lass (Josr Algarhoud). February 24. Eighth foal. 50,000Y. Tattersalls October Book 2. Sackville/Donald. Half-brother to 5 winners including the fairly useful 6f (at 2 yrs) and Listed 10f winner Cruck Realta, the quite useful 13f and 14f winner Davy's Dilemma (both by Sixties Icon), the fair 7f and 1m winner Bridie ffrench (by Bahamian Bounty) and the fair 7f (at 2 yrs) and 6f winner Universal Circus (by Imperial Dancer). The dam, a modest 10f seller winner, is a half-sister to 3 minor winners. The second dam, Silannka (by Slip Anchor), a moderate 12f and 13f winner, is a half-sister to 5 winners. (Manor House Stables LLP). *"A nice horse, he'll probably want six furlongs, he's not over-big but very genuine. He's not really sharp enough for five furlongs and he'll be a mid-May 2-y-o to start with; I'll be surprised if he can't win races".*

496. TIDAL POINT (IRE) ★★

br.c. Sea The Moon – Centred (Dalakhani). March 20. Second foal. 5,000Y. Tattersalls December. Sleeve It Ltd. The dam, a quite useful 10f winner, is a half-sister to the smart 1m (at 2 yrs) and Group 2 10f Blandford Stakes winner Eleanora Duse, the Listed 10f winner and Group 1 Irish Oaks second Scottish Stage and the fairly useful 10f winner and subsequent Australian Group 3 placed Voice Coach. The second dam, Drama Class (by Caerleon), a useful 10.2f winner, is a half-sister to 6 winners including the Group 2 10.3f winner Stage Gift. (Sleeve It Ltd). *"A big, tall, angular, weak horse that'll be trained with next year in mind. He's not ready to do any more than a canter at the moment but he'll be fine if we give him time".*

497. WILD EDRIC ★★

ch.c. Equiano – Lady Red Oak (Medicean). February 7. First foal. 6,500Y. Goffs UK Autumn. Not sold. The dam, a modest 6f (at 2 yrs) and 9f placed maiden, is a half-sister to 5 winners including the French Listed winner Matin De Tempete. The second dam, Nuit Sans Fin (by Lead On Time), is an unplaced half-sister to 9 winners. (Mr D. R. Passant). *"This colt came in late and although he's behind some of the others he's done so well physically that he must have put on 40-60 kilos and looks magnificent now. So now he's ready to be trained. He's a home-bred, we trained the dam and now we'll see how we get on with him".*

498. UNNAMED ★★★

ch.f. Lope De Vega – Ballymore Celebre (Peintre Celebre). March 19. Tenth foal. 155,000Y. Tattersalls October Book 1. Creighton, Schwartz, Sackville, Donald. Half-sister to 7 winners including the quite useful 2017 2-y-o dual 5f winner Awesome, the smart 2-y-o Group 2 6f July Stakes winner Anjaal (both by Bahamian Bounty), the quite useful 2-y-o 7f winner Samharry (by Exceed And Excel) and the fair 7f winner Hitman (by Canford Cliffs). The dam won twice at 3 yrs in France and is a half-sister to 10 winners including the Irish triple Group 3 winner Nysaean. The second dam, Irish Arms (by Irish River), won once in France and is a half-sister to 9 winners including the US Grade 2 winner Morold. (Mr J E Dance). *"She's literally only just arrived here so I can't tell you anything about her other than she's been in pre-training and cantering away".*

499. UNNAMED ★★★★

b.c. Kodiac – Motion Lass (Motivator). March 9. First foal. £48,000Y. Goffs UK Premier (Doncaster). Sackville/Donald. The dam, a modest 1m placed 2-y-o, is a half-sister to 9 winners including the Group 3 Darley Stakes winner and dual Group 1 third Enforcer. The second dam, Tarneem (by Zilzal), a quite useful 3-y-o 1m winner, is a half-sister to 4 minor winners abroad. *"A very nice colt, he's the only one we haven't sold and I have no idea why. Kodiac is a great sire and we've had a lot of success with him. This colt goes like a rocket and the worst case scenario is that Manor House Stables will own and run him".*

500. UNNAMED ★★

b.c. Zoffany – Mount Crystal (Montjeu). March 7. Third foal. 100,000Y. Tattersalls October Book 1. Sackville/Donald. Half-brother to the quite useful 1m to 10.5f winner of 3 races Al Neksh (by Zoffany). The dam, a modest 12f winner, is a half-sister to 8 winners. The second dam, State Crystal (by High Estate), winner of the Group 3 12f Lancashire Oaks and placed in the Yorkshire Oaks and the Prix Vermeille, is a half-sister to 6 winners including the Group 1 Fillies' Mile winner Crystal Music and the Group 3 winners Dubai Success and Solar Crystal. (Mr A. E. Peterson). *"A lovely individual, he's going to take time and probably wants a mile later on in the season, but he's grown nicely and we're just cantering away for now. He's got no problems and we're just looking after him for now because he's a horse that'll hopefully be with us for a few years. We should see him out in the second half of the season over seven furlongs and a mile".*

501. UNNAMED ★★★

b.f. Elusive Quality – Wall Of Sound (Singspiel). January 28. The dam, a useful dual Listed-placed 9f and 10f winner of 3 races here and subsequently third in a US Grade 2 stakes, is a half-sister to the Group 3 7f and Listed 6f winner and Group 1 July Cup second The Cheka. The second dam, Veiled Beauty (by Royal Academy), is an unplaced half-sister to 6 winners including the French Listed winner Arabride and the dam of the Group 1 Haydock Park Sprint Cup winner Regal Parade. (Chasemore Farm). *"A home-bred filly of Andrew Black's, we trained the dam and this filly only came in a couple of weeks ago. She's as hard as nails and everyone that rides her thinks she can go a bit, but she hasn't done anything more than a canter. She'll probably start in midsummer but will want a mile later on and she has a lot of strengthening up to do".*

ED DUNLOP

502. ALAMEERY ★★★

b.c. Kingman – Zacheta (Polish Precedent). March 26. Tenth foal. 160,000Y. Tattersalls October Book 2. Shadwell Estate Co. Half-brother to the Group 2 Joel Stakes and Group 3 Earl Of Sefton Stakes winner Ransom Note (by Red Ransom), to the fairly useful 1m and 10f winner of 4 races Shargiah (by New

Approach), the quite useful 11.5f winner Dawn Sky (by Fantastic Light) and the fair dual 1m winner Nice Thoughts (by Shamardal). The dam is an unraced half-sister to 6 winners including Marienbard (Prix de l'Arc de Triomphe). The second dam, Marienbad (by Darshaan), a French 1m winner at 2 and 3 yrs, is a half-sister to 6 winners. (Hamdan Al Maktoum). *"A nice horse, probably for the second half of the season, he's good-looking and relatively precocious. He's one we like and ought to be one for six/seven furlongs I should think".*

503. ARCTIC SPIRIT ★★★

b.f. Intello – Tahirah (Green Desert). March 26. Tenth foal. 15,000Y. Tattersalls October Book 2. Not sold. Half-sister to 6 winners including the useful dual 6f winner and Group 2 Richmond Stakes second Louie De Palma (by Pastoral Pursuits), the fairly useful 9f and 10f winner Little Rocky (by Cadeaux Genereux), the fairly useful dual 6f winner Bahamian Heights (by Bahamian Bounty) and the quite useful 6f winner Edward Lewis (by Kyllachy). The dam, a useful 7f and 1m winner, was Listed-placed twice and is a sister to one winner and a half-sister to 5 winners. The second dam, Kismah (by Machiavellian), a very useful dual 1m winner, is a half-sister to 10 winners. (Colin Murfitt, Edwin Lee). *"I like her; she's small and racy, looks to have some speed and will probably start at six furlongs which is a surprise for an Intello".* TRAINER'S BARGAIN BUY

504. ATWAAR ★★★

b.f. Slade Power – Musharakaat (Iffraaj). March 28. Fourth foal. Half-sister to the quite useful 2-y-o 6f winner Alqubbah (by Arcano). The dam, a fairly useful 7f winner, was third in the Group 2 1m May Hill Stakes and is a half-sister to 4 winners. The second dam, Gift Of Spring (by Gilded Time), placed at 3 yrs in France, is a half-sister to 7 winners including the Listed-placed and smart broodmare Witch Of Fife (the dam of three stakes winners). (Hamdan Al Maktoum). *"She's precocious, quite speedy-looking, probably a six furlong 2-y-o and goes OK. Hasn't done fast work yet but looks to show some speed".*

505. DANCINGWITHWOLVES (IRE) ★★

b.c. Footstepsinthesand – Clodovina (Rock

Of Gibraltar). February 23. Seventh foal. €125,000Y. Goffs Orby. Charlie Gordon-Watson. Half-brother to the French 10f winner and US Grade 1 10f second Canndal (by Medicean) and to the minor French winner Clariyn (by Acclamation). The dam, a French Listed-placed winner, is a half-sister to 5 winners including the French 2,000 Guineas winner and sire Clodovil and the Group 3 10f Gordon Richards Stakes winner Colombian. The second dam, Clodora (by Linamix), won the Group 2 9.3f Prix de l'Opera. (Mrs Susan Roy). *"A big, tall, seven furlong horse for later in the year. A nice colt, but not early"*.

506. GLOBAL COMMAND (IRE) ★★★
b.c. War Command – Parsley (Zebedee). March 24. First foal. £75,000Y. Goffs UK Premier (Doncaster). Blandford Bloodstock. The dam, a useful 2-y-o 5f and 6f winner, was second in the Group 3 6f Firth Of Clyde Stakes and is a half-sister to the Group 3 Italian 2,000 Guineas winner Anda Muchacho. The second dam, Montefino (by Shamardal), is an unraced half-sister to 2 minor winners. (Dr Johnny Hon). *"He's had a bit of a hiccup but he'll be over it shortly and we like him. He did his first bit of half-speed and went well; a strong, mature horse and probably one for six furlongs when he's ready"*.

507. GLOBAL DESTINATION (IRE) ★★★ ♣
b.c. Slade Power – Silk Trail (Dubai Destination). March 6. Fourth foal. 260,000Y. Tattersalls October Book 1. Charlie Gordon-Watson. Half-brother to the fair 2-y-o 7f winner Terhaal (by Raven's Pass). The dam, a fair 7f winner, is a half-sister to 6 winners including the Group 1 6f Middle Park Stakes winner Lujain, the dual Listed winner Lilium and the useful 2-y-o 6f winner and Group 3 6f Coventry Stakes second Botanical. The second dam, Satin Flower (by Shadeed), won the Group 3 7f Jersey Stakes, was second in the Grade 1 9f Queen Elizabeth II Challenge Cup and is a half-sister to 7 winners including the US Grade 1 Santa Anita Handicap winner Martial Law. (Dr Johnny Hon). *"A very nice horse, I think he was the most expensive Slade Power at the sales, he's good-looking, scopey and will probably be fast when he's ready to run. One for six furlongs, he's nice and we like him. The sire got better with age, but this colt will be a well-made horse later in the year"*.

508. GLOBAL FREEDOM ★★★★
b.c. Maxios – Modesty's Way (Giant's Causeway). April 3. Second foal. €130,000Y. Goffs Orby. Blandford Bloodstock. Half-brother to Bhodi (by Dark Angel), unplaced in one start at 2 yrs in 2017. The dam, a minor French 3-y-o winner, is a half-sister to 3 winners including the French Listed 9f winner and Group 3 11f Prix Cleopatre second Poupee Flash. The second dam, Modesty Blaise (by A P Indy), placed at 2 yrs in France, is a sister to the stakes winner Tomisue's Indy and a half-sister to the triple US Grade 1 winner (over 7f and 1m) Aldebaran, the Canadian Grade 1 Atto Mile winner Good Journey and the US Grade 3 winner Sea Of Showers. (Dr Johnny Hon). *"We like him, he's one for seven furlongs this year and he's a good-looking, quality colt; he's not going to be early but he's got some class"*.

509. GLOBAL GIFT ★★★
b.c. Invincible Spirit – Special Gift (New Approach). February 10. First foal. €200,000Y. Arqana Deauville August. Charlie Gordon-Watson. The dam is an unraced half-sister to 11 winners including the Group 3 6f Prix de Meautry winner Do The Honours and the Listed Chesham Stakes winner Seba. The second dam, Persian Secret (by Persian Heights), a fairly useful 2-y-o 6f winner here and a Listed winner in France, is a half-sister to the dual Group 2 winning sprinter and smart broodmare Cassandra Go (dam of the dual Group 1 winner Halfway To Heaven) and to the Group 3 Coventry Stakes winner and sire Verglas. (Dr Johnny Hon). *"A good-looking colt, he's not an early type but he has some quality; a late maturing horse that goes well"*.

510. GLOBAL MYTH ★★★ ♣
b.c. Scat Daddy – Excelente (Exceed And Excel). May 9. Fifth foal. €320,000Y. Arqana Deauville August. Blandford Bloodstock. Brother to the quite useful dual 5f winner at 2 and 3 yrs Little Voice and half-brother to the quite useful 10f and 11.5f winner Lemoncetta (by Lemon Drop Kid). The dam, a fairly useful Listed-placed Irish 2-y-o 7f winner, subsequently won twice in the USA and is a half-sister to 3 winners including the useful 1m and Listed 15f winner Anousa and the useful 7f (at 2 yrs) and 11f winner

Prince Nureyev. The second dam, Annaletta (by Belmez), a minor French 12f winner and Listed-placed in Germany, is a half-sister to 7 winners. (Dr Johnny Hon). *"I thought he would be relatively early despite the fact he's a May foal and John Gosden has entered the 3-y-o half-brother in the Wood Ditton. He's a very good-moving horse, very athletic, racy-looking and goes well. He's done one half-speed which we liked".*

511. GLOBAL WARNING ★★★★

b.c. Poet's Voice – Persario (Bishop Of Cashel). April 19. Ninth foal. 155,000Y. Tattersalls October Book 1. Charlie Gordon-Watson. Half-brother to the Group 1 Diamond Jubilee Stakes and Group 1 British Champions Sprint winner The Tin Man (by Equiano), to the Group 2 6f Qipco British Champions Sprint and triple Group 3 sprint winner Deacon Blues (by Compton Place), the fairly useful 2-y-o 6f winner Hilario (by Sepoy), the fairly useful 5f winner of 4 races and dual Listed-placed Holley Shiftwell (by Bahamian Bounty) and the fair 6f winner of 4 races If So (by Iffraaj). The dam, a quite useful 6f and 7f winner, is a half-sister to 3 winners including the triple Group 3 winner and Group 1 Prix de la Foret third Warningford. The second dam, Barford Lady (by Stanford), a fairly useful 7f and 1m winner, is a half-sister to 5 winners. (Dr Johnny Hon). *"A quality horse, the pedigree suggests time but he's done everything well so far. He hasn't done any fast work but he's a good-looking horse that we like".*

512. HALLALULU ★★★

b.f. Kyllachy – Cat O' Nine Tails (Motivator). February 18. Third foal. €60,000Y. Arqana Deauville August. Rabbah Bloodstock. Half-sister to the fair 1m and 8.5f winner of 3 races Al Nafoorah (by Bated Breath). The dam, a fair 12f and 14f winner of 4 races, is a half-sister to 5 winners including the dual Group 3 winner Purr Along. The second dam, Purring (by Mountain Cat), a quite useful 7f winner, is a half-sister to the Group 2 1m Falmouth Stakes and Group 3 1m Prix de Sandringham winner Ronda (herself dam of a US dual Group 3 winner) and to the smart 1m (at 2 yrs) and Listed 2m winner Silver Gilt. (Mr Mohammed Jaber). *"A good-looking filly, her half-sister won three for us last year. This filly is probably*

more precocious, is one for six/seven furlongs and she goes OK. We haven't been able to get going properly with our 2-y-os yet because of the bad weather and I suspect most trainers are in the same boat".

513. HOMESICK BOY ★★

b.c. Data Link – Don't Cry For Me (Street Cry). March 28. Third foal. 47,000Y. Tattersalls October Book 2. Blandford Bloodstock. Half-brother to the minor US 3-y-o 1m winner Let's Get Loud (by More Than Ready). The dam won two minor races at 5 yrs in the USA and is a half-sister to 4 winners. The second dam, Sobinka (by Sadler's Wells), won 3 races in France at 3 yrs including over 11f and is a half-sister to 3 other minor winners. (The Old Etonian Racing Syndicate III). *"A fine, good-looking horse for seven furlongs later in the year. He goes well but just needs time".*

514. INSPIRATIONAL (IRE) ★★★

b.f. Slade Power – Refuse To Give Up (Refuse To Bend). April 17. Fifth foal. 82,000Y. Tattersalls October Book 2. Charlie Gordon-Watson. Half-sister to the fairly useful 5f (at 2 yrs) and 6f winner of 4 races and Listed-placed Snap Shots, to the fairly useful 2-y-o 5f winner and Listed 6f second Spy Ring (by Bushranger) and the quite useful dual 6f winner Zebedaios (by Zebedee). The dam ran once unplaced and is a half-sister to 2 winners including the Group 2 Sun Chariot Stakes and Group 3 Matron Stakes winner of 4 races Independence (herself dam of the dual Group 1 winner Mount Nelson and the Group 2 winner Monitor Closely). The second dam, Yukon Hope (by Forty Niner), was a fair 6f to 1m placed maiden. (Cliveden Stud). *"A good-looking filly, she'll probably need a bit of time and she's been turned out for a bit but before her break she was going well. She's one for later on, we like her and she'll be quick when her time comes".*

515. JABALALY (IRE) ★★★

b.c. Moohaajim – Bahati (Intikhab). April 4. Fourth foal. £85,000Y. Goffs UK Premier (Doncaster). Shadwell Estate Co. Half-brother to the very useful Listed 7f and Listed 1m winner Tabarrak and to the quite useful 2-y-o Listed-placed 5f and 6f winner The Wagon Wheel. The dam, a quite useful Listed-placed

2-y-o 6f winner, is a half-sister to 9 winners including the Irish 7f (at 2 yrs) to 10f and subsequent Hong Kong stakes winner Solid Approach. The second dam, Dawn Chorus (by Mukaddamah), is an unraced half-sister to 7 winners. (Hamdan Al Maktoum). *"A half-brother to two quite good horses, he's precocious looking but is probably one for six furlongs in the middle of the season. He goes OK, I haven't done any fast work with him yet but he'll be a strong colt. It's too early to tell but he'll be OK".*

516. KHANMURJAN (USA) ★★
b.c. Scat Daddy – Late Day Sun (Montjeu). April 11. Second foal. 130,000Y. Tattersalls October Book 1. Charlie Gordon-Watson. The dam, a 1m (at 2 yrs) and 10f winner, is a half-sister to 4 winners. The second dam, Where We Left Off (by Dr Devious), a US Grade 3 9f winner, is a half-sister to 6 winners including the Australian Group 2 10f winner Rekindled Interest and the French Listed 11f winner Porticcio. (Mr Mohammed Jaber). *"A tall, leggy colt that probably needs time".*

517. MAQAADEER ★★★
b.c. Mukhadram – Burnt Fingers (Kheleyf). January 23. First foal. 48,000 foal. Tattersalls December. Shadwell Estate Co. The dam, a modest 1m winner at 4 yrs, s a half-sister to 4 winners including the Listed winner and Group 3 third Millbag. The second dam, Play With Fire (by Priolo), a minor French 3-y-o winner, is a half-sister to 6 winners. (Hamdan Al Maktoum). *"I like him very much but he's going to need time. A big, very mature horse that won't be rushed and he's one for the second part of the season, probably over seven furlongs to begin with".*

518. MAWSOOL (IRE) ★★★
b.c. Kodiac – Habaayib (Royal Applause). April 9. Half-brother to the fair 1m and subsequent UAE 5f winner Ejbaar (by Oasis Dream). The dam, a useful 2-y-o Group 3 6f Albany Stakes winner, was second in the Group 2 Cherry Hinton Stakes and is a sister to a winner. The second dam, Silver Kestrel (by Silver Hawk), a minor winner of 2 races at 3 and 4 yrs in the USA, is a half-sister to 5 winners. (Hamdan Al Maktoum). *"Most of the family are precocious but this colt has more*

scope and seems to have a better temperament than most of them. He hasn't been here long and he's only cantered so far".

519. RAINBOW SPIRIT ★★
b.f. Charm Spirit – Navajo Rainbow (Rainbow Quest). April 1. Seventh foal. 10,000 foal. Tattersalls December. Not sold. Half-sister to the dual Listed 1m winner of 8 races Navajo Chief (by King's Best), to the quite useful 10f winner Navajo War Dance (by Makfi), the fair 1m 5f and 2m winner Imphal (by Nathaniel) and a minor winner in Italy by Dr Fong. The dam, is an unraced half-sister to 8 winners including the 2-y-o Group 1 1m National Stakes winner Mus-If and the very smart 1m (at 2 yrs) and triple Listed 10f winner Jammaal. The second dam, Navajo Love Song (by Dancing Brave), placed once at 4 yrs, is a half-sister to 5 minor winners in France and Italy. (Geoffrey Bishop). *"A nice filly that we liked early on, she's tall and having a break at the moment. It's not a precocious family and she's not going to be an early 2-y-o".*

520. ROXY ART (IRE) ★★★★
ch.f. Dutch Art – Chicago Girl (Azamour). April 27. First foal. 175,000Y. Tattersalls October Book 1. Michael Roy. The dam, a Group 3 7f C L Weld Park Stakes second, is a half-sister to 8 winners including the Listed winner Army Of Angels and the dam of the Group 1 Cheveley Park Stakes winner Serious Attitude. The second dam, Angelic Sounds (by The Noble Player), a minor 2-y-o 5f winner, is a half-sister to 8 winners including the Group 1 Prix de la Foret winner Mount Abu. (Mrs Susan Roy). *"A nice, strong, powerful, good-looking filly. She's racy and relatively precocious but won't be rushed".*

521. SAN DIACO ★★★
gr.c. Kodiac – Cland Di San Jore (Lando). January 23. Ninth foal. 33,500Y. Tattersalls October Book 2. Ed Dunlop. Half-brother to 6 winners in Italy including the Group 3 10f and dual Listed 10f winner So Many Shots (by Duke Of Marmalade), the 9f and hurdles winner and 13f Listed-placed Meganisi (by Galileo) and the Listed-placed Batezar (by Oratorio). The dam won 5 minor races at 3 and 4 yrs in Italy and is a half-sister to 9 winners including the dam of the Italian

Group 1 winners Jakkalberry and Crackerjack King. The second dam, Claw (by Law Society), a winner of 7 races in Italy and Listed-placed twice, is a half-sister to 5 winners. (Miltil Consortium). *"A seven furlong horse from an Italian family, he's strong, good-looking and probably a July/August type. He's tough-looking but has done no more than one half-speed where he went OK".*

522. SINJAARI (IRE) ★★★
b.c. Camelot – Heavenly Song (Oratorio). March 19. Second foal. 110,000Y. Tattersalls October Book 2. Charlie Gordon-Watson. Half-brother to the fair 2-y-o 5.5f winner Calypso Choir (by Bahamian Bounty). The dam ran twice unplaced and is a half-sister to 5 winners and to the unraced dam of the Group 2 winner Norse King. The second dam, Lochangel (by Night Shift), a very smart winner of the Group 1 5f Nunthorpe Stakes, is a half-sister to the champion sprinter Lochsong. (Mr Mohammed Jaber). *"A nice colt but being by Camelot he's one for later on over seven furlongs plus. A good-looking horse, he's strong, powerful and all is well with him so far".*

523. TORO DORADO ★★★
b.c. Toronado – Rawoof (Nayef). February 24. First foal. €48,000Y. Goffs Orby. Blandford Bloodstock. The dam, a quite useful 11.5f winner, is a sister to the Listed-placed Zahoo and a half-sister to 6 winners including the smart Group 3 14f winner Tactic and the French Listed 12f winner Yaazy and to the dam of the high-class miler Ribchester. The second dam, Tanaghum (by Darshaan), a useful Listed-placed 10f winner, is a half-sister to 8 winners including the Group 2 10f Premio Lydia Tesio winner Najah. *"I like him; he's very racy, very athletic and probably speedier than you'd think being out of a mare that was relatively backward. He goes OK and should be a six/seven furlong 2-y-o".*

524. VENEDEGAR (IRE) ★★
b.c. Dubawi – Cara Fantasy (Sadler's Wells). May 10. Brother to the useful 2-y-o Listed 1m winner Prince Gagarin and half-brother to 6 winners including the very smart 2-y-o Group 3 7f Acomb Stakes and Group 3 1m Craven Stakes winner and Group 1 Racing Post Trophy second Elusive Pimpernel (by Elusive Quality),

the smart 1m (at 2 yrs), Group 3 10f Strensall Stakes and Listed 9f winner Palavicini (by Giant's Causeway), the quite useful 1m (at 2 yrs) and 12f winner Oasis Fantasy (by Oasis Dream) and the fair 10f winners Invincible Cara (by Invincible Spirit) and Miss Topsy Turvy (by Mr Greeley). The dam, a quite useful dual 12f winner, is a half-sister to the Group 2 Topkapi Trophy winner Lucky Guest. (Windflower Overseas Holdings & j Dunlop OBE). *"A late foal, he's a well-bred, good-looking horse but he's not done anything more than cantering as yet and will definitely be a seven furlongs plus 2-y-o. A strong, powerful colt, he's not the biggest and not as big as his brothers, but he hasn't been a problem so far".*

525. YES CAN DO ★★★
b.f. No Nay Never – Sheba's Humor (Distorted Humor). March 1. First foal. £50,000Y. Goffs UK Premier (Doncaster). Blandford Bloodstock. The dam is an unraced half-sister to 3 winners. The second dam, Sheba Gold (by Sadler's Wells), is an unplaced sister to the US Grade 1 1m winner Perfect Soul and a half-sister to 3 winners. (Milmo, Sturgess, White). *"I like her but she's not that precocious. Quite scopey, she has a very good temperament and is a good-looking filly. We like her but she's one for later on".*

526. YOUARESTAR ★★★★
b.c. Sea The Stars – Alumna (Mr Greeley). February 20. First foal. 145,000Y. Tattersalls October Book 1. Charlie Gordon-Watson. The dam, a 1m and 10f winner and third in the Group 3 10f Prix de Psyche, is a half-sister to 2 minor winners. The second dam, Alma Mater (by Sadler's Wells), a fairly useful French Listed 12.5f winner, is a half-sister to 8 winners including the dual Champion Stakes winner Alborada and the triple German Group 1 winner Albanova. (Mr Mohammed Jaber). *"A nice horse but very big and he won't be rushed. One for seven furlongs in August or September, he's a good-looking horse that we like".*

527. UNNAMED ★★
b.c. Tertullian – Anatola (Tiger Hill). April 28. Eighth foal. €80,000Y. Baden Baden. Tina Rau. Half-brother to 4 winners including the Group 1 Melbourne Cup and Group 1 Tancred Stakes winner Almandin and to the German Group

2 12f winner Atempo (both by Monsun). The dam, a Listed 12f winner in Germany, is a half-sister to 6 winners including the Greoup 1 German Derby winner Amarette French Derby third Arras. The second dam, Avocette (by Kings Lake), a German Listed winner, is a half-sister to 10 winners including Aviso (Group 2 German 2,000 Guineas). (OTI Racing). *"He's just arrived and is a half-brother to the Melbourne Cup winner. A beautifully-bred horse and he's very nice from what I've seen but he's one for much later on. I like him".*

HARRY DUNLOP

528. BLACK ABBEY (FR) ★★★
b.c. Hannouma – Alta Stima (Raven's Pass). March 10. Second foal. €40,000Y. Arqana Deauville October. Stroud/Coleman & H Dunlop. The dam won the Listed Prix Solitude and is a half-sister to 10 winners including Kreem (Group 3 Prix du Lys) and the Listed winners and Group placed Sardaukar, Rostrum and Kindjhal. The second dam, En Public (by Rainbow Quest), is a placed half-sister to 8 winners including the Group 1 Gran Criterium winner Will Dancer. (D. MacAuliffe, Anoj Don & Etreham Partnership). *"He looks a nice colt, he's done a certain amount of faster work and we'll probably be mixing English and French racing. The sire, a son of Anabaa, won the Group 1 Criterium de Saint-Cloud. He's had a few runners and stands in France at €3,000".*

529. BROOKLYN BOY ★★★★
b.c. Camelot – Tan Tan (King's Best). March 1. Fifth foal. 68,000Y. Tattersalls October Book 2. Stroud/Coleman & H Dunlop. Half-brother to the fair 2017 2-y-o 5f winner Revived (by Dark Angel), to the fair 7f and 1m winner German Whip (by Zoffany) and the moderate 2-y-o 6f winner Music Stop (by Iffraaj). The dam, a minor French 3-y-o winner, is a half-sister to 6 winners including the Group 2 Flying Childers Stakes winner Land Of Dreams (dam of the multiple Group 1 winner Dream Ahead). The second dam, Sahara Star (by Green Desert), winner of the Group 3 5f Molecomb Stakes, was third in the Group 2 Lowther Stakes and is a half-sister to 6 winners including the Group 3 7f Greenham Stakes winner Yalaietanee. (Daniel MacAuliffe & Anoj Don). *"We did well with our Camelot colt last year Fighting Irish and this horse would be a bigger version of*

him. He's quite strong and I should imagine he'll be out around July time over seven furlongs. He looks a nice colt at the moment and we're very pleased with him".

530. BUG BOY (IRE) ★★★
b.c. Big Bad Bob – Velvetina (Barathea). March 20. Second foal. €1,500. Tattersalls Ireland November. Not sold. Brother to the 2017 Irish dual 1m placed 2-y-o Bring On The Band. The dam, a fair 10f and 12f winner, is a half-sister to 4 winners. The second dam, Pershaan (by Darshaan), a quite useful 12f winner, is a half-sister to 3 winners including the very useful Listed 11.5f winner of 6 races Persian Lightning. (Windflower Overseas Holdings Inc). *"I trained the dam who was pretty smart. This colt is a bonny type and he'll be running early, probably in May. He was bought back cheaply at the sale, but he's worth putting in the book".*

531. CRANEUR ★★★
ch.c. Showcasing – Paris Winds (Galileo). January 24. Fifth foal. 12,500Y. Tattersalls October Book 2. Harry Dunlop Racing. Half-brother to the quite useful 1m and subsequent US winner Stableford (by Smart Strike) and to the fair 1m winner Calima Breeze (by Oasis Dream). The dam, a useful 1m winner here and a stakes winner in the USA, was third in the Group 2 10f Blandford Stakes and is a half-sister to 5 winners. The second dam, Lil's Jessy (by Kris), won 4 races at 2 and 3 yrs including the Group 3 7f Nell Gwyn Stakes and is a half-sister to 9 winners including the smart French 1m Listed winner Lone Bid. (Be Hopeful Partnership). *"A nice, big, strong colt, I would envisage him starting at seven furlongs in July and hopefully he'll be one we could have a bit of fun with".*

532. FLYING MOON (GER) ★★
b.br.c. Sea The Moon – Finity (Diesis). March 31. €28,000Y. Baden Baden. Blandford Bloodstock. Half-brother to 6 winners including the quite useful 7f to 8.5f winner Finelcity (by Elusive City), the fair 2-y-o 6f winner Flintlock (by Oasis Dream) and the fair 12f winner Finity Run (by Hurricane Run). The dam, a useful 2-y-o 7f winner, was third in the Group 3 7f C L Weld Park Stakes and is a half-sister to 4 winners including Cavalryman

(Group 1 Grand Prix de Paris). The second dam, Silversword (by Highest Honor), a winner at 3 yrs in France and second in the Group 3 Prix de Royaumont, is a full or half-sister to 6 winners including the Group 2 Goodwood Cup second Double Honour. (Crimbourne Stud). *"A half-brother to a horse we had called Finelcity who did well, this horse is quite backward but he's showing some pace and ability. So hopefully he won't be too late in the season and I'm hoping he'll be a mid-season 2-y-o. More immature than Finelcity was at this stage though".*

533. FREQUENCE ★★
b.f. Equiano – Iridescence (Dutch Art). February 11. Second foal. 14,000Y. Tattersalls October Book3. Not sold. Half-sister to the useful 2017 2-y-o Listed 7f winner Raydiance (by Mayson). The dam, a fair 8.5f and 10f winner, is a half-sister to 2 winners. The second dam, Radiate (by Sadler's Wells), is an unraced half-sister to 7 winners including the Group 3 winner and Group 1 Haydock Park Sprint Cup third Strath Burn. (Emma Hunter). *"One for six/ seven furlongs in mid-season".*

534. GORA BERE (FR) ★★
b.br.c. Pedro The Great – Monatora (Hector Protector). April 30. Tenth foal. €27,000Y. Arqana. Stroud/Coleman & Harry Dunlop. Half-brother to 6 winners including the 2017 French 2-y-o 7f and Listed 1m winner Francesco Bere, the modest 8.5f winner Betty Bere (both by Peer Gynt), the French 7.5f (at 2 yrs) and Listed 1m winner of 3 races Hurricane (by Hurricane Run) and the French 2-y-o 6.5f and 7.5f winner Atora Bere (by Della Francesca). The dam, a French 2-y-o 6f winner, is a half-sister to 6 winners including the 2-y-o Group 2 5f Flying Childers Stakes winner and sire Sir Prancealot and the French Listed 10f winner Nice Applause. The second dam, Mona Em (by Catrail), a Listed sprint winner, is a half-sister to 4 winners. (Daniel MacAuliffe & Anoj Don). *"By the French sire Pedro The Great, this colt is quite immature and at this stage I don't know much about him. He's cantering away nicely but we're not likely to get him out until later on, probably over seven furlongs".*

535. KYAT KHAN (FR) ★★★
b.c. Palace Episode – Kensita (Soviet Star).

January 28. Sixth foal. €20,000Y. Arqana Deauville August V2. Stroud/Coleman & Harry Dunlop. Half-brother to the 2017 French 2-y-o 6.5f winner Fatou (by Penny's Picnic) and to the fair 6f (including at 2 yrs) and 7f winner of 5 races Veena (by Elusive City). The dam is an unraced half-sister to 3 winners including Keraka (Group 3 Anglesey Stakes and herself the dam of a Listed winner). The second dam, Kerita (by Formidable), winner of the Group 3 7f Supreme Stakes and third in the Group 2 Challenge Stakes, is a half-sister to 3 winners. *"A sharp little horse, we're hoping to start him over five furlongs in April and then we'll race him in France because he's French-bred and he qualifies for the premiums. We should have some sport with him early on, especially as he was an early foal".* The sire, winner of the Group 1 Racing Post Trophy at two, has only had a handful of runners. He stands in France at €3,000.

536. LAURA KENNY (IRE) ★★★
b.f. Dutch Art – Lottie Dod (Invincible Spirit). March 8. Second foal. The dam, a fairly useful Irish 4-y-o 6f winner, was third in the 2-y-o Group 1 Phoenix Stakes and is a half-sister to the very useful 2-y-o 6f winner and Group 2 Railway Stakes second Rockaway Valley. The second dam, Sharapova (by Elusive Quality), a quite useful 3-y-o 7f winner, is a half-sister to 6 winners including the US stakes winner and Grade 1 second Tamweel. (Velocity Racing). *"She's owned by my cycling syndicate and hence the name Laura Kenny! She looks like being a five furlong filly, has done a fair amount of faster work already and I can see her being out by early May. We like her so far".*

537. UNNAMED ★★★
b.c. Whipper – Ellary (Equerry). March 31. Third foal. €29,000Y. Arqana Deauville October. Stroud/Coleman & H Dunlop. Half-brother to the 2-y-o Listed 7f winner of 4 races Ella Diva (by Heliostatic). The dam was a minor 2-y-o winner in France. The second dam, Ella Nico (by Archway), won the 2-y-o Group 3 Prix d'Arenburg. *"The sire gets speedy types and I'm very pleased with this horse, he should be racing in August and he's a nice colt".*

538. UNNAMED ★★★
b.br.f. Iffraaj – Merry Diva (Bahamian Bounty).

March 21. Sixth foal. 20,000Y. Tattersalls October Book 2. Not sold. Half-sister to the quite useful 2-y-o triple 5f winner Merry Banter (by Bated Breath), to the fair 2-y-o 6f winner Belvoir Diva (by Exceed And Excel) and the fair 7f winner Concrete Mac (by Machiavellian). The dam, a fair 2-y-o 6f winner, is sister to the dual Listed winner and Group 3 third Paradise Isle and a half-sister to 8 winners. The second dam, Merry Rous (by Rousillon), won once at 2 yrs and is a half-sister to 5 winners including the dual Group 3 winning sprinter Tina's Pet. (Windsor House Stables). *"She took some time to break and get going and as a result I don't know an awful lot about her, but there are plenty of 2-y-o winners in the pedigree and the sire has certainly done very well. So she should have every chance and all is well with her. I can see her being out by mid-season and she looks like a sprinter".*

539. UNNAMED ★★
ch.f. Australia – Peace Palace (Archipenko). February 6. First foal. 22,000Y. Tattersalls December. Stroud/Coleman & H Dunlop. The dam ran once unplaced and is a half-sister to 5 winners including the Group 3 Princess Margaret Stakes and Group 3 Nell Gwyn Stakes winner Osaila and the Group 3 9f Dance Design Stakes winner Obama Rule. The second dam, Mennetou (by Entrepreneur), is an unraced half-sister to 5 winners including the 'Arc winner Carnegie. *"A filly that's going to take some time, but she's a lovely mover. I should think she'll want seven furlongs to a mile from September onwards".* TRAINER'S BARGAIN BUY

540. UNNAMED ★★★
b.f. Rock Of Gibraltar – Seasonal Cross (Cape Cross). April 10. Fourth foal. Sister to the quite useful 1m (at 2 yrs) and 8.5f winner Storm Rock and to the moderate 4-y-o 6f winner Hurricane Rock and half-sister to the fair 2-y-o 6f winner Coastal Cyclone (by Canford Cliffs). The dam, a fair 1m winner of 4 races, is a half-sister to 5 winners including the very useful 6f to 12f winner of 4 races (including the Listed Galtres Stakes) Brushing. The second dam, Seasonal Blossom (by Fairy King), is an unplaced half-sister to 7 winners including the US Grade 2 winner Wait Till Monday and the Irish Group 3 winner Token Gesture

(dam of the Grade 1 winner Relaxed Gesture). (Malcolm & Alicia Aldis). *"She's not in the yard yet but she's a sister to a good horse we had called Storm Rock and from what I've seen of her she's a nice filly that'll take a bit of time".*

TIM EASTERBY
541. AMADEUS GREY (IRE)
gr.c. Zebedee – Benedicte (Galileo). April 5. Fifth foal. £30,000Y. Goffs UK Premier (Doncaster). Tim Easterby. Half-sister to the quite useful 11f winner High Language (by Lawman) and to a winner in Qatar by Acclamation. The dam, a fairly useful 10f winner, is a half-sister to 5 winners including the Group 1 Middle Park Stakes, Group 2 Duke Of York Stakes and Group 2 Gimcrack Stakes winner Amadeus Wolf and the Group 3 Sirenia Stakes winner Rouleau. The second dam, Rachelle (by Mark Of Esteem), a minor winner in Italy at around 1m, is a half-sister to 2 winners. (Ontoawinner 10 & Partner).

542. DREAM OF HONOUR (IRE)
b.c. Dream Ahead – Pernica (Sir Percy). February 4. First foal. £70,000Y. Goffs UK Premier (Doncaster). Highflyer Bloodstock. The dam, a fair 10f winner, is a half-sister to 8 winners including the German Group 1 winner Neatico and the US Grade 2 1m winner Beautyandthebeast. The second dam, Nicola Bella (by Sadler's Wells), an Irish 9.6f winner, is a sister to the winner and Group 1 Irish Oaks third Sister Bella and a half-sister to 4 winners. (Mr & Mrs J. D. Cotton).

543. DREAMSELLER (IRE)
ch.c. Dream Ahead – Picture Of Lily (Medicean). March 3. Fourth foal. 31,000Y. Tattersalls October Book 3. Tim Easterby. Half-brother to the useful 2017 2-y-o 7f winner and Group 3 Killavullan Stakes second Mcmunigal (by Epaulette). The dam, a modest 1m placed 2-y-o, is a half-sister to 5 winners including the very smart dual Listed middle-distance winner of 12 races and dual Group 1 placed Scott's View and the Italian 2-y-o Listed 7.5f winner Mac Melody. The second dam, Milly Of The Vally (by Caerleon), a fairly useful 12f winner, is a half-sister to 9 winners including the Listed winner and Group 3 third Bosham Mill. (Ryedale Partners No. 2).

544. LADY CALCARIA
b.f. Mayson – Ride The Wind (Cozzene). March 12. Fourth foal. £32,000Y. Goffs UK Silver (Doncaster). Ontoawinner/ Tim Easterby. Half-brother to the modest 7f winner Bahamian Bird (by Bahamian Bounty) and to a minor 2-y-o winner in the USA by Kheleyf. The dam, a modest 1m and 9.5f placed maiden, is a half-sister to one winner. The second dam, Wind Surf (by Lil's Lad), a minor stakes winner in North America, is a half-sister to 3 winners. (Ontoawinner 10 & Partner).

545. RAQUELLE (IRE)
b.f. Requinto – Zuccini Wind (Revoque). January 26. Eleventh foal. £25,000Y. Goffs UK Premier. Tim Easterby & Reality Partnerships). Half-sister to the fairly useful 5f and 6f winner of 6 races (including at 2 yrs) and dual Listed placed Favourite Girl (by Refuse To Bend) and to a minor winner abroad by Balmont. The dam, a winner of 8 races from 2 to 4 yrs in Scandinavia, is a half-sister to 8 winners including the smart Irish 5f and Listed 6f winner Rolo Tomasi. The second dam, Elegant Bloom (by Be My Guest), a quite useful Irish 2-y-o 6f winner, stayed 7f and is a full or half-sister to 12 winners. (Reality Partnerships X).

546. SEPERABLE
ch.c. Sepoy – Poyle Meg (Dansili). March 7. Fourth foal. £28,000Y. Goffs UK Premier. Not sold. Half-brother to the modest 5f winner Jess (by Equiano) and to the moderate dual Hong Kong 1m winner Win For Charity (by Equiano). The dam, a 1m and 10f winner, is a half-sister to 3 winners. The second dam, Lost In Lucca (by Inchinor), a fair 12f winner, is a half-sister to 3 winners including the Group 2 Lowther Stakes winner Jemima. (Habton Farms).

547. UNNAMED
ch.c. Pivotal – Fondled (Selkirk). March 2. Seventh foal. 30,000Y. Tattersalls October Book 2. Robin O'Ryan. Brother to 3 winners including the useful Listed-placed 7f to 8.5f winner Keystroke and the fairly useful 1m to 10.5f winner Cosseted and half-brother to the quite useful dual 10f winner Indulged (by Teofilo). The dam, a quite useful dual 1m winner, is a half-sister to 8 winners including the fairly useful 7f to 9f winner Tartan Gunna. The second dam, Embraced (by Pursuit Of Love), a useful Listed 1m winner, is a half-sister to 7 winners including the Group 2 Summer Mile winner Cesare and the Group 3 12f Prix la Force winner and French Derby second Nowhere To Exit. (David Scott & Partner).

548. UNNAMED
ch.c. Reliable Man – Hamloola (Red Ransom). March 27. Fourth foal. 30,000Y. Tattersalls October Book 2. Peter Molony. Half-brother to the fair 7f (at 2 yrs) and 10f winner Shufoog (by Mawatheeq). The dam, a quite useful 7f and 1m winner, is a half-sister to 7 winners. The second dam, Dusty Answer (by Zafonic), a quite useful Listed-placed 2-y-o 7f winner, is a half-sister to 5 winners including the Listed 1m and subsequent US Grade 2 winner Spotlight and the dam of Zoffany (Group 1 Phoenix Stakes winner). (Qatar Racing Ltd).

DAVID ELSWORTH

549. ARABIAN KING ★★★★
ch.c. New Approach – Barshiba (Barathea). February 28. Half-sister to the fair 2017 6f and 8.5f placed 2-y-o Cosmopolitan Queen, to the Group 1 10.5f Juddmonte International and Group 2 6f Duchess Of Cambridge Stakes winner Arabian Queen (both by Dubawi) and to the fairly useful 1m winner Australian Queen (by Fastnet Rock). The dam, a dual Group 2 Lancashire Oaks winner of 7 races, is a half-sister to several winners including the useful 2-y-o Listed 1m winner Doctor Dash and the fairly useful 1m (at 2 yrs) and 10f winner Dashing Star. The second dam, Dashiba (by Dashing Blade), a useful 9f and 10f winner, is a half-sister to several winners including the fairly useful 10f and 12f winner Smart Blade. (J C Smith). *"A nice, big horse that I'd like to think will come to the fore next year but I'll be hoping for some encouragement from him as a 2-y-o over seven furlongs or a mile. The dam was a very versatile racemare and she was so good over a mile it took me a while to raise her in trip so she could win the Lancashire Oaks twice".*

550. DANDHU ★★★★
ch.f. Dandy Man – Poldhu (Cape Cross). February 25. 75,000Y. Tattersalls October Book 2. Suzanne Roberts. Half-sister to the fairly useful 2-y-o 6f and 7f winner Dutch Courage (by Dutch Art), to the fairly useful 6f (at 2

yrs) and 7f winner and Listed-placed Maid A Million (by Kyllachy) and the quite useful 10.5f winner Gustavus Vassa (Equiano). The dam is an unraced half-sister to 3 winners including the Group 1 Falmouth Stakes winner Rajeem. The second dam, Magic Sister (by Cadeaux Genereux), a modest 3-y-o 7f placed maiden, is a sister to the very smart 2-y-o Group 1 6f Prix Morny and Group 3 5f Molecomb Stakes winner Hoh Magic and a half-sister to 5 winners. (Mrs Anne Coughlan& Mr D Elsworth). *"She should be one of our stars a bit later in the season. I couldn't get her going early because of a few little issues but it's a very good family and I would have paid more for her if I had to. She's a good-looking, imposing filly that'll make a 2-y-o in the second half of the season".*

551. DARWIN DREAM ★★★
b.c. Australia – Snoqualmie Girl (Montjeu). April 9. Half-brother to the fair 7f winner Snow Squaw (by Excelebration). The dam, a very useful Listed 1m (at 2 yrs) and Listed 10f winner, is a sister to the smart Listed 10f winner and Group 2 Dante Stakes third Snoqualmie Boy and a half-sister to 6 winners including the fairly useful 2-y-o 7f winner Seattle Drive. The second dam, Seattle Ribbon (Seattle Dancer), placed over 9f and 10f at 3 yrs, is a sister to the 2-y-o Group 1 1m winner Seattle Dancer. (J C Smith). *"A good-looking colt with a strong pedigree and the potential to be a good 3-y-o".*

552. ENDEAVOURING (IRE) ★★
b.c. Shamardal – La Divina (Sadler's Wells). February 4. Fifth foal. 80,000Y. Tattersalls October Book 1. Suzanne Roberts. The dam, unplaced in one start, is a sister to 6 winners including the multiple Group 1 winner Islington, the smart stayer Election Day and the German Group 1 winner Greek Dance and half-brother to the Group 1 Grand Prix de Saint-Cloud winner Mountain High. The second dam, Hellenic (by Darshaan), won the Yorkshire Oaks and the Ribblesdale Stakes and is a half-sister to 8 winners. (Mr B C M Wong). *"I think he was cheap, but maybe that's because the dam hasn't bred a winner yet. He's very well-related and although he'll be better next year he's a good-looking horse and I'd like to think he'll do something this year".*

553. HARRY THE NORSEMAN ★★
ch.c. Norse Dancer – Titled Lady (Sir Percy). March 21. First foal. £5,500Y. Tattersalls Ireland Ascot. Not sold. The dam, a fair 7f placed 2-y-o, is a half-sister to 3 minor winners here and abroad. The second dam, May West (by Act One), is an unraced half-sister to 10 winners including the Listed winner and Group 3 third Bosham Mill. (Elsworth & Nettlefold). *"It's a strong female line although it's watered down to some extent because the dam split a pastern before I could get her to win and the second dam, who was as wild as a hawk, did the same."*

554. MARTINI MAGIC ★★★
ch.f. Norse Dancer – Premier Prize (Selkirk). April 9. Eighth foal. Half-sister to the useful 2-y-o 1m winner, Group 3 1m Prix des Reservoirs second and Group 3 12f St Simon Stakes third Cocktail Queen (by Motivator), to the fairly useful dual 1m winner (including at 2 yrs) Gold Prince (by Nayef), the fair 7f and 1m winner Hidden Fire (by Alhaarth) and the modest 10f winner Prize Diva (by Motivator). The dam, a useful 7f (at 2 yrs) and Listed 10f winner, was third in the Group 2 Sandown Mile and is a half-sister to 7 winners including the Group 2 15f Prix Kergorlay winner Gold Medallist. The second dam, Spot Prize (by Seattle Dancer), a useful filly, won over 5f at 2 yrs and was fourth in the Oaks. (J C Smith). *"The owner sportingly sent the sire a couple of good mares to give him the chance of getting a nice horse and this filly is a good mover I can see being suited by a mile".*

555. NO NONSENSE ★★★
b.c. Acclamation – Gift Of Music (Cadeaux Genereux). March 14. Second foal. Half-brother to Musical Dream (by Dream Ahead), unplaced on her only start at 2 yrs in 2017. The dam, a modest 2-y-o 6f winner, is a half-sister to 2 winners. The second dam, Loch Verdi (by Green Desert), a useful Listed 5f winner of 4 races, is a half-sister to 4 winners including the smart Listed 6f winner of 5 races Lochridge. (J C Smith). *"He's a big horse but he's by a sire that gets speedy horses and I'd like to think he'll make a 2-y-o".*

556. ROCKET ACTION ★★★★
b.c. Toronado – Winning Express (Camacho).

April 6. The dam, a very useful 2-y-o Listed 6f winner of 3 races, was second in the Group 1 Cheveley Park Stakes and is a half-sister to 3 winners. The second dam, Lady Fabiola (by Open Forum), won 2 races at 2 and 3 yrs in Italy and is a half-sister to 7 winners. (Mr R Ng). *"He looks a 2-y-o type and he's out of a bloody good mare that was trained by Ed McMahon. I bought her at the sales for a hundred grand after her racing career was over. She has a Dark Angel yearling but unfortunately she's subsequently had to be put down. This colt is a real goer".*

557. SONGKRAN (IRE) ★★★★
b.c. Slade Power – Choose Me (Choisir). April 13. Fifth foal. €100,000Y. Goffs Orby. Sackville/Donald. Half-brother to the Group 1 1m Queen Elizabeth II Stakes winner of 6 races Persuasive (by Dark Angel), to the useful Listed 1m winner of 5 races Tisbutadream (by Dream Ahead) and the fairly useful 6f and 7f winner of 5 races Amazour (by Azamour). The dam, a very useful 6f (at 2 yrs) to 10f winner of 4 races including a Listed 7f event in Ireland, was third in the Group 2 Blandford Stakes and is a half-sister to 5 winners including the Listed winner Shanghai Glory. The second dam, Hecuba (by Hector Protector), a fairly useful 10f winner, is a half-sister to 7 winners including the German Group 2 winner Bad Bertrich Again and the Group 3 Scottish Classic winner Prolix. (King Power Racing Co Ltd). *"This colt is out of a very good family and the mare is worth a fortune. He's small and looks like a 2-y-o, so for me he could be quite early".*

558. UNNAMED ★★★
b.f. Tamayuz – Lovers Peace (Oratorio). March 12. Third foal. 21,000Y. Tattersalls October Book 3. D Elsworth. Half-sister to the fair 2017 Irish 2-y-o 7f winner Beach Wedding (by Footstepsinthesand). The dam, a fair 12f and 13f winner, is a half-sister to 9 winners including the useful Listed 5f winner and Group 2 5f Flying Childers Stakes second Emerald Peace (herself dam of the 2-y-o Listed winner Vital Statistics). The second dam, Puck's Castle (by Shirley Heights), a fairly useful 2-y-o 1m winner and third in the Listed 10f Zetland Stakes, is a half-sister to 6 winners including the champion 2-y-o filly and Cheveley Park

Stakes winner Embassy and to the Group 2 Pretty Polly Stakes winner Tarfshi. (Mr D R C Elsworth). *"A small, early type, I'll be getting after him soon".*

559. UNNAMED ★★★
b.c. Swiss Spirit—Moment In The Sun (Dubai Destination). April 15. The dam, a modest 1m to 10f winner, is a half-sister to 2 winners. The second dam, Special Moment (by Sadler's Wells), a modest 11f to 14f placed maiden, is a sister to 2 winners including the Listed 1m winner and Irish 1,000 Guineas third Starbourne and a half-sister to 3 winners. (Roscommon Syndicate). *"A nice little home-bred horse that was sent to me. We're pleased with his progress and although he's one of the lesser lights on pedigree they're all flyers at this stage. Doing everything we're asking of him".*

560. UNNAMED ★★★
gr.c. Alhebayeb – Peacemaker (High Chaparral). February 20. First foal. 40,000Y. Tattersalls October Book 3. Suzanne Roberts. The dam, a fair 2-y-o 7f winner, is a half-sister to 3 winners including the useful 10f and 12f winner Senate. The second dam, Sauterne (by Rainbow Quest), a Listed winner of 3 races from 7f to 10f, is a half-sister to 6 winners including the smart 2-y-o Group 3 6f Cherry Hinton Stakes winner Applaud. (Mr D R C Elsworth). *"By a first season sire and the first foal of his dam, so I'm guessing a bit but he looks a 2-y-o type".*

RICHARD FAHEY
562. ABSOLUTE DREAM (IRE)
ch.c. Dream Ahead – Absolute Diamond (Monsieur Bond). March 6. First foal. €62,000Y. Goffs Orby. Robin O'Ryan. The dam, a moderate 7f winner, is a sister to 2 winners including the useful Group 3 5f Prix du Petit Couvert and Listed 5f winner of 9 races Move In Time and a half-sister to 3 winners. The second dam, Tibesti (by Machiavellian), is an unraced sister to the UAE Group 3 winner and Group 1 second Tropical Star.

563. AMBERSAND (IRE)
b.f. Footstepsinthesand – Miss Sally (Danetime). March 7. Seventh foal. €50,000Y. Goffs Sportsmans. Robin O'Ryan. Half-sister to the useful 1m and 9f winner of 3 races

Masteroftherolls (by Refuse To Bend) and to the fair 9f winner Wyldfire (by Raven's Pass). The dam, winner of the Group 3 7f Brownstown Stakes and the Group 3 7.5f Concorde Stakes, is a half-sister to 5 winners. The second dam, Evictress (by Sharp Victor), was placed three times from 6f (at 2 yrs) to 1m in Ireland and is a half-sister to 8 minor winners.

564. ANGEL SARAH (IRE)
b.f. Dark Angel – Padma (Three Valleys). January 15. First foal. £80,000Y. Goffs UK Premier (Doncaster). Robin O'Ryan. The dam is an unraced half-sister to 3 winners including Winsili (Group 1 Nassau Stakes). The second dam, Winter Sunrise (by Pivotal), a useful dual 10f winner, is a half-sister to 6 winners including the Group 2 10f Prix Greffulhe winner Ice Blue.

565. BENJI
b.c. Magician – Penny Sixpence (Kheleyf). February 24. First foal. 70,000Y. Tattersalls December. Robin O'Ryan. The dam, a minor US 3-y-o winner, is a sister to the Group 2 Criterium de Maisons-Laffitte winner Penny's Picnic. The second dam, Zerky (by Kingmambo), a modest 1m placed 2-y-o, is a sister to the triple Group 3 winner Penny's Gold and a half-sister to the dam of the Japanese Group 1 winner Curren Black Hill.

566. CADEAU D'AMOUR (IRE)
b.c. Camacho – Perfect Pose (Amadeus Rose). March 28. Second foal. £35,000Y. Goffs UK Premier (Doncaster). Robin O'Ryan/MPR. The dam, a modest 9f placed maiden, is a half-sister to 5 winners including the fairly useful 6f (at 2 yrs) and subsequent US stakes winner and Grade 1 placed Rinterval. The second dam, Interpose (by Indian Ridge), is an unraced half-sister to 7 winners including the French Group 3 winner Short Pause, the French 1m Listed winner Cheyenne Dream and the dams of the Group 1 winners Continent and Zambezi Sun.

567. CAMBER ♠
b.c. Garswood – Topflightcoolracer (Lujain). April 2. Third foal. 60,000Y. Tattersalls October Book 2. John & Jake Warren. Half-brother to the fair 2-y-o 6f winner Top Flight Princess (by Cockney Rebel). The dam, a quite useful 2-y-o dual 5f winner, is a half-sister to 4 winners. The second dam, Jamarj (by Tyrnavos), won 9 races at 2 and 3 yrs including the Listed October Stakes the Listed Sceptre Stakes and is a half-sister to 4 winners.

568. COLLEGIAN
b.c. Mayson – Graduation (Lomitas). February 8. Sixth foal. £34,000Y. Goffs UK Premier (Doncaster). Not sold. Half-brother to the quite useful 9.5f and 10f winner Marma's Boy (by Duke Of Marmalade), to the useful Listed-placed 7f and 1m winner of 4 races Certificate (by Pivotal) and a winner in Sweden by Sakhee. The dam, a fairly useful 1m winner, was Listed-placed. The second dam, Ceremonial (by Lion Cavern), a fair 1m winner, is a half-sister to 6 winners including the Group 2 Great Voltigeur Stakes and Group 2 Prix Jean de Chaudenay winner Sacrament. (Cheveley Park Stud).

569. COMMANDER SOLO (IRE)
b.c. Elzaam – Gangster Squad (Astronomer Royal). March 6. First foal. €40,000Y. Goffs Sportsmans. Robin O'Ryan. The dam, a fair 2-y-o 1m winner in France, is a half-sister to 8 winners in France and the USA. The second dam, Cobblestone Road (by Grindstone), a Listed-placed dual winner at 3 yrs in the USA, is a half-sister to 5 winners.

570. DEFENCE TREATY (IRE)
b.c. Dandy Man – Just Like Ivy (Street Cry). March 26. Fifth foal. £100,000Y. Goffs UK Premier (Doncaster). Robin O'Ryan. Half-brother to the modest Irish dual 12f winner Creeping Ivy (by Mustameet) and to a hurdles winner by Elusive City. The dam, a moderate Irish 14f winner, is a half-sister to 3 winners including the US stakes winner and Grade 3 placed Galina Point. The second dam, Celtic Craft (by Danehill), a minor US 3-y-o winner, is a half-sister to 5 winners including the US Grade 2 winner Kara's Orientation.

571. FINAL ACT
b.f. Lethal Force – Enact (Kyllachy). April 9. Half-sister to the 2017 2-y-o winner Validator (by Kodiac), to the fair 7f winner Dubai Art (by Dubawi) and the fair 7f (at 2 yrs) and dual 1m winner Star Of The Stage

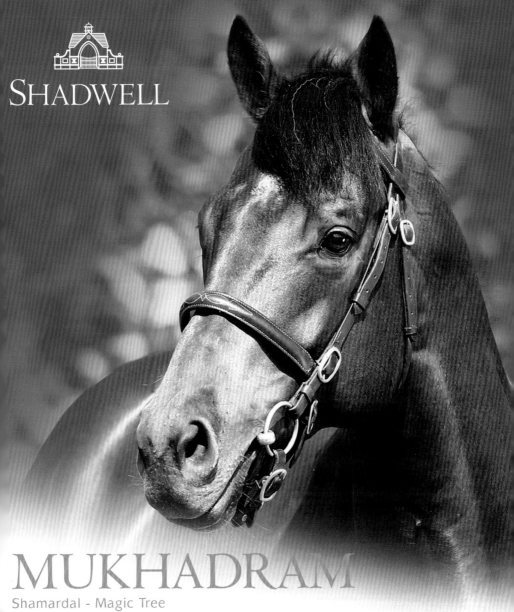

MUKHADRAM

Shamardal - Magic Tree

FIRST 2YOS IN 2018

First juveniles with top trainers including Karl Burke, Roger Charlton, William Haggas and Richard Hughes

£7,000 (1st JAN, SLF) Call the nominations team to discuss terms

Discover more about the Shadwell Stallions at www.shadwellstud.com
Or call Richard Lancaster, James O'Donnell or Tom Pennington on 01842 755913
Email us at: nominations@shadwellstud.co.uk

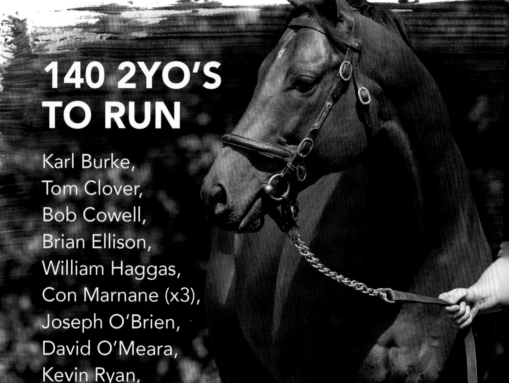

Budding talent

Two young sprint sires whose stud careers are set to blossom

GARSWOOD	TWILIGHT SON
Group 1 winning sprinter and Stakes winning 2yo	Dual **Group 1** winning sprinter by **KYLLACHY**
First crop yearlings made up to **140,000gns** and averaged over 8x his fee.	An immediate hit with breeders, with **142 mares** booked in his first season.
First crop 2yos in 2018	*First crop foals in 2018*
2018 fee: **£4,000** (1st Oct. SLF)	2018 fee: **£10,000** (1st Oct. SLF)

Their future's looking rosy...

Cheveley Park Stud

Duchess Drive, Newmarket, Suffolk CB8 9DD
+44 (0)1638 730316 • enquiries@cheveleypark.co.uk
www.cheveleypark.co.uk • ✵@CPStudOfficial

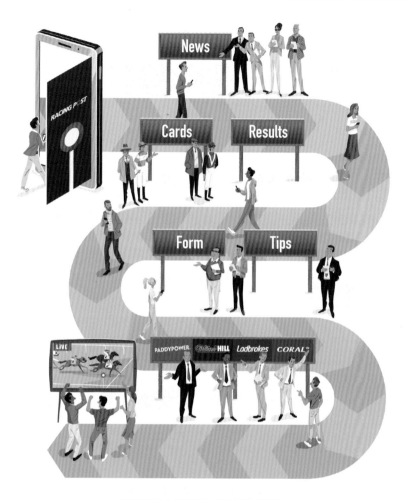

THE RACING POST APP.
EVERYTHING YOU NEED TO INFORM YOUR BET,
AND YOUR CHOICE OF BOOKIE TO PLACE IT.

Why continuously flit between apps when racing's best information and top bookies are sat side by side in one place? It only takes a couple of taps to log in to your account and, to top it all off, you can remain logged in to all four bookies at once. Placing an informed bet with the best odds has never been easier.

RACING POST

**WHEN YOU BET ON RACING,
YOU CAN BET ON RACING POST.**

(by Invincible Spirit). The dam, a fairly useful dual 6f winner (including at 2 yrs), was Listed-placed twice and is a full or half-sister to 5 winners. The second dam, Constitute (by Gone West), a quite useful 1m winner, is a half-sister to 8 winners including the smart Group 3 10f Select Stakes second Battle Chant. (Cheveley Park Stud).

572. GET THE RHYTHM
b.c. Garswood – Star Kodiak (Kodiac). February 22. Second foal. £50,000Y. Goffs UK Premier (Doncaster). Robin O'Ryan. The dam, an Italian 2-y-o Listed 6f winner, is a half-sister to 3 winners. The second dam, Red Fanfare (by First Trump), a moderate 4-y-o 7f winner, is a half-sister to one winner.

573. GINGER MAX
b.c. Garswood – Miss Bunter (Bahamian Bounty). February 24. Second foal. 68,000Y. Tattersalls October Book 2. Robin O'Ryan. Half-brother to the useful 2017 2-y-o Listed 6f winner Alwasmiya (by Kyllachy). The dam, a fair 5f and 6f winner at 3 and 4 yrs, is a half-sister to 4 winners including the Group 3 Flying Five and Listed Rous Stakes winner Dutch Masterpiece. The second dam, The Terrier (by Foxhound), a fair 2-y-o 5f winner, is a half-sister to 7 minor winners.

574. GUZMAN (IRE)
b.c. Camacho – Casablanca Jewel (Kalanisi). April 30. Sixth foal. €48,000Y. Goffs Orby. Robin O'Ryan. Brother to the fair 2017 2-y-o 5f and 6f winner Guzman and half-brother to the fair Irish 2-y-o dual 1m winner Catch A Wave (by Approve), the minor Italian winner of 7 races Super Alessandro (by Oratorio) and to the fair 7f and 1m winner Ibergman (by Big Bad Bob). The dam, a fair 2-y-o 1m winner, is a half-sister to 5 winners including the Group 3 July Stakes winner and Group 1 Middle Park Stakes third Fallow and the Hong Kong Listed winner Lucky Six. The second dam, Cartier Bijoux (by Ahonoora), a fairly useful 2-y-o 5f winner, is a half-sister to 7 winners including the Group 3 Jersey Stakes winner Miss Silca Key (herself dam of the Group 3 winner Central City).

575. INAUGURATE
b.f. Garswood – Constitute (Common

Grounds). March 29. Half-sister to 6 winners including the fairly useful 6f and 7f winner and Listed-placed Enrol, the fair dual 6f winner Comprise (both by Pivotal), the fairly useful Listed-placed dual 6f winner at 2 and 3 yrs Enact and the fair 2-y-o 6f and subsequent German winner Assembly (both by Kyllachy). The dam, a quite useful 1m winner, is a half-sister to 7 winners including the Listed winner and Group 3 second Battle Chant. The second dam, Appointed One (by Danzig), a Grade 3 placed US stakes winner, is a sister to the Group 2 1m Lockinge Stakes winner Emperor Jones and a half-sister to the Group 1 William Hill Futurity Stakes winner Bakharoff. (Cheveley Park Stud).

576. JIMMY GREENHOUGH
gr.c. Dream Ahead – Expedience (With Approval). April 10. Eighth foal. 37,000Y. Tattersalls December. Robin O'Ryan. Half-brother to the minor Italian 2-y-o winner Azamourday (by Azamour), to the modest 10f and 12f winner Clenymistra (by Poet's Voice) and two minor winners abroad by Exceed And Excel and Bahamian Bounty. The dam, a fair 1m winner, is a half-sister to 8 winners including the 2-y-o Group 3 Autumn Stakes winner and Group 1 Racing Post Trophy second Fantastic View. The second dam, Promptly (by Lead On Time), a quite useful 6f winner here, also won a minor 1m stakes in the USA and is a half-sister to 7 winners.

577. LIGHTNING ATTACK
b.c. Lethal Force – Afrodita (Montjeu). April 7. Fourth foal. 58,000Y. Tattersalls October Book 2. Robin O'Ryan. Half-brother to the modest UAE 6f winner Ajwad (by Rock Of Gibraltar). The dam ran once unplaced and is a half-sister to 8 winners including the Group 1 placed and smart broodmare Dance To The Top and the Listed winner and Australian Group 1 placed Polar Bear. The second dam, Aim For The Top (by Irish River), won the Group 3 7f Premio Chiusura and is a half-sister to 6 winners including the Gimcrack Stakes winner Splendent.

578. MENIN GATE (IRE)
gr.c. Farhh – Telegraphy (Giant's Causeway). February 20. First foal. 100,000Y. Tattersalls October Book 2. Robin O'Ryan. The dam was

placed fourth twice over 12f. The second dam, Cable (by Dynaformer), won two races at 3 yrs in the USA and was placed in three Grade 3 events and is a half-sister to 7 winners including the US Grade 2 Tom Fool Handicap winner Exchange Rate and the Group 3 10.5f Rose Of Lancaster Stakes winner Sabre d'Argent.

579. METATRON (IRE)
gr.c. Dark Angel – Orikawa (Gold Away). March 10. £120,000Y. Goffs UK Premier (Doncaster). Robin O'Ryan. The dam, a minor French placed 3-y-o, is a half-sister to 6 winners including the UAE Group3 winner Allybar. The second dam, Irika (by Irish River), a Minor French 3-y-o winner, is a half-sister to 6 winners including the French dual Group 2 winner Athyka.

580. MORE THAN THIS
b.c. Dutch Art – Striving (Danehill Dancer). March 1. Seventh foal. 40,000Y. Tattersalls October Book 2. Robin O'Ryan. Brother to the 2017 2-y-o 1m winner from two starts Preening , closely related to the fair 6f (including at 2 yrs) and 7f winner Best Endeavour and the minor winner of 9 races abroad Streamer (both by Medicean) and half-brother to the quite useful 8.5f winner Staunch (by Pivotal) and the quite useful 2-y-o 6f winner Showpiece (by Kyllachy). The dam, a modest 1m and 10f placed maiden, is a sister to the Listed 1m winner Pirateer and a half-sister to 6 winners including Wannabe Grand (Group 1 6f Cheveley Park Stakes). The second dam, Wannabe (by Shirley Heights), a quite useful 1m and 10f winner, is a half-sister to the Group 1 Cheveley Park Stakes second Tanami.

581. NICKI'S ANGEL (IRE)
gr.f. Dark Angel – Titova (Halling). March 1. Fourth foal. 62,000Y. Tattersalls October Book 2. Robin O'Ryan. Half-sister to a minor winner abroad by Sir Percy. The dam won 2 minor races at 3 yrs in Italy and is a half-sister to 7 winners including the Group 1 Prix de la Foret and Group 2 Prix d'Astarte winner Field Of Hope (herself the dam of 3 stakes winners). The second dam, Fracci (by Raise A Cup), was an Italian Listed winner of 4 races and Group 3 placed twice.

582. NOBLE CROWN
ch.f. Lethal Force – Noble Descent (Pivotal). February 10. First foal. The dam, a modest 1m placed maiden, is a sister to the quite useful 10f winner and Swedish Group 3 12f second Court Circle and a half-sister to 2 winners. The second dam, Noble Lady (by Primo Dominie), a fair 3-y-o dual 6f winner, is a full or half-sister to 6 winners including the useful dual 5f winner Noble One (herself dam of the dual Group 1 winner Peeress). The second dam, Noble Destiny (by Final Straw), was a fairly useful 2-y-o 7f winner. (Cheveley Park Stud).

583. OUT OF CONTROL (IRE)
b.f. Sir Percy – Barawin (Hawk Wing). March 8. Fourth foal. 80,000Y. Tattersalls October Book 1. Robin O'Ryan. Sister to the useful 7f (at 2 yrs) and 12f winner and Group 2 Royal Lodge Stakes third Sir Jack Leyden and half-sister to the quite useful 5f and 6f winner Family Fortunes (by Paco Boy) and the modest 11f and 12f winner Kelvin Hall (by Halling). The dam, a quite useful 2-y-o 1m winner, is a half-sister to 4 winners. The second dam, Cosabawn (by Barathea), is an unplaced half-sister to 7 winners.

584. PARION
b.f. Mayson – Delft (Dutch Art). Third foal. March 6. Half-sister to the fair 1m winner Faience (by Holy Roman Emperor). The dam, a quite useful 7f (including at 2 yrs) and 6f winner of 3 races, is a half-sister to one winner. The second dam, Plucky (by Kyllachy), a quite useful 7f winner, is a half-sister to 7 winners including the 2-y-o Group 2 5f Flying Childers Stakes and Group 3 5f Molecomb Stakes winner Wunders Dream and the Group 3 Ridgewood Pearl Stakes winner Grecian Dancer. (Cheveley Park Stud).

585. PESCI (IRE)
b.c. Elzaam – Siansa (Teofilo). March 16. Second foal. £35,000Y. Goffs UK Premier (Doncaster). Robin O'Ryan. Half-brother to Morgan Blond (by Intense Focus), a winner of 4 races in France and Italy at 2 and 3 yrs. The dam is an unplaced half-sister to 2 winners. The second dam, Arjooch (by Marju), was unraced.

586. RAPTURE
b.f. Dutch Art – Adore (Oasis Dream). March
21. First foal. The dam, a modest 8.5f winner,
is a half-sister to 2 winners including the
fairly useful 1m winner and Listed-placed
Illusion. The second dam, Fantazie (by Groom
Dancer), a useful 7f (at 2 yrs) and 1m Listed
winner, is a half-sister to the Group 3 6f Cherry
Hinton Stakes winner and 1,000 Guineas
third Dazzle and to the 2-y-o Listed 7f winner
Hypnotize. (Cheveley Park Stud).

587. RARE EMERALD ♠
ch.f. Dutch Art – Bahia Emerald (Bahamian
Bounty). March 14. Fourth foal. Half-sister to
the fair 2017 2-y-o 6f and 7f winner Crown Of
Cortez (by Pivotal) and to the modest 2-y-o
5f winner Emerald Bay (by Kyllachy). The dam,
a modest dual 6f winner, is a sister to one
winner and a half-sister to 6 winners including
the Listed 6f winner and Group 3 Princess
Margaret Stakes second Vital Statistics. The
second dam, Emerald Peace (by Green Desert),
a useful Listed 5f winner of 4 races and second
in the Group 2 5f Flying Childers Stakes, is a
half-sister to 9 winners. (Cheveley Park Stud).

588. ROSEBANK
b.f. Kyllachy – Dutch Courage (Dutch Art).
February 9. First foal. The dam, a fairly useful
2-y-o 6f and 7f winner, is a half-sister to 2
winners including the fairly useful 6f (at 2
yrs) and 7f winner and Listed-placed Maid A
Million. The second dam, Poldhu (by Cape
Cross), is an unraced half-sister to the Group
1 Falmouth Stakes winner Rajeem. (Cheveley
Park Stud).

589. ROYAL DESTINY
b.f. Garswood – Regina (Green Desert).
March 23. Ninth foal. Half-sister to 5 winners
including the fairly useful 2-y-o 5f winner and
6f Listed-placed Survived (by Kyllachy), the
fair dual 6f winner King Of Spin (by Pivotal)
and the quite useful 5f and 6f winner of 10
races from 2 to 7 yrs Six Wives (by Kingsalsa).
The dam, a fairly useful 2-y-o dual 5f winner,
is a half-sister to 5 winners. The second dam,
Dazzle (by Gone West), winner of the Group 3
6f Cherry Hinton Stakes and third in the 1,000
Guineas, is a half-sister to 3 Listed winners
including Hypnotize (dam of the Group 1
Cheveley Park Stakes winner Hooray) and
to the placed dam of the Group 2 winner

Danehurst. (Cheveley Park Stud).

590. SILVER DUST (IRE)
gr.c. Clodovil – Silesian (Singspiel). March 22.
Ninth foal. 57,000Y. Tattersalls October Book 2.
Robin O'Ryan. Half-brother to the fairly useful
10f winner and Listed-placed Nurture, to the
modest dual 6f and dual 7f winner Cliff (both
by Bachelor Duke), the fair Irish 12f winner
Upper Silesian and a minor winner in Italy
(both by Lawman). The dam is an unraced
half-sister to the US stakes winner and Grade 2
placed Sol Mi Fa. The second dam, Sil Sila (by
Marju), won the Group 1 Prix de Diane and is
a half-sister to 2 winners including the Group
1 placed 2-y-o Frequent Flyer.

591. ZIP
gr.c. Kyllachy – Flycatcher (Medicean). April
5. First foal. £30,000Y. Goffs UK Premier
(Doncaster). Robin O'Ryan. The dam, a fair 7.5f
and 1m winner, is a half-sister to 8 winners
including the useful Listed 10f winner and US
dual Grade 2 placed Rosa Grace. The second
dam, Night Haven (by Night Shift), a fairly
useful Listed-placed 5f (at 2 yrs) and 6f winner,
is a sister to 3 winners including the French
2-y-o Listed 5f winner Shoalhaven.

592. UNNAMED
b.c. Alhebayeb – America Alone (Dalakhani).
March 20. Second living foal. €40,000Y. Goffs
Orby. Robin O'Ryan. The dam is an unraced
half-sister to 2 winners including the Group 3
7f Prix du Calvados second Sara Lucille. The
second dam, Magic America (by High Yield),
a 2-y-o Group 3 7f Prix Miesque winner and
second in the Group 1 6f Prix Morny, is a half-
sister to 4 winners.

593. UNNAMED
b.c. Kingman – Gaditana (Rainbow Quest).
April 15. Fourth foal. 40,000Y. Tattersalls
December. Robin O'Ryan. The dam ran
once unplaced and is a full or half-sister to
6 winners including the 2-y-o Group 1 1m
Racing Post Trophy winner and St Leger
second Armiger, the very useful 10.2f winner
Migration and the 2-y-o 1m and 8.5f winner
and Group 2 Royal Lodge Stakes third Besiege.
The second dam, Armeria (by Northern
Dancer), a fair 3-y-o 10f winner, is a half-sister
to the Park Hill Stakes winner I Want To Be.

594. UNNAMED

ch.c. Dragon Pulse – St Edith (Desert King). April 8. Eleventh foal. £35,000Y. Goffs UK Premier (Doncaster). Robin O'Ryan / MPR. Half-brother to the fair 2-y-o 6f and 1m winner That's Dangerous (by Three Valleys), to the moderate 6f (at 2 yrs) to 1m winner It's All A Game (by Sleeping Indian), the Italian Listed-placed winner Furia Ceca (by Mujahid), the modest 7f (at 2 yrs) to 12f winner Kemsing (by Footstepsinthesand) and a hurdles winner by Haafhd. The dam, placed fourth once over 1m, is a half-sister to 7 winners. The second dam, Carnelly (by Priolo), an Irish 9f winner, was Listed-placed and is a sister to the winner and Group 3 placed Wenda.

CHARLIE FELLOWES

595. CAVALRY PARK ★★★

b.c. Epaulette – Sarah Park (Redback). April 20. Fourth foal. 20,000Y. Tattersalls October Book 3. Charlie Gordon-Watson / C Fellowes. Half-brother to the fair 2017 2-y-o 6f winner Titchy Digits (by Helmet) and to the fair 7f winner Delilah Park (by Delegator). The dam, a quite useful 7f to 8.5f winner of 6 races and is a half-sister to 2 minor winners. The second dam, Brillano (by Desert King), a modest 2-y-o 7f winner, is a sister to a French Listed winner and a half-sister to 6 winners. (Never So Bold – Aquino). *"I like this horse. He wasn't expensive and was quite a late foal and yet he's one of our more forward 2-y-o's. Not early enough for Royal Ascot, but he's very uncomplicated, a nice type and he'll be a sprinter – I'd say six or maximum seven furlongs. I've put him in a lot of those sales races at the end of the year because he won't carry much weight and he'll be the ideal type for them. I like him quite a lot".* TRAINER'S BARGAIN BUY

596. CRIMEAN QUEEN ★★★

b.f. Iffraaj – Victoria Cross (Mark Of Esteem). February 15. Ninth foal. Half-sister to 8 winners including the dual Group 2 12f winner Bronze Cannon, the US Grade 3 winner Valiant Girl (both by Lemon Drop Kid), the Group 2 12f King Edward VII Stakes winner Across The Stars (by Sea The Stars), the useful 2-y-o dual 7f winner Elusive Award (by Elusive Quality) and the fairly useful Listed-placed 2-y-o 7f winner Valiance (by Horse Chestnut). The

dam, a Listed-placed 7f winner, is a half-sister to the US Grade 2 winner Prize Giving and to the dam of the dual US Grade 1 winner Alpride. The second dam, Glowing With Pride (by Ile de Bourbon), a 7f and 10.5f winner, was second in the Park Hill Stakes. (A. E. Oppenheimer). *"She's the best-bred of my 2-y-o's. There's not much of her, she's relatively forward and will be ready to run in May over six furlongs, but she's a bit of a madam apart from when out exercising. A forward-going filly and despite not being the most impressive physically there's no doubt there's an engine there".*

597. DIVINE GIFT ★★★

b.c. Nathaniel – Souter's Sister (Desert Style). March 23. Fourth foal. 44,000Y. Tattersalls October Book 3. Not sold. Half-brother to the fair 1m and 10.5f winner of 4 races Mia Tesoro (by Danehill Dancer). The dam, a useful 2-y-o Group 3 7f Oh So Sharp Stakes winner, is a half-sister to 4 winners including the fairly useful 5f (at 2 yrs) to 7f winner of 3 races Premier Fantasy. The second dam, Hemaca (Distinctly North), was unraced. (Deron Pearson). *"I've trained every member of the family and his sister Mia Tesoro in particular has done really well for the yard. The Mastercraftsman 3-y-o has just started to pull herself together, so they both improved with age and yet we now have this Nathaniel 2-y-o that's as sharp as anything which is not what you'd expect! He's small, I've just backed off him because of sore shins but he will be a 2-y-o and finds everything pretty easy. I won't be in a rush with him and he's a nice, straightforward little colt".*

598. FRENCH MONTANA ★★★★

ch.c. Showcasing – Moving Sea (Rock Of Gibraltar). February 6. Third foal. 58,000Y. Tattersalls October Book 2. Charlie Gordon-Watson / C Fellowes. The dam is an unraced half-sister to 6 winners including the Group 3 Prix de Guiche winner Mister Sacha, the Listed winner Mister Charm and the Listed-placed Tahrir (dam of the multiple Group 1 winning sprinter Muhaarar). The second dam, Miss Sacha (by Last Tycoon), a Listed sprint winner, is a half-sister to 6 winners. (Never So Bold & Sohi). *"A belter – he's the one that stands out at the moment. He was quite a strong, well-made individual when I bought him but he's shot up and as a result he's weakened, so although he finds everything easy I've backed off him. He's one of those that catches your eye going up the hill but he can lull you into thinking he could be early when he's not. He's not going to be an Ascot 2-y-o so there's no need to rush him and he'll be a July or early August type. A colt with a lovely way of going, he's a beautiful mover and I like him".*

599. GARRYOWEN ★★★

b.c. Garswood – Lomapamar (Nashwan). March 20. Ninth foal. 17,000Y. Tattersalls October Book 2. Charlie Gordon-Watson/ Fellowes. Half-brother to 5 winners including the useful 2-y-o 6f and 7f winner and Group 1 Fillies' Mile third Urban Fox (by Foxwedge), the fair 1m (at 2 yrs) to 14f winner Getaway Car (by Medicean), the fair 2-y-o 6f winner Ghost Cat (by Equiano) and the moderate 1m and hurdles winner Mister Fantastic (by Green Tune). The dam, a fair 10f winner, is a half-sister to 8 winners including the 2-y-o Group 2 1m Royal Lodge Stakes winner Mons and the Irish Oaks third Inforapenny. The second dam, Morina (by Lyphard), won over 11f in France and is a half-sister to 10 winners. (Mrs Emma Capon, Tom Wilson, John Eastwood). *"A nice, big, well put-together 2-y-o, I'm surprised he didn't make more money because his pedigree isn't bad and his half-sister Urban Fox was very good. He's had sore shins so I backed off him and I'd say he'll make a 2-y-o in the second half of the season. Very laid-back and with a lovely attitude, I quite like him".*

600. LORD HALIFAX (IRE) ★★

b.c. Famous Name – Neutral (Beat Hollow). March 15. Fifth foal. €22,000Y. Tattersalls Ireland September. Charlie Gordon Watson & C Fellowes. Half-brother to the fairly useful Irish Listed-placed 2-y-o 7f winner Play The Game (by Lawman), to the fair 1m winner of 4 races Dark Ocean (by Dylan Thomas) and a winner in Poland by Duke Of Marmalade. The dam is an unraced half-sister to 5 winners including the 2-y-o Group 2 7f Debutante Stakes winner Silk And Scarlet (herself dam of the UAE and Japanese Group 1 winners Master Of Hounds and Eishin Apollon). The second dam, Danilova (by Lyphard), is an unraced half-sister to the French Derby and

Prix d'Ispahan winner Sanglamore. (Never So Bold – Aquino). *"He's likely to be gelded soon but that's no reflection on his ability or his temperament because both are very good, he's just very backward and he's unlikely to have any more than one or two runs at the back-end. I do like him and he's a nice type, but more of a 3-y-o".*

601. MAYFAIR POMPETTE ★★★★

ch.f. Toronado – Tipsy Me (Selkirk). February 4. Sixth foal. €40,000Y. Arqana Deauville August. Charlie Gordon-Watson. Half-sister to the quite useful 2-y-o dual 7f winner Just Fabulous (by Sakhee) and to the quite useful dual 12f winner Wrangler (by High Chaparral). The dam, a modest 1m placed maiden, is a half-sister to 7 winners including the Group 2 12f King Edward VII Stakes winner Plea Bargain and the Listed winners Lay Time and Jira. The second dam, Time Saved (by Green Desert), a fairly useful 10f winner, is a sister to the useful 1m winner and Listed-placed Illusion and a half-sister to 5 winners including Zinaad and Time Allowed, both winners of the Group 2 12f Jockey Club Stakes and the dams of the Group winners Anton Chekhov, First Charter, Plea Bargain and Time Away. (Joe & Mason Soiza). *"A lovely, big, scopey filly. I fell in love with her at the sales and if you'd given me a choice after the sales she would have been my pick. She's a big girl and may have a break for a few weeks now so she can put on a bit of weight, but she will be a 2-y-o. A big, flashy chestnut with a white face and white socks, she'll make a lovely 3-y-o as well. She has a beautiful stride on her and could do a dressage test!"*

602. MAYFAIR SPIRIT ★★★

b.c. Charm Spirit – Sassy Gal (King's Best). March 18. Sixth foal. 42,000Y. Tattersalls October Book 2. Not sold. Half-brother to the fair 2-y-o 1m winner Dreamy Gal (Dream Ahead) and to the fairly useful 5f (at 2 yrs) and 6f winner of 3 races Ben Hall (by Bushranger). The dam, a quite useful 1m (at 2 yrs) and 7f winner, is a half-sister to 9 winners including the very useful 6f (at 2 yrs) to 10f winner and Group 3 placed Firebet. The second dam, Dancing Prize (by Sadler's Wells), a useful maiden and third in the Listed Lingfield Oaks Trial, is a sister to 3 winners including the Group 1 Fillies Mile second and good broodmare Dance To The Top and a half-sister to 6 winners. (Ed Player, Whatton Manor Stud). *"A nice horse and my most forward colt. If I have one that could be ready in time for Royal Ascot it's him – but I don't mean quality-wise. He's very uncomplicated, well-made and a good size but strong. He canters beautifully and finds Warren Hill very easy and he'll be out in late April or early May".*

603. RUDY LEWIS (IRE) ★★★
b.c. Excelebration – Bless You (Bahamian Bounty). January 27. Third foal. €45,000Y. Tattersalls Ireland September. Charlie Gordon-Watson / C Fellowes. Half-brother to the quite useful 2017 2-y-o 5f winner Wings Of The Rock (by Rock Of Gibraltar) and to the useful 2-y-o Listed 5f winner and Group 3 5f Curragh Stakes third Yulong Baobei (by Choisir). The dam, a quite useful 6f winner, is a half-sister to 3 winners. The second dam, Follow Flanders (by Pursuit Of Love), a fairly useful dual 5f winner, is a full or half-sister to 10 winners including the top-class Group 1 5f Nunthorpe Stakes winner Kyllachy. *"I really liked his half-sister Wings Of The Rock at the sales and nearly bought her. She was small and sharp but this colt has a bit of size about him and he won't be as early as some other members of the family. I wouldn't be surprised if he turned out to be a seven furlong/miler in the end. One for the back-end of the season because he's got plenty of scope and a bit of quality about him".*

604. SNAZZY ★★★★ ♠♠
b.f. Kodiac – Tilthe End Of Time (Acclamation). February 23. Fourth foal. €40,000Y. Tattersalls Ireland September. Charlie Gordon-Watson. The dam is an unraced half-sister to 3 winners. The second dam, Neverletme Go (by Green Desert), a fairly useful dual 5f winner at 3 yrs, is a sister to one winner and a half-sister to 4 winners including the triple Group 1 winner Halfway To Heaven (dam of the Group 1 Fillies' Mile winner Rhododendron) and the Group 3 winners Tickled Pink and Theann (dam of the US dual Grade 1 winner Photo Call). (Highclere Thoroughbred Racing-JustWannaHaveFun). *"She's by Kodiac out of an Acclamation mare and she does exactly what it says on the tin. She's ready to go. There's a five furlong conditions race for fillies at Newcastle*

on Good Friday and we might go there. I think she's quite smart, she did a nice piece of work the other day, she's pretty straight and has been a dream to train. She could be quite nice and might end up at Royal Ascot". As Charlie intimated, Snazzy won on her debut in early April.

605. URBAN SCENE ★★
b.f. Cityscape – Fashionable Gal (Galileo). March 11. The dam, a fair triple 10f and hurdles winner, is a half-sister to 2 winners. The second dam, Fashion (by Bin Ajwaad), a fair 1m (at 2 yrs) and 10f winner, is a half-sister to 5 winners including the Group 1 Italian Oaks winner Bright Generation. (Mr J. C. Webb). *"I've turned her out to give her a break. She was cantering away and I'm quite happy with her but she'll benefit from some spring grass and we'll look to get her back in by early summer and get a couple of runs out of her before the end of the season. A very uncomplicated filly but very immature at this stage".*

JAMES GIVEN
606. FAROL ★★
br.f. Kuroshio – Spate Rise (Speightstown). March 22. Fourth foal. Half-sister to the fair 2017 1m and 8.5f placed 2-y-o Creel (by Aussie Rules). The dam is an unraced half-sister to two minor winners in the USA and to the modest 2-y-o 6f winner X Raise. The second dam, Raise (by Seattle Slew), a minor US winner at 4 yrs, is a half-sister to 7 winners including the Irish Group 2 Railway Stakes winner Lizard Island and to the dams of the US Grade 1 winner Corinthian and the Group 3 Ballycorus Stakes winner Six Of Hearts. (Mr P Onslow). *"The sire was an Australian sprinting son of Exceed And Excel. This is a big filly that's still growing, she moves well and when she's finished growing she'll cover the ground because she's got a big old stride on her. It's hard to say what trip she'll want, but one would expect her to be a sprinting type. One for midsummer onwards, she's not strong enough to be doing too much at the moment".*

607. GARSBAY ★★★
ch.c. Garswood – Marmot Bay (Kodiac). March 4. Second foal. £38,000Y. Goffs UK Premier

(Doncaster). Cool Silk & Stroud/Coleman. Half-brother to the quite useful dual 5f winner at 2 and 3 yrs Cool Spirit (by Swiss Spirit). The dam, a modest 2-y-o triple 6f winner, is a half-sister to 4 minor winners. The second dam, Tides (by Bahamian Bounty), is an unplaced half-sister to 5 winners including the Listed winner Amazing Bay. (The Cool Silk Partnership). *"By the first season sire Garswood whose best run was over seven furlongs, this colt is a half-brother to a 3-y-o of ours, Cool Spirit and this is a speedy pedigree. This is a big horse and he's just started to grow again, he's not backward and he's cantering away every day, but he'll take a bit of time to fill his frame. He'll be a nice, big 2-y-o later on".*

608. GINVINCIBLE ★★★
gr.f. Zebedee – Gone Sailing (Mizzen Mast). March 12. Fourth foal. £26,000Y. Goffs UK Premier (Doncaster). James Given. Sister to the fairly useful 5f (including at 2 yrs) and 6f winner of 4 races Major Jumbo and half-sister to the moderate triple 6f winner Goadby (by Kodiac). The dam is an unraced half-sister to one minor winner. The second dam, Shoot (by Barathea), a fair 3-y-o 7f winner here, later won in the USA and is a half-sister to 6 winners including the Australian triple Group 1 winner Foreteller, the Group 2 winner Modern Look and the Listed winner Arabesque (dam of the Group winners and sires Showcasing and Camacho). (Roy Tozer & Team Given 2). *"She was doing some nice bits of work before she had a growth spurt and she shows a good bit of speed. If the weather does improve and we can start doing more with her she should be out in May over five furlongs and she should get six in time".* TRAINER'S BARGAIN BUY

609. JUST JOSEPHINE (IRE) ★★
b.f. Arakan – Salingers Star (Catcher In The Rye). April 1. Third foal. Sister to the modest 2017 5f placed 2-y-o Mount Victoria. The dam, a fair 2-y-o 6f winner, is a sister to one winner and a half-sister to 4 winners. The second dam, Head For The Stars (by Head For Heights), is an unplaced half-sister to 2 minor winners. (D Gibbons, T Gaunt Partnership). *"The dam won first time out and this filly is bigger than her 3-y-o half-sister was at this stage. Hopefully she can emulate her mother and win reasonably early. I see her being a*

2-y-o to start in June because she has some furnishing still to do".

610. MENDELEEV ★★
b.g. Hellvelyn – Wightgold (Golden Snake). February 13. First foal. £4,500Y. Goffs UK Autumn. Not sold. The dam, a moderate 12f to 2m placed maiden, is out of Main Brand (by Main Reef), a 2-y-o 1m winner on her only start on the Flat and herself a half-sister to several winners. (Team Given 1). *"A home-bred that's been leased to us, the dam was a stayer but the sire is an influence for precocious speed. We gelded him early on but he's a sensible, decent-sized horse and we should be running him early once we get some better weather; a straightforward horse that shows a bit of speed and is there to be got on with".*

611. ORANGE BLOSSOM ★★★★ ♠
ch.f. Showcasing – Satsuma (Compton Place). January 29. £65,000Y. Goffs UK Premier (Doncaster). Cool Silk & Stroud/Coleman. The dam, a quite useful 2-y-o 5f winner, is a half-sister to 3 winners. The second dam, Jodrell Bank (by Observatory), a modest 6f placed 3-y-o, is a sister to the winner and subsequent Grade 1 Hollywood Derby second Sebastian Flyte and a half-sister to 3 winners including the dual 5f (at 2 yrs) and Group 3 6f Ballyogan Stakes winner Age Of Chivalry. (The Cool Silk Partnership). *"A lovely filly, the mother was called Satsuma because her backside is like two oranges stuck together! She's a big, bright chestnut with a big backside on her and this daughter of hers seems to be going the same way. I think she's a very nice filly, five furlongs should suit her, the sire is doing well and she was an early foal. So all she needs is some decent weather because she's done some good bits of work, the penny's dropping and we like her very much".*

612. PIPOCA ★★
ch.f. Archipenko – Trick Or Treat (Lomitas). March 27. Sister to the very useful 7f (at 2 yrs) and Listed 11f winner and dual Group 3 third Medrano and half-sister to the quite useful dual 12f winner Guising (by Manduro), the quite useful 2-y-o 1m winner Hollowina (by Beat Hollow) and the fair 8.5f winner Maahir (by Cape Cross). The dam, a winner of 7 races including the Group 3 12f Princess

Royal Stakes and the Listed Pinnacle Stakes, was third in the Group 1 Yorkshire Oaks and is a half-sister to 3 winners. The second dam, Trick Of Ace (by Clever Trick), a stakes-placed winner of 4 races in the USA over 1m or more, is a half-sister to 5 winners including the US Grade 2 La Prevoyante Handicap winner Prospectress. (Peter Onslow). *"The dam is an old favourite of ours and sadly she passed away last year. This filly is in the middle of a growth spurt at present, she has a great temperament like her mother – and indeed the sire gets them that way as well. She's going to be one for the second half of the season at least and should be progressive into her third and fourth years. A nice racing filly I would think".*

613. RUSSIAN RUM ★★★

b.c. Archipenko – Bebe De Cham (Tragic Role). February 25. Half-brother to 3 winners including the fair 2-y-o 1m and jumps winner Cava Bien (by Bien Bien) and the modest 2-y-o 7f winner Punch Drunk (by Beat Hollow and herself dam of the fairly useful 2-y-o Listed 7f winner of 3 races Russian Punch (by Archipenko)). The dam, a fair 2-y-o 5f and 6f winner, is a half-sister to several minor winners. The second dam, Champenoise (by Forzando), a 1m seller winner at 4 yrs, is a half-sister to 3 winners. (Lovely Bubbly Racing). *"We trained the closely related Russian Punch who won the Radley Stakes as a 2-y-o but didn't really train on. This colt has more scope than she had so I'm hopeful that we'll get a good 2-y-o career out of him but also a 3-y-o career as well. He was a bit behind the others but he's catching up quickly, seems to have a nice mind on him and moves pretty well, so I should think he'll be out in midsummer".*

614. SANTANA SLEW ★★★

b.f. Gregorian – Saratoga Slew (Footstepsinthesand). March 31. Third foal. 4,500 foal. Tattersalls December. Not sold. Half-sister to the quite useful 5f and 6f winner of 3 races at 2 and 3 yrs Savannah Slew (by Kheleyf). The dam, a fair 7f winner, is a half-sister to 3 winners including the French winner of 8 races (including twice at 2 yrs over 6f) Wild Horse (by Kheleyf). The second dam, Life Rely (by Maria's Mon), is an unraced half-sister to 3 winners including the Group 1 Italian

Oaks winner and Group 1 Moyglare Stud Stakes third Menhoubah. (Dachel Stud). *"A big filly, she's by first season sire Gregorian so we're guessing a bit, but she's athletic, wants to get on with life and is still a bit unfurnished. She'll be a six/seven furlong horse I should think. She was injured at the sale and as a result didn't sell; hence the breeders decided to put her in training themselves".*

615. SIRIUS SLEW ★★★

b.c. Epaulette – Slewtoo (Three Valleys). April 16. First foal. £16,000Y. Goffs UK Silver (Doncaster). James Given. The dam, a fair 2-y-o 7f winner, is a half-sister to 2 winners. The second dam, Red Slew (by Red Ransom), is an unraced half-sister to 5 winners including the Listed winner Ahla Wasahl. (Dachel Stud). *"He looks like he'll be a six/seven furlong 2-y-o ultimately, but he could well start over five. He's quite forward and has done plenty of work already but his work suggests he'll benefit by moving up to six furlongs pretty quickly".*

616. SISTER OF THE SIGN (IRE) ★★★

b.f. Kodiac – Summer Magic (Desert Sun). March 30. Fifth foal. 58,000Gs. Tattersalls October Book 3. Cool Silk Partnership/Stroud/ Coleman. Sister to the fairly useful 5f and 6f winner of 5 races from 2 to 4 yrs Sign Of The Kodiac and to the quite useful 7f (at 2 yrs) and 1m winner Vector Force. The dam, a quite useful 6f to 1m winner of 6 races, is a half-sister to a hurdles winner and to the dam of the Irish Group 3 winner Ansgar. The second dam, Cimeterre (by Arazi), is a placed half-sister to 4 winners including the dam of the dual Group 3 winning sprinter Captain Gerrard. (The Cool Silk Partnership). *"We had her good half-brother Sign Of The Kodiac who wasn't the most precocious of horses and I suspect she'll be quite similar to him. She'll be a sprinter in time but she won't be early".*

617. THE LAST UNICORN ★★★

b.c. Bated Breath – Rohlindi (Red Ransom). March 2. Third foal. 125,000Y. Tattersalls October Book 2. Cool Silk & Stroud/Coleman. Brother to the fairly useful 2017 2-y-o Listed-placed maiden Mistress Of Venice and half-brother to the quite useful 8.5f winner War Of Succession (by Casamento). The dam, a modest 5.5f placed maiden, is a half-sister to 8 winners including the Listed 7f winner Kalindi (herself the dam of 3 stakes winners) and the useful Group 3 placed Tayseer. The second dam, Rohita (by Waajib), a fairly useful 2-y-o 5f and 6f winner, was third in the Group 3 6f Cherry Hinton Stakes and is a half-sister to 5 winners. (The Cool Silk Partnership). *"A full-brother to Mistress Of Venice who ran some very good races in Group company for us last year, when we were all a bit surprised at her precocity. This colt is going to take a little bit of time because he's still growing so we just don't know about him yet; he's likely to be one for the middle of the season onwards".*

618. TUNKY ★★
gr.f. Gregorian – Alushta (Royal Applause). March 8. Fourth foal. £12,000Y. Goffs UK Silver (Doncaster). James Given. Half-sister to the modest 2017 6f and 7f placed 2-y-o Elysee Star (by Champs Elysees). The dam ran once unplaced and is a sister to the Group 2 6f Richmond Stakes winner Mister Cosmi and to the smart 2-y-o Listed 6f winner Auditorium and a half-sister to 2 winners. The second dam, Degree (by Warning), a quite useful 4-y-o 1m winner, is a half-sister to 2 winners. (R. C. Spore). *"She had a slight setback which will put her back a little bit and she is growing, but she's done a few bits of galloping already and shown a bit of speed so hopefully we'll have her out from late May onwards".*

619. UNNAMED ★★★
b.f. Sir Prancealot – Ballet Of Doha (Zebedee). February 7. First foal. £28,000 2-y-o. Tattersalls Ireland Ascot Breeze Up. Cool Silk & Stroud/ Coleman. The dam ran once unplaced and is a half-sister to 2 winners including the very useful dual 7f (at 2 yrs) and Listed 1m winner Baltic Knight (by Baltic King). The second dam, Night Of Joy (by King's Best), a fairly useful 2-y-o dual 1m winner, is a half-sister to 6 winners. (Cool Silk Partnership). *"A recent breeze-up purchase, she's a bit on her toes as you might expect having been a breeze-up horse. Her breeze was good in atrocious ground at Ascot and we would hope to have her out within a month, but we don't really know much about her yet".*

620. UNNAMED ★★
b.f. Havana Gold – Sunseek (Rail Link). April

9. Third foal. £1,500Y. Goffs UK Autumn. Not sold. The dam, placed at 3 yrs in France, is a half-sister to 9 winners including Meteor Storm (Grade 1 10f Manhattan Handicap), Polish Summer (Group 1 Dubai Sheema Classic) and the French Group 3 2m winner Host Nation. The second dam, Hunt The Sun (by Rainbow Quest), was placed at 3 yrs in France and is a sister to the high-class Rothmans International, Prix Royal-Oak and Prix Kergorlay winner Raintrap and to the very smart Criterium de Saint-Cloud and Prix du Conseil de Paris winner Sunshack. (C. G. Rowles Nicholson). *"A nice physical specimen with a nice head on her, she's going to take a bit of time. It's hard to judge at the moment but I would say she's one for midsummer onwards over six/seven furlongs".*

JOHN GOSDEN

621. ALFAATIK ★★
b.c. Sea The Stars – Biz Bar (Tobougg). April 26. Seventh foal. 850,000Y. Tattersalls October Book 2. Shadwell Estate Co. Half-brother to 4 winners in Italy including the Group 1 Gran Premio di Milano and Group 2 Italian Derby winner Biz The Nurse (by Oratorio), the Group 2 Premio Gran Criterium winner Biz Heart (by Roderic O'Connor), the Group 3 Premio Guido Berardelli winner Misterious Boy (by Arcano) and the Italian 2-y-o Listed winner Biz Power (by Power). The dam, a 2-y-o Listed winner in Italy, is a half-sister to 2 winners. The second dam, Ulanova (by Trempolino), won 3 minor races at 3 and 4 yrs in Italy and is a half-sister to 6 winners. (Hamdan Al Maktoum). *"A big, rangy horse that hasn't some to me from Shadwell yet, he was in Book 2 at Tattersalls and I should think he pretty much topped that sale. From an Italian family, I haven't seen enough of him to comment really but I should think he'll take time".*

622. ALNORAS ★★★
b.f. Kingman – Kareemah (Peintre Celebre). April 3. Sixth foal. Half-sister to the quite useful 1m winner Ehtiraas (by Oasis Dream) and to the fair 12f winner Saraha (by Dansili). The dam, a French Listed 10f winner, is a half-sister to 4 winners including the French Listed 9f and subsequent US Grade 1 10f and Grade 1 11f winner Lahudood. The second dam, Rahayeb (by Arazi), a fair 12.3f winner,

is a full or half-sister to 4 winners. (Hamdan Al Maktoum). *"A good mover, she looks an athletic type and is hopefully one to start in the middle of the season".*

623. ALRAJAA ★★★
b.c. Dubawi – Ethaara (Green Desert). March 1. Half-brother to the useful Listed 1m winner of 4 races Etaab (by Street Cry), to the fairly useful triple 1m winner Estiqaama (by Nayef) and the quite useful 6f winner, from two starts, Farsakh (by Smart Strike). The dam, a useful Listed 6f winner, is closely related to the very useful 2-y-o Listed 7f Star Stakes winner and Group 3 7f Prestige Stakes second Mudaaraah and a half-sister to the useful 2-y-o Listed 7f winner Sudoor. The second dam, Wissal (by Woodman), is an unraced sister to the high-class 2-y-o Group 2 7f Laurent Perrier Champagne Stakes winner Bahhare and a half-sister to the Group 1 1m St James's Palace Stakes and Group 1 1m Queen Elizabeth II Stakes winner Bahri. (Hamdan Al Maktoum). *"A strong colt that moves pretty well, he looks the sort for July onwards. He's got a nice way about him and carries himself well".*

624. AMBLING ★★★ ♠
b.f. Lope De Vega – Royale Danehill (Danehill). March 26. Half-sister to the fair 2017 2-y-o 5.5f winner Magnus (by Makfi), to the quite useful 2-y-o 6f winner Bircham (by Dubawi) and the quite useful triple 6f winner from 2 to 4 yrs Souville (by Dalakhani). The dam won two minor races at 4 yrs in France including over 7.5f at Deauville and is a half-sister to 6 winners including the Group 3 placed Juliet Capulet and the Listed-placed Fly To The Moon. The second dam, Royal Ballerina (by Sadler's Wells), winner of the Group 2 12f Blandford Stakes and second in the Oaks, is a half-sister to 7 winners including the dual Group 2 10f Sun Chariot Stakes winner Free Guest (herself dam of the Group 1 Fillies Mile winner and Oaks second Shamshir). *"A good filly that goes nicely, she's very much one for August or September time but she's a nice type".*

625. ANGEL'S HIDEAWAY ★★★★ ♠
gr.f. Dark Angel – The Hermitage (Kheleyf). April 2. Fifth foal. €390,000Y. Goffs Orby. Cheveley Park Stud. Sister to the 2017 6f and

7f placed 2-y-o Modern Love, to the fairly useful 2-y-o 6f winner and Group 2 Mill Reef Stakes second Perfect Angel and the fair 6f winner Where's Sue. The dam, a quite useful Listed-placed 2-y-o 5f winner, is a half-sister to 9 winners including the Listed winners and Group 1 placed Crown Of Light and Alboostan. The second dam, Russian Countess (by Nureyev), a useful French 2-y-o 1m winner, was Listed-placed twice and is a half-sister to 5 winners. *"She's a neat, racy, very active filly and light on her feet. She won't be backward by any means and I can see her being out in May".*

626. ARABIST ★★★ ♠
b.c. Invincible Spirit – Highest (Dynaformer). February 2. Third foal. Half-brother to the 2017 2-y-o 8.5f winner, from two starts, Antonian (by Intello). The dam, a fairly useful Listed-placed 12f winner, is a half-sister to 5 winners including the French Listed 12f and US Grade 2 12f Long Island Handicap winner Olaya and the smart Listed-placed 7f (at 2 yrs) to 10f winner Wasan. The second dam, Solaia (by Miswaki), winner of the Listed Cheshire Oaks and second in the Group 3 12f Lancashire Oaks, is a half-sister to 3 winners. *"A strong, good-looking horse that goes fine, but being out of that mare he may take some time to come to hand".*

627. AZANO ★★★
b.c. Oasis Dream – Azanara (Hurricane Run). February 9. Third foal. The dam is an unplaced half-sister to 10 winners including the high-class Group 1 Prix Ganay and Group 2 Prix d'Harcourt winner Astarabad and the useful Irish winner at up to 10f Asmara (herself dam of the top-class colt Azamour). The second dam, Anaza (by Darshaan), only ran at 2 yrs when she was a useful winner of the Listed Prix Herbager and is a half-sister to 2 winners. *"A nice type of colt, he's cantering away for now and quite aggressive in everything he does. Well-balanced and a good mover".*

628. CALYX ★★★★
b.c. Kingman – Helleborine (Observatory). April 25. Half-brother to the fair 2017 1m fourth placed 2-y-o Orchid Lily (by Dansili). The dam, a 2-y-o Group 3 1m Prix d'Aumale winner, is a sister to the Group 1 6f Sprint Cup and Listed 7f winner African Rose. The

second dam, New Orchid (by Quest For Fame), a useful 10f winner and third in the Group 3 Lancashire Oaks, is a half-sister to 3 winners including the champion 2-y-o and Group 1 7f Dewhurst Stakes winner Distant Music. (Khalid Abdullah). *"He goes well and is a nice type of horse with plenty of character. He has a good action and we'll wait for the six furlong maidens. A colt with a nice way about him".*

629. CHANDERI ★★★
ch.f. Dubawi – Silk Sari (Dalakhani). March 27. First foal. 1,300,000Y. Tattersalls October Book 1. Godolphin. The dam, a smart Group 2 14.5f Park Hill Stakes winner and second in the Group 1 British Champions Fillies/Mare Stakes, is a half-sister to 3 winners. The second dam, So Silk (by Rainbow Quest), is an unraced half-sister to 6 winners including Ibn Khaldun (2-y-o Group 1 Racing Post Trophy). *"A nice type, she's quite big and will take some time but she's a nice filly and we won't be in a rush".*

630. CORDELHIA (IRE) ★★★
b.f. Australia – Chrysanthemum (Danehill Dancer). January 21. Third foal. Closely related to the 2017 dual 6f placed 2-y-o on both his starts Cassini (by Galileo) and to the useful 2-y-o 6f winner and triple Listed-placed Cunco (by Frankel). The dam, a winner of 5 races including the 2-y-o Group 3 7f C L Weld Park Stakes and the Group 3 Park Express Stakes, was third in the Group1 Pretty Polly Stakes and is a half-sister to 2 winners. The second dam, Well Spoken (by Sadler's Wells), a jumps winner in France, is a half-sister to 6 winners. *"She came into the yard late but she's a nice type of filly. From what we've seen of Australia's produce we like them and this is a neat filly but probably one for a bit later in the season".*

631. DAAFR ★★★
b.c. Invincible Spirit – Kitty Love (Kitten's Joy). May 6. Second foal. €350,000Y. Goffs Orby. Shadwell Estate Co. The dam, a minor US dual winner at 3 yrs, is a half-sister to 6 winners including the Group 1 Ascot Gold Cup and Group 1 Irish St Leger winner Order Of St George, the French Group 3 1m winner Asperity and the US Grade 3 9f winner Angel Terrace. The second dam, Another Storm (by Gone West), a minor US 2-y-o winner, is a

half-sister to 4 winners. *"He's grown a lot, has a nice action and a good temperament and is a promising colt for mid-season".*

632. DAARIK ★★★★
b.c. Tamayuz – Whip And Win (Whipper). February 18. Second foal. 325,000Y. Tattersalls October Book 2. Shadwell Estate Co. Half-brother to the French dual 1m (at 2 yrs) and Listed 7f winner Pas De Soucis (by Footstepsinthesand). The dam, a French 2-y-o Listed 1m winner and Group 3 placed, is a half-sister to 3 minor winners. The second dam, Queensalsa (by Kingsalsa), a dual 2-y-o winner in France and second in the Group 2 Prix Robert Papin, is a half-sister to 5 winners. *"He's pretty active, looks quite sharp and well-made with a good action. One of our earlier types".*

633. DAMON RUNYON ★★★★
b.c. Charm Spirit – Tawaasul (Haafhd). February 7. Third foal. 70,000Y. Tattersalls October Book 2. Norris/Huntingdon. Half-brother to the modest 1m placed 2017 2-y-o Baasha (by Havana Gold) and to the quite useful 2-y-o 6f winner of 4 races Tawny Port (by Arcano). The dam, a fair 1m winner, is a half-sister to 3 winners. The second dam, Muwakleh (by Machiavellian), a dual winner and second in the Newmarket 1,000 Guineas, is a sister to the Dubai World Cup and Prix Jean Prat winner Almutawakel and the useful 10f winner Elmustanser and a half-sister to 11 winners including the smart Group 3 placed 10f winner Inaaq. *"A nice horse, he's very likeable and I can see him being out in July, probably over seven furlongs. He goes well, has a good attitude and is a nice-moving colt".*

634. ELISHEBA ★★★★
b.f. Australia – Laugh Out Loud (Clodovil). March 31. Second foal. 200,000Y. Tattersalls October Book 2. Blandford Bloodstock. Closely related to the Irish 2017 2-y-o 1m winner Platinum Warrior (by Galileo). The dam, a winner of 4 races including the Group 2 1m Prix de Sandringham, is a half-sister to 7 winners including the dual Listed winner Suzi's Decision. The second dam, Funny Girl (by Darshaan), was placed from 7f to 9f and is a half-sister to 3 winners. *"A neat, very 'together'*

filly with a quick action. Her mother was very talented and this looks a nice filly for July/August".

635. ENTITLE
b.f. Dansili – Concentric (Sadler's Wells). February 18. Sixth foal. Half-sister to the outstanding filly Enable (by Nathaniel), a winner of five Group 1 races over 12f including the Oaks, the King George VI and the 'Arc', to the French 1m 7f winner and Group 2 second Contribution (by Champs Elysees) and the quite useful triple 1m winner Tournament (by Oasis Dream). The dam, a useful French Listed 10f winner, was second in the Group 3 10.5f Prix de Flore and is a sister to the Group 2 12.5f Prix de Royallieu winner Dance Routine, closely related to the dual Group 3 1m winner Apsis and a half-sister to the Listed 12f winner Space Quest. The second dam, Apogee (by Shirley Heights), won the Group 3 12f Prix de Royaumont and is a half-sister to the Group 2 12f Grand Prix de Chantilly winner Daring Miss. (Khalid Abdullah). *"Not in training yet".*

636. EVER CHANGING (USA) ★★★ ♠
ch.c. Tapit – Rainbow View (Dynaformer). March 8. Third foal. The dam won the Group 1 Fillies' Mile and the Group 1 1m Matron Stakes and is a half-sister to the Canadian Grade 1 winner Just As Well, the 7f (at 2 yrs) and US Grade 2 8.5f winner Utley and the US Grade 3 9f and Grade 3 12f winner Winter View. The second dam, No Matter What (by Nureyev), winner of the Grade 1 Del Mar Oaks, is a half-sister to the Grade 2 Suburban Handicap and Grade 2 Dwyer Stakes winner E Dubai. *"A nice type of colt that moves well. He's not going to be precocious like his mother and we'll probably see him starting off around September time".*

637. FABULIST ★★
b.f. Dubawi – Melodramatic (Sadler's Wells). April 11. Fourth living foal. Half-sister to the smart 10f and 11f winner and Group 2 Hardwicke Stakes third Almodovar (by Sea The Stars). The dam, a useful 1m winner and second in the Listed Ballymacoll Stud Stakes, is closely related to the Group 1 6f Haydock Sprint Cup winner Tante Rose and a half-sister to 5 winners including the dam of the Group

1 winners Make Believe and Dubawi Heights. The second dam, My Branch (by Distant Relative), winner of the Listed 6f Firth Of Clyde Stakes (at 2 yrs) and the Listed 7f Sceptre Stakes, was second in the Group 1 Cheveley Park Stakes and is a half-sister to 7 winners. (Bjorn Nielsen). *"A nice type of filly with a good temperament. A little immature at this stage, she's gone through a growing phase and I very much feel she'll benefit from patience".*

638. FAILAISE ★★
b.br.f. War Front – La Conseillante (Elusive Quality). May 7. Eighth foal. $750,000Y. Keeneland September. Cheveley Park Stud. Sister to the 6f (at 2 yrs) and 1m winner and Group 2 Champagne Stakes second War Envoy and to the minor French 8.5f winner Beychevelle. The dam, a French Listed 1m winner, is a half-sister to 6 minor winners. The second dam, Stormin Winnie (by Storm Cat), is an unraced daughter of the Kentucky Derby winning filly Winning Colors. *"She hasn't arrived here yet so I can't say a lot except that she's a tall, backward type for later in the season".*

639. FALSEHOOD ★★★
gr.c. Kingman – Half Truth (Verglas). February 18. The dam, a fair 2-y-o 6f winner, is a half-sister to the Group 1 6f July Cup and dual Group 2 winner Fleeting Spirit and the fairly useful Irish 6f to 1m winner of 7 races and Listed-placed Alone He Stands. The second dam, Millennium Tale (by Distant Relative), is an unraced half-sister to 5 winners. *"A nice colt and a good mover with good scope about him. He goes well, needs to strengthen and he'll be a mid-season horse".*

640. FIGHTWITHME ★★★
b.c. Shamardal – Music Show (Noverre). April 28. Third foal. Half-brother to the 2017 2-y-o 7f winner on his only start New Show (by New Approach). The dam won 5 races including the Group 1 Falmouth Stakes, the Group 2 Rockfel Stakes and Group 3 Nell Gwyn Stakes and was Group 1 placed three times. She is a half-sister to the useful winner and triple Listed-placed Fantasia Girl. The second dam, Dreamboat (by Mr Prospector), a fair 7f winner, is a sister to the French Listed-placed winner Sweetheart and a half-sister to 5 winners including the

Listed 7f winner and Group 2 placed Stunning. *"He was a little immature but he's improving all the time and he goes nicely in his canters. A likeable colt and one for the mid-season onwards".*

641. FIRST IN LINE ★★★

ch.c New Approach – Hidden Hope (Daylami). March 31. Brother to the quite useful 12f and 13.5f winner of 3 races Dawn Horizons and half-brother to the useful 1m (at 2 yrs), 10f and Listed 12f winner Our Obsession (by Shamardal), to the fairly useful dual 1m winner Westwiththenight (by Cape Cross) and the modest 11f winner Fine Style (by Pivotal). The dam, a useful Listed 11.4f Cheshire Oaks winner, is a half-sister to 9 winners including Rebecca Sharp (Group 1 1m Coronation Stakes) and the Group 3 Lingfield Derby Trial winner Mystic Knight. The second dam, Nuryana (by Nureyev), a useful winner of the Listed 1m Grand Metropolitan Stakes, is a half-sister to 5 winners. (Mr A E Oppenheimer). *"A tall, good-looking colt, he's straightforward and will be an August or September 2-y-o. A nice type, he needs to strengthen but he's got quality".*

642. FLY THE FLAG ★★

gr.f. Australia – Approach (Darshaan). April 8. Closely related to the Group 2 Irish Derby Trial winner, Irish Derby second and St Leger second Midas Touch, to the quite useful 10f winner Murgan (both by Galileo) and half-sister to 3 winners including the smart 1m (at 2 yrs) and Group 2 12f Ribblesdale Stakes winner Coronet (by Dubawi) and the useful 10f winner and Group 3 third Streetcar To Stars (by Sea The Stars). The dam, a 7.5f (at 2 yrs) and Listed 10f winner, was second in a US Grade 2 event and the Group 3 May Hill Stakes and is a full or half-sister 7 winners including the French 2,000 Guineas and US Grade 1 winner Aussie Rules. The second dam, Last Second (by Alzao), a dual Group 2 10f winner and second in the Group 1 Coronation Stakes, is a half-sister to the dams of the Group 1 winners Albanova, Alborada, Allegretto, Yesterday and Quarter Moon. (Denford Stud). *"A nice type of filly that's grown a lot, she's a little unfurnished at this stage but has a good temperament. It's a good staying family".*

643. FRISELLA ★★★

b.f. Frankel – Panzanella (Dansili). April 11. Half-sister to the quite useful 2-y-o 7f winner Blending (by Medicean). The dam, a quite useful 7f winner, is a sister to the smart Group 3 10f winner of 3 races Remote and a half-sister to the high-class Group 1 1m Irish 2,000 Guineas, St James's Palace Stakes, Sussex Stakes and Prix Jacques le Marois winner Kingman. The second dam, Zenda (by Zamindar), won the French 1,000 Guineas, was second in the Coronation Stakes and the Grade 1 Queen Elizabeth II Challenge Cup at Keeneland and is a half-sister to the July Cup and Nunthorpe Stakes winner Oasis Dream and the dual Listed 1m winner Hopeful Light. (Khalid Abdullah). *"She canters fine, has no problems and I'm happy enough with her. A nice type for the mid-season onwards".*

644. FRONTMAN ★★★

b.c. Kingman – Winter Sunrise (Pivotal). March 2. Half-brother to the 7f (at 2 yrs) and Group 1 10f Nassau Stakes winner Winsili (by Dansili), to the quite useful 1m (at 2 yrs) and 10f winner Melting Dew (by Cacique) and a Listed 6f winner in Scandinavia by Oasis Dream. The dam, a useful dual 10f winner, is a half-sister to 5 winners including the Group 2 10f Prix Greffulhe winner Ice Blue. The second dam, Winter Solstice (by Unfuwain), a French 2-y-o 1m winner and second in the Group 3 1m Prix d'Aumale, is a half-sister to the Grade 1 Manhattan Handicap winner Meteor Storm, to the Group 2 12.5f Grand Prix de Deauville winner Polish Summer, the Group 3 2m winner Host Nation and the French 10f Listed winner Morning Eclipse. (Khalid Abdullah). *"He's a nice type of colt, he canters fine and I'm perfectly happy with him. One for the middle of the season to start with".*

645. FUGHETTA ★★★

br.f. Dubawi – The Fugue (Dansili). January 17. First foal. The dam was a top-class winner of 6 races including the Group 1 Prince Of Wales's Stakes, Nassau Stakes, Yorkshire Oaks and Irish Champion Stakes. She is a sister to one winner and a half-sister to another. The second dam, Twyla Tharp (by Sadler's Wells), a useful 9f winner and second in the Group 2 12f Ribblesdale Stakes, is a half-sister to 7 winners including the Group 1 winners Compton

Admiral and Summoner. *"She's an active filly, quite strong and 'together' with a lot of spirit about her. I can see her running over seven furlongs in mid-season".*

646. GANTIER ★★★

b.c. Frankel – Kid Gloves (In The Wings). March 9. Half-brother to 5 winners including the Group 2 12f Prix de Malleret and US Grade 2 11f Sheepshead Bay Stakes winner Treat Gently (by Cape Cross), the French 1m and 9f winner and Listed-placed Ideology, the French 7f winner Warm Hands (both by Oasis Dream) and the modest 6.5f to 10f winner of 4 races Handheld (by Observatory). The dam, a minor French 11f winner, is a half-sister to several winners and to the outstanding broodmare Hasili. The second dam, Kerali (by High Line), a quite useful 7f winner, is a half-sister to the Group 1 Nunthorpe Stakes winner So Factual and the Group 3 6f July Stakes winner Bold Fact. (Khalid Abdullah). *"He goes fine and is just cantering at the moment. A mid-season type 2-y-o for seven furlongs to begin with, he does everything OK and he's a pleasing colt to be around".*

647. GODHEAD ★★★★

b.c. Charm Spirit – Hello Glory (Zamindar). February 17. Second foal. 85,000Y. Tattersalls October Book 2. Blandford Bloodstock. The dam, a fairly useful 2-y-o 6f winner and third in the Group 2 Lowther Stakes, is closely related to the useful 2-y-o Listed 6f and 7f winner Bibury Flyer and the useful 10f and 11.8f winner Mojalid (both by Zafonic) and a half-sister to 8 winners. The second dam, Affair Of State (by Tate Gallery), a very useful Irish 2-y-o 6f winner, is a half-sister to 7 minor winners. *"He's settled in well, has a quick action and we're happy with him. We like both our Charm Spirits at this stage. A good-bodied horse and very active".*

648. GOLD STICK ★★★★

b.c. Dubawi – Gamilati (Bernardini). February 6. Second foal. Half-brother to the quite useful 2-y-o 6f winner Nasimi (by Shamardal). The dam won the 2-y-o Group 2 6f Cherry Hinton Stakes and UAE Listed 1m 1,000 Guineas and is a half-sister to the French 7f (at 2 yrs) and 6f winner and Listed-placed Late Romance. The second dam, Illustrious Miss (by Kingmambo),

a smart Group 3 7f Chartwell Stakes winner, was third in the Irish 1,000 Guineas and is a half-sister to 3 winners including the Grade 3 Regret Stakes and Grade 3 Lake George Handicap winner Nani Rose. *"He moves well, has a great attitude and has a good mind on him. He's grown recently but he looks a very nice colt for mid-season. A nice colt with quality".*

649. INFORMED FRONT ★★★

b.c. War Front – Informed Decision (Monarchos). March 9. Third foal. The dam won 10 races in the USA including three Grade 1's over 7f. (George Strawbridge). *"A lengthy colt with a good temperament and a nice action. He needs to strengthen but he's a pleasing colt at this stage and one for the middle of the season".*

650. INTRICATE ★★★★ ♠

b.f. Showcasing – Last Slipper (Tobougg). April 3. Fifth foal. 240,000Y. Tattersalls October Book 2. John & Jake Warren. Half-sister to the French 3-y-o 1m winner and German Listed-placed Slippers Best (by Mount Nelson). The dam is an unraced half-sister to 7 winners including the Listed winner Dansili Dancer. The second dam, Magic Slipper (by Habitat), a useful 10f and 11.5f winner, is a half-sister to 6 winners including the 1,000 Guineas winner Fairy Footsteps and the St Leger winner Light Cavalry. *"A racy, well-balanced, forward filly and a good mover. You'd have to think about her as a possible for Royal Ascot if she showed up in her work because she's very clued up. She has a good mind on her, we like her and she'll probably start out at six furlongs".*

651. INVALUABLE ★★★

b.f. Invincible Spirit – Prima Luce (Galileo). February 29. Sixth foal. €580,000Y. Goffs Orby. Cheveley Park Stud. Sister to the useful dual 7f winner at 2 and 3 yrs Emmaus (by Invincible Spirit) and half-sister to the quite useful dual 1m winner Dawn Mirage (by Oasis Dream). The dam, winner of the Group 3 7f Athasi Stakes and second in the Group 3 Solonaway Stakes, is a half-sister to 6 winners. The second dam, Ramona (by Desert King), is an unraced half-sister to 9 winners including the Group 2 5f Kings Stand Stakes winner Cassandra Go (herself dam of the triple Group 1 winner

Halfway To Heaven) and the smart Group 3 6f Coventry Stakes winner and Irish 2,000 Guineas second Verglas. *"A good-bodied, athletic filly in her exercise and she looks a nice type for mid-season".*

652. JADEERAH ★★★★

b.f. Frankel – Maqaasid (Green Desert). January 26. Fourth foal. Half-sister to the 2017 2-y-o 7f winner, from two starts, Nawassi (by Dubawi). The dam, a very useful 2-y-o Group 2 5f Queen Mary Stakes winner, was third in the Group 1 6f Cheveley Park Stakes. The second dam, Eshaadeh (by Storm Cat), unplaced in 2 starts, is a half-sister to 7 winners including the 1,000 Guineas and Coronation Stakes winner Ghanaati and the Group 3 12f Cumberland Lodge Stakes winner Mawatheeq. (Hamdan Al Maktoum). *"She's done everything fine so far and we're happy with her. She's strong with a good action and is very competitive. Quite a sharp type like her mother who won the Queen Mary".*

653. JAHAFIL ★★★

b.f. Kingman – Taghrooda (Sea The Stars). February 25. First foal. The dam, a 1m (at 2 yrs), Group 1 12f Epsom Oaks and Group 1 12f King George VI winner, is a sister to one winner. The second dam, Ezima (by Sadler's Wells), a smart 1m, Listed 10f and Listed 12f winner, is a full or half-sister to 3 winners including the Listed placed Ezalli. (Hamdan Al Maktoum). *"A nice filly that's strengthening all the time, she'll be one for September time like her dam".*

654. KESTA ★★★★

ch.f. Australia – Caserta (Dansili). January 10. Second foal. 300,000 foal. Tattersalls December. Blandford Bloodstock. The dam, a French 1m and 9.5f winner, is a half-sister to 7 winners including the French Listed winner Destruct and the Group 3 Musidora Stakes second Quickfire. The second dam, Daring Miss (by Sadler's Wells), won 4 races in France including the Group 2 12f Grand Prix de Chantilly and is a half-sister to 5 winners including the Group 3 12f Prix de Royaumont winner Apogee. (George Strawbridge). *"A straightforward, strong-bodied, very nice filly that goes well. She's a quality filly and we're very happy with her".*

655. KING OF COMEDY (IRE) ★★★ ♠

b.c. Kingman – Stage Presence (Selkirk). May 16. Half-brother to the Group 1 10.5f Prix de Diane winner Star Of Seville (by Duke Of Marmalade), to the Group 3 7f Sweet Solera Stakes winner and Group 1 Fillies' Mile third English Ballet (by Danehill Dancer), the useful triple 1m winner Sacred Act (by Oasis Dream) and the quite useful 2-y-o 5f winner Spectacular Show (by Spectrum). The dam, a quite useful 7f and 1m winner, is a half-sister to 5 winners including the 6f (at 2 yrs) and Group 3 7f Ballycorus Stakes winner Rum Charger. The second dam, Park Charger (by Tirol), a useful winner over 1m and 10f at 3 yrs in Ireland, was Listed-placed 4 times and is a half-sister to 9 winners. *"An active, likeable colt and a good mover, there's quite a bit of 'get up and go' about him. He's one for mid-season onwards".*

656. LENYA ★★★

gr.f. Dark Angel – Lixirova (Slickly). April 4. Fourth foal. Half-sister to the quite useful dual 1m winner Mudallel (by Invincible Spirit). The dam won 3 races in France at 2 yrs including the Group 3 7f Prix Miesque and is a half-sister to 2 winners. The second dam, Linorova (by Trempolino), is an unraced half-sister to 5 winners. *"An angular sort of filly, she goes nicely on the canters and I see her being out around June time hopefully".*

657. LYRA'S LIGHT ★★★

b.f. Lope De Vega – Diamond Sky (Montjeu). March 17. Second foal. 360,000Y. Tattersalls October Book 1. Cheveley Park Stud. Half-sister to the unplaced 2017 2-y-o Faughill (by Lawman). The dam was second in the 2-y-o Group 2 Debutante Stakes in Ireland and is a sister to the fairly useful Scandinavian dual Group 3 and Chester Listed 13f winner Berling and a half-sister to 3 winners including the Group 1 Dewhurst Stakes and Group 1 Lockinge Stakes winner Belardo. The second dam, Danaskaya (by Danehill), a useful Irish 2-y-o 6f winner and third in the Group 1 6f Cheveley Park Stakes, is a half-sister to 7 winners including the triple Listed 7f winner Modeeroch. *"A close coupled filly that goes nicely, we're happy with her".*

658. MARHABA MILLIAR ★★★
b.c. Kodiac – Lady Of The Desert (Rahy).
January 31. Third foal. Half-brother to the
smart 2-y-o Group 2 6f Lowther Stakes and
3-y-o Listed 6f winner Queen Kindly (by
Frankel). The dam, a Group 2 6f Lowther
Stakes, Group 3 6f Princess Margaret Stakes
and Group 2 6f Diadem Stakes winner, is a
half-sister to 6 winners including the fairly
useful dual 10f winner Prince Of Stars. The
second dam, Queen's Logic (by Grand Lodge),
a champion 2-y-o filly and winner of the
Group 1 6f Cheveley Park Stakes and the
Group 2 6f Lowther Stakes, is a half-sister to
6 winners including the top-class multiple
Group 1 winner Dylan Thomas. *"He's quite a
nice type that goes well. A likeable, well-made
athletic colt with a good attitude".*

659. MARY SOMERVILLE ★★★
ch.f. Galileo – Maureen (Holy Roman
Emperor). March 12. First foal. 800,000Y.
Tattersalls October Book 1. Godolphin. The
dam, a Group 3 6f Princess Margaret Stakes
and Group 3 Fred Darling Stakes winner, was
second in the Group 2 Cherry Hinton Stakes
and is a half-sister to 4 winners. The second
dam, Exotic Mix (by Linamix), placed once at 3
yrs in France, is a full or half-sister to 8 winners
including the Group winners Spinola and Shot
To Fame. *"We like her, she's done everything
fine so far and is nicely proportioned with a
good action. She's been a straightforward filly
and will make a 2-y-o a bit later on".*

660. MAXIMUM EFFECT ★★★★
ch.f. Iffraaj – Dubai Bounty (Dubai
Destination). February 6. Third foal. 120,000Y.
Tattersalls October Book 2. Hugo Lascelles.
Half-sister to the Group 3 5f Molecomb Stakes
winner (at 2 yrs) and Group 1 Commonwealth
Cup second Kachy (by Kyllachy). The dam,
a fair 8.5f (at 2 yrs) to 12.5f winner, is a half-
sister to one winner. The second dam, Mary
Read (by Bahamian Bounty), a useful 2-y-o
dual 5f winner, was second in the Group 3
Molecomb Stakes and is a full or half-sister
to 8 winners. *"She's a strong filly and she's
done very well since she's been with us. She
could well be starting over six furlongs because
there's speed on the dam's side and she's very
'together' with a good, positive attitude".*

661. MILLICENT FAWCETT ★★★
b.f. Kingman – Mainstay (Elmaamul). March
7. Half-sister to the Group 2 7f Hungerford
Stakes winner of 3 races Richard Pankhurst
(by Raven's Pass) and to the 2-y-o Group 3
7f Horris Hill Stakes winner of 3 races Crazy
Horse (by Sleeping Indian). The dam, a quite
useful 1m winner, is a sister to the 1m (at 2
yrs), Group 3 9f Prix Daphnis and Listed 10.5f
winner Lateen Sails and a half-sister to 3 minor
winners here and abroad. The second dam,
Felucca (by Green Desert), a fairly useful 2-y-o
6f winner, is a half-sister to 5 winners including
the Group 2 10f Prix Eugene Adam winner
Radevore. (Rachel D S Hood). *"Owned by my
wife and named after a suffragette whose
statue has just been erected in Parliament
Square. This is a nice filly and I can see her
being out around July time over seven furlongs.
She goes well".*

662. MISS MOROCCO ★★★
b.f. Nathaniel – Morocco Moon (Rock Of
Gibraltar). February 9. First foal. The dam, a
quite useful dual 5f winner, is a half-sister to 2
winners. The second dam, One Giant Leap (by
Pivotal), a modest 7f winner, is a half-sister to
9 winners including the useful 2-y-o Group 3
7f C L Weld Park Stakes winner Rag Top and
the dam of the 2-y-o Listed winner Elhamri.
(Lady Bamford). *"A strong, good-bodied filly
and a nice mover that covers a lot of ground. A
nice type of filly".*

663. OUSELL FALLS ★★★
b.f. Invincible Spirit – Too The Stars (Sea The
Stars). January 29. First foal. The dam, a fair
2-y-o 10f winner, is a half-sister to 2 winners
including the 2-y-o Group 2 1m Beresford
Stakes winner Ol' Man River. The second dam,
Finsceal Beo (by Mr Greeley), winner of the
Prix Marcel Boussac, 1,000 Guineas and Irish
1,000 Guineas, is a half-sister to the German
Group 2 1m winner Frozen Power. (George
Strawbridge). *"A nice filly that goes well, she
has a good attitude and a good stride on her.
She won't be early but she's a likeable filly for
June/July".*

664. PRIVATE SECRETARY ★★★
b.c. Kingman – Intrigued (Darshaan). March
20. Ninth foal. Half-brother to 5 winners
including the Listed 11f winner and Group 1

St Leger third Michelangelo, the fairly useful triple 12f winner No Heretic, the fair 14f winner Blue Chip (all by Galileo) and the fair 8.5f winner All The Rage (by Dubawi). The dam, a very useful Listed-placed 2-y-o 8.5f winner, is a sister to the Listed 10f winner and US Grade 2 second Approach (dam of the Group 2 Irish Derby Trial winner Midas Touch) and a half-sister to the French 2,000 Guineas and US Grade 1 winner Aussie Rules. The second dam, Last Second (by Alzao), won the 10f Nassau Stakes and the 10f Sun Chariot Stakes and is a half-sister to the dams of the Group 1 winners Albanova, Alborada, Allegretto, Yesterday and Quarter Moon. *"A medium-sized, very straightforward colt that canters fine".*

665. PROMISSORY ★★★
b.f. Dubawi – Seal Of Approval (Authorized). February 20. First foal. 1,100,000Y. Tattersalls October Book 1. Godolphin. The dam won four races including the Group 1 12f British Champions Fillies/Mare Stakes and is a half-sister to 4 winners including the French Listed 2m winner Gale Force. The second dam, Hannda (by Dr Devious), a winner over 10f in Ireland from 2 starts, is a half-sister to 5 winners including the Group 3 7.5f Concorde Stakes winner Hamairi and the Listed 6f winner Hanabad. *"A nice, quality filly out of a mare that stayed well, she's a bit weak at this stage so we'll give her time. There's some quality there".*

666. QUESTIONARE ★★★
b.c. Galileo – Dream Peace (Dansili). February 17. The dam, a Group 2 10f Prix de la Nonette winner, was Grade 1 placed three times in North America and is a half-sister to French 2,000 Guineas second Catcher In The Rye. The second dam, Truly A Dream (by Darshaan), won the Grade 2 10f E P Taylor Stakes and is a half-sister to 7 winners including the Group 2 winner Wareed and the good broodmare Solo de Lune (dam of the Group 1 winners Moonstone and Cerulean Sky). (Lady Bamford). *"A good mover, he's a strong colt and not the biggest but he moves well and has a nice attitude".*

667. SHAMBOLIC ★★★
b.f. Shamardal – Comic (Be My Chief). March

12. Half-sister to 7 winners including the US dual Grade 1 winner Laughing (by Dansili), the Listed winner of 5 races here and Hong Kong dual Grade 1 winner Viva Pataca (by Marju), the quite useful 10f to 14f and hurdles winner Comedy Act (by Motivator) and the fair 2-y-o 8.5f winner Nice Future (by Dubawi),. The dam, a quite useful 10f and 11.5f winner, is a half-sister to 4 winners including the 2-y-o Group 3 Solario Stakes and multiple US Grade 2 winner Brave Act. The second dam, Circus Act (by Shirley Heights), is an unraced sister to the Listed winner Lady Shipley and a half-sister to the Listed winner Ellie Ardensky. (Duke Of Devonshire). *"A nice, promising filly that moves well and has a good attitude. I can see her running in mid-season".*

668. SHE'S GOT YOU ★★★
b.f. Kingman – Without You Babe (Lemon Drop Kid). May 3. Half-sister to the 2017 2-y-o 1m debut winner Without Parole (by Frankel) and to the Grade 1 Breeders Cup Dirt Mile and UAE triple Group 3 winner Tamarkuz (by Speightstown). The dam is an unraced half-sister to 7 winners including the stakes winners and Grade 1 placed Andromeda's Hero, Stay Thirsty and Superfly. The second dam, Morozia (by Storm Bird), a fair 12f winner, is a half-sister to 4 winners. *"A nice, racy filly, we like her and she's done very well. Good tempered and plenty to like about her".*

669. SPANISH ARIA ★★★
b.f. Lope De Vega – Woodland Aria (Singspiel). January 29. First foal. The dam, a useful 7f and 9.5f winner, was third in the Group 3 Musidora Stakes and is a half-sister to the Group 1 Eclipse Stakes, Group 2 York Stakes and Group 3 Brigadier Gerard Stakes winner Mukhadram. The second dam, Magic Tree (by Timber Country), ran once unplaced and is a half-sister to the Group 1 winner Gran Criterium winner Kirklees and the St Leger winner Mastery. *"She canters well, shows quite a fiery temperament and is medium-sized, nice type of filly".*

670. VALENTINE'S DAY ★★★
b.f. Galileo – L'Amour De Ma Vie (Dansili). February 12. First foal. €1,200,000Y. Goffs Orby. Godolphin. The dam won 3 races in France and the UAE including the Group 2

9f Balanchine Stakes, was Group 2 placed twice and is a half-sister to the US Grade 2 and Grade 3 winner Scuba. The second dam, Cuaba (by Smoke Glacken), won four races in the USA and was Grade 2 placed. *"She's a nice, quality filly for the autumn and for middle-distances at three".*

671. VANDELLA ★★★★
b.f. Invincible Spirit – Lady Livius (Titus Livius). April 14. Eighth foal. 280,000Y. Tattersalls October Book 1. Blandford Bloodstock. Half-sister to the smart 2-y-o Group 3 7f Sirenia Stakes winner Burnt Sugar (by Lope De Vega), to the 2-y-o Group 3 5f Molecomb Stakes and Group 3 Sirenia Stakes winner Brown Sugar (by Tamayuz), the quite useful 6f (at 2 yrs) and 7f winner Elle Woods and the minor French 4-y-o winner Widyaan (both by Lawman). The dam, a fairly useful 5f winner of 3 races from 2 to 4 yrs, is a half-sister to 5 winners including the Group 2 6f Mill Reef Stakes winner and Group 1 placed Galeota. The second dam, Refined (by Statoblest), a fairly useful dual 5f winner, is a half-sister to 6 winners including Pipe Major (Group 3 7f Criterion Stakes). *"An active filly with a good stride, she's quite forward and I can see her being out in May. A nice type".*

672. VEGTINA ★★★
b.f. Lope De Vega – Valtina (Teofilo). January 26. First foal. 220,000Y. Tattersalls October Book 1. Blandford Bloodstock. The dam, a quite useful 1m winner, is a half-sister to 5 winners including the Group 3 Phoenix Sprint Stakes winner Girouette, the Group 3 second Prince d'Alienor and the Listed-placed Paraphernalia. The second dam, Vassiana (by Anabaa), a Listed-placed French 3-y-o winner, is a sister to the Group 3 Prix d'Arenburg winner Villadolide and to the French dual Listed winner Victorieux. *"Straightforward, she does everything fine and is a medium-sized filly for July and seven furlongs".*

673. WHIMBREL ★★★★
gr.f. Dark Angel – Seagull (Sea The Stars). February 7. First foal. €375,000Y. Goffs Orby. Godolphin. The dam, a quite useful 12f winner, is a half-sister to 7 winners including the Irish 1,000 Guineas winner Nightime (dam of the Grade 1 Man O'War Stakes winner Zhukova).

The second dam, Caumshinaun (by Indian Ridge), won 5 races from 6f to 1m in Ireland at 3 and 4 yrs including a Listed event and is a half-sister to one winner. *"A nice filly, she's well-balanced and moves well. A good type, I'd love to have her out in May".*

674. WHITE COAT ★★★
gr.c. Dansili – Clinical (Motivator). February 20. Half-brother to the fair 2017 6f placed 2-y-o Procedure (by Invincible Spirit) and to the useful 2-y-o 7f winner and Group 1 National Stakes third Lockheed (by Exceed And Excel). The dam, a very useful Group 3 9f and triple Listed 1m winner, is a half-sister to 9 winners including the smart Group 3 7f Horris Hill Stakes winner of 7 races Cupid's Glory, the Listed 1m and 10f winner of 6 races Courting and the fairly useful Listed 6f winner of 5 races Prescription. The second dam, Doctor's Glory (by Elmaamul), a fairly useful 5.2f (at 2 yrs) and 6f winner, is a half-sister to 6 winners. (Cheveley Park Stud). *"A good-topped colt that looks a mid-season type, especially judging by his sire. He's done nothing wrong and goes nicely in his canters".*

675. WILL OF IRON ★★★
b.c. Invincible Spirit – Astronomy Domine (Galileo). April 4. Third foal. Half-brother to the fairly useful 2-y-o 7f winner and 3-y-o 10f Listed-placed Astronomy's Choice (by Redoute's Choice). The dam, unplaced on her only start, is a half-sister to 4 winners including Pacifique (Group 3 Prix du Lutece) and the Listed winner Prudenzia (dam of the Irish Oaks winner Chicquita). The second dam, Platonic (by Zafonic), a minor winner in France, is a half-sister to 7 winners including the Group 2 Lancashire Oaks winner Pongee. *"He's growing and filling out his frame, canters fine at this stage and has a good temperament".*

676. UNNAMED ★★★
gr.f. Kingman – Cozy Maria (Cozzene). February 21. Closely related to the 2-y-o Group 2 5f Flying Childers Stakes and Group 3 5f Molecomb Stakes winner of 6 races Zebedee and to the fair 2-y-o 7f winner Auntinet (both by Invincible Spirit) and half-sister to the fair 7f winner Pategonia (by Oasis Dream) and a jumps winner by

Authorized. The dam, a useful 10f winner, was Listed-placed twice and is a half-sister to 7 winners. The second dam, Mariamme (by Verbatim), won twice at 3 yrs in the USA and is a half-sister to 7 winners including the Grade 1 Breeders' Cup Turf winner Miss Alleged. *"A racy, nice type of filly, we're happy with her. She's got good depth and a nice action"*.

677. UNNAMED ★★★★★
gr.c. Kitten's Joy – Cozzy Street (Street Cry). February 9. First foal. $435,000Y. Keeneland September. Godolphin. The dam was placed at 4 yrs in the USA and is a half-sister to one winner. The second dam, Real Cozzy (by Cozzene), won the Grade 2 Fairgrounds Oaks and was Grade 1 placed three times. *"A grand colt, we like him and he does everything very comfortably. He looks a nice horse that should start his career in mid-season, has a good temperament and I'd be disappointed if he doesn't make up into a nice horse"*.

678. UNNAMED ★★★ ♠
b.f. No Nay Never – Danehill's Dream (Danehill). February 9. Eighth foal. 155,000Y. Tattersalls October Book 1. Blandford Bloodstock. Half-sister to the fairly useful Listed-placed 12f to 14f winner of 6 races Viking Storm (by Hurricane Run), to the quite useful 11f winner Maldowney (by Dalakhani) and the fair dual 1m winner at 2 and 3 yrs Dream Of Summer (by Canford Cliffs). The dam is an unraced sister to the 2-y-o winner and Group 1 Criterium de Saint-Cloud second Summerland and a half-sister to 2 minor winners. The second dam, Summerosa (by Woodman), a fair 3-y-o 8.5f winner, is a half-sister to 4 winners including the Group 1 Racing Post Trophy third Zind and to the unraced dam of the Derby winner Dr Devious. *"A well-grown filly, a little bit backward at this stage but a nice filly for the future"*.

679. UNNAMED ★★★
b.f. Galileo – Dank (Dansili). March 4. First foal. 4,000,000Y. Tattersalls October Book 1. Godolphin. The dam won 7 races including the Grade 1 Beverly D Stakes and the Grade 1 Breeders' Cup Filly and Mare Turf and is a half-sister to 5 winners including the 2-y-o Group 1 1m Prix Marcel Boussac winner and triple Group 1 placed Sulk and the Group 1

10f Hong Kong Cup and dual Group 2 winner Eagle Mountain. The second dam, Masskana (by Darshaan), a minor 9f and 10f winner, is a half-sister to 3 winners including Massyar (Group 2 Gallinule Stakes) and Madjaristan (Grade 3 Arcadia Handicap). *"A lovely filly and a good mover with a good attitude, she's grown a fair bit and will be a late summer or autumn filly over seven furlongs plus"*.

680. UNNAMED ★★★
b.c. Dubawi – Dar Re Mi (Singspiel). March 27. Fifth foal. Brother to the very smart 1m (at 2 yrs) and Group 3 10.5f Musidora Stakes winner and Group 1 Prix de l'Opera third So Mi Dar and half-brother to the 7f (at 2 yrs) and 10f winner and multiple Group 3 placed De Treville (by Oasis Dream). The dam won the Pretty Polly Stakes, Dubai Sheema Classic and Yorkshire Oaks (all Group 1 events) and is a half-sister to 9 winners including the Group 1 winners Rewilding, Diaghilev and Darazari. The second dam, Darara (by Top Ville), won the Group 1 Prix Vermeille and is a half-sister to 11 winners including the French Derby winner and high-class sire Darshaan. *"He's going along fine but he hasn't arrived here from pre-training yet so I can't say a lot about him"*.

681. UNNAMED ★★★ ♠
b.c. Australia – Dorothy B (Fastnet Rock). January 18. First foal. 350,000Y. Tattersalls October Book 2. Blandford Bloodstock. The dam, a very useful Listed-placed 2-y-o 6f winner, is a half-sister to 3 winners. The second dam, Slow Sand (by Dixieland Band), ran twice unplaced and is a half-sister to 5 winners including the French Derby 3 and Listed winner Slow Pace. *"A nice colt, he's well-balanced and a good mover. A strong colt, I'm pleased with him and I can see him being out in mid-season over seven furlongs"*.

682. UNNAMED ★★★★
b.f. Iffraaj – Ego (Green Desert). March 6. Tenth living foal. Half-sister to 8 winners including the useful 7f (at 2 yrs) and 1m winner and Listed-placed Chef, the fair 7f winner I'm Sensational (both by Selkirk), the quite useful Listed-placed 2-y-o 7f winner Self Centred (by Medicean), the quite useful 7f and 1m winner Simply Me (by New Approach) and

the fair 7f winner of 4 races (including at 2 yrs) Cut And Thrust (by Haafhd). The dam, a dual Listed-placed 2-y-o dual 6f winner, is a half-sister to 3 winners. The second dam, Myself (by Nashwan), won the Group 3 7f Nell Gwyn Stakes and is a half-sister to 12 winners including the Group 3 Princess Margaret Stakes winner Bluebook. *"A very well-balanced, good-moving filly with a good attitude. I would hope that she could run in May or June. A nice type".*

683. UNNAMED ★★★
b.c. Noble Mission – Fashion Insider (Indian Charlie). March 11. Third foal. $85,000Y. Keeneland September. Not sold. Half-brother to the fair 7f winner Secret Insider (by Elusive Quality). The dam, placed over 1m at 2 yrs from two starts here, won minor races at 3 and 4 yrs in the USA and is a half-sister to 6 winners including the US Grade 2 Amsterdam Stakes winner Bwana Charlie, the US Grade 2 Super Derby winner My Pal Charlie (both by Indian Charlie), the US Grade 3 winner Bwana Bull (by Holy Bull) and the US stakes-placed winner Ten Halos (by Marquetry). The second dam, Shahalo (by Halo), was unplaced in 2 starts. *"Owned by myself and three mates, this is a very good-looking colt and a good walker. A lovely horse for the second half of the season and we're pleased with him at this stage".*

684. UNNAMED ★★★
gr.f. Mastercraftsman – Front House (Sadler's Wells). February 20. Sixth foal. 180,000Y. Tattersalls October Book 2. Blandford Bloodstock. Half-sister to the fair 1m winners Balcony and Casla (both by Fastnet Rock). The dam, a South African and UAE Grade 2 12f winner, is a half-sister to 7 winners including the Listed Marble Hill Stakes and Group 1 Phoenix Stakes second Access All Areas. The second dam, Adjalisa (by Darshaan), was placed once over 7f at 5 yrs and is a half-sister to 5 winners including the Irish Listed winner and Group 1 placed Adjareli. *"She's done very well, she's got a good attitude and moves well. A very likeable individual for seven furlongs from mid-season onwards".*

685. UNNAMED ★★★
ch.c. Pivotal – Gull Wing (In The Wings). April 14. Brother to the high-class Group 2

12f King Edward VII Stakes winner Eagle Top, to the Group 2 10.5f Dante Stakes winner and Group 1 King George VI fourth Wings Of Desire and the very useful 1m (at 2 yrs) and Group 2 Park Hill Stakes winner The Lark. The dam, a 10f and Listed 14f winner, is a half-sister to the 7f (at 2 yrs), Epsom Oaks and Irish Oaks winner Sariska. The second dam, Maycocks Bay (by Muhtarram), a useful 14f Listed winner, is a half-sister to several winners including the useful 7f and 1m winner (at 2 yrs) and Listed 10.3f placed 3-y-o Indian Light. (Lady Bamford). *"A lovely model of a colt, he's a lovely horse to be around and we know the family very well. It's going to be all about the autumn and next year for him but he's got quality".*

686. UNNAMED ★★★
b.c. Dansili – Igugu (Galileo). February 18. The dam won 10 races in South Arica including four Group 1's from 9f to 11f and is a half-sister to the Australian Group 3 10f winner Honorius. *"A nice type of colt out of a very tough racemare, he's one for mid-season over seven furlongs".*

687. UNNAMED ★★★★★
b.br.c. War Front – Lerici (Woodman). April 28. Eighth foal. $995,000Y. Godolphin. Brother to the US Grade 1 Rodeo Drive Stakes winner Avenge and half-brother to 4 winners including the US Listed winner Lira (by Giant's Causeway). The second dam, Balinese (by Nijinsky), a minor dual winner in the USA, is a sister to the St Leger winner Mashaallah and the US Grade 1 winner Folk Art. *"He's a nice type of colt, he's strong, moves well and we're happy with him. He's got some class and quality about him".*

688. UNNAMED ★★★ ♠
b.c. Frankel – Marine Bleue (Desert Prince). April 7. Eighth foal. Half-brother to 5 winners including the French Listed 12f winner Marina Piccola (by Halling), the quite useful 2-y-o 6f winner and UAE Group 3 1m third Wednaan (by Dubawi) and the fair 10f winner Adalene (by Makfi). The dam, a German Group 3 and Listed 1m winner at 3 yrs, is a half-sister to 5 winners including the French Listed winner Mystic Spirit. The second dam, Mirina (by Pursuit Of Love), a minor French 3-y-o winner,

is a half-sister to 6 winners including the dam of the Group 1 Grand Prix de Paris winner Mirio. *"A nice type for the second half of the season".*

689. UNNAMED ★★★
b.c. Holy Roman Emperor – Midnight Partner (Marju). April 17. Tenth foal. 210,000Y. Tattersalls October Book 1. China Horse Club. Half-brother to 8 winners including the US Grade 3 winner Lilbourne Eliza (by Elusive City), the fair 2-y-o 1m winner Escholido (by Noverre), the modest 9f and 10f winner of four races Buona Sarah (by Bertolini) and the German and Italian Listed-placed Terre Neuve (by Verglas). The dam is an unraced half-sister to the winner of 5 races and Group 1 Criterium International second Top Seed. The second dam, Midnight Heights (by Persian Heights), an Italian dual Listed winner, was second in the Group 2 10f Premio Lydia Tesio and is a half-sister to the Group 3 Sandown Classic Trial winner Galitzin. *"Quite a forward, active colt and I'd like to have him out in May".*

690. UNNAMED ★★★
b.c. Australia – Nobilis (Rock Of Gibraltar). January 22. Second foal. The dam, a 3-y-o winner in France and placed in the Group 2 Prix de Malleret and Group 3 Prix Minerve, is a half-sister to 4 winners including the Group 2 Lonsdale Cup second Drill Sergeant. The second dam, Dolydille (by Dolphin Street), won 7 races including two Listed events from 9f to 12f and is a half-sister to 9 winners including the Irish Listed 1m winner La Meilleure (the dam of four stakes winners). (China Horse Club). *"A likeable, active colt that moves well".*

691. UNNAMED ★★★
b.c. Kodiac – Querulous (Raven's Pass). April 24. Second foal. 100,000Y. Tattersalls October Book 2. Not sold. Brother to the unraced 2017 2-y-o Breaking Records. The dam is an unraced half-sister to one minor winner in the USA. The second dam, Contentious (by Giant's Causeway), a useful 1m winner and Listed placed here, subsequently won in the USA at 4 yrs, was Group 3 placed in Germany and is a half-sister to the US dual Grade 2 winner Gone Astray. *"He's active, strong, uncomplicated and*

forward-going. He gets on with the job and should be starting his career over five furlongs".

692. UNNAMED ★★★
b.c. Dubawi – Tasaday (Nayef). February 28. First foal. The dam, winner of the Group 2 12f Prix de la Nonette, the Group 3 1m Prix des Reservoirs and Group 3 10f Prix de Psyche, is a half-sister to the Group 3 1m Desmond Stakes winner Tribal Beat. The second dam, Tashelka (by Mujahid), a dual Group 3 10f winner in France, is a half-sister to 4 winners including the Listed 1m winner Tashkandi. *"A nice colt, he's active, a good mover and has a lovely mind on him. One for July onwards I'd say".*

693. UNNAMED ★★★
b.f. Kingman – The Gold Cheongsam (Red Clubs). January 22. First foal. The dam, a useful Listed-placed 6f and 7f winner of 4 races at 2 and 3 yrs, is a half-sister to one winner. The second dam, Fuerta Ventura (by Desert Sun), a useful Listed-placed Irish 1m to 9.5f winner of 3 races, and is a half-sister to 3 winners including the useful 2-y-o Listed 6f winner and Group 2 6f Mill Reef Stakes second Sir Xaar. *"She's a nice, active filly and I'm happy with her".*

694. UNNAMED ★★★
gr.f. Dark Angel – Umneeyatee (Encosta De Lago). February 19. Second foal. Half-sister to the fair 2017 7f placed 2-y-o Taghee (by Acclamation). The dam is a half-sister to 3 winners including South African Grade 2 1m winner Amanee. The second dam, Moon Is Up (by Woodman), a Listed 1m winner and Group 3 placed in France, is closely related to the French 2,000 Guineas, the St James's Palace Stakes and Prix du Moulin winner Kingmambo and the smart Group 3 6f winner Miesque's Son and a half-sister to the high-class triple Group 1 winner East of the Moon. *"A nice, athletic type, she's improved physically and looks to be fairly forward".*

RAE GUEST
695. BRICKLEBRIT ★★
ch.f. Sir Percy – Blush's Gift (Cadeaux Genereux). February 20. Second foal. 7,000Y. Tattersalls October Book 3. Rae Guest Racing. The dam is an unraced sister to the Listed winner Rambling Rose (herself dam of the

triple Group 1 winner and sire Notnowcato) and a half-sister to 7 winners. The second dam, Blush Rambler (by Blushing Groom), a 12f winner in Ireland, is a half-sister to 5 winners. (Mr Enno Albert). *"She didn't cost a lot of money but like all Sir Percy fillies she's a little bit small, but she's got a lot of character, moves well and is going well. She won't be running until later in the season over seven furlongs, but she hasn't had any problems so we're pleased with her".*

696. DEPTFORD MICK (IRE) ★★★

br.c. Bated Breath – Be Joyful (Teofilo). April 5. Third foal. 11,000Y. Tattersalls October Book 3. Rae Guest. Half-brother to the quite useful 2-y-o 7f winner Time Zone (by Kheleyf). The dam is an unraced half-sister to 8 winners the smart 6f (at 2 yrs) and Listed 8.3f winner Army Of Angels, the Group 1 Lowther Stakes second Seraphina and the dam of the dual Group 1 winner Serious Attitude. The second dam, Angelic Sounds (by The Noble Player), a minor 2-y-o 5f winner, is a half-sister to 8 winners including the Group 1 Prix de la Foret winner Mount Abu. (Mr Derek J. Willis). *"A very nice colt, he's big but not backward and this is a family we know very well. He wasn't expensive and he's grown into a nice horse now so we're very pleased with him. He's got a lucky owner so he's got a lot going for him and he'll be one for six furlongs in mid-season to start with".* TRAINER'S BARGAIN BUY

697. DIVIDING LINE ★★

b.c. Heeraat – Elfine (Invincible Spirit). April 25. Fourth foal. Half-brother to the fair 5f and 6f winner Defining Moment (by Camacho). The dam, a fair 1m (at 2 yrs) and 10f placed maiden, is a half-sister to 3 winners. The second dam, Donnelly's Hollow (by Docksider), a modest 1m placed Irish maiden, is a half-sister to 5 winners including the Group 1 12f Italian Derby winner and King George VI and Queen Elizabeth Stakes second White Muzzle and the Group 2 German St Leger winner Fair Question and the Listed 10f winner Elfaslah (dam of the Dubai World Cup winner Almutawakel). (Mr Derek J. Willis). *"By a first season sire whose yearlings sold very well, we've got a half-sister to him, Defining Moment, that's won a couple of races and is fast. So this colt should be fast too, but he was*

a fairly late foal and at the moment he's a big, gangly, backward horse. So it might take a bit of time before the penny drops".

698. FEEL THE NOIZE ★★★

br.f. Slade Power – Sugar Free (Oasis Dream). February 12. Sixth foal. 14,000Y. Tattersalls October Book 3. Storm Again Syndicate. Half-sister to the fair Irish 1m winner Calorie (by Sea The Stars) and to the modest 2-y-o dual 5f winner True Course (by Dubawi). The dam, a useful Listed 5f winner and third in the Group 3 Flying Five is a sister to one winner and a half-sister to 4 winners including the useful 1m (at 2 yrs) and 9f winner High Twelve. The second dam, Much Faster (by Fasliyev), won the Group 2 6f Prix Robert Papin and the Group 3 5f Prix du Bois, was second in the Group 1 Prix Morny and is a half-sister to 5 winners. (The Storm Again Syndicate). *"A very nice filly from the first crop of her sire, she's out of a Listed winning mare who had previously visited stallions with a lot more stamina than Slade Power. So hopefully this will be a good cross. One for mid-season, I'm very pleased with her and she looks a nice 2-y-o type for five furlongs".*

699. UNNAMED ★★

b.f. Roderic O'Connor – California Rose (Oratorio). April 15. Second foal. 4,000Y. Tattersalls October Book 3. Rae Guest. The dam, a moderate Irish 1m and 8.5f winner of 3 races at 3 and 4 yrs, is a half-sister to 3 other minor winners. The second dam, Asi (by El Prado), won once at 3 yrs in France and is a sister to the US Grade 1 winner Asi Siempre (herself dam of the Grade 1 winner Outstrip) and a half-sister to 3 winners. *"A nice filly we got very cheap, she was a fairly late foal and is going to take some time. I like Oratorio as a broodmare stallion because everything we've had out of an Oratorio mare has done well. She's a sprinter but she's not going to be early".*

700. UNNAMED ★★

b.c. Camelot – Gaselee (Toccet). April 11. Fourth foal. Half-brother to the minor French 10.5f winner Millepassi (by Holy Roman Emperor). The dam, a fair 9f and 2m winner, is a half-sister to 4 winners including the very useful 12f winners Sayadaw and Year Two Thousand. The second dam, Vingt Et Une (by

Sadler's Wells), a minor French 3-y-o winner, is a sister to the very useful Group 1 10.5f Prix Lupin and US Grade 2 1m winner Johann Quatz and to the smart French 10.5f to 13.5f Listed winner Walter Willy and a half-sister to the top-class middle-distance colt Hernando, winner of the Group 1 Prix du Jockey Club and Group 1 Prix Lupin. (Paul Smith & Rae Guest). *"A very nice horse, he looks the part but he's backward and immature. The dam didn't do anything until she got a trip and this colt will want middle distances in time too. Hopefully we'll get a run or two out of him this year but he's a very nice horse and one we'll be looking forward to being a half decent 3-y-o".*

701. UNNAMED ★★★

b.f. Born To Sea – Rhapsodize (Halling). April 20. Eighth foal. 6,000Y. Tattersalls October Book 3. Rae Guest. Half-sister to 6 winners including the quite useful triple 1m winner Lawmans Thunder (by Lawman), the fair 5f winner Nawarah (by Acclamation), the modest triple 5f winner (including at 2 yrs) Melodize (by Iceman) and the moderate 7f (at 2 yrs) and dual 1m winner Improvized (by Authorized). The dam is an unraced half-sister to 6 winners including the Group 1 Cheveley Park Stakes winner Hooray and the useful 2-y-o Listed 8.3f winner Hypnotic. The second dam, Hypnotize (by Machiavellian), a useful 2-y-o Listed 7f winner, is closely related to 2 winners including Dazzle (Group 3 6f Cherry Hinton Stakes) and a half-sister to 6 winners including the useful 1m Listed winner Fantasize. (The Reprobates). *"Another one we bought cheaply at the sales, she's doing very well and has grown quite a bit since we bought her. She moves well and will want six/seven furlongs in mid-season. I think she'll win this year but a bit later on".*

702. UNNAMED ★★★

b.f. Bated Breath – Ruffled (Harlan's Holiday). April 10. Second foal. Half-sister to the quite useful 2017 2-y-o 9f winner Ship Of The Fen (by Champs Elysees). The dam, a fair 9.5f winner, is a half-sister to the very smart 9f (at 2 yrs) and Group 3 9f winner of 4 races Monarchs Glen and to the quite useful 5f and 6f winner Cordial. The second dam, Mirabilis (by Lear Fan), a Listed 7f winner in France, was third in the Group 1 7f Prix de la Foret

and subsequently won a Grade 3 event in the USA over 1m at 4 yrs. She is a half-sister to the Group 1 1m Prix du Moulin and Group 1 10.5f Prix de Diane winner Nebraska Tornado and the Group 2 10f Prix Eugene Adam winner Burning Sun. (Mr Colin J. Murfitt). *"A very nice, well-bred filly from a very good Juddmonte family, she's going to take a bit of time because the family gets better as it gets older. The sire's stock were struggling to sell but then he had a very good end to the season and all of a sudden he's over-subscribed with mares by a couple of hundred! How things change".*

WILLIAM HAGGAS

703. ALKAAMEL ★★★

b.c. Havana Gold – Grace And Glory (Montjeu). February 19. Second foal. 250,000Y. Tattersalls October Book 2. Shadwell Estate Co. Half-brother to the quite useful 2-y-o 7.5f winner Give And Take (by Cityscape). The dam is an unraced sister to 3 winners including the Irish Derby winner Fame And Glory and a half-sister to 6 winners including the dam of the triple Group 1 winner Legatissimo. The second dam, Gryada (by Shirley Heights), a fairly useful 2-y-o 7f and 8.3f winner, was third in the Group 3 1m Premio Dormello and is a full or half-sister to 4 winners. (Hamdan Al Maktoum). *"We have the 3-y-o out of the mare called Give And Take and we hope she'll develop into a stakes filly. We have two Havana Gold's and we like them both, but having said that I think this horse made too much. He's a nice horse that's having a break at the moment and he won't be that early".*

704. ASCENDED ★★★

gr.f. Dark Angel – Mamma Morton (Elnadim). April 16. Eighth foal. 68,000Y. Tattersalls October Book 2. John & Jake Warren. Half-sister to the 2-y-o Listed 6f winner and Group 2 Mill Reef Stakes and Group 2 Richmond Stakes second Master Of War (by Compton Place), to the quite useful dual 6f (including at 2 yrs) Muaamara (by Bahamian Bounty), the quite useful dual 7f winner Mr McLaren (by Royal Applause), the fair 2-y-o 5f winner Marigot Bay (by Paco Boy) and the Irish 2-y-o 6f winner Aca Awesome (by Makfi). The dam, a fair 10f and 11f placed maiden, is a half-sister to 11 winners. The second dam, Gharam (by Green Dancer), a very useful 2-y-o 6f winner and third in the French 1,000 Guineas, is a half-sister to the US Grade 1 9f winner Talinum. (Mike & Michelle Morris). *"Plain, strong and well-made, she looks very solid and has a good backside on her. Looks workmanlike and I'm sure she'll be a runner".*

705. ASTRONAUT ★★★
ch.c. Olympic Glory – Gimme Some Lovin (Desert Style). March 7. Third foal. £55,000Y. Goffs UK Premier (Doncaster). Not sold. Half-brother to the quite useful 2-y-o 5f and 6f winner Thammin (by Dark Angel). The dam, a modest 6f winner here, later won 14 races in Greece and is a half-sister to 8 winners including the Group 1 Golden Shaheen winner Muarrab and the dual 2-y-o Group 3 winner Bungle Inthejungle. The second dam, Licence To Thrill (by Wolfhound), a quite useful dual 5f winner, is a half-sister to 4 winners. (Chris Wright & Jeremy Fox). *"I think there's a lot of speed there and he goes well. I think he'll make a 2-y-o all right".*

706. BAIDDAA ★★★
b.f. Dubawi – Ferdoos (Dansili). March 14. Third foal. Sister to the very smart Group 1 10f Pretty Polly Stakes and Listed 10f winner Nezwaah. The dam, a smart 10f and Listed 12f winner, is a half-sister to the German dual Listed winning stayer Brusco. The second dam, Blaze Of Colour (by Rainbow Quest), a quite useful dual 12f winner, was Listed-placed and is a half-sister to 5 winners including the Group 3 placed Equity Princess. (Sheikh Ahmed Al Maktoum). *"She has a real, old-fashioned, genuine head on her. A good, solid filly, she's not going to be early so we'll give her the time she needs. She could be a Classic filly next year".*

707. BIBLIC (IRE) ★★★
b.f. New Approach – Savannah Belle (Green Desert). January 24. Twelfth foal. 210,000Y. Tattersalls October Book 1. Jill Lamb. Half-sister to 10 winners including the Group 2 Celebration Mile and dual Listed winner and English and Irish 2,000 Guineas second Dubawi Gold, the 7f (at 2 yrs) and Listed 1m winner and Group 3 third Fort Knox, the very useful Listed 1m winner D'Bai, the useful Listed-placed 10f winner Savannah Storm (all by Dubawi), the fairly useful 6f (at 2 yrs) and

7f winner Campanology (by Royal Applause) and the quite useful 7f to 9f winner of 14 races Salient (by Fasliyev). The dam, a quite useful 2-y-o 5f winner, is a half-sister to 5 winners. The second dam, Third Watch (by Slip Anchor), a Group 2 12f Ribblesdale Stakes winner, is a half-sister to the Group winners Richard of York, Three Tails (the dam of three Group winners) and Maysoon. (Graham Smith-Bernal). *"One for the back-end, she's not here yet but we really liked her as a yearling, she's a lovely filly that needs time and she'll make a lovely 3-y-o".*

708. BOERHAN ★★★
b.c. Sea The Stars – Greenisland (Fasliyev). May 15. Fifth foal. 270,000Y. Tattersalls October Book 1. Shadwell Estate Co. Half-brother to the 2-y-o Listed 5f winner of 6 races Shamshon, to the minor French 6f winner Shajjy (both by Invincible Spirit) and the fair 7f winner Carpe Diem Lady (by Acclamation). The dam, a fairly useful 1m (at 2 yrs) and 7f winner, was Listed-placed three times and is a half-sister to 7 winners including the Listed winner Ithoughtitwasover. The second dam, Green Castle (by Indian Ridge), was placed once over 1m at 4 yrs in Ireland from only 2 starts and is a half-sister to 12 winners. (Sheikh Ahmed Al Maktoum). *"I liked him at the sales even though he was a very immature yearling, but he's really done well physically. He'll want at least seven furlongs this year and is much more of a 3-y-o type".*

709. BREAK OF DAY ★★★★
b.f. Shamardal – Dawn Glory (Oasis Dream). January 31. Third foal. Half-sister to the fair 2017 2-y-o 6f winner First Drive (by Street Cry). The dam, a modest 6f placed maiden, is a half-sister to 5 winners including the Australian Group 1 10f winner of 7 races My Kingdom Of Fife and the useful 1m (including at 2 yrs) and 7f winner of 6 races and Group 3 1m Autumn Stakes third Four Winds. The second dam, Fairy Godmother (by Fairy King), a Listed 10f winner, is a half-sister to several winners including the Group 2 12f Jockey Club Stakes winner Blueprint. (The Queen). *"I like her very much, she's from a family that do better with age but she's built like a fast filly. I suspect she'll start over six furlongs. A nice filly".*

710. CAPPTOO (IRE) ★★★

b.c. Dark Angel – Charlotte Rua (Redback). April 19. First foal. 120,000Y. Tattersalls October Book 2. Shadwell Estate Co. The dam, a modest 1m placed Irish maiden, is a half-sister to 7 winners including the Listed 6f winner and Irish 1,000 Guineas second Dimenticata and the useful Listed 6f winner Master Fay. The second dam, Non Dimenticar Me (by Don't Forget Me), a modest 5f winner, is a half-sister to 7 winners. (Sheikh Ahmed Al Maktoum). *"He's a nice horse, he got very sick in the winter but he's recovered well and he's doing well. Should make a mid-season 2-y-o".*

711. CARRIES VISION ★★★

b.f. Oasis Dream – Lacarolina (Charge D'Affaire). March 27. First foal. 50,000Y. Tattersalls October Book 1. Not sold. The dam won four races at 2 yrs in France including the Group 3 7f Prix Miesque and is a half-sister to 2 minor winners in France. The second dam, Malinday (by Lord Of Men), a minor French 3-y-o winner, is a half-sister to 9 winners including the dual Group 3 winner in France Myasun. (Ivis Size). *"She's a strong filly and I'll be trying a win a bonus race with her. She'll probably be quite early too".*

712. COUP DE GOLD (IRE) ★★

b.c. Maxios – Astroglia (Montjeu). February 12. First foal. €155,000Y. Goffs Orby. John Clarke. The dam, a minor winner at 4 yrs in France, is a half-sister to 3 winners including the dam of the multiple US Grade 1 winner Emollient. The second dam, Glia (by A P Indy), won the Listed Prix Imprudence and a minor stakes event in the USA and was second in the Grade 2 Revere Stakes and the Group 3 Prix Miesque. She is a sister to the US triple Grade 3 winner Snake Mountain, closely related to the Group 3 Prix de Cabourg winner Loving Kindness and a half-sister to the Group 1 Prix Marcel Boussac winner Denebola and to the dam of the Group 1 winners Bago and Maxios. (Sunderland Holding Inc). *"He's got a really interesting pedigree because the third dam is related to Maxios (the sire of this colt) so he's in-bred to the top-class broodmare Coup de Genie. That was one of the reasons we were keen on him. He's not very big but he's very strong and he's going to stay middle-distances next year".*

713. DALAALAAT (IRE) ★★

b.c. Kingman – Gile Na Greine (Galileo). May 16. Fourth foal. Closely related to the modest 2017 2-y-o 8.5f winner Ghanimah (by Invincible Spirit) and half-brother to the quite useful 8.5f winner Alwahsh and the quite useful 9f winner Mawjood (both by Dubawi). The dam, an Irish 2-y-o 7f winner, was second in the Group 1 Coronation Stakes and third in the 1,000 Guineas and is a sister to the 2-y-o dual Group 3 6f winner and 1,000 Guineas second Cuis Ghaire and the Group 3 9f Meld Stakes winner Scintillula. The second dam, Scribonia (by Danehill), is an unraced half-sister to 6 winners including the 2-y-o Listed 6f winner and dual Group 1 placed Luminata. (Hamdan Al Maktoum). *"We've had all the progeny out of the mare and they've all been useful without being top-class. This is a lovely horse but he was a late foal so he's one for the back-end".*

714. DASHWOOD BEAU (IRE) ★★★

b.f. Kodiac – High Dasher (High Chaparral). April 5. Third foal. €28,000Y. Tattersalls Ireland September. Amanda Skiffington. The dam is an unraced half-sister to 3 winners including the dual Listed-placed Bear Behind. The second dam, Gerobies Girl (by Deposit Ticket), a quite useful 1m winner in Ireland, is a half-sister to 8 winners including the Group 3 winner and Group 1 placed Santillana. (Sheikh Juma Dalmook Al Maktoum). *"Very racy, she was a bit small as a yearling but she's grown and is now medium-sized. I think she was cheap for what she cost".* TRAINER'S BARGAIN BUY

715. DESERT CARAVAN ★★★

b.c. Oasis Dream – Sequence (Selkirk). March 12. Second foal. The dam, a fairly useful 10f and 12f winner, is a half-sister to numerous winners including the top-class middle-distance colt Sinndar, winner of the Derby, the Irish Derby and the Prix de l'Arc de Triomphe. The second dam, Sinntara (Lashkari), won 4 races in Ireland at up to 2m. (The Queen). *"A home bred of the Queen's, I like him. He's just a little immature looking at the moment but I think when we get to July/August he'll be a smashing looking horse. He's just a baby at the moment but he's nice".*

716. EXOPTABLE ★★★
b.gr.f. Dark Angel – Executrix (Oasis Dream). February 11. First foal. The dam, a modest 1m and 10f placed maiden, is a half-sister to the Group 1 1m Matron Stakes and Group 2 Celebration Mile winner Echelon and the dual Group 2 1m winner Chic. The second dam, Exclusive (by Polar Falcon), winner of the Group 1 1m Coronation Stakes, is a half-sister to 9 winners including the 2,000 Guineas winner and Derby fourth Entrepreneur, the smart Cheshire Oaks winner and Epsom Oaks second Dance a Dream, the very useful middle-distance Listed winner Sadler's Image and the useful French 2-y-o Listed 7f winner Irish Order. (Cheveley Park Stud). *"She should be a 2-y-o, very much so, because she was an early foal and she's quite strong. It's a good family and she's not small".*

717. EYELOOL (IRE) ★★★
b.g. Dragon Pulse – Lady Heartbeat (Avonbridge). February 7. Third foal. 80,000Y. Tattersalls October Book 2. Shadwell Estate Co. The dam, a moderate 5.5f placed 2-y-o, is a half-sister to 6 winners including the Listed-placed dual 10f winner Lonely Heart (dam of the Group 3 Tetrarch Stakes winner Leitrim House). The second dam, Take Heart (by Electric), a quite useful 7f to 10f winner, is a half-sister to 3 winners. (Sheikh Ahmed Al Maktoum). *"I like him, he's fast and he was a lovely yearling. We really liked him at the sales but he got a bit above himself so he's recently been gelded and we'll have to see how he comes on for that.*

718. FANAAR (IRE) ★★★★
b.c. Dark Angel – Inca Trail (Royal Academy). March 12. Fourth foal. £240,000Y. Goffs UK Premier (Doncaster). Shadwell Estate Co. Half-brother to the fair 2-y-o 1m winner Al Rayyan (by Danehill Dancer). The dam is an unraced half-sister to 8 winners including the French Listed 10f winner Indian Choice. The second dam, Cheyenne Dream (by Dancing Brave), a French Listed 1m winner and Group 3 placed twice, is a half-sister to the French Group 3 winner Short Pause and to the dam of the Group 1 winner Continent. (Mr Hamdan Al Maktoum). *"A strong, well-made colt, perhaps a bit heavy but he was a lovely yearling and he goes well. I like him and he's one of the more*

natural ones. We'll have to see, but he could develop into a Royal Ascot 2-y-o. He's strong, his knees are mature and he'll take the work".

719. FAYLAQ ★★★
b.c. Dubawi – Danedream (Lomitas). March 2. Third foal. 1,500,000Y. Tattersalls October Book 1. Shadwell Estate Co. The dam, a top-class winner of 8 races from 6f (at 2 yrs) to 12f including the Group 1 King George VI and the Prix de l'Arc de Triomphe, is a half-sister to 4 winners including Venice Beach (Group 3 Chester Vase). The second dam, Danedrop (by Danehill), is an unraced half-sister to 7 minor winners. (Hamdan Al Maktoum). *"He was a lovely yearling and he's a lovely horse. It's a pleasure to have him and this is what we're trying to do – to get horses like him. He should stay well in time and I hope he'll be a big, strong horse as a 3-y-o".*

720. FLAREPATH ★★★★
b.f. Exceed And Excel – Fiery Sunset (Galileo). February 3. First foal. The dam, a winner, a quite useful 12f winner, is a half-sister to 3 winners. The second dam, Five Fields (by Chester House), a quite useful 10f winner, is a half-sister to numerous winners including the US dual Grade 1 winner Senure. (The Queen). *"I like her, she's an attractive filly with a bit of size and scope. Looks well, goes well and just does everything right. A midsummer 2-y-o I should think".*

721. FRANKELLINA ★★★ ♠
ch.f. Frankel – Our Obsession (Shamardal). January 27. First foal. The dam, a useful 1m (at 2 yrs), 10f and Listed 12f winner, is a half-sister to the fairly useful dual 1m winner Westwiththenight (by Cape Cross), the quite useful dual 12f winner Dawn Horizons (by New Approach) and the modest 11f winner Fine Style (by Pivotal). The second dam, Hidden Hope (by Daylami), a useful Listed 11.4f Cheshire Oaks winner, is a half-sister to 9 winners including Rebecca Sharp (Group 1 1m Coronation Stakes) and the Group 3 Lingfield Derby Trial winner Mystic Knight. (Mr A E Oppenheimer). *"Mr Oppenheimer kindly offered this filly to us when she was a foal and she looks very like her mum. Very strong and well-made, she could be anything but she's going to stay well next year".*

722. ICE GALA ★★★
b.f. Invincible Spirit – Ice Palace (Polar Falcon). March 18. Half-sister to the dual Listed 12f winner Queen Of Ice (by Selkirk), to the quite useful 10f winner Frosting (by Kyllachy), the quite useful 1m to 11f winner Gone Dutch (by Dutch Art) and the modest French 1m winner Medici Palace (by Medicean). The dam, a useful 1m and Listed 10f winner, is a half-sister to 7 winners including the useful Listed 10f winner Portal and the dam of the Group 2 1m May Hill Stakes winner and 1,000 Guineas second Spacious. The second dam, White Palace (by Shirley Heights), a quite useful 3-y-o 8.2f winner, is a half-brother to one winner abroad. (Cheveley Park Stud). *"She's a half-sister to a useful filly we had called Queen Of Ice who stayed well. This filly looks much sharper and I would think she'll be a mid-season 2-y-o. She'll be the first 2-y-o winner the dam has bred".*

723. JIRNAAS ★★★ ♠
ch.c. Showcasing – Stresa (Pivotal). February 16. Second foal. 85,000 foal. Tattersalls December. Shadwell Estate Co. The dam, a quite useful 1m winner, is a half-sister to 3 winners including the fairly useful 2-y-o dual 6f winner Mezmaar. The second dam, Bay Tree (by Daylami), a useful 2-y-o Listed 7f winner, was third in the Group 3 Musidora Stakes and is a half-sister to 4 winners including the Group 1 6f Haydock Sprint Cup winner Tante Rose. (Hamdan Al Maktoum). *"He was bought as a foal and he's a strong, very well-made horse. I don't think his legs are quite strong enough to carry his body at the moment and we're just going quietly with him but when his time comes I think he'll come together quite quickly. A nice-looking horse".*

724. KODINAR ★★★
b.f. Kodiac – Miss Queen (Miswaki). April 2. Eleventh foal. Half-sister to 8 winners including the very useful 2-y-o Group 2 5f Flying Childers Stakes and subsequent Hong Kong winner Chateau Istana (by Grand Lodge), the very useful 2-y-o Group 3 6f Sirenia Stakes winner of 5 races Prince Of Light (by Fantastic Light), the very useful 1m Britannia Handicap winner and Listed-placed Mandobi (by Mark Of Esteem) and the quite useful 7f winner Druids

Ridge (by Paco Boy). The dam, a minor US 6f winner, is a half-sister to 8 winners including the useful 2-y-o Group 3 6f Princess Margaret Stakes winner Tajannub. The second dam, Empress Jackie (by Mount Hagen), won 8 races in the USA including two stakes and is a half-sister to the Derby and Irish Derby third Star Of Gdansk and the US Grade 3 winner W D Jacks. (Abdulla Al Khalifa). *"She'll be our first 2-y-o runner, in mid-April. She did a bit upsides the other day and did better than the other one. She's very small and is clearly sharp".*

725. LUXOR ★★★
b.c. Oasis Dream – Eminently (Exceed And Excel). January 22. Second foal. £190,000Y. Goffs UK Premier (Doncaster). John & Jake Warren. The dam, a fair 2-y-o 6f winner, is a half-sister to 9 winners including the high-class Haydock Park Sprint Cup and the Nunthorpe Stakes winner Reverence and the very useful 2-y-o Listed 7f Chesham Stakes and 5-y-o 1m winner and 1m Britannia Handicap second Helm Bank. The second dam, Imperial Bailiwick (by Imperial Frontier), won 3 races around 5f including the Group 2 Flying Childers Stakes, was placed in the Molecomb Stakes and the Prix du Petit-Couvert and is a half-sister to 3 winners in France. (Highclere Thoroughbred Racing). *"A nice horse, he's a little bit 'up behind' at the moment but he goes well and I think these quicker mares are what Oasis Dream wants. He's strong and he'll be a really nice 3-y-o, but I hope there's a bit of mileage in him at two and the family is all about speed. That may not be until the second half of the season though".*

726. MAGNETIC CHARM ★★★★
b.f. Exceed And Excel – Monday Show (Maria's Mon). April 27. Half-sister to the Group 2 1m Duke Of Cambridge and Group 2 9f Dahlia Stakes winner Usherette and to the German Listed 9f winner Show Day (both by Shamardal). The dam, Listed-placed over 11f in Germany, is a sister to the US Grade 2 11f winner Expansion. The second dam, La Sylphide (by Barathea), won the Group 3 Prix Penelope and is a half-sister to 9 winners including the Group 1 Grand Prix de Paris and Group 1 Prix Jean Prat winner Vespone and the Listed Glorious Stakes winner and Melbourne Cup second Purple Moon. (The

Queen). *"I like this filly, she was a gift from Sheikh Mohammed to Her Majesty and she goes very nicely. Possibly an Ascot 2-y-o because she's got a bit of quality, a bit of size and a bit of speed".*

727. MALBAS ★★★

b.c. Mukhadram – Violet (Mukaddamah). February 3. Fourteenth foal. 85,000Y. Tattersalls October Book 2. Shadwell Estate Co. Half-brother to 8 winners including the dual 6f and subsequent US Grade 2 winner and Grade 1 second Starlarks (by Mujahid), the quite useful 1m to 9.3f winner of 5 races Boo (by Namaqualand), the fair dual 1m winner Mutineer (by Sepoy) and the modest 7f and 1m winner Kannon (by Kyllachy). The dam, a fair 6f and 8.5f winner, is a full or half-sister to 8 winners including the 10.4f John Smiths Handicap and triple Hong Kong stakes winner and Group 2 third Sobriety. The second dam, Scanno's Choice (by Pennine Walk), a middle-distance placed maiden, is a half-sister to 6 winners including the US Grade 2 winner Dilmoun. (Hamdan Al Maktoum). *"He doesn't look too backward and he goes well. He might change a bit but he's always gone well and he was a relatively early foal so I would hope we'd get something out of him at two. We'd like to get the sire going with a 2-y-o winner or two from his first crop".*

728. MAQSAD (FR) ★★★

b.f. Siyouni (FR)—Amerique (IRE) (Galileo). January 22. Second foal. 750,000 foal. Goffs November. Shadwell Estate Co. The dam, a French dual Listed-placed 3-y-o winner, is a half-sister to 4 winners including the Listed winner and Group 1 Prix de Romanet second Ame Bleue. The second dam, Aquarelliste (by Danehill), won three Group 1's in France and is a half-sister to 5 winners. (Hamdan Al Maktoum). *"A very attractive filly and a very expensive purchase at the foal sales".*

729. MARMOOQ (USA) ★★★

ch.c. Tamayuz—Bashoosha (USA) (Distorted Humor). February 12. Third living foal. The dam is a US placed half-sister to one winner. The second dam, Ask Me No Secrets (by Seattle Slew), a US Grade 3 winner and Grade 2 placed, is a half-sister to 5 winners. (Hamdan Al Maktoum). *"A nice horse, he's very strong, well-made and will make a 2-y-o".*

730. MOFTRIS ★★★★★

b.c. Iffraaj – Baheeja (Dubawi). February 25. Third foal. Brother to Romaana, placed fourth over 7f on her only start at 2 yrs in 2017 and half-brother to the quite useful 2-y-o 8.5f winner Dowayla (by Sepoy). The dam, a fairly useful winner of 4 races over 7f, was Listed-placed and is a half-sister to 2 winners including the useful 5f and 6f winner of 6 races (including at 2 yrs) Grigorovitch. The second dam, Hasty Words (by Polish Patriot), won over 6f (at 2 yrs) and the Listed Doncaster Mile at 4 yrs and was third in the Group 2 7f Rockfel Stakes. (Sheikh Ahmed Al Maktoum). *"A nice horse that deserves five stars in your book and he may be an Ascot 2-y-o. He may want six furlongs but he'll be running around May time, I like him and he's a strong, well-made horse. He goes well too".*

731. NAPLES (IRE) ★★★

b.c. Clodovil – Annamanamoux (Leroidesanimaux). April 27. Fourth foal. 65,000Y. Tattersalls October Book 2. Jill Lamb. Half-brother to the fair 2-y-o 7f winner Annie Fior (by Finsceal Fior) and to a minor 2-y-o winner abroad by Vocalised. The dam is an unraced half-sister to 5 winners including Carelaine (the dam of three stakes winners in France). The second dam, Annoconnor (by Nureyev), won three Grade 1 events in the USA and is a half-sister to 10 winners including the Melbourne Cup winner At Talaq. (Graham Smith-Bernal). *"A good-moving horse, he always catches my eye. He's a bit juvenile at the moment, a bit of a lad, but I like the look of him and I think he's all right. He's got a bit of scope, he's changed already and he'll improve and mature as the season goes on. Not bad at all".*

732. POLITICISE (IRE) ★★★★

b.c. Camelot – Politesse (Barathea). February 28. Half-brother to the very smart Group 1 6.5f Prix Maurice de Gheest and Group 2 6f Diadem Stakes winner of 7 races King's Apostle (by King's Best), to the fairly useful 6f and 7f winner of 4 races Cape Classic (by Cape Cross), the 7f to 10f winner of 7 races Kalk Bay (by Hawk Wing) and the 6f and 7f winner Floating Along (by Oasis Dream) – both quite useful. The dam is an unraced half-sister to 4 minor winners out of the Group 1

6f Cheveley Park Stakes winner Embassy (by Cadeaux Genereux), herself a half-sister to 6 winners including the Group 2 Pretty Polly Stakes winner Tarfshi. (Mr B. Kantor). *"This is a lovely horse. Obviously Camelot is an influence for stamina and this colt is probably a seven furlong 2-y-o, but looks quite fast and he could well start over six at Newmarket's July meeting. The dam's offspring tend to need time but this colt doesn't look like he does. A nice horse".*

733. RED HUT RED (IRE) ★★★★
b.f. Kodiac – Happy Land (Refuse To Bend). April 4. Fifth foal. 60,000Y. Tattersalls October Book 1. William Haggas. Half-sister to 4 winners including the useful 1m Britannia Stakes winner Bless Him (by Sea The Stars), to the fair 10f winner Thunder In Myheart (by Mastercraftsman) and the minor German 3-y-o winner Dime Dancer (by Azamour). The dam is an unraced half-sister to 10 winners including the US 2-y-o Grade 1 8.5f Starlet Stakes winner Creaking Board (herself dam of the US Grade 3 winner Crowd Pleaser), the Group 2 German 1,000 Guineas winner Dakhla Oasis and the Group 3 6f Prix de Seine-et-Oise and German Group 3 6f Benazet-Rennen winner Dyhim Diamond. The second dam, Happy Landing, was placed at 3 yrs in France. (Mr Tim Bridge). *"I thought she was quite well-bought. She looks quite a strong, racy 2-y-o and she goes well. So I hope she'll develop into a useful 2-y-o but whether she's an Ascot type we'll have to see. A neat, racy filly".*

734. SEA OF REALITY ★★★
b.f. Born To Sea – Girouette (Pivotal). April 14. Third foal. Sister to the useful 2017 2-y-o 7f winner and Group 1 Moyglare Stud Stakes fourth Muirin. The dam, a Group 3 Phoenix Sprint Stakes winner of 3 races, is a half-sister to numerous winners including the French 1m winner of 7 races and Group 3 second Prince d'Alienor. The second dam, Vassiana (by Anabaa), a French 3-y-o winner, was Listed-placed and is a sister to the Group 3 Prix d'Arenburg winner Villadolide and to the French dual Listed winner Victorieux. (Sunderland Holding Ltd). *"She's not a big filly but she's got a good frame to her and I think she'll be nice in time. Could be a 2-y-o too".*

735. SEA WINGS ★★★ ♠♠
ch.c. Sea The Stars – Infallible (Pivotal). March 1. Brother to the Group 2 Summer Mile winner and US Grade 1 Woodbine Mile third Mutakayyef and half-brother to the useful Irish Listed 1m winner and Group 3 9.5f third Intimation (by Dubawi) and the useful 6f winner of four races Intrinsic (by Oasis Dream). The dam, a very smart 7f (at 2 yrs) and Group 3 7f Nell Gwyn Stakes winner, was second in the Group 1 Coronation Stakes and the Group 1 Falmouth Stakes and is a full or half-sister to 3 winners. The second dam, Irresistible (by Cadeaux Genereux), was a fairly useful 5f (at 2 yrs) and Listed 6f winner and is a half-sister to 2 winners. (Cheveley Park Stud). *"He's immature and hasn't come in yet, but he's not as big and immature as his brother Mutakayyef was at this stage. He's a lovely horse of course, but he's still in pre-training".*

736. SENZA LIMITI (IRE) ★★★★
ch.c. Lope De Vega – Senza Rete (Barathea). March 1. Second foal. 100,000Y. Tattersalls October Book 1. Highflyer Bloodstock. The dam, a Listed 1m winner in Italy, is a half-sister to 6 winners. The second dam, Lyrical Dance (by Lear Fan), a minor winner at 4 yrs in the USA, is a sister to the French Listed 10.5f winner Shaal and a half-sister to 6 winners including the Group/Grade 1 winners Black Minnaloushe, Pennekamp and Nasr El Arab and the placed dam of the US dual Grade 1 winner Round Pond. (Simon Munir & Isaac Souede). *"He goes well, he's grown a bit but has always shown a bit of speed. He should be a July/August 2-y-o and he's a nice, solid horse. He was well bought".*

737. SKARDU ★★★★
ch.c. Shamardal – Diala (Iffraaj). April 1. First foal. The dam, a fairly useful 2-y-o 7f winner, is a half-sister to one winner. The second dam, Quaich (by Danehill), a fair 7f winner, is a half-sister to 3 winners including the German 3-y-o winner and Group 3 1m second Lukretia. (Abdulla Al Khalifa). *"Quite a strong, well-made colt, I trained the mother who was a bit disappointing but looked really promising. I like this colt, he'll like fast ground and should be a 2-y-o".*

738. SOLOIST ★★★★
b.f. Camelot – Ayshea (Mr Greeley). March 8.
Third foal. 100,000Y. Tattersalls October Book
1. John & Jake Warren. Half-sister to a minor
2-y-o winner abroad by Holy Roman Emperor.
The dam is an unraced half-sister to 4 minor
winners. The second dam, Be My Queen (by
Sadler's Wells), an Irish Listed-placed 1m
winner, is a half-sister to 6 winners including
the Group 1 5f Prix de l'Abbaye winner
Imperial Beauty. (Highclere Thoroughbred
Racing). *"A beautiful filly but one for the
autumn. A lovely mover, she has great presence
and stands out. One for seven furlongs and a
mile this year".*

739. SPACE WALK ★★
b.c. Galileo – Memory (Danehill Dancer).
March 29. Fourth foal. Brother to the smart
2-y-o Group 3 7f Acomb Stakes winner
Recorder and to the Listed 14f winner Call To
Mind and closely related to the fairly useful
2017 2-y-o Listed-placed 7f winner Learn By
Heart (by Frankel). The dam won the Group 2
6f Cherry Hinton Stakes and is a sister to one
winner and a half-sister to 5 winners including
the 2-y-o Group 3 Tyros Stakes winner
Remember Alexander. The second dam,
Nausicaa (by Diesis), won 3 races at 2 and 3
yrs in France and the USA over 7f and 1m, was
third in the Grade 3 Miesque Stakes and is a
half-sister to 3 winners. (The Queen). *"He's a
full brother to a good stayer Call To Mind and
he's quite like him so he'll take time to develop.
The other full brother Recorder was a neater
colt and he had speed. This is an immature
horse at present".*

740. SPOTTON (IRE) ★★★★
b.c. Tamayuz – Farbenspiel (Desert Prince).
March 31. Sixth foal. 330,000Y. Tattersalls
October Book 1. Shadwell Estate Co. Half-
brother to 4 winners including the quite useful
5f winner of 4 races at 2 and 3 yrs Coolfitch
(by Roderic O'Connor), the fair 6f winner
Sand Boy (by Footstepsinthesand) and the
fair 7f winner Excellent Royale (by Excellent
Art). The dam won once at 3 yrs in Germany
and is a half-sister to 10 winners including
the Group 1 Haydock Sprint Cup winner G
Force and the US Grade 3 Miesque Stakes
winner Louvain. The second dam, Flanders (by
Common Grounds), a very useful sprint winner

of 6 races including the Listed Scarbrough
Stakes, was second in the Group 2 Kings
Stand Stakes and is a half-sister to 8 winners.
(Sheikh Ahmed Al Maktoum). *"He was a lovely
yearling and he's now a strong, well-made type
that should make a 2-y-o. It's a good, speedy
family".*

741. SQUELCH ★★
b.f. Dark Angel – Blancmange (Montjeu).
March 13. Fourth foal. Half-sister to the fairly
useful 1m and 8.5f winner Mange All (by
Zamindar). The dam is an unraced half-sister
to 2 winners. The second dam, Blue Dream
(by Cadeaux Genereux), a useful 6f winner,
was Listed-placed and is a half-sister to 5
winners including the 1m (at 2 yrs) and 9.2f
winner and Listed-placed Equity Princess. (J
B Haggas). *"Quite a tall, leggy filly, she's not a
typical Dark Angel filly but they can go on at
three as Persuasive showed. She'll need some
time".*

742. SWISS AIR ★★★ ♠
b.f. Oasis Dream – Swiss Lake (Indian Ridge).
April 13. Eleventh foal. Sister to the useful
triple Listed 6f winner Swiss Dream and half-
sister to 8 winners including the Group 3 6f
Prix de Meautry and Group 3 5f Prix de Petit
Couvert winner Swiss Diva (by Pivotal), the
very useful 6f (at 2 yrs) and Group 3 5f winner
Swiss Spirit (by Invincible Spirit) and the 2-y-o
5f winner and triple Group 2 placed Swiss
Franc (by Mr Greeley). The dam, a dual Listed
5f winner and second in the Group 2 Flying
Childers, is a half-sister to 4 winners. The
second dam, Blue Iris (by Petong), was a useful
Listed-placed winner of 5 races over 5f and 6f.
(Lordship Stud). *"She's a bit of a madam but
we like the look of her and she'll be a 2-y-o too.
Very much a sprinting type".*

743. TAPISSERIE ★★★★
ch.f. Le Havre – Miss Work Of Art (Dutch Art).
April 11. Second foal. 95,000Y. Tattersalls
October Book 2. John & Jake Warren. Half-
sister to the modest 2-y-o 5f winner Spin Top
(by Acclamation). The dam, a useful 2-y-o
Listed 5f winner of 3 races and second in the
3-y-o Group 3 6f Firth of Clyde Stakes, is a
half-sister to 3 winners including the fairly
useful 2-y-o 1m winner and Group 3 Musidora
Stakes second Romantic Settings. The second

dam, Lacework (by Pivotal), a fairly useful 7f (at 2 yrs) to 10f winner, is a sister to the Scandinavian Group 3 winner Entangle and a half-sister to 4 winners. (Isa Salman). *"I like her, she's fast. Although she's by Le Havre her dam was a speedy 2-y-o and this is a strong filly – maybe a little bit long if you were critical, but she goes well".*

744. THE NIGHT WATCH ★★★

b.c. Dutch Art – Scarlet Runner (Night Shift). May 4. The dam, a very useful Group 3 Princess Margaret Stakes (at 2 yrs) and Group 3 7f Nell Gwyn Stakes winner, is a half-sister to 2 winners. The second dam, Sweet Pea (by Persian Bold), a quite useful 1m winner of 4 races, is a half-sister to numerous winners including the Listed 6f winner Star Tulip. (Mr Nicholas Jones). *"The dam was good but so far she hasn't been a great breeder. This colt was a late foal but he's done OK and he's strong. I hope he'll be a 2-y-o but most Dutch Art's take a bit of time".*

745. TIANADARGENT (FR) ★★★

b.f. Kendargent – Restia (Montjeu). March 22. Seventh foal. 90,000Y. Tattersalls October Book 1. Not sold. Sister to three winners including Restiadargent (Group 2 6f Criterium de Maisons-Laffitte) and the Listed 10f winner and Group 3 second Restiana. The dam is an unraced half-sister to 2 minor winners in France. The second dam, Restifia (by Night Shift), a Listed winner in France, is a half-sister to 3 winners. (Guy Pariente). *"I was surprised she didn't make more at the sales and she's done well since. A nice filly that goes well, she's a little bit keen but she could be a 2-y-o".*

746. TWO BIDS ★★★

b.c. Dalakhani – Echelon (Danehill). April 8. Seventh foal. 375,000Y. Tattersalls October Book 1. Shadwell Estate Co. Brother to the Group 1 Falmouth Stakes and Group 1 Sun Chariot Stakes winner Integral and half-brother to the useful Listed-placed 7f and 1m winner Provenance, the modest 12f winner Elysian (both by Galileo), the quite useful dual 10f winner Entity (by Shamardal) and the fair 8.5f winner Jabbaar (by Medicean). The dam won the Group 1 1m Matron Stakes, the Group 2 Celebration Mile and four Group 3 events and is a half-sister to 5 winners

including the dual Group 2 Celebration Mile winner Chic. The second dam, Exclusive (by Polar Falcon), won the Group 1 1m Coronation Stakes and is a half-sister to 9 winners including the 2,000 Guineas winner Entrepreneur. (Sheikh Ahmed Al Maktoum). *"It's certainly nice to have a well-bred colt like this. It's an interesting mating and the dam has been around a while now but it's a hell of a family and there's no reason why he couldn't be a good horse. He's going to want a mile this year and he'll probably get further at three".*

747. WINGREEN (IRE) ★★★★

ch.f. Lope De Vega – Relation Alexander (Dandy Man). January 19. First foal. €88,000Y. Goffs Orby. John & Jake Warren. The dam, a fair dual 7f at 2 and 3 yrs, is a half-sister to 9 winners including the useful triple 6f (including at 2 yrs) and UAE Listed 5f winner Taqseem and the 2-y-o 7f winner and Group 2 Rockfel Stakes third Desert Blossom. The second dam, Elshamms (by Zafonic), a fairly useful 2-y-o 7f winner and third in the Group 3 Prestige Stakes, is a half-sister to 10 winners. (Mr Isa Salman). *"I like her, she has a plain head but that's very typical of the sire, she goes well and could be a 2-y-o. Very much so".*

748. UNNAMED ★★ ♠

b.f. Slade Power – Bedouin Dancer (Pivotal). March 26. First foal. 85,000Y. Tattersalls October Book 2. Rabbah Bloodstock. The dam is an unplaced sister to the Listed 7f Radley Stakes (at 2 yrs) and the Group 3 7f Oak Tree Stakes winner Summer Fete and a half-sister to 4 winners. The second dam, Tamarillo (by Daylami), a fairly useful 2-y-o 8.3f and UAE 3-y-o winner, is a half-sister to 7 winners. (Sheikh Juma Dalmook Al Maktoum). *"A little more backward than I thought, she's grown a bit which is probably a good thing but it means she won't be that early. This is the only Slade Power we've got and I know he was at his best as a five-year-old, but he did win late on at two".*

749. UNNAMED ★★★

b.c. Dandy Man – Celtic Lynn (Celtic Swing). February 23. Third living foal. 110,000Y. Tattersalls October Book 2. Blandford Bloodstock. Half-brother to the fair 9f winner Sahara (by Clodovil). The dam, a fair 6f and 7f winner, is a half-sister to 5 winners including the Group 3 Middleton Stakes third Flying Clarets. The second dam, Sheryl Lynn (by Miller's Mate), won 2 races at 3 and 4 yrs in Germany and is a half-sister to 3 winners. (Sheikh Rashid Dalmook Al Maktoum). *"We bought him because he was a ringer for the horse Squats who had the same sire, owner and trainer and won three times as a 2-y-o. He looks just like him but he's a little bit flat of his withers still and I'm not sure how early he'll be".*

750. UNNAMED ★★★★
b.c. Sea The Stars – Chiosina (Danehill Dancer). February 26. Ninth foal. 310,000Y. Tattersalls October Book 1. Amanda Skiffington. Brother to the fairly useful 2-y-o 1m winner Naseem and half-brother to the French Listed 6f and Listed 7f winner and Group 2 placed Mixed Intention, to the French 7f and 1m winner Mixed Evidence (both by Elusive City), the quite useful 2-y-o 5f and 6f winner Meritocracy and the poor 6f winner Kerfuffle (both by Kheleyf). The dam is an unraced half-sister to 4 winners including the Italian Listed winner and Group 2 placed Aria Di Festa. The second dam, Alarme Belle (by Warning), a useful Irish dual 6f winner, was Listed-placed and is a half-sister to 4 winners. (Fiona Carmichael). *"A lovely horse, he's really done well since we bought him and he's got a bit of speed for a Sea The Stars which is usually a good sign with that sire. I'm hoping he'll develop into a 2-y-o by late summer or the autumn".*

751. UNNAMED ★★★
b.c. Camelot – Coppertop (Exceed And Excel). April 4. Third foal. 62,000Y. Tattersalls October Book 2. Stroud/Coleman. Half-brother to a minor Italian 3-y-o winner by Dragon Pulse. The dam, a moderate 7f and 1m placed maiden, is a half-sister to 3 minor winners. The second dam, Fresh Mint (by Sadler's Wells), was a fair 11f and 12f winner of 4 races. (Mr B Kantor). *"Lovely. We're quite keen on the sire and we like this horse, he's a little bit slack of his pasterns but he's got great presence. He showed us lots when he was here, we've sent him out for a break but he should be back in a month's time. He'll be a September 2-y-o and he has lots of scope".*

752. UNNAMED ★★★
br.f. Showcasing – Dance Pearl (Danehill Dancer). April 23. First foal. 330,000Y. Tattersalls October Book 1. John & Jake Warren. The dam is an unraced half-sister to 4 winners including Group 2 Champagne Stakes winner and 2,000 Guineas second Vital Equine. The second dam, Bayalika (by Selkirk), is an unraced half-sister to 6 winners. (Mike & Michelle Morris). *"A lovely filly, she was expensive but she's got lots of quality and is a nice walker and mover. I had a Showcasing last year that I tried to make into a 2-y-o but that didn't work out, so I'm trying not to train this filly too early. She'll be given the chance to develop".*

753. UNNAMED ★★★★
gr.f. Galileo – Fork Lightning (Storm Cat). April 4. Third foal. 280,000Y. Tattersalls October Book 1. Rabbah Bloodstock. The dam, a fairly useful 9f winner, is a half-sister to 9 winners including the French 2,000 Guineas and US Grade 1 winner Aussie Rules and the Listed 10f winner and US Grade 2 second Approach. The second dam, Last Second (by Alzao), winner of the Group 2 10f Nassau Stakes and the Group 2 10f Sun Chariot Stakes, is a half-sister to 7 winners and the dam of the Group 1 winners Albanova, Alborada, Allegretto, Yesterday and Quarter Moon. (Sheikh Juma Dalmook Al Maktoum). *"She was quite expensive but I think she's really nice, she's done really well and I'm very pleased with the way she's improved. I don't think she's that backward either because she's quite strong, there's a bit of speed in the pedigree and I can see her running by July".*

754. UNNAMED ★★★★
b.c. No Nay Never – Gilded Vanity (Indian Ridge). January 20. Tenth foal. 210,000Y. Tattersalls October Book 2. Blandford Bloodstock. Half-brother to 6 winners including the useful 6f (at 2 yrs) to 1m winner of 8 races and Group 2 Superlative Stakes second Birdman, the fairly useful dual 7f winner Predominance, the quite useful 7f winner Golden Glimmer (all by Danehill Dancer), the fair 2-y-o 5f winner Roman Seal (by Holy Roman Emperor) and the fair 6f winner of 4 races Desert Icon (by Desert Style). The dam, an Irish 5f winner, is a sister

to the Irish 2,000 Guineas second Fa-Eq and a half-sister to 5 winners. The second dam, Searching Star (by Rainbow Quest), was a modest 6f to 11.3f placed half-sister to 8 winners. (Sheikh Juma Dalmook Al Maktoum). *"This colt is really nice – probably the nicest by a first season stallion that we've got. We trained the half-brother Predominance who rated about 100. This horse is strong and well-made, has quite immature joints at the moment but I think he'll be a 2-y-o and he goes well".*

755. UNNAMED ★★★
b.f. War Command – High Figurine (High Chaparral). April 19. Fourth foal. Half-sister to the fair 2-y-o 7f and 1m winner Under Control (by Power) and to the quite useful 2-y-o 6f winner Shaka Zulu (by Holy Roman Emperor). The dam, a quite useful 11f and 12f winner, is a half-sister to several winners including the dual Listed winner Craig's Falcon. The second dam, Royale Figurine (by Dominion Royale), was a useful Listed 6f winner. *"A strong, quite racy, well-grown filly that moves well. The dam stayed well so I'm not sure what they were trying to breed here but the sire is a beautiful looking horse. This is quite a strong filly and she surprised me when she came in because I thought she looked good, so I hope she'll be a 2-y-o".*

756. UNNAMED ★★★
b.c. Lope De Vega – Mickleberry (Desert Style). February 6. Second foal. 125,000Y. Tattersalls October Book 1. Westwood Bloodstock. The dam, a moderate 5f winner, is a half-sister to 6 winners including the Group 2 July Stakes winner Alhebayeb. The second dam, Miss Indigo (by Indian Ridge), is a placed half-sister to 8 winners including the useful Listed 10f Pretty Polly Stakes winner and Group 2 placed Musetta. (Fiona Carmichael). *"A nice horse, we had a few issues with him in the spring but we've ironed them out now and I like him. He's well-made and goes well".*

757. UNNAMED ★★★
b.c. Zoffany – Polly Perkins (Pivotal). April 12. Seventh foal. €50,000Y. Goffs Orby. China Horse Club. Half-brother to the 2-y-o Group 3 Anglesey Stakes winner Final Frontier (by Dream Ahead), to the useful 2-y-o 7f winner

and Group 3 7f C L & M F Weld Park Stakes second Lola Beaux (by Equiano) and the fair triple 7f winner Marmarus (by Duke Of Marmalade). The dam, a useful 2-y-o dual Listed 5f winner, is a half-sister to 2 winners. The second dam, Prospering (by Prince Sabo), a moderate 7f winner at 3 yrs, is a half-sister to 6 winners. (China Horse Club). *"He's done really well since the sale and he goes very nicely. A nice horse you should add to the list".*

758. UNNAMED ★★★★
b.br.f. Shamardal – Sentaril (Danehill Dancer). January 8. Second foal. The dam, a useful dual 7f and Listed 1m winner, was second in the Group 3 7f Jersey Stakes and is a sister to one winner and a half-sister 6 winners including the very smart Group 3 5f Molecomb Stakes and Group 3 5f King George Stakes winner Enticing. The second dam, Superstar Leo (by College Chapel), won 5 races the Group 2 5f Flying Childers Stakes and the Weatherbys Super Sprint and is a full or half-sister to numerous winners. (Lael Stable). *"Lovely. I loved the dam and she was a pretty good filly too. This filly was an early foal, she has a bit of quality and could be anything".*

MICHAEL HALFORD
759. BALEFIRE ★★★★
b.c. Shamardal – Patent Joy (Pivotal). April 6. First foal. The dam, placed twice over 10f in France, is a half-sister to 3 winners. The second dam Kitty Matcham (by Rock Of Gibraltar), winner of the 2-y-o Group 2 7f Rockfel Stakes, is a sister to the Irish 10f winner and dual Group 1 placed Red Rock Canyon, closely related to the 2-y-o Group 1 7f Prix Jean Luc Lagardere winner Horatio Nelson and a half-sister to the UAE Group 2 winner and Group 1 Eclipse Stakes third Viscount Nelson. (Godolphin). *"Not over-big, but he's a horse that's done very well and he's typical of the sire in that he's tough and likes to get on with the job. He's started to come together recently and I think he'll go six furlongs. We like him, he's a well-balanced horse with a good attitude".*

760. CARTESIENNE ★★★★
ch.f. Pivotal – Modern Ideals (New Approach). March 19. First foal. The dam, unplaced in one start, a half-sister to numerous winners including the Group 1 Prix Jean-Luc Lagardere

winner Ultra and the Group 3 Prix Minerve winner Synopsis. The second dam, Epitome (by Nashwan), is a placed half-sister to 7 winners. (Godolphin). *"A lovely filly that'll take a bit of time but we've liked her from the beginning and she's one of our nicer fillies. She'll make a 2-y-o from July onwards, probably over seven furlongs".*

761. DESIGNATION ★★★

b.f. Acclamation – Delira (Namid). February 29. Fourth foal. €105,000Y. Goffs Orby. M Halford. Closely related to the quite useful 2-y-o 1m winner Wahash (by Dark Angel). The dam, a modest 5.5f winner, is a half-sister to 6 winners including Barrier Reef, a winner of 8 races and second in the Group 3 Beresford Stakes. The second dam, Singing Millie (by Millfontaine), won twice in Ireland at 3 yrs and is a half-sister to 7 winners. (Imperial Racing Syndicate). *"She's out having a break now getting some spring grass but she's a nice filly with a good action and a good attitude, she'll be one for the second half of the season and she goes well. She's typical of the sire but we haven't got a lot done with her yet because of the bad weather. She might have enough pace to start at six furlongs before stepping her up to seven".*

762. LETHAL TURBO ★★★

gr.c. Lethal Force – Privet (Cape Cross). February 12. Fifth foal. €50,000Y. Goffs Orby. McKeever/Ferguson. Half-brother to the quite useful 7f (at 2 yrs) and 1m winner Cryptic (by Lord Shanakill), to the fair UAE 6f and 7f winner Just A Penny (by Kodiac), the fair 6f (at 2 yrs) and 7f winner Hedging (by Mastercraftsman)and the minor French 7f winner Bilge Kagan (by Whipper). The dam, a fair 6f (at 2 yrs) to 1m placed maiden, is a sister to the German 2-y-o Group 2 winner Mokabra and a half-sister to 6 winners. The second dam, Pacific Grove (by Persian Bold), a fairly useful 2-y-o Listed-placed winner of 3 races from 7f to 1m, is a half-sister to 5 winners including the Listed winners Mauri Moon and Kimbridge Knight. *"He's a smashing horse with a good attitude; a good mover, he'll be ready to start off in May, he's a good, strong horse, very straightforward and loves his work. As soon as the six furlong maidens start he'll be ready to get going and I'd say he'll probably be suited by a bit of ease in the ground".*

763. MALVOLIO ★★★

ch.c. Farhh – Philae (Seeking The Gold). April 16. Sixth foal. Half-brother to the French 2-y-o 1m winner Historic Find and to the fair UAE 6f winner Ru'Oud (both by Pivotal) and the fairly useful French 7.5f and 1m winner Philosopher (by Shamardal). The dam is an unplaced sister to the outstanding Dubai Millennium, winner of the Dubai World Cup, the Prix Jacques le Marois, the Prince Of Wales's Stakes and the Queen Elizabeth II Stakes (all Group 1 events) and a half-sister to the Group 2 10.5f Prix Greffuhle second Denver County. The second dam, Colorado Dancer (by Shareef Dancer), winner of the Group 2 13.5f Prix de Pomone, is closely related to the Grade 1 Gamely Handicap winner Northern Aspen, to the Group 1 July Cup winner Hamas and the Group 1 Grand Prix de Paris winner Fort Wood and a half-sister to the Prix d'Astarte winner Elle Seule (herself dam of the Irish 1,000 Guineas winner Mehthaaf) and the champion US 2-y-o colt Timber Country. (Godolphin). *"A lovely, scopey horse with a great attitude and we like him. He's grown and changed a lot since he's been here but he does everything well. He'll make a 2-y-o from the middle of the season onwards, he's furnishing well all the time and is one of our nicer 2-y-o's".*

764. MY AQUARIAN ★★

b.f. Dubawi – My Renee (Kris S). May 2. Ninth foal. €150,000Y. Goffs Orby. BBA (Ire). Half-sister to 5 winners including the Group 2 Ribblesdale Stakes and Group 2 Royal Whip Stakes winner of 7 races Banimpire (by Holy Roman Emperor), the fairly useful 8.5f to 10f winner and dual Listed-placed My Spirit (by Invincible Spirit) and the fair dual 1m winner Dream On Buddy (by Oasis Dream). The dam, a very useful dual Listed 12f winner, was second in the Group 3 Princess Royal Stakes and is a half-sister to 5 winners. The second dam, Mayenne (by Nureyev), is an unraced three-parts sister to the Prix de l'Arc de Triomphe winner Carnegie and to the smart Group 2 10f Prix Guillaume d'Ornano winner Antisaar. (Mr Y. Zhang). *"A May foal, she's just been ticking over and we haven't done much with her yet because she's still a bit immature. She has a good attitude and she'll be a nice filly in the second half of the year over seven* furlongs. She'll come to hand at the back-end of the year but a lot of these fillies could do with the sun on their backs".

765. OLYMPIC HEROINE ★★★★
b.f. Olympic Glory – Hideaway Heroine (Hernando). April 23. Tenth foal. €85,000Y. Goffs Orby. S Kirk. Half-sister to 4 winners including the French dual Group 3 1m winner Maimara (by Makfi), the Group 3 1m Premio Dormello winner Ombrage (by Orpen) and the Italian Listed 1m winner Cisneros (by Johannesburg). The dam, a useful Listed-placed 7f winner, is a half-sister to 3 minor winners. The second dam, Dulcinea (by Selkirk), a fair 7f and 1m winner, is a half-sister to 6 winners including the French Listed winner Amato. (Imperial Racing Syndicate). *"A lovely filly, she's quite tall and one of the more forward of our fillies. She has a lovely attitude, pleases us in her work and she's one for the middle of the season. Very straightforward and a filly we like a lot".*

766. SAGITTARIAN WIND ★★★
b.f. Iffraaj – Bahia Breeze (Mister Baileys). March 2. Sixth foal. €52,000Y. Goffs Orby. BBA (Ire). Sister to the promising 2017 2-y-o 6f winner Beshaayir and to the quite useful 7f winner Khalaas and half-sister to the quite useful 2-y-o 6f winner Alsaaden (by Acclamation), the Polish winner and French Listed 9f second Brioniya (by Pivotal) and the fair 6f winner of 4 races Kaeso (by Excelebration). The dam, a very useful 6f (at 2 yrs) and 1m dual Listed winner, was second in the Group 2 Betfred Mile and the Group 2 Prix Jean Romanet and is a half-sister to 3 winners. The second dam, Ring Of Love (by Magic Ring), a fair 5f winner of 4 races (including at 2 yrs), is a half-sister to 7 winners. (Y. Zhang). *"We like her, she's a filly with size and scope, we've starting stepping up her work and she's doing everything nicely. A filly that'll run in mid-season and what we've seen we like".*

767 TAKE SILK ★★★★
b.f. Shamardal – Raw Silk (Malibu Moon). May 14. Fifth foal. Half-sister to the quite useful 2-y-o 6f winner Tailor's Row, to the fair 8.5f to 12f winner of 4 races Filament Of Gold (both by Street Cry) and the US 2-y-o 1m winner Wedding Dress (by Medaglia d'Oro). The dam won the Grade 2 9f Sands Point

Stakes in the USA. The second dam, Silken Sash (by Fairy King), was a quite useful 5f winner. (Godolphin). *"She was a late foal but she's a filly we really like. She's forward-going, has a good attitude and she's been showing us a nice bit despite her immaturity. A filly to start off in mid-season, she goes well and might be quick enough to start over six furlongs".*

768. VIDIYNI ★★★
b.c. Siyouni – Virana (King's Best). May 9. Fifth foal. Half-brother to the minor French 12f winner Viyana (by Azamour) and to a hurdles winner by Sinndar. The dam, a Listed 9.5f placed maiden in France, is a half-sister to one winner. The second dam, Vereva (by Kahyasi), won the Group 1 10.5f Prix de Diane. (H H Aga Khan). *"He'll be one of our earlier ones, has a great attitude, well-balanced and goes well. A nice horse that'll be ready to start when the six furlong races appear, so for a colt from one of the Aga Khan families he's quite precocious".*

769.WILD MUSTANG ★★★
b.c. Invincible Spirit – Propaganda (Sadler's Wells). April 7. Eighth foal. €55,000Y. Goffs Orby. BBA (Ire). Brother to the quite useful 2017 multiple 7f placed 2-y-o Porth Swtan and to the useful 2-y-o 7f winner and Group 2 May Hill Stakes third Shagah and half-brother to the quite useful 12f and hurdles winner Swnymor (by Dylan Thomas). The dam, a fair Irish 11f winner at 4 yrs, is a half-sister to 5 winners including the German Group 3 winner Pearl Banks. The second dam, Pearly Shells (by Efisio), won the Group 1 Prix Vermeille and the Group 2 Prix de Malleret and is a half-sister to 4 winners including the US Grade 1 Hollywood Turf Handicap winner Frenchpark. *"He only arrived about six weeks ago but he's a nice colt with a good attitude, well-balanced and has a good way of going. We've recently started to increase his work and he's one for mid-season".*

770. UNNAMED ★★★★
b.c. Bated Breath – Adelfia (Sinndar). March 5. Eighth foal. €75,000Y. Tattersalls Ireland September. BBA (Ire). Half-brother to the quite useful 2-y-o 1m winner Adelana (by Manduro), to the fairly useful 1m (at 2 yrs) and 9f winner Adilapour (by Azamour)

and a hurdles winner by Nayef. The dam, a quite useful 12f winner, is a half-sister to 3 winners including the smart dual Group 3 winner Adilabad. The second dam, Adaiyka (by Doyoun), was a smart winner of the Group 3 9f Prix Chloe. (Copper Beech Racing Syndicate). *"A lovely horse and one of our nicer colts, he's straightforward and has a good attitude. A half-brother to two 2-y-o winners we trained, he'll be racing in May or June over six furlongs and I'm sure he'll get seven. We like him a lot".*

771. UNNAMED ★★★
b.c. Iffraaj – Burke's Rock (Cape Cross). February 23. Second foal. €40,000Y. Goffs Orby. McCarthy Bloodstock. Half-brother to the fairly useful 1m winner Shaaqaaf (by Sepoy). The dam, a fairly useful Listed 1m winner of 4 races, is a half-sister to 2 winners. The second dam, Miss Lacey (by Diktat), is an unplaced half-sister to 8 winners including the Group 2 Superlative Stakes and Group 2 Bosphorus Cup winner Halicarnassus. (Knockenduff Stud). *"A very tall horse but he's a lovely, well-balanced colt and everything we've asked him to do he's done well. We like him".*

772. UNNAMED ★★★
b.f. Born To Sea – Kalidaha (Cadeaux Genereux). February 12. Fourth foal. The dam, a useful 7f (at 2 yrs) and 1m winner, was third in the Group 3 Brownstown Stakes and is a half-sister to 3 winners including the useful Listed UAE 1m winner Burano. The second dam, Kalimanta (by Lake Coniston), ran twice unplaced and is a half-sister to 6 winners including the top-class Champion Stakes and Breeders Cup Turf winner Kalanisi and the high-class 1m Listed winner and Group 1 St James's Palace Stakes second Kalaman. (H H Aga Khan). *"A good-looking filly for the second half of the year, the little we've done with her we like and she's taking her training really well".*

773. UNNAMED ★★★
b.c. So You Think – Karawana (King's Best). March 1. Ninth foal. Closely related to the French dual Group 3 10f winner Karaktar (by High Chaparral) and half-brother to the fairly useful Irish 2-y-o 6f winner Karamaya (by Invincible Spirit) and the fairly useful 10f

winner Karatash (by Halling). The dam, a fairly useful Irish 1m and 10f winner, is a half-sister to 3 winners. The second dam, Karaliyfa (by Kahyasi), a quite useful 9f winner, is a half-sister to 6 winners including the 2-y-o Group 3 1m May Hill Stakes winner Karasta and to the Group 2 2m 2f Doncaster Cup dead-heat winner Kasthari. (H H Aga Khan). *"A lovely, big, well-balanced horse, there's plenty of size and scope about him. Even though he's quite big he'll make a 2-y-o in the second half of the year and I like him".*

774. UNNAMED ★★★
ch.c. Exceleberation – Kerisa (Azamour). March 30. Second foal. The dam, a quite useful 10f and 12f winner, is a half-sister to the useful Irish 2-y-o 7f winner and Group 3 9f Kilboy Estates Stakes second Kirinda and the fairly useful 7f (at 2 yrs) and Listed 12f winner Karasiyra. The second dam, Kerania (by Daylami), unplaced in one start, is a half-sister to the useful Irish 12f winner and Group 2 placed and dual Australian Group 2 placed Kerdem. (H H Aga Khan). *"He's done particularly well lately, strengthening and developing, his work has improved and he enjoys it, so he's one that's going forward and showing promise even though he probably wants seven furlongs".*

775. UNNAMED ★★★
b.c. Rock Of Gibraltar – Lidaya (Elusive Quality). April 21. Third foal. Half-brother to the French 10f winner Lasspour (by Dalakhani). The dam is an unraced half-sister to 5 winners including the German Group 1 and Italian Group 1 winner of 11 races Linngari. The second dam, Lidakiya (by Kahyasi), a useful 10f and 12f winner, is a half-sister to 8 winners including the Irish triple Listed winner Livadiya. (H H Aga Khan). *"A very straightforward colt with a good attitude, he's one for the second half of the year and everything we've asked him to do he's done it well".*

776. UNNAMED ★★★
ch.f. Frankel – Maids Causeway (Giant's Causeway). March 18. Seventh foal. Half-sister to the quite useful 10f and hurdles winner Jameel (by Monsun), to the minor French 10f winner Spirit Ditty (by Singspiel), the fair

2-y-o 6f winner Gmaash and the dual hurdles winner Mountainside (both by Dubawi). The dam, winner of the Group 1 1m Coronation Stakes, is a half-sister to 3 winners including the Irish 7f winner and Group 3 placed Uimhir A Haon. The second dam, Vallee Des Reves (by Kingmambo), is an unraced half-sister to the Group 2 Prix du Muguet winner Vetheuil, the Group 3 Prix de l'Opera winner Verveine (dam of the Grade 1 winners Vallee Enchantee and Volga) and the dam of the Grand Prix de Paris winner Vespone. (Godolphin). *"A big, scopey filly, she's well-balanced, has a great action and is one for the second half of the year. For the little we've done with her we like her a lot".*

777. UNNAMED ★★★
br.c. Power – Money Penny (Montjeu). April 4. Sixth foal. €36,000Y. Tattersalls Ireland September. BBA (Ire). Half-brother to the quite useful 9f winner Wild As The Wind (by Approve). The dam, placed twice at 3 yrs in Italy, is a half-sister to 6 winners. The second dam, Miss Marisa (by Beldale Flutter), a minor winner in Italy, is a half-sister to 10 winners including Don Orazio (Group 1 Italian Derby). (Copper Beech Racing Syndicate). *"A big, scopey horse, we're just increasing his work now and he's going well. A horse for the second half of the year over seven furlongs".*

778. UNNAMED ★★★★
b.c. Elzaam – Playamongthestars (Galileo). April 1. Third foal. €40,000Y. Tattersalls Ireland September. BBA (Ire). The dam is an unraced half-sister to 4 winners in Australia. The second dam, Moon Magic (by Casual Lies), a winner in New Zealand and third in the Group 1 New Zealand 1,000 Guineas, is a half-sister to 5 winners. (Copper Beech Racing Syndicate). *"A gorgeous horse, big, scopey with a great action. We like him plenty, he probably wants seven furlongs but he's doing everything right".*

779. UNNAMED ★★★
b.c. Cape Cross – Rayna (Selkirk). February 18. First foal. The dam, a quite useful 11f and 12f winner of 4 races, is a half-sister to 2 winners. The second dam, Raydiya (by Marju), a useful Listed 12f winner in Ireland, is a half-sister to one winner. (H H Aga Khan). *"A lovely horse*

that's just started to come forward lately, he likes to please in his work and he's very straightforward".

780. UNNAMED ★★★
gr.f. Dark Angel – Riyaba (Dalakhani). April 4. Second foal. Half-sister to the 2017 2-y-o Listed 7f winner Riyazan (by Iffraaj). The dam is an unraced half-sister to 5 winners including Riyalma (Listed 10f Pretty Polly Stakes). The second dam, Riyafa (by Kahyasi), was a Listed 12f winner at Ascot. (H H Aga Khan). *"A nice, straightforward filly with a good attitude, we like her but the fillies are a shade behind in their work on account of the bad weather. She'd be one of our nicer fillies, has plenty of strength about her and I'd expect her to make a 2-y-o all right".*

781. UNNAMED ★★
b.c. Lope De Vega – Shamooda (Azamour). January 20. Second foal. Half-brother to the minor French 1m winner Shemda (by Dutch Art). The dam, a fair Irish dual 12f winner, is a half-sister to 4 winners including the French Group 3 10f and Group 3 15f winner Shemima and the French Listed winners Shemaya and Shemala. The second dam, Shemaka (by Nishapour), won the Group 1 10.5f Prix de Diane, the Group 3 10f Prix de la Nonette and the Group 3 9f Prix de Conde. (H H Aga Khan). *"A lovely, very big horse with a great action and a good attitude. He's one for the back-end and he'll be a nicer 3-y-o. For what he's done you'd like him but he'll take plenty of time".*

782. UNNAMED ★★★
ch.c. Rip Van Winkle – Shebella (Dubai Destination). February 24. Third foal. The dam, a useful 7f winner, was Group 3 placed over 9.5f and is a half-sister to the smart 11f winner and Group 3 placed Shikarpour. The second dam, Shibina (by Kalanisi), a quite useful 10f and 12f winner, is a half-sister to 6 winners including the Irish Derby third Shalapour. (H H Aga Khan). *"A lovely, well-balanced horse with a great action, even though he's one for seven furlongs in the second half of the year we like him. There's a bit of style about him".*

783. UNNAMED ★★★
gr.f. Dark Angel – Sinaniya (More Than Ready).

March 19. First foal. The dam, a quite useful 2-y-o 7f winner, is a half-sister to the fairly useful 1m (at 2 yrs) and 10f winner Sindjara. The second dam, Sindirana (by Kalanisi), won over 7f (at 2 yrs) and the Listed 11f Lingfield Oaks Trial and is a half-sister to 2 winners. (H H Aga Khan). *"She's doing half-speeds now and is very willing and well-balanced. I'd expect her to be running in mid-season but we haven't pressed any buttons with her yet".*

784. UNNAMED ★★★

b.c. Poet's Voice – Talkative (Oasis Dream). April 3. Fourth foal. €18,000Y. Tattersalls Ireland September. BBA (Ire). Half-brother to Good To Talk (by Camacho), a winner of 4 races in France at 2 yrs in 2017 over 5.5f and 6f, and to a hurdles winner by Champs Elysees. The dam is an unraced half-sister to 6 winners including the US Grade 1 Matriarch Stakes winner Price Tag. The second dam, Tarocchi (by Affirmed), a minor French 3-y-o winner, is a half-sister to 8 winners including the French Group 2 winner Privity. (Copper Beech Racing Syndicate). *"A smashing horse, he's very straightforward, has a good attitude and shows plenty of promise. He has a good way of going and will be one of the earlier ones. I'd say he has enough pace for six furlongs and he's been going well".* TRAINER'S BARGAIN BUY

785. UNNAMED

b.c. Camelot – Zerkeriya (Soviet Star). April 23. Fifth foal. Half-brother to the French 1m winner Ziriyan (by Zamindar) and to 2 minor winners by Cape Cross and Shamardal. The dam, a French 12f winner, is a half-sister to 4 winners notably Zarkava – a multiple Group 1 winner from 1m to 12f. The second dam, Zarkasha (by Kahyasi), is an unraced half-sister to the Group 3 Prix de Sandringham winner and French 1,000 Guineas fourth Zarkiya and the French Listed-placed winner Zariyan. The second dam, Zarkana (by Doyoun), won over 1m in France and is a half-sister to the smart French 7f and 1m winner Zarannda. (H H Aga Khan). *"A nice horse, being by Camelot he'll take a bit of time but he's a good-moving horse and has been pleasing us for what we've asked him. He'll be fine over seven furlongs in the second half of the year".*

RICHARD HANNON

786. ACTIVE POWER (FR) ★★★★

b.f. Le Havre – Sun Seeker (Galileo). January 9. Second foal. €90,000Y. Arqana Deauville August. Peter & Ross Doyle. Half-sister to the 2017 French 2-y-o 7f winner Action Parfaite (by Air Chief Marshal). The dam ran once unplaced and is a half-sister to 7 winners, two of them Group 3 placed. The second dam, Sharakawa (by Darshaan), is an unraced half-sister to 4 winners. *"A nice filly with a good action and a good shape to her so she's one we should have plenty of fun with this year".*

787. AIM POWER (IRE) ★★★

gr.f. Zebedee – Montefino (Shamardal). March 5. Fourth foal. 160,000Y. Tattersalls October Book 2. Sackville/Donald. Sister to the useful 2-y-o 5f and 6f winner of 3 races and Group 3 6f Firth Of Clyde Stakes second Parsley and half-sister to the Italian Group 2 10f and dual Group 3 winner Anda Muchacho (by Helmet). The dam is an unraced half-sister to 2 minor winners. The second dam, Monturani (by Indian Ridge), winner of the Group 2 10f Blandford Stakes and two Listed events over 1m and 10f, is a half-sister to 8 winners including the Listed winners Monnavanna and Mill Springs. *"She did her first half speed yesterday and she's a very nice filly. A good, strong, early type, she'll be racing in April but it's a case of finding a race for her – there are so few at this time of the year. We're pleased with her".*

788. AIR BENDER ★★★

b.c. Garswood – Swanky Lady (Cape Cross). May 5. Fifth foal. 70,000Y. Tattersalls October Book 2. Peter & Ross Doyle. The dam, a quite useful 2-y-o 7f winner, is a half-sister to 3 winners including the useful Listed 6f (at 2 yrs) and Listed 7f winner Selinka. The second dam, Lady Links (by Bahamian Bounty), a dual Listed 6f winner (including at 2 yrs), is a half-sister to 5 winners. *"A lovely, big horse that's gone a bit backward on us. A good mover, we'll wait for the six/seven furlong races with him".*

789. AMOROUSLY (IRE) ★★

b.f. Australia – Know Me Love Me (Danehill Dancer). March 19. First foal. €85,000Y. Goffs Orby. Peter & Ross Doyle. The dam is an unraced sister to the South African winner and dual Group 2 third Berry Blaze and a half-sister to 3 winners. The second dam, Strawberry Roan (by Sadler's Wells), an Irish Listed winner over 7f and 1m, was second in the 1,000 Guineas and is a sister to the Irish 1,000 Guineas and Epsom Oaks winner and good broodmare Imagine and a half-sister to Generous, winner of the Derby, the Irish Derby, the King George VI and Queen Elizabeth Diamond Stakes and the Dewhurst Stakes. *"She seems to be doing everything nicely at the moment, she's a good size, strong and won't be early but she's a nice filly. Doing everything asked of her so far".*

790. BADER ★★★
b.c. Elusive City – Golbahar (Holy Roman Emperor). January 22. First foal. £70,000Y. Goffs UK Premier (Doncaster). Peter & Ross Doyle. The dam, a Listed-placed winner of 4 races in France at 2 and 3 yrs, is a half-sister to 5 winners. The second dam, Grosgrain (by Diesis), a minor French 3-y-o winner, is a half-sister to 7 winners. *"A big, strong horse, he's grown a lot having looked like he might be early. We'll definitely wait for the six furlong races for him now".*

791. BEAUTY CONCEPT ★★★
b.c. Heeraat – Contenance (Dansant). April 1. First foal. 26,000Y. Tattersalls December. Peter & Ross Doyle. The dam ran twice unplaced and is a half-sister to 8 winners including Les Fazzani, a winner of four Listed events over 10f and 12f, and third in the Group 1 10f Premio Lydia Tesio and the German Listed winner and Group 3 6f placed Miss Lips. The second dam, Massada (by Most Welcome), a Listed-placed 7f and 1m winner at 2 yrs in Germany, is a half-sister to 3 minor winners. *"A good, strong horse, he's a bit leggy, does everything easily and has a very good way about him".*

792. BEECHWOOD JAMES (FR) ★★★
b.c. Sunday Break – Mururoa (Great Journey). April 22. Second foal. €9,000Y. Osarus September. F Barberini/MPR. The dam is an unraced half-sister to 2 winners including the French Group 3 1m and Hong Kong winner Mr Bond. The second dam, Melodya (by Great Palm), a minor French winner, is a half-sister to 7 other minor winners there, including over

jumps. *"A nice colt that's doing half-speeds now, he's grown a bit and done very well".* TRAINER'S BARGAIN BUY

793. BIG BABY BULL ★★★★
ch.c. Tagula – Grotta Del Fauno (Galileo). March 12. Third foal. £70,000Y. Goffs UK Premier (Doncaster). Peter & Ross Doyle. Half-brother to the Italian winner, including at 2 yrs, Guntur (by Notnowcato). The dam is an unraced half-sister to 4 minor winners in Italy. The second dam, Conca Peligna (by Persian Bold), a minor winner at 3 yrs in Italy, is a half-sister to 7 winners including Duca D'Atri (Group 2 Premio Ribot). *"He's a nice horse, physically he looks great and we're very happy with him. He's got good conformation, he's a likeable type and we'll probably wait for six furlongs with him".*

794. BRIAN EPSTEIN (IRE) ★★★
b.c. Dark Angel – Jewel In The Sand (Bluebird). April 3. Eighth foal. £140,000Y. Goffs UK Premier (Doncaster). Peter & Ross Doyle. Half-brother to 5 winners including the quite useful 10f winners Bedouin (by High Chaparral) and Falkirk (by Montjeu), the fair 2-y-o 5f winners The Rising (by Pivotal) and Dansili Dual (by Dansili), and the moderate 5f winner Fearbuster (by Fastnet Rock). The dam, a winner of 4 races including the Group 2 6f Cherry Hinton Stakes and the Albany Stakes, is a half-sister to 4 winners including the German 3-y-o Listed 6f winner Davignon. The second dam, Dancing Drop (by Green Desert), a useful dual 2-y-o 6f winner, was Listed-placed and is a half-sister to 9 winners. *"A lovely horse that cost a lot but you can see the money in him. We're in no hurry with him whatsoever but he looks like he's a bit classy. The Coventry has been suggested for him and although it's early days you wouldn't look silly at the moment for thinking about it".*

795. CANTON QUEEN (IRE) ★★★
b.f. Shamardal – Hana Lina (Oasis Dream). February 19. First foal. 110,000Y. Tattersalls October Book 1. Sackville/Donald. The dam, a modest 7f and 1m placed maiden, is a half-sister to 8 winners including the Group 2 6f Lowther Stakes, Group 3 6f Princess Margaret Stakes and Group 2 6f Diadem Stakes winner Lady Of The Desert. The second dam, Queen's

Logic (by Grand Lodge), a champion 2-y-o filly and winner of the Group 1 6f Cheveley Park Stakes and the Group 2 6f Lowther Stakes, is a half-sister to 6 winners including the top-class multiple Group 1 winner Dylan Thomas and the 1,000 Guineas winner Homecoming Queen. *"A lovely filly, she's grown and turned into a nice, straightforward filly for later on".*

796. CASTING (IRE) ★★★
b.c. Society Rock – Suffer Her (Whipper). April 12. Sixth foal. £160,000Y. Goffs UK Premier (Doncaster). Peter & Ross Doyle. Half-brother to the quite useful 2017 2 y o 5.5f and 6f winner Mraseel (by Sir Prancealot), to the quite useful 2-y-o dual 5f winner Tahoo (by Zebedee), the quite useful 2-y-o 5f winner Sarista (by Kodiac) and the fair dual 5f winner Vodka Chaser (by Baltic King). The dam is an unraced half-sister to 4 winners including the useful 2-y-o dual 6f winner and Listed-placed Campbeltown. The second dam, Jallaissine (by College Chapel), placed twice at 2 yrs in France, is a half-sister to the smart 12f Listed winner Riyafa. *"He looks an early type like a lot of the Society Rock's were last year, he's done a half-speed this morning and he's one we'll be looking to crack on with".*

797. CHATHAM HOUSE ★★
gr.c. Dark Angel – Timely (Pivotal). March 4. First foal. The dam is an unraced half-sister to 9 winners including the French 2,000 Guineas and US Grade 1 winner Aussie Rules and the Listed winner and US Grade 2 second Approach. The second dam, Last Second (by Alzao), a dual Group 2 10f winner and second in the Group 1 Coronation Stakes, is a half-sister to the dams of the Group 1 winners Albanova, Alborada, Allegretto, Yesterday and Quarter Moon. *"A big, long horse with a massive action. We've been caught out a few times trying to get these Dark Angel's ready early and they show a bit but then go weak. So he's one for the longer term, maybe the back-end of the season".*

798. CHONBURI ★★★
b.f. Lawman – Expected Dream (Galileo). April 3. First foal. 55,000Y. Tattersalls December. Sackville/Donald. The dam is an unraced half-sister to 4 winners including Group 1 1m Prix Jean Prat winner of 5 races

Havana Gold. The second dam, Jessica's Dream (by Desert Style), a very smart sprinter, won the Group 3 Ballyogan Stakes and the Group 3 Premio Omenoni and is a half-sister to the Listed winner and dual Group 1 placed Majors Cast. *"A very nice filly, being by Lawman you wouldn't be pushing her too early but she's a good, straightforward filly and a good mover with a good temperament".*

799. COCO CHEVAL (IRE) ★★★
ch.f. Kyllachy – Chant De Sable (IRE) (Oasis Dream). February 3. First foal. €57,000Y. Arqana Deauville August. De Burgh Equine. The dam, placed twice at 3 yrs in France, is a half-sister to 6 winners including Delfos (Group 2 Prix d'Harcourt) and Balius (UAE Group 2 winner). The second dam, Akhla (by Nashwan), a minor winner in the USA, is a half-sister to 6 winners. *"She's done a bit of work this morning and could be starting over six furlongs – maybe even five".*

800. COOL KITTY ★★★★
b.f. Kodiac – Ligeia (Rail Link). February 7. First foal. 35,000Y. Tattersalls October Book 2. Peter & Ross Doyle. The dam, a useful dual 6f (at 2 yrs) and 8.5f winner, is a half-sister to 2 winners including the Group 3 1m Prix d'Aumale winner Shahah. The second dam, Elegant Beauty (by Olden Times), is an unraced half-sister to 8 winners including the champion 2-y-o Grand Lodge and the Listed winners La Persiana and Papabile. *"She's done really well actually. Since she's been in she's strengthened up a lot and has a bit of an attitude like most Kodiacs, but that's not a problem. A good-moving filly, hopefully she'll be fairly early and is probably one to get out in May over six furlongs. A grand filly".*

801. CRACKING SPEED (IRE) ★★★
gr.c. Alhebayeb – Summer Glow (Exceed And Excel). March 26. First foal. €70,000Y. Goffs Orby. Peter & Ross Doyle. The dam, a moderate 10f winner, is a half-sister to 2 other minor winners. The second dam, In The Ribbons (by In The Wings), was a quite useful Irish Listed-placed 12f winner. *"A big horse like all of them by this sire – the ones we have anyway. We'll definitely be waiting for the six furlong races with him but there's plenty of strength about him".*

802. CROWN OF FLOWERS ★★★
ch.f. Garswood – Ring Of Love (Magic Ring).
April 17. Twelfth foal. 98,000Y. Tattersalls
October Book 1. Peter & Ross Doyle. Closely
related to a 3-y-o winner in Hong Kong by
Dutch Art and half-sister to the very useful
6f (at 2 yrs) and 1m dual Listed winner and
dual Group 2 placed Bahia Breeze (by Mister
Baileys), the fair dual 6f winner Proper Charlie
(by Cadeaux Genereux) and the fair dual 5f
winner Ring For Baileys (by Kyllachy). The
dam, a fair 5f winner of 4 races (including at
2 yrs), is a half-sister to 7 winners. The second
dam, Fine Honey (by Drone), a fairly useful
2-y-o 5f winner, is a half-sister to 7 winners.
*"A very strong, good-sized filly with an awful
lot to like about her. We'll be waiting for the
six/seven furlong races with her".*

803. DANCING SPEED (IRE) ★★★
br.c. Dandy Man – Air Maze (Dansili). April
28. Fifth foal. €60,000Y. Tattersalls Ireland
September. Peter & Ross Doyle. Half-brother
to the quite useful 7f (including at 2 yrs) and
8.5f winner of 6 races Harlequin Striker (by
Bahamian Bounty). The dam, a fair 9f and 10f
winner, is a half-sister to 3 winners. The second
dam, Begueule (by Bering), a quite useful 7f
and 1m winner at 2 and 3 yrs in France, was
Listed-placed twice and is a half-sister to 10
winners. *"A leggy colt, a good sort and a very
good mover. Even though he's by Dandy Man I
don't think we'll be in a big hurry with him and
he's a six furlong type".*

804. DAWN TREADER (IRE) ★★★
b.c. Siyouni – Miss Elena (Invincible Spirit).
March 19. First foal. 60,000Y. Tattersalls
October Book 2. Sackville/Donald. The dam,
a minor 2-y-o winner in France, is a half-sister
to four other minor winners abroad. The
second dam, New Largue (by Distant View),
was placed at 2 and 3 yrs in France and is a
half-sister to 4 winners including the French
Group2 and Group 3 winner New Girlfriend.
*"A lovely big horse, we'll be in no hurry with
him at all and he'll wait for the six/seven
furlong races".*

805. DIRTY RASCAL ★★★
b.c. Acclamation – Refusetolisten (Clodovil).
March 25. First foal. 58,000Y. Tattersalls
October Book 2. Peter & Ross Doyle. The
dam, a fair Irish 7f winner, is a half-sister to

3 other minor winners. The second dam,
Smoken Rosa (by Smoke Glacken), placed 3
times in the USA, is a half-sister to 4 winners
including Snowdrops (three Graded 3 stakes
wins). *"A typical Acclamation in that he's very
long but looks strong and is probably more like
a six furlong colt than five. He's nice and we'll
hopefully have a bit of fun with him".*

806. DIXIELAND ★★★
b.c. Red Jazz – Signora Lina (High Chaparral).
April 20. Third foal. £60,000Y. Goffs UK
Premier (Doncaster). Peter & Ross Doyle. The
dam is an unraced half-sister to 6 winners
including the French Listed winner and US
Grade 3 second Polygreen. The second dam,
Yxenery (by Sillery), a dual Listed 1m winner in
France, is a half-sister to 2 minor winners.
*"He's looking like being one of our first runners,
he looks sharp, has plenty of speed and he's
fairly straight. So hopefully he'll be winning
fairly early".*

807. DOUGHAN ALB ★★★
b.c. Havana Gold – Sandtime (Green Desert).
February 1. Seventh foal. 30,000Y. Tattersalls
October Book 3. Khalifa Al-Attiya. Half-
brother to the fair 2-y-o 1m winner Deerfield
(by New Approach) and to the modest 7f
winner Ioannou (by Excellent Art). The dam,
a Listed-placed 1m winner in Ireland, is a full
or half-sister to 6 winners. The second dam,
Key Change (by Darshaan), won the Group 1
Yorkshire Oaks and is a half-sister to 7 winners.
*"A big, strong colt and a good-moving type
with a real nice way about him. He'll be a six
furlong 2-y-o".*

808. EDDIE COCHRAN (IRE) ★★★
bl.c. Society Rock – Crossreadh (Sahm). April
2. Fourth foal. €44,000Y. Tattersalls Ireland
September. Peter & Ross Doyle. Half-brother
to a 2-y-o winner in Russia by Ad Valorem.
The dam is an unplaced sister to the Irish
triple Listed winner Red Maloney and a half-
sister to 10 winners. The second dam, Roja
(by L'Enjoleur), was placed once at 2 yrs in the
USA and is a half-sister to 2 minor winners.
*"He's doing half-speeds now and doing it very
nicely. We'll be looking for the first six furlong
races with him, he's a bit bigger than most
Society Rock's but he's a nice colt and doing
everything well".*

809. ELSAABLQAAT ★★★
b.f. Invincible Spirit – Fleeting Smile (Distorted Humor). March 21. First foal. The dam was a fairly useful dual 7f winner at 2 and 3 yrs. The second dam, Fleet Indian (by Indian Charlie), a champion older mare in the USA, won 13 races including the Grade 1 Beldame Stakes and the Grade 1 Personal Ensign Stakes and is a half-sister to 2 winners. (Hamdan Al Maktoum). *"She looks like an early type who could be ready to start over six furlongs. A small filly, but strong and very well-built".*

810. ENTERTAINING ★★★
b.c. Dandy Man – Letizia Sophia (Shamardal). March 25. Second foal. 92,000Y. Tattersalls October Book 1. Peter & Ross Doyle. The dam is an unraced half-sister to 3 minor winners. The second dam, Tralanza (by Traditionally), a fair 7f (at 2 yrs) and 10f placed maiden, is a half-sister to 3 minor winners. *"A big 2-y-o, he's a nice, good-moving colt for the six/seven furlong races and we wouldn't be in a hurry with him".*

811. EQUAL SUM
br.f. Paco Boy – Hypoteneuse (Sadler's Wells). March 6. Half-sister to the fairly useful 7f and 1m winner of 3 races Pythagorean (by Oasis Dream), to the quite useful 2-y-o 7.5f and 1m winner Maths Prize (by Royal Applause) and the modest 11.5f winner Longside (by Oasis Dream). The dam, a fair 12f winner, is a sister to 4 winners including the Oaks second Flight Of Fancy and the dual Listed 7f winner Golden Stream and a half-sister to 4 winners. The second dam, Phantom Gold (by Machiavellian), a very useful winner from 1m (at 2 yrs) to 12f including the Group 2 Ribblesdale Stakes and the Group 3 St Simon Stakes, is a sister to the Listed 10f winner Fictitious and a half-sister to the 1m winner and dual Listed-placed Tempting Prospect. *"A nice, big filly of The Queen's, she's quite leggy and will take time but has a good action and once she's strengthened up we'll have a bit of fun with her".*

812. EXTREME (IRE) ★★★★
br.c. No Nay Never – Mixed Blessing (Lujain). May 3. Fifth living foal. €280,000Y. Goffs Orby. Stephen Hillen. Half-brother to the useful Group 3 12f winner Apphia (by High Chaparral), to the useful 1m winner (at 2 yrs) and Listed 2m placed Century, to the Australian 12f winner and Group 3 third Our Century (both by Montjeu) and the minor French 2-y-o winner Privy Garden (by Oasis Dream). The dam, a 2-y-o Group 3 6f Princess Margaret Stakes winner, is a half-sister to 3 minor winners. The second dam, Marjorie's Memory (by Fairy King), a fair 5f winner at 2 and 3 yrs, is a half-sister to 4 winners. *"A lovely big colt that cost a lot of money in Ireland, he's got a hell of a way about him, you'd love him. A nice horse, he might be sharp enough for six furlongs but he'll really come into his own over seven. We like the No Nay Never's a lot".*

813. FLOATING ARTIST ★★★
b.c. Nathaniel – Miss Kenton (Pivotal). February 29. First foal. 80,000Y. Tattersalls October Book 2. Will Edmeades. The dam is an unplaced half-sister to 4 winners including the French Group 3 second Woven Lace. The second dam, Do The Honours (by Highest Honor), winner of the Group 3 6f Prix de Meautry, is a half-sister to 10 winners including the 2-y-o Listed Chesham Stakes winner and US Grade 1 third Seba. *"A lovely big horse, he's a good mover with a good temperament. We're not in a hurry with him but he'll be a lovely horse for the seven furlong races".*

814. FOX HAPPY (IRE) ★★★
b.c. Showcasing – Roo (Rudimentary). April 18. Twelfth living foal. 150,000Y. Tattersalls October Book 2. Sackville/Donald. Half-brother to 8 winners including the very smart 6f (at 2 yrs) and 7f winner and Group 1 Prix Morny second Gallagher (by Bahamian Bounty), the very useful 7f (including at 2 yrs) to 10f winner and Listed-placed Quick Wit (by Oasis Dream), the useful 5f (at 2 yrs) and 7f winner and Listed-placed Roodeye (by Inchinor and dam of the dual Grade 2 winner Prize Exhibit) and the quite useful 2-y-o winners Cockney Dancer (by Cockney Rebel) and Roodolph (by Primo Valentino). The dam, a Listed-placed 2-y-o 5f and 6f winner, is a half-sister to 6 winners including Bannister (Group 2 6f Gimcrack Stakes). The second dam, Shall We Run (by Hotfoot), a 5f placed 2-y-o, is a half-sister to the Group 1 6f Cheveley Park Stakes winner Dead Certain.

"He looked like he was going to be one of our first runners but he's grown again since so we won't be in a rush with him. That's no problem at all and he looks a proper 2-y-o".

815. FOX KASPER (IRE) ★★★

ch.c. Society Rock – Easy Times (Nayef). February 25. Second foal. 220,000Y. Tattersalls October Book 2. Sackville/Donald. Half-brother to the fairly useful dual 1m (at 2 yrs) and 12f winner and Listed-placed Al Hamdany (by Kodiac). The dam is an unraced half-sister to 4 winners. The second dam, Easy To Love (by Diesis), a quite useful 4-y-o 11.5f winner, is a sister to the Oaks winner Love Divine (herself dam of the St Leger winner Sixties Icon) and a half-sister to 5 winners including the Listed winners Dark Promise and Floreeda. *"A lovely big colt, he'll take time but he's got plenty of size and strength. A good mover and one for a bit later on".*

816. FOX POWER (IRE) ★★★

gr.c. Dark Angel – Zenella (Kyllachy). April 4. Fourth foal. 450,000Y. Tattersalls October Book 1. Sackville/Donald. Half-brother to the fair 2-y-o 7f winner Dark Crescent (by Elnadim) and to the modest 7f winner Art's Desire (by Dutch Art). The dam, a fairly useful 2-y-o Listed 1m winner, is a half-sister to 4 minor winners. The second dam, West One (by Gone West), ran twice unplaced and is a half-sister to 2 winners. *"A lovely big horse, he's a good-looking and good-moving 2-y-o like all our Dark Angel's and we wouldn't in any hurry with him at all. Seven furlongs should suit him in the second half of the season".*

817. GALILEO JADE ★★★

b.f. Australia – Dusty In Memphis (Broken Vow). April 5. Second foal. €67,000Y. Goffs Orby. Peter & Ross Doyle. The dam, a fair Irish 3-y-o 7f winner, is a half-sister to 4 winners including the Canadian 2-y-o Grade 3 1m winner Prussian. The second dam, Crystal Downs (by Alleged), a useful Irish 2-y-o 7f winner, was second in the Prix Marcel Boussac and third in the Moyglare Stud Stakes and is a half-sister to 5 winners including the Group 2 Geoffrey Freer Stakes winner and Prix de l'Arc de Triomphe second Mubtaker. *"She's not overly big but she has a good action and she's been upsides a few times and shown a bit, so*

we'll probably get a run into her in mid-season. We're happy with where she's at".

818. GINGER FOX ★★★

ch.c. Iffraaj – Rimth (Oasis Dream). April 1. Fourth foal. Half-brother to the 2017 2-y-o 7f winner, from two starts, Bullingdon (by Dansili), to the quite useful 1m and 10f winner Garrick and a winner over jumps (both by Galileo). The dam, a winner over 5f (at 2 yrs) and the Group 3 7f Fred Darling Stakes, was second in the Group 1 Cheveley Park Stakes. The second dam, Dorelia (by Efisio), a fair 1m winner, is a half-sister to 3 winners including the smart Group 2 5f Kings Stand Stakes and Group 3 5f Cornwallis Stakes winner Dominica. *"A lovely horse, he carries a bit of weight but he goes very well and has a really good way about him. Definitely a six furlong 2-y-o".*

819. GINGER NUT (IRE) ★★★

ch.f. Sir Prancealot – Applauding (Royal Applause). March 13. Eighth foal. £23,000Y. Goffs UK Silver. Peter & Ross Doyle. Half-sister to the 6f and 7f winner Loud (by Dutch Art), to the 1m and 10f winner Stoneboat Bill (by Virtual) and the 2-y-o 5f winner Jonnysimpson (by Zebedee) – all three only modest. The dam is an unraced half-sister to 9 winners including the German Listed 10f winner Metaxas. The second dam, Miller's Melody (by Chief Singer), a fair 6f and 7f placed maiden, is a half-sister to 7 winners including the Group 3 10f Royal Whip Stakes winner Kamakura and to the dams of the Group winners Blew By Em and Tioman Island. *"She reminds us a bit of Stormy Clouds who was by the same sire and was trained here to win two races. She looks sharp, isn't very big but should be early".*

820. GLORIOUS DANE ★★★★★

b.c. Olympic Glory – Kaminari (Sea The Stars). April 25. Second foal. €85,000Y. Goffs Orby. Peter & Ross Doyle. The dam, a quite useful Irish 2-y-o 1m winner, is a half-sister to 4 winners including the Group 1 Prix Marcel Boussac second On Verra. The second dam, Karmifira (by Always Fair), winner of the Listed Prix Finlande and second in the French 1,000 Guineas, is a half-sister to 5 winners including the Listed 1m Prix Coronation winner Kart Star. *"He's a very nice horse with a good action, a good way of going and a great attitude. He's* one we could have a lot of fun with come May and six furlongs. We like him a lot".

821. GLORY ★★★

b.c. Olympic Glory – Updated (New Approach). February 11. First foal. 38,000Y. Tattersalls December. Woodstock /Peter & Ross Doyle. The dam is an unplaced half-sister to 8 winners including the Group 3 Dee Stakes and Listed Magnolia Stakes winner South Easter. The second dam, Dance Treat (by Nureyev), won the Group 3 10f La Coupe and the Group 3 10.5f Prix de Flore and is a half-sister to 4 winners. *"A lovely horse, I think her owner Julie Wood did well buying him. He's got plenty of strength and looks more a six furlong 2-y-o than five but he's done a couple of bits upsides and shows plenty. We like him".*

822. GOD HAS GIVEN ★★★

b.c. Nathaniel – Langs Lash (Noverre). March 22. Third foal. 350,000Y. Tattersalls October Book 2. China Horse Club. Brother to the 2017 2-y-o 1m winner, from two starts, The Kid Bobby G and half-brother to the 2-y-o Listed 7.5f winner Waipu Cove (by Equiano). The dam, winner of the 2-y-o Group 2 5f Queen Mary Stakes and third in the Group 2 Lowther Stakes, is a half-sister to 3 winners. The second dam, Temple Street (by Machiavellian), is an unraced half-sister to 4 winners and to the placed dam of the French 1,000 Guineas winner Elusive Wave. *"He seems to be doing everything really well at the moment. His dam won the Queen Mary so hopefully he'll be a six furlong colt and we'll probably work him in the next few weeks to see where we are with him".*

823. GOOD LUCK FOX (IRE) ★★★

b.c. Society Rock – Violet Ballerina (Namid). March 29. Seventh foal. 180,000Y. Tattersalls October Book 2. Sackville/Donald. Half-sister to the fair 7f winner of 4 races Fab Lolly (by Rock Of Gibraltar), to the fair 7f and 8.5f winner Wolfie (by Duke Of Marmalade) and 2 minor winners in Germany by Cape Cross and Cadeaux Genereux. The dam, a fair 7f (at 2 yrs) and 6f winner, is a half-sister to 3 winners including the very useful 2-y-o Group 2 6f Richmond Stakes winner Carizzo Creek. The second dam, Violet Spring (by Exactly Sharp), a 5-y-o 2m winner in Ireland, is a half-sister to 3 other minor winners. *"A horse with a good*

action, he's doing everything nicely at the moment and he'll be slightly sharper than Fox Kasper (another Society Rock 2-y-o that's here). A mid-season type 2-y-o".*

824. GRACEFUL (IRE) ★★

b.f. Zoffany – Tahara (Caerleon). March 21. Fifteenth foal. 72,000Y. Tattersalls October Book 2. Not sold. Half-sister to 8 winners including the Group 1 5f Prix de l'Abbaye and Group 3 Ballyogan Stakes winner Gilt Edge Girl (by Monsieur Bond), the Group 2 5f Flying Childers Stakes winner Godfrey Street (by Compton Place) and the quite useful 7f winner Always Ready (by Best Of The Bests). The dam is an unplaced half-sister to 3 winners and to the unraced dam of the Group 1 Prix Morny winner Arcano. The second dam, Tarwiya (by Dominion), winner of the Group 3 C L Weld Park Stakes and third in the Group 1 Irish 1,000 Guineas, is a half-sister to 5 winners. *"Not over-big, but she does everything nicely enough and we'll crack on with her in the first few months of the season and see what we've got".*

825. HERMOCRATES (FR) ★★★

b.c. Farhh—Little Shambles (Shamardal). March 26. First foal. £82,000Y. Goffs UK Premier. Peter & Ross Doyle. The dam, a quite useful triple 7f winner, is a half-sister to 4 winners including the smart 2-y-o 6f winner and Group 1 French 1,000 Guineas third Rahiyah and the useful 5f (at 2 yrs) and 6f winner League Champion. The second dam, Meiosis (by Danzig), a useful 7f winner, is a half-sister to 6 winners. *"A lovely, sharp colt and a good mover, he'll want six/seven furlongs this year".*

826. HE'ZANARAB (IRE) ★★★

b.c. Footstepsinthesand – Ziggy's Secret (Sakhee's Secret). February 17. First foal. £30,000Y. Goffs UK Premier (Doncaster). Peter & Ross Doyle. The dam, a fair 5f (at 2 yrs) and 7f winner, is a half-sister to 3 minor winners. The second dam, Ziggy Zaggy (by Diktat), is an unraced half-sister to 7 winners including the Group 1 Premio Roma winner Imperial Dancer. *"A good sized colt, he's got good strength too and is one for the second half of the season. He covers the ground well and hopefully we'll have some fun with him".*

827. HUA HIN (IRE) ★★★
ch.c. Dandy Man – Midnight Oasis (Oasis Dream). February 6. Fifth foal. €70,000Y. Goffs Orby. Sackville/Donald. Half-brother to the useful 6f winner of 5 races at 3 and 4 yrs Mr Win (by Intikhab), to the fairly useful 6f winner of 5 races at 2 and 3 yrs George Bowen (by Dark Angel) and the quite useful 6f, 7f (both at 2 yrs) and 1m winner Mutahaady (by Elzaam). The dam is an unplaced half-sister to 8 winners including Miss Anabaa (Group 3 Ballyogan Stakes). The second dam, Midnight Shift (by Night Shift), a fair dual 6f winner at 3 yrs, is a half-sister to 8 winners including the Group 1 6f July Cup winner Owington. *"He's sharp, working well and showing plenty. He's got a lovely action, not overly-big but has plenty of strength and I should think he'll be racing in April. He knows his job".*

828. JAAYIZ (IRE) ★★★
b.c. Zoffany – So Devoted (Holy Roman Emperor). March 31. Second foal. 68,000Y. Tattersalls October Book 2. Peter & Ross Doyle. The dam, a modest Irish 6f winner at 4 yrs, is a half-sister to 5 winners including the Listed winner Bon Nuit. The second dam, Pray (by Priolo), is an unraced half-sister to 4 winners including the Group 3 and US Grade 2 winner Anshan. *"Not a big colt but he's likeable, has a good attitude and he'll be racing in May or June, probably over six furlongs. He's fine and doing everything nicely".*

829. JUNGLE WARFARE ★★★
ch.c. Bungle Inthejungle – Fanditha (Danehill Dancer). March 2. Third foal. £56,000Y. Goffs UK Premier (Doncaster). Peter & Ross Doyle. Half-brother to the fair 2-y-o 6f and 7f winner Cuppatee (by Canford Cliffs). The dam, a quite useful 7f (at 2 yrs) to 11f winner of 4 races, was Listed-placed over 10f and is a half-sister to 6 winners. The second dam, Splendid (by Mujtahid), placed third once over 6f at 2 yrs, is a half-sister to 3 winners including the very useful 1m (at 2 yrs) and 12f winner Peking Opera. *"He's a likeable type and hopefully he'll be fairly early, but whether it's five or six furlongs we'll see once we start to work him along. He's a good size, a good shape and the sire has plenty of 2-y-os running already so they look sharp, as a type. He's doing everything we want so far".*

830. KHIBRAH ★★★
b.f. Dark Angel – Mi Anna (Lake Coniston). April 27. Thirteenth foal. 140,000Y. Tattersalls October Book 2. Shadwell Estate Co. Half-sister to 10 winners here and abroad including the German dual Group 2 1m winner Mi Emma (by Silvano), the useful 1m winner and Group 1 Criterium International second Anna's Pearl (by Pivotal), the German winner and 7f Listed-placed Mi Rubina (by Rock Of Gibraltar) and the quite useful dual 7f winner Flourishing (by Exceed And Excel). The dam a German 2-y-o Listed winner, is a half-sister to 3 winners. The second dam, Medicenal (by Robellino), won 4 races in Germany and is a half-sister to 3 winners. *"A nice bay filly that's set for the six/seven furlong races, she's a good-moving filly that's doing everything well but she wasn't an early foal and we'll take our time with her".*

831. KINGS ROYAL HUSSAR (FR) ★★
b.c. Zebedee – Ile Rouge (Red Ransom (USA). March 30. Third foal. €40,000Y. Arqana Deauville August V2. Highflyer/Shefford. The dam, placed twice at 3 yrs in France, is a half-sister to 4 winners including the US Grade 2 Del Mar Derby and dual Grade 3 winner Inesperado. The second dam, Ile Mamou (by Ela-Mana-Mou), won twice at 3 yrs in Germany and is a half-sister to 2 winners. *"Even though he's a big horse and so one of the bigger Zebedee's he shows a lot of speed and he just might be ready for a six furlong race. A nice horse, when you see him he looks a bit big, but he goes very nicely".*

832. LADY SCATTERLEY (FR) ★★★★
ch.f. No Nay Never – Camdara (Hawk Wing). February 17. Second foal. The dam is a half-sister to the dam of the Group 1 6f Cheveley Park Stakes and Group 2 5.5f Prix Robert Papin winner Vorda. The second dam, Viavigoni (by Mark Of Esteem), is a daughter of the Italian 1,000 Guineas and Italian oaks winner Val d'Erica. *"A very nice, strong filly that's built like a colt. There's plenty of strength about her, she goes very well and is one for six furlongs. We think a lot of her".*

833. LEOUBE (IRE) ★★★★
b.f. Kodiac – Sojitzen (Great Journey). February 24. First foal. 120,000Y. Tattersalls

October Book 1. Peter & Ross Doyle. The dam, a minor French placed maiden, is a half-sister to 6 winners including the German Group 3 winner Lady Deauville. The second dam, Mercalle (by Kaldoun), won 8 races including the Group 1 Prix du Cadran and is a half-sister to 2 winners. *"A lovely filly that's shown us plenty already. We'll definitely wait for the six furlong races with her but she's very nice".*

834. LONDON ROCK (IRE) ★★★

b.c. Society Rock – Scottish Exile (Ashkalani). May 16. Eighth foal. €57,000Y. Tattersalls Ireland September. Peter & Ross Doyle. Half-brother to the smart 5f and 6f 2-y-o winner and multiple Group 3 second Bonnie Charlie (by Intikhab) and to the modest 2-y-o 6f seller winner Jimmy's Girl (by Equiano). The dam, a fair triple 5f winner, is a sister to the fairly useful 6f winner of 11 races and Listed-placed Million Percent and a half-sister to 7 winners. The second dam, Royal Jade (by Last Tycoon), a fairly useful 7f winner, is a half-sister to 6 winners including the Group 3 5f King George Stakes winner Averti. *"He worked the other day and looked sharp but being a May foal we won't kick on with him yet. We'll take our time and let him find his own way".*

835. MAGICAL WISH (IRE) ★★★

b.c. Heeraat – Tomintoul Magic (Holy Roman Emperor). March 2. Second foal. £48,000Y. Goffs UK Premier (Doncaster). Peter & Ross Doyle. The dam, a modest 6f placed 3-y-o, is a half-sister to 7 winners including the Listed winners Abbeyside and Flat Spin. The second dam, Trois Graces (Alysheba), a French 1m winner, is a half-sister to the Group 3 winners Rami and Crack Regiment and to the Prix de l'Abbaye second La Grand Epoque. *"A big, tall horse, he's quite leggy (some of these Heeraats are like that) but he's a nice, big horse with plenty to like about him. He'll definitely be waiting for the six furlong races".*

836. MAHBOB (IRE) ★★

b.c. Toronado – Lily Link (Rail Link). February 16. First foal. 100,000Y. Tattersalls October Book 1. Al Shaqab /Mandore. The dam is an unraced half-sister to 3 winners including Redwood (Canadian Grade 1 12f Northern Dancer Turf Stakes and Group 3 12f Glorious Stakes). The second dam, Arum

Lily (by Woodman), a minor French 1m and 9f winner, is a half-sister to 3 winners out of the Prix de Diane and Prix Vermeille winner Jolypha. *"A big, leggy colt, we wouldn't be in a hurry with him and we wouldn't want to run him any sooner than when the seven furlong races come along".*

837. MERSEY (IRE) ★★★

gr.f. Kodiac – Wylye (Dalakhani). March 13. First foal. The dam, a fair but lightly raced 2-y-o 1m winner, is a half-sister to one winner. The second dam, Tavy (by Pivotal), is an unraced half-sister to 4 winners including the Group 3 Prix du Palais Royal winner Frenchman's Bay. *"She looks sharp and does everything very easily, so she could be one to go with pretty early".*

838. MOLAAHETH ★★★

b.c. Heeraat – All Fur Coat (Multiplex). February 12. Third foal. £150,000Y. Goffs UK Premier (Doncaster). Shadwell Estate Co. Half-brother to the moderate 2017 5f placed 2-y-o Mocead Cappall and to the fair 2-y-o 5f winner Gerrard's Fur Coat (both by Captain Gerrard). The dam, a quite useful 2-y-o 5f winner, is a half-sister to 2 winners. The second dam, Elegant Lady (by Selkirk), a quite useful 6f winner, is a half-sister to 4 winners. *"He's another colt that's started to grow recently so we won't be in a hurry with him. We don't know about the sire because this is his first season, but this colt is the type for six furlongs".*

839. MONDAKHAR (IRE) ★★★

b.c. Battle Of Marengo (IRE) – Lost Highway (IRE) (Danehill Dancer). March 20. Third foal. £85,000Y. Goffs UK Premier. Shadwell Estate Co. Half-brother to the fair 2017 2-y-o 7f winner Painting Pictures (by Roderic O'Connor) and to the modest dual 1m winner Cliff Bay (by Elzaam). The dam, a moderate 9.5f and 12f placed maiden, is a half-sister to 4 winners including the Group 3 Gordon Stakes winner Rebel Soldier. The second dam, En Garde (by Irish River), a quite useful 2-y-o 5.7f winner, is a half-sister to 7 winners including the top-class Group 1 1m Queen Elizabeth II Stakes and Group 1 9.3f Prix d'Ispahan winner Observatory and the Group 2 Prix de Malleret winner High Praise. *"He's done very well and matured into a nice horse. We wouldn't be in a hurry but he'll be ready for the six furlong races".*

840. MORDRED (IRE) ★★★

b.c. Camelot – Endure (Green Desert). March 23. Ninth foal. 175,000Y. Tattersalls October Book 1. Peter & Ross Doyle. Brother to the fair 2017 7f placed 2-y-o Camomile Lawn and half-brother to 5 winners including the very useful 2-y-o Listed 7f winner Bunker (by Hurricane Run), the fairly useful Listed placed dual 5f winner Imtiyaaz (by Starspangledbanner), the quite useful 2-y-o 6f winner Atacama Crossing and the fair 2-y-o 5f and 6f winner of 4 races at 2 and 3 yrs Beach Candy (both by Footstepsinthesand). The dam was an unplaced half-sister to 7 winners including the Canadian Grade 3 winner Alexis and the Irish Listed winners Miss Helga and Freshwater Pearl. The second dam, Sister Golden Hair (by Glint Of Gold), a Listed-placed winner at 2 yrs in Germany, is a half-sister to 2 winners. *"We trained the half-brother Bunker who was a good horse. This colt has a better temperament than him, he does everything nicely but he's big and is one for later on over seven furlongs".*

841. MOSHARAKKA (IRE) ★★★

b.c. Alhebayeb – Azia (Desert Story). April 28. Eighth foal. 105,000Y. Tattersalls October Book 2. Shadwell Estate Co. Half-brother to the fair 2017 2-y-o 6f winner Chess Move (by Kodiac), to the useful Listed Ripon Champion 2-y-o Trophy winner Hold Your Colour, the modest 11f to 14f and hurdles winner Taste The Wine (both by Verglas) and the quite useful dual 1m winner at 2 and 4 yrs Arcano Gold (by Arcano). The dam, a 2-y-o 7f winner in Ireland, is out of the unraced Safdara (by Shahrastani), herself an unraced half-sister to 10 winners including the Group 2 Lockinge Stakes winner Safawan. *"He's turned the corner and is doing well. We're not sure about the sire because this is his first season but they're all a good size, we won't be chasing any of them up early and they'll all definitely be six/seven furlong horses".*

842. MOYASSAR ★★★

ch.c. Tamayuz – Catwalk (Pivotal). March 10. Third foal. 85,000 foal. Tattersalls December. Shadwell Estate Co. The dam, a quite useful 6f winner, is a half-sister to 6 winners including the 2-y-o Group 2 5f Flying Childers Stakes winner Sir Prancealot (by Tamayuz) and the

French Listed 10f winner of 10 races Nice Applause. The second dam, Mona 'Em (by Catrail), a Listed sprint winner, is a half-sister to 4 winners. *"Not over-big but there's plenty to like about him, he's very strong and he'll be a six furlong 2-y-o".*

843. MY BABYDOLL (IRE) ★★★

b.f. Slade Power – Keilogue (Invincible Spirit). April 9. Second foal. €55,000Y. Goffs Orby. Peter & Ross Doyle. The dam, a fair 1m placed maiden, is a half-sister to 7 winners including the Group 2 Prix de Pomone winner Bernimixa, the Group 3 Prix Gladiateur winner Miraculous and the French Listed winner and Group 2 Prix de Nieuil second Winkle. The second dam, Bernique (by Affirmed), a winner of 5 races in the USA and Grade 3 placed, is a half-sister to 10 winners. *"She looks sharp enough, not over-big and does everything easily. We'll crack on with her when the six furlong races come around".*

844. NAUGHTY RASCAL ★★★

ch.c. Kyllachy – Gerika (Galileo). April 7. Third foal. 19,000Y. Tattersalls December. Peter & Ross Doyle. Half-brother to the fair 2-y-o 7f winner Pirate Look (by Canford Cliffs). The dam, a 10f winner in Italy, is a half-sister to 6 winners including the Italian triple Listed 1m winner Donoma and the Italian dual Listed 10f winner Right Connection. The second dam, Green Tern (by Miswaki Tern), won once at 2 yrs in Italy and is a full or half-sister to 8 winners including the Group 3 Italian St Leger winner Green Senor. *"He didn't cost very much but he's a likeable type that's done plenty of growing, he's strengthened up now and is probably one to start in mid-season. He looks the part, has a good action and covers the ground".*

845. OONA (IRE) ★★★

b.f. Kodiac – Society Pearl (Kheleyf). February 5. First foal. 75,000Y. Tattersalls October Book 1. R Hannon. The dam, a fair 1m and 12f placed maiden, is a half-sister to 4 winners including the very smart 1m (at 2 yrs) and Group 2 Lancashire Oaks winner and dual Group 1 second Endless Time. The second dam, Mamonta (by Fantastic Light), placed once over 2m, is a half-sister to 8 winners including the Group 2 12.5f Prix de Royallieu winner and smart broodmare Mouramara. *"Not over-big but looks a bit sharp, we'll be having a look at her for the six furlong races".*

846. OUZO ★★★
b.c. Charm Spirit – Miss Meltemi (Miswaki Tern). April 7. Thirteenth foal. 95,000Y. Tattersalls October Book 2. Peter & Ross Doyle. Half-brother to 7 winners including the very useful 7f (at 2 yrs) and Listed 1m winner and Group 3 Dahlia Stakes third Don't Dili Dali, the useful Listed-placed 7f to 8.5f winner Balducci, the fairly useful Listed-placed 1m winner Ada River (all by Dansili), the quite useful 2-y-o 5f winner Haigh Hall (by Kyllachy) and the quite useful 12f winner Zafarana (by Tiger Hill). The dam, a dual 2-y-o winner in Italy and third in the Group 1 Italian Oaks, is a half-sister to 3 winners. The second dam, Blu Meltemi (by Star Shareef), a winner of 5 races at 2 and 3 yrs in Italy and second in the Italian Oaks, is a half-sister to 3 winners. *"A lovely, big horse that looks like one with plenty of class. We won't be in a hurry with him and he could be one of the nicer horses that we'll be looking at towards the back-end".*

847. PESTO ★★★★
br.c. New Approach – Pickle (Piccolo). April 2. Sixth foal. 80,000Y. Tattersalls October Book 2. John & Jake Warren. Closely related to the smart winner of four Listed races over 6f (including at 2 yrs) and 7f Gusto (by Galileo) and half-brother to the US Listed stakes winner Beauly (by Sea The Stars), the fair triple 6f winner Love Oasis (by Oasis Dream) and the fair 2-y-o 7f winner Pinter (by Exceed And Excel). The dam won 7 races here and in the USA including the Grade 3 Wilshire Handicap and the Grade 3 Yerba Buena Breeders Cup Handicap and is a half-sister to 5 winners. The second dam, Crackle (by Anshan), a quite useful 5.7f (at 2 yrs) to 10f winner, is a half-sister to 5 winners including the Listed winner Ronaldsay. *"He's doing half-speeds on the gallops now and we think he could be out early even though he's a New Approach. He's got a lot of class, he could be one to start in June and does show a lot of speed".*

848. PIMLICO PLEASER (IRE) ★★★
b.f. Zebedee – Pretty Bonnie (Kyllachy). April 14. Third foal. £34,000Y. Goffs UK Premier

(Doncaster). Sackville/Donald. The dam, a quite useful 5f and 6f winner of 6 races, was Listed placed and is a half-sister to 2 minor winners. The second dam, Joonayh (by Warning), a quite useful 2-y-o 6f winner is a half-sister to 6 winners including Millennium Force (Group 3 Gladness Stakes). *"She's working well now and we'll be looking for a race for her in April. She'll be fast enough for five furlongs".*

849. PIRATE ★★★★
b.c. Dark Angel – Rum Raisin (Invincible Spirit). April 9. Fifth foal. £67,000Y. Goffs UK Premier (Doncaster). Peter & Ross Doyle. The dam, a modest 6.5f winner, is a half-sister to 6 minor winners in Europe. The second dam, Femme Femme (by Lyphard), placed in France at 3 and 4 yrs, is a half-sister to the multiple Group 1 winning filly Ma Biche. *"He's quite an early type because he's not over-big but he's very strong. Hopefully we'll work him along in a few weeks and he could even be sharp enough for five furlongs. I'm very happy with him, he has a good action and a good attitude".*

850. PRODUCTION ★★★
b.c. Oasis Dream – Pure Excellence (Exceed And Excel). March 1. First foal. 85,000Y. Tattersalls October Book 2. John & Jake Warren. The dam, a quite useful 2-y-o Listed 1m winner of 3 races, is a half-sister to one winner. The second dam, Albavilla (by Spectrum), a fair 14f winner, is a half-sister to 9 winners including the Listed winner and Group 2 third Barolo. *"He's quite big for an Oasis Dream but he's a very good, extravagant mover. We wouldn't be in a rush with him but I'd say he'll be ready for the six furlong races".*

851. QUICK ★★★
b.f. Olympic Glory – The Giving Tree (Rock Of Gibraltar). March 11. Second foal. 13,000Y. Tattersalls October Book 3. Woodstock. The dam, a fair dual 8.5f winner including at 2 yrs, is a half-sister to 2 winners including the Group 3 Park Express Stakes third Starbright. The second dam, Starry Messenger (by Galileo), a fair 12f winner, is a half-sister to the US Grade 1 Gamely Handicap winner Tuscan Evening and the dual Listed winner Barbican. *"She's a nice filly, probably the type to start at six furlongs in May or June, has a good action*

and goes up the hill nicely. She's similar to the other Olympic Glory filly we have, Ventura Glory".

852. REGENT (IRE) ★★★★
b.f. War Command – Regency Girl (Pivotal). April 5. Third foal. £95,000Y. Goffs UK Premier (Doncaster). Peter & Ross Doyle. Half-sister to the 2017 US 2-y-o 5f winner and Group 3 Prix du Bois second Elizabeth Darcy (by Camacho). The dam, a modest 12f placed maiden, is a half-sister to 5 winners including the Listed-placed This Is The Day and Vanity Rules. The second dam, Miss Pinkerton (by Danehill), a useful 6f (at 2 yrs) and Listed 1m winner, is a half-sister to 5 winners including the smart 7f (at 2 yrs) and 10f winner and Group 2 placed Grand Central. *"A lovely, strong filly with a good attitude and a good way of going. All the War Command 2-y-o's are strong and they should be fairly sharp too because he was a fast horse. One for six furlongs and you'd like her a lot".*

853. RITCHIE VALENS (IRE) ★★★★
ch.c. Helmet – Miss Cape (Cape Cross). February 9. First foal. 47,000Y. Tattersalls October Book 2. Peter & Ross Doyle. The dam is an unraced half-sister to 2 winners including the useful dual 1m winner Masteroftherolls. The second dam, Miss Sally (by Danetime), winner of the Group 3 7f Brownstown Stakes and the Group 3 7.5f Concorde Stakes, is a half-sister to 5 winners. *"Being a Helmet you wouldn't be in a hurry with him, but he has a very good way of going and even now you can see he's got a nice cruising speed and he's a hell of a mover. Maybe he'll come a bit earlier than we expected".*

854. ROONG ROONG (IRE) ★★★★
gr.f. Dark Angel – Cut No Ice (Verglas). January 31. Second foal. 825,000Y. Tattersalls October Book 1. Sackville/Donald. Sister to the smart 2017 2-y-o 5f winner and Group 2 Prix Robert Papin second Frozen Angel. The dam, a fair 2-y-o 5f winner, is a half-sister to 12 winners including the Group 1 6f Haydock Park Sprint Cup and Group 3 5f Palace House Stakes winner Pipalong, the Listed winner Out Of Africa and the useful 2-y-o 5f winner and Group 2 5f Flying Childers Stakes second China Eyes. The second dam, Limpopo (by

Green Desert), a poor 5f placed 2-y-o, is a half-sister to 8 winners here and abroad. *"A sister to Tom Dascombe's filly, Frozen Angel, she cost a fortune but she's very nice and obviously we won't be in a hurry with her. A very good-moving filly, there's an awful lot to like about her, but being by Dark Angel we just have to wait a bit".*

855. SOGANN (FR) ★★★
b.c. Frankel – Rumored (Royal Academy). March 25. Eleventh foal. €550,000Y. Arqana Deauville August. Richard Knight. Half-brother to 6 winners including the Group 1 Prix Morny and Group 1 Prix Jean-Luc Lagardere winner Dabirsim (by Hat Trick), the US stakes-placed winner Preferred Yield (by High Yield), the French 6f (at 2 yrs) and 1m winner Pompilius (by Holy Roman Emperor) and the minor French 2-y-o 1m winner Zirgon (by New Approach). The dam is a placed half-sister to 8 winners out of the Italian Oaks winner and Group 1 Moyglare Stud Stakes second Bright Generation (by Rainbow Quest). *"A lovely, big horse that cost a few quid, he's grown a lot and we're in no rush. A very nice horse".*

856. SPELL ★★★
b.f. Slade Power – Jeanie Johnston (One Cool Cat). February 18. Second foal. £47,000Y. Goffs UK Premier (Doncaster). Peter & Ross Doyle. The dam, a fairly useful 2-y-o 6f winner, was Listed placed and is a half-sister to 3 winners including the Group 3 placed Switcher. The second dam, Bahamamia (by Vettori), won over 1m at 2 yrs in France and is a half-sister to 4 winners including the German Group 2 winner Accento. *"She looks fairly sharp, whether she's one for five furlongs or six we'll have to see once we start to work her along, but she's likeable, has a good action and I like her".*

857. ST OUEN ★★★ ♠
b.c. Alhebayeb – Heat (King's Best). April 8. Fifth foal. €50,000Y. Tattersalls Ireland September. Amanda Skiffington. Half-brother to the fairly useful Irish 10.5f, 12f and hurdles winner Cardinal Palace (by Papal Bull) and to the fair 9.5f winner Hot Sauce (by Peintre Celebre). The dam is an unraced half-sister to the Group 1 King's Stand Stakes winner Prohibit, to the French 7f (at 2 yrs) and Listed

6.5f winner Prior Warning and the French Listed 6f winner and dual Group 3 placed Emergency. The second dam, Well Warned (by Warning), a useful 2-y-o 6f winner, was third in the Group 3 6f Cherry Hinton Stakes and is a full or half-sister to 7 winners. *"He's done really well in the last month, strengthened up a lot, looks the part and put a lot of condition on. He's cantering away and we're waiting a bit longer with him but we're happy with where we're at".*

858. SWIPER (IRE) ★★★★
b.c. Clodovil – Hawk Dance (Hawk Wing). April 8. Fourth foal. £40,000Y. Goffs UK Premier (Doncaster). Peter & Ross Doyle. Half-brother to the fair 10.5f winner Clayton Hall (by Lilbourne Lad) and to the modest 1m seller winner Glorvina (by Dragon Pulse). The dam, a modest 12f placed maiden, is a half-sister to 4 winners. The second dam, Dancingintheclouds (by Rainbow Quest), is an unplaced sister to the Group 1 St Leger winner Millenary and the Group 3 Princess Royal Stakes winner Head In The Clouds. *"A lovely big colt, we'll not be going early with him and he's probably one to start at six and then move up to seven furlongs. He's got a good attitude and we're happy with him at the moment. We all like him a lot".*

859. THE PADDOCKS ★★★★
b.c. Charm Spirit – Miss Plimsoll (Arch). March 22. Second foal. €120,000. Arqana Deauville August. Peter & Ross Doyle. The dam, a minor winner in the USA, is a sister to the Group 2 Lancashire Oaks winner Pomology. The second dam, Sharp Apple (by Diesis), a US stakes winner of 4 races at 4 yrs, is a half-sister to 5 winners. *"A lovely colt that looks precocious, he's sharp and doing everything well up the hills with a good action and a great attitude. Knows what he's doing".*

860. TIME FOR BED (IRE) ★★★
b.f. Zebedee – Violet Flame (Kalanisi). April 9. Fifth foal. 7,500Y. Tattersalls October Book 3. Woodstock. Half-sister to the fair 2017 2-y-o 6f winner Episcia (by Arcano), to the fair 8.5f winner Kubali (by Approve) and the minor Italian winner of 5 races Full Recovery (by Intense Focus). The dam is an unplaced half-sister to 2 winners including the 2-y-o

Grade 1 8.5f Breeders Cup Juvenile and Listed 7f Stardom Stakes winner Vale Of York. The second dam, Red Vale (by Halling), is an unraced half-sister to 9 winners including the fairly useful 10f and subsequent US Grade 3 winner Uraib. *"A sharp filly, she could well start at five furlongs and she's gone up the hill well a few times, so she's a nice enough filly with good strength and size to her".* TRAINER'S BARGAIN BUY

861. TYPHOON TEN (IRE) ★★★★
b.c. Slade Power – Cake (Acclamation). February 19. Fifth foal. Half-brother to the fairly useful Listed-placed 5f and 5.5f winner of 4 races at 2 and 3 yrs Tomily (by Canford Cliffs) and to the useful 2-y-o 5f and Listed 6f winner Fig Roll (by Bahamian Bounty). The dam, a useful 2-y-o Listed 5f winner of 4 races, is a full or half-sister to 6 winners. The second dam, Carpet Lady (by Night Shift), a fair dual 6f placed 2-y-o, is a half-sister to 5 winners including the Hong Kong stakes winner Classic Fountain. *"He's from a very fast family and in fact two of them won last week. This colt is a bit bigger than those two, which is good, but he shows a lot of toe and you'd be thinking that either five or six furlongs would be fine for him".*

862. VENTURA GLORY ★★★
b.f. Olympic Glory – Fringe Success (Selkirk). April 11. Fifth foal. £42,000Y. Goffs UK Premier (Doncaster). Peter & Ross Doyle / B O'Ryan / MPR. Half-sister to the quite useful dual 10f winner Rib Reserve and the minor French 4-y-o winner Zafri (both by Azamour). The dam ran once unplaced and is a half-sister to 7 winners including the Group 2 10.3f winner Stage Gift. The second dam, Stage Struck (by Sadler's Wells), a quite useful 12f winner, is a sister to the Group 1 7f Dewhurst Stakes winner (in a dead-heat) Prince of Dance. *"She's got a great action on her, really stretches out and puts her head down and does everything really well. So she looks a nice filly, probably the type to start over six furlongs, and she's a likeable type".*

863. WAREEDA (IRE) ★★★★
b.f. War Command – Areeda (Refuse To Bend). February 17. Third foal. 140,000Y. Tattersalls October Book 1. Stephen Hillen. Half-sister to

the useful 2-y-o Group 3 7f Prix du Calvados winner of 3 races Great Page (by Roderic O'Connor). The dam, a fair 3-y-o 7f winner, is a half-sister to 10 winners, two of them Listed-placed. The second dam, Raindancing (by Tirol), a fairly useful 2-y-o 6f winner, was third in the Group 3 6f Princess Margaret Stakes and is a sister to the smart 7f (at 2 yrs) to 10f winner and Group 1 National Stakes third Mountain Song and a half-sister to 7 winners including the Group 2 Cherry Hinton Stakes winner Please Sing. *"A very big, strong filly that looks like a colt. She's a very good mover with a bit of class about her, we'll wait for six furlongs but when those races appear she'll be more than ready for them. There's a lot to like about her and she'll be very easy to work with".*

864. WE LIKE HER A LOT (IRE) ★★★
ch.f. No Nay Never – Alamouna (Indian Ridge). February 16. Seventh foal. €76,000Y. Goffs Orby. Peter & Ross Doyle. Half-sister to the French 1m and 9f winner Almoradi (by Barathea), to the quite useful dual 12f winner Humble Hero (by High Chaparral) and the minor French 11f winner Almadan (by Azamour). The dam, a quite useful 10f winner, is a half-sister to 8 winners including the useful 7f (at 2 yrs) and Listed 1m winner Alasha (herself the dam of two stakes winners). The second dam, Alasana (by Darshaan), won twice in France over 1m and 9f and is a half-sister to 8 winners including the French dual Group 2 winner Altayan. *"She's doing half-speeds, doing it well and is a lovely, classy filly. I like her".*

865. WELL DONE FOX ★★★
b.c. Acclamation – Excelette (Exceed And Excel). January 28. Second foal. 255,000Y. Tattersalls October Book 2. Sackville/Donald. Half-brother to the quite useful 2017 2-y-o 5f winner Excellently Poised (by Sepoy). The dam, a Listed 5f winner of 3 races, is a half-sister to 3 winners. The second dam, Madam Ninette (Mark Of Esteem), is an unraced half-sister to 9 winners including the very smart King's Stand Stakes and Temple Stakes winner Bolshoi and the useful sprinters Mariinsky, Great Chaddington and Tod. *"A nice horse, he's very strong and heavy so he carries a bit of weight. Probably a six furlong type, he shows plenty of speed".*

866. UNNAMED ★★★
b.f. Kodiac – Alina (Galileo). April 15. Third foal. 400,000Y. Tattersalls December. David Redvers. Half-sister to the Group 1 St James's Palace Stakes winner and 2,000 Guineas second Barney Roy (by Excelebration). The dam, unplaced, is out of smart Irish Group 3 7f and Group 3 1m winner Cheyenne Star, herself a half-sister to 4 winners and to the unraced dam of the dual Group 1 sprint winner Gordon Lord Byron. *"A nice filly and a half-sister to Barney Roy, she's still a bit weak but she's a very good mover and has a good temperament. Does everything nicely but we won't be in a hurry with her".*

867. UNNAMED ★★★
b.c. Kodiac – Bailonguera (Southern Halo). April 25. Ninth living foal. €280,000Y. Arqana. Peter & Ross Doyle. Half-brother to 7 winners including the French Listed 9.5f winner Bayargal (by Bernstein) and the French Listed-placed winners Bulliciosa (by Successful Appeal) and Bargouzine (by Stravinsky and herself dam of the French Grade 3 winner Baghadur). The second dam, Balromana (by Logical), won once in Argentina and is a half-sister to 4 winners. *"A nice, good-moving horse, he always looked sharp but then he grew and got a bit weak. He's one you'd like a lot but we'll be waiting for the six furlong races with him".*

868. UNNAMED ★★★
b.f. Kodiac – Big Boned (Street Sense). January 22. First foal. €85,000Y. Goffs Orby. Mayfair / Peter & Ross Doyle. The dam, a modest 6f placed 2-y-o, is a half-sister to 4 winners including the US Listed stakes winner and Grade 2 second Cool Bullet. The second dam, Lizzy Cool (by Saint Ballado), a US Listed stakes winner, is a half-sister to 8 winners including the Irish Listed 9f winner Sense Of Honour. *"She's not overly big but she's done well in the last couple of weeks. She's got a Kodiac attitude which isn't a bad thing and I think they're the best ones to have. She's grand and doing everything we need at the moment".*

869. UNNAMED ★★★
b.f. Zoffany – Idle Curiosity (Red Clubs). February 20. First foal. £75,000Y. Goffs UK Premier (Doncaster). Peter & Ross Doyle. The dam, a modest 6f and 7f winner, is a half-sister

to 6 winners. The second dam, Idle Fancy (by Mujtahid), a fair Irish 3-y-o 1m winner, is a half-sister to 7 winners including the French Listed 1m winner Danish Field and the dam of the Lancashire Oaks winner Ela Athena. *"A nice filly, she's not over-big, looks to have plenty of speed about her and will be running in the six furlong races".*

870. UNNAMED ★★★

ch.f. Teofilo – Katdogawn (Bahhare). February 25. Seventh foal. €36,000Y. Tattersalls Ireland September. Peter & Ross Doyle. Half-sister to the modest 5f to 7.5f winner of 6 races Oor Jock (by Shamardal). The dam, a 2-y-o 6f winner here, subsequently won three Grade 2 events over 1m and 9f in the USA and is a half-sister to 3 winners. The second dam, Trempkate (by Trempolino), a French 2-y-o 9f winner, is a half-sister to 7 winners including the Group winners King Jock and Perfect Touch. *"We've trained a lot of the family and they're all decent. She could be sharp, she'll definitely run over six furlongs and might even be ready for five. She does have a bit of speed about her".*

871. UNNAMED ★★★

b.c. Dark Angel – Lady Marita (Dandy Man). February 29. First foal. 80,000Y. Tattersalls October Book 2. Charlie Gordon-Watson. The dam, a modest 5f placed 2-y-o, is a half-sister to 3 winners including 2-y-o Group 3 6f Prix de Cabourg and 3-y-o Listed 6f winner Mazameer and to the unraced dam of the French Group 3 winner and Group 1 second Vue Fantastique. The second dam, Straight Miss (by In The Wings), is an unraced half-sister to 9 winners including the 2-y-o Group 1 Prix Jean-Luc Lagardere winner Naaqoos and the Group 3 Prix la Force winner Barastraight. *"He's a nice colt, very quiet in the string and you don't see a huge amount of him which is a good thing. He looks the part, has a good action and does everything nicely. Probably one for six or seven furlongs".*

872. UNNAMED ★★★

b.f. Charm Spirit – Mill Guineas (Salse). March 25. Twelfth foal. €80,000Y. Goffs Orby. David Redvers. Half-sister to 6 winners including the Listed Scandinavian winner Mill Marin (by Pivotal), the fairly useful dual 12f winner

Monotype (by Makfi), the French 2-y-o 7f and 1m winner and Listed placed Olvia (by Giant's Causeway) and the quite useful 11f winner Deadly Silence (by Diesis). The dam, a Listed-placed maiden in France, is a half-sister to 3 winners including Ronda (Group 2 Falmouth Stakes). The second dam, Memory's Gold (by Java Gold), a modest 3-y-o 7.6f winner, is a half-sister to 5 winners including the German Group 3 winner Fields Of Spring. *"A nice filly, she looks the part and just has a bit of strengthening up to do. Hopefully we'll have a bit of fun with her, she has a great attitude and a great action. At the moment all looks well".*

873. UNNAMED ★★★

b.c. Gale Force Ten – Queen Myrine (Oratorio). February 9. Third foal. €28,000Y. Tattersalls Ireland September. Peter & Ross Doyle. Half-brother to the useful 6f to 1m winner of 3 races at 2 and 3 yrs Mutawatheb (by Dark Angel) and to the fair Irish 7f (at 2 yrs) and 10f winner Roibeard (by Big Bad Bob). The dam ran twice unplaced and is a half-sister to 4 winners including the Grade 1 Hollywood Turf Cup winner Boboman. The second dam, Slewvera (by Seattle Slew), a winner and Group 3 second in France, subsequently won and was Grade 2 second in the USA. *"Not a bad sort, he'll take a little bit of time because he's got a bit of strengthening up to do, but it looks like he's nice at the moment. He's cantering away, has a good action and there are no problems with him".*

874. UNNAMED ★★★

b.f. Dark Angel – Waveband (Exceed And Excel). April 24. Fifth foal. €80,000Y. Tattersalls Ireland September. Peter & Ross Doyle. Half-sister to the quite useful 2017 2-y-o 7f winner Sallab (by Havana Gold) and to the fair 5f winner of 3 races at 2 and 4 yrs Archimedes (by Invincible Spirit). The dam, a fairly useful Listed 6f winner of 4 races, is a sister to the smart 2-y-o dual Group 3 5f winner Bungle Inthejungle and a half-sister to 7 winners including the Group 1 Golden Shaheen winner Muarrab and the Group 2 5f King George Stakes second Group Therapy. The second dam, Licence To Thrill (by Wolfhound), a quite useful dual 5f winner, is a half-sister to 4 winners. *"A sharp filly, she's a half-sister to Sallab who looked like he wanted a trip when he raced on Saturday. This filly shows a lot more speed than he did and she'll be ready for the six furlong races – maybe even five".*

JESSIE HARRINGTON

875. BODAK (IRE) ★★★
b.f. Kodiac – Arty Crafty (Arch). April 3. Sixth foal. €180,000Y. Goffs Orby. BBA (Ire). Half-sister to the fairly useful Irish triple 10f winner Pincheck (by Invincible Spirit) and to the quite useful 2-y-o 7f winner Enraptured (by Oasis Dream). The dam, a modest 10f and 12f winner of 4 races, is a sister to the US Grade 1 11f winner Prince Arch and a half-sister to the Group 1 National Stakes winner Kingsfort. The second dam, Princess Kris (by Kris), a quite useful 3-y-o 1m winner, is half-sister to 8 winners including the Group 3 May Hill Stakes winner Intimate Guest and to the placed dam of the US Grade 1 winner Luas Line. *"A lovely filly, she wasn't very big but she's done a lot of growing and now she's a good, big, strong filly with an easy action".*

876. BOSTON BRUIN (IRE) ★★★★
b.c. Kodiac – Sovana (Desert King). March 2. Eleventh foal. 160,000Y. Tattersalls October Book 1. BBA (Ire). Half-brother to 7 winners including the Group 2 Kilboy Estate Stakes and Group 2 Dance Design Stakes winner Bocca Baciata (by Big Bad Bob), the Group 3 Prix Miesque winner and French 1,000 Guineas third Topeka, the Group 3 Prix Edmund Blanc winner Kalsa (both by Whipper) and the quite useful dual 7f winner Suvenna (by Arcano). The dam, a 3-y-o winner in France and third in the Group 3 Prix Minerve, is a half-sister to 5 winners including Perugina (2-y-o Group 3 Prix Eclipse Stakes). The second dam, Piacenza (by Darshaan), a minor French 3-y-o winner, is a half-sister to 5 winners. *"A nice horse, not as big as his half-sister Bocca Baciata but he goes well and I can see him being out in late May over six furlongs. He's a typical Kodiac as far as his size is concerned and he's a 2-y-o type".*

877. CHICAS AMIGAS (IRE) ★★★
b.f. Dragon Pulse – Veronica Falls (Medicean). March 4. Second foal. €25,000Y. Goffs Orby. BBA (Ire). The dam, a fair 1m winner, is a half-sister to 5 other minor winners. The second dam, Red Peony (by Montjeu), a useful 7f (at 2 yrs) and 12f winner and Group 3 7f Prestige Stakes third, is a half-sister to 4 winners. *"She'll*

probably be my first filly to run. One for five/six furlongs, she's a big, strong 2-y-o".

878. DAME KYTELER (IRE) ★★★
b.f. Acclamation – Irish Flower (Zieten). February 19. Tenth foal. €115,000Y. Goffs Orby. BBA (Ire). Half-sister to the Italian Listed-placed 2-y-o 6f winner Shishangaan (by Mujadil), to the French 7f winner and Listed-placed Mister Ryan (by Acclamation), the French Listed-placed 2-y-o winner Parker's Way (by Pivotal) and three minor French winners by Big Bad Bob, Saddex and Verglas. The dam, a Listed-placed winner of 4 races in France, is a half-sister to 9 winners. The second dam, Sally St Clair (by Sallust), a minor US 3-y-o winner, is a half-sister to 7 winners including the Group 2 Flying Childers Stakes winner Superlative. *"She's a big, strong, slightly long filly and a lovely mover that might take a bit of time, but she's very nice".*

879. DINGLE BAY (IRE) ★★
gr.c. Alhebayeb – Lady Rockfield (Rock of Gibraltar) May 14. Sixth foal. €8,000Y. Goffs Sportsmans. Kate Harrington. Half-brother to the fair 9.5f and 10f winner Cape Crystal (by Cape Cross) and to the modest 6f winner Belle Dormant (by Rip Van Winkle). The dam, a modest 1m placed maiden, is a half-sister to 6 winners including the 2-y-o Group 3 7f C L Weld Park Stakes and 3-y-o Listed 6f winner and Group 1 7f Moyglare Stud Stakes second Ugo Fire. The second dam, Quiet Mouse (by Quiet American), is an unraced half-sister to 7 winners including the smart broodmare Witch Of Fife (the dam of 3 stakes winners). *"He's pretty good and forward; a nice colt bought by Kate my daughter, he's tall with plenty of presence about him and a good mover. He'll be ready to go very shortly".* TRAINER'S BARGAIN BUY

880. FANCY FOOTINGS (IRE) ★★
b.c. Dandy Man – Mystical Past (Majestic Missile).April 8. First foal. The dam, a moderate Irish 4-y-o 7f winner, is a half-sister to 3 other minor winners. The second dam, Opari (by Night Shift), a French 2-y-o 6f winner, is a half-sister to one winner. *"Bought privately, he's a sharp, typical Dandy Man with a bit of body about him. He looks like he's ready to go and he'll start at five furlongs".*

881. FOR YOUR EYES (IRE) ★★★★

b.f. Iffraaj – Armoise (Sadler's Wells). January 16. Third foal. Half-sister to the quite useful 10f and 12f winner Regicide (by Archipenko). The dam, a fair 11.5f winner, is a half-sister to 5 winners including the French Listed winner Toi Et Moi. The second dam, Di Moi Oui (by Warning), won the Group 3 Prix Chloe and the Group 3 Prix de la Nonette and is a half-sister to 5 winners. *"A very big filly, she's a very easy mover and reminds me a bit of my smart 2-y-o Listed winner from last year Alpha Centauri. Does everything very easily but due to her size you wouldn't know at this point when she'll run sooner or later. A lovely, big filly".*

882. HARLISTON TOWER (IRE) ★★★

gr.c. Mastercraftsman – Bayberry (Bering). March 8. Eighth foal. Half-brother to the fairly useful 9f and 10f winner Eddystone Rock (by Rock Of Gibraltar), to the French 2-y-o 9.5f winner Ketchikan, the French Listed-placed 1m winner Myrica (both by Dansili) and the fair 7f winner Maximus Daia (by Holy Roman Emperor). The dam, a fairly useful 10f winner, was Listed-placed and is a half-sister to 3 winners including the Group 3 1m Prix d'Aumale winner Birthstone and the Listed 14f winner Songcraft. The second dam, Baya (by Nureyev), a very useful Group 3 1m Prix de la Grotte winner, was second in the Group 1 10.5f Prix de Diane. *"He's a fine, big colt and a typical Mastercraftsman; a good mover, strong-bodied and a seven furlong 2-y-o".*

883. INDIGO BALANCE (IRE) ★★★★

b.c. Invincible Spirit – Rose De France (Diktat). March 6. Sixth foal. €155,000Y. Goffs Orby. BBA (Ire). Brother to the Group 2 Challenge Stakes and Group 3 John Of Gaunt Stakes winner and Group 1 7f Dewhurst Stakes second Cable Bay and to the fair 5f winner Tanghan and half-brother to the useful 5f, 7f (including at 2 yrs) and 1m winner of 6 races Sea Wolf (by Amadeus Wolf) and the fair 5f and 6f winner May Rose (by Lawman). The dam, placed four times at 3 yrs in France, is a half-sister to 6 winners including the Group 3 winner and French 2,000 Guineas third Bowman and the dam of the Group 1 winners Kirklees and Mastery. The second dam, Cherokee Rose (by Dancing Brave), won

the Group 1 Haydock Park Sprint Cup and the Group 1 Prix Maurice de Gheest and is a half-sister to 4 winners. *"A very nice colt, he's forward-going, a good mover and light on his feet. A six furlong type 2-y-o, at least to begin with".*

884. INVINCIBLE KARMA (IRE) ★★★

b.c. Invincible Spirit – Bratislava (Dr Fong). February 10. Eighth foal. €300,000Y. Goffs Orby. BBA (Ire). Half-brother to the useful triple Listed 6f winner (including at 2 yrs) Katla (by Majestic Missile), to the fair 7f and 1m winner Slovak (by Iffraaj), the fair Irish 1m winner Derulo (by Arakan) and a minor winner in the USA by Diamond Green. The dam is an unplaced half-sister to 9 winners including the Group 1 7f Prix Jean-Luc Lagardere winner Wootton Bassett. The second dam, Balladonia (by Primo Dominie), a useful 9f winner, was Listed-placed twice over 10f and is a half-sister to 5 winners. *"He's a strong, blocky colt that goes nicely and he should be racing in May over six furlongs".*

885. KLUTE (IRE) ★★★

br.c. Kodiac – Fonda (Quiet American). April 16. Fifth foal. €120,000Y. Goffs Orby. BBA (Ire). Half-brother to the fairly useful 2-y-o 6f winner Ribaat (by Invincible Spirit) and to the quite useful 7f winner Musaaid (by Lawman). The dam ran once unplaced and is a half-sister to 4 winners including the Group 3 Prix de Cabourg and Group 3 Sovereign Stakes winner and dual Group 1 placed Layman. The second dam, Laiyl (by Nureyev), won over 10f and is a half-sister to 3 winners including Allurement (Group 3 Prix Cleopatre). *"He's a very nice colt and he could be quite early. He's a typical Kodiac, has a low to the ground action, a great attitude and he's a good mover".*

886. MARSHALL LAW (IRE) ★★★

b.c. Bated Breath – Art Of Dance (Medicean). March 17. Second foal. 72,000Y. Tattersalls October Book 2. BBA (Ire). The dam, placed at 2 to 4 yrs in France, is a half-sister to 4 winners including the French Listed winner and Group 3 placed Rainbow Dancing. The second dam, Danceabout (by Shareef Dancer), won the Group 2 Sun Chariot Stakes and the Listed Oak Tree Stakes and is a half-sister to the dual Group 3 winner Pole Position. *"He looked like he'd be early but he's done a lot of growing lately. He might wait for six furlongs at the end of May and he's a nice horse".*

887. MR SECRETARY (IRE) ★★
b.c. Sea The Stars – Oui Say Oui (Royal Applause). February 8. Fourth foal. €225,000Y. Goffs Orby. BBA (Ire). The dam, a useful 2-y-o 6f winner and second in the Group 2 7f Debutante Stakes, is a half-sister to 7 winners including the smart 2-y-o Group 3 6f Sirenia Stakes and Group 3 1m Joel Stakes winner Satchem and the Group 3 Ballyroan Stakes winner Eye Of The Storm. The second dam, Mohican Princess (by Shirley Heights), fourth over 10f on her only start, is a half-sister to 5 winners. *"A typical Sea The Stars in that he'll take a bit of time and won't be out before August time over six/seven furlongs".*

888. NAILED IT (IRE) ★★★
ch.c. Helmet – Il Palazzo (Giant's Causeway). May 15. Second foal. Half-brother to the 2017 2-y-o 1m winner Still Standing (by Mastercraftsman). The dam is a placed half-sister to 4 winners. The second dam, Starlight Night (by Distant View), is a placed half-sister to 9 winners including the dual US Grade 1 winner Senure. *"A late foal, he's a half-brother to a 3-y-o of ours I like a lot called Still Standing; this is a lovely, big, easy-moving colt for six/seven furlongs".*

889. PLEASUREABLE (IRE) ★★★★
b.f. Camelot – Notable (Zafonic). May 3. €75,000Y. Arqana. Private Sale. Eighth foal. Closely related to the Group 2 13f Prix de Royallieu winner Maria Royal and to the useful 11.5f and 12f winner and German Group 1 second Red Cardinal (both by Montjeu) and half-sister to the quite useful 2018 3-y-o 10f winner Proschema (by Declaration Of War). The dam is an unraced half-sister to 3 winners including the Group 3 Prix de Sandringham winner and smart broodmare Orford Ness. The second dam, Nesaah (by Topsider), a fairly useful Listed-placed 10f and 10.5f winner, is a half-sister to 8 winners including the Group winners Privity and Zindari. *"She's a lovely filly and despite being by Camelot looks like being early, so she could be racing as soon as the six furlong races start; a nice, very well-balanced filly".*

890. PURSUIT OF MAGIC (IRE) ★★★
b.f. Kingman – Three Mysteries (Linamix). March 24. Tenth foal. Half-sister to 3 winners including the French Listed winner and Group 2 Prix Guillaume d'Ornano second Three Bodies (by Domedriver). The dam, a minor winner in France, is a half-sister to 7 winners including the Group 2 Premio Regina Elena winner Erin Bird. The second dam, Maid Of Erin (by Irish River), is an unplaced sister to the dam of the Champion Stakes winner Spectrum. *"She's a very nice filly, probably not an early type – she's out of a Linamix mare after all, but she's likely to be out in June or July; a good-looking, good-moving filly".*

891. SNEAKY SNOOZE (IRE) ★★★
b.f. Exceed And Excel – Crossanza (Cape Cross). May 12. Fifth foal. €40,000Y. Goffs Orby. Knockarigg Stud (private sale). Half-sister to the quite useful Listed 6f winner Cape Factor (by Oratorio), to the quite useful 1m and 9f winner Benzanno (by Refuse To Bend) and the fair 7f winner Hidden Belief (by Holy Roman Emperor). The dam is an unraced half-sister to two minor winners. The second dam, Alegranza (by Lake Coniston), a winner over 5f at 3 yrs, was Listed-placed and is a full or half-sister to 7 winners including the Listed winner Army Of Angels and the dam of the Group 1 Cheveley Park Stakes and Canadian Grade 1 6f winner Serious Attitude. *"She was a very late foal but she's a nice filly I wouldn't expect to be running until May/June. She goes nicely".*

892. SPARKLE'N'JOY ★★★★
ch.f. Sepoy – Silent Secret (Dubai Destination). March 27. Sixth foal. €40,000Y. Goffs Orby. BBA (Ire). Half-sister to the modest dual 6f winner at 2 and 3 yrs Boolass (by Bushranger) and to the modest Irish 2-y-o 5f winner Gwen Lady Byron (by Dandy Man). The dam, a fair 2-y-o 5f winner, is a half-sister to 4 winners including the smart Irish Group 3 7f and Group 3 1m winner Cheyenne Star and to the dam of the triple Group 1 winner Gordon Lord Byron. The second dam, Charita (by Lycius), a Listed 1m winner in Ireland, is a half-sister to 4 winners including the Italian Group 2 winner Stanott. *"A lovely filly, she's going very nicely and I'd expect her run in May over six furlongs. I'm very happy with her, she's a nice moving filly and she's done a bit of growing lately, so we have to wait a bit longer for her".*

893. SERVALAN (IRE) ★★★
b.f. No Nay Never – Catch The Eye (Oratorio). April 14. Fourth foal. €50,000Y. Goffs Orby. BBA (Ire). Half-sister to a minor 3-y-o winner abroad by Power. The dam, a fairly useful Irish Listed-placed 7f and 8.5f winner, is a half-sister to 4 winners. The second dam, Lexy May (by Lear Fan), a minor winner at 3 yrs in the USA, is a half-sister to 6 winners including Secret History (Group 3 Musidora Stakes). *"She's a nice filly, not over-big but strong and could be racing in May. She's got a bit of speed so she'll go five/six furlongs".*

894. SWEET DIME ★★★
b.f. Toronado – Rainbow's Edge (Rainbow Quest). April 6. Seventh foal. €58,000Y. Goffs Orby. BBA (Ire). Half-sister to the very useful 2-y-o 6f (at 2 yrs) and Listed 10f winner and Group 3 second Peacock (by Paco Boy), to the quite useful 10f to 2m winner of 4 races Purple Spectrum (by Verglas), the fair 12f, 2m and hurdles winner Discovery Bay (by Dansili) and the fair 13f and 2m winner Clear Evidence (by Cape Cross). The dam, a fair 12f winner, is a half-sister to 3 winners including the 2-y-o Listed 7f winner Free Agent. The second dam, Film Script (by Unfuwain), a useful 10f and 12f Listed winner, was a half-sister to 5 winners. *"A very solid, great-bodied, workmanlike filly that takes a good bit of work; a nice mover that does everything right".*

895. TRETHIAS ★★★★★
b.f. Invincible Spirit – Evita (Selkirk). February 10. Sixth foal. 400,000Y. Tattersalls October Book 1. BBA (Ire). Half-sister to the useful Listed 1m winner of 4 races from 2 to 4 yrs Moohaarib (by Oasis Dream) and to a minor winner in France by Galileo. The dam, a modest 9f and 12f placed maiden, is a half-sister to 10 winners including the triple Group 1 winner Da Re Mi, the Group 1 Prince Of Wales's Stakes and Dubai Sheema Classic winner Rewilding, the Hong Kong Group 1 winner Diaghilev and the Australian Group 1 winner Darazari. The second dam, Darara (by Top Ville), won the Group 1 12f Prix Vermeille and is a half-sister to 11 winners including the Prix du Jockey Club winner and high-class sire Darshaan. *"A lovely filly that should be out around July time, she's a very good-moving, medium-sized filly and light on her feet".*

896. WEAVING SILK ★★★★
b.f. Mastercraftsman – Apparel (Cape Cross). January 17. Third foal. €100,000Y. Goffs Orby. BBA (Ire). The dam, a modest 12f winner, is a half-sister to 7 winners including the Group 1 1m Criterium International and Group 1 Eclipse Stakes winner and sire Mount Nelson and the 1m (at 2 yrs) and Group 2 12f Great Voltigeur Stakes winner and St Leger third Monitor Closely. The second dam, Independence (by Selkirk), won four races at 3 yrs from 7f to 1m including the Group 2 Sun Chariot Stakes and the Group 3 Matron Stakes and is a half-sister to one winner. *"A nice, strong, medium-sized filly for six/seven furlongs".*

897. UNNAMED ★★★
b.c. Dark Angel – Gorband (Woodman). April 29. Tenth foal. 130,000Y. Tattersalls October Book 1. Willow Spring Stable. Closely related to the quite useful 2017 2-y-o 7f winner Mutakatif and to the 2-y-o Group 2 6f Richmond Stakes winner Harbour Watch (both by Acclamation) and half-brother to the South African Grade 1 10f winner Europe Point (by Rock Of Gibraltar), the quite useful triple 6f winner Ghalib (by Lope De Vega) and the quite useful UAE triple 7f winner Cross Grain (by Cape Cross). The dam is a placed half-sister to 7 winners including the dual Group 2 winner Kabool. The second dam, Sheroog (by Shareef Dancer), a fair 1m winner, is a sister to the dam of Dubai Millennium, closely related to the Group/Grade 1 winners Hamas, Northern Aspen and Fort Wood and a half-sister to the Grade 1 winner Timber Country. *"A gorgeous colt, he's very nice and will be racing in May/June over six furlongs. He's quite a tall son of Dark Angel".*

898. UNNAMED ★★★
b.c. Kodiac – Oasis Sunset (Oasis Dream). February 7. Fifth foal. 220,000Y. Tattersalls October Book 2. Amanda Skiffington. Half-sister to the quite useful 7f and 1m winner Sunset Dream (by Acclamation). The dam, a fair 7f winner at 2 yrs, is a half-sister to 5 winners including the 2-y-o Group 1 6f Cheveley Park Stakes winner Seazun. The second dam, Sunset Cafe (by Red Sunset), a minor Irish 12f winner, is a sister to the Group 3 Prix Foy winner Beeshi and a half-sister to

8 winners including the John Smiths Magnet Cup winner Chaumiere. *"He's a grand horse, quite tall for a Kodiac, but a lovely-moving horse that might not run until midsummer over six/seven furlongs".*

CHARLIE HILLS

899. ALANDALOS ★★★
b.f. Invincible Spirit – Ghanaati (Giant's Causeway). April 23. Half-sister to the fairly useful 2017 2-y-o 7f winner Wafy, to the quite useful 7f to 8.5f winner of 4 races Alnashama (by Dubawi), the fairly useful dual 1m winner Afaak (by Oasis Dream and the modest 1m winner Almuhalab (by Dansili). The dam, winner of the 1,000 Guineas and Coronation Stakes, is a half-sister to 6 winners including the Group 3 12f Cumberland Lodge Stakes winner and Group 1 Champion Stakes second Mawatheeq and the useful 1m (at 2 yrs) and Listed 9f winner Rumoush. The second dam, Sarayir (by Mr Prospector), winner of a Listed 1m event, is closely related to the Champion Stakes winner Nayef and a half-sister to Nashwan and Unfuwain. (Hamdan Al Maktoum). *"The first filly out of the mare – the rest have all been colts. A nice, rangy filly, she'll probably be a seven furlong 2-y-o but she's not short of speed.*

900. ARTISTIC RIFLES (IRE) ★★★★
b.c. War Command – Chatham Islands (Elusive Quality). February 25. Seventh foal. €60,000Y. Goffs Orby. Sackville/Donald. Half-brother to the useful 6f (at 2 yrs) and Group 3 Superior Mile winner of 7 races Balty Boys (by Cape Cross), to the quite useful 5.5f and 6f winner of 4 races Shore Step (by Footstepsinthesand) and the minor 10f winner from two starts Catsbury (by Teofilo). The dam, a fair 2-y-o 6f winner, is a half-sister to 6 winners including the French Group 3 winner Time Prisoner and the 2-y-o Listed 6f winner and Group 2 6f Cherry Hinton Stakes second Pearl Grey. The second dam, Zelanda (by Night Shift), a Listed 6f winner of 4 races, is a half-sister to 6 winners including the Group 3 1m Prix des Reservoirs winner and smart broodmare Emily Bronte. *"A big, well-made horse, I think he's a bit bigger than his half-brother Balty Boys who was a good horse for us. He has a good constitution and hopefully we should be in for a good year with him".*

901. ASHCOMBE (FR) ★★★
b.c. Le Havre – Cape Magic (Cape Cross). February 5. First foal. 85,000Y. Tattersalls October Book 1. John & Jake Warren. The dam, an Italian Listed 10f winner, is a half-sister to the smart Listed 10f winner and Group 3 9f Meld Stakes second Portage. The second dam, Galley (by Zamindar), placed at 3 yrs in France, is a half-sister to 10 winners including Wharf (Group 3 July Stakes) and the dams of the Prix de l'Arc de Triomphe winner Rail Link and the Group 1 Criterium de Saint-Cloud winner Linda's Lad. *"A lovely, strong colt, his knees are still open which has held us back a bit, but he's a beautiful looking horse to look at. I'm sure he'll come good later on in the year".*

902. BRAWNY ★★★★
b.c. Dark Angel – Natty Bumppo (Kheleyf). February 16. Second foal. 200,000Y. Tattersalls October Book 1. Richard Knight. The dam is an unraced half-sister to 4 winners including the Group 3 winners Astrophysical Jet and Coral Wave. The second dam, Common Knowledge (by Rainbow Quest), is an unraced half-sister to 6 winners including the Group 2 12f Jockey Club Stakes and dual US Grade 2 winner Blueprint and the Listed 10f winner Fairy Godmother. *"I loved this horse at the sales, he's grown over the winter and now he's a really nice looking colt. I'm looking forward to running him and I see him starting at six furlongs".*

903. BURNING LAKE (IRE) ★★★★
b.c. Le Havre – Baby Houseman (Oasis Dream). February 2. Fifth foal. €310,000Y. Goffs Orby. Sackville/Donald. Half-brother to the French 6f (at 2 yrs) and Listed 1m winner Baby Foot (by Footstepsinthesand) and to the French 5f Listed-placed winner Plaza Mayor (by Kyllachy). The dam, a fairly useful 7f winner, is a half-sister to 3 other minor winners. The second dam, Photogenic (by Midyan), a fairly useful 6f and Listed 7f winner at 2 yrs, is a half-sister to 6 winners including the Listed winner and Group 1 placed Mona Lisa and the Group 2 1m Falmouth Stakes second Croeso Cariad. *"He looks like he's got plenty of speed and he's not backward either, so there's every chance he'll be racing in May over six furlongs. The mare's been a pretty good producer and the sire is certainly well thought of".*

904. CAESONIA ★★★
ch.f. Garswood – Agrippina (Timeless Times).
March 25. Eighth foal. 35,000Y. Tattersalls
October Book 2. Not sold. Half-sister to the
dual Listed 6f winner and Group 3 third
Cartimandua, to the modest 7f winner
Chelabella (both by Medicean), the useful 5f
winner of 5 races (including at 2 yrs) Terentia
(by Diktat), the fair 2-y-o 9f winner Sejanus
(by Dubai Destination) and the moderate 1m
winner Jay Jays Joy (by Diktat). The dam, a
useful 2-y-o Listed 7f winner, is a half-sister to
2 winners. The second dam, Boadicea's Chariot
(by Commanche Run), an Irish 12f and hurdles
winner, is a half-sister to 6 winners. *"A strong-
looking filly, she's going to make a 2-y-o, has a
good attitude and will probably prefer a bit of
cut in the ground. A mid-season type 2-y-o".*

905. CLEMATIS (USA) ★★★
b.br.f. First Defence – Faraway Flower (Distant
View). March 4. Half-sister to the fairly useful
1m (at 2 yrs) to 1m 6f winner of 5 races Sepal
(by Afleet Alex). The dam, a useful 2-y-o 6f
winner, is a half-sister to 2 winners. The second
dam, Silver Star (by Zafonic), won over 1m at
2 yrs in France, was Listed-placed over 1m at
3 yrs and is a sister to the champion European
2-y-o Xaar (winner of the Group 1 Dewhurst
Stakes and the Group 1 Prix de la Salamandre)
and a half-sister to the Group 3 10.5f Prix
Corrida winner Diese and the Group 3 1m Prix
Quincey winner Masterclass. (Khalid Abdullah).
*"She's a scopey filly with a big action; one for
the second half of the year and seven furlongs".*

906. CHUCK WILLIS (IRE) ★★★★
b.c. Kodiac – Xinji (Xaar). March 10. Fifth
foal. €55,000Y. Goffs Orby. Sackville/Donald.
Half-brother to the fairly useful Irish 10f to 12f
winner of 3 races Xebec (by Mizzen Mast), to
the modest Irish 10f winner Castle Of Argh
and the minor US dual winner Archiboldo
(both by Arch). The dam, a fairly useful Irish
dual 7f winner (including at 2 yrs), is a full
or half-sister to 4 minor winners here and
abroad. The second dam, Hero's Pride (by
Hero's Honor), won four races in France and
the USA and was second in the Grade 2 All
Along Stakes and is a half-sister to 2 minor
winners. *"A very attractive looking colt and
a good mover, he'll be running by the end of
April, has a nice action and is still a bit 'up*

*behind' so I think he has some scope. He's a
horse that I like".*

907. COOL POSSIBILITY (IRE) ★★★
b.br.c. Dark Angel – Pink Diva (Giant's
Causeway). March 6. Third foal. Brother to the
unplaced 2017 2-y-o Makambe. The dam,
a fair 2-y-o 1m winner, is a half-sister to 3
winners including the useful 1m (at 2 yrs) and
Listed 7f winner Requisition. The second dam,
Saoire (by Pivotal), winner of the Irish 1,000
Guineas and third in the Group 1 Moyglare
Stud Stakes, is a half-sister to 6 winners. (Mrs
Fitri Hay). *"A nice, attractive looking horse with
plenty of size and scope and a good action;
he'll make a 2-y-o and will be out in mid-
season".*

908. DARK JEDI (IRE) ★★★
b.c. Kodiac – Whitefall (Street Cry). March 10.
First foal. 68,000Y. Tattersalls October Book
2. Sackville/Donald. The dam, a moderate
10f winner, is a half-sister to 3 winners. The
second dam, Nalani (by Sadler's Wells), a
French Listed 12f winner, is a half-sister to 7
winners including the French Group 2 winner
Affadavit. *"A colt with plenty of spirit, he's a
bit temperamental but the lads like him. He's
a good-looking colt with plenty of size and
scope".*

909. DELICIOUS ★★★
gr.f. Olympic Glory – You Look So Good
(Excellent Art). February 15. Second foal.
68,000Y. Tattersalls October Book 2. Sackville/
Donald. The dam, a modest 7f winner, is
a sister to the useful 2-y-o 6f winner and
Group 2 Rockfel Stakes third Gray Pearl and a
half-sister to 6 winners including the German
Group 2 6f Goldene Peitsche winner of 5
races Electric Beat. The second dam, Divine
Grace (by Definite Article), ran unplaced twice
and is a half-sister to 2 minor winners. *"She's
a nice-actioned filly, seems to have a good
temperament and we'll be hoping to start her
over seven furlongs in mid-season. We have
two 2-y-o's by Olympic Glory and they both
seem to go nicely".*

910. DEVILS ROC ★★
gr.f. Lethal Force – Ring For Baileys (Kyllachy).
April 2. 18,000Y. Tattersalls October Book 3.
Crimbourne Bloodstock. Half-sister to the

quite useful 5f (including at 2 yrs in 2017) and 6f winner of 5 races Rock On Baileys (by Rock Of Gibraltar). The dam, a quite useful dual 1m winner at 3 yrs, is a half-sister to 3 winners including the dual Listed winner Bahia Breeze. The second dam, Ring Of Love (by Magic Ring), a fair 5f winner of 4 races (including at 2 yrs), is a half-sister to 7 winners. *"She's done a couple of bits of work and will be running in April but she'll improve as the year goes on".*

911. DRUMNADROCHIT ★★★
b.c. Coach House – Blissamore (Kyllachy). February 17. Second foal. 28,000Y. Tattersalls October Book 2. Sackville/Donald. The dam is an unplaced half-sister to 5 winners. The second dam, Tremiere (by Anabaa), was placed 9 times in France and is a half-sister to 9 winners. *"He has plenty of size and scope, is quite laid-back in his work and is one for six furlongs around June/July time".*

912. FRAGRANT DAWN ★★★
b.f. Iffraaj – Festivale (Invincible Spirit). April 2. Half-sister to four winners including the quite useful dual 10f winner Carnevale (by New Approach), the quite useful 10f and 11.5f winner Fashion Parade (by Fastnet Rock) and the fair 10f winner Winterval (by Dubawi). The dam, a useful 6f (at 2 yrs) and Listed 1m winner, was third in the Group 3 7f Nell Gwyn Stakes and is a full or half-sister to 4 winners including the French Listed winner Invincible Dragon. The second dam, Cephalonie (Kris S), a French 12f winner, is a half-sister to 3 winners including the Japanese stakes winner Fifty Oner. *"The nicest one the mare has had, she's got size and scope, has a little bit of an attitude which is good and she's had no problems. She'll get a trip I think, at least seven furlongs".*

913. GLOBAL FALCON ★★★★ ♠
ch.c. Siyouni – Maggi Fong (Dr Fong). January 31. Third foal. 115,000Y. Tattersalls October Book 2. Sackville/Donald. Brother to the French 6.5f winner Fongani. The dam won 2 minor races in France at 2 and 5 yrs and is a half-sister to 4 winners including the French Listed winner Cadeau For Maggi. The second dam, Maggi For Margaret (by Shavian), a French 2-y-o Listed 5f winner, is a half-sister to 5 winners. *"He's a very attractive colt with*

plenty of size and scope, has a good attitude and he's a horse I like. He's not going to be early and will probably go a mile at the end of the season. A very nice horse and one you'd pick out in the string".*

914. GLOBAL QUALITY ★★★
ch.c. No Nay Never – Dynacam (Dynaformer). April 7. Eighth foal. 80,000Y. Tattersalls October Book 2. Sackville/Donald. Half-brother to the quite useful 2-y-o 7f and subsequent Hong Kong winner Ensuring (by New Approach) and to a minor winner abroad by Shamardal. The dam, a quite useful 2-y-o 10f winner, is a half-sister to 3 winners including the champion US 2-y-o colt and Breeders Cup Juvenile winner Action This Day. The second dam, Najecam (by Trempolino), a winner over 6f at 2 yrs and later a smart US 1m/9f winner, was placed in two Grade 2 events in the USA and is a full or half-sister to 6 winners. *"A big-striding colt with a nice attitude, he'll be running by the end of May".*

915. GLOBAL SHIFT (IRE) ★★★
ch.g. Dandy Man – Am I (Thunder Gulch). March 15. Seventh foal. 50,000Y. Tattersalls October Book 2. Sackville/Donald. Half-brother to the smart 1m (at 2 yrs) and Group 3 9f Earl Of Sefton Stakes winner and Group 2 second Questioning (by Elusive Quality) and a minor winner abroad by Dylan Thomas. The dam, a minor 2-y-o winner in the USA, is a half-sister to 6 winners including the US Grade 3 winner Certainly Classic and the French Group 3 winner Mahfooth. The second dam, I Certainly Am (by Affirmed), a minor winner in the USA, is a sister to the Group 2 Premio Lydia Tesio winner Medi Flash and a half-sister to 7 winners including the US Grade 1 Flower Bowl Invitational winner Laugh And Be Merry. *"He's just been a little bit tricky and we've gelded him. He's bred for speed and I would think we'll see him out in May".*

916. GLORIOUS SUNSHINE (IRE) ★★★★
br.c. Bated Breath – Brilliant Sunshine (Pivotal). February 25. Second foal. 75,000Y. Tattersalls October Book 2. Sackville/Donald. The dam is an unraced half-sister to the Listed winners Ferdoos and Brusco. The second dam, Blaze Of Colour (by Rainbow Quest), a quite useful dual 12f winner, was Listed-placed and is a

half-sister to 5 winners. *"A big, strapping colt that had a little niggling problem but he's OK now. All the lads like him, Bated Breaths take a little bit of time and he's out of a Pivotal mare as well, so I see him being out in mid-season and he'll probably prefer some cut in the ground".*

917. GLORY FIGHTER ★ ★ ★ ♠
b.c. Kyllachy – Isola Verde (Oasis Dream). April 7. Second foal. 95,000Y. Tattersalls October Book 2. Sackville/Donald. The dam, a fair 6f winner, is a half-sister to 3 minor winners. The second dam, Firenze (by Efisio), a dual Listed 6f winner, was third in the Group 2 5f Temple Stakes and is a sister to the Group 1 July Cup winner Frizzante and a half-sister to 3 winners including the Stewards Cup winner Zidane. *"He's a nice, sharp horse, that'll be racing in mid-April, he has a good temperament and does everything right".*

918. HAWAYEL (IRE) ★ ★ ★
b.f. Dandy Man – Dissonance (Rossini). February 18. 19,000Y. Tattersalls Ireland September. R Knight / Sheikh Abdullah al Sabah. Half-sister to the fairly useful 2-y-o 5f winner Disko (by Kodiac), to the modest Irish dual 7f winner Consonance and a minor 2-y-o winner in Italy (both by Chineur). The dam is an unraced sister to the 2-y-o Group 3 Firth Of Clyde Stakes winner Golden Legacy and a half-sister to a winner in Italy. The second dam, Dissidentia (by Dancing Dissident), won four races in Belgium and France and is a half-sister to 4 winners abroad. *"She's going to run in April, she goes nicely and has a good attitude".*

919. HEROIC ★ ★ ★
b.c. Heeraat – Aquasulis (Titus Livius). March 8. Second foal. 31,000Y. Tattersalls October Book 3. J K Powell. Half-brother to the fair 9.5f winner Things Happen (by Captain Gerrard). The dam, a fair 2-y-o 5f and 6f winner of 4 races, is a full or half-sister to 9 winners. The second dam, Christoph's Girl (by Efisio), a Belgian 6f and 7f Listed winner, is a sister to the Group 1 5f Prix de l'Abbaye winner Hever Golf Rose and a half-sister to 7 winners. *"He could be a fast horse but his knees are bit immature yet so we haven't asked him too many questions. He's come a long way since he's been here".*

920. KHAADEM (IRE) ★ ★ ★ ★
br.c. Dark Angel – White Daffodil (Footstepsinthesand). April 18. Fifth foal. 750,000Y. Tattersalls October Book 1. Shadwell Estate Co. Brother to the smart 2-y-o 5f and Listed 6f winner and multiple Group 2 placed Log Out Island. The dam, a modest 5f (at 2 yrs) and 6f winner, is a half-sister to 5 winners including the dual Listed 6f winner (including at 2 yrs) Lady Links (herself dam of the dual Listed winner Selinka). The second dam, Sparky's Song (by Electric), a moderate 10.2f and 12f winner, is a half-sister to the very smart Group 1 6.5f winner Bold Edge and to the Listed winner and Group 3 5f Temple Stakes second Brave Edge. *"A very athletic horse, he looks a natural to me and we'll get him out before Royal Ascot to see if he's good enough to go there. One to follow".*

921. LYRICAL BALLAD (IRE) ★ ★ ★
b.f. Dark Angel – Iffraaj Pink (Iffraaj). February 13. First foal. The dam, a quite useful 8.5f winner, is a half-sister to the 2-y-o Grade 1 8.5f Breeders Cup Juvenile and Listed 7f Stardom Stakes winner Vale Of York. The second dam, Red Vale (Halling), is an unraced half-sister to 9 winners including the fairly useful 10f and subsequent US Grade 3 winner Uraib. *"She's on the weak side at the moment and is going to need a bit of time, but she's very athletic, has a good action and I'm in no rush with her".*

922. MOONGAZER ★ ★ ★ ★
br.f. Kuroshio – Sonnellino (Singspiel). February 28. Second foal. 5,500 foal. Tattersalls December. Crimbourne Stud. The dam is an unplaced half-sister to 5 winners including the smart German Group 2 12f winner Baroon, the Group 2 Goldene Peitsche winner Vision Of Night and the smart Group 3 5f Prix de Saint-Georges winner Struggler. The second dam, Dreamawhile (by Known Fact), a quite useful 3-y-o 7f winner, is a half-sister to 5 winners including the Group 1 Italian Derby winner My Top and the Hoover Fillies Mile second Mountain Memory. *"A lovely filly with size and scope, she's attractive, has a nice action and I like her, she's really nice. One for six/seven furlongs".* TRAINER'S BARGAIN BUY

923. MR SPIRIT (IRE) ★★★★
b.c. Invincible Spirit – Sharapova (Elusive Quality). April 26. Seventh foal. 150,000Y. Tattersalls October Book 1. Richard Knight. Brother to the quite useful Irish 4-y-o 6f winner and 2-y-o Group 1 Phoenix Stakes third Lottie Dod and to the minor French 3-y-o winner Floriade and half-sister to the very useful 2-y-o 6f winner and Group 2 Railway Stakes second Rockaway Valley and the modest 6f winner Evies Wish (both by Holy Roman Emperor). The dam, a quite useful 3-y-o 7f winner, is a half-sister to 6 winners including the US stakes winner and Grade 1 placed Tamweel. The second dam, Naazeq (by Nashwan), a quite useful 10.5f winner, is a sister to the very useful 10f winner and Group 3 second Shaya and a half-sister to 9 winners. *"He's done a few bits of work and he's a well-balanced, neat colt with a good action. A nice horse that should start at six furlongs".*

924. MUNHAMEK ★★★
b.c. Dark Angel – Cadenza (Dansili). March 11. Half-brother to the fair 1m winner Anif (by Cape Cross) and to the minor French 11.5f winner Ladheeda (by Halling). The dam is an unraced half-sister to 6 winners including the Group 3 winners Kandidate and Star Valley. The second dam, Valleyrose (by Royal Academy), a minor winner of 2 races at 3 yrs in France, is a half-sister to 5 other minor winners in France. *"A strong-bodied colt with plenty of bone, I haven't done much with him yet but he'll probably be a June type 2-y-o and he looks like being a sprinter".*

925. MUTARAFFA ★★★
b.c. Acclamation – Excellent View (Shamardal). March 3. First foal. 70,000Y. Tattersalls October Book 2. Shadwell Estate Co. The dam, placed once at 3 yrs in France, is a half-sister to 3 minor winners. The second dam, Pearl Grey (by Gone West), a useful 2-y-o Listed 6f winner and second in the Group 2 6f Cherry Hinton Stakes, is a full or half-sister to 6 winners including the French Group 3 5f winner Time Prisoner. *"A big horse that's going to need a bit of time but he's got a good action and I've been really pleased with him over the last few weeks. One for the second half of the season, he's got plenty of scope".*

926. MUTAWAFFER (IRE) ★★★ ♠
b.c. Kodiac – Golden Flower (Royal Applause). April 15. Third foal. 160,000Y. Tattersalls October Book 2. Shadwell Estate Co. The dam, a fair dual 5f winner (including at 2 yrs), is a sister to the 2-y-o Group 3 6f Albany Stakes winner and Group 2 Cherry Hinton Stakes second Habaayib. The second dam, Silver Kestrel (by Silver Hawk), a minor winner of 2 races at 3 and 4 yrs in the USA, is a half-sister to 5 winners. *"He's going to be quick and will be racing just after his second birthday. He looks very sharp".*

927. NASSAM (IRE) ★★★
br.c. New Approach – Moon's Whisper (Storm Cat). April 7. Brother to the 2-y-o 8.5f winner Atnab and half-brother to the smart Listed 7f winner and Group 2 Champagne Stakes second Ibn Malik (by Raven's Pass), the dual 1m winner Yazamaan (by Galileo), the quite useful 5f and 6f winner of 5 races Mutafaakir (by Oasis Dream) and the fair 2m winner Hamsat Elqamar (by Nayef). The dam is an unraced half-sister to the 2-y-o Group 3 5.5f Prix d'Arenburg winner Moon Driver and the US winner and Grade 2 second Mojave Moon. The second dam, East Of The Moon (by Private Account), won the French 1,000 Guineas, Prix de Diane and Prix Jacques le Marois and is a half-sister to the top class miler and sire Kingmambo. *"A small, neat horse, he's quite nice and seven furlongs should suit him".*

928. NUBOUGH (IRE) ★★★
b.c. Kodiac – Qawaasem (Shamardal). January 14. The dam, a useful 2-y-o 6f winner and second in the Group 3 7f Prestige Stakes, is a half-sister to 2 winners. The second dam, Misdaqeya (by Red Ransom), a useful 2-y-o 7f winner, was second in the Group 3 Sweet Solera Stakes and is a half-sister to one winner. *"A strong-looking colt with a good action, he won't be too backward but needs a little bit more time to shape up".*

929. OCEAN PARADISE ★★★
b.f. New Approach – Tropical Paradise (Verglas). April 5. Fourth foal. 115,000Y. Tattersalls October Book 1. Jamie Lloyd. Half-sister to the quite useful 6f and 7f winner Coral Sea (by Excelebration). The dam won 6

races including the Group 3 7f Oak Tree and Group 3 7f Supreme Stakes and is a half-sister to 5 winners including the Italian Group 3 winner Harlem Shake. The second dam, Ladylishandra (by Mujadil), an Irish 2-y-o 6f winner, is a half-sister to 7 winners. *"Looks a bit on the weak side at the moment but she has a lovely action and to me she looks the nicest out of the mare so far. One for the second half of the season".*

930. PENRHOS ★★★

b.c. Kodiac – Bereka (Firebreak). February 25. First foal. 70,000Y. Tattersalls October Book 2. Jill Lamb. The dam, a modest 6f and 7f placed maiden, is a sister to the Group 1 Gran Criterium winner and Group 1 St James Palace Stakes third Hearts Of Fire and a half-sister to 3 winners. The second dam, Alexander Ballet (by Mind Games), an Irish 3-y-o 5f winner, is a half-sister to 8 winners (three of them Listed-placed). *"He hasn't come in his coat yet but he looks sharp and he's going to be a 2-y-o for six furlongs".*

931. PHOENIX OF SPAIN (IRE) ★★★

gr.c. Lope De Vega – Lucky Clio (Key Of Luck). February 17. Seventh foal. 220,000Y. Tattersalls October Book 1. Howson & Houldsworth. Half-brother to the useful dual 5f (at 2 yrs) and 6f winner and dual Listed-placed Lucky Beggar (by Verglas), to the useful 1m (at 2 yrs) and 10f winner and Group 3 Dee Stakes third Kingsdesire (by King's Best), the useful triple 10f winner Central Square (by Azamour), the quite useful dual 1m winner War Of Art (by Tamayuz) and the fair 1m winner Karisma (by Lawman). The dam was placed 3 times at 3 yrs and is a half-sister to 3 winners including Special Kaldoun, a winner of 9 races including the Group 2 Prix Daniel Wildenstein Casino Barriere (twice). The second dam, Special Lady (by Kaldoun), was placed at 2 yrs in France and is a half-sister to 5 minor winners. *"A very big horse with a plain head and he's a lovely bodied horse. He's not short of speed but we'll wait until the seven furlong races start".*

932. RED BRAVO (IRE) ★★★★

b.c. Acclamation – Vision Of Peace (Invincible Spirit). April 12. Fourth foal. 75,000Y. Tattersalls October Book 2. BBA (Ire). Half-brother to the fairly useful 5f and 6f winner of 5 races at 2

and 3 yrs Aguerooo (by Monsieur Bond). The dam is an unraced half-sister to 3 winners including the Group 3 Premio Tudini winner Victory Laurel. The second dam, Special Cause (by Fasliyev), won once over 7f at 3 yrs in France and is a half-sister to 6 winners including the smart broodmare Shy Lady (dam of the Group 1 St James's Palace Stakes winner Zafeen). *"A good-looking colt that I like very much, he's doing well and he'll be one for June/ July time over six furlongs".*

933. RHYDWYN (IRE) ★★★★

b.c. Kodiac – Pilates (Shamardal). February 22. First foal. 170,000Y. Tattersalls October Book 2. Jill Lamb. The dam, a modest 7f and 1m winner, is a half-sister to 4 winners including the 2-y-o Listed 5f winner Knavesmire. The second dam, Caribbean Escape (by Pivotal), is an unraced half-sister to 8 winners. *"It looks like he's going to be sharp and make a nice 2-y-o. He's still a bit behind in his coat at the minute, but he'll be a fast horse".*

934. RING OUT THE BELLS (IRE) ★★★★

b.f. Kodiac – Newlywed (Authorized). January 9. First foal. 75,000Y. Tattersalls October Book 2. BBA (Ire). The dam is an unraced half-sister to 4 winners including the useful Listed 1m winner of 7 races Yamal. The second dam, Pioneer Bride (by Gone West), is an unplaced half-sister to 7 winners including Faithful Son (Group 2 10f Prince of Wales's Stakes), Always Fair (Group 3 Coventry Stakes) and the dams of the Irish Oaks winner Lailani and the Group winners Keep The Faith and Naheef. *"She's done a couple of bits of work already, I think she should be running around May and she's a small, athletic type. Hopefully one for Royal Ascot".*

935. RIQAABY (USA) ★★★

b.f. New Approach – Aqsaam (Dynaformer). February 7. Second foal. Half-sister to the fairly useful triple 6f winner Thafeera (by War Front). The dam was Grade 3 placed over 12f in the USA and is a half-sister to the US dual Grade 2 placed Lady Lumberjack. The second dam, Harbor Blues (by Petionville), is a half-sister to the US Grade 2 winner Night Patrol (Hamdan Al Maktoum). *"She's only been here a week but she's a lovely, scopey filly that looks to have plenty of class".*

936. SAIKUNG (IRE) ★★★★
b.f. Acclamation – Glitter Baby (Danehill Dancer). April 29. Fourth foal. 42,000Y. Tattersalls October Book 2. Sackville/Donald. Sister to the French 6.5f winner Gloss (by Acclamation) and closely related to the minor French winner of 3 races at 3 yrs Luire (by Dark Angel). The dam, a fairly useful 12f and 2m winner, was Listed-placed and is a half-sister to 6 winners including the useful 2-y-o 7f winner and Group 2 Beresford Stakes third Going Public. The second dam, Gifts Galore (by Danehill Dancer), is a placed full or half-sister to 7 winners. *"She's a typical Acclamation, has a nice, big action and we all like her. Attractive looking, she's likely to be a six/seven furlong 2-y-o".*

937. SHANGHAI GRACE ★★★★
b.c. Kyllachy – Lavinia's Grace (Green Desert). February 18. Seventh living foal. 68,000Y. Tattersalls October Book 2. Sackville/Donald. Half-brother to the fairly useful 7f to 8.5f winner of 9 races Justonefortheroad (by Domedriver), to the quite useful dual 6f winner Jubilante (by Royal Applause), the fair 2-y-o 6f winner Magique Touch (by Equiano) and a winner in Greece by Compton Place. The dam, a minor 2-y-o winner in France, is a half-sister to 3 winners including the dual Listed-placed Guilia (dam of the US Grade 2 winner Goodyearforroses). The second dam, Lesgor (by Irish River), won over 10f in France, was third in the Group 3 10f Prix de Psyche and is a half-sister to 3 winners. *"He could be sharp, he's done a couple of bits of work upsides, he's a good-looking horse, has a good action and we all like him".*

938. SUPERSEDED (IRE) ★★★★
gr.c. Exceed And Excel – Satwa Ruby (Verglas). April 4. Second foal. €62,000Y. Goffs Orby. Kennet Valley Thoroughbreds. Half-brother to the quite useful 2017 2-y-o 1m winner Che Bella (by Holy Roman Emperor). The dam, a 10.5f and 11.5f winner in France, is a half-sister to 3 winners including the Group 1 Criterium de Saint-Cloud winner Morandi. The second dam, Vezina (by Bering), is a French placed full or half-sister to 13 winners. *"He's a nice horse, all the lads like him and he won't be too backward. He's athletic and looks a speedy type".*

939. TADAABEER ★★★★
b.f. Dubawi – Thakafaat (Unfuwain). April 7. Half-sister to the useful 1m and 10f winner of 4 races Taqleed (by Shamardal), to the quite useful 2m 2f winner Mashaari (by Monsun) and a jumps winner by Dalakhani. The dam, a very useful 7f (at 2 yrs), 10f and Group 2 12f Ribblesdale Stakes winner, is a half-sister to the Grade 1 E P Taylor Stakes winner Curvy and to the Group 1 National Stakes and Irish 2,000 Guineas winner Power. The second dam, Frappe (by Inchinor), a fairly useful 2-y-o 6f winner, is a half-sister to the Group 1 winners Footstepsinthesand and Pedro The Great. (Hamdan Al-Maktoum). *"I think she's got quite a bit of speed this filly, she reminds of the Dubawi filly Kiyoshi who won two Group 3's for us. One for six/seven furlongs, she's not overly big but she's strong – a typical Dubawi really".*

940. TEMUJIN (IRE) ★★★★
b.c. Moohaajim – Alhena (Alhaarth). February 16. Fourth foal. £55,000Y. Goffs UK Premier (Doncaster). Highflyer Bloodstock. Half-brother to a minor winner abroad by Bushranger. The dam is an unplaced half-sister to 3 winners including the Group 1 7f Moyglare Stud Stakes winner and Coronation Stakes third Mail The Desert. The second dam, Mail Boat (by Formidable), is an unraced half-sister to 4 winners including the Group 3 Chester Vase winner and St Leger third Dry Dock and the dam of the dual Group 3 winner and multiple Group 1 placed Norse Dancer. *"A lovely, well-balanced colt. We always loved him as a yearling, he has a good attitude, he's a good model and I think he'll be a six/seven furlong 2-y-o from the middle of the year".*

941. YNYS MON (IRE) ★★★
b.c. Olympic Glory – Russian Spirit (Falbrav). March 14. Third foal. 85,000Y. Tattersalls October Book 1. B W Hills. Half-brother to the 2017 2-y-o 6f winner, from two starts, Foreseeable Future (by Harbour Watch). The dam, a fairly useful Listed 6f winner of 3 races, is a half-sister to 2 winners. The second dam, Russian Rhapsody (by Cosmonaut), a fairly useful Listed-placed 7f and 1m winner, is a half-sister to 3 winners. *"I think he's above average. He's had one run but got stuck in the mud and we'll get him out again at Newmarket's Craven meeting".*

942. UNNAMED ★★★ ♠
b.f. Charm Spirit – Air Biscuit (Galileo). February 28. 30,000 foal. Tattersalls December. Half-sister to the useful 6 and 7f winner of 5 races from 2 to 5 yrs Solar Flair (by Equiano) and to the fairly useful Irish 7f (at 2 yrs) and 1m winner Warbird (by Royal Applause). The dam, a quite useful 1m and 10f winner of 3 races, is a half-sister to 6 winners including the Group 3 5f Prix du Bois and Group 3 5f Prix du Petit-Couvert winner Ziria. The second dam, Surprise Visitor (by Be My Guest), was placed once in France and is a half-sister to 9 winners including the dual German Listed winner Mirage (herself dam of the Group 2 winner Swallow Flight) and the champion Scandinavian older horse Red Hero. *"We've done a little bit of work with her, she shows speed, I like her and she's one for six/seven furlongs. I think these Charm Spirits could be quite nice".*

943. UNNAMED ★★★
b.c. Mayson – Aromatherapy (Oasis Dream). February 27. Half-brother to the fair 2017 2-y-o 5f and 6f winner Queen Of Kalahari (by Lethal Force), to the modest 5f winner Pieman's Girl (by Henrythenavigator) and the moderate 10f winner Scent Of Power (by Authorized). The dam, a quite useful dual 1m winner at 3 yrs, is a half-sister to one winner. The second dam, Fragrant View (by Distant View), a useful 10.3f winner, is a sister to the champion 2-y-o Distant Music, winner of the Group 1 7f Dewhurst Stakes, the Group 2 7f Champagne Stakes and the Group 2 9f Goffs International Stakes and a half-sister to the useful 10f winner and Group 3 Lancashire Oaks third New Orchid (herself dam of the Group 1 Sprint Cup winner African Rose). *"A half-brother to a 2-y-o winner we had last year, Queen Of Kalahari, this colt is a bit bigger and stronger. He has plenty of scope and has done nothing wrong at all".*

944. UNNAMED ★★★
b.f. Zebedee – Fonseca (Red Clubs). January 31. Second foal. £40,000Y. Goffs UK Premier (Doncaster). Sackville/Donald. The dam is an unplaced half-sister to 4 winners including the very useful dual Listed winner and Group 1 Sussex Stakes third Gabrial. The second dam, Guajira (by Mtoto), a minor French 11f

winner of 3 races, is a half-sister to 9 winners including the US Grade 2 winners Jaunatxo and Iron Deputy and the dam of the Italian Group 1 winner Shamalgan. *"A very strongly made filly, she's not short of speed, should be on the track in May and we've had no problems with her up to now".*

945. UNNAMED ★★★
b.c. Exceed And Excel – Hecuba (Hector Protector). April 28. Tenth foal. 60,000Y. Tattersalls October Book 2. Sackville/Donald. Brother to the useful Listed 6f winner of 4 races at 2 and 3 yrs Shanghai Glory and half-brother to 5 winners including the very useful Listed 7f winner of 4 races and Group 2 Blandford Stakes third Choose Me (by Choisir), the fairly useful Irish dual 10f winner Spirit Of Cuba (by Invincible Spirit) and the quite useful 7f (at 2 yrs) and 1m winner of 4 races Aeronwyn Bryn (by Dylan Thomas). The dam, a fairly useful 10f winner, is a half-sister to 7 winners including the German Group 2 winner Bad Bertrich Again and the Group 3 Scottish Classic winner Prolix. The second dam, Ajuga (by The Minstrel), was a useful 6f and 7f winner. *"He looks like he's going to be a speed horse, he's very athletic and very similar to his brother Shanghai Glory. He's done nothing wrong, we'll take our time with him but he should be fast".*

946. UNNAMED ★★★
b.f. Dark Angel – Illuminating Dream (High Chaparral). February 14. First foal. €100,000Y. Goffs Orby. BBA (Ire). The dam, a quite useful 2-y-o 7f winner, is a half-sister to 7 winners including the very smart 1m (at 2 yrs) and multiple Listed winner from 10f to 12f Les Fazzani. The second dam, Massada (by Most Welcome), a Listed-placed 7f and 1m winner at 2 yrs in Germany, is a half-sister to 3 minor winners. *"A nice, strong filly that's done nothing wrong up to now and has a nice attitude. Pretty scopey, we haven't done much with her yet".*

947. UNNAMED ★★★
b.f. Dark Angel – Littlepromisedland (Titus Livius). April 4. Fourth foal. £56,000Y. Goffs UK Premier. Sackville/Donald. Closely related to the fairly useful 2017 2-y-o dual 6f winner Elizabeth Bennet (by Acclamation). The dam,

a poor 1m placed maiden, is a half-sister to 2 winners including the Group 1 July Cup and Group 1 Diamond Jubilee Stakes winner Lethal Force. The second dam, Land Army (by Desert Style), ran once unplaced and is a sister to a French Listed winner and a half-sister to 8 winners including the Listed winner Flanders (dam of the Group 1 winning sprinter G Force). *"Not as big as her sister Elizabeth Bennet, she has a good attitude, moves nicely and we're just waiting for a bit of sun with her".*

948. UNNAMED ★★
ch.f. Showcasing – Love And Cherish (Excellent Art). February 15. Second foal. 70,000Y. Tattersalls October Book 1. B W Hills. The dam, a fairly useful Listed-placed 1m (at 2 yrs) and 10f winner, is a half-sister to one winner. The second dam, Party Feet (by Noverre), is an unraced half-sister to the Group 2 Sun Chariot Stakes and Group 3 Matron Stakes winner of 4 races Independence (herself dam of the dual Group 1 winner Mount Nelson and the Group 2 winner Monitor Closely). *"A nice filly with plenty of size and scope, she's not looking an obvious 2-y-o yet but I'm sure she'll come good in the second half of the year".*

949. UNNAMED ★★★
b.f. Camacho – Royal Majestic (Tobougg). April 28. Fourth foal. €44,000Y. Tattersalls Ireland September. Richard Knight. Half-sister to the fairly useful 2-y-o triple 5f winner Big Time Baby (by Dandy Man) and to the minor Italian 2-y-o winners Ultimo Respiro (by Kheleyf) and Charline Royale (by Zebedee). The dam, a fair 7f and 1m winner at 2 yrs, is a half-sister to 3 minor winners. The second dam, Golden Symbol (by Wolfhound), is an unplaced half-sister to 4 minor winners. *"She's got a great attitude, isn't backward and we'll be running her in May. We've had no problems with her".*

RICHARD HUGHES
950. AMBITION ★★★
ch.f. Dubawi – Talent (New Approach). March 18. First foal. The dam, a 7f (at 2 yrs) and Group 1 12f Oaks winner, is a sister to one winner and a half-sister to 2 winners including the smart 7f and 1m winner and Listed-placed Skilful. The second dam, Prowess (by Peintre Celebre), a fairly useful 12f winner, was Listed-

placed and is a half-sister to the fairly useful 11.5f winner and Listed placed Genoa and the useful 2-y-o 1m winner and Listed-placed Clipper. (Mr Mark Dixon & Mr J Roswell). *"What a pedigree, it's a privilege to have her and she's the best-bred horse in the yard! She's petite, so she's not made like a middle-distance filly and it wouldn't surprise me if she was racing in June. We're just ticking along quietly with her for now and she'll tell me when she's ready, but she looks more mature than the pedigree would suggest".*

951. ANTIDOTE (IRE) ★★★
gr.c. Dark Angel – Mood Indigo (Indian Ridge). March 13. Eleventh foal. 100,000Y. Tattersalls October Book 1. Hillen & Hughes. Half-brother to the Group 3 7f Silver Flash Stakes winner Luminous Eyes (by Bachelor Duke), to the quite useful Irish 1m winner Michikabu (by Grand Lodge),the modest 7f and 1m winner of 4 races Janaab (by Nayef) and the minor French 11f winner Indigo King (by Danehill Dancer). The dam, an Irish 7f winner, is a half-sister to 2 winners including the minor US stakes winner Got A Crush (herself dam of the US Grade 3 winner Palmilla). The second dam, Glowing Ardour (by Dancing Brave), won the Group 3 1m Silken Glider Stakes and is a half-sister to 7 winners including the top-class Breeders Cup Turf, Japan Cup, Champion Stakes and Eclipse Stakes winner Pilsudski. (Mr Anthony Hogarth). *"A big horse we bought from Book One, we'll have to take our time with him but I see him coming out around July/August time. He's a beautiful mover and has a great mind".*

952. BALLYLEMON (IRE) ★★★
b.c. Champs Elysees – Athreyaa (Singspiel). April 11. Fourth foal. 75,000Y. Tattersalls October Book 2. Hillen/Hughes. Half-brother to the fairly useful dual 6f (at 2 yrs) and dual 7f winner Dawaa (by Tamayuz) and to the fair 1m winner Inaad (by New Approach). The dam is an unraced half-sister to 4 winners including the Group 2 Doncaster Cup winner Honolulu and the unraced Hit The Sky (the dam of three Group winners). The second dam, Cerulean Sky (by Darshaan), a 1m (at 2 yrs) and Group 1 10f Prix Saint-Alary winner, is a sister to 2 winners including the 7f (at 2 yrs) and Listed 12f winner and Breeders' Cup Filly

& Mare second L'Ancresse and a half-sister to 8 winners including the Group 1 Irish Oaks winner Moonstone. (Graham Doyle & Hazel Lawrence). *"A beautiful moving horse, he's probably one for a nursery at the back-end and he'll only be any good when he's going a trip. Has a great chance of being a winner at two, even though we bought him to be a 3-y-o".*

953. CANFORD DANCER ★★★

b.f. Canford Cliffs – Petite Nymphe (Golan). February 25. Fifth foal. 25,000Y. Tattersalls October Book 2. Hillen/Hughes. Half-sister to the fairly useful 2017 1m placed 2-y-o Lubinka (by Mastercraftsman) and to the quite useful 2-y-o 7f winner Paulownia (by Nathaniel). The dam, a minor 3-y-o winner in France, is a half-sister to 11 winners including the French 1,000 Guineas and Prix de la Foret winner Danseuse Du Soir (herself dam of the Group 1 Gran Criterium winner Scintillo). The second dam, Dance By Night (by Northfields), won twice over 7f at 2 yrs and is a half-sister to 3 winners. (The Lakota Partnership & Mrs J. Blake). *"She was quite cheap, the 2-y-o last year Lubinka finished sixth in the Fillies' Mile after we bought her. It's a very good family but she's a little bit weak so we'll wait on her and she could be out around July time".*

954. DANDY LAD (IRE) ★★★

b.c. Dandy Man – Lucky Pipit (Key Of Luck). May 5. Ninth living foal. 32,000Y. Tattersalls October Book 2. Hillen/Hughes. Half-brother to the useful Listed 7f winner Haalick (by Roderic O'Connor) and to 5 minor winners in North America (by Mr Greeley (2), Rahy and Student Council) and Germany (by Arcano). The dam, a useful 2-y-o 7f Listed winner, is a half-sister to 5 winners. The second dam, Meadow Pipit (by Meadowlake), a smart winner of 4 races at 4 yrs from 7f to 10f including a Listed event, is a half-sister to 9 winners. (Mr Peter Crane). *"Physically he looks really early but he's a May foal and his knees are a bit open. He's showed us enough to say we like him and he's grown a lot in the last couple of weeks. I don't think he'd be the same price now if he went to the breeze-ups".*

955. KADIZ (IRE) ★★★

b.f. Lope De Vega – Looby Loo (Kyllachy). April 14. Fifth foal. £50,000Y. Goffs UK Premier.

Half-sister to the quite useful 7f winner Whaleweigh Station (by Zamindar). The dam, placed once over 5f at 2 yrs, is a half-sister to 4 winners including the 2-y-o Group 1 Middle Park Stakes and Group 1 Prix Morny winner Dutch Art and the Group 2 10f Blandford Stakes winner Up. The second dam, Halland Park Lass (by Spectrum), ran 3 times unplaced and is a half-sister to 5 winners including the Scandinavian Group 3 winner King Quantas. (The High Flyers). *"She'll be the first of our fillies to run; she's small and goes well, has a great mind on her and hasn't put a foot wrong yet. She just eats and sleeps and has a great pedigree behind her".*

956. LIGHT UP OUR STARS (IRE) ★★★

b.c. Rip Van Winkle – Shine Like A Star (Fantastic Light). March 7. Sixth foal. 30,000Y. Tattersalls October Book 3. Not sold. Half-brother to 4 winners including the useful 7f (at 2 yrs) and Listed 1m winner and multiple Group 3 placed Light Up Our World (by Zoffany), the useful 2-y-o 6f and 7f winner and Group 2 May Hill Stakes third Light Up My Life (by Zamindar) and the quite useful 2-y-o 6f winner Money Never Sleeps (by Kyllachy). The dam is an unplaced half-sister to 4 winners including the Group 1 Coronation Stakes winner Fallen For You, the Listed 1m winner Fallen Idol and the useful 2-y-o 1m winner and Group 2 12f Lancashire Oaks second Fallen In Love. The second dam, Fallen Star (by Brief Truce), a Listed 7f winner and Group 3 placed twice, is a half-sister to 7 winners including the Group 1 7f Lockinge Stakes winner Fly To The Stars. (Dereck Boocock). *"A big, backward horse and yet he took my eye cantering the other morning and he shouldn't be able to do that yet. It's a good pedigree and I can see him racing in July/August".*

957. MISS ENIGMA (IRE) ★★★

b.f. Kodiac – Mysteriousness (Beat Hollow). March 17. Second foal. €50,000Y. Goffs Orby. Stephen Hillen/ Richard Hughes. The dam won 2 minor races at 3 yrs in France and is a half-sister to the French Listed winner Three Bodies. The second dam, Three Mysteries (by Linamix), a minor French 4-y-o winner, is a half-sister to 7 winners including the Group 2 Italian 1,000 Guineas winner Erin Bird. *"She's the last 2-y-o I sold and luckily enough I kept a leg because she looks very nice. She's a beautiful-moving filly".*

958. PRETTY EYES (IRE) ★★★★
b.f. Kodiac – Maoin Dor (Manduro). February 15. Third foal. £70,000Y. Goffs UK Premier (Doncaster). Hillen/Hughes. The dam is an unraced half-sister to one winner. The second dam, Royal Alchemist (by Kingsinger), a winner over 6f (at 2 yrs) and two Listed events over 1m and 9f, was placed in four Group events and is a half-sister to 3 winners. (Cedar Investments Ltd & Mr M Burke). *"A very strong-looking filly, she'll probably run in May. She's going quite nicely and she's by a great sire in Kodiac who can't go wrong. Not a tall filly, but she's as wide as she is tall and she's a typical 2-y-o – this is her year".*

959. PRINCE OF ROME ★★★
b.c. Lethal Force – Garraun (Tamayuz). March 9. First foal. €37,000Y. Goffs Orby. Stephen Hillen/Richard Hughes. The dam, a modest 2-y-o 6f placed maiden, is a half-sister to 4 winners including the 2-y-o Group 3 second Fort Bastion. The second dam, French Fern (by Royal Applause), placed at 2 yrs in Ireland and a minor US dual 4-y-o winner, is a half-sister to 4 winners including the Group 2 Criterium de Maisons-Laffitte winner Captain Marvelous. (John & Jordan Lund). *"He has a lovely pedigree and I bought him because at the sales he was such a loose mover. He grew a little bit more than I expected when we got him home which was no harm. We're trying to slow him down at the moment because his knees are little immature, but he'll be ready when he's more mature".*

960. QUEEN SHAAHD (IRE) ★★★★
b.f. Kodiac – Cherika (Cape Cross). April 28. Second foal. £40,000Y. Goffs UK Premier (Doncaster). Rabbah Bloodstock. The dam is an unraced half-sister to 5 winners including the smart Irish Group 3 7f and Group 3 1m winner Cheyenne Star and to the dam of the triple Group 1 winner Gordon Lord Byron. The second dam, Charita (by Lycius), a Listed 1m winner in Ireland, is a half-sister to 4 winners including the Italian Group 2 winner Stanott. (Mr Jaber Abdullah). *"This filly really covers an awful lot of ground, she'll be early enough and she's definitely one for five/six furlongs. A real good-moving filly".*

961. RAGSTONE COWBOY (IRE) ★★★
b.c. Slade Power – Three Decades (Invincible Spirit). January 29. Fifth foal. 140,000Y. Tattersalls October Book 2. Gallagher/ Hillen. Half-brother to the modest 2017 dual 7f placed 2-y-o Corazon Espinado (by Iffraaj), to the Listed Bosra Sham Stakes winner and Group 3 Fred Darling Stakes third Melbourne Memories (by Sleeping Indian) and the modest 1m, 9f and hurdles winner Big McIntosh (by Bushranger). The dam, a quite useful 2-y-o 6f winner, is a half-sister to 6 winners including the South African Group 2 and Group 3 winner Gorongosa. The second dam, Parvenue (by Ezzoud), a quite useful 2-y-o 6f winner, is a half-sister to 6 winners. (Gallagher Bloodstock Limited). *"A nice horse, he just does what you ask him every time but he hasn't let us down yet. A beautiful looking horse I'm hoping will be out in May, he was an early foal and he's very strong".*

962. SAEDI SHAAHD ★★★
ch.c. Coach House – Martha (Alhaarth). March 20. Sixth foal. £15,000Y. Goffs UK Premier (Doncaster). Hillen/Hughes (private sale). The dam, placed once over 5f at 3 yrs, is a sister to the Group 2 5f Kings Stand Stakes and Group 3 5f Cornwallis Stakes Dominica and a half-sister to 3 winners including the dam of the Group 3 winner Rimth. The second dam, Dominio (by Dominion), a 2-y-o Listed 5f winner, was second in the Group 2 5f Temple Stakes and is a half-sister to 6 winners including the very smart Group 1 5f Nunthorpe Stakes winner Ya Malak. (Mr Jaber Abdullah). *"He was ready to go very early on but he just had a small problem and I backed off him a bit. I'm still hoping he'll be early though and he was very cheap for what he's shown me. A real 2-y-o".*

963. SWISS PRIDE ★★★
b.c. Swiss Spirit – Encore Encore (Royal Applause). February 11. First foal. 35,000Y. Tattersalls October Book 3. Hillen/Hughes. The dam, a modest 2-y-o 8.5f winner, is a half-sister to 6 winners including the fairly useful 2-y-o 7f winner and Group 3 7f Sweet Solera Stakes third Kay Es Jay. The second dam, Angel Rose (by Definite Article), won twice at 2 yrs in Sweden and is a half-sister to 8 winners. *"He's an early 2-y-o, a good-looking horse and he goes nicely. One for five and six furlongs".*

964. UM SHAMA (IRE) ★★★
ch.f. Helmet – Night Club (Mozart). March 22. Eighth foal. £9,000Y. Goffs UK Premier (Doncaster). Hillen/Hughes. Half-sister to 5 winners including the quite useful 12f, 14f and hurdles winner Sebastian Beach (by Yeats), the quite useful 10f and 12f winner Wefait (by Harbour Watch), the fair dual 1m winner Opening Nite (by Azamour) and the modest 2-y-o 5f and 6f winner Dunmore Boy (by Iffraaj). The dam is an unplaced half-sister to 12 winners including the French 1,000 Guineas and Group 1 7f Prix de la Foret winner Danseuse du Soir (herself dam of the Group 1 Gran Criterium winner Scintillo). The second dam, Dance By Night (by Northfields), a quite useful 2-y-o dual 7f winner, is a half-sister to 3 winners. (Mr Jaber Abdullah). *"She's just started to come now, when we bought her she was very small and she has a white patch over one eye which would have put some people off. I couldn't believe I got her so cheaply and thought there must be something wrong with her, but there's not. She's grown into a nice filly, did her first bit of work the other morning and if she continues to do well she'll run in April or May".*

965. UNCLE JERRY ★★★
b.c. Kyllachy – News Desk (Cape Cross). March 27. Third foal. 20,000Y. Tattersalls October Book 3. Richard Hughes. Half-brother to the modest 8.5f and 10f winner Broughtons Story (by Royal Applause). The dam, a modest 10f winner, is a half-sister to one winner. The second dam, La Presse (by Gone West), a useful 2-y-o 6f winner, was third in the Group 3 6f Firth Of Clyde Stakes and is a half-sister to 6 winners. (Thames Boys). *"A little smasher, the best value horse I bought last year I think. I actually told the owner that if he doesn't win a race I'd give up! A gorgeous little horse and he'll be early, hasn't put a foot wrong and goes well".* TRAINER'S BARGAIN BUY

966. WINTER LIGHT ★★★
ch.f. Bated Breath – Moonglow (Nayef). February 14. Third foal. Half-sister to the fairly useful 2017 2-y-o 6f winner Zap (by Mayson) and to the moderate 1m and jumps winner Crucial Moment (by Pivotal). The dam, a modest 11f fourth placed 3-y-o, is a half-sister to 5 winners including the Group 1 Eclipse

Stakes and Group 1 Lockinge Stakes winner and sire Medicean. The second dam, Mystic Goddess (by Storm Bird), a fairly useful 2-y-o Listed 7f Sweet Solera Stakes winner, was placed in the Queen Mary Stakes, the Cherry Hinton Stakes and the Rockfel Stakes and is a half-sister to 4 winners including the Group 1 Gran Criterium winner Sanam and the South African Grade 2 winner Shaybani. (Cheveley Park Stud). *"A very nice filly that covers a lot of ground, we thought she'd be backward but she's rushed to the front of the pile and she'll be out in June. She's quite nice and does everything easily, so we like her".*

967. WOLF HUNTER (IRE) ★★★
ch.c. Sir Prancealot – Sunny Hollow (Beat Hollow). April 11. Second foal. £9,000Y. Goffs UK Premier (Doncaster). Richard Hughes. Half-brother to the fair 2017 2-y-o 6f winner Alaska (by Kodiac). The dam, a moderate 5.5f and 6f placed maiden, is a half-sister to 5 winners including the 2-y-o Group 2 6f July Stakes winner Nevisian Lad. The second dam, Corndavon (by Sheikh Albadou), a fairly useful 6f winner of 3 races, is a sister to 2 winners. (Mr Jaber Abdullah). *"He'll be my first runner and he's a horse with a bit of character – cheeky but he'll get better with racing. A very cheap colt, he'll have no problem winning a race".*

968. UNNAMED ★★
b.f. Paco Boy – Goldamour (Fasliyev). March 22. Fourth foal. Half-sister to the fair 2017 2-y-o 6f and 7f winner Bath And Tennis (by Footstepsinthesand) and to the modest 6f to 1m winner of 5 races Big Amigo (by Bahamian Bounty). The dam, placed at 3 yrs in France, is a half-sister to 3 minor winners. The second dam, Glamadour (by Sanglamore), a winner over 11.5f in France, is a half-sister to 11 winners including the outstanding multiple Group 1 winner Goldikova and the Group 1 Prix Vermeille winner Galikova. (Richard Hughes Racing Club). *"A beautiful looking filly with a few Paco Boy traits that I know very well! The owner has leased her to us and I can understand why he wants to keep her".*

969. UNNAMED ★★★
ch.f. Showcasing – Magic Art (Nayef). February 7. First foal. €60,000Y. Goffs Orby.

Not sold. The dam won 4 races at 2 and 3 yrs in Germany and Austria and is a half-sister to 3 winners including the Italian and German Group 3 10f winner Magic Artist. The second dam, Artisti (Cape Cross), is an unraced half-sister to 5 winners including the Group 1 winner Gran Criterium winner Kirklees and the Group 1 St Leger and Hong Kong Vase winner Mastery and to the dam of the Group 1 Eclipse Stakes winner Mukhadram. (C. McHale & The Rat Pack Partnership). *"A real 2-y-o that's done nothing but improve since she came in and she's really starting to do well now. She'll run in May, hopefully".*

970. UNNAMED ★★★
b.c. Dark Angel – Mythicism (Oasis Dream). March 28. Sixth foal. 48,000Y. Tattersalls October Book 2. Hillen/Hughes. Half-brother to 4 winners including the very useful Group 2 Prix Robert Papin winner Tis Marvellous (by Harbour Watch), the useful triple Listed-placed 6f winner of 6 races Mythmaker (by Major Cadeaux) and the moderate 2-y-o 5f winner Kinkohyo (by Indesatchel). The dam, a fair 2-y-o 6f winner, is a half-sister to 5 other minor winners. The second dam, Romantic Myth (by Mind Games), winner of the Group 3 5f Queen Mary Stakes, is a half-sister to 12 winners including another Queen Mary winner in Romantic Liason. (M Clarke, P Munnelly & D Waters). *"A strong little horse, we're hoping to try and get him out early but he's had a few little issues since we bought him. He's made to be a 2-y-o because he's not over-big".*

971. UNNAMED ★★★★
b.f. No Nay Never – Sparkling Rock (Rock Of Gibraltar). May 3. Third foal. €42,000Y. Goffs Sportsmans. Hillen/Hughes. Half-sister to the fairly useful 2017 Irish 2-y-o 6.5f winner Eire Rock (by Most Improved) and to a minor 2-y-o winner abroad by Born To Sea. The dam is an unplaced half-sister to 5 winners including the 2-y-o Listed winner Al Aasifh. The second dam, Urgele (by Zafonic), a French Listed 1m winner and third in the Group 3 Prix Miesque, is a half-sister to 7 winners. (M Clarke, P Munnelly & D Waters). *"Based on her I think No Nay Never will make it as a stallion. She's a filly with an awful lot of quality and I'd say she could be ready whenever I want her to be. She does everything so easy and nothing fazes*

her, but I'm aware that she's a May foal so I'm hovering! She could be running tomorrow even though she's a big 2-y-o. Probably the pick of the fillies at this stage and if she's good she'll be an Ascot filly".

972. UNNAMED ★★★★
b.c. Olympic Glory – Miss Hygrove (Exceed And Excel). March 5. Third foal. €31,000Y. Arqana Deauville August V2. Hillen/Hughes. The dam is an unraced half-sister to 6 minor winners. The second dam, Durrah Green (by Green Desert), a quite useful Irish 3-y-o 5f winner, is a half-sister to 6 winners. (Robin Heffer). *"A very nice horse bought very cheaply at Deauville, he's a beautiful mover and we might start him off in May. He's one to look out for".*

WILLIAM JARVIS

973. FIRE AND FURY ★★★
b.c. Equiano – Luanshya (First Trump). May 4. Tenth foal. 16,000Y. Tattersalls December. William Jarvis. Brother to the fair 6f (at 2 yrs) and 7f winner Luna Moon and half-brother to 6 winners including the Listed 6f Rose Bowl Stakes winner and Group 2 Mill Reef takes third Saigon (by Royal Applause), the useful 2-y-o Listed 5f Roses Stakes and 3-y-o 6f winner of 5 races Tabaret (by Bertolini), the modest 5f (at 2 yrs) and 6f winner African Breeze (by Atraf) and the modest 1m and 9f winner of 5 races Aussie Blue (by Bahamian Bounty). The dam, a fair 3-y-o 6f winner, is a half-sister to 4 winners. The second dam, Blues Indigo (by Music Boy), won over 6f and was second in the Group 3 Palace House Stakes and is a half-sister to 5 winners. (The Marine Team). *"A May foal and possibly a bit weak at the moment, but he's a half-brother to a good horse in Saigon. We'll take our time but he's bred to be quick and there's no reason why he won't get into the winner's enclosure. I know the dam has had plenty of foals but most of them have won and I think this colt was a good buy".* TRAINER'S BARGAIN BUY

974. GREAT SUSPENSE ★★★
b.c. Bated Breath – Gimasha (Cadeaux Genereux). January 31. Seventh living foal. 52,000Y. Tattersalls October Book 3. William Jarvis. Half-brother to the fairly useful 2-y-o 6f winner and 3-y-o 6f Listed-placed Samminder

(by Red Ransom), to the fairly useful triple 6f winner at 2 and 3 yrs Queen's Pearl (by Exceed And Excel) and the 7f winner Platinum Pearl (by Shamardal). The dam, a useful 5f and 6f winner of 5 races, is a half-sister to 9 winners including the very useful triple 1m winner Atlantic Rhapsody and the Group 3 Prix Thomas Bryon third Gaitero. The second dam, First Waltz (by Green Dancer), winner of the Group 1 6f Prix Morny, was second in the Cheveley Park Stakes. (Mr Clive Washbourn). *"I trained the dam who was very quick and quite a smart handicapper. This colt has a lovely temperament but he's a big horse and will probably take a bit of time so we're looking at the second half of the season with him".*

975. LESTRADE ★★★★
b.c. Lawman – Ninas Rainbow (Rainbow Quest). April 7. Third foal. 65,000Y. Tattersalls October Book 2. James Toller. Half-brother to the French 2-y-o 1m winner Normandie (by Redoute's Choice). The dam, a minor German 4-y-o winner, is a half-sister to the German dual Listed winner Nina Celebre. The second dam, Next Gina (by Perugino), won the Group 1 German Oaks and is a half-sister to 7 winners including the Group 1 German Derby winner Next Desert. (Mr Clive Washbourn). *"A very nice horse, I like him and the Lawman/ Rainbow Quest nick has worked before. He has a lovely way of going, I can see him being a 2-y-o from July onwards, he's really nice and we like him. A good, strong sort who will be a ten furlong horse next year".*

976. MICHAEL'S CHOICE ★★★
b.c. War Command – Todber (Cape Cross). March 25. Third living foal. 62,000Y. Tattersalls October Book 2. James Toller. Half-brother to the modest 6f winner Bandolier (by Bahamian Bounty. The dam, a modest 5f and 6f winner of 3 races, is a half- sister to 2 winners. The second dam, Dominica (by Alhaarth), winner of the Group 2 5f Kings Stand Stakes and the Group 3 Cornwallis Stakes, is a half-sister to 3 winners including the Listed-placed sprinter Bowness. (The Music Makers). *"A strong colt, he looks very wintry at the moment but when he starts to look a bit better we'll go a bit faster with him. He's a no-nonsense, decent-sized colt and he's got a chance".*

977. NO THANKS ★★★
b.c. Pour Moi – Miss Fifty (Whipper). March 21. Second foal. 40,000Y. Tattersalls October Book 3. James Toller. The dam was placed 10 times from 2 to 4 yrs in France including when second in the Group 3 Prix du Calvados and third in the Group 3 Prix Imprudence. The second dam, Annatto (by Mister Baileys), is a placed half-sister to 8 winners including the Group 3 Norfolk Stakes winner Rosselli. (P. C. J. Dalby & R. D. Schuster). *"He's out of a very quick mare so it's interesting with Pour Moi on top, but he's not over-big and he points his toe nicely. At the moment he's only cantering away but he does everything very easily so there's no reason why he shouldn't be a winner. He'll probably have the speed for six and could be an early summer 2-y-o".*

978. UNNAMED ★★
gr.f. Nathaniel – All Hallows (Dalakhani). January 31. Fourth foal. €140,000Y. Goffs Orby. Ric Wylie. Half-sister to the fairly useful 2-y-o 1m winner and Listed-placed Temple Church (by Lawman). The dam is an unraced half-sister to 7 winners including the Group 1 Prix Royal-Oak winner Allegretto. The second dam, Alleluia (by Caerleon), won the Group 3 Doncaster Cup and is a half-sister to 7 winners including the Nassau Stakes and Sun Chariot Stakes winner Last Second (dam of the French 2,000 Guineas winner Aussie Rules) and the dams of the Group 1 winners Alborada, Albanova, Yesterday and Quarter Moon. (Mr Kevin Hickman). *"She's backward, as you'd expect from the pedigree, but she's quite nice and just going through the motions at the moment. One for the second half of the season, she has a lovely pedigree and her owner generally races them here and then takes them home to his stud in New Zealand".*

979. UNNAMED ★★★
ch.f. Starspangledbanner – Alpine Belle (Rock Of Gibraltar). March 5. Fourth foal. £29,000Y. Goffs UK Premier. Not sold. Half-sister to two minor winners in Australia by Artie Schiller and Statue Of Liberty. The dam, unplaced in Australia, is a half-sister to 5 winners including the New Zealand Group 2 winner Hasselhoof and the NZ Group 2 placed Vercors. The second dam, Alpine (by Zabeel), was placed in Australia and is a full or half-sister to 5

winners including the NZ Group 1 winner Lord Ted. (Mr Kevin Hickman). *"A likeable filly with a good temperament, she's doing nothing wrong at the moment and should be on the racecourse by the middle of June. I like her and we're looking forward to running her"*.

980. UNNAMED ★★★

b.f. Sir Percy – Katy O'Hara (Komaite). April 21. Sister to the useful 5f, 6f (both at 2 yrs here) and US 6.5f and 1m winner Kune Kune and half-sister to the fair 6f winner of 4 races Katy's Secret (by Mind Games) and the modest 2-y-o 5f winner Mademoiselle Bond (by Monsieur Bond). The dam, a modest 2-y-o dual 5f winner, is a half-sister to one winner. The second dam, Amy Leigh (by Imperial Frontier), was a moderate 5f (including at 2 yrs) and 6f winner. (Mrs S E Hall). *"She was bred by my aunt, Sally Hall, so the pressure's on! The dam has done OK and in particular with this filly's full sister Kune Kune who was pretty smart. Sally tells me that this filly is even nicer than Kune Kune was at this stage. So far she's settled in nicely, she gets up the hill well and I can see her taking after her dam and being a 2-y-o type over five and six furlongs"*.

981. UNNAMED ★★★★

b.f. Acclamation – Lovely Thought (Dubai Destination). March 7. Fifth foal. 200,000Y. Tattersalls October Book 1. James Toller. Closely related to the 2017 2-y-o 5f winner, on her only start, Gisele's Angel (by Dark Angel) and half-sister to the useful 5f winner of 5 races here and subsequent UAE 6f winner High On Life (by Invincible Spirit) and the fairly useful 6f (at 2 yrs) and 5f winner Vibrant Chords (by Poet's Voice). The dam, a quite useful Listed placed 7f (at 2 yrs) and dual 6f winner, is a half-sister to the Group 2 7f Challenge Stakes and Group 3 7f Jersey Stakes winner Just James and to the Listed winner Blue Jack. The second dam, Fairy Flight (by Fairy King), an Irish 2-y-o 6f winner, is a half-sister to the Listed winners Titled Ascent and Northern Tide. (Ms E. L. Banks). *"Our most expensive filly, she was lovely as a yearling and she still is. She's just gone through a weak stage but I should think she's going to give her owner Emma Banks a lot of fun this year for sure. She'll be like her siblings and be a speedy 2-y-o"*.

982. UNNAMED ★★★★

b.f. Nathaniel – Maglietta Fina (Verglas). April 22. Second foal. 82,000Y. Tattersalls October Book 2. James Toller. Half-sister to the 2017 2-y-o Listed 6f winner Speak In Colours (by Excelebration). The dam, a minor Italian winner of 5 races at 2 and 5 yrs, is a half-sister to 4 winners including the dual Group 2 and dual Group 3 winner Tullius. The second dam, Whipped Queen (by Kingmambo), won 2 minor races at 3 and 4 yrs in the USA and is a half-sister to 9 winners including the Group 1 Prix Jean Prat placed Monsagem and the US Grade 3 winner Pie In Your Eye. (Ms E L Banks). *"We got lucky with this filly because we loved her at the sales and two weeks after we bought her her half-brother Speak In Colours won a Listed race. So we're on the front foot with her straight away and from what we've seen so far she's a filly full of quality. We rate her highly, she's a pretty nice filly by a very good sire and she's showing me enough to suggest she'll be a July 2-y-o"*.

983. UNNAMED ★★★

b.f. Holy Roman Emperor – Quilita (Lomitas). March 8. Second foal. €85,000Y. Baden Baden. Not sold. The dam, placed in a Group 3 over 10f in Germany, is out of Quirigua (by Lomitas). (Mr Kevin Hickman). *"She's not over-big so she wants to be running reasonably early, but she's quite sharp and quite speedy. She'll be out in May and there's nothing not to like about her other than she's just shy of an inch. Otherwise she's not a problem"*.

EVE JOHNSON HOUGHTON
984. BUCKINGHAM ★★

gr.c. Clodovil – Lizzy's Township (Delaware Township). March 31. Seventh foal. €13,000Y. Tattersalls Ireland September. Eve Johnson-Houghton. Half-brother to the minor French winner of two races at 3 and 4 yrs Kaniza (by Myboycharlie). The dam, a Listed stakes winner of three races at 2 and 3 yrs in the USA, is a half-sister to 8 winners including two US stakes winners. The second dam, Tarahumara (by Black Tie Affair), is an unraced half-sister to 4 minor winners. *"He's just started growing recently so he won't be quite as early as we thought, but he won't take long and just needs to regain his strength a bit. He's done everything right so far and done it nicely too. He's likely to be out in May"*.

985. CANAVESE ★★★
ch.f. Mastercraftsman – Rivara (Red Ransom). February 12. Fourth foal. £22,000Y. Tattersalls Ireland Ascot. Eve Johnson Houghton. Half-sister to the quite useful 2-y-o 7f winner Farandine (by Rock Of Gibraltar). The dam is an unraced half-sister to 10 winners including the Group 2 Prix de Pomone winner Armure and the Listed winners Affirmative Action, Berlin Berlin, Gravitas and Seta. The second dam, Bombazine (by Generous), a useful 10f winner, is a half-sister to 7 winners including the Group 1 winners Barathea and Gossamer (dam of the Group 1 winner Ibn Khaldun) and the US Grade 3 winner Free At Last (dam of the US multiple Grade 2 winner Coretta). (The Chriselliam Partnership). *"A big, long-striding filly, she goes very nicely but won't be early; does everything very easily".*

986. DARYANA ★★★★
b.f. Dutch Art – Darysina (Smart Strike). February 12. Second foal. 20,000Y. Tattersalls October Book 1. Highflyer/Eve Johnson Houghton. Half-sister to the promising 2017 2-y-o winner on her only Ejtyah (by Frankel). The dam, placed over 10.5f at Saint-Cloud, is a half-sister to four stakes winners including Daryakana (Group 1 Hong Kong Vase and dam of the Group 1 winner Dariyan) and Daramsar (Group 2 Prix du Conseil de Paris). The second dam, Daryaba (by Night Shift), won the Group 1 Prix de Diane and the Prix Vermeille and is a half-sister to 7 winners. (Lionel Godfrey & Peter Wollaston). *"She has a great pedigree and I can't understand why she was so cheap. There's nothing wrong with her, she has the 25 grand and +10 bonuses to go for and even if she never runs she's worth at least three times what she cost. A nice, straightforward filly, she's a typical Dutch Art in that she only does as much as she has to. The more you ask the more she gives and I like that. She's one to start around June/July over six/seven furlongs and then go up from there".*

987. DOUBLE ESPRIT ★★
b.c. Invincible Spirit – Nature Spirits (Beat Hollow). March 20. Third foal. 100,000Y. Tattersalls October Book 1. Highflyer Bloodstock. Half-brother to Ghostwatch (by Dubawi), placed twice over 1m at 2 yrs in 2017. The dam, a French 10f and Listed 12f

winner, is a half-sister to 3 winners including the Group 2 1m Beresford Stakes and Group 3 10f Mooresbridge Stakes winner Curtain Call and the French dual Listed winner Launched. The second dam, Apsara (by Darshaan), a minor French placed maiden, is a half-sister to 10 winners including the Group 1 10.5f Prix Lupin and US Grade 2 1m winner Johann Quatz and the Group 1 Prix du Jockey Club and Group 1 Prix Lupin winner Hernando. (Mr Simon Munir & Mr Isaac Souede). *"A nice horse but he's a baby and very backward, so you won't see him until September".*

988. GAMBON ★★★★
b.c. Dutch Art – Guajara (Montjeu). March 7. First foal. 52,000Y. Tattersalls October Book 1. Highflyer /Eve Johnson Houghton. The dam, an Italian Listed winner of four races, is a half-sister to 3 winners including the German Group 3 winner Goathemala. The second dam, Global World (by Big Shuffle), a Listed-placed winner in Germany, is a sister to the German Group 2 winner Global Dream. (Mr A. Pye-Jeary). *"I've gone long on Dutch Art this year because they were very buyable. This colt looks a classy, very good-looking type and very straightforward; just a real nice horse".*

989. GARRISON COMMANDER (IRE) ★★★
b.c. Garswood – Malea (Oratorio). March 6. Second foal. £32,000Y. Goffs UK Premier (Doncaster). Highflyer BS/Shefford BS. The dam, a minor French winner of 3 races at 3 and 4 yrs, is a half-sister to 6 winners. The second dam, Don't Worry Me (by Dancing Dissident), won 9 races including the Group 2 King's Stand Stakes and is a half-sister to 4 winners. (HP Racing). *"He's got sore shins and he's growing so we're leaving him alone for now, but I think we'll see him out around July time. Originally we thought he'd be early, particularly as he's done everything nicely. I think the first-season sire Garswood is going to be all right".*

990. JUMEIRAH (IRE) ★★★
b.f. Acclamation – Scarlet Plum (Pivotal). January 5. First foal. 33,000Y. Tattersalls October Book 2. Eve Johnson Houghton/J Reid. The dam, a modest 7f placed maiden, is out of the very useful Group 3 Princess Margaret Stakes (at 2 yrs) and Group 3 7f Nell

Gwyn Stakes winner Scarlet Runner (by Night Shift). (Mr S. Almuhairi). *"She's not very big but that's a family trait, she's very racy though and I wouldn't think she'd take too long. I had to stop with her because she had a cough, otherwise she'd have been out very early. I'm really pleased with her, she's sharp and racy".*

991. KWELA ★★★

b.f. Kodiac – Funday (Daylami). March 15. Fifth foal. 50,000Y. Tattersalls October Book 1. Highflyer /Eve Johnson Houghton. Half-sister to the quite useful 12f winner Miss Giler (by High Chaparral). The dam, a quite useful Listed-placed 10f and 12f winner, is a half-sister to 8 winners including the very smart Group 2 1m Royal Lodge Stakes winner Mons and the smart 10f winner and Irish Oaks third Inforapenny. The second dam, Morina (by Lyphard), won over 11f in France and is a half-sister to 10 winners. (Mrs J. Blyth Currie). *"She's sharp and should be out in April, so she seems to take after the sire rather than the dam. Probably one for five/six furlongs, she's very straightforward, knows her job and enjoys it".*

992. LIVELY LYDIA ★★★

b.f. Charm Spirit – Coventina (Daylami). April 22. Ninth foal. 11,000Y. Tattersalls October Book 2. Highflyer/Eve Johnson Houghton. Half-sister to 5 winners including the useful 9f to 12f winner Conduct (by Selkirk), the fair 1m winner Further Detail (by Verglas), the fair 7f (at 2 yrs) and 10f winner Celestation (by Excelebration) and the fair triple 2m winner Aiyana (by Indian Haven). The dam, a useful 1m (at 2 yrs) and 2m winner, was Listed-placed and is a half-sister to 3 winners. The second dam, Lady Of The Lake (by Caerleon), a useful Listed 2m winner of 4 races, is a half-sister to 5 winners including the Italian Group 3 winner Guest Connections and the dam of the Group 1 Irish St Leger winner Sans Frontieres. (Mr Khalifa Dasmal). *"She's 'up behind' at the moment and needs to grow into herself, but I like her a lot. I'd hope to get her out around June time, probably over six furlongs".*

993. LOLITA PULIDO ★★★

b.f. Toronado – Myth And Magic (Namid). March 26. Sixth foal. 40,000Y. Tattersalls October Book 1. Highflyer/Eve Johnson

Houghton. Half-brother to two minor winners in Germany (by Duke Of Marmalade) and the USA (by Danehill Dancer). The dam is an unraced half-sister to 11 winners including the Grade 1 9f Matriarch Stakes and Group 2 1m Sun Chariot Stakes winner Dress To Thrill and the dam of the Group 1 Prince Of Wales's Stakes winner Free Eagle. The second dam, Trusted Partner (by Affirmed), winner of the Group 3 7f C L Weld Park Stakes (at 2 yrs) and the Irish 1,000 Guineas, is a full or half-sister to 10 stakes winners including Easy to Copy (herself the dam of 3 stakes winners). (Galloway, Page, Pritchard, Hobson & Thomas). *"She looked a backward filly, but she's just started to come together well. She's a nice, classy horse, doing nice bits of work now and I'm thrilled to bits with her".*

994. MADAME TANTZY ★★★

b.f. Champs Elysees – Roodle (Xaar). February 24. Half-sister to the smart Listed-placed 6f and 7f winner of 4 races at 2 and 3 yrs winner Accidental Agent (by Delegator). The dam, the quite useful 5f (at 2 yrs) and 7f winner, is a half-sister to 6 winners including the fairly useful 2-y-o 7f and 7.5f winner Harbour Master (by Harbour Watch), the US Grade 2 and Grade 3 winner Prize Exhibit, the Hong Kong 6f winner Super Sixteen (both by Showcasing), and the fair 2-y-o 6f winner Must Be Me (by Trade Fair). The second dam, Roodeye (by Inchinor), a useful 5f (at 2 yrs) and 7f winner, was Listed-placed and is a half-sister to 6 winners including the Group 1 Prix Morny second Gallagher. (Mrs R. F. Johnson Houghton). *"Closely related to a good horse of ours, Accidental Agent (Dansili is the grandsire of them both), she was home-bred here and isn't going to be early but she's strong, well-made and lovely. Only cantering away at the moment, she's one for the back-end of the season".*

995. MASTER MILLINER (IRE) ★★

ch.c. Helmet – Aqualina (King's Theatre). April 8. Seventh foal. €26,000Y. Tattersalls Ireland September. Eve Johnson-Houghton. Half-brother to the fairly useful 10f and 11f winner of 3 races Silver Ghost (by Dark Angel), to the quite useful dual 1m winner Mister Ross (by Medicean) and the modest 12f winner Breakwater Bay (by Lilbourne Lad). The dam, a 7f (at 2 yrs) and 1m winner in Ireland, was second in the Group 3 Irish 1,000 Guineas Trial and is a half-sister to 7 winners including the Group 3 Anglesey Stakes winner and Group 1 National Stakes second Malvernico. The second dam, Malvern Beauty (by Shirley Heights), a useful 10.5f winner, is a half-sister to 2 winners. (Mrs Jennifer Simpson Racing). *"A half-brother to a nice horse I trained, Silver Ghost, this colt is a lovely, long-striding horse who is one for the back-end of the season, probably starting at seven furlongs".*

996. MY STYLE (IRE) ★★★

bl.c. Holy Roman Emperor – That's My Style (Dalakhani). March 8. Second foal. 30,000Y. Tattersalls October Book 1. Highflyer / Eve Johnson Houghton. The dam, a fair 7f placed 3-y-o here and a minor 4-y-o winner in Germany, is a half-sister to 5 winners including Sparkling Beam (Group 3 Prix Chloe) and the 2-y-o Group 1 Prix Marcel Boussac third Rainbow Springs. The second dam, Pearl Dance (by Nureyev), a useful 2-y-o 6f winner and third in the Group 1 Moyglare Stud Stakes, is a half-sister to 7 winners including the dam of the Melbourne Cup winner Delta Blues. *"A really nice horse with a good temperament, he's racy and won't take too long, so I should think he'll be out in April or May over six furlongs. He's a nice horse".*

997. OBERYN MARTELL ★★★

b.c. Charm Spirit – Nickels And Dimes (Teofilo). February 1. Second foal. £28,000Y. Goffs UK Premier. Highflyer /Nick Bradley. The dam, a fair 9.5f winner, is a half-sister to 4 winners including the Listed winner and UAE Group 2 placed Kalahari Gold. The second dam, Neat Shilling (by Bob Back), is an unraced sister to the winner and dual Group 3 placed Fill The Bill and a half-sister to 6 winners including the US Grade 3 winner Riddlesdown. (Nick Bradley Racing). *"He was going really nicely but then got sore shins so I had to leave him alone for a bit. I like him a lot and I think he'll be a five/six furlong 2-y-o".*

998. PARISEAN ARTISTE (IRE) ★★★

ch.f. Zoffany – Meeting In Paris (Dutch Art). February 21. Second foal. €38,000Y. Tattersalls Ireland September. Not sold. Sister to the quite useful 2017 Irish 2-y-o 7f winner

Masucci. The dam, a modest 6f (including at 2 yrs) and 5f placed maiden, is a half-sister to a winner in Germany. The second dam, Sharplaw Star (by Xaar), a fairly useful 2-y-o dual 5f winner, was third in the Group 3 5f Queen Mary Stakes and is a half-sister to 2 winners. (Mr A. R. W. Marsh). *"There's not much of her, she's quite light-boned but a great mover and knows her job. Goes better than her looks would suggest, I'm pleased with her and she'll be a five/six furlong 2-y-o".*

999. PEGASUS BRIDGE ★★★

b.c. Camacho – Fire Line (Firebreak). April 8. Third foal. £35,000Y. Goffs UK Premier (Doncaster). Highflyer / Shefford. Half-brother to the fair 7f winner Grinty (by Elnadim). The dam, a minor French 3-y-o winner, is a sister to the Group 1 Gran Criterium winner and Group 1 St James Palace Stakes third Hearts Of Fire and a half-sister to 2 winners. The second dam, Alexander Ballet (by Mind Games), an Irish 3-y-o 5f winner, is a half-sister to 8 winners (three of them Listed-placed). (HP Racing). *"A nice, big, strong horse that'll be racing in May over six furlongs I should think".*

1000. RESOLUTE BAY ★★★

b.f. Showcasing – Confusing (Refuse To Bend). February 4. Second foal. 30,000Y. Tattersalls October Book 2. Highflyer /Eve Johnson Houghton. The dam, a modest 1m winner, is a half-sister to 3 winners. The second dam, Ruse (by Diktat), is a placed half-sister to 9 winners including the very useful Group 3 7f Jersey Stakes winner Ardkinglass. (Mrs Jennifer Simpson Racing). *"A filly I like a lot, she's really nice and definitely a 2-y-o. She should be sharp enough for six furlongs around May or June time and then we'll go on with a bit of luck".*

1001. SHORTER SKIRT ★★★

ch.f. Showcasing – Heading North (Teofilo). April 6. Second foal. 70,000 foal. Tattersalls December. Airlie Stud. The dam, a quite useful 2-y-o 7f winner, is a half-sister to one winner. The second dam, Round The Cape (by Cape Cross), a quite useful 1m winner, is a half-sister to 4 winners including the useful Listed 1m winner and Group 2 Falmouth Stakes second Heavenly Whisper and the Listed winner Gipsy Moth (dam of the Group 2 Goodwood Cup winner Illustrious Blue). (Hot to Trot).

"A well-named filly, I haven't had her in long but everything she's done, she's done nicely. She's well-made and just needs to learn her job now but she looks quite sharp to me". You'd have to say she was well-named!

1002. SMITH (IRE) ★★★★

ch.c. Dawn Approach – Alazeya (Shirocco). January 16. Second foal. 32,000Y. Tattersalls October Book 1. Highflyer/Eve Johnson-Houghton. The dam, a fair 2-y-o 8.5f placed maiden, is a half-sister to 5 winners including the smart dual Group 3 7f and dual Listed winner Alanza and the Listed winner Alonsoa. The second dam, Alasha (Barathea), a useful 7f (at 2 yrs) and Listed 1m winner, was Group 1 placed twice and is a half-sister to 8 winners including the Irish Listed winner Alaiyma. (Mr A. J. Pye-Jeary). *"A tough, hard-knocking sort, he's really nice and does what it says on the tin. The sire didn't do too well with his first crop last year but they started to improve at the back-end and I like this colt. One for six or seven furlongs".* It only dawned on me after my interview with Eve that the horse is named after the late comedian Mel Smith who was a long-standing owner of Eve's. ST.

1003. TIN HAT (IRE) ★★★

ch.c. Helmet – Precautionary (Green Desert). March 20. Eighth foal. 30,000Y. Tattersalls October Book 2. Highflyer / Eve Johnson-Houghton. Half-brother to the quite useful 2017 2-y-o 6f and 7f winner Curiosity (by High Chaparral), to the fair 5f winner of 5 races from 2 to 4 yrs Best Be Careful (by Exceed And Excel) and the modest 2-y-o 7f winner Summer Stroll (by Hurricane Run). The dam, a modest 2-y-o 6f and 7f placed half-sister to the Group 1 King's Stand Stakes winner Prohibit, to the French 7f (at 2 yrs) and Listed 6.5f winner Prior Warning and the French Listed 6f winner and dual Group 3 placed Emergency. The second dam, Well Warned (by Warning), a useful 2-y-o 6f winner, was third in the Group 2 6f Cherry Hinton Stakes and is a full or half-sister to 7 winners. (Eden Racing III). *"He might be my first 2-y-o runner and I really like him. He's a good sort and will probably be able to start at five furlongs and then step up. He's short coupled, not very big, but solid and with a great backside on him".* TRAINER'S BARGAIN BUY

MARK JOHNSTON

1004. ACCORDANCE

b.f. Archipenko – Moi Aussi (USA) (Aussie Rules). January 28. Sister to the useful Irish 2-y-o 8.5f winner and Group 2 1m Beresford Stakes second Clonard Street and to a winner over jumps by Aussie Rules. The dam, a moderate 7f winner, is a half-sister to 4 winners including the useful 2-y-o dual 7f winner and Listed-placed Oblige. The second dam, Acquiesce (by Generous), is an unraced half-sister to 4 winners including the Group 1 Prix Morny second Endless Summer. (Miss K Rausing).

1005. ASHBAAL (IRE)

ch.c. Pivotal – Ghostflower (Dansili). March 4. First foal. 170,000Y. Tattersalls October Book 2. Shadwell Estate Co. The dam, a minor 4-y-o winner in France, is a half-sister to 2 other minor winners. The second dam, Silkwood (by Singspiel), a winner of 3 races including the Group 2 12f Ribblesdale Stakes, is a sister to one winner and a half-sister to 4 winners including Silent Honor (2-y-o Group 2 6f Cherry Hinton Stakes). (Hamdan bin Rashid Al Maktoum).

1006. ASIAN ANGEL (IRE)

b.c. Dark Angel – Chiang Mai (Sadler's Wells). February 17. Tenth foal. €45,000Y. Goffs Orby. Mark Johnston. Half-brother to five winners by Dalakhani including the Group 1 Pretty Polly Stakes and Group 2 Blandford Stakes winner Chinese White, the Irish Listed-placed Highly Toxic and the quite useful 10f winner Raushan and to the quite useful 1m and 10f winner Daira Prince (by Dubawi). The dam won the Group 3 12f Blandford Stakes and is a half-sister to 9 winners including the Group 1 10.5f Prix de Diane winner Rafha (the dam of four stakes winners including Invincible Spirit). The second dam, Eljazzi (by Artaius), a fairly useful 2-y-o 7f winner, is a half-sister to the high-class miler Pitcairn. (Dr J Walker).

1007. BLOWN BY WIND

b.c. Invincible Spirit – Discourse (Street Cry). March 16. Third foal. Half-brother to the fairly useful 2017 2-y-o Listed 1m winner Hadith (by New Approach) and to the German Listed 1m winner Discursus (by Dubawi). The dam, a smart 2-y-o Group 3 7f Sweet Solera Stakes winner, is a sister to one winner and half-sister 8 winners including the US Grade 1 and Grade 3 winner Bandini. The second dam, Divine Dixie (by Dixieland Band), a stakes-placed winner of 2 races at 3 yrs in the USA, is a half-sister to 4 winners including the stakes winner and sire Stormy Atlantic and to the unraced dam of the Group/Grade 2 winners Incanto Dream and Atlando. (Sheikh Hamdan Al Maktoum).

1008. CUPBOARD LOVE

b.f. Iffraaj – Sri Kandi (Pivotal). March 6. Fifth foal. 65,000Y. Tattersalls October Book 2. Axom. Half-brother to a winner in Sweden by High Chaparral. The dam, a fair 2-y-o 7.5f winner, is a half-sister to 5 winners including the Group 1 1m Gran Criterium winner Pearl Of Love and the dual US Grade 3 winner Social Charter. The second dam, Aunt Pearl (by Seattle Slew), a winner at up to 7f in the USA, is a half-sister to 7 winners. (Owners Group 004).

1009. GRAVISTAS

b.c. Dansili – Gaze (Galileo). April 14. Seventh foal. 100,000Y. Tattersalls October Book 1. Not sold. Half-brother to 5 winners including the useful 2-y-o 1m and subsequent Australian Listed 9f winner Greatwood (by Manduro), the quite useful dual 12f winner Musaanada (by Sea The Stars), the fair 6f and 7f winner Ganymede (by Oasis Dream) and the fair 12f to 14f winner Bridgehampton (by Lando). The dam, placed over 10f and 12f here, won twice in Germany and is a half-sister to 9 winners including the Irish Derby winner Fame And Glory. The second dam, Gryada (by Shirley Heights), a fairly useful 2-y-o 7f and 8.3f winner, was third in the Group 3 1m Premio Dormello and is a full or half-sister to 4 winners. (China Horse Club).

1010. HARD FOREST (IRE) ♠

b.f. Hard Spun – Moojha (Forest Wildcat). February 1. Second foal. 50,000Y. Tattersalls October Book 1. Richard Knight. Half-sister to the US stakes winner of 3 races at 3 yrs Big Handsome (by Street Boss). The dam, a minor French 3-y-o winner, is a half-sister to 3 winners including the US Grade 3 winner Kiss Moon and to the unraced dam of the Group 2

Lowther Stakes winner Besharah. The second dam, Kiss The Devil (by Kris S), a US Grade 3 winner of 6 races from 3 to 5 yrs, is a half-sister to 4 winners. (Mr H. A. Lootah).

1011. I AM A DREAMER

b.c. Dream Ahead – Alexander Ballet (Mind Games). February 27. Tenth living foal. 62,000Y. Tattersalls October Book 2. Mark Johnston. Half-brother to the Group 1 Gran Criterium winner and Group 1 St James Palace Stakes third Hearts Of Fire, to the minor French 3-y-o winner Fire Line (both by Firebreak), the useful 7f winner and Listed-placed Kenny Powers (by Vital Equine) and the fair triple 5f winner September Issue (by Dutch Art). The dam, an Irish 3-y-o 5f winner, is a half-sister to 8 winners (three of them Listed-placed). The second dam, Dayville (by Dayjur), a quite useful triple 6f winner, is a half-sister to 4 winners including the Grade 1 Yellow Ribbon Handicap winner Spanish Fern and to the unraced dams of the Group/Grade 1 winners Lord Shanakill and Heatseeker. (Mr M. Doyle).

1012. KING SHAMARDAL

b.c. Shamardal – Model Queen (Kingmambo). May 7. Thirteenth foal. 100,000Y. Tattersalls October Book 1. Mark Johnston. Half-brother to 8 winners including the Group 1 Haydock Sprint Cup and Group 1 Prix Maurice de Gheest winner Regal Parade (by Pivotal), the Group 3 7f Acomb Stakes winner and Group 2 7f Champagne Stakes third Entifaadha (by Dansili), the useful 1m (at 2 yrs) and 10f winner and triple Group 3 placed Hot Prospect (by Motivator), the quite useful 1m winner Commander (by Frankel) and the French Listed-placed 11f and 12f winner Mount Helicon (by Montjeu). The dam, a fair 7f winner, is a half-sister to 5 winners including the Listed winner Arabride. The second dam, Model Bride (by Blushing Groom), is an unraced half-sister to the dams of the Group 1 winners Elmaamul, Reams Of Verse, Zafonic and Zamindar. (K. F. Leung).

1013. LOVE KISSES (IRE)

b.c. Dream Ahead – Coconut Kisses (Bahamian Bounty). April 16. Second foal. €52,000Y. Goffs Orby. Mark Johnston. Half-brother to the 2017 2-y-o Listed 5f winner and Group 3 5f Prix du

Bois third Ardenode (by Hellvelyn). The dam, a modest dual 5f winner, is a half-sister to 3 winners. The second dam, Royal Mistress (by Fasliyev), a 2-y-o 6f winner and Listed-placed in France, is a half-sister to 5 winners including the dam of the US Grade 2 winner Friendly Island.

1014. MAYDANNY (IRE)
b.c. Dubawi – Attraction (Efisio). February 25. Ninth foal. 1,350,000Y. Tattersalls October Book 1. Shadwell Estate Co. Half-brother to 7 winners including the smart 2017 2-y-o Group 3 7f Tattersalls Stakes winner Elarqam (by Frankel), the useful 10f winner and US dual Grade 3 second Cushion (by Galileo), the useful 5f (at 2 yrs) and Group 3 5f winner Fountain Of Youth, the fairly useful 1m winner of 4 races Huntlaw (both by Oasis Dream), the quite useful 2-y-o 1m winner Devastation (by Montjeu) and the fair 2-y-o 7f winner Elation (by Cape Cross). The dam, a high-class 1,000 Guineas, Irish 1,000 Guineas, Coronation Stakes, Matron Stakes and Sun Chariot Stakes winner, is a half-sister to 5 winners. The second dam, Flirtation (by Pursuit Of Love), is an unplaced half-sister to 4 winners. (Hamdan bin Rashid Al Maktoum).

1015. MEMPHIS BLEEK
ch.c. Olympic Glory – Party (Cadeaux Genereux). March 4. Fourth foal. 65,000Y. Tattersalls October Book 2. Mark Johnston. Half-brother to the useful Listed 11f and subsequent Australian Group 3 winner Observational (by Galileo) and to the quite useful multiple 12f winner Party Line (by Montjeu). The dam won the 2-y-o Listed 7f Radley Stakes and is a half-sister to 2 winners. The second dam, Forty Belles (by Forty Niner), was placed 6 times in France and is a half-sister to 8 winners including the French Group 3 winner In Clover. (Sohi & Sohi).

1016. NAME THE WIND
b.c. Toronado – Trust The Wind (Dansili). March 31. Second foal. 62,000Y. Tattersalls October Book 1. Rabbah Bloodstock. The dam was a modest 1m winner at 3 yrs. The second dam, Hypnology (by Gone West), is an unraced half-sister to 7 winners including the Group 3 winners Gentleman's Deal and Hathal. (Sheikh R. D. Al Maktoum).

1017. NATALIE'S JOY
b.f. Lope De Vega – Semaphore (Zamindar). April 2. Seventh foal. 35,000Y. Tattersalls October Book 2. Mark Johnston. Half-sister to 5 winners including the useful 2-y-o 7f winner and Group 3 7f Oh So Sharp Stakes third Annie's Fortune (by Montjeu), the quite useful triple 6f winner at 2 to 4 yrs Reputation (by Royal Applause), the quite useful triple 1m winner Semaral (by High Chaparral) and the fair 2-y-o 6f winner Deep Blue Sea (by Rip Van Winkle). The dam is an unraced half-sister to 3 winners including the dam of the Group 3 winners Fantasia and Pink Symphony. The second dam, Blue Duster (by Danzig), winner of the Group 1 6f Cheveley Park Stakes, is a sister to the smart Group 1 6f Middle Park Stakes winner Zieten and a half-sister to 9 winners.

1018. NO LIPPY (IRE)
b.f. Oasis Dream – Freedonia (Selkirk). February 19. Sixth foal. €55,000Y. Goffs Orby. Mark Johnston. Sister to the very useful 6f winner of 4 races at 3 and 4 yrs and Group 3 Bengough Stakes third Polybius. The dam won the Group 3 12.5f Prix de Pomone and is a half-sister to 3 minor winners. The second dam, Forest Rain (by Caerleon), won 2 minor races at 3 yrs in France and is a half-sister to 6 winners including Domedriver (Grade 1 Breeders' Cup Mile). (Barbara & Alick Richmond).

1019. PANZANO
b.c. Dutch Art – Special Meaning (Mount Nelson). February 6. First foal. 68,000Y. Tattersalls October Book 2. Mark Johnston. The dam, a fairly useful Listed 12f winner of 6 races and Group 3 second in Germany, is a half-sister to 9 winners including the 1,000 Guineas and Group 2 Rockfel Stakes winner Speciosa and the US Grade 3 stakes winner and Grade 1 placed Major Rhythm. The second dam, Specifically (by Sky Classic), a US 2-y-o winner, is a half-sister to 11 winners including the triple Group 1 winner Pride. (P. D. Savill).

1020. PORT OF LEITH (IRE)
b.c. Dark Angel – Tender Is Thenight (Barathea). March 30. Fourteenth foal. €70,000Y. Goffs Orby. Mark Johnston.

Brother to a minor 3-y-o winner in France and half-brother to 6 winners including the French 1,000 Guineas winner Tie Black (by Machiavellian), the French Listed 1m winner Besotted (by Dutch Art) and the useful 9.5f and 10.5f winner Razor Wind (by Dubawi). The dam, a minor French 3-y-o winner, is a half-sister to 10 winners including the dual Group 1 winner Last Tycoon, the Group 2 winner Astronef and the dams of the Group 1 winners Sense Of Style, Valentine Waltz and Immortal Verse. The second dam, Mill Princess (by Mill Reef), a French 10f winner, is a half-sister to the Irish Derby winner Irish Ball and the dam of classic winners Assert, Bikala and Eurobird. (Jane Newett & Dougie Livingston).

1021. SAPA INCA (IRE)
b.f. Galileo – Inca Princess (Holy Roman Emperor). January 18. Third foal. 200,000Y. Tattersalls October Book 1. Form Bloodstock. Sister to the 2-y-o Group 1 7f Criterium International winner and Group 1 Racing Post Trophy second Johannes Vermeer and to the Group 2 Kilboy Estate Stakes winner Elizabeth Browning. The dam, a quite useful Irish 2-y-o 6f winner, is a half-sister to 2 winners including the smart Irish 10f and 13f winner Changingoftheguard. The second dam, Miletrian (by Marju), a smart Group 2 Ribblesdale Stakes and Group 3 Park Hill Stakes winner, is a sister to one winner and a half-sister to the Group 2 Geoffrey Freer Stakes winner Mr Combustible. (China Horse Club).

1022. SIR RON PRIESTLEY
ch.c. Australia – Reckoning (Danehill Dancer). March 11. Second foal. 70,000Y. Tattersalls October Book 2. Mark Johnston. Half-brother to Day Of Reckoning (by Dawn Approach), unplaced in two starts at 2 yrs in 2017. The dam, a fairly useful 2-y-o 1m winner, was Listed-placed three times at around 10f and is a half-sister to 4 winners including the US winner and Grade 3 8.5f second Hope Cross. The second dam, Great Hope (by Halling), a quite useful Irish dual 1m winner, is a half-sister to 5 winners. (Mr P Dean).

1023. TANAAWOL
b.c. Dansili – Eshaadeh (Storm Cat). April 2. Half-brother to the very useful 2-y-o Group 2 5f Queen Mary Stakes winner and Group 1 6f Cheveley Park Stakes third Maqaasid (by Green Desert). The dam, unplaced in two starts, is a half-sister to 7 winners including the 1,000 Guineas and Coronation Stakes winner Ghanaati and the Group 3 12f Cumberland Lodge Stakes winner Mawatheeq. The second dam, Sarayir (by Mr Prospector), a Listed 1m winner, is closely related to the top-class Champion Stakes winner Nayef and a half-sister to the 2,000 Guineas, Eclipse, Derby and King George winner Nashwan. (Hamdan Al Maktoum). (Hamdan bin Rashid Al Maktoum).

1024. UNNAMED
b.f. Slade Power – Embassy (Cadeaux Genereux). March 26. Half-sister to 8 winners including the useful 2-y-o 7f winner Grosvenor Square (by Dubai Millennium), the fairly useful 6f and 7f winner Felicitous, the quite useful 7f and 1m winner King's Pavilion (both by King's Best), the fair dual 7f winner Gleneagles (by Pivotal) and the modest 7f and 1m winner of 6 races Diplomatic (by Cape Cross). The dam, a champion 2-y-o filly and winner of the Cheveley Park Stakes, is a half-sister to the smart 7f (at 2 yrs) and Group 2 Pretty Polly Stakes winner Tarfshi and the fairly useful 2-y-o 1m winner Puck's Castle. The second dam, Pass The Peace (by Alzao), won the Cheveley Park Stakes, was second in the French 1,000 Guineas and is a half-sister to 3 winners. (Sheikh Hamdan bin Mohammed Al Maktoum).

1025. UNNAMED
b.f. Iffraaj – Honky Tonk Sally (Dansili). February 13. Sixth foal. 250,000Y. Tattersalls October Book 2. Rabbah Bloodstock. Sister to the fairly useful 2-y-o triple 5f winner and Listed-placed Umneyati and half-sister to the fairly useful 7f (at 2 yrs) and 9.5f winner Tonkinese (by Authorized) and the modest 2-y-o 7f winner Ragtime Dancer (by Medicean). The dam, a quite useful 2-y-o 7f winner, is a half-sister to 7 winners including the Group 3 1m Prix Saint-Roman winner Eco Friendly. The second dam, Flower Girl (by Pharly), a winner of 5 races including the Group 3 6f Goldene Peitsche and the Listed 6f Sandy Lane Stakes, is a sister to the Listed 9.4f winner Farmost and a half-sister to 3 winners. (Sheikh Hamdan Bin Mohammed Al Maktoum).

1026. UNNAMED
b.f. Dubawi – Mondalay (Monsun). April 1.
Third foal. Half-sister to the quite useful 2-y-o
6f winner Romantic View (by Shamardal). The
dam is a half-sister to 6 winners including the
sire Manduro, a triple Group 1 winner from
1m to 10f (including the Prince Of Wales's
Stakes) and the German Listed 11f winner and
Group 2 placed Mandela. The second dam,
Mandellicht (by Be My Guest), a winner and
Listed-placed in Germany, is a half-sister to 6
winners. (Sheikh Hamdan Bin Mohammed Al
Maktoum).

1027. UNNAMED ♠
b.c. Dutch Art – Privacy Order (Azamour).
February 17. Third foal. 57,000Y. Tattersalls
October Book 1. Mark Johnston. Half-brother
to the useful 2-y-o Listed 6f winner Private
Matter (by Mayson). The dam is an unplaced
half-sister to the Listed winner Red Box and
to the French 10f winner and Group 2 Prix
Greffulhe second Untold Secret. The second
dam, Confidential Lady (by Singspiel), winner
of the Group 3 7f Prix du Calvados (at 2 yrs)
and the Group 1 10.5f Prix de Diane, is a half-
sister to 5 winners. (Mr A. Al Mansoori).

1028. UNNAMED
ch.c. Dubawi – Shumoos (Distorted Humor).
March 15. Second foal. 350,000Y. Tattersalls
October Book 1. Rabbah Bloodstock. The dam,
a 2-y-o Group 3 Sirenia Stakes winner, was
placed in the Group 2 Queen Mary Stakes and
the Group 2 Cherry Hinton Stakes. The second
dam, Wile Cat (by Storm Cat), is an unraced
sister to the Grade 2 La Canada Stakes winner
Cat Fighter and a half-sister to the Group 3
winner and sire Ishiguru. (Mr A. Al Mansoori).

WILLIAM KNIGHT
1029. CHINESE ALPHABET
b.c. Leroidesanimaux – Kesara (Sadler's Wells).
February 20. Sixth foal. 30,000Y. Tattersalls
October Book 2. Richard Knight. Half-brother
to the fairly useful 10f winner Night Of Glory
(by Sea The Stars), to the fair 10f and 12f
winner Apparatchika, the moderate Irish 9.5f
winner Kandahari (both by Archipenko) and
a winner in Singapore by Selkirk. The dam, a
minor dual winner at 4 yrs in France, is a half-
sister to 6 winners including the dual French
Listed winner Persona Grata. The second dam,
Kaldounya (by Kaldoun), a minor US 3-y-o

winner, is a full or half-sister to 5 winners
including the Italian dual Group 1 winner
Altieri. (Mr C K R Cheung).

1030. DANCING WARRIOR
b.f. War Command – Corps De Ballet (Fasliyev).
May 1. 12,000 foal. Tattersalls December. T
G Roddick. Half-sister to the 2-y-o 6f and
subsequent Hong Kong winner Georges Lane
(by Diamond Green), to the quite useful 5f
and 6f winner of 13 races (including at 2 yrs)
Dark Lane (by Namid), the quite useful triple
7f winner Dance Company (by Aussie Rules)
the quite useful 6f and 7f winner Compton
Park (by Compton Place) and the fair 6f
winner of 4 races at 2 and 3 yrs Gold Waltz (by
Acclamation). The dam, a fairly useful 5f (at 2
yrs) and 6f winner, is a half-sister to 7 winners
including the prolific Hong Kong winner of 8
races and £750,000 Quick Action. The second
dam, Dwell (by Habitat), was a fairly useful
Listed-placed 1m winner. (Mr T. G. Roddick).

1031. ENGLISH HEROINE
ch.f. Nathaniel – Merton Matriarch (Cadeaux
Genereux). January 27. Second foal. Half-sister
to the fair 2-y-o 5.5f winner English Hero (by
Royal Applause). The dam, placed second over
6f on her only start at 2 yrs, is a half-sister to 4
winners. The second dam, Tesary (by Danehill),
a useful 5f (at 2 yrs) to 7f winner, is a half-sister
to 5 winners. (Mr P. Winkworth).

1032. GOODWOOD SONNET (IRE)
b.c. Lope De Vega – Surface Of Earth (Empire
Maker). February 14. First foal. 48,000Y.
Tattersalls October Book 2. R Frisby. The
dam is an unplaced half-sister to 9 winners
including the US Grade 2 Dahlia Handicap
winner Surya (herself dam of the US Grade 2
winner Aruna). The second dam, Wild Planet
(by Nureyev), won at 2 yrs here and the Listed
Prix Coronation in France, was third in the
Group 3 Prestige Stakes and is a half-sister
to 6 winners. (Goodwood Racehorse Owners
Group (25)).

1033. LOCO AMOR
b.c. Es Que Love – Larghetto (Giant's
Causeway). March 14. First foal. €10,500Y.
Goffs Sportsmans. Richard Knight. The dam,
a modest 6f to 1m winner of 3 races, is a
half-sister to 4 winners including the US Grade

3 placed Clyde's Image. The second dam, Marquetessa (by Marquetry), is an unplaced half-sister to 7 winners including the US Listed winner Sassy Pants (the dam of two US Grade 1 winners). (Angmering Park Thoroughbreds V).

1034. SEA ART
b.c. Born To Sea – Kekova (Montjeu). May 10. Fifth foal. The dam, a French 3-y-o 14f winner, is a half-sister to 2 winners including the Group 3 Dahlia Stakes second Casilda. The second dam, Koniya (by Doyoun), a minor French 3-y-o winner, is a half-sister to 7 winners. (Mr T. G. Roddick).

1035. SIR BUSKER
b.c. Sir Prancealot – Street Kitty (Tiger Hill). March 20. Fourth foal. €25,000Y. Tattersalls Ireland September. Kern/Lillingston. Half-brother to the fair 5f and 6f winner of 7 races (including at 2 yrs) Nag's Wag (by Approve). The dam is an unraced half-sister to one winner abroad. The second dam, Fascination Street (by Mujadil), a modest 7f winner at 3 yrs, is a half-sister to 6 winners including the US triple Grade 1 winner from 9f to 10f Golden Apples and the Group 3 Park Hill Stakes winner Alexander Three D. (Kennet Valley Thoroughbreds XI).

1036. WINTER GLEAM (IRE)
b.f. Kodiac – Boo Boo Bear (Almutawakel). March 19. Fourth foal. 55,000Y. Tattersalls October Book 2. Will Edmeades. Half-sister to the useful Listed 6f winner Letters Of Note (by Azamour), to the quite useful 2-y-o Listed-placed dual 7f winner Island Vision (by Arcano) and the minor French 4-y-o winner Victoria Bear (by Lope De Vega). The dam, a fair Irish 1m winner, is a sister to the winner and dual Listed placed Eddie Jock and a half-sister to 3 winners including the 2-y-o winner and Group 2 Beresford Stakes second Mawaakef. The second dam, Al Euro (by Mujtahid) a moderate 6f placed 2-y-o, is a half-sister to 5 winners including the Group 1 1m Queen Elizabeth II Stakes winner Air Express. (Mrs E. Roberts).

DANIEL KUBLER

1037. ARISHKA (IRE) ★★★
b.f. Dandy Man – Symbol Of Peace (Desert Sun). March 12. Seventh foal. £24,000Y.

Goffs UK Premier (Doncaster). Kubler Racing. Half-sister to the fairly useful 2-y-o Group 3 7f Acomb Stakes winner Treaty Of Paris (by Haatef), to the fairly useful 8.5f and 10f winner White Poppy (by Frozen Power), the fairly useful 7f and 1m winner Mustarrid (by Elzaam) and the fair 1m winner All Nighter (by Bertolini). The dam, a fair 9.5f winner, is a half-sister to 5 other minor winners. The second dam, Rosy Lydgate (by Last Tycoon), is a placed half-sister to 5 winners including the US Grade 3 winner Supreme Sound. *"The dam's done well and this filly goes well too. She'll be early and she's strong enough to start at the end of April. I haven't asked her any massive questions but we're pleased with what we're seeing, she's a nice filly. Has an entry in the Supersprint".* TRAINER'S BARGAIN BUY

1038. CASTELO ★★★★
b.f. Casamento – Fortress (Generous). April 7. Fifth foal. £8,500Y. Goffs UK Silver. Kubler Racing Ltd. Half-sister to the fair 2-y-o 7f winner Mersad (by Shamardal) and to a 2-y-o winner in Italy by Sir Prancealot. The dam, a modest 6f winner, is a half-sister to 9 winners including the high-class sprinter Reverence, winner of the Haydock Park Sprint Cup and the Nunthorpe Stakes and the very useful 2-y-o Listed 6f Chesham Stakes winner Helm Bank. The second dam, Imperial Bailiwick (by Imperial Frontier), was a useful winner of 3 races at around 5f including the Group 2 Flying Childers Stakes, was Group 3 placed twice and is a half-sister to 3 winners in France. *"It's a fast family so she should be quick although Casamento will probably add a touch more stamina. She's definitely a 2-y-o type and she's doing easy, fast work so we're looking at late May/early June with her. She's got an entry in the Supersprint".*

1039. CHAMOMILE ★★
b.f. Teofilo – Al Joza (Dubawi). January 17. Fifth foal. 85,000Y. Tattersalls October Book 1. Kubler Racing. Sister to the useful Listed-placed 1m and 9.5f winner of 3 races Festive Fare. The dam, a modest 1m winner, is a half-sister to 11 winners including the very smart Group 1 1m Racing Post Trophy and Group 2 10.4f Dante Stakes winner Dilshaan and the smart 7f (at 2 yrs) and Listed 10f winner and Group 1 1m Prix Marcel Boussac

second Darrfonah. The second dam, Avila (by Ajdal), a fair 7f placed maiden, is a half-sister to the smart middle-distance colts Alleging, Monastery and Nomrood. (Mr & Mrs G. Middlebrook). *"She's a big filly and probably more of a 3-y-o type but she's done a couple of nice bits and I think she's a nice horse for the back-end".*

1040. CHITRA ★★★
b.f. Sea The Moon – Persian Star (Shamardal). February 15. Third foal. 10,000Y. Tattersalls Book 3. Not sold. The dam is an unraced half-sister to 3 winners including the very useful 2-y-o 7f winner and Group 3 1m Autumn Stakes second Prompter and the multiple Listed-placed Penny Drops. The second dam, Penny Cross (by Efisio), a useful 7f to 8.5f winner of 3 races, was Listed placed twice and is a half-sister to 7 winners including the Group 2 Celebration Mile winner Priors Lodge. (Mr & Mrs G Middlebrook). *"I reckon she'll be the sire's first runner, so if I'm right she'll be out in April. Physically she's not typical of the Sea The Moon's I saw at the sales, I think she's more to the dam's side of the pedigree. That's where the precocity must be coming from and we'll start her over five furlongs because she's ready, but we'll go longer as those races come along".*

1041. FREESIA GOLD (IRE) ★★★
ch.f. Havana Gold – Secret Happiness (Cape Cross). March 4. Third foal. £22,000Y. Goffs UK Premier (Doncaster). Kubler Racing. The dam is an unraced half-sister to 4 winners including the Listed winners Beauly and Gusto. The second dam, Pickle (by Piccolo), won 7 races here and in the USA including the Grade 2 Wilshire Handicap and the Grade 3 Yerba Buena Breeders Cup Handicap and is a half-sister to 5 winners. *"A nice, racy, compact filly. I haven't done a lot with her but she's not overly big and will make a 2-y-o. Early on she was a bit immature both mentally and physically but she's caught up well. I'll get cracking with her shortly and I can see her being out in June".*

1042. ZEPHYRINA (IRE) ★★★
b.f. Big Bad Bob – Western Sky (Barathea). February 26. Eighth foal. €13,000Y. Tattersalls Ireland September. Kubler Racing Ltd. Half-sister to the German dual Group 3 1m winner

(including at 2 yrs) and Group 1 11f German Oaks second Djumama (by Aussie Rules), to the quite useful 2m and hurdles winner of 5 races Alfredo (by Arcano) and four minor winners abroad. The dam, placed fourth once over 6f at 3 yrs from two starts, is a sister to the Group 3 Greenham Stakes winner and triple Group 1 placed Barathea Guest and a half-sister to 5 winners. The second dam, Western Heights (by Shirley Heights), is an unraced half-sister to 6 winners including the Listed Galtres Stakes winner Startino. (Mr P J H Whitten). *"She's quite a good-looking filly and the sire gets plenty of winners but doesn't seem to be fashionable. She's quite precocious and bred on the same lines as the Group 3 winner Berg Bahn as they're both by Big Bad Bob and out of Barathea mares who are both out of Shirley Heights mares. She's not a five furlong horse but she's quite forward and a six/seven furlong 2-y-o type".*

1043. UNNAMED ★★
ch.c. Paco Boy – Free Falling (Selkirk). March 27. First foal. The dam, a moderate 12f and dual hurdles winner, is a half-sister to one winner. The second dam, Free Flying (by Groom Dancer), unplaced in two starts, is a half-sister to numerous winners including the Group 1 Fillies Mile winner and Oaks second Shamshir. (A.C. Entertainment Technologies Ltd). *"He'll need plenty of time and if I get one run into him at the back-end I'd be happy".*

1044. UNNAMED ★★★
b.c. Toronado – Jules (Danehill). February 24. Twelfth foal. £28,000Y. Goffs UK Premier (Doncaster). Kubler Racing. Closely related to the modest 1m to 14f winner of 8 races The Blue Dog (by High Chaparral) and half-brother to 7 winners including the useful 6f and 7f winner of 9 races including at 2 yrs Golden Desert (by Desert Prince), the quite useful 5f (at 2 yrs) and 6f winner Jule On The Crown (by Harbour Watch), the quite useful dual 7f winner (including at 2 yrs) Romantic Wish (by Hawk Wing) and the quite useful 7f and 1m winner of 5 races Stosur (by Mount Nelson). The dam, a fair 7f winner, is a half-sister to 10 winners including the dam of the Australian Group 1 winner Prowl. The second dam, Before Dawn (by Raise A Cup), a champion US 2-y-o filly, won two Grade 1 events. *"A nice*

horse that's done some quicker bits of work. I think six furlongs will be fine to start with but he'll progress to seven and a mile as the season goes on. Very straightforward and with a very good mind, he goes nicely and should be out in May or June. I think the sire will do better than some might think and he has a lot of 2-y-o's as well".

1045. UNNAMED ★★★★
b.f. Kyllachy – Welsh Angel (Dubai Destination). April 23. Fifth foal. 95,000Y. Tattersalls October Book 1. Kubler Racing. Sister to the useful 2-y-o 7f and 8.5f winner Commander Cole and half-sister to the very useful 7f (at 2 yrs) and 12f winner of 5 races and Group 3 third Scarlet Dragon (by Sir Percy). The dam is an unraced half-sister to 7 winners including the Listed winner and Group 2 6f Mill Reef Stakes third Nantyglo. The second dam, Bright Halo (by Bigstone), a minor French 3-y-o 9f winner, is a half-sister to 10 winners including the Group 1 Irish Oaks winner Moonstone, the Breeders Cup second L'Ancresse and the Group 1 10f Prix Saint-Alary winner Cerulean Sky (herself dam of the Group 2 Doncaster Cup winner Honolulu). (Newclose Properties Ltd). *"A very nice filly, she looks smart in everything she does. She's a big filly but balanced and 'together', we won't force her but she's doing quicker bits and showing promise".*

1046. UNNAMED ★★
gr.f. Cacique – Tibouchina (Daylami). April 21. Eighth foal. €20,000Y. Tattersalls Ireland September. Kubler Racing Ltd. Half-sister to the Italian and Australian winner of 4 races and Group 2 Italian Derby second Wish Come True (by Aussie Rules) and the fair 2-y-o 1m winner Viking Hoard (by Vale Of York). The dam, a modest 4-y-o 11.5f and 12f winner, is a half-sister to 3 other minor winners. The second dam, Kalimar (by Bigstone), is an unplaced half-sister to 5 winners including Karliyka (the dam of three Group winners). *"A seven furlong/mile type 2-y-o for later on and probably a 10f type next year".*

1047. UNNAMED ★★
b.c. Camelot – Love Everlasting (Pursuit Of Love). April 8. Half-brother to 6 winners including the fairly useful 12f winner and

Listed Cheshire Oaks second Acquainted (by Shamardal), the quite useful 2-y-o dual 7f winner Penny Rose (by Danehill Dancer), the fair 10f winner Covenant (by Raven's Pass) and the fair 2m winner Yours Ever (by Dansili). The dam, a 7.5f (at 2 yrs) and Group 3 12f Princess Royal Stakes winner of 6 races, is a half-sister to 6 winners including the smart Group 3 10f Scottish Classic winner Baron Ferdinand. The second dam, In Perpetuity (by Great Nephew), a fairly useful 10f winner, is a half-sister to 6 winners including the Derby winner Shirley Heights. (Mr & Mrs G. Middlebrook). *"Likely to be much more of a 3-y-o type than two, but he's athletic and sadly the mare died foaling him so he was fostered. He's having a break now so he can grow and develop, so we're just taking our time with him".*

DAVID LANIGAN

1048. CORINTHIAN GIRL (IRE) ★★★
ch.f. Raven's Pass – Elegant Beauty (Olden Times). April 4. Eighth foal. 60,000Y. Tattersalls October Book 2. Not sold. Half-sister to the Group 3 1m Prix d'Aumale winner Shahah (by Motivator), to the quite useful dual 6f (at 2 yrs) and 8.5f winner Ligeia (by Rail Link) and the fair 5f and 6f winner Royal Guinevere (by Invincible Spirit). The dam is an unraced half-sister to 8 winners including the champion 2-y-o Grand Lodge and the Listed winners La Persiana and Papabile. The second dam, La Papagena (by Habitat), is an unraced half-sister to 7 winners including the Listed winners Lost Chord and Eagling. *"A nice, compact filly that should be able to make a 2-y-o. She's strong, does everything right and it'll be interesting to see what she does. She could start at six furlongs".*

1049. DEADLY FORCE ★★
b.c. Lethal Force – Dream Belle (Oasis Dream). May 18. Fifth foal. 35,000Y. Tattersalls October Book 3. J Brummitt. Half-brother to 2 minor winners in Italy by Poet's Voice and Notnowcato. The dam is an unraced half-sister to 6 winners including Es Que (dam of the Group 1 winner Dominant and the Group 2 winner Es Que Love). The second dam, Bellona (by Bering), a Listed 11f winner in France, is a half-sister to 7 winners including the Group 2 Prix de Flore winner In Clover (dam of the Group 1 Prix de l'Opera winner We Are). *"A*

lovely horse I bought myself on spec at the sales, he's grown a bit but he's very strong and has a huge chest on him. A smashing horse, I love him but he's a late foal and although he's probably more of a 3-y-o he could be anything".

1050. DREAMINGOFDIAMONDS (IRE) ★★
b.f. Alhebayeb – Jemima's Art (Fantastic Light). February 29. Fifth foal. £13,500Y. Goffs UK Silver. Diamond Racing. Closely related to the quite useful 2-y-o 1m winner Shalimah (by Dark Angel) and half-sister to the winner of 3 races at 3 and 4 yrs Maulesden May (by Dark Angel). The dam, a moderate 10f winner, is a half-sister to 11 winners including the US dual Grade 2 10f winner Battle Of Hastings and the smart Listed 12f winner Villa Carlotta. The second dam, Subya (by Night Shift), was a very useful winner of 5 races from 5f (at 2 yrs) to 10f including the Lupe Stakes, the Masaka Stakes and the Star Stakes (all Listed events). *"Not a bad-looking filly, she's done very well since she came in and she's quite a good, strong filly. She came in quite late so she may not be ready to race until around September time".*

1051. GOLD ARCH ★★★
b.c. Archipenko – Goldrenched (Montjeu). April 20. Sixth foal. 35,000Y. Tattersalls October Book 3. J Brummitt. Half-brother to the fair 7f winner Fei Kuai, to the moderate 12f winner of 4 races Esspeegee (both by Paco Boy) and the minor German winner of 3 races at 2 and 4 yrs Goldbraid (by Exceed And Excel). The dam, a modest 2m winner, is a half-sister to one other minor winner. The second dam, Sundrenched (by Desert King), a useful 2-y-o Listed 1m winner, is a half-sister to 7 winners including the Group 1 placed Bonnard. *"One for August/September time, I've had a lot of luck with the sire and this is a big, strong, good-looking horse. He does everything very nicely and he's improved a lot since the sales. He'll be starting off over seven furlongs or a mile".*

1052. IRISH ART (IRE) ★★★
b.c. Dutch Art – Slieve Mish (Cape Cross). February 2. Fifth foal. 20,000Y. Tattersalls October Book 2. David Lanigan. The dam, a fairly useful 3-y-o 7f and 1m winner, is a half-sister to 5 winners including the Irish 2-y-o 7f

winner and dual Group 3 placed Chivalrous. The second dam, Aspiration (by Sadler's Wells), a 10f winner in Ireland, is a sister to the Group 1 1m Gran Criterium winner Sholokhov and a half-sister to the Listed winners Zavaleta, Napper Tandy and Affianced (herself dam of the Irish Derby winner Soldier Of Fortune). *"A very nice horse, he's a little effeminate looking but quite scopey. He goes well and we were lucky to pick him up for what he cost because I think he was in the wrong part of the sale. A straightforward horse, he should be able to start off around June time and be a seven furlong type 2-y-o".*

1053. UNNAMED ★★
b.f. Champs Elysees – Al Cobra (Sadler's Wells). March 19. Seventh foal. 30,000Y. Tattersalls October Book 3. Not sold. Half-sister to the fair triple 7f and subsequent minor US winner Macaabra (by Exceed And Excel) and to the fair dual 10f winner Sampera (by Iffraaj). The dam is an unplaced half-sister to 6 winners including the Group 1 12f Prix de l'Arc de Triomphe and dual German Group 1 winner Marienbard. The second dam, Marienbard (by Darshaan), a French 1m winner at both 2 and 3 yrs, is a half-sister to 6 winners including the French and Italian Listed winner Kentucky Coffee. *"The mare was very light and not a lot to look at, but this would be as nice a foal as she's delivered. This is a nice horse, he's strong but more of a 3-y-o type".*

1054. UNNAMED ★★★
ch.c. Lope De Vega – Autumn Leaves (Muhtathir). March 10. Third foal. 35,000Y. Tattersalls October Book 2. Jamie Lloyd. The dam, a minor French 2-y-o winner, is a half-sister to 11 winners including Capal Garmon (Group 3 Jockey Club Cup). The second dam, Elevate (by Ela-Mana-Mou), a Listed-placed dual 12f winner, is a half-sister to 4 winners including the Group 1 winners Sun Princess and Saddlers' Hall. *"A lovely horse, at the sales I thought he was a bit plain but he's become more athletic and is pleasing us more now. Size-wise he screams 2-y-o at you and he should be able to start any time from August onwards, although he should be even better next year. He's nicely made, has a lot of scope about him and he'd be the most improved of all of them since he came in".*

1055. UNNAMED ★★★
ch.c. Showcasing – Cockney Dancer (Cockney Rebel). May 4. Second foal. 20,000Y. Tattersalls December. Not sold. The dam, a quite useful 6f (at 2 yrs) and dual 7f winner, is a half-sister to 6 winners including the very smart 6f (at 2 yrs) and 7f winner and Group 2 Prix Morny second Gallagher and the Listed-placed Quick Wit and Roodeye (herself dam of the dual US Grade 2 winner Prize Exhibit). The second dam, Roo (by Rudimentary), a quite useful Listed-placed 2-y-o 5f and 6f winner, is a half-sister to the Group 2 6f Gimcrack Stakes winner Bannister. *"A nice, strong colt that's done nothing wrong, he moves very well and is one for August or September".*

1056. UNNAMED ★★★
b.c. Galileo – Gooseberry Fool (Danehill Dancer). April 26. Second foal. $75,000Y. Keeneland September. Rabbah Bloodstock. Brother to the 2017 Irish 2-y-o 8.5f winner, from two starts, Amedeo Modigliani. The dam, the fairly useful 2-y-o 7f winner, was third in the Group 3 Silver Flash Stakes and is a half-sister to 9 winners including the French 2,000 Guineas and US Grade 1 winner Aussie Rules, and the Listed 10f winner and US Grade 2 second Approach (dam of the Group 2 winners Coronet and Midas Touch). The second dam, Last Second (by Alzao), winner of the Group 2 10f Nassau Stakes and Sun Chariot Stakes, is a half-sister to 7 winners and the dams of the Group 1 winners Albanova, Alborada, Allegretto, Yesterday and Quarter Moon. *"His year older brother is apparently highly thought of at Ballydoyle and this colt is a nice horse. Just like the mare he's not very big, but he doesn't lack strength. He wasn't expensive at the sales, there's nothing wrong with him and he's very straightforward".*

1057. UNNAMED ★★★★
b.f. Australia – Have Faith (Machiavellian). February 3. Ninth foal. €100,000Y. Arqana Deauville August. J Brummitt. Half-sister to the quite useful Listed-placed 7f and 1m winner Faithful One (by Dubawi), to the quite useful 6f and 7f winner of 7 races Believe It (by Rip Van Winkle), the modest 7f winner Nur Jahan (by Selkirk), the modest 5f winner Fly True (by Raven's Pass) and a winner in Qatar by Cape Cross. The dam, a quite useful 2-y-o 7f

winner, is a sister to the useful UAE winner of 7 races and Group 3 third Opportunist and a half-sister to the Group 1 Nassau Stakes winner Favourable Terms and the French Listed winner Modern History. The second dam, Fatefully (by Private Account), won two Listed events over 1m and is a half-sister to 6 winners including the Canadian Grade 2 winner Points Of Grace. *"A smashing filly, she'll be at her best next year but she's as nice a filly as I've had for some time as far as a specimen is concerned. She does everything easily, has gone through a little growth spurt so she's gone a bit weak on me, but she's a gorgeous model. When you look at the stallions at Coolmore Australia is the standout – I think he's the second coming! We just need to mind this filly for now but if she comes out in July I'll be getting excited about her".*

1058. UNNAMED ★★★
b.c. Zoffany – Millestan (Invincible Spirit). February 7. Fifth foal. 130,000Y. Tattersalls October Book 2. Rabbah Bloodstock. Half-brother to the fairly useful Listed-placed 1m and 10f winner Weetles (by High Chaparral) and to the moderate 6f winner Seraphima (by Fusaichi Pegasus). The dam, a quite useful 2-y-o 8.3f and subsequent US winner, is a half-sister to 6 winners including the useful French 9.5f (at 2 yrs) to 15f winner and Listed-placed Grey Mystique. The second dam, Atnab (by Riverman), a modest 12f winner, is a half-sister to 6 winners including the Listed winner Dansili Dancer. *"He was a very attractive yearling and he's cantering now after a few niggling problems. A nice type of horse, we like to think he's got a bit of speed and quality".*

1059. UNNAMED ★★★★
b.f. Giant's Causeway – Sarah Lynx (Montjeu). January 25. Third foal. The dam, winner of the Grade 1 12f Canadian International and Group 2 12.5f Prix de Pomone, is a half-sister to 3 winners including the Group 3 10f Classic Trial winner Sugar Boy. The second dam, Steel Princess (by Danehill), a winner of 3 races including the Group 3 10.5f Prix Cleopatre, is a sister to one winner and a half-sister to 7 winners including the US Grade 1 placed Falcon Rock. *"A really lovely filly, I bought her myself privately after the Keeneland sale. She's strong, athletic and built like a colt. She should make a 2-y-o but she'll train on as a 3-y-o".*

1060. UNNAMED ★★
ch.c. Iffraaj – Spirit Of Winning (Invincible Spirit). February 3. First foal. 18,000Y. Tattersalls October Book 3. Not sold. The dam, placed once at 3 yrs over 8.5f from two starts, is a half-sister to 3 winners including the very smart 6f (at 2 yrs) and Listed 1m winner and Group 2 July Stakes second Neebras. The second dam, Crossmolina (Halling), a minor winner at 3 yrs in France, is a sister to the dual Listed 10f winner Foodbroker Fancy (the dam of two stakes winners) and a half-sister to the Listed winner Femme Fatale. *"Not a bad looking colt, he does everything right and goes well. The Iffraaj horses are all good-looking. He's strong and there's nothing wrong with him, so hopefully he'll be able to do something this year".*

1061. UNNAMED ★★★
ch.f. Slade Power – Star Studded (Cadeaux Genereux). April 2. Tenth foal. 28,000Y. Tattersalls December. Rabbah Bloodstock. Half-sister to 5 winners including the useful 2-y-o 6f winner and dual Group 3 7f placed Zumbi (by Dubawi), the useful 1m winner and triple Listed-placed Say No Now, the fair 5f winner Dream Cast (both by Refuse To Bend) and the quite useful Irish and Hong Kong 6f winner Full Steam Ahead (by Rock Of Gibraltar). The dam is an unraced sister to the Group 2 5f Flying Childers Stakes and Group 3 5f King George V Stakes winner Land Of Dreams (herself dam of the multiple Group 1 winner Dream Ahead) and a half-sister to 6 winners. The second dam, Sahara Star (by Green Desert), won the Group 3 5f Molecomb Stakes, was third in the Lowther Stakes and is a half-sister to 6 winners. *"A lovely filly that's related to Say No Now, she's a smaller version so although I've had a few niggles with her I'd like to think she could be a 2-y-o. She does everything nicely and she's very strong and racy".*

1062. UNNAMED ★★
b.f. Mayson – Sunset Avenue (Street Cry). April 16. Fifth foal. 10,000Y. Tattersalls October Book 3. Not sold. Half-sister to a minor winner in Greece by Teofilo. The dam, a fair 2-y-o 7f winner on her only start, is a half-sister to 6 winners including the Listed winner subsequent US dual Grade 2 second True

Cause. The second dam, Dearly (by Rahy), won the Group 3 Blandford Stakes and is a half-sister to 4 winners including the US Grade 1 Frizette Stakes winner Balletto. *"She looks like she could be a 2-y-o, she's quite forward, mature and goes about her business very well. She was an April foal so might take a bit of time to get her out".*

1063. UNNAMED ★★★★
b.f. Sepoy – Threetimesalady (Royal Applause). February 2. First foal. 60,000Y. Tattersalls October Book 2. Rabbah Bloodstock. The dam, a fair 2-y-o dual 6f winner, is a half-sister to 8 winners including the Listed 10.5f winner Trinity Joy. The second dam, Triple Joy (by Most Welcome), a useful 6f and 7f winner and second in the Listed Abernant Stakes, is a half-sister to 7 winners including the Sun Chariot Stakes winner and useful broodmare Talented. *"A lovely filly, I'm hoping she'll be a 2-y-o because she goes very nicely. A nice model that does everything well, she's a good, strong filly. You'd like to think she'd be a six furlong 2-y-o like her dam".*

GER LYONS

1064 ANDRE AMAR (IRE) ★★★
b.c. Dandy Man – Heaven's Vault (Hernando). March 23. Fourth foal. €38,000Y. Tattersalls Ireland September. Gaelic Bloodstock. Half-brother to the fair 5f (at 2 yrs) to 7f winner of 4 races Buccaneer's Vault (by Dandy Man). The dam, placed third in the Group 3 Prix Cleopatre, is a half-sister to 5 winners here and abroad. The second dam, Neutrina (by Hector Protector), is an unraced half-sister to 7 winners including the Group 1 Breeders' Cup Mile winner Domedriver. *"A grand little colt, he's not far off running and is likely to be out in May. Typical of the sire, he's sharp and precocious".*

1065. BAILLY ★★★
b.f. Charm Spirit – Czarna Roza (Polish Precedent). March 16. Ninth foal. 100,000Y. Tattersalls October Book 1. Gaelic Bloodstock. Half-sister to 6 winners including the very smart Listed 1m winner of 9 races, Group 2 Topkapi Trophy third and Group 3 Diomed Stakes third Mabait, to the fair 6f and 7f winner of 5 races Jay Bee Blue (both by Kyllachy) and the fair 1m winners Cape To

Cuba (by Harbour Watch) and Gypsy Carnival (by Trade Fair). The dam is an unraced half-sister to 9 winners including the dam of the Group 2 Queen Mary Stakes winner Elletelle. The second dam, Nemesia (by Mill Reef), a very useful Listed 13f winner, is a full or half-sister to 8 winners including Elegant Air (Group 2 Tattersalls Rogers Gold Cup). *"I won't run her on this bad ground we have at the moment but as soon as it dries up she'll start. A five/six furlong 2-y-, she's sharp, early and ready to go".*

1066. CALIFORNIA DADDY (USA) ★★★★★
ch.c. Scat Daddy – Sulis (Maria's Mon). April 12. Fourth foal. $325,000Y. Fasig-Tipton Saratoga. Asian Bloodstock Services. Bother to the minor US winner Conquest Slayer. The dam, a minor winner at 2 and 3 yrs in Canada, is a half-sister to 9 winners including three US stakes winners. The second dam, Medicine Woman (by Dr Blum), was a Grade 3 winner of 7 races in the USA at 4 and 5 yrs. *"A beautiful colt, everything is real easy for him, he has quality written all over him and although I'd like to wait for seven furlongs he's so precocious I might be tempted to start him over six on a good track. Ideally though, he's a seven furlong/mile 2-y-o. A lovely horse".*

1067. CALONNE (IRE) ★★★
bl.c. Alhebayeb – Lady Pastrana (Key Of Luck). March 28. First foal. 50,000Y. Tattersalls October Book 2. Gaelic Bloodstock. The dam, a fair 2-y-o 7f winner, is a half-sister to one winner. The second dam, Caribbean Queen (by Celtic Swing), is an unraced half-sister to 3 winners. *"We broke him, put him away at the farm so he could grow and he's certainly done a lot of that. He's back in training now, he's a fine looking colt and everything he's done I've liked but I can't imagine him being anything other than a seven furlong plus type".*

1068. CHAFFI WOODS (IRE) ★★★
b.c. Acclamation – So Dandy (Oratorio). February 8. Second foal. €100,000Y. Goffs Orby. Gaelic Bloodstock. The dam, a minor French 2-y-o winner, is a half-sister to 8 winners including the 2-y-o Listed 7f Prix Herod winner and smart hurdler Power Elite and the German Listed winner La Sylvia. The second dam, Hawas (by Mujtahid), a 1m

winner at 3 yrs in Ireland, is a sister to the Listed winner Mutakarrim and a half-sister to 7 winners including the Listed winner Nafisah. *"He's just come back in from having a break and he's a fine, big colt that'll want six/seven furlongs. We're in no rush with him and you won't see him before June. He hasn't done any fast work but he's a fine stamp of a horse and I look forward to seeing what he's like when I step him up".*

1069. DUMOURIEZ (IRE) ★★★
b.c. Elzaam – Kolkata (Rainbow Quest). April 25. Fourth foal. €40,000Y. Tattersalls Ireland September. Gaelic Bloodstock. Half-brother to 2 minor winners including the Italian 2-y-o winner Kundalina (by Gold Away). The dam, placed at 3 yrs in France, is a half-sister to 6 winners including two Listed winners in France and Italy. The second dam, City Centre (by Be My Guest), is an unplaced half-sister to 7 winners including the Group 1 Prix du Cadran winner Sought Out (dam of the Derby winner North Light). *"A lovely Elzaam colt who was doing everything I wanted including fast work, but he's a bit 'on the leg' so he's gone out for a break to allow him to grow. He has shown ability, he's a six/seven furlong horse for the middle of the summer onwards and is typical of the sort I buy".*

1070. ERICH BLOCH (IRE) ★★★★
b.c. Dandy Man – Star Bonita (Invincible Spirit). February 13. Third foal. £100,000Y. Goffs UK Premier (Doncaster). Gaelic Bloodstock. The dam is an unplaced half-sister to 2 winners. The second dam, Honour Bright (by Danehill), is an unraced half-sister to 5 winners including the Listed 10f Ballyroan Stakes winner and Group 3 placed Dabtiya. *"A gorgeous colt named after a German I once met on holiday who was very inspirational. This colt could run early if the ground dries up a bit, he's a quality horse and I always seem to buy a nice horse off Mark Dwyer. He's a smart, sharp, gorgeous looking horse and I'd be disappointed if he wasn't above average".*

1071. FEMME ARGENT (IRE) ★★★
b.f. Dark Angel – Havin' A Good Time (Jeremy). March 27. Third foal. €160,000Y. Goffs Orby. BBA (Ire). The dam, a fair triple 5f winner, is a half-sister to 10 winners including

the Group 1 Haydock Park Sprint winner G Force, the US Grade 3 Miesque Stakes winner Louvain (herself dam of the dual Group 1 winner Flotilla) and the useful Listed 10f winner Laajooj. The second dam, Flanders (by Common Grounds), winner of the Listed Scarbrough Stakes and second in the Group 2 Kings Stand Stakes, is a half-sister to 8 winners and to the dam of the dual Group 1 winning sprinter Lethal Force. *"She only arrived a few weeks ago from her owner's farm. With the few pieces she's done she shows ability but she isn't a sharp type and I can't imagine her being out before mid-season. Not pretty to look at, but typical of the sire in that she can gallop".*

1072. HAZARAGULA (IRE) ★★★
b.f. Tagula – Hazarayna (Polish Precedent). February 28. Seventh foal. €50,000Y. Goffs Orby. M O'Toole. Half-sister to the quite useful 10f (here) and Australian Group 2 13f winner Swashbuckling (by Raven's Pass). The dam, a modest dual 10f placed maiden, is a half-sister to 7 winners including the Group 3 winners Hazariya and Hazarista. The second dam, Hazaradjat (by Darshaan), won twice at 2 and 3 yrs and is a full or half-sister to 10 winners including the Flying Childers and Middle Park Stakes winner Hittite Glory. *"I've been taking things easy with her because she's a fine big, strapping filly and not unlike the Tagula filly I had last year, Ball Girl, who won and was Group placed. She'll probably start around the same time, June/July and I won't rush her".*

1073. HELEN OF ALBANY (IRE) ★★★★★
b.f. Exceed And Excel – Harmonic Note (Nayef). April 26. Second foal. €220,000Y. Goffs Orby. BBA (Ire). The dam, a quite useful Listed-placed dual 1m winner, is a half-sister to 4 winners including the fairly useful 2-y-o 6f winner Haadeeth. The second dam, Musical Key (by Key Of Luck), a fair maiden, was fourth twice over 5f at 2 yrs and is a half-sister to 6 winners including the high-class Hong Kong horses Mensa and Firebolt and the dam of the Group 2 Flying Childers winner Wunders Dream. *"She's a smart filly and a complete opposite to the dam, who I also trained. We like everything she's doing and I would hope that she's above average. She'll start once the ground dries up, then go for a Listed race at Naas and if all goes to plan she'll go for the Queen Mary – she's nice".*

1074. INFLECTION POINT (IRE) ★★
br.c. Invincible Spirit – Danuta (Sunday Silence). January 20. Half-brother to the US 2-y-o 7f and UAE 3-y-o Listed 9f winner Devotee (by Elusive Quality), to the fairly useful 10f winner Flight Officer (by New Approach), the quite useful 2-y-o 6f winner Evening Rain, the fair 1m winner Wave Runner (both by Raven's Pass) and the quite useful dual 7f winner Discoverer (by Bernardini). The dam, a US 1m and UAE 1m and 9f winner, is a half-sister to numerous winners including the UAE Listed 1m and Listed 9f winner Folk. The second dam, Polish Style (by Danzig), was a French Listed 6f winner. *"He was doing everything grand but he's having an easy month now. A nice horse, he'll be out in the second half of the year".*

1075. INVASION DAY ★★★★
b.c. Footstepsinthesand – Van De Cappelle (Pivotal). April 27. Eighth foal. €100,000Y. Tattersalls Ireland September. Joe Foley. Half-brother to the quite useful 2-y-o 6f winner Art Nouvelle (by Art Connoisseur), to the fair 2-y-o 7f winner Vegas Rebel (by Alfred Nobel) and a winner in Germany by High Chaparral. The dam is an unraced half-sister to 6 winners. The second dam, Sea Picture (by Royal Academy), is a placed half-sister to 9 winners including the Group 1 Yorkshire Oaks winner Hellenic (dam of the top-class filly Islington and the Group 1 winners Greek Dance and Mountain High). *"An above average horse, he's everything I want and I'm delighted to have him. With his sire you can either be lucky or unlucky and I think he's one of the good ones".*

1076. KINCH (IRE) ★★★★
b.c. Dark Angel – Lapis Blue (Invincible Blue). March 27. Second foal. £95,000Y. Goffs UK Premier. Gaelic Bloodstock. Brother to the 2017 2-y-o winner Dark Blue. The dam, a fair 4-y-o 6f winner, is a half-sister to 5 winners including the Irish Listed winner Go For Goal. The second dam, Triple Try (by Sadler's Wells), a quite useful Irish dual 10f winner, is a sister to the Irish Oaks and Tattersalls Gold Cup winner Dance Design and a half-sister to 4 winners. *"A lovely horse, he has a lot of quality about him and is up there in our top half a dozen. He's smart, one that I like and could be an Ascot 2-y-o if he's good enough, but Ascot*

isn't the be all and end all; I've got bigger fish to fry over here".

1077. MERRICOURT (IRE) ★★★
gr.c. Mizzen Mast – Elite (Invincible Spirit). March 1. Third foal. 65,000Y. Tattersalls October Book 1. Gaelic Bloodstock. Half-brother to the French 1m winner Different Views (by Proud Citizen). The dam, a modest maiden, was placed fourth four times from 5f to 7f and is a half-sister to 6 winners including the Group 1 9f Prix Jean Prat winner Olden Times and the Listed 6f winner and Group 1 Cheveley Park Stakes third Festoso. The second dam, Garah (by Ajdal), a very useful winner of 4 races over 6f and second in the Group 3 5f Duke Of York Stakes, is a half-sister to 6 winners. *"A horse I loved at the start and I really liked him all the way along but he's going through a growing spurt at the moment. He was definitely in my top half a dozen a month or two ago, so what I saw early doors I liked. If he comes back to that I'll be happy".*

1078. MORAVIA ★★★★
b.f. Siyouni – Demeanour (Giant's Causeway). March 1. Third foal. £80,000Y. Goffs UK Premier (Doncaster). Gaelic Bloodstock. Half-sister to the modest French 10f winner Talento (by Azamour) and to the minor French and Norwegian winner Swedish Dream (by Helmet). The dam, a fair Scandinavian Listed 12f winner, is a half-sister to 6 winners. The second dam, Akuna Bay (by Mr Prospector), a 2-y-o 7f winner, is a half-sister to 3 winners including the Ribblesdale Stakes second Gothic Dream (herself the dam of two Listed winners). *"A beautiful filly, she's ready to run. I have a lovely bunch of fillies and she'd be up there with the best. One for five/six furlongs".*

1079. NEVER SHY AWAY (IRE) ★★
b.f. Zoffany – Shy Bride (Excellent Art). April 28. Second foal. €155,000Y. Goffs Orby. Empire Bloodstock. The dam, a fair 2-y-o 7f winner, is a half-sister to 9 winners including the Group 2 and triple Group 3 winning miler Gold Away and the Group 3 winners Blushing Gleam and Danzigaway (dam of the dual Grade 2 winner Silent Away). The second dam, Blushing Away (by Blushing Groom), was a French Listed-placed 3-y-o winner. *"She was doing everything I wanted but needs a bit of*

time because she's not precocious. I wanted to let her have some time off to fill her frame, so she's back at the farm doing that. I like what I've seen without getting carried away".

1080. NICKAJACK CAVE (IRE) ★★★★
gr.c. Kendargent – Could You Be Loved (Montjeu). March 9. First foal. £65,000Y. Goffs UK Premier (Doncaster). Gaelic Bloodstock. The dam was unraced. The second dam, Light My Way (by Polish Precedent), is an unraced half-sister to 12 winners including the multiple Group 1 winner Pride (Champion Stakes, etc) and the dam of the 1,000 Guineas winner Speciosa. *"A beautiful colt, he's just getting his act together and you'll see him around June time. He wins his maiden all day long and hopefully he's better than that".*

1081. PYTHION (FR) ★★★★
b.c. Olympic Glory – Paragua (Nayef). March 31. Third foal. 85,000Y. Tattersalls October Book 2. Gaelic Bloodstock. Half-brother to the 2017 French 2-y-o 1m winner Para El Futoro (by Maxios). The dam won two minor races at 2 and 3 yrs in Germany and is a half-sister to 4 winners including the Group 1 Criterium de Saint-Cloud winner Paita, the Group 2 German Oaks winner Puntilla and the dam of the Group 1 Premio Roma winner Potemkin. The second dam, Prada (by Lagunas), a German 3-y-o Listed winner, is a half-sister to 7 winners. *"A very smart, gorgeous individual, there's plenty of size and scope about him and definitely in the top half dozen of my 2-y-o's. A horse I like a lot, he has a lot of quality and I'd be very positive about him".*

1082. QUEEN MEDB (IRE) ★★★
br.f. Kodiac – Alizaya (Highest Honor). April 2. Seventh foal. £36,000Y. Goffs UK Premier (Doncaster). Gaelic Bloodstock. Half-brother to 4 winners including the fairly useful triple 10f winner Shabbah (by Sea The Stars), the quite useful 7f (at 2 yrs) to 10f winner of 5 races Ingleby Symphony and the minor French 3-y-o winner Oratello (both by Oratorio). The dam is an unraced half-sister to 7 winners including the Group 1 Irish St Leger and Group 1 Prix du Cadran winner Alandi and the Irish Listed 12f winner Aliyfa. The second dam, Aliya (by Darshaan), a dual 12f winner in Ireland, is a

sister to the Group 3 12f Lingfield Oaks Trial winner and disqualified Epsom Oaks winner Aliysa and a half-sister to 7 winners. *"She's not in the main yard because she's been backward but she'll be joining the main team soon and being a typical Kodiac you'd like to see her out from July onwards. She's nice but hasn't done any fast work yet. The name Medb is Gaelic and is pronounced Mave".*

1083. RITA LEVI (IRE) ★★★
b.f. Kodiac – Pioneer Alexander (Rip Van Winkle). March 6. First foal. €90,000Y. Goffs Orby. Gaelic Bloodstock. The dam is an unplaced half-sister to 7 winners including the very useful Listed 6f winner and Group 2 Richmond Stakes second Bannock and the Australian Listed winner Moulin Lady. The second dam, Laoub (by Red Ransom), a winner in the UAE at 3 yrs, is a half-sister to 9 winners including Never Retreat (US Grade 1 First Lady Stakes). *"She's precocious but needs to put on a bit of weight. I have a good bunch of fillies and they all look like they'll win their maiden. This filly is a few weeks behind my really early types, but her time will come soon enough".*

1084. ROMME ★★★★
b.f. Society Rock – River Style (Desert Style). April 24. Fourth foal. Half-sister to the modest 6f winner on her only start Starsovertheriver and to the modest 6f winner Monashka Bay (both by Kodiac). The dam is an unplaced half-sister to 6 winners including the very useful 2-y-o Listed 5f winner of 7 races Star Rover. The second dam, Charlene Lacy (by Pips Pride), won once over 5f at 2 yrs and is a half-sister to 4 winners. *"She had her first run at Dundalk in early April where she finished second. The horse in third came out and beat one of Aidan O'Brien's next time out. So the form is working out and all our early fillies are of a similar standard. There's no reason why she won't improve, win her maiden and then we'll take it from there".*

1085. SINGER ★★★★
b.c. Oasis Dream – Caponata (by Selkirk). January 11. Second foal. The dam, a Listed 9.5f and Listed 10f winner, was second in the Group 2 10f Blandford Stakes and is a half-sister to the Group 2 1m Lanwades Stud

Stakes winner Brooch. The second dam, Daring Diva (by Dansili), a French 2-y-o Listed 5f winner, is a sister to the Group 1 1m Matron Stakes and multiple Group 3 winner Emulous and a half-sister to the fairly useful 2-y-o 6f winner Striking Spirit. *"A beautiful filly by Oasis Dream from Juddmonte, she's only just got over a dirty nose so she hasn't done any fast work, but everything about her is quality. A big, scopey filly, there's no rush with her and she'll be out in the second half of the season. She has a lot of character about her".*

1086. WARTIME HERO (IRE) ★★★★
b.c. Kodiac – Spring Surprise (Hector Protector). April 4. Fifth living foal. £210,000Y. Goffs UK Premier (Doncaster). Ger Lyons. Half-brother to the smart 2-y-o Group 2 6f Mill Reef Stakes winner Toocoolforschool (by Showcasing), to a minor winner abroad by Bertolini and a hurdles winner by Doyen. The dam, a fair 2-y-o 7f winner, is a half-sister to 10 winners including the useful 6f (at 2 yrs) to 1m and hurdles winner and Listed Heron Stakes second Tucker. The second dam, Tender Moment (by Caerleon), a fair triple 7f winner, is a half-sister to 6 winners. *"He was entered to run early but got sore shins, so he's just getting over it now. He looks above average, is a typical Kodiac for five/six furlongs and he'll win his maiden all day long. Hopefully he's even better than that".*

1087. UNNAMED ★★★
b.c. Exceed And Excel – Crying Shame (Street Cry). February 8. First foal. 110,000Y. Tattersalls October Book 1. Gaelic Bloodstock. The dam won 3 minor races at 4 yrs in France and is a half-sister to 5 winners including the US Grade 2 winner and Grade 1 third Dancing House. The second dam, Tout Charmant (by Slewvescent), won the Grade 1 Del Mar Oaks and the Grade 1 Matriarch Stakes and is a half-sister to 10 winners including the US Grade 3 winner Forest Grove. *"A gorgeous, big horse, he's in the main string, everything he does at the minute is good, without any bells and whistles. A mid-season type of horse and I'm very happy with what I'm seeing".*

1088. UNNAMED ★★★
gr.c. Dark Angel – Lightwood Lady (Anabaa). May 5. Eighth foal. 180,000Y. Tattersalls

October Book 1. Gaelic Bloodstock. Half-brother to the fairly useful 1m winner of 4 races Express Himself (by Dylan Thomas), to the quite useful 6f (at 2 yrs) and 5f winner Munshid (by Dutch Art), the quite useful 2-y-o 5f winner (on her only start) Its Alright (by King's Best), the fair 1m and subsequent US winner Totheendoftheeearth (by Hurricane Run) and the minor French dual 3-y-o winner Halendale (by Elusive City). The dam, a fair Irish 6f winner, is a half-sister to 6 winners. The second dam, Lyrical Dance (by Lear Fan), a minor winner at 4 yrs in the USA, is a full or half sister to 7 winners including the Group/Grade 1 winners Black Minnaloushe, Pennekamp and Nasr El Arab. *"He's done everything I want up to now but needs a bit of time to grow up. He's in the second yard, I'm happy with him and hopefully he's a good one but he won't be rushed".*

1089. UNNAMED ★★★
b.f. Oasis Dream – Noyelles (Docksider). March 10. Seventh foal. 340,000Y. Tattersalls October Book 1. Meridian / David Redvers. Half-sister to the Group 3 7f and triple Listed winner of 10 races and Group 1 placed Lily's Angel (by Dark Angel) and to the useful 7f (at 2 yrs) and 1m winner Zurigha (by Cape Cross). The dam is an unraced half-sister to 8 winners including the Group 3 Prix de Flore winner In Clover and the French Listed winners Bayourida and Bellona. The second dam, Bellarida (by Bellypha), won the Group 3 Prix de Royaumont and is a half-sister to 2 winners. *"A beautiful half-sister to Lily's Angel, she came in to me late but is catching up. She has a good attitude, definitely has an engine and I'd like to get her out from mid-season onwards".*

GEORGE MARGARSON
1090. MODEL GUEST ★★★ ♠
ch.f. Showcasing – Looks All Right (Danehill Dancer). March 1. Third foal. 135,000Y. Tattersalls October Book 2. Amanda Skiffington /John Guest. Half-sister to the modest 2017 dual 5f placed 2-y-o Bodybuilder (by Power) and to minor Italian 2-y-o winner Oakville (by Arcano). The dam is an unplaced sister to the Group 3 7f C L Weld Park Stakes winner Venturi and the French Listed winner and Group 1 third Feels All Right and a half-sister to 2 winners. The

second dam, Zagreb Flyer (by Old Vic), is an unraced half-sister to 8 winners. (John Guest Racing Ltd). *"She's a filly that was bought to be a midsummer type, she's doing two strong canters a day and pleasing us because she goes up Warren Hill very easily. She has a good temperament and her knees are mature so I can see her being out in May but if she needs more time she'll get it. It's early days but I'd say she'll be above average and obviously at this time of year you have hopes of Royal Ascot, but it's too early to make a decision on that".*

1091. SPIRITED GUEST ★★★
b.c. Swiss Spirit – Choisette (Choisir). February 4. Sixth foal. £45,000Y. Goffs UK Premier (Doncaster). Amanda Skiffington. Half-brother to the fairly useful 6f winner of 5 races Flying Pursuit (by Pastoral Pursuits) and to the quite useful triple 6f winner from 2 to 4 yrs Straightothepoint (by Kyllachy). The dam, a modest triple 5f winner (including at 2 yrs), is a half-sister to 2 winners. The second dam, Final Pursuit (by Pursuit Of Love), a fairly useful 2-y-o 5.7f winner, is a half-sister to 10 winners including the Group 3 Coventry Stakes second Sir Nicholas (subsequently very successful in Hong Kong), the smart sprint winner and Ayr Gold Cup second Double Action and the very useful 2-y-o Listed 6f Sirenia Stakes winner Lipstick. (John Guest Racing Ltd). *"He's done bits of work, he's well forward and looks well. A big horse that was bought with next year in mind, I wouldn't be surprised if he got seven furlongs and a mile. Big and strong, he could be out by the end of July or early August. He's come in his coat already and looks great".*

1092. STAR TRACKER ★★★
ch.c. Universal – New Falcon (New Approach). February 22. Second foal. 22,000Y. Tattersalls October Book 3. George Margarson. Half-brother to the fair 2017 2-y-o 7f placed 2-y-o Falcon's Vision (by Iffraaj). The dam, a fair 2-y-o 7f winner, is a half-sister to 5 winners including the Group 3 second Sharnberry. The second dam, Wimple (by Kingmambo), a useful 5f and 6f winner at 2 yrs, was Listed-placed and is a half-sister to 3 winners. (Mr A. Al Mansoori). *"He's a 2-y-o for late April or early May because he's a very forward horse. There are no temperament issues, he's already*

been upsides and been through the stalls, so if he wasn't a Universal you'd be saying this is a sharp, early sort. As soon as he comes in his coat we'll get him on the track to try and get him to win before the end of May and I'd be surprised if he couldn't win when the six furlong races comes out".

1093. WINDY GUEST ★★★

b.c. Toronado – Enliven (Dansili). February 1. First foal. £42,000Y. Goffs UK Premier (Doncaster). Amanda Skiffington. The dam, a fair 7f winner, is a half-sister to two minor winners abroad. The second dam, Aurore (by Fasliyev), was placed over 6f and 7f in France at 2 yrs and is a half-sister to 6 winners including the triple Group 1 winner Aquarelliste and the dual US Grade 1 10f winner Artiste Royal. (John Guest Racing Ltd). "He's by the first season sire Toronado and if this colt is anything to go by he'll be a successful stallion. He was very small when I bought him, but he's now a proper, compact 2-y-o type. He's a bull of a horse, strong and powerful and he's done plenty of work. All being well he should be out by late April or early May. He's had no issues at all and he should be a proper five/six furlong 2-y-o and I'd be surprised if I couldn't win with him first or second time out".

1094. UNNAMED ★★★

ch.c. Universal – Regal Sultana (New Approach). February 16. First foal. 10,000Y. Tattersalls October Book 3. George Margarson. The dam was unraced. The second dam, Calakanga (by Dalakhani), a quite useful 12f winner, is a half-sister to 11 winners including the very smart Group 1 1m Racing Post Trophy and Group 2 10.4f Dante Stakes winner Dilshaan and the Listed winner and Group 1 second Darrfonah. (Mr A. Al Mansoori). "A really nice horse and a big, powerful brute that goes easily. I've brought him along with a couple of proper 2-y-o types and he still goes easily with them. I've not asked him to quicken up but he would do and I'm thinking of him as a summer horse. He's grown, levelled out and has a hell of a good temperament. A seven furlong or mile 2-y-o in the making".

MARTYN MEADE

1095. ACHIEVABLE (IRE) ★★★★

br.f. No Nay Never – Always A Way (Danehill Dancer). May 14. Fourth foal. €30,000Y. Goffs Orby. D Farrington. Half-sister to a minor winner abroad by Dream Ahead. The dam ran once unplaced and is a half-sister to 5 winners including the Group 2 Prix Robert Papin winner Never A Doubt. The second dam, Waypoint (Cadeaux Genereux), a fairly useful 6f and 7f winner, is a half-sister to 5 winners including the Group 2 Diadem Stakes winner and high-class sire Acclamation. "A smashing filly, she's got plenty of bone and enormous presence. Of all the 2-y-o's she was showing the most early on but she's a mid-May foal and we had to back off. Physically she's one of the picks and there's plenty of her as well. We might get her going before mid-season and she's done nothing wrong so far". TRAINER'S BARGAIN BUY

1096. ADVERTISE ★★★★

b.c. Showcasing – Furbelow (Pivotal). February 23. Third foal. £60,000Y. Goffs UK Premier (Doncaster). Dermot Farrington. Half-brother to the quite useful 2017 2-y-o 7f winner Flavius Titus (by Lethal Force). The dam, a quite useful 6f winner, is a sister to the US Listed stakes winner Red Diadem and a half-sister to 5 winners including the dam of the Group 2 Richmond Stakes winner Saayerr. The second dam, Red Tiara (by Mr Prospector), a moderate 7.6f fourth-placed maiden, is closely related to the Japanese sprint stakes winner Meiner Love and a half-sister to 4 winners. "We like this colt, he's a big, strong type, probably 16.2 hands and if all goes well he's a Royal Ascot type. A horse that's done very well, we managed to get on with him early in the year and he's certainly going the right way".

1097. AIRWAVES ★★

b.f. Monsieur Bond – Forever Bond (Danetime). March 21. Tenth foal. Sister to the triple Group 3 Summer Stakes winner Ladies Are Forever, to the 6f Stewards Cup winner of 11 races and Group 1 Haydock Sprint Cup third Hoof It and the fair 5f and 6f winner of 8 races Forever's Girl and half-sister to the 5f and 6f winner of 6 races Bop It (by Misu Bond) and the fair 6f to 9f winner of 7 races Chosen

Forever (by Choisir). The dam is an unraced half-sister to 7 winners including Group 3 5.2f winner Ratio. The second dam, Owdbetts (by High Estate), a fair 7f to 10.2f winner of 4 races, is a half-sister to 5 minor winners. *"A horse that was sent to us by the owner, she's a light-framed filly and should be a midsummer type for sprint distances. She's done very well considering she didn't undergo any sales preparation".*

1098. ASSUMING ★★
ch.f. Ruler Of The World – Bold Assumption (Observatory). March 25. Eighth foal. 30,000Y. Tattersalls December. Dermot Farrington. Half-sister to the 2-y-o Listed 1m winner, Group 1 French 1,000 Guineas second and Group 1 Sun Chariot Stakes third Irish Rookie (by Azamour), to the fairly useful 1m and hurdles winner Altruism (by Authorized), the Irish 3-y-o 1m winner, from two starts, Harmonyofthestars (by Lope De Vega) and the modest 7f winner Alice Rose (by Manduro). The dam is an unraced half-sister to 5 winners and to the unraced dams of the German/Italian Group winners Daring Love and Exhibit One. The second dam, Bold Empress (by Diesis), a fairly useful 2-y-o 6f winner, is a half-sister to 8 winners including the champion 2-y-o and 3-y-o and sire Zafonic. *"A sentimental one for us because she's a half-sister to Irish Rookie whom we trained to be Group 1 placed twice. She's not going to be early and is probably one for September time. She's a strong filly with plenty of bone and from the first crop of a Derby winner. Naturally we won't rush her".*

1099. CONFIDING ★★★★
b.c. Iffraaj – Entre Nous (Sadler's Wells). March 5. Sixth foal. €47,000Y. Tattersalls Ireland September. D Farrington. Half-brother to the quite useful Irish 1m winner Royal Memory (by Invincible Spirit). The dam is an unplaced sister to the Listed 12f winner Scriptwriter and a half-sister to 7 winners including the Group 2 Grand Prix de Deauville winner Courteous and the dam of the Group 1 Premio Roma winner Hunter's Light. The second dam, Dayanata (by Shirley Heights), is an unraced sister to the French Derby winner and high-class sire Darshaan and a half-sister to 11 winners including the Prix Vermeille winner Darara (the dam of four Group 1 winners)

and the dam of the Group 1 Coronation Cup winner Daliapour. *"He's very nice, we like him and he'll be racing in the early part of the season but will stay further in time. Going really well, he's a nice, big, strong horse and doing nothing wrong at the moment".*

1100. FOX VARDY (USA) ★★★★
b.c. Frankel – Dance With Another (Danehill Dancer). January 17. First foal. 210,000Y. Tattersalls October Book 1. Sackville/Donald. The dam, a quite useful Irish 2-y-o 1m winner, is a half-sister to 7 winners including the Group 1 Pretty Polly Stakes winner Diamondsandrubies and to the dam of the Group 2 winner and Derby fourth Eminent. The second dam, Quarter Moon (by Sadler's Wells), winner of the Group 1 7f Moyglare Stud Stakes and second in the Irish 1,000 Guineas, the Oaks and the Irish Oaks, is a sister to 4 winners including the Irish 1,000 Guineas winner Yesterday. *"This colt has a very distinctive look to him in that he has an old-fashioned, honest head. His dam is a half-sister to the dam of our good colt Eminent, so we rather like that. He's a strong, compact colt that may take a bit of time but that's not a problem".*

1101. FRILLY ★★★
ch.f. Frankel – Ladies Are Forever (Monsieur Bond). April 4. First foal. £180,000Y. Goffs UK Premier (Doncaster). Dermot Farrington. The dam, a triple Group 3 Summer Stakes winner, is a sister to the 6f Stewards Cup winner of 11 races and Group 1 Haydock Sprint Cup third Hoof It and a half-sister to 3 winners. The second dam, Forever Bond (by Danetime), is an unraced half-sister to 9 winners including Group 3 5.2f winner Ratio. *"She's a small filly and not typical of the sire but she has a great pedigree. A strong filly, she'll take a bit of time".*

1102. GLENN MILLER ★★★
b.c. Exceed And Excel – Tupelo Honey (Sadler's Wells). March 7. Third foal. 32,000Y. Tattersalls October Book 2. Dermot Farrington. The dam, a fair 10f winner, is closely related to 2 winners including the 2-y-o Group 2 1m Beresford Stakes and Group 3 Rose Of Lancaster Stakes winner and Group 1 7f National Stakes third David Livingston. The second dam, Mora Bai (by Indian Ridge), is an unraced full or

half-sister to 9 winners including the multiple Group 1 winner and sire High Chaparral and the Group 2 Dante Stakes winner Black Bear Island. *"A big, strong colt that's going really nicely, he's the strongest of all our colts at the moment. We should be able to get him out relatively early, probably in May".*

1103. HEADLAND ★★★
b.c. Harbour Watch – Bazzana (Zebedee). February 13. First foal. The dam was a fairly useful 2-y-o 6f winner. The second dam, Bazelle (by Ashkalani), a fair 8.5f and 9.5f winner, is a half-sister to 5 other minor winners. *"We trained the mare who won as a 2-y-o at Windsor by about ten lengths on her second start. This is her first foal and he'll be racing in the early part of the season. He'll probably be our first 2-y-o runner".*

1104. LOVING GLANCE ★★★★ ♣
b.f. Invincible Spirit – Kissable (Danehill Dancer). January 10. Second foal. 200,000Y. Tattersalls October Book 1. D Farrington. Half-sister to the fair 2017 6f and 7f placed maiden Amandine (by Shamardal). The dam, a smart Irish 2-y-o 7f winner, was third in the Group 1 Moyglare Stud Stakes and won a Listed stakes event in the USA and is a half-sister to 5 winners. The second dam, Kitty O'Shea (by Sadler's Wells), won twice over 1m including at 2 yrs and a Listed event at 3 yrs and is a sister to 2 winners including the Group 1 Racing Post Trophy and Group 1 St Leger winner Brian Boru and a half-sister to 4 winners including the Group 2 winners Sea Moon and Moon Search and to the unraced dam of the Derby winner Workforce. *"A filly with a fantastic pedigree and she's really well put-together. Probably the nicest 2-y-o filly we've got, you couldn't knock her, she has a great stride, a good temperament and is a real eye-catcher. One for seven furlongs this year probably".*

1105. PHOSPHOR ★★★
b.c. Havana Gold – Luminous Gold (Fantastic Light). April 7. Fifth foal. 50,000Y. Tattersalls October Book 2. Dermot Farrington. Half-brother to the fairly useful 2-y-o 6f winner and Group 3 Prestige Stakes third Zifena (by Zamindar), to the quite useful triple 7f winner at 2 and 3 yrs Aventinus (by Zoffany)

and the modest 1m winner Paved With Gold (by Champs Elysees). The dam, a fair 5f and 6f winner of 3 races from 2 to 5 yrs, is a half-sister to 7 winners including the Group 2 5f Flying Childers Stakes third Kissing Lights. The second dam, Nasaieb (by Fairy King), a fairly useful 2-y-o 5f winner, was third in the Listed 5f National Stakes and is a half-sister to 5 winners including the Group 3 7f Solario Stakes winner Raise A Grand. *"A nice colt that was going well early on, but he's going through a growth spurt at the moment. He'll come out of it pretty quickly and will make a 2-y-o by June/July time".*

1106. SEA STORM ★★★
b.f. Monsieur Bond – Chez Cherie (Wolfhound). February 21. Sister to the fairly useful 7f to 9.5f winner of 10 races, including a Listed 1m event, Alfred Hutchinson and to the fair 9.5f and 11f winner Kingthistle and half-sister to a minor 5-y-o winner in the USA by Proud Citizen. The dam, a useful 2-y-o 7f winner, was third in the Group 3 Lancashire Oaks and is a half-sister to 4 winners including the Hong Kong Listed winner Golconda. The second dam, Gerante (by Private Account), is an unplaced half-sister to 7 minor winners. *"She's a bit of a character and I think the only way to deal with that is a bit of graft and she's been going really well. A compact 'ready to go' sort, she's showing she needs to get on with it".*

1107. UNNAMED ★★★
gr.f. Dark Angel – Abeille (Alhaarth). April 15. Fourth foal. €27,000Y. Arqana Deauville October. Private sale. The dam was placed over 12f in France and is a half-sister to 5 winners including Quest For Honor (Group 2 Greffulhe). The second dam, Quest For Ladies (by Rainbow Quest), a US Listed stakes winner, is a half-sister to 3 winners. *"A nice, tall filly, she's strong and a proper piece of kit. She's developed since the sale and will probably want seven furlongs to begin with".*

1108. UNNAMED ★★
ch.c. Iffraaj – Alabelle (Galileo). April 12. Fourth foal. €36,000Y. Tattersalls Ireland September. D Farrington. Half-brother to the quite useful 1m winner A L'Anglaise (by Invincible Spirit). The dam, a fair 10f winner, is a half-sister to 4 winners including the Derby second

Dragon Dancer. The second dam, Alakananda (by Hernando), a fairly useful dual middle-distance winner, is a sister to one winner and a half-sister to 7 winners including the dual Champion Stakes winner Alborada and the triple German Group 1 winner Albanova. *"He's small and a bit weak and immature at the moment so we'll be taking our time with him. He was doing well but his knees were open so we've had to leave him alone for now. We won't get going again with him now until midsummer which is annoying because you'd expect to crack on with a small Iffraaj".*

1109. UNNAMED ★★★

b.f. Zoffany – Arcangela (Galileo). March 10. Fifth foal. €45,000Y. Arqana Deauville October. D Farrington. Half-sister to a minor winner abroad by Rock Of Gibraltar. The dam, a poor 1m 6f placed maiden, is a half-sister to 6 winners. The second dam, Crafty Buzz (by Crafty Prospector), a US 2-y-o Listed winner, is a half-sister to 7 winners including the US Grade 3 winner Gone For Real. *"A typical Zoffany, she walks beautifully, has plenty of bone and we bought her purely on looks, partly because she reminds us of our Lancashire Oaks winner Wilamina who is by the same sire. One for September time to start off with I should think".*

1110. UNNAMED ★★

b.c. Cape Cross – Argent Du Bois (Silver Hawk). May 14. Ninth foal. 50,000Y. Tattersalls October Book 2. D Farrington. Half-brother to 7 winners including the 2-y-o 6.5f and 7f and subsequent US dual Grade 1 winner Ticker Tape (by Royal Applause), the Group 1 Prix Maurice de Gheest winner Brando (by Pivotal), the quite useful dual 6f winner (including at 2 yrs) and Canadian Listed-placed Sant Elena (by Efisio and herself dam of the dual Group 1 winner Reckless Abandon) and the fair French 2-y-o 1m winner Woodland Faery (by Act One). The dam was placed five times in France and is a half-sister to 9 winners including the 2-y-o Group 1 Racing Post Trophy winner Crowded House. The second dam, Wiener Wald (by Woodman), is an unplaced half-sister to 6 winners abroad. *"Not terribly tall but really well put-together, we've just had a small setback with him. Being a mid-May foal he'll need a bit of time so he's one for the back-end.*

He has a very good pedigree and just needs us to look after him for a few months".

1111. UNNAMED ★★★

b.f. Slade Power – Aris (Danroad). March 29. Fourth foal. Half-sister to the Group 1 7f Prix de la Foret, Group 2 7f Park Stakes and Group 2 7f Challenge Stakes winner Aclaim (by Acclamation). The dam, a Listed-placed 7f winner, is a half-sister four winners including Again (Irish 1,000 Guineas and Moyglare Stud Stakes) and the Group 3 Give Thanks Stakes third Arkadina. The second dam, Cumbres (by Kahyasi), is an unraced half-sister to Montjeu. *"A half-sister to a very good horse we had, Aclaim, she's very similar in looks despite being a filly. She'll take a bit of time, he only started his career in November as a 2-y-o and she certainly won't be an early bird either".*

1112. UNNAMED ★★

gr.c. Mastercraftsman – Arosa (Sadler's Wells). January 20. Seventh foal. €40,000Y. Goffs Orby. D Farrington. Half-brother to the useful triple 1m winner at 2 and 3 yrs and Group 3 third Water Hole (by Oasis Dream) and to two minor winners in France and Ireland by Fastnet Rock. The dam, a fairly useful Irish 9f and subsequent US stakes winner, is a sister to the German Group 2 8.5f and Italian Group 2 1m winner Crimson Tide and to the Group 3 12f Give Thanks Stakes winner Tamarind and a half-sister to the US Grade 2 and Group 3 Prix de Sandringham winner Pharatta and the US stakes winner and Grade 2 placed La Vida Loca. The second dam, Sharata (by Darshaan), is an unraced half-sister to Shahrastani. *"He's a tall colt but I think he'll be out a bit earlier than you might expect. He knows the job and he'll probably be racing as soon as the first seven furlong races come out".*

1113. UNNAMED ★★

b.c. Dubawi – Casual Look (Red Ransom). May 6. Tenth foal. Brother to the quite useful 12f winner Eyeshine and half-brother to 4 winners including the US Grade 3 9f winner Casual Smile (by Sea The Stars), the fairly useful 1m to 10f winner of 4 races Mushreq (by Distorted Humor) and the US dual 1m winner and Listed-placed Casual Trick (by Bernardini). The dam, an Epsom Oaks winner, was second in the Group 1 Fillies' Mile and is a sister to the Listed Prix de Liancourt winner and Grade 1 Yellow Ribbon Stakes third Shabby Chic and a half-sister to 5 winners including the US winner and Grade 2 placed American Style. The second dam, Style Setter (by Manila), a stakes-placed winner of 3 races at 2 and 3 yrs in the USA, is a half-sister to the US stakes winner and Grade 1 placed Fashion Delight. *"A beautifully-bred colt, he's a typical Dubawi. He's compact but the dam wanted middle-distances and he was a May foal, so we'll give him plenty of time. Much more likely to show his best form next year".*

1114. UNNAMED ★★★
ch.c. Champs Elysees – Galicuix (Galileo). March 14. Fourth foal. 120,000Y. Tattersalls October Book 1. Not sold. Half-brother to the Group 1 2,000 Guineas and Group 1 St James's Palace Stakes winner Galileo Gold and to the quite useful 2-y-o 7f winner Choumicha (both by Paco Boy). The dam ran twice unplaced and is a half-sister to the Group 1 Prix de l'Abbaye and Group 1 King's Stand Stakes winner Goldream. The second dam, Clizia (by Machiavellian), is an unraced half-sister to 3 winners including the multiple Listed winner and Group 2 placed Mont Rocher. *"A strong colt, the sire certainly stamps his stock and this colt is typical – a chestnut with a white face and lots of bone. He's obviously not going to be a sharp 2-y-o like his half-brother Galileo Gold".*

1115. UNNAMED ★★
b.c. Dalakhani – Montbretia (Montjeu). March 8. Fourth foal. €24,000Y. Tattersalls Ireland September. D Farrington. Half-brother to the fair 6f to 8.5f winner of 4 races Specialv (by Big Bad Bob). The dam, a fairly useful 10f winner, is a half-sister to 6 winners. The second dam, Bayswater (by Caerleon), a fair 12.3f winner, is a sister to the high-class Group 1 1m Ciga Grand Criterium and Group 2 10.4f Dante Stakes winner Tenby, to the very useful 1m (at 2 yrs) and 10f winner Bright Water and a half-sister to the Listed winner Bristol Channel. *"A smallish colt, he's a bit of a boyo which isn't surprising given his sire and damsire, but he's nice and will obviously want a bit of a trip even though he isn't behind the other two-year-olds of ours at the moment. He's well put-together but with his pedigree we have to be patient with him".*

1116. UNNAMED ★★
b.f. Exceed And Excel – Myrine (Sadler's Wells). April 27. Fifth foal. 22,000Y. Tattersalls December. Salcey Forest Stud. Half-brother to a minor winner in Denmark by Sea The Stars. The dam, a fairly useful 14f and 2m winner, is a sister to the 2-y-o 1m winner, Group 3 Chester Vase second and subsequent Hong Kong winner Almighty and a half-sister to 7 winners including the Prix de l'Arc de Triomphe winner Sagamix, the Group 1 Criterium de Saint-Cloud winner Sagacity and the Group 2 Prix de Malleret winner Sage Et Jolie (dam of the Group 1 Prix d'Ispahan winner Sageburg). The second dam, Saganeca (by Sagace), won the Group 2 12.5f Prix de Royallieu. *"A relatively late foal, she just appeared good value for what she cost. Not a great eye-catcher – hence the relatively low purchase price – but we just thought that she was worth taking a chance with".*

1117. UNNAMED ★★★
b.f. Lawman – Rising Wind (Shirocco). March 25. Fourth foal. €36,000Y. Goffs Orby. D Farrington. Half-sister to the fairly useful Listed-placed 2-y-o dual 1m winner Rioja (by Jeremy) and to a minor French 3-y-o winner by Acclamation. The dam, an Irish 2-y-o 1m winner, was Listed placed over 1m and is a half-sister to 3 winners. The second dam, Right Key (by Key Of Luck), a very useful Irish 7f (at 2 yrs) and dual Group 3 winner over 10f and 12f, is a full or half-sister to 5 winners including the Irish dual 7f (at 2 yrs) and Listed 1m winner and dual Group 2 placed Wrong Key. *"A really nice horse, she has plenty of bone and presence and she's ready to go on but we'll wait for the seven furlong races".*

1118. UNNAMED ★★★
b.c. Toronado – Sparkling Eyes (Lujain). April 11. Sixth foal. €42,000Y. Tattersalls Ireland September. D Farrington. Half-brother to the quite useful 6f (at 2 yrs) to 1m winner of 3 races Wimpole Hall (by Canford Cliffs), to the quite useful 6f and subsequent Hong Kong winner Blurred Vision (by Royal Applause) and the quite useful 5.5f (at 2 yrs) and 6f winner of 5 races Pea Shooter (by Piccolo). The dam, a fairly useful dual 5f winner (including at 2 yrs), was fourth in the Group 2 5f Queen Mary Stakes, is a half-sister to 3 winners here and abroad. The second dam, Lady Georgia (by

Arazi), was a useful 3-y-o 7.8f winner. *"A big horse but he has a great stride and everything seems effortless. We haven't turned the screws yet because of his size, but he's not immature".*

1119. UNNAMED ★★★
b.c. Acclamation – With Colour (Rainbow Quest). April 18. Seventh foal. €78,000Y. Tattersalls Ireland September. D Farrington. Brother to the useful 2-y-o 5f and 6f winner Pearl Acclaim and half-brother to the fair 1m to 10f and hurdles winner Our Phylli Vera (by Motivator) and the modest 9f and 10f winner Quest Of Colour (by Iffraaj). The dam is an unplaced half-sister to 9 winners including the smart 7f (at 2 yrs) and Listed 10f winner With Interest. The second dam, With Fascination (by Dayjur), won the Group 3 6f Prix de Cabourg and was Group 2 placed twice at 2 yrs and is a half-sister to 5 winners including the US multiple Grade 1 winner With Anticipation. *"A typical Acclamation, he'll be racing in April because he's ready to go".*

ROD MILLMAN
1120. ARDIMENTO (IRE) ★★
b.c. Roderic O'Connor – Begin The Beguine (Peintre Celebre). April 13. €29,000 foal. Goffs. Howson & Houldsworth. Brother to the quite useful 7f and 1m winner of 5 races Sir Roderic and half-brother to the quite useful 9f to 12f winner Dew Line (by Vale Of York), the Italian 2-y-o winner La Grande Jatte and the minor French 3-y-o winner Beyond Time (both by Key Of Luck). The dam, a fair 10f winner, is a half-sister to 6 winners including Group 1 Phoenix Stakes second Big Time and the Irish 2-y-o 5f and 7f winner and Listed-placed Master Papa. The second dam, Beguine (by Green Dancer), is an unplaced half-sister to the champion two-year-old and high-class sire Grand Lodge and to the Listed winners La Persiana and Papabile. (David Little, The Links Partnership). *"A full brother to Sir Roderic who was a good horse of mine. This colt is leggy and isn't as strong as his brother, so he's out in a field at the moment because he needs time to develop. He'll come back into training much later in the season for a back-end/all-weather campaign".*

1121. BONNY BLUE ★★★
b.f. Harbour Watch – Bonnie Grey (Hellvelyn).

March 12. First foal. The dam, a fairly useful 2-y-o 5f winner and second in the Group 3 7f Prestige Stakes, is a half-sister to numerous winners including the useful 2-y-o 5f and 6f winner Cop Hill Lad and the fairly useful Listed 7f winner Clifton Dancer. The second dam, Crofters Ceilidh (by Scottish Reel), a Listed-placed winner of 3 races over 5f including at 2 yrs, is a half-sister to 4 winners including the Group 2 placed Lord Kintyre. (Howard Barton Stud). *"Not as forward as his mother who won first time out. She's a bit weak at the moment but she's got a bit of quality and won't be quite as early as her dam, probably one for six furlongs to start with".*

1122. GREELEY (IRE) ★★★★
b.c. Sir Prancealot – Hannah Greeley (Mr Greeley). April 10. Fourth foal. £18,000Y. Goffs UK Silver (Doncaster). Howson & Houldsworth / Rod Millman. Half-brother to the minor Italian 2-y-o winner Sharming Girl (by Zebedee) and to a winner in Qatar by Kodiac. The dam ran twice unplaced and is a half-sister to 3 minor winners in the USA and Mexico. The second dam, Miss Hannah (by Deputy Minister), a minor US 3-y-o winner, is a half-sister to 6 winners. (B R Millman). *"A very good-looking horse, he does look the part. This is a racy colt and is entered in the Supersprint but I think he's probably a six furlong 2-y-o. I thought he was the pick of the Silver sale at Doncaster".*

1123. GREYZEE ★★★
gr.c Zebedee – Curl (Duke of Marmalade). March 29. Second foal. The dam, a modest 11f seller winner, is a half-sister to 3 winners including the useful Listed 1m winner of 6 races Master Carpenter. The second dam, Fringe (by In The Wings), a quite useful 10f winner, is a half-sister to the French Listed winner Mount Elbrus. (David Little, The Links Partnership). *"He's out of Master Carpenter's sister and this is quite a nice horse, a good size and not over-tall but solid. Very much like Master Carpenter except he's grey!"*

1124. LADY WOLF ★★
b.f. Kuroshio – Angry Bark (Woodman). April 5. Half-sister to the fair 7.5f (at 2 yrs) to 2m and hurdles winner Arthur's Secret (by Sakhee's Secret), to the fair 2-y-o 9f winner Mattoral

(by High Chaparral), the fair 9f winner Plutocraft (by Starcraft) and the moderate 12f winner Ablaze (by Arcano). The dam, placed over 9f, is a half-sister to 4 winners including the French Listed winner and US Grade 2 placed Cyrillic. The second dam, Polemic (by Roberto), a 2-y-o 6.5f winner and second in the Prix Saint-Alary, also won a Grade 3 and was Grade 1 third in the USA and is a sister to the Group 3 winner Tralos. (Howard Barton Stud). *"This filly has really improved since she arrived, she's quite nice and should win races. I should imagine we'll start her off over five furlongs in May".* The sire, a son of Exceed And Excel, won a Group 2 and a Group 3 over 5f in Australia.

1125. MAWDE (IRE) ★★★
ch.f. Sir Prancealot – Rise Up Lotus (Zebedee). January 20. First foal. £8,000Y. Goffs UK Premier (Doncaster). Howson & Houldsworth / Rod Millman. The dam, a fair 2-y-o dual 5f winner, is a half-sister to four 2-y-o winners including the useful 5f and 6f winner and Group 2 7f Superlative Stakes second Roi de Vitesse. The second dam, Face The Storm (by Barathea), a fair 2-y-o 1m winner, is a half-sister to 3 winners including the Listed winner Santa Isobel. (The Mow Partnership). *"A very correct filly, she's quite sharp and will be out soon. The dam is a half-sister to Roi de Vitesse who was a good 2-y-o for us and continues to run well in Dubai at a ten year old. This filly is well-mannered, very correct and coming along nicely. She'll be out in May and she's a five/six furlong 2-y-o".* We've had such bad weather this spring my whole string is behind at the moment". TRAINER'S BARGAIN BUY

1126. POWER SEEKER ★★★
b.c. Power – Eclat Royale (Royal Applause). March 17. Second foal. The dam as an unraced half-sister to one winner. The second dam, Maramkova (by Danehill Dancer), is an unraced half-sister to the very useful 2-y-o 5f, 6f Listed and 6.5f Watership Down Stud Sales Race winner and dual Group 3 placed Nyramba and to the Listed 10f winner and Group 3 placed Cape Amber. (Five Horses Ltd). *"The first and second dams all showed speed at home but didn't get to the track. This is quite a good-looking individual, he's sharp and will be out in late April. Not over-big but well put-together".*

1127. SKI MIST ★★
gr.f. Hellvelyn – Piste (Falbrav). March 29. Second foal. £3,000Y. Goffs UK Autumn. Not sold. Half-sister to the modest 2017 6f placed 2-y-o Equilibrium (by Equiano). The dam, a modest dual 5f winner at 3 and 6 yrs, is a half-sister to 3 winners including the useful dual 1m winner and Group 3 1m Atalanta Stakes third Black Cherry and the useful 2-y-o 1m winner Alfathaa. The second dam, Arctic Char (by Polar Falcon), a useful Listed 7f winner, is a half-sister to 7 winners including the Group 2 winners Barrow Creek and Last Resort and the dam of the Group 2 winner Trans Island. (Miss G J Abbey). *"A very big filly, she's 'up behind' and she's thrown a splint, so she'll won't be ready until much later on. Probably more of a 3-y-o type".*

1128. STEEVE ★★★
ch.c. Lethal Force – Club Tahiti (Hernando). March 31. Second foal. Half-brother to the modest triple 6f winner at 2 and 3 yrs Tahiti One (by Bertolini). The dam, a quite useful 2-y-o 7f winner, is a half-sister to the Group 3 12f St Simon Stakes and Listed 10f winner and Group 1 placed Clowance and is a half-sister to 3 winners. The second dam, Freni (by Sternkoenig), a German Group 2 11f winner, is a half-sister to the smart German 10f performer Ferrari. (Seasons Holidays). *"Not over-big but very racy and keen to get on with it, she'll start at five furlongs and will stay six. Not a bad sort and quite sharp".*

1129. SUFFICIENT ★★★
gr.f. Showcasing – Good Enough (Mukaddamah). April 14. Half-sister to the useful 7f (at 2 yrs) and Listed 6f winner of 6 races Oasis Dancer (by Oasis Dream), the very useful 1m winner and subsequent Scandinavian Listed winner of 6 races Smart Enough (by Cadeaux Genereux), the fair 2-y-o 5f winner Grey Street (by Royal Applause), the fair 2-y-o 1m winner Bright Enough (by Fantastic Light) and the fair 10f winner Arcamist (by Arcano). The dam won once at 3 yrs in the USA, was third in the Group 1 Prix Saint-Alary and is a half-sister to the Group 3 Molecomb Stakes winner Classic Ruler. The second dam, Viceroy Princess (by Godswalk), a modest 2-y-o 7f seller winner, is a half-sister to 7 winners. (Whitsbury Manor & Heather

Slade). *"This is a nice filly, quite tall with a bit of quality and she wants six furlongs plus. So she won't be out until June, but she's going quite nicely".*

1130. UNNAMED ★★★
b.g. Intello – Aneedah (Invincible Spirit). February 29. Fourth foal. 75,000Y. Tattersalls October Book 2. Howson & Houldsworth / Rod Millman. Half-brother to the quite useful dual 6f winner at 2 and 3 yrs Gorgeous Noora (by Raven's Pass). The dam, a fairly useful 2-y-o 1m winner, was Listed-placed and is a half-sister to 2 winners including the dual Group 2 winning sprinter Muthmir and the 2-y-o Group 3 7f C L Weld Park Stakes winner My Titania. The second dam, Fairy Of The Night (by Danehill), an Irish 7f Listed and 9.5f winner, is a sister to one winner and a half-sister to 3 winners including the US Grade 3 12f and Irish Listed 11f winner Dress Rehearsal. (E J S Gadsden). *"A good-looking horse that was quite expensive for us, he had a little setback in the spring so he'll be a mid-season 2-y-o. A quality horse, very solid and he'll want seven furlongs plus".*

STAN MOORE
1131. ATHENA STAR ★★★
b.f. War Command – Angie And Liz (Spectrum). May 12. Seventh foal. Half-sister to the fairly useful 2-y-o 6f winner and Group 3 Brownstown Stakes second Song Of Time, to the quite useful Irish 2-y-o 7f winner Caprella (both by Kheleyf) and the modest 6f winner Oliveraie (by Dutch Art). The dam, a moderate 6f (at 2 yrs) and 5f winner, is a half-sister to 2 winners. The second dam, Mary Magdalene (by Night Shift), a fair 5f winner, is a half-sister to 2 winners. (Elvyn & Tom Yates, J S Moore). *"She shows nice paces, will probably be better at six furlongs than five and I think War Command will be a successful stallion".*

1132. DELTA BRAVO ★★★
b.f. Mastercraftsman – Rhiannon (High Chaparral). January 8. First foal. €15,000Y. Tattersalls Ireland September. Not sold. The dam, placed fourth over 9f once from 8 starts, is a half-sister to 4 winners including the 2-y-o Listed second Hollow Ridge. The second dam, Bolas (by Unfuwain), a very smart winner of the Group 1 Irish Oaks and the Group 2

Ribblesdale Stakes and is a full or half-sister to 7 winners. (Eventmasters Racing). *"A big, strong filly, she'll be one for seven furlongs and a mile. There's plenty of strength about her, probably won't run until June over six/seven furlongs and she's by a good sire in Mastercraftsman. She's done everything asked of her, moves well and we'll be hoping for nice things from her".*

1133. MAGNETIC (IRE) ★★
b.g. Alhebayeb – Telltime (Danetime). April 21. Seventh foal. £7,000Y. Goffs UK Silver. Not sold. Half-brother to three winners in Italy by Iffraaj, Vale Of York and Redback. The dam, a fair 5.5f and 6f winner, is a half-sister to 4 winners in Japan. The second dam, Tesla (by Fayruz), is an unplaced half-sister to 7 winners including the Grade 1 Santa Anita Derby winner the Deputy. (Mrs Wendy Jarrett & J S Moore). *"I thought he was going to be early but he's grown a bit on me. He has the makings of a very nice horse, I'll start him at six furlongs around July/August time but he'll end up getting seven or a mile. Goes nicely and will win his races".*

1134. NAKAKANDE ★★
b.f. Bungle Inthejungle – Tallawalla (Oratorio). April 4. €1,000Y. Goffs Open. Not sold. Half-brother to the modest 2-y-o 5.5f winner Quick Skips Lad (by Lilbourne Lad). The dam, a moderate 1m winner at 3 yrs, is half-sister to one winner out of the placed Edetana (by Diesis), herself a half-sister to 4 winners. (Keiron Badger & J S Moore). *"She's already had a run when she was fifth at Bath. Although she didn't cost much her sire has had a good start to his career and I trained her sister who won for us a 2-y-o and she was a tough, hardy horse. I think she's got a little bit about her and she'll win races".* TRAINER'S BARGAIN BUY.

1135. UNNAMED ★★
gr.c. Alhebayeb – Cape Violet (Cape Cross). March 16. Third foal. £10,000Y. Goffs UK Doncaster Breeze Up. Not sold. The dam won four races in Belgium and Germany and is a half-sister to 3 winners. The second dam, Violet Ballerina (by Namid), a fair 7f (at 2 yrs) and 6f winner, is a half-sister to 3 winners including the very useful 2-y-o Group 2 6f Richmond Stakes winner Carizzo Creek. *"A good, strong colt, he goes really well, has*

good paces and will be running in May over five furlongs but will probably be better at six. He has the makings of a good horse and I think the sire will do well this year".

1136. UNNAMED ★★
b.g. Sayif – Pose (Acclamation). February 11. Third foal. 3,000Y. Tattersalls October Book 3. Not sold. The dam, a fair dual 6f winner, is a full or half-sister to 3 winners. The second dam, Lyca Ballerina (by Marju), a fair 7f winner at 3 yrs, is a half-sister to 7 winners. (The Moore The Merrier). *"A good stamp of a horse, he'll be a six/seven furlong 2-y-o from mid-season onwards. The dam won twice and there seems to be a lot of Acclamation about him".*

1137. UNNAMED ★★★
b.f. Sayif – Shohrah (Giant's Causeway). February 12. Half-sister to the quite useful 2-y-o 9f winner Shaayeq (by Dubawi), to the fair 2017 2-y-o 7f winner Wahoo (by Stimulation) and the fair 2-y-o 1m winner Bronte Flyer (by Nayef). The dam, a useful 2-y-o 6f winner, is a half-sister to 6 winners including the useful 7f winner and 1m Listed second Ma-Arif. The second dam, Taqreem (by Nashwan), was second four times over middle-distances and is a half-sister to the high class middle distance colt Ibn Bey, winner of 4 Group 1 events including the Irish St Leger and second in the Breeders' Cup Classic and to the very smart Group 1 Yorkshire Oaks winner Roseate Tern. *"The sire gets winners but he isn't popular but the mare has bred three winners from three and this filly is a fantastic mover. She's one for six/seven furlongs and might get a mile later on. Does everything nicely and will hopefully one of my nicer ones".*

1138. UNNAMED ★★★
ch.f. Dandy Man – Validate (Alhaarth). February 20. Seventh foal. £9,000Y. Goffs UK Doncaster Breeze Up. Not sold. Half-brother to the quite useful 2-y-o 5f winner Little Lion Man (by Kyllachy), to the quite useful dual 7f winner (including at 2 yrs) Personal Touch (by Pivotal), the quite useful dual 7f winner Carnival King (by Arcano), the modest 2m winner Kirkman (by Virtual) and the moderate dual sprint winner Bushwise (by Bushranger). The dam is an unraced half-sister to 4 winners including the fairly useful dual 6f winner

(including at 2 yrs) and Listed-placed Enact. The second dam, Constitute (by Gone West), a quite useful 1m winner, is a half-sister to 7 winners including the dual Listed winner and Group 3 10f Select Stakes second Battle Chant. *"A good little filly, she's strong, one for six furlongs and she goes along nicely. I hope to have her running fairly soon and I think she'll progress to be one of our nicest".*

HUGHIE MORRISON
1139. BARBEGAZI ★★★★
b.c. Swiss Spirit – Belle Des Airs (Dr Fong). April 14. Fifth foal. 31,000Y. Tattersalls October Book 3. H Morrison. Half-brother to the fair 2017 2-y-o 6f winner Airshow (by Showcasing), to the quite useful 6f (at 2 yrs) and dual 7f winner Scofflaw (by Foxwedge) and the quite useful 2-y-o 5.5f winner Air Of Mystery (by Sakhee's Secret). The dam, a quite useful 6f (at 2 yrs) and 7f winner, is a half-sister to 5 minor winners. The second dam, Belle Reine (by King Of Kings), is an unraced half-sister to 6 winners. (Mr M. Kerr-Dineen, Mr D. Fass, Viscount Trenchard). *"Quite forward-going, he's not a particularly robust horse but you'd hope he'd be out by midsummer if all went well. A nice athlete, he's a really easy-moving horse so he could be quite a fun 2-y-o".*

1140. CRASTER ★★★
b.c. Sea The Stars – Coquet (Sir Percy). February 22. Second foal. 85,000Y. Tattersalls October Book 1. Not sold. Half-brother to the quite useful 2017 2-y-o 1m winner Glencadam Master (by Mastercraftsman). The dam, a useful Listed 1m (at 2 yrs) and Listed 10f winner, was third in the Group 3 Newbury Arc Trial and is a half-sister to 2 winners. The second dam, One So Marvellous (by Nashwan), a fair 10f winner, is a sister to the Juddmonte International winner One So Wonderful (dam of the US Grade 2 winner Sun Boat) and a half-sister to 7 winners including Alnasr Alwasheek (Group 2 Dante Stakes) and Relatively Special (Group 3 Rockfel Stakes). (Lord Margadale, Mr A. Scott, Mr M. Kerr-Dineen). *"I doubt he'll be out before September, we had the dam who won a Listed at two and we could have run her in the summer but we waited and we'll do the same with him. A nice, typical Sea The Stars, he's not over-big at the moment but I suspect he'll grow a lot".*

1141. INDIAN VICEROY ★★★
b.c. Kodiac – Broadlands (Kheleyf). March 24. Third foal. 30,000Y. Tattersalls October Book 2. H Morrison. Half-brother to the minor 2017 French 2-y-o winner Castlewarden (by Henrythenavigator). The dam is an unraced half-sister to 4 winners including the useful Listed 14f winner and Group 3 14f Lillie Langtry Stakes third Twitch. The second dam, Blinking (by Marju), is an unraced sister to Viva Pataca, a winner of 18 races and nearly £6 million in prize money here and in Hong Kong from 6f (at 2 yrs) to 12f and a half-sister to 6 winners including the US dual Grade 1 winner Laughing. (Mr Simon Malcolm, Mr Harry & Mrs Julie Parkes). *"A forward-going colt that takes everything in his stride, he's growing a bit at the moment and hopefully he'll run in the summer. Last year I bought quite a few 2-y-o's where the pedigree had been upgraded with a winner after the catalogue was printed. This was one of them".* TRAINER'S BARGAIN BUY

1142. KORCHO ★★★
b.c. Toronado – Locharia (Wolfhound). April 10. Thirteenth foal. 50,000Y. Tattersalls October Book 1. Charlie Gordon-Watson. Half-brother to 8 winners including the fairly useful 2-y-o 5f winner and Group 3 6f second Seafront (by Foxwedge), the quite useful 6f to 9f and hurdles winner of 7 races Credit Swap (by Diktat), the quite useful 7f and 1m winner of 9 races Lochantanks (by Compton Place), the fair 5f winner Yanza (by Bahamian Bounty), the fair 2-y-o 6f winner Woodland Girl (by Kyllachy) and the fair 7f and 10f winner Lady Loch (by Dutch Art). The dam was a fairly useful 2-y-o 5f winner. The second dam, Lochbelle (by Robellino), a fair 10.2f winner, is a half-sister to the champion sprinter Lochsong and the Nunthorpe Stakes winner Lochangel. (Mr M. Kerr-Dineen, Mr M. Hughes & Mr W. Eason). *"Having looked a scopey type he's stopped growing now and he's looking mature, so I'm quite happy with him. He probably won't be out before midsummer but you never know he could be one of those that come very quickly. A nice sort, there's nothing flashy about him and he'll make a 2-y-o but not a 'cheap speed' type of 2-y-o".*

1143. MAJESTIC MAC ★★★
b.c. Cape Cross – Talent Spotter (Exceed And Excel). January 29. First foal. 40,000Y. Tattersalls October Book 2. H Morrison. The dam, a modest maiden, was placed fourth twice over 5f and 6f. The second dam, Sophie's Girl (by Bahamian Bounty), a quite useful 2-y-o dual 5f winner, is a sister to the Listed winner and Group 3 placed Paradise Isle and a half-sister to 8 winners. (Mr A. McAlpine). *"He's quite neat and it's a sharp family so I'd like to think he'll be out in late summer. Quite forward-going, he'll hopefully be out in July".*

1144. MUMS HOPE ★★★
gr.f. Lethal Force – Jadwiga (Pivotal). March 11. Fourth foal. 23,000Y. Tattersalls October Book 3. H Morrison. Half-sister to the fair 2017 2-y-o 7f winner Autumn Leaves (by Helmet) and to two minor winners in Italy by Royal Applause and Paco Boy. The dam is an unraced half-sister to 3 minor winners. The second dam, Queen Of Poland (by Halling), a very useful 2-y-o Listed 7f winner and second in the Group 2 1m May Hill Stakes, is a full or half-sister 8 winners. (Mr Martin Hughes). *"Lethal Force is quite a nice 'buyable' stallion and this is a nice, strong-looking filly. I haven't done anything with her yet because she's had a bit of a virus but she's fine now and I see her as a seven furlong type 2-y-o".*

1145. REQUITED ★★★★
b.c. Requinto – Joyfullness (Dixieland Band). April 28. Eleventh foal. 50,000Y. Tattersalls October Book 2. Sackville/Donald, H Morrison. Half-brother to 7 winners including the quite useful 2017 2-y-o Listed-placed 6f winner Academy House (by Kodiac), the Italian Listed-placed 2-y-o winner Flying Teapot (by King Charlemagne), the quite useful Irish 1m winner Song In My Heart (by Spartacus), the fair 7f winner of 6 races Khajaaly (by Kheleyf) and the fair 2-y-o 1m winner Sir Trevor (by Refuse To Bend). The dam is an unraced half-sister to 11 winners including the dam of the Group 2 Royal Lodge Stakes winner Mons. The second dam, Arewehavingfunyet (by Sham), won the Grade 1 Oak Leaf Stakes and is a half-sister to 6 winners. (Mr M. Kerr-Dineen, Mr W. Eason, Mr D. Malpas). *"Quite forward and mature, he's got speed and could be a May 2-y-o. He looks sharp, speedy and physically quite strong".*

1146. SANDYMAN ★★

ch.c. Footstepsinthesand – Quiz Mistress (Doyen). January 23. First foal. The dam, a useful 9.5f (at 2 yrs) and French triple Listed middle-distance winner, is a half-sister to 6 winners including the smart Group 3 11.5f Lingfield Derby Trial winner Saddler's Quest and the French Listed middle-distance winner Seren Hill. The second dam, Seren Quest (by Rainbow Quest), was a fairly useful 10f winner. (The Fairy Story Partnership). *"A lovely-looking, scopey horse, he's only just arrived and looks like a proper staying sort, so if he runs before the autumn I'd be amazed. He'll be a better 3-y-o and physically he's a lovely horse, but he's big and weak at the moment".*

1147. SPARGROVE ★★★

b.c. Cacique – Capriolla (In The Wings). February 14. Eighth foal. 70,000Y. Tattersalls October Book 2. Not sold. Half-brother to 5 winners including the Group 3 Henry II Stakes winner and Group 2 Prix Chaudenay second Vent De Force (by Hurricane Run), the Group 3 Prix de Barbeville winner and Group 2 second Marmelo (by Duke Of Marmalade), the quite useful 2-y-o 6f winner Valerius Maximus (by Spartacus) and the fair 2-y-o 1m winner Halling's Quest (by Halling). The dam, a modest 10f placed maiden, is a half-sister to 6 winners including the smart Group 3 11.5f Lingfield Derby Trial winner Saddler's Quest and the French Listed middle-distance winners Quiz Mistress and Seren Hill. The second dam, Seren Quest (by Rainbow Quest), was a fairly useful 10f winner. (Selwood Bloodstock & Mrs S Read). *"A lovely horse that came in about a month ago, he's very big but has a very nice character. He'll probably have a break now until May and we'll see him racing in the autumn".*

1148. TARTLETTE ★★★

b.f. Champs Elysees – Tottie (Fantastic Light). April 21. Fourth foal. Half-sister to the quite useful 2-y-o 7.5f winner Column (by Mount Nelson). The dam, a fairly useful Listed-placed 1m winner here and a US Grade 3 9f winner, is a half-sister to the fairly useful 1m (at 2 yrs) and 10f winner Mister Impatience. The second dam, Katy Nowaitee (by Komaite), a useful Listed 10f winner, is a half-sister to 3 winners. (J H Richmond-Watson). *"She's quite*

'together' for a Champs Elysees and I can't see why she wouldn't be running in August or September. The dam did well but not all of her offspring have. There's every chance she could win at two".

1149. TELECASTER ★★★

b.c. New Approach – Shirocco Star (Shirocco). February 9. Second foal. 180,000Y. Tattersalls October Book 1. Not sold. Half-brother to the 2017 1m and 9f placed 2-y-o Starcaster (by Dansili). The dam, a 2-y-o 1m winner, was second in the Oaks and the Irish Oaks. The second dam, Spectral Star (by Unfuwain), a fair 11.8f winner, is a half-sister to 8 winners including the Group 3 7f Tetrarch Stakes winner and Irish 2,000 Guineas second France. (Castle Down Racing). *"A lovely, big, strong colt and typical of the family, I'd be surprised if we see him before the autumn over a mile and he'll like a bit of dig in the ground. He came here with a bit of an excitable reputation but it's so far so good. He could be very nice in time and I'd like to think he'll make a lovely staying 3-y-o".*

1150. UNNAMED ★★★

b.c. Havana Gold – Jasmeno (Catcher In The Rye). April 28. Fourth foal. Half-brother to the quite useful 2017 2-y-o 7f winner Escape The City (by Cityscape) and to the fair 11f and 12f winner Pastoral Music (by Pastoral Pursuits). The dam, a modest 12f and 13f winner, is a half-sister to the useful 7f (at 2 yrs) and 1m winner and dual Group 3 placed Sagramor. The second dam, Jasmick (by Definite Article), a quite useful 10f and 14f winner, is a half-sister to 2 winners. (MNC Racing). *"A nice little horse that'll be racing in July. We had last year's 2-y-o out of the dam, Escape The City, who won in August".*

1151. UNNAMED ★★★

ch.f. Dutch Art – Strictly Lambada (Red Ransom). April 20. Fifth foal. 50,000Y. Tattersalls October Book 1. R Frisby. Half-sister to the useful Listed-placed 2-y-o 1m winner Last Tango Inparis (by Aqlaam), to the fair 12f winner Hawridge Flyer (by Sir Percy) and the fair dual 12f and hurdles winner Sleep Easy (by Rip Van Winkle). The dam, a fair 10f and 12f placed maiden, is a half-sister to 6 winners including the Listed 10f winner Marsh

Daisy. The second dam, Bella Lambada (by Lammtarra), a quite useful 10.4f winner, is a half-sister to 6 winners including the Group 2 10f Prince of Wales's Stakes and dual US Grade 2 winner Stagecraft and the Group 3 winner Mullins Bay and to the unraced dam of the triple Group 2 winner Caspar Netscher. (Sir Francis Brooke, Mr R Pilkington, Mr A Rogers). *"The type to make a late summer 2-y-o, a nice soft ground maiden in September should be fine for her. I think she was well-bought, it's a nice pedigree and we know the family well as we've won with a few of them. I'm sure she'll be a nice filly".*

WILLIAM MUIR

1152. JACK'S POINT ★★★★
b.c. Slade Power – Electra Star (Shamardal). February 25. Fourth foal. 120,000Y. Tattersalls October Book 1. Willie Muir. Half-brother to the quite useful 2-y-o dual 5f winner Starlight Mystery (by Iffraaj), to the fair dual 7f winner Electra Voice (by Poet's Voice) and the fair 7f (at 2 yrs) and 1m winner Native Soldier (by Sepoy). The dam, a fairly useful triple 1m winner, is a half-sister to 6 winners including the useful 2-y-o 5f and 7f winner Asia Winds and the useful 2-y-o dual 6f winner Fancy Lady. The second dam, Ascot Cyclone (by Rahy), a fairly useful 5.7f (at 2 yrs) and 7f winner, is a full or half-sister to 13 winners including the Group 1 7f Prix de la Salamandre second Bin Nashwan and the US Grade 2 winner Magellan. (C L A Edginton). *"I really like this horse, he's big, strong and shows ability already. He's growing a bit so I wouldn't be in a rush to get him out and on his page you'd say he'd want six furlongs, but he shows speed. The dam's first three foals have all won and I guarantee he will too; he's one of those that makes you want to get out of bed in the morning".*

1153. JUST HUBERT (IRE) ★★
b.c. Dunaden – La Tulipe (Authorized). January 25. First foal. 20,000Y. Tattersalls October Book 3. Not sold. The dam, a winner of 3 races at 3 and 4 yrs in France including over 1m 5f, is a half-sister to one winner. The second dam, Tulipe Royale (by Java Gold), a dual 2-y-o winner, was third in the Group 1 Prix Marcel Boussac and is a half-sister to 9 winners. (Foursome Thoroughbreds). *"A lovely individual we bought as a foal, we put him in Book 3 as a yearling where fortunately he wasn't so sold and now he's qualified for auction races. His owner bred Red Cadeaux who was only beaten by a pixel by this colt's sire Dunaden in the Melbourne Cup, so of course that race will be his long-term aim. He's a lovely big individual with loads of scope".*

1154. SO CLAIRE ★★★
br.f. Kyllachy – If So (Iffraaj). March 27. Second foal. 50,000Y. Tattersalls December. Not sold. The dam, a fair 6f winner of 4 races at 3 and 4 yrs, is a half-sister to 4 winners including the dual Group 1 sprint winner The Tin Man and the Group 2 and triple Group 3 sprint winner Deacon Blues. The second dam, Persario (by Bishop Of Cashel), a quite useful 6f and 7f winner, is a half-sister to 3 winners including the triple Group 3 winner and Group 1 Prix de la Foret third Warningford. (Foursome Thoroughbreds). *"A really nice filly out of a half-sister to The Tin Man. The dam's first foal Worthington was big and backward but I know they like him. This filly would have been in Book One but for a cut on a leg and if she'd gone there she'd have made 250,000. She shows me she's got everything but the family all take a little bit of time and I'm respectful of that, so she should be fast but not early; she'll still be a 2-y-o later on though".*

1155. SUNVISOR (IRE) ★★★
ch.c. Helmet – Island Sunset (Trans Island). February 1. Third foal. €14,000Y. Tattersalls Ireland September. Not sold. Half-brother to the fair 7f (at 2 yrs) to 8.5f winner of 3 races Sunnua (by Dark Angel). The dam, a fairly useful 7f (at 2 yrs) to 10f winner of 5 races, is a half-sister to 6 winners. The second dam, Islandagore (by Indian Ridge), a 3-y-o 7f winner in Ireland, was second in a Listed event over 9f on her only other start and is a half-sister to the 2-y-o Listed 6f winner Lady Of Kildare. (Muir Racing Partnership – Leicester). *"I really like him – he probably could have won the Brocklesby but he started to grow. On his page I don't think he should be an early 2-y-o but he shows natural talent. I've seen the dam's other two foals and I think this one is the best of them because he's got a bit more size. I've yet to press the button though".* TRAINER'S BARGAIN BUY

1156. UNNAMED ★★★
b.c. Nathaniel – Danehill Dreamer (Danehill). April 10. Eighth foal. 40,000Y. Tattersalls October Book 2. Willie Muir. Half-brother to the fair 2017 2-y-o 7f winner Fille De Reve (by Iffraaj), to the fairly useful 6f (at 2 yrs) and 7f winner Sulaalaat (by New Approach), the fairly useful 2-y-o 1m winner Madeed and the Qatar winner Khudoua (both by Nayef). The dam is an unraced half-sister to 8 winners including Compton Admiral (Group 1 Coral Eclipse Stakes), Summoner (Group 1 Queen Elizabeth II Stakes) and the dam of the multiple Group 1 winner The Fugue. The second dam, Sumoto (by Mtoto), a useful 6f (at 2 yrs) and 7f winner, is a half-sister to 5 winners. (O'Mulloy, Schwartz). *"I really like him, bought him from Watership Down Stud and he's the cheapest one out of the mare. He's got a great attitude, a great mind, moves well and he'll be a middle-distance horse next year. So he's a typical Nathaniel in that he'll take a bit of time and will want seven furlongs to start with in the second part of the season. Andre Fabre has the 4-y-o full-brother that cost 675,000 and was bought to win the Derby but that didn't happen. Maybe the cheapest one out of the mare will do that instead".*

1157. UNNAMED ★★★
b.c. Bated Breath – Effervesce (Galileo). February 19. Fourth foal. 45,000Y. Tattersalls December. Willie Muir. Half-brother to the 2-y-o Listed 7f winner Cristal Fizz (by Power) and to the fairly useful 2-y-o 6f winner Qeyaadah (by Acclamation). The dam, a fair 10f winner, is a half-sister to 4 winners including the dual Group 3 6f Greenlands Stakes and UAE Group 3 6f winner of 11 races (including at 2 yrs) Hitchens. The second dam, Royal Fizz (by Royal Academy), won once over 6.5f at 2 yrs in France and is a half-sister to 7 winners here and abroad including the £1.4m Hong Kong earner Floral Pegasus. (Muir Racing Partnership – St Cloud). *"He'll probably be my first 2-y-o to run, he shows ability and is just getting going now. He's just about the right size for a 2-y-o, he's big and strong and I like him. He's just started fast work and if he can take it we'll continue".*

1158. UNNAMED ★★
b.g. Mount Nelson – London Welsh (Cape Cross). March 5. Third foal. 14,000 foal. Tattersalls December. Not sold. Half-brother to the fairly useful 2-y-o Listed 6f winner of 3 races Wick Powell (by Sakhee's Secret). The dam ran once unplaced and is a half-sister to 4 minor winners. The second dam, Croeso Cariad (by Most Welcome), a very useful 2-y-o 5f and 7f Italian Listed winner, was second in the Group 2 1m Falmouth Stakes and is a half-sister to 6 winners including the Irish Listed winner and multiple Group 1 placed Mona Lisa. (Mr M. P. Graham). *"He was a big, backward home-bred, he came in and we broke him in, gelded him and now he's a lovely, big individual but he'll take time".*

1159.UNNAMED ★★
b.c. Lilbourne Lad – Ornellaia (Mujadil). March 20. Seventh foal. Half-brother to the fairly useful 1m (at 2 yrs) and 10.5f winner Black Schnapps, to the quite useful dual 10f winner Angrywhitepyjamas (both by Manduro), to the fairly useful 7.5f, 1m (both at 2 yrs) and 10f winner of 5 races Hi There, the modest 2-y-o 5f winner Slipstream Angel (both by Dark Angel) and the fair 2-y-o 5f winner Super Tuscan (by Fath). The dam, placed fourth once over 6f at 2 yrs, is a half-sister to 5 winners including the useful 2-y-o 6f and Listed 1m winner Henri Lebasque. The second dam, Almost A Lady (by Entitled), placed over 7f and 1m at 2 yrs, is a half-sister to 5 winners including the dual Group 2 winner Insatiable. *"A family we know well, he'll take time like they did. So we won't rush him and we'll keep him ticking along for now".*

JEREMY NOSEDA
1160. DEARLY BELOVED (USA)
b.f. Scat Daddy – Beloveda (Ghostzapper). March 16. Third foal. $1,000,000Y. Keeneland September. Kerri Radcliffe. The dam won 13 races in North America, was second in the Grade 3 Rampart Stakes and is a half-sister to the Grade 3 winner Golden Mystery. The second dam, Mysterious Angel (by Saint Ballado), won in the USA and is a half-sister to the English and French Group 3 winner Voyagers Quest.

1161. DURESS (USA)
b.c. Violence – Mattieandmorgan (Smart Strike). February 2. Fourth foal. $210,000Y.

Keeneland September. Marc Keller. Half-brother to a minor US 3-y-o winner by Giant's Causeway. The dam, placed at 4 yrs in the USA, is a half-sister to 4 stakes winners including the US Grade 1 winners Shakespeare and Perfect Shirl. The second dam, Lady Shirl (by That's A Nice), won the Grade 1 Flower Bowl Handicapand the Grade 2 E.P. Taylor Stakes.

1162. LOST IN ALASKA (USA)
b.c. Discreet Cat – Truly Blushed (Yes It's True). February 23. Fifth foal. $35,000Y. Fasig-Tipton Kentucky. Michael Roy. Brother to the fairly useful 7f (at 2 yrs) to 10f winner Abe Lincoln and half-brother to the US stakes-placed winner Truly Marie (by Hard Spun) and a minor US winner by Street Sense. The dam, a Canadian stakes winner at 2 yrs, is a half-sister to the minor stakes winner Fishin Frank. The second dam, Easytoblush (by Blushing John), was placed at 3 yrs.

1163. NO TROUBLE (IRE)
b.c. No Nay Never – Lady Babooshka (Cape Cross). March 2. First foal. 120,000Y. Tattersalls October Book 1. Norris/Huntington. The dam is an unraced half-sister to 5 winners including the UAE Grade 2 and Group 3 Select Stakes winner Alkaadhem. The second dam, Balalaika (by Sadler's Wells), a useful 4-y-o Listed 9f winner, is a sister to the high-class Group 2 10f Prince of Wales's Stakes and dual US Grade 2 winner Stagecraft and a half-sister to 5 winners including the Group 3 Strensall Stakes winner Mullins Bay.

1164. POET'S CORNER
b.c. Poet's Voice – Helter Helter (Seeking The Gold). February 27. Fifth foal. 30,000Y. Tattersalls October Book 2. Charlie Gordon-Watson. Half-brother to the fair 13f and 2m winner Trafalgar Rock (by Mount Nelson) and to a winner in Japan by Pivotal. The dam, a 12f winner of 3 races in France, is a half-sister to 6 winners including the US Grade 3 winner Beauty Parlor. The second dam, Moon Queen (by Sadler's Wells), won the Group 2 Prix de Royallieu and a US Grade 3 stakes and is a full or half-sister to 10 winners including the US Grade 2 winner Innuendo.

1165. SETENTA (IRE)
b.c. Canford Cliffs – Sentimental (Galileo). March 17. Fifth foal. The dam is an unraced half-sister to 5 winners including the French Listed winners Bermuda Rye and Bermuda Grass and the dam of the Group 2 Royal Lodge Stakes winner Foundation. The second dam, Alleluia Tree (by Royal Academy), a French 2-y-o winner, is a half-sister to 7 winners and to the unraced dam of the triple Group 1 winner Scorpion.

1166. UNNAMED
b.br.f. Scat Daddy – Auction (Mr Greeley). March 18. First foal. $800,000Y. Saratoga August. Kerri Radcliffe. The dam, a fairly useful winner of 3 races at 3 yrs over 7f and 1m and Listed-placed, is a half-sister to 2 winners. The second dam, Exhibit One (by Silver Hawk), a smart Italian Group 3 10f and 12f winner, was third in the Group1 Gran Premio di Milano and is a half-sister to 4 winners.

1167. UNNAMED
b.br.c. Union Rags – Caragh Queen (Hard Spun). April 4. Third foal. $130,000Y. Keeneland September. Michael Roy. The dam is an unraced half-sister to 7 winners including the Kentucky Derby winner Always Dreaming and the Grade 1 Spinaway Stakes winner Hot Dixie Chick. The second dam, Above Perfection (by In Excess), won the US Grade 3 Las Flores Handicap and is a half-sister to another US stakes winner.

1168. UNNAMED
b.c. War Front – Dynamic Feature (Rahy). March 30. Fifth foal. $1,100,000Y. Keeneland September. Kerri Radcliffe. Half-brother to the US Grade 2 Royal Heroine Stakes and triple Grade 3 winner and triple Grade 1 placed Parranda. The dam, a minor US dual winner at 3 yrs, is a half-sister to the US Grade 3 winner Sisterly Love. The second dam, Odylic (by Dixieland Band), unplaced in one start, is a sister to the US Grade 1 Metropolitan Handicap winner Dixie Brass and a half-sister to the Grade 2 winner Odyle.

1169. UNNAMED
b.f. Dansili – Instance (Invincible Spirit). April 5. Second foal. Half-sister to the 2017 2-y-o 6f winner, from two starts, Betty F (by

Frankel). The dam, a fairly useful 6f (including at 2 yrs) and 7f winner, is a half-sister to the Group 1 12f British Champions Fillies and Mares winner Seal Of Approval and the useful Listed 2m winner Gale Force. The second dam, Hannda (by Dr Devious), a winner over 10f in Ireland from 2 starts, is a half-sister to 5 winners including the Group 3 7.5f Concorde Stakes winner Hamairi and the Listed 6f winner Hanabad.

1170. UNNAMED
b.c. No Nay Never – Jessica Rocks (Fastnet Rock). April 14. First foal. €480,000Y. Arqana Deauville August. Kerri Radcliffe. The dam is an unraced half-sister to 4 winners including the Group 1 Prix Jean Prat winner and sire Havana Gold. The second dam, Jessica's Dream (by Desert Style), a very smart sprinter, won the Group 3 Ballyogan Stakes and the Group 3 Premio Omenoni and is a half-sister to the Listed winner and dual Group 1 placed Majors Cast.

1171. UNNAMED
ch.c. Scat Daddy – Miss Lamour (Mr Greeley). March 5. First foal. $950,000Y. Keeneland September. Kerri Radcliffe. The dam, a US stakes-placed winner at 2 and 3 yrs, is a half-sister to the winner and multiple Grade 3 placed Tejida. The second dam, Betique (by Storm Cat), won three US Grade 3 stakes events and is a half-sister to 4 winners including the dam of the Group 1 Eclipse Stakes winner Hawkbill.

1172. UNNAMED
b.c. Acclamation – Queen Of Power (Medicean). January 25. First foal. 100,000Y. Tattersalls October Book 2. Not sold. The dam, a fairly useful 7f winner, is a half-sister to 2 minor winners. The second dam, Danamight (by Danetime), a modest 1m (at 2 yrs) and 10f placed maiden, is a half-sister to 6 winners.

1173. UNNAMED
b.f. Dark Angel – Warshah (Shamardal). February 11. Third foal. 400,000Y. Tattersalls October Book 2. Blandford Bloodstock. Sister to the useful 2017 2-y-o dual 7f winner Al Hajar and to the fair 7f and 1m winner Volition. The dam is an unraced half-sister to 3 winners including Group 1 Prix de l'Opera and Group

2 1m May Hill Stakes winner Kinnaird (herself dam of the 2-y-o Group 2 Royal Lodge Stakes winner Berkshire) and the Group 3 Chester Vase winner Mickdaam. The second dam, Ribot's Guest (by Be My Guest), ran unplaced in Italy and is a half-sister to 6 winners.

1174. UNNAMED
b.c. Into Mischief – Yes Liz (Yes It's True). February 21. First foal. $500,000Y. Saratoga August. Kerri Radcliffe. The dam, a US 2-y-o winner and Listed-placed, is a half-sister to one winner. The second dam, For Scarlett (by Red Ransom), placed at 3 yrs, is a half-sister to 2 winners.

AIDAN O'BRIEN

1175. AFLOAT (IRE)
b.f. Galileo – Pikaboo (Pivotal). March 19. Sixth foal. Half-sister to the 2-y-o Group 2 6f Duchess Of Cambridge Stakes and Group 2 6f Lowther Stakes winner Lucky Kristale (by Lucky Story), to the fair 2-y-o 6f winner Mon Visage (by Ishiguru) and the fair dual 5f winner (including at 2 yrs) I See You (by Sleeping Indian). The dam is a placed half-sister to 7 winners including Arabian Gleam (Group 2 Challenge Stakes and Group 2 Park Stakes, twice). The second dam, Gleam Of Light (by Danehill), won over 7f and is a full or half-sister to 4 winners.

1176. ALBUQUERQUE (IRE)
b.c. Galileo – Looking Back (Stravinsky). February 11. Ninth foal. Brother to the Sussex Stakes, Queen Elizabeth II Stakes and Juddmonte International winner Rip Van Winkle, to the quite useful 9f and 10f winner Illusive and the fair 1m winner A Star Is Born and a half-brother to the Italian Group 3 1m winner Le Vie Infinite (by La Vie Dei Colori). The dam, an Italian winner of 2 races at 2 and 3 yrs and Listed-placed, is a half-sister to 2 winners. The second dam, Mustique Dream (by Don't Forget Me), a quite useful dual 1m winner, is a half-sister to 6 winners.

1177. ALL THE KING'S MEN (IRE)
b.br.c. No Nay Never – Chaibia (Peintre Celebre). January 21. €400,000Y. Arqana Deauville August. Mayfair/Peter & Ross Doyle/ M V Magnier. Half-brother to 4 winners including the minor French triple 9f winner

Primus Incitatus (by Mastercraftsman) and the French 2-y-o 9.5f winner Salorina (by A P Indy). The dam won the Group 3 Prix de Psyche and is a half-sister to one winner. The second dam, Mawhiba (by Dayjur), is an unplaced half-sister to 7 winners including the Derby winner Erhaab.

1178. BECHSTEIN (USA)
b.br.c. Scat Daddy – Dreams Of Fire (Dynaformer). April 23. Third foal. $500,000Y. Keeneland September. M V Magnier. Half-brother to the quite useful Irish 6f winner Solar Halo (by Harlan's Holiday). The dam, a fair 2-y-o 1m winner, is a half-sister to numerous winners including the Derby winner Kris Kin and the French winner and Group 2 10f placed Bravodino. The second dam, Angel In My Heart (by Rainbow Quest), dam won the Group 3 10f Prix de Psyche and was second in the Matriarch Stakes, the Yellow Ribbon Stakes, the Santa Ana Handicap (all Grade 1 events) and the Group 2 Prix de l'Opera. She is a half-sister to the Group 1 Prix de la Salamandre winner and useful sire Common Grounds.

1179. BLENHEIM PALACE (IRE)
ch.c. Galileo – Meow (Storm Cat). March 5. Fourth foal. Brother to the Churchill, a winner of four Group 1's – the Dewhurst Stakes, National Stakes (both at 2 yrs), 2,000 Guineas and Irish 2,000 Guineas and to the 2-y-o Group 1 6f Cheveley Park Stakes winner Clemmie. The dam, a useful 2-y-o Listed 5f winner, was second in the Group 2 5f Queen Mary Stakes and is a half-sister to 2 winners including the Group 3 9f winner Aloof. The second dam, Airwave (by Air Express), a champion 2-y-o filly and winner of 6 races including the Group 1 6f Cheveley Park Stakes, is a half-sister to 6 winners.

1180. CAPE OF GOOD HOPE (IRE)
b.c. Galileo – Hveger (Danehill). May 6. Eighth foal. 240,000Y. Tattersalls October Book 1. MV Magnier. Brother to the multiple Group 1 winner (Breeders Cup Turf, King George VI etc,) Highland Reel, to the Group 2 Great Voltigeur and Group 2 Hardwicke Stakes winner Idaho and half-brother to the Australian winner and dual Group 1 second Valdemoro (by Encosta De Lago). The dam

won once in Australia and was Group 1 placed and is a sister to the multiple Group 1 winner Elvstroem and a half-sister to the Group 1 Queen Anne Stakes and dual Australian Group 1 winner Hardasun. The second dam, Circles Of Gold (by Marscay), won the Group 1 AJC Oaks in Australia and is a half-sister to the Australian Group 2 winner Gold Wells.

1181. CARDINI
b.c. Magician – Perfect Step (Iffraaj). March 13. First foal. 210,000Y. Tattersalls October Book 2. Amanda Skiffington. The dam, a quite useful 7f winner, is a full or half-sister to 4 winners. The second dam, Spiritual Air (by Royal Applause), a fairly useful 2-y-o 6f winner, subsequently won at 4 yrs in the USA and is a half-sister to 3 winners including the multiple Group 2/Group 3 placed 2-y-o Mystical Land.

1182. CIRCUS MAXIMUS (IRE)
b.c. Galileo – Duntle (Danehill Dancer). February 8. First foal. The dam, winner of the Group 2 1m Duke Of Cambridge Stakes, was Group 1 placed three times and is a half-sister to 5 winners. The second dam, Lady Angola (by Lord At War), a quite useful 12f winner, is a half-sister to 6 winners including the dam of the US Grade 1 winner Honor In War.

1183. CORAL BEACH (IRE)
b.f. Zoffany – Abbasharjah (Tiger Hill). April 13. Sixth foal. 90,000Y. Tattersalls October Book 2. MV Magnier. Half-sister to the German 4-y-o 10f winner and Group 1 German Oaks third Amona (by Aussie Rules). The dam is an unraced sister to the German dual Group 3 winner Abbashiva and a half-sister to the German dual Group 3 winner Abbadjinn. The second dam, Abba (by Goofalik), won twice at 3 yrs in Germany and is a sister to the German Group 2 winner Acambaro and a half-sister to 9 winners.

1184. CYCLAMEN (USA)
b.f. War Front – Marvellous (Galileo). January 22. First foal. The dam, a Group 1 Irish 1,000 Guineas winner, is a sister to the 2017 2-y-o Group 1 Moyglare Stud Stakes and Group 1 Prix Jean-Luc Lagardere winner Happily, the National Stakes (at 2 yrs), 2,000 Guineas, Irish 2,000 Guineas and St James's Palace Stakes winner Gleneagles, the Australian Group

2 12f winner The Taj Mahal and the 2-y-o Group 3 7f CL & MF Weld Park Stakes winner Coolmore,. The second dam, You'resothrilling (by Storm Cat), winner of the Group 2 Cherry Hinton Stakes, is a sister to several winners and a half-sister to the multiple Group 1 winner Giant's Causeway.

1185. DUNKIRK HARBOUR (USA)

gr.c. Declaration Of War – Goodness Gray (Pulpit). May 1. First foal. $185,000Y. Keeneland September. M V Magnier. The dam was placed in the USA and is a half-sister to the US dual Grade 1 winner General Quarters and the Japanese Grade 2 A Shin Top. The second dam, Ecology (by Unbridled's Song), is an unplaced half-sister to a stakes winner.

1186. EMPIRE STATE (USA)

b.br.c. Scat Daddy – Love's Blush (Not For Love). April 24. Fourth foal. $275,000Y. Keeneland September. M V Magnier. Half-brother to a minor winner at 3 and 4 yrs in the USA by Giant's Causeway. The dam, a stakes winner of 5 races in the USA, is a half-sister to 3 minor winners. The second dam, Blushing Broad (by Broad Brush), a stakes-placed winner of 3 races in the USA, is a sister to the US Grade 3 winner Brushing Groom and a half-sister to 7 winners.

1187. FAIRYLAND (IRE)

b.f. Kodiac – Queenofthefairies (Pivotal). January 14. Fourth foal. 925,000Y. Tattersalls October Book 1. MV Magnier / Mayfair / Peter & Ross Doyle. Sister to the fairly useful 6f and 7f winner Atletico and half-sister to the Group 3 Irish 1,000 Guineas and Australian Group 2 7f winner Now Or Later (by Bushranger). The dam is an unraced half-sister to 5 winners including the multiple Group 1 winner Dream Ahead and the dual Listed winner Into The Dark. The second dam, Land Of Dreams (by Cadeaux Genereux), won the Group 2 5f Flying Childers Stakes and the Group 3 5f King George V Stakes and is a half-sister to 6 winners.

1188. FANTASY (IRE)

b.f. Invincible Spirit – Cassandra Go (Indian Ridge). April 19. Twelfth foal. 1,600,000Y. Tattersalls October Book 1. MV Magnier. Sister to the very useful Group 3 5f and Group 3 6f winner Tickled Pink and half-sister to 5

winners including the Irish 1,000 Guineas, Nassau Stakes and Sun Chariot Stakes winner Halfway To Heaven (by Pivotal and herself dam of the Group 1 winner Rhododendron), the Group 3 6f Summer Stakes winner Theann (by Rock Of Gibraltar), the fairly useful triple 1m winner Jayed Jidan (by Teofilo) and the fairly useful dual 5f winner Neverletme Go (by Green Desert). The dam won the Group 2 5f Kings Stand Stakes and is a half-sister to 8 winners including Verglas (Group 3 6f Coventry Stakes). The second dam, Rahaam (by Secreto), a fairly useful 7f winner, is a half-sister to 8 winners.

1189. FIRE FLY (IRE)

ch.f. Galileo – Massarra (Danehill). April 9. Sister to the 2017 Group 2 7f Superlative Stakes winner Gustav Klimt, to the 2-y-o Listed 6f winner Cuff, the 2-y-o Group 3 7f Silver Flash Stakes winner Wonderfully, the Irish 2-y-o 7f winner and Group 1 St James's Palace Stakes third Mars and the fairly useful 2-y-o 7f winner Toscanelli and half-sister to 3 winners including the 2-y-o Group 1 1m Gran Criterium winner Nayarra (by Cape Cross). The dam, a useful Listed 6f winner and second in the Group 2 Prix Robert Papin at 2 yrs, is a sister to one winner, closely related to the Group 1 6f Haydock Park Sprint Cup winner Invincible Spirit and a half-sister to the Group 3 winners Acts Of Grace and Sadian. The second dam, Rafha (by Kris), won the Group 1 10.5f Prix de Diane, the Group 3 Lingfield Oaks Trial and the Group 3 May Hill Stakes and is a half-sister to 9 winners.

1190. FLYING (IRE)

b.f. Galileo – Butterfly Cove (Storm Cat). February 14. Sister to the 2-y-o Group 1 1m Prix Marcel Boussac winner and 1,000 Guineas second Ballydoyle, to the Group 1 Moyglare Stud Stakes, Prix Marcel Boussac (both at 2 yrs), Irish 1,000 Guineas and Pretty Polly Stakes winner Misty For Me and the useful 7f (at 2 yrs) and Listed 9f winner and dual Group 3 placed Twirl. The dam is an unraced sister to the Irish 1,000 Guineas Trial winner Kamarinskaya and a half-sister to the champion 2-y-o colt Fasliyev. The second dam, Mr P's Princess (by Mr Prospector), is an unraced half-sister to the US Grade 1 winners Menifee and Desert Wine.

1191. FROSTY (IRE)
ch.f. Galileo – Laddies Poker Two (Choisir). May 1. Sister to the multiple Group 1 1m and 10f winner Winter. The dam, a useful triple 6f winner at 3 and 5 yrs, is a full or half-sister to 4 winners. The second dam, Break Of Day (by Favorite Trick), is an unraced half-sister to 5 winners including the Group 2 Gimcrack Stakes second Ma Yoram.

1192. GODDESS (IRE)
b.f. Galileo – Penchant (Kyllachy). January 16. Fifth foal. Half-sister to the Group 1 6.5f Prix Maurice de Gheest and Group 2 7f Lennox Stakes winner Garswood (by Dutch Art). The dam is an unraced half-sister to 5 winners including the Group 3 7f Nell Gwyn Stakes winner and dual Group 1 placed Infallible. The second dam, Irresistible (by Cadeaux Genereux), a fairly useful 5f (at 2 yrs) and Listed 6f winner, was Group 3 placed and is a half-sister to 2 winners.

1193. GOSSAMER WINGS (IRE)
b.br.f. Scat Daddy – Lavender Baby (Rubiano). May 14. Ninth foal. $500,000Y. Keeneland September. M V Magnier. Sister to the stakes winner Lavender Chrissie and half-sister to 5 winners including the US Grade 3 winner Baby J (by J Be K) and the US stakes winner and Grade 1 third Laureate Conductor (by Bernstein). The dam won 8 minor races in the USA from 4 to 6 yrs. The second dam, Mighty Milk (by Hero's Honor), won 5 minor races in the USA at 3 and 4 yrs and is a half-sister to 2 stakes winners.

1194. I REMEMBER YOU (IRE)
b.f. Australia – Remember You (Invincible Spirit). January 25. The dam, a fairly useful 2-y-o 6f winner, was third in the Group 3 6f Round Tower Stakes. The second dam, Miss Dela (by King's Best), a modest Irish 7f placed maiden, is a half-sister to 6 winners including the 2-y-o Group 3 7f winner and Group 1 placed Governor Brown and the Listed 1m (at 2 yrs) and Listed 10.4f winner Hataab.

1195. ISLE OF INNISFREE
b.c. Scat Daddy – Dream The Blues (Oasis Dream). January 21. Third foal. Brother to the 2017 2-y-o Group 1 6f Phoenix Stakes winner Sioux Nation. The dam, a 3-y-o 6f winner on

her only start, is a half-sister to numerous winners. The second dam, Catch The Blues (by Bluebird), a smart 5f to 7f winner of 3 races including the Group 3 5f Ballyogan Stakes, was third in the Group 1 Haydock Park Sprint Cup and is a half-sister to 6 winners.

1196. JAPAN (IRE)
b.c. Galileo – Shastye (Danehill). February 22. Ninth foal. 1,300,000Y. Tattersalls October Book 1. MV Magnier / Mayfair / Peter & Ross Doyle. Brother to the Group 2 10.5f Middleton Stakes and dual Listed winner and Group 1 Oaks second Secret Gesture and to the Group 3 International Stakes and Listed winner Sir Isaac Newton and half-brother to the Australian Listed winner Maurus (by Medicean) and the fair 10f winner Secret Sense (by Shamardal). The dam, a useful Listed-placed 12f and 13f winner, is a half-sister to 8 winners including Sagamix (Prix de l'Arc de Triomphe), Sagacity (Group 1 Criterium de Saint-Cloud) and the Group 2 Prix de Malleret winner Sage Et Jolie (dam of the Group 1 winner Sageburg). The second dam, Saganeca (by Sagace), won the Group 3 12.5f Prix de Royallieu.

1197. LAND FORCE (IRE)
b.c. No Nay Never – Theann (Rock Of Gibraltar). February 22. Seventh foal. €350,000Y. Goffs Orby. Magnier/Mayfair. Half-brother to 3 winners including the US Grade 1 Rodeo Drive Stakes and Grade 1 First Lady Stakes winner Photo Call and the modest Irish dual 12f winner Pincode (both by Galileo). The dam, winner of the Group 3 6f Summer Stakes, is a half-sister to 5 winners including the Irish 1,000 Guineas, Nassau Stakes and Sun Chariot Stakes winner and high class broodmare Halfway To Heaven. The second dam, Cassandra Go (by Indian Ridge), a very smart winner of the Group 2 5f Kings Stand Stakes, is a full or half-sister to 8 winners including the smart Group 3 6f Coventry Stakes winner and Irish 2,000 Guineas second Verglas.

1198. MONA LISA'S SMILE (USA)
b.br.f. War Front – Imagine (Sadler's Wells). April 27. Sister to the fairly useful 7f (at 2 yrs) and 1m winner General Macarthur and half-sister to numerous winners including the 2-y-o Group 1 7f Prix Jean Luc Lagardere winner

Horatio Nelson, the UAE Group 2 winner and Group 1 Eclipse Stakes third Viscount Nelson, the 2-y-o Group 2 7f Rockfel Stakes winner Kitty Matchem and the US Grade 3 winner Point Piper. The dam won the Irish 1,000 Guineas and the Epsom Oaks and is a half-sister to the top-class Generous. The second dam, Doff The Derby (by Master Derby), is an unraced half-sister to the Prix Ganay winner Trillion (herself dam of the outstanding racemare Triptych).

1199. MOUNT TABORA

b.c. Scat Daddy – Canterbury Lace (Danehill). February 6. Half-brother to the Group 1 1m Matron Stakes and Group 2 7f Lennox Stakes winner Chachamaidee, to the Group 3 7f Oak Tree Stakes winner J Wonder (both by Footstepsinthesand), the quite useful 12f to 14f winner Hassle (by Montjeu) and the fair 7f (at 2 yrs) and 1m winner of four races Maybe I Will (by Hawk Wing). The dam is an unraced sister to the Group 3 Gallinule Stakes winner and Irish Derby second Alexander Of Hales and to the 2-y-o 1m winner and Group 1 1m Criterium International second Chevalier and a half-sister to the 1,000 Guineas winner Virginia Waters. The second dam, Legend Maker (by Sadler's Wells), won the Group 3 10.5f Prix de Royaumont and is a half-sister to the Group 2 12f King Edward VII Stakes winner Amfortas.

1200. NEVER NO MORE (IRE)

ch.c. No Nay Never – Law Of The Jungle (Catcher In The Rye). March 11. Fourth foal. €300,000Y. Goffs Orby. Magnier /Mayfair / Doyle. The dam, a modest 9.5f placed maiden, is a half-sister to 5 winners including the dual Group 3 7f winner Eastern Appeal. The second dam, Haut Volee (by Top Ville), a German 2-y-o 6f and 1m winner, is a half-sister to 9 winners.

1201. NORWAY (IRE)

ch.c. Galileo – Love Me True (Kingmambo). April 18. Brother to the Epsom Derby winner Ruler Of The World and to the 2-y-o 1m winner and Group 1 Irish Derby third Giovanni Canaletto, closely related to the quite useful 2-y-o 7f winner So In Love With You (by Sadler's Wells) and half-brother to 3 winners including the multiple Group 1 10f to 12f winner Duke Of Marmalade (by Danehill).

The dam, an Irish 1m winner and third in the Group 3 Killavullan Stakes, is a half-sister to US Grade 2 winner Bite The Bullet and the Listed 10f winner Shuailaan. The second dam, Lassie's Lady (by Alydar), a stakes-placed winner in the USA, is a half-sister to 10 winners including the high-class sprinter Wolfhound.

1202. SAN ANDREAS (IRE)

b.c. Dark Angel – Last Bid (Vital Equine). February 28. Second foal. £250,000Y. Goffs UK Premier. Sackville/Donald. Brother to the fairly useful 2017 Listed-placed 2-y-o 5f winner Maggies Angel. The dam, a fairly useful Listed-placed 2-y-o triple 5f winner, is a half-sister to 4 minor winners. The second dam, Manderina (by Mind Games), is an unplaced half-sister to 5 winners.

1203. SERGEI PROKOFIEV (USA)

b.br.c. Scat Daddy – Orchard Beach (Tapit). February 5. First foal. $1,100,000Y. Keeneland September. MV Magnier. The dam was placed once at 3 yrs in Canada and is a half-sister to the US Grade 3 winner Necessary Evil. The second dam, Song And Danz (by Unbridled's Song), was unplaced in one start and is a half-sister to a stakes winner.

1204. SO PERFECT (USA)

b.br.f. Scat Daddy – Hopeoverexperience (Songandaprayer). February 1. Third foal. $400,000Y. Keeneland September. MV Magnier. Sister to the Japanese stakes-placed winner Scat Eddie. The dam, a minor US winner at 3 yrs, is a half-sister to the US Grade 2 and Grade 3 winner Cowtown Cat. The second dam, Tom's Cat (by Storm Cat), was a minor US 4-y-o winner.

1205. SYDNEY OPERA HOUSE (IRE)

ch.c. Australia – Sitara (Salse). March 28. Ninth foal. 525,000Y. Tattersalls October Book 1. M V Magnier /Mayfair /Peter & Ross Doyle. Closely related to the Group 1 2m, Melbourne Cup winner Rekindling, to the Group 3 12f Chester Vase winner and Irish Derby second Golden Sword, the fair triple 12f winner All Body And Soul (all by High Chaparral) and the quite useful 10f and 13f winner Harrison's Cave (by Galileo) and half-brother to the minor French 3-y-o winner Bitooh (by Diktat). The dam, a fair 12f winner, is a half-sister to 10 winners including the very useful Listed 12f winner Puce (dam of the Group 3 Lancashire Oaks winner Pongee) and the fairly useful 10.5f winner Shouk (dam of the Oaks winner Alexandrova and the Cheveley Park Stakes winner Magical Romance). The second dam, Souk (by Ahonoora), a fairly useful 7f winner, was Listed placed over 1m and is a half-sister to 3 winners.

1206. SYMPHONY ORCHESTRA (USA)

b.c. Scat Daddy – Bailzee (Grand Slam). April 4. Third foal. $300,000Y. Saratoga August. M V Magnier. The dam, a US stakes-placed winner, is a half-sister to 4 winners. The second dam, Golden Gale (by Summer Squall), won the US Grade 2 Beaumont Stakes and is a half-sister to 9 winners.

1207. TEN SOVEREIGNS (IRE)

b.c. No Nay Never – Seeking Solace (Exceed And Excel). March 28. Fourth foal. 200,000Y. Tattersalls October Book 2. Charlie Gordon-Watson. The dam, a French Listed-placed 10f winner, is a half-sister to 5 winners including the UAE Group 2 placed Flash Fire. The second dam, Flamelet (by Theatrical), an Irish 7.5f winner, was Group 3 placed and is a half-sister to 7 winners including the French 7f Listed winner Bezrin.

1208. THE IRISH ROVER (IRE)

b.c. No Nay Never – Shelley Beach (Danehill Dancer). January 14. Third foal. 150,000Y. Tattersalls October Book 1. MV Magnier / Mayfair / Peter & Ross Doyle. Closely related to the quite useful 2017 2-y-o 7f and 8.5f winner West Palm Beach (by Scat Daddy). The dam, a fair 6f and 7f placed 2-y-o, is a half-sister to 3 winners including the Australian dual Listed winner Skiddaw Peak. The second dam, River Flow (by Affirmed), is an unraced half-sister to 5 winners including the Group 1 placed King Sound and to the unraced dam of the French 2,000 Guineas and US Grade 1 winner Landseer.

1209. TRACING (IRE)

b.f. Galileo – Ishvana (Holy Roman Emperor). April 3. The dam, a very useful 5f (at 2 yrs) and Group 3 7f Jersey Stakes winner, is a half-sister to one winner. The second dam, Song Of The Sea (by Bering), placed fourth once over 12f, is a half-sister to 5 winners.

1210. USS MICHIGAN (USA)

gr.c. War Front – Photograph (Unbridled's Song). May 22. Brother to the French Group 3 9f winner of 7 races Green Dispatch and to the French 2-y-o 6.5f and 7.5f winner and 3-y-o Group 3 second General Patton. The dam is an unraced half-sister to several stakes winners here and abroad out of Black Speck (by Arch).

1211. VAN BEETHOVEN (USA)

b.br.c. Scat Daddy – My Sister Sandy (Montbrook). February 19. Second foal. The dam, a minor US 4-y-o winner, is a sister to the US stakes winner and Grade 3 third Exotic Bloom (herself dam of the US triple Grade 1 winner Stopchargingmaria). The second dam, Melegant (by Kris S), a minor US 3-y-o winner, is a half-sister to 3 winners.

1212. WESTERN AUSTRALIAN (IRE)

ch.c. Australia – What A Treasure (Cadeaux Genereux). April 6. Sixth foal. 260,000Y. Tattersalls October Book 1. MV Magnier/ Mayfair/ Peter & Ross Doyle. Half-brother to the fairly useful 7f, 1m (both at 2 yrs) and Listed 10f winner Hoarding (by Elusive Quality) and to the fair 7f winner Strada Facendo (by Street Cry). The dam, a fair dual 7f winner, is a sister to the Group 1 Prix de la Foret winner Toylsome and a half-sister to 6 winners including Coral Mist (Group 3 Firth of Clyde Stakes). The second dam, Treasure Trove (by The Minstrel), is a placed half-sister to the US Graded stakes winners Dance Parade and Ocean Queen.

1213. ZAGITOVA

b.f. Camelot – Cherry Hinton (Green Desert). February 27. Closely related to the Group 1 Irish Oaks winner Bracelet and to the 2-y-o Group 2 7f Rockfel Stakes winner Wading (both by Montjeu) and half-sister to the fairly useful Listed-placed 5f winner Simply A Star (by Giant's Causeway). The dam, a useful maiden, was second in the Group 3 10f Blue Wind Stakes and third in a Listed event over 9f in Ireland. She is closely related to the outstanding colt Sea The Stars (winner of the 2,000 Guineas, Derby, Prix de l'Arc de Triomphe etc) and a half-sister to 6 winners including the top-class dual Derby and King George VI winner and sire Galileo, and the dual Group 1 winner Black Sam Bellamy. The second dam, Urban Sea (by Miswaki), won the Group 1 Prix de l'Arc de Triomphe, is closely related to the 2,000 Guineas winner King's Best and a half-sister to numerous winners.

1214. UNNAMED

b.f. Galileo – Again (Danehill Dancer). February 28. Fourth foal. Sister to the 2017 2-y-o 1m winner and Group 2 1m Beresford Stakes second Delano Roosevelt and to the 2-y-o Listed 7.5f winner Indian Maharaja. The dam won the 2-y-o Group 1 Moyglare Stud Stakes and the Irish 1,000 Guineas and is closely related to 2 winners including the fairly useful 9f winner and Group 3 12f third Arkadina. The second dam, Cumbres (by Kahyasi), is an unraced half-sister to Montjeu.

1215. UNNAMED

b.c. Galileo – Aleagueoftheirown (Danehill Dancer). May 7. Sixth foal. Brother to 4 winners including the Group 1 Falmouth Stakes, Group 1 Sun Chariot and Group 1 Matron Stakes winner Alice Springs, the fairly useful 12f winner and Group 2 12f Ribblesdale Stakes third Criteria and the useful Irish 2-y-o 7f winner and Group 3 Tyros Stakes third Kingston Jamaica. The dam, a useful Irish 9f winner, was Listed-placed and is a half-sister to 2 winners. The second dam, Golden Coral (by Slew O'Gold), is an unplaced sister to the Group 1 Coronation Stakes winner Golden Opinion and a half-sister to 7 winners.

1216. UNNAMED

b.f. Galileo – Beauty Is Truth (Pivotal). May 6. Sister to the Group 1 1m Matron Stakes and Group 1 British Champions Fillies' and Mares Stakes winner Hydrangea, to the 7f (at 2 yrs), Group 3 10f and Australian Group 2 12.5f winner The United States and the useful 2-y-o 9f winner Buonarotti and half-brother to the triple Group 3 6f winner and dual Group 1 placed Fire Lily (by Dansili). The dam, winner of the Group 2 5f Prix de Gros-Chene, is a half-sister to numerous winners including the French Listed 9f winner Glorious Sight. The second dam, Zelda (by Caerleon), a French 6.5f winner, is closely related to the dam of the French 1,000 Guineas winner Valentine Waltz and a half-sister to the dual Group 1 winner Last Tycoon and the Group winners Astronef and The Perfect Life.

1217. UNNAMED

b.f. Galileo – Lillie Langtry (Danehill Dancer). May 27. Fifth foal. Sister to the top-class multiple Group 1 winner at 2 and 3 yrs Minding and to the Group 3 1m Irish 1,000 Guineas Trial winner Kissed By Angels. The dam, a very smart winner of 5 races including the Group 1 1m Coronation Stakes and Group 1 1m Matron Stakes, is a half-sister to 2 winners including the very useful 3-y-o Listed 1m winner and 2-y-o Group 3 6f Anglesey Stakes third Count Of Limonade. The second dam, Hoity Toity (Darshaan), is an unraced half-sister to 5 winners.

1218. UNNAMED

b.c. Australia – Peeping Fawn (Danehill). February 29. Fourth foal. Half-brother to the 2017 2-y-o Listed 7f winner and triple Group 1 placed September and the useful 12.5f winner Wisconsin (both by Deep Impact) and to the useful 2-y-o 6f winner and Group 2 Coventry Stakes third Sir John Hawkins (by Henrythenavigator). The dam won the Pretty Polly Stakes, Irish Oaks, Nassau Stakes and Yorkshire Oaks (all Group 1 events) and is a half-sister to the very smart 2-y-o Group 1 Criterium International winner Thewayyouare. The second dam, Maryinsky (by Sadler's Wells), a 2-y-o 7f winner, was second in the Group 1 Fillies Mile and is a half-sister to the Grade 2 9f Demoiselle Stakes winner Better Than Honour, the smart Group 2 1m Beresford Stakes winner Turnberry Isle and the Group 2 1m Prix d'Astarte winner Smolensk.

1219. UNNAMED

b.c. Dubawi – Sky Lantern (Red Clubs). January 19. First foal. 2,000,000Y. Tattersalls October Book 1. MV Magnier/ Mayfair/ Peter & Ross Doyle. The dam won 6 races including 4 Group 1 events (1,000 Guineas, Coronation Stakes, Moyglare Stud Stakes and Sun Chariot Stakes) and is a half-sister to 9 winners including the 2-y-o Group 3 6f Round Tower Stakes winner Arctic and the Group 3 Queen's Vase winner Shanty Star. The second dam, Shawanni (by Shareef Dancer), a useful 2-y-o 7f winner, is a half-sister to the Group 3 winners Blatant and Songlark.

JOSEPH O'BRIEN

1220. BUCKHURST (IRE)

b.c. Australia – Artful (Green Desert). March 7. Sixth foal. 70,000Y. Tattersalls October Book 1. Joseph O'Brien. Half-brother to the 2-y-o Listed 6f winner Duplicity (by Cadeaux Genereux). The dam, a minor 3-y-o winner in France, is a half-sister to 4 winners including the Irish Group 3 C L Weld Park Stakes winner Chintz (dam of the dual Group 1 winner The Gurkha). The second dam, Gold Dodger (by Slew O'Gold), a Listed 10f winner of 2 races in France, is a half-sister to 11 winners including the Prix de l'Arc de Triomphe winner Solemia and the Group winners Prospect Wells and Prospect Park.

1221. CLARENDON (IRE)

b.c. Australia – Lady Gloria (Diktat). February 21. Second living foal. €65,000Y. Goffs Orby. Lloyd Williams. Half-brother to the modest 4-y-o triple 1m winner Buzz Lightyere (by Royal Applause). The dam was a smart winner of 6 races at 3 and 4 yrs including the Group 3 8.5f Princess Elizabeth Stakes and the Group 3 10f Select Stakes and is a half-sister to 4 winners. The second dam, Tara Moon (by Pivotal), was unraced.

1222. DELGANY (IRE)

b.c. Camelot – Tadris (Red Ransom). April 9. Ninth foal. 77,000Y. Tattersalls October Book 2. Joseph O'Brien. Half-brother to the useful 2-y-o 1m winner and Group 3 1m Craven Stakes third Yaseer (by Dansili), to the quite useful 7f and 1m winner Elmraan (by Shamardal) and the minor French 1m winner Thakerah (by New Approach). The dam, a dual Listed 1m winner, is a half-sister to the US dual Grade 3 winner Mustanfar and to the dam of the Group 2 Temple Stakes winner Hot Streak. The second dam, Manwah (by Lyphard), was placed four times at 3 yrs and is a three-parts sister to Unfuwain and a half-sister to Nashwan and Nayef.

1223. DOM CARLOS (IRE)

b.c. Gale Force Ten – Fancy Feathers (Redback). March 27. Sixth foal. £45,000Y. Goffs UK Premier (Doncaster). Joseph O'Brien. Half-brother to the fair 2017 2-y-o dual 5f winner Elnadim Star (by Elnadim), to the fairly useful 6f winner of 5 races Red Pike (by Kheleyf) and the fair 2-y-o 5f winner Just Past Andover (by Amadeus Wolf). The dam, a fair 1m winner, is a half-sister to 6 winners. The second dam, Idle Fancy (by Mujtahid), a fair Irish 3-y-o 1m winner, is a half-sister to 7 winners including the dam of the Lancashire Oaks winner Ela Athena.

1224. EAGLE SONG (IRE)

b.c. No Nay Never – Al Ihsas (Danehill). May 2. Twelfth foal. €240,000Y. Goffs Orby. Stephen Hillen. Half-brother to 4 winners including the minor US winner of 4 races El Medwar (by Elusive Quality) and the quite useful 1m and hurdles winner Jinsha Lake (by Galileo). The dam, a useful 3-y-o dual 7f winner and second in the Group 3 5f Queen Mary Stakes, is a full or half-sister to 8 winners including Windsor Palace (Group 3 Mooresbridge Stakes) and the Listed winner Anna Karenina. The second dam, Simaat (by Mr Prospector), a fair 1m winner, is a half-sister to 2 winners.

1225. GOOD ANSWER

b.c. Iffraaj – Cool Question (Polar Falcon). April 21. Ninth living foal. 70,000Y. Tattersalls October Book 3. Tom Malone. Half-brother to 5 winners including the very smart Group 1 6f Golden Shaheen winner of 11 races Krypton Factor (by Kyllachy). the quite useful dual 5f winner (including at 2 yrs) Fairfield Princess (by Inchinor), the quite useful 2-y-o dual 6f winner Haven't A Clue (by Red Ransom) and the modest 1m winner North Pole (by Compton Place). The dam, a useful 2-y-o 5f and Listed 6f winner, is a half-sister to 5 winners. The second dam, Quiz Time (Efisio), a fairly useful 2-y-o 5f winner, was second in the Listed St Hugh's Stakes and is a half-sister to 6 winners including the Group 3 Premio Dormello winner Brockette.

1226. JUPITER ROAD

b.c. Charm Spirit – Thankful (Diesis). April 17. Sixth foal. 210,000Y. Tattersalls October Book 2. MV Magnier. Half-brother to the useful 2-y-o Listed-placed 7f winner Morning Post (by Acclamation), to the fair 7f and 1m winner Always Thankful and the fair 7f winner Munfarrid (both by Showcasing). The dam is an unplaced half-sister to the Listed-placed winner Jo'burg. The second dam, La Martina (by Atraf), a useful 7f winner at 2 yrs in Italy and subsequently a dual stakes winner in the USA, is a half-sister to 5 winners.

1227. LARMOUR (IRE)
b.c. Dark Angel – C'Est Ma Souer (Oratorio). February 14. First foal. €65,000Y. Tattersalls Ireland September. Joseph O'Brien. The dam, a modest dual 7f winner, is a half-sister to 4 winners including the useful 2-y-o 6f winner and Listed-placed Emperor Hadrian. The second dam, Gilded Edge (by Cadeaux Genereux), a fairly useful 2-y-o 6f winner, is a half-sister to 4 winners including the champion Swedish 2-y-o 5f to 1m winner King Quantas and to the unplaced dam of the high-class sprinter Dutch Art.

1228. MILLSWYN (IRE)
b.c. Camelot – Condition (Deploy). April 24. Ninth foal. €77,000Y. Goffs Orby. Lloyd Williams. Half-brother to Gardens Of Babylon (by Camelot) placed third over 1m on his only start at 2 yrs in 2017, to the French Listed 1m winner Dreamt (by Oasis Dream) and the French 10f winner and Listed-placed Homepage (by Dansili). The dam, a Listed-placed 11f winner, is a half-sister to 3 winners including the French Listed and US stakes winner Night Chapter. The second dam, Context (by Zafonic), placed five times in France at around 1m, is a half-sister to 4 winners including the US Grade 2 winner Bon Point.

1229. NO NEEDS NEVER (IRE)
br.c. No Nay Never – Opera Fan (Cape Cross). March 15. First foal. €65,000Y. Goffs Orby. Joseph O'Brien. The dam, a fair 10f and 12f winner, is a half-sister to 4 winners including the Group 2 Prix de Sandringham winner Volta and the French dual Group 3 winner and Group 1 placed Calvados Blues. The second dam, Persian Belle (by Machiavellian), is an unraced sister to the US Grade 2 1m winner Beautyandthebeast and a half-sister to 8 winners including the German 2-y-o Group 3 8.5f winner Neatico.

1230. OZONE (IRE)
b.c. Camelot – Moore's Melody (Marju). March 2. Seventh foal. 90,000Y. Tattersalls October Book 2. Joseph O'Brien. Half-brother to the very useful 2-y-o Group 3 7f Solario

Stakes and 3-y-o Listed 1m winner Talwar, to the modest 2-y-o 5f winner Men United (both by Acclamation) and the French 6f winner Dark Orbit (by Dark Angel). The dam won twice over 1m at 3 and 4 yrs in France and is a sister to the Irish Listed winner Bruges and a half-sister to 2 winners. The second dam, Liege (by Night Shift), is an unraced half-sister to 2 winners including the dam of the multiple Group 1 winner Moonlight Cloud.

1231. PARISIAN EXPRESS (IRE)
b.c. Zoffany – Desert Darling (Green Desert). April 30. Twelfth living foal. €55,000Y. Goffs Orby. Joseph O'Brien. Half-brother to 5 minor winners in Australia and New Zealand by Zabeel (3), Fusaichi Pegasus and Show A Heart including the dam of the Australian Group 1 winner Humidor. The dam, a modest 5f placed 2-y-o, is a half-sister to 2 winners including the dam of the New Zealand Group 2 winner Lafleur and to the placed dam of the German and Italian Group 1 winner Morshdi. The second dam, Habibti (by Habitat), an outstanding sprinter and winner of three Group 1 events, is a half-sister to 3 winners and to the unplaced Eight Carat (the dam of five Group 1 winners in Australia and New Zealand.

1232. PASLEY (IRE)
b.c. Camelot – Lesson In Life (Duke Of Marmalade). April 5. First foal. €85,000Y. Goffs Orby. Lloyd Williams. The dam, a moderate 11f placed maiden, is a half-sister to 6 winners including the Group 3 6f Ballyogan Stakes winner and Group 1 second Lesson In Humility, the Group 3 Oh So Sharp Stakes winner Poet's Vanity and Listed winner Boastful. The second dam, Vanity (by Thatching), a fair 5f and 6f placed maiden, is a half-sister to 6 winners including the Listed winner Ffestiniog (herself the dam of 3 stakes winners).

1233. RECOVERY ROAD (IRE)
br.c. No Nay Never – Hannahs Turn (Dubai Destination). April 16. First foal. £62,000Y. Goffs UK Premier (Doncaster). M V Magnier. The dam, a fair 5f and 6f winner of 7 races, is out of the minor German 2-y-o winner Fontaine House (by Pyramus), herself a half-sister to 2 winners.

1234. REST BAY (IRE)

ch.c. Dandy Man – Why Now (Dansili). March 25. Eighth foal. €46,000Y. Tattersalls Ireland September. Donnacha O'Brien. Half-brother to the quite useful 5f and 6f winner of 5 races (including at 2 yrs) Here Now And Why, to the fair 2-y-o winner Woodland Mill (both by Pastoral Pursuits), the quite useful 2-y-o 6f winner What About You (by Statue Of Liberty), the fair 5f (including at 2 yrs) and 6f winner of 4 races Rosealee (by Zebedee) and the fair 5f to 1m winner Al Freej (by Iffraaj). The dam, a fair 5f and 6f winner, is a half-sister to 4 winners. The second dam, Questionable (by Rainbow Quest), is an unraced sister to the Group 3 15f Prix Berteux winner Ecologist and a half-sister to 7 winners including the Group 1 placed Greensmith and Infrasonic.

1235. STAYCATION (IRE)

b.c. Acclamation – Staceymac (Elnadim). April 20. Ninth foal. 42,000Y. Tattersalls October Book 2. Nick Bradley. Closely related to the smart dual Listed 5f winner and Group 2 Queen Mary Stakes second Easton Angel (by Dark Angel). The dam, a modest 5f winner at 3 yrs, is a half-sister to 4 winners including the Listed 7f winner Kalahari Gold. The second dam, Neat Shilling (by Bob Back), is an unraced full or half-sister to 7 winners including the US Grade 3 winner Riddlesdown.

1236. UNNAMED

ch.c. Sea The Moon – Kensington Gardens (Oasis Dream). March 22. Second foal. 48,000Y. Tattersalls October Book 2. Stamina Turf. Half-brother to the quite useful 2017 2-y-o 7f winner Royal Parks (by Bated Breath). The dam, a moderate 9f placed maiden, is a sister to the very smart Group 2 10f Prix Guillaume d'Ornano, Group 2 York Stakes and dual Group 3 winner Sri Putra and a half-sister to 3 winners. The second dam, Wendylina (by In The Wings), is an unraced half-sister to 9 winners including the Group 1 10.5f Prix de Diane winner Caerlina.

1237. UNNAMED

b.c. Frankel – L'Ancresse (Darshaan). April 9. Eleventh foal. Closely related to the useful Irish dual Listed 12f winner Chamonix (by Galileo) and half-brother to the minor French 12f winner Allez Y (by Rip Van Winkle) and two jumps winners by Sadler's Wells and Rip Van Winkle. The dam, a 7f (at 2 yrs) and Listed 12f winner, was second in the Irish Oaks and the Breeders Cup Filly & Mare Turf and is a sister to the Group 1 10f Prix Saint-Alary winner Cerulean Sky (dam of the Group 2 winner Honolulu) and a half-sister to the Group 1 Irish Oaks winner Moonstone (dam of the Derby second US Army Ranger). The second dam, Solo de Lune (by Law Society), a French 11f winner, is a half-sister to the Group/Grade 2 winners Truly A Dream and Wareed.

1238. UNNAMED

b.c. Fast Company – Mawu (Pivotal). February 23. First foal. 50,000Y. Tattersalls October Book 2. Joseph O'Brien. The dam is an unplaced half-sister to a minor winner in France. The second dam, Fortunate Isles (by Seeking The Gold), a minor 2-y-o winner in France, is a half-sister to 5 winners.

1239. UNNAMED

ch.c. Iffraaj –Miss You Too (Montjeu). February 10. Second foal. 95,000Y. Tattersalls October Book 2. Joseph O'Brien. Half-brother to the 2017 1m placed 2-y-o (from two starts) Te Koop (by Mastercraftsman). The dam, a Listed 10f winner and third in the Group 1 10f Criterium de Saint-Cloud, is a half-sister to the useful Irish 2-y-o 7f winner and Group 3 7f Killavullan Stakes second Vitruvian Man. The second dam, Portrait Of A Lady (by Peintre Celebre), a fairly useful Listed-placed 12f winner of 3 races, is a half-sister to 4 winners including the dam of the dual Group 1 winner Covert Love.

1240. UNNAMED

b.f. Holy Roman Emperor – Moonstone Magic (Trade Fair). January 25. Second foal. €55,000Y. Goffs Orby. Joseph O'Brien. Half-sister to the fair 7f winner Moonwise (by Exceed And Excel). The dam was a very useful Group 3 7f Fred Darling Stakes winner of 3 races. The second dam, Woodcock Moon (by Kyllachy), is an unraced half-sister to 10 winners including the very useful 6f and 7f (at 2 yrs) and subsequent US stakes winner Steelaninch.

JAMIE OSBORNE

1241. BRAINS ★★★

b.c. Dandy Man – Pure Jazz (Marju). April

1. Fifth foal. €21,000Y. Tattersalls Ireland September. F Barberini. Half-brother to the fair 1m winner Pure Action (by Haatef) and to the fair 7f winner Granny May (by Holy Roman Emperor). The dam, placed over 1m on her only start, is a half-sister to 3 winners including the Group 3 7f C L Weld Park Stakes and Group 3 7f Athasi Stakes winner Jazz Princess. The second dam, Jazz Up (by Cadeaux Genereux), is an unraced half-sister to 5 winners including the dual Italian Listed winner Mister Cavern. (The Judges). *"A lovely horse, he's not totally typical of the sire because he has a bit more scope than most of them. For that reason he's not going to happen in the first half of the year but he has a lot of quality and we like him".*

1242. ETOILE FILANTE ★★★
b.f. So You Think – Alpha Lupi (Rahy). March 12. Seventh foal. 58,000Y. Tattersalls October Book 1. Not sold. Half-sister to the 2017 2-y-o Listed 6f winner and Group 3 Albany Stakes second Alpha Centauri (by Mastercraftsman), to the useful 2-y-o Listed 7f winner and Group 2 Royal Lodge Stakes second Tenth Star (by Dansili) and the French 7f winner Elitist (by Danehill Dancer). The dam is an unraced half-sister to 3 winners including the 2-y-o Group 3 5.5f Prix d'Arenburg winner Moon Driver and to the placed dam of the Group 3 winners Autocratic and Evasive. The second dam, East Of The Moon (by Private Account), won the French 1,000 Guineas, the Prix de Diane and the Prix Jacques le Marois and is a half-sister to the top class miler and sire Kingmambo and to the smart Miesque's Son. (Flaxman Stables Ireland Ltd and Partner). *"I know the stallion has been a failure in the northern hemisphere but I really like this filly. She's got a lovely pedigree, she's strong, a good mover and looks like a 2-y-o. If we can forgive the sire she's got a chance".*

1243. JERSEY WONDER (IRE) ★★★
ch.c. Zoffany – Magena (Kingmambo). February 14. Third foal. 40,000Y. Tattersalls October Book 2. F Barberini. Half-brother to the quite useful 9.5f and 11f winner Bush House and to the fair 2-y-o 7f winner Poplar Close (both by Canford Close). The dam is an unraced half-sister to 8 minor winners here and abroad. The second dam, Vingt Et Une (by Sadler's Wells), a minor French 3-y-o winner, is

a sister to the Group 1 10.5f Prix Lupin and US Grade 2 1m winner Johann Quatz and a half-sister to Hernando, winner of the Group 1 Prix du Jockey Club and the Group 1 Prix Lupin. *"He's done well; he was a slightly plain looking yearling that's turned into a very good-looking 2-y-o and a good mover. He hasn't galloped yet but he could probably cope with it now so it won't be long before I kick on a bit with him".*

1244. LOVING LIFE (IRE) ★★★
b.f. Society Rock – Edelfa (Fasliyev). March 27. Fifth foal. €24,000Y. Tattersalls Ireland. F Barberini. Half-sister to the fairly useful 6f (including at 2 yrs) and 7f winner of 4 races Stamp Hill (by Zoffany), to the fair 7f to 8.5f winner of 5 races Italian Beauty (by Thewayyouare) and a winner in Italy by Aussie Rules. The dam won four minor races in Italy and is a half-sister to 7 winners. The second dam, Daziyra (by Doyoun), is an unplaced half-sister to 4 winners. (Bashir, Deerman, Ridout). *"She's done well since we bought her, the Society Rock's weren't easy to buy last autumn and she was a relatively cheap one. A good mover and a sharp-looking filly, she should be racing in the first couple of months of the season".*

1245. RIVIERA CLAIRE ★★
b.f. Showcasing – Seldemosa (Selkirk). May 13. Sixth foal. 16,000Y. Tattersalls October Book 3. F Barberini. Half-sister to 4 winners including the quite useful 6f (at 2 yrs) and 10f winner Lucky Henry (by Lucky Story), the quite useful dual 1m winner Imperial State (by Holy Roman Emperor) and the modest 6f to 1m winner of 6 races Lady Bayside (by Ishiguro). The dam, a modest 8.5f winner, is a half-sister to 4 winners including the very useful 7f winner of 4 races here and in the UAE Sirocco Breeze. The second dam, Baldemosa (by Lead On Time), won over 1m in France at 3 yrs and is a half-sister to 4 winners including the Group 1 5.5f Prix Robert Papin winner Balbonella (herself dam of the top-class sprinter Anabaa and the French 1,000 Guineas winner Always Loyal). (Mr & Mrs I Barratt). *"She's done a fair bit of growing and she was a late foal so probably won't be as early as I would have liked. We like the stallion and she's a lovely mover so she has a chance and hopefully won't be too backward".*

1246. USANECOLT (IRE) ★★★
b.c. Olympic Glory – Never Busy (Gone West).
March 25. Fourth foal. £40,000Y. Goffs UK
Premier (Doncaster). F Barberini. Half-brother
to a minor winner in France and the USA
by Giant's Causeway. The dam is a placed
half-sister to 5 winners including three
French Listed winners. The second dam, Pas
De Reponse (by Danzig), won the Group 1
Cheveley Park Stakes and is a half-sister to the
Group 1 French 2,000 Guineas winner Green
Tune. (Homecroft Wealth Racing). *"It's hard to
know what the first-season sire Olympic Glory
2-y-o's are going to be but I like this horse, he's
done very well since the sale and grown quite
a lot. A strong, good-looking horse and he'll be
a 2-y-o".*

1247. UNNAMED ★★★
b.c. Sir Prancealot – Balamiyda (Ashkalani).
March 21. Tenth foal. 10,000Y. Tattersalls
October Book 3. F Barberini. Half-brother
to 5 winners including the Irish 2-y-o 1m
and subsequent Hong Kong winner Pearl
Music (by Oratorio), the Italian winner of 4
races from 2 to 4 yrs and dual Listed-placed
Escalada (by American Post) and the minor
French dual winner (including at 2 yrs) Hidden
Magic (by Bering). The dam is an unraced half-
sister to 6 winners including Balakheri (Group
2 10f King Edward VII Stakes) and Baliyana
(Group 3 Irish 1,000 Gns Trial). The second
dam, Balanka (by Alzao), a French Listed
winner and third in the Group 2 9.2f Prix de
l'Opera, is a half-sister to 7 winners. *"I thought
he was relatively cheap, he's strong and goes
nicely. Could be one of our earliest 2-y-o's".*

1248. UNNAMED ★★★
b.f. Power – Break Of Day (Favorite Trick).
March 23. Eighth foal. Half-sister to 6 winners
including the 2017 2-y-o 7f winner on her
only start Lush Life (by Mastercraftsman), the
useful triple 6f winner at 3 and 5 yrs Laddies
Poker Two, the quite useful triple 6f winner at
2 to 4 yrs Chooseday (both by Choisir) and the
quite useful 1m winner One Good Emperor
(by Antonius Pius) and the fair 2-y-o dual 6f
winner Rock Ace (by Verglas). The dam is an
unraced half-sister to 5 winners including the
Group 2 Gimcrack Stakes second Ma Yoram.
The second dam, Quelle Affaire (by Riverman),
was placed three times at 2 yrs in France and

is a sister to the Irish Group 3 winner Rami
and a half-sister to the French Group 3 winner
Crack Regiment. (Mrs P Shanahan). *"A half-
sister to Lush Life who we like for this year that
won her only start for us at the back-end as a
2-y-o. This filly is a more likely 2-y-o because
she's a different type. She's stronger and more
forward-looking than her half-sister, so I'd
hope she'll be out in the first half of the year. I
haven't galloped her yet but she looks OK".*

1249. UNNAMED ★★★
ch.c. No Nay Never – Brigids Cross (Sadler's
Wells). January 25. Seventh foal. €75,000Y.
Goffs Orby. F Barberini. Half-sister to the
useful 8.5f (at 2 yrs) and Listed 10f winner
Weareninety (by Thewayyouare) and to
the quite useful dual 6f winner Lady Brigid
(by Holy Roman Emperor). The dam is an
unraced sister to the Group 1 7f Moyglare
Stud Stakes winner Sequoyah (the dam of
Henrythenavigator) and to the 2-y-o Group 1
Fillies' Mile winner Listen and a half-sister to
the Listed winner Oyster Catcher. The second
dam, Brigid (by Irish River), a minor French 1m
winner, is a sister to the French Listed winner
Or Vision (dam of the Group/Grade 1 winners
Dolphin Street, Insight and Saffron Walden)
and a half-sister to 5 winners. (Mr Michael
Buckley). *"Quite a big colt but he's very strong-
looking and a good mover. Hopefully he's one
for midsummer, there are good reports on the
sire and this horse has a good brain on him".*

1250. UNNAMED ★★★
b.c. Requinto – Cadescia (Cadeaux Genereux).
March 31. Fifth foal. £25,000Y. Goffs UK
Premier. F Barberini. Half-brother to a minor
winner in Italy by Excellent Art and to a
hurdles winner by Casamento. The dam is an
unraced half-sister to 5 winners. The second
dam, Pescia (by Darshaan), a winner over 10f
and 12f in France, was Group 3 placed and is
a half-sister to 4 winners. *"I know the stallion
isn't fashionable but this is a very good-
looking colt and a lovely mover. He seems very
straightforward and we'll be breezing him
shortly, so he'll be one of the earlier ones".*

1251. UNNAMED ★★★
b.c. Dream Ahead – Daganya (Danehill
Dancer). March 3. Ninth foal. £35,000Y. Goffs
UK Premier (Doncaster). F Barberini. Half-

brother to the fairly useful 7f to 10.5f winner of 8 races Akasaka (by King's Best), to the dual 12f winner Cape Of Good Grace (by Cape Cross), the 5f and 6f winner Kernoff (by Excellent Art) – all fairly useful, the fair 6f (at 2 yrs) and 5f winner Dancing Years (by Iffraaj), the fair dual 5f winner Jashma (by Power) and the modest dual 6f winner Chasca (by Namid). The dam, a Listed 6f event in Ireland, was second in the Group 2 5f Flying Five. She is a sister to the Listed 5f winner Snaefell and a half-sister to 4 winners. The second dam, Sovereign Grace (by Standaan), won over 5f in Ireland and is a half-sister 9 winners. (Ian Barratt, Adam Signy, Ben Spiers). *"Very strong, he's done very well over the winter and I really like him. He's about to start breezing and has gone the right way since the sale".*

1252. UNNAMED ★★
b.f. Camacho – Dancing Lauren (Oratorio). April 11. Fourth foal. £16,000Y. Tattersalls Ireland Ascot. F Barberini. The dam is an unraced half-sister to 6 winners including the 2-y-o Group 2 Superlative Stakes second Birdman and the 2-y-o Group 3 placed A Mind Of Her own. The second dam, Gilded Vanity (by Indian Ridge), an Irish 5f winner, is a sister to the Irish 2,000 Guineas second Fa-Eq and a half-sister to 5 winners. (Five Grand Fillies Partnership). *"Very strong, she could be one of the earlier 2-y-o's and has started doing little breezes. She's as wide as she's tall and she'll come early enough".*

1253. UNNAMED ★★
b.f. Dream Ahead – Dartrix (Dutch Art). February 2. First foal. £18,000Y. Goffs UK Silver. F Barberini. The dam, a modest 5f and 6f winner of 3 races at 4 yrs, is a half-sister to the Listed-placed winner of 10 races Spinatrix. The second dam, Shrink (by Mind Games), a modest triple 5f winner at 3 and 4 yrs, is a half-sister to 6 winners. (Five Grand Fillies Partnership). *"She's sharp enough and we've had a bit of luck with the stallion. Has the chance of being an early 2-y-o".*

1254. UNNAMED ★★★
gr.c. Kendargent – Desca (Cadeaux Genereux). March 16. Seventh foal. €32,000Y. Goffs Orby. F Barberini. The dam won 2 minor races at 3 yrs in Germany and is a half-sister to 10

winners including the Group 2 German 1,000 Guineas winner Diacada and the German Group 3 winner Desidera. The second dam, Diasprina (by Aspros), a champion German 2-y-o filly, is a half-sister to 6 winners. (Ian Barratt, Adam Signy, Ben Spiers). *"He's got quite a nice pedigree and we like the stallion; he's gone very well, is about to start breezing and he's a strong 2-y-o type".*

1255. UNNAMED ★★★★
b.f. War Command – Highindi (Montjeu). April 6. Seventh foal. €40,000Y. Goffs Orby. G Troeller. Half-sister to the quite useful triple 10f winner Windsor Beach (by Starspangledbanner), to the fair 5f (at 2 yrs) to 7f winner of 3 races Victorious Secret (by Holy Roman Emperor) and the modest Irish 10f winner Salacious Sally (by Excellent Art). The dam ran once unplaced and is a half-sister to the Grade 2 La Prevoyante Handicap winner and Group 1 10f Prix Saint-Alary third Arvada and to the Group 3 7f Craven Stakes winner Adagio. The second dam, Lalindi (by Cadeaux Genereux), a fair middle-distance winner of 7 races, is a half-sister to 5 winners including the dam of the Group 1 winners Summoner and Compton Admiral. *"A beautiful filly and a lovely mover, she's very strong and doesn't get tired. I really like her, she's got a bit of scope so I'm not going to be getting her ready too soon but she's one of my favourites".*

1256. UNNAMED ★★★
ch.c. Mastercraftsman – High Praise (Quest For Fame). April 11. Ninth foal. €48,000Y. Goffs Orby. Not sold. Half-brother to 5 winners including the useful 11f winner and Listed-placed Sight Unseen (by Sadler's Wells), the fairly useful 10f winner Eagles Peak (by Galileo), the quite useful triple 12f winner Grandiloquent (by Rail Link) and the quite useful 12f winner Critical Acclaim (by Peintre Celebre). The dam, winner of the Group 2 Prix de Malleret, is a half-sister to 7 winners including the top-class Group 1 1m Queen Elizabeth II Stakes and Group 1 9.3f Prix d'Ispahan winner Observatory. The second dam, Stellaria (by Roberto), won from 5f to 8.5f including the Listed 6f Rose Bowl Stakes and is a half-sister to 8 winners. (T Hyde and Partner). *"He's done well, typical of the sire in that he's slightly plain but he's a lovely mover.*

More likely to be a 3-y-o type but there's plenty about him".

1257. UNNAMED ★★★
b.c. Lope De Vega – Liberating (Iffraaj). January 29. First foal. 60,000Y. Tattersalls October Book 1. Not sold. The dam, a fairly useful 2-y-o 5f winner, was Listed-placed twice and is a half-sister to 5 winners including the dam of the Group 3 winners Eastern Impact and Miss Katie Mae. The second dam, Ros The Boss (by Danehill), a quite useful 7f and 1m winner, is a half-sister to 9 winners including the 2-y-o Listed 9f winner and Group 1 second Yehudi. (Airlie Stud and Partner). *"A sharp colt, he's not overly-big but forward-looking for a Lope De Vega. The dam was very quick and this colt has a speedy look to him as well, so we could get him going reasonably early".*

1258. UNNAMED ★★★
b.f. Camelot – Lily Of Kenmare (Exceed And Excel). March 31. Second foal. €35,000Y. Tattersalls Ireland September. F Barberini. The dam, a fair 7f and 1m winner, is a half-sister to 4 winners including the useful Irish 5f (at 2 yrs) and Listed 6f winner and Group 3 placed Croisultan. The second dam, Zoudie (by Ezzoud), a fair 10f winner, is a half-sister to 7 winners including the dual Group 3 winner Redback. *"She's unusual in that although the Camelots are tending to take a bit of time she looks quite sharp. Maybe she's just confusing me at the moment, but she's a beautiful mover and I'll kick on. She looks like a filly that might come in the first half of the season, so maybe the damsire Exceed And Excel is influencing that".*

1259. UNNAMED ★★★
b.c. Declaration Of War – Memories For Us (Street Cry). March 29. Seventh foal. €50,000Y. Goffs Orby. F Barberini. Half-brother to two minor 2-y-o winners in the USA by Hard Spun and Perfect Soul. The dam is an unraced half-sister to four stakes winners including the dual US Grade 1 winner Winter Memories and the US Grade 3 winner La Cloche. The second dam, Memories Of Silver (by Silver Hawk), won the Grade 1 Beverly D Stakes and the Grade 1 Queen Elizabeth II Challenge Cup Stakes and is a half-sister to 8 winners.

(Ian Barratt, Adam Signy, Ben Spiers). *"He's a big colt but a beautiful mover and is probably going to take a bit of time. A quality horse that has the look of a good horse about him, so it's fingers crossed that he will be"*

1260. UNNAMED ★★
b.c. Dream Ahead – Nurture (Bachelor Duke). February 20. Fifth foal. €22,000Y. Tattersalls Ireland September. F Barberini. The dam, a fairly useful Listed-placed 10f winner, is a half-sister to 3 winners. The second dam, Silesian (by Singspiel), is an unraced half-sister to the US stakes winner and Grade 2 placed Sol Mi Fa. (Helen Allenson). *"A big, strong horse that's done really well since the sale. He doesn't seem to tire which is a good sign and although he's big he'll probably be a first half of the season 2-y-o".* TRAINER'S BARGAIN BUY

1261. UNNAMED ★★★
b.c. Kyllachy – Pious (Bishop Of Cashel). April 6. Thirteenth foal. 100,000Y. Tattersalls October Book 2. John Ferguson. Brother to 3 winners including the Group 2 Sandown Mile and Group 2 Joel Stakes winner Penitent and the 2-y-o Group 2 Mill Reef Stakes winner Supplicant and half-brother to 8 winners including the quite useful 5f winner of 10 races Solemn, the quite useful 7f winners Blithe (at 2 yrs) and Anoint and the fair 5.5f to 7f winner of 7 races Divine Call (all by Pivotal). The dam, a fair dual 6f winner at 2 and 3 yrs, is a half-sister to 5 winners. The second dam, La Cabrilla (by Carwhite), a 2-y-o 5f and 6f winner and third in the Group 3 Princess Margaret Stakes, is a half-sister to 6 winners including the Group 1 Nunthorpe Stakes winner Ya Malak. (Mr Michael Buckley). *"He'll be a 2-y-o, most of the family has done better with time but he's very straightforward, nice and solid. The cross has worked before and I'd be hopeful of him being a nice 2-y-o for the second half of the season".*

1262. UNNAMED ★★★
ch.f. No Nay Never – Sliabh Na Mban (Sadler's Wells). January 7. Second foal. The dam is an unraced sister to the jumps winner Chesapeake and a half-sister to 4 winners including the 1,000 Guineas, Oaks and US Grade 1 Flower Bowl Invitational winner Kazzia (herself the dam of three stakes winners

including the Group 1 Dubai Sheema Classic winner Eastern Anthem) and the German Listed winner Kimbajar. The second dam, Khoruna (by Lagunas), won 2 minor races at 2 and 4 yrs in Germany and is a half-sister to one winner. *"She came in a bit later than some of the others so she's playing catch-up a little bit, but like the other No Nay Never 2-y-o we have she appears to have a good brain and she's very strong".*

1263. UNNAMED ★★★
b.c. Lope De Vega – Sound Of Guns (Acclamation). April 2. First foal. €50,000Y. Goffs Orby. F Barberini. The dam, a very useful 2-y-o 6f winner, was third in the Group 2 5f Flying Childers Stakes and is a half-sister to 2 winners. The second dam, Eastern Lily (by Eastern Echo), a minor stakes-placed winner of 3 races in the USA, is a half-sister to 10 winners. (Mr Michael Buckley). *"A raw, slightly plain-headed, old fashioned looking Lope De Vega but a great mover. The dam was quite quick and I think a lot of these Lope De Vega's do work at shorter trips even though he was a French Derby winner. A nice, second half of the season type 2-y-o".*

1264. UNNAMED ★★★
b.f. Australia – Teddy Bears Picnic (Oasis Dream). April 26. Seventh foal. €60,000Y. Goffs Orby. F Barberini. Half-sister to the fairly useful 2-y-o 6f and 7f winner and Group 3 Somerville Tattersall Stakes third Nezar (by Mastercraftsman), to the quite useful Irish 1m winner Ottilie and a minor 10f winner abroad (both by Hurricane Run). The dam is an unraced half-sister to 5 winners. The second dam, Jackie's Opera (by Indian Ridge), is an unraced half-sister to 5 winners including the dual French Listed winner Arabian King. *"A sweet filly, she's done very well and certainly has the look of a 2-y-o so I'll be getting on with her. It's hard to know what an Australia is, because it's his first season and he was a Derby winner of course".*

1265. UNNAMED ★★★★
b.c. Sea The Stars – Wizz Kid (Whipper). April 27. Third foal. 155,000Y. Tattersalls October Book 1. F Barberini. The dam, winner of the Group 1 5f Prix de l'Abbaye and the Group 2 5f Prix du Gros-Chene (twice), is a half-sister to

the Listed 10f winner Mustaheel. The second dam, Lidanski (Soviet Star), a fairly useful Irish 7f winner, was Listed-placed and is a half-sister to 7 winners including the Listed winner Yaa Wayl. (Mr Michael Buckley and Ballylinch Stud). *"He has an unusual pedigree, by an Arc winner out of an Abbaye winner. He's definitely more Wizz Kid than Sea The Stars, he's not over-big but a real quality horse and he's about to start breezing because he looks very mature. An out-and-out 2-y-o and we'll be kicking on with him".*

JOHN OXX

1266. ACED IT (IRE) ★★★★
b.c. Lope De Vega – Farranjordan (Galileo). March 29. Fourth foal. Half-brother to the quite useful Irish 6f (at 2 yrs) and 7f winner Red Marvel (by Invincible Spirit). The dam is an unraced half-sister to 4 winners including the useful Listed 1m (at 2 yrs) and Listed 10f winner and Group 3 placed Coquet. The dam, a fair 10f winner, is a sister to the Group 1 10.4f Juddmonte International Stakes winner One So Wonderful (herself dam of the US Grade 2 winner Sun Boat) and a half-sister to 7 winners including the Group 2 Dante Stakes and Group 3 Craven Stakes winner Alnasr Alwasheek and the Group 3 Rockfel Stakes winner Relatively Special. *"A nice horse that hasn't been here too long, he's very good-looking, big and strong. His half-brother Red Marvel won as a 2-y-o but he was by Invincible Spirit who is a stronger influence for precocity than Lope De Vega. This colt is probably one for the autumn but he's a particularly good looker and a good mover with a nice pedigree".*

1267. AZOPHI ★★★
b.f. Sea The Stars – Beta (Selkirk). April 5. Eighth foal. Closely related to the French dual Listed-placed 10f winner Bedale (by Cape Cross). The dam, a French 2-y-o Listed 5f winner, is a half-sister to 6 winners including the Prix de l'Arc de Triomphe winner Bago, to the Group 3 1m Prix Thomas Bryon winner Maxios and the French 2-y-o 6f and 7f winner Million Wishes. The second dam, Moonlight's Box (by Nureyev), is an unraced half-sister to the Group 1 Prix Marcel Boussac winner Denebola and to the Group 3 Prix de Cabourg winner Loving Kindness. *"She's going to take a bit of time of course, but she's a good-looking*

filly, correct and a good mover. Quite a heavy, blocky filly, she could be nice in the autumn".

1268. BASALAH ★★
b.f. Afleet Alex – Circleofinfluence (Eurosilver). January 26. Second foal. €42,000Y. Goffs Orby. MAS. The dam, a minor US 2-y-o winner, is a half-sister to 9 winners including the Grade 1 Hopeful Stakes winner Dublin. The second dam, Classy Mirage (by Storm Bird), won the Grade 1 Ballerina Stakes and four Grade 2 events and is a half-sister to 4 winners including the dual Grade 1 winner Missy's Mirage. *"Quite a nice filly, she's OK and whatever she's capable of we should see it at two".*

1269. CLOCKERS CORNER ★★★
ch.c. No Nay Never – Starlight Night (Distant View). April 19. Ninth foal. €115,000Y. Goffs Orby. Sackville/Donald. Half-brother to 4 winners including the Irish 2-y-o 6f winner and Group 3 Irish 1,000 Guineas Trial third Divine Night (by Danehill), the quite useful 13f and hurdles winner Hallmark (by Montjeu) and the fair Irish 11f winner Lost Generation (by Giant's Causeway). The dam is a placed half-sister to 9 winners including the dual US Grade 1 winner Senure. The second dam, Diese (by Diesis), won the Group 3 Prix Corrida and is a half-sister to 13 winners including the champion 2-y-o Xaar. *"A nice, well-grown, good moving, good tempered horse. He wouldn't be real early because he's quite a biggish horse. You'd expect the sire to get 2-y-o's so hopefully this colt will debut in the summer and we like him. He'll probably start at six furlongs but you only get a proper feel for them when they've started working and he hasn't yet".*

1270. MONTY'S MIRACLE ★★★
b.f. Shamardal – Monty's Girl (High Chaparral). March 28. Half-sister to the Listed 13f winner Naughty Or Nice (by Fastnet Rock), to the fairly useful 11f to 14f winner and Group 3 12f second Dark Crusader (by Cape Cross) and the quite useful 12f and 13f winner Cailini Alainn (by Danehill Dancer). The dam, a minor Irish 13f winner, is a full or half-sister to 7 winners including the US Grade 1 Gulfstream Park Breeders Cup Handicap and Group 2 King Edward VII Stakes winner Subtle Power.

The second dam, Mosaique Bleue (by Shirley Heights), is an unraced half-sister to the Prix Royal-Oak winner Mersey and to the 10f Prix Saint-Alary winner Muncie. *"She's just arrived recently, I've had two of her siblings and the family aren't early horses, but the people who broke her at home think she's a 2-y-o type. She might have ability, she's a nice-looking filly and she should appear later on all right and could make a 2-y-o too. A very good mover and a strong filly, she's medium-sized and lengthy; you'd like her".*

1271. NOVA AQUILAE ★★★
b.f. Sea The Stars – Irish History (Dubawi). March 30. Third foal. The dam, a useful 8.5f winner, was third in the Group 1 Coronation Stakes and is a half-sister to the Group 2 1m and Group 3 1m and 9f winner Echo Of Light, the useful 10f winner and Group 2 12f Ribblesdale Stakes second Flame Of Gibraltar and the smart dual 12f Listed winner Akarem. The second dam, Spirit Of Tara (by Sadler's Wells), a 12f winner and second in the Group 2 Blandford Stakes, is a sister to the multiple Group 1 winner Salsabil and a half-sister to the St James's Palace Stakes winner Marju. *"She's a medium-sized, well-made, quality filly and a good mover. She'll run at two because she's not really backward but you wouldn't rush her".*

1272. O'CAROLAN ★★
b.c. Sea The Stars – History Note (Azamour). March 7. Second foal. The dam, a very useful Irish 2-y-o 7f winner, was third in the Group 3 1,000 Guineas Trial and is a sister to 2 winners including the fairly useful dual 1m winner Stepwise and a half-sister to 2 winners. The second dam, Cadence (by Cadeaux Genereux), was a quite useful Irish 9f winner. *"A backward colt, he's a fine looking horse with a good temperament and the second biggest 2-y-o I have. He's a good-moving colt but he'll take a bit of time to fill his frame".*

1273. PENLIGHT ★★
b.f. Shamardal – Porto Roca (Barathea). May 1. Half-sister to 7 winners including the Group 1 10f Dubai World Cup and dual Group 2 12f winner Monterosso, the fair 7f and 8.5f winner Pietrafiore (both by Dubawi), the fairly useful 1m (at 2 yrs) and 12f winner Expert Fighter (by Dubai Destination), the fair 2-y-o 1m

winner Heat Of The Day (by Raven's Pass) and the fair 9f winner Fossola (by Elusive Quality). The dam, an Australian Group 1 7.5f winner, is a half-sister to the Australian Group 1 10f winner Bluebird the Word. *"Quite a big filly, she's growing a lot at the moment so she'll be a back-end 2-y-o. A nice filly, I like her, she's very strong and well-made but growing a lot".*

1274. SCHERZANDO ★★★★
b.c. Shamardal – Sea Chanter (War Chant). March 11. Sixth foal. Half-brother to the quite useful 9f and 10f winner Outre Mer (by Raven's Pass), to the US 9.5f winner Ocean Telegraph (by Street Cry) and the French 10f winner Seafire (by Lonhro). The dam was a US 2-y-o Group 3 1m and Listed 1m winner out of the US Grade 1 second Smooth Charmer (by Easy Goer). *"A nice colt, quite sharp-looking and although I don't have very early 2-y-o's he'd be one of the earlier ones. He's well put-together, a good mover and a 2-y-o type to look at, so we'll aim at getting him out in mid-season".*

1275. SNOW OCEAN ★★★
b.c. Exceed And Excel – Callistan (Galileo). April 6. First foal. €130,000Y. Goffs Orby. Sackville/Donald (private sale). The dam, a fair 12f winner, is a half-sister to 3 winners. The second dam, Alabastrine (by Green Desert), placed over 7f at 2 yrs, is a half-sister to 8 winners including the Nassau Stakes and Sun Chariot Stakes winner Last Second (dam of the French 2,000 Guineas winner Aussie Rules) and the dams of the Group 1 winners Alborada, Albanova, Allegretto, Yesterday and Quarter Moon. *"A very nice colt and a super mover, he had a setback and he's grown a lot so he's missed a few months. A big, long-striding horse that may need seven furlongs plus this season, he's one for later in the year but he's certainly a nice horse and hopefully he can do something by the end of the season".*

1276. SOFTLY STRONG ★★★★
b.f. Sea The Stars – Society Hostess (Seeking The Gold). February 4. Fifth foal. Half-sister to the useful Listed-placed 6f winner Sailors Swan (by Henrythenavigator). The dam, a US Grade 3 7f and German Listed winner, is a half-sister to several winners. The second dam, Touch Of Truth (by Storm Cat), a minor

US winner of 2 races at 4 yrs, is a half-sister to 8 winners including the US Grade 1 winner Twilight Agenda and the dams of the Group/Grade 1 winners Refuse To Bend, Media Puzzle and Go And Go. *"A nice filly, she's strongly made and moves well. The dam had speed and this filly might make a 2-y-o – I wouldn't rule it out".*

1277. UNNAMED ★★
b.f. Galileo – Catch The Moon (Peintre Celebre). May 9. Eighth foal. 350,000Y. Tattersalls October Book 1. BBA (Ire). Half-sister to 6 winners including the promising 2017 Irish 2-y-o 1m winner The King (by Mastercraftsman), the very useful Group 3 6f Bengough Stakes winner Lightning Moon (by Shamardal), the useful Irish 2-y-o Listed 6f winner Song Of My Heart (by Footstepsinthesand), the quite useful 6f and 7f winner Orbit The Moon (by Oratorio) and the 2-y-o 6f winners Gift From Heaven (by Excellent Art) and Catskill Mountain (by One Cool Cat). The dam, a minor French 3-y-o 9f winner, is a half-sister to one other minor winner. The second dam, Sensitivity (by Blushing John), a Listed winner in France and second in the Group 3 Prix Chloe, is a half-sister to 7 winners including the US Grade 3 winner Luftikus. *"An expensive Galileo filly for later in the year, she was a late foal and I haven't got her here yet".*

1278. UNNAMED ★★★★
b.c. Shamardal – Crinoline (Street Cry). April 8. Fourth foal. Half-brother to the fairly useful 2-y-o 7f winner Quality Time (by Exceed And Excel). The dam is an unraced half-sister to the Group 1 Moyglare Stud Stakes and Group 1 Phoenix Stakes winner and 1,000 Guineas third Saoirse Abu. The second dam, Out Too Late (by Future Storm), is an unraced half-sister to the dam of the Oaks and Irish Derby winner Balanchine. *"He's quite well-made and looks like he could make a 2-y-o. A nice tempered horse and a good mover, I'll be hoping to crack on with him early enough. He could be a nice horse for the middle of the year and if he has any ability he'll do it at two".*

1279. UNNAMED ★★★
gr.f. Dark Angel – Elshamms (Zafonic). February 28. Twelfth foal. €190,000 foal.

Goffs November. Richard Knight. Half-sister to 10 winners including the 2-y-o 6f winner Flaming Spear (by Lope De Vega), the 2-y-o 7f winner and Group 2 Rockfel Stakes third Desert Blossom (by Shamardal) and the useful triple 6f (including at 2 yrs) and UAE Listed 5f winner Taqseem (by Fantastic Light). The dam, a fairly useful 2-y-o 7f winner and third in the Group 3 Prestige Stakes, is a half-sister to 10 winners. The second dam, Gharam (by Green Dancer), a 2-y-o 6f winner and third in the French 1,000 Guineas, is a half-sister to the US Grade 1 winner Talunim. *"She certainly looks like a 2-y-o, like most Dark Angel's, built like a 2-y-o, she's good-looking, nice tempered and one of the earlier ones".*

1280. UNNAMED ★★★
ch.c. Super Saver – Hafifah (Machiavellian). May 5. Ninth foal. $115,000Y. Keeneland September. Margaret O'Toole. Half-brother to 4 winners including the US Grade 3 1m winner Devious Intent (by Dixie Union) and the US stakes-placed winner Devious d'Oro (by Medaglia d'Oro). The dam is an unraced half-sister to 3 winners including the US Grade 3 winner Runspastum. The second dam, Erandel (by Danzig), won twice at 4 yrs and is a sister to the US Grade 3 winner Lech. *"A nice horse, he came from Keeneland and he's done well since he's been here. He's grown a lot and is one for the second half of the year; a good-looking horse and you'd like him".* The sire won the Kentucky Derby and has sired three Grade 1 winners from four crops.

1281. UNNAMED ★★★
b.f. Nathaniel – Intiba (Street Cry). April 2. Second foal. The dam, a fair 2-y-o 7f winner, is a half-sister to the Group 1 12f Dubai Sheema Classic and multiple Hong Kong Group 1 winner Vengeance Of Rain and the Australian Group 1 10f winner Dizelle. The second dam, Daneleta (by Danehill), a 2-y-o 7f winner and third in the Group 3 Railway Stakes, is a sister to the Group 3 12f Noblesse Stakes winner Danelissima and a half-sister to 7 winners. *"She's probably bred to take a bit of time but she's actually quite sharp looking. A medium-sized, very good moving filly and forward going, she'll be running from the midsummer onwards. Time will tell, but you'd like the look of her at the moment".*

1282. UNNAMED ★★★
b.c. Sea The Moon – Mouriyana (Akarad). February 6. Thirteenth foal. €90,000Y. Goffs Orby. Emerald Bloodstock. Half-brother to 7 winners including the Group 3 Prix Edmund Blanc winner Skins Game (by Diktat), the useful French Listed 10.5f winner Epatha (by Highest Honor), the quite useful 12f winner Cerutty (by Shamardal), the fair 2-y-o 9f winner Oasis Storm (by Oasis Dream) and the minor French 2-y-o winner Golden Thai (by Red Ransom). The dam won once over 1m at 2 yrs in France and is a half-sister to 7 winners including the Group 2 12.5f Prix de Royallieu winner Mouramara. The second dam, Mamoura (by Lomond), won over 10f and 12f in Ireland and is a half-sister to 5 winners. *"A nice, medium-sized, lengthy colt and a good mover, he's done plenty and looks like a horse that'll run in mid-season. Not a backward type even though his pedigree would probably suggest he wouldn't have much of a 2-y-o career. If they have ability the pedigree wouldn't stop them from doing it as 2-y-os".*

1283. UNNAMED ★★★
b.f. Shamardal – Munaafasat (Marju). April 24. Second foal. €32,000Y. Goffs Open. BBA (Ire). The dam is an unplaced half-sister to 7 winners including the dual Listed winner My Renee. The second dam, Mayenne (by Nureyev), is an unraced three-parts sister to the Prix de l'Arc de Triomphe winner Carnegie and to the smart Group 2 10f Prix Guillaume d'Ornano winner Antisaar. *"She's quite a nice, sharp sort, not backward at all and we'll keep moving with her. A compact filly and if she's got ability she'll show it this year. We'll get her out around June time".*

1284. UNNAMED ★★★★
b.f. Sea The Stars – Ragsah (Shamardal). March 27. Third foal. The dam, a fairly useful 2-y-o 7f winner, was second in the Group 3 6f Firth Of Clyde Stakes. She is a half-sister to Dubai Millennium, winner of the Dubai World Cup, the Prix Jacques le Marois, the Prince Of Wales's Stakes and the Queen Elizabeth II Stakes (all Group 1 events) and a half-sister to the Group 2 10.5f Prix Greffuhle second Denver County. The second dam, Colorado Dancer (by Shareef Dancer), won the Group 2 13.5f Prix de Pomone and the Group 3 12f

Prix de Minerve, is closely related to the US Grade 1 winner Northern Aspen, to the July Cup winner Hamas and the Grand Prix de Paris winner Fort Wood and a half-sister to the Prix d'Astarte winner Elle Seule (dam of the Irish 1,000 Guineas winner Mehthaaf) and the champion US 2-y-o colt Timber Country. *"This is a nice filly with a great pedigree. Medium-sized, well made and a very fluent mover, she's a clever filly in that she's a quick learner. We'll see her out in the second half of the year".*

1285. UNNAMED ★★★
b.c. Gale Force Ten – Rosa Grace (Lomitas). January 28. Third foal. €18,000 foal. Tattersalls December. PF Bloodstock. The dam, a useful 2-y-o 7f and Listed 10f winner, was Grade 2 placed twice in the USA and is a half-sister to 5 winners including the fairly useful 5f and 6f winner and Listed-placed Secret Night. The second dam, Night Haven (by Night Shift), a fairly useful 5f (at 2 yrs) and 6f winner and 6f Listed-placed, is a sister to 3 winners including the French 2-y-o Listed 5f winner Shoalhaven. *"He's a nice horse that didn't cost a lot at the sales, he's lengthy, good-moving and one of those we'll crack on with. He's not a bad sort at all – he has a really good stride to him, seems to be on the ball and wants to be a 2-y-o".*

HUGO PALMER
1286. ALMUFTI ★★★
b.c. Toronado – Green Tern (Miswaki). February 5. Twelfth foal. 120,000Y. Tattersalls October Book 1. Al Shaqab Racing. Half-brother to 7 winners including the Italian Listed winners Cromo (by Grand Lodge), Donoma and Right Connection (both by Beat Hollow). The dam won once at 2 yrs in Italy and is a full or half-sister to 8 winners including the Group 3 Italian St Leger winner Green Senor. The second dam, Green Leaves (by Rheingold), was a Listed-placed winner in Italy. (Al Shaqab Racing UK Limited). *"A really strong, hard knocking brute of a horse at this stage. He has a high opinion of himself, very willing to please and show off and he looks like his sire Toronado, very forward going and moves well. So I'm happy with him in all respects".*

1287. BAREND BOY ★★★★
b.c. Oasis Dream – Scarborough Fair (Pivotal). February 9. Second foal. 60,000Y. Tattersalls October Book 2. Hugo Palmer. The dam is an unraced half-sister to 4 winners including the Group 2 Royal Lodge Stakes winner Berkshire and the dam of the dual Group 2 winning 2-y-o Ivawood. The second dam, Kinnaird (by Dr Devious), won 6 races including the Group 1 Prix de l'Opera and the Group 2 May Hill Stakes and is a half-sister to the Group 3 Chester Vase winner Mickdaam. *"Very strong and muscular, I think he's going to be sharp and he's doing everything I want him to do. I love him and he's got very natural speed so he could be an early season 2-y-o".*

1288. BIRDCAGE WALK ★★★
b.f. Sea The Moon – Baisse (High Chaparral). February 7. Half-sister to the smart 2-y-o Group 2 1m Royal Lodge Stakes winner Best Of Days (by Azamour). The dam, fair 11f and subsequent German Listed 1m winner, is a half-sister to the Listed 7f (at 2 yrs), Group 3 Dee Stakes and Group 3 Sandown Classic Trial winner Azmeel. The second dam, an Irish 7f (at 2 yrs) and 1m winner, was Listed-placed and is a half-sister to 7 winners including the Irish Group 3 winner Grand Ducal and the useful 2-y-o 6f winner and Listed-placed Hurricane Floyd. (Mr G. Schoeningh). *"I've got two by Sea The Moon and I like them both. He was a good two-year-old, this is a sister to a Royal Lodge winner and she looks the part. I should imagine she'd be one for seven furlongs from July onwards".*

1289. BLONDE WARRIOR (IRE) ★★★★ ♠
b.c. Zoffany – Dame Blanche (Be My Guest). February 8. Ninth living foal. €210,000Y. Arqana Deauville August. Amanda Skiffington. Half-brother to the fairly useful 7f and1m winner of 5 races Fastnet Tempest, to the quite useful French 10f winner and Group 3 Prix Cleopatre third Excellent Girl, the quite useful 5f to 1m winner of 6 races at 2 to 4 yrs Moon River (both by Exceed And Excel), the minor Italian winner of 4 races Tempesta d'Amore (by Oratorio) and a winner in Qatar by Xaar. The dam, a modest 1m placed 3-y-o, is a half-sister to 6 winners including the US Grade 1 winner and Irish 1,000 Guineas third Luas Line and the Group 2 second Lost In The Moment.

The second dam, Streetcar (by In The Wings), fourth once at 2 yrs over 1m, is a half-sister to 9 winners. (Mrs F. J. Carmichael). *"A lovely colt, probably the most expensive of mine from the sales and he's solid, forward, a good mover and has a good attitude. He's very hard to dislike at this stage. I think he'll be a nice 2-y-o and he should progress".*

1290. CLOUD SURFING ★★★

b.f. Oasis Dream – Hasten (IRE) (Montjeu). March 26. Third foal. 200,000Y. Tattersalls October Book 1. Not sold. The dam is an unplaced sister to 2 winners including the 2-y-o Group 1 1m Criterium International winner and Irish Derby third Jan Vermeer and a three-parts sister to the 2-y-o Group 3 7f Silver Flash Stakes winner, multiple Group 1 placed and subsequent US Grade 1 9f winner Together and the fairly useful 2-y-o 7f and 1m winner and Listed-placed Terrific. The second dam, Shadow Song (by Pennekamp) won once at 3 yrs in France and is a half-sister to 7 winners including the Group 3 May Hill Stakes winner Midnight Air (herself dam of the Group 3 and US Grade 2 winner Midnight Line) and to the placed dam of the Group 1 Prix de l'Abbaye winner Imperial Beauty. (Al Asayl Bloodstock Ltd). *"She's beautiful, I loved her at the sales where she didn't reach her reserve and she's turned herself inside out since she's been in work. It's early days but I can't see why she wouldn't be nice by August".*

1291. CROCHET (USA) ★★

b.br.f. First Defence – Magic Motif (Giant's Causeway). March 2. First foal. The dam, placed from 7f (at 2 yrs) to 9f in France, is a half-sister to the smart 10f and 12f winner and Group 2 Hardwicke Stakes second Barsanti and to the useful 2-y-o 6f winner Faraway Flower. The second dam, Silver Star (by Zafonic), won over 1m at 2 yrs in France, was Listed-placed over 1m at 3 yrs and is a sister to the champion European 2-y-o Xaar (winner of the Group 1 Dewhurst Stakes and the Group 1 Prix de la Salamandre) and a half-sister to the Group 3 10.5f Prix Corrida winner Diese and the Group 3 1m Prix Quincey winner Masterclass. (Khalid Abdullah). *"She's gorgeous but she's big and rangy so she won't be early. A scopey middle-distance type, she should have two or three runs this year over seven furlongs or a mile".*

1292. DEBBONAIR (IRE) ★★★

b.c. Slade Power – Bryanstown Girl (Kalanisi) April 13. The dam is an unraced half-sister to 3 minor winners. The second dam, Stiletta (by Dancing Brave), is an unraced sister to the Epsom and Irish Derby winner Commander In Chief and a half-sister to the champion 2-y-o and miler Warning, the US Grade 1 winner Yashmak, the Irish Derby second Deploy and the Great Voltigeur Stakes winner Dushyantor. (Commission Air Limited). *"He was bought almost on a whim and he's done incredibly well despite being small as a yearling. He goes very nicely and I think he'll be one for six/seven furlongs from July onwards. I think he'll get plenty of runs this year and I like him".*

1293. DESERT WAR (USA) ★★★★

gr.c. Oasis Dream – Gracie Square (Awesome Again). April 13. Third foal. 38,000Y. Tattersalls October Book 1. Sackville/Donald. The dam is an unraced half-sister to 7 winners including the US Graded stakes winners Teammate, Ecclesiastic and War Front. The second dam, Starry Dreamer (by Rubiano), won three Listed stakes in the USA and was Grade 1 placed and is a half-sister to 9 winners. (Mr Martin Hughes & Lord de La Warr). *"I adore this colt. Statistically speaking the sire is exceptional and the dam is a sister to War Front. I love to see speed being bred to speed. He looks fast, has lots of natural muscle and a lot of style and quality about him. I think he was incredibly well-bought and believe he had travel sickness on his way over from America, so maybe he didn't look his best at the sale. Gai Waterhouse had a champion called Desert War and I hope I can too".*

1294. DOMBRA ★★★★

b.c. Frankel – Chigun (Oasis Dream). January 11. Second foal. The dam, a smart Irish Group 3 1m and Newmarket Listed 1m winner, is a half-sister to 2 winners. The second dam, Stormy Weather (by Nashwan), is an unraced half-sister to 8 winners including the Group 3 Prix d'Arenberg winner Starlit Sands and the smart broodmare Summer Night (the dam of four stakes winners). (Mr V I Araci). *"He's not a big colt and looks a real 2-y-o. He's done everything to suggest he's forward and if he turned out to be an Ascot 2-y-o it wouldn't surprise me".*

1295. DRAGON KUZA ★★★
b.c. Dragon Pulse – Mylaporyours (Jeremy).
April 3. First foal. 28,000Y. Goffs UK Premier.
Not sold. The dam, a fair 2-y-o 5f winner, is a
half-sister to one winner abroad. The second
dam, Kuwinda (by Hunting Lion), ran twice
unplaced and is a half-sister to 8 winners. *"He's
a solid, strong colt that's done plenty and he's a
forward 2-y-o with five furlong speed. Barring
injury I think he'll be our first runner"*.

1296. EAGLE HUNTER ★★★★★
b.c. Dansili – Zeva (Zamindar). April 23. Second
foal. Half-brother to the fair 2017 2-y-o 7f and
1m winner Trumps Up (by Cape Blanco). The
dam, placed third over 7f on her only start
at 2 yrs, was placed at 3 yrs in the USA and
is a half-sister to 3 winners. The second dam,
Mennetou (by Entrepreneur), is an unraced
half-sister to 5 winners including the Prix de
l'Arc de Triomphe winner Carnegie, the Group
2 10f Prix Guillaume d'Ornano winner Antisaar
and the Group 3 St Simon Stakes winner
Lake Erie. (Al Asayl Bloodstock Ltd). *"He's a
bit of a standout at this stage because he's a
phenomenal mover and I like everything about
him. I think he'll be a second half of the season
horse, but it wouldn't surprise me if he were to
make a start a bit sooner than that"*.

1297. EVERYMANANEMPROR ★★★
br.c. Gregorian – Winterbourne (Cadeaux
Genereux). April 1. Fourth foal. £37,000Y.
Goffs UK Premier (Doncaster). Sackville/
Donald. Half-brother to a minor winner in Italy
by Sakhee's Secret. The dam is an unplaced
half-sister to 4 winners including the Group
2 Prix du Gros-Chene winner of 11 races The
Trader. The second dam, Snowing (by Tate
Gallery), a quite useful dual 5f winner at 3 yrs,
is a half-sister to 2 minor winners. (Mr G. M.
Richardson). *"I really like this horse, he's strong
and looks forward and sharp. He could be
rattling along in late May or early June. There's
plenty of him too, so he could very easily train
on to be a 3-y-o"*.

1298. FENJAL (IRE) ★★★★
gr.c. Kodiac – Spinamix (Spinning World).
February 14. Twelfth foal. 160,000Y. Tattersalls
October Book 1. Al Shaqab Racing. Half-
brother to 9 winners including the French
Listed 10f winner and subsequent Hong Kong

Group 1 Hong Kong Derby second Some
World (by Hawk Wing), the smart dual Listed
5f winner Spin Cycle (by Exceed And Excel),
the useful Group 3 7f winner San Sicharia (by
Daggers Drawn), the useful 2-y-o Listed 1m
winner Spinacre (by Verglas), the 2-y-o 7f
winner and 3-y-o US Grade 3 third Spinamiss
(by Lilbourne Lad) and the fairly useful 2-y-o
6f winner and subsequent US Grade 3 placed
Codeword (by Dansili). The dam, placed at
2 yrs in France, is a half-sister to 4 winners.
The second dam, Vadsagreya (by Linamix),
a French Listed-placed 7f (at 2 yrs) and 1m
winner, is a half-sister to 12 winners including
the dams of the French 1,000 Guineas winner
Vahorimix and the Breeders' Cup Mile winner
Val Royal. (Al Shaqab Racing UK Limited). *"He
looks like a proper early season runner and
the sire is arguably the most phenomenal sire
of 2-y-o's we've seen in some time. This colt is
strong with a good action and is forward going.
He looks the part to me"*.

1299. GEORGE FORMBY ★★★
ch.c. Mayson – Supa Sal (King's Best). March
10. Fifth foal. €36,000Y. Tattersalls Ireland
September. Amanda Skiffington. Half-brother
to the fair 4-y-o 10f winner Be My Rock (by
Rock Of Gibraltar). The dam, a fair dual 7f
winner (including at 2 yrs), is a half-sister to 6
winners including the useful dual 1m winner
and Group 2 third Supaseus. The second dam,
Supamova (by Seattle Slew), a quite useful 8.5f
winner at 3 yrs, is a sister to the very smart
Group 1 7f Prix de la Foret winner Septieme
Ciel and a half-sister to 7 winners including
the Group 1 1m Prix Marcel Boussac winner
Macoumba. (Chelsea Thoroughbreds).
*"I adored him at the sales because he reminded
me of Galileo Gold. He's changed a bit now and
looks less like him but no less nice. He's done
nothing wrong and he's a 2-y-o for the second
half of the season"*.

1300. GOLD FLEECE ★★★
b.f. Nathaniel – Conquete (Kyllachy). March 31.
First foal. 26,500Y. Tattersalls December. Hugo
Palmer /Mark McStay. The dam, placed over
7.5f and 1m at 2 yrs in France, is a half-sister
to 3 minor winners. The second dam, Chesnut
Bird (by Storm Bird), a dual Listed 10f winner,
is a half-sister to 4 winners including the
French Group 3 winner and Group 2 placed

Caesarion. (Lady Mary Manton). *"This filly is a bit more forward than my other Nathaniel filly but that doesn't mean she's going to be out any time soon. One of the deeper fillies we have and a seven furlong to a mile type from midsummer onwards".*

1301. HAPPY FACE ★★★

b.f. Kingman – Intense Pink (Pivotal). January 25. First foal. 47,000Y. Tattersalls October Book 1. Rabbah Bloodstock. The dam, a fairly useful Listed 7f winner, was third in the Group 3 Chartwell Stakes and is a half-sister to 8 winners including the smart 2-y-o 6f winner and Group 1 1m Racing Post Trophy third Henrik and the useful 2-y-o 6f winner and Group 2 6f Gimcrack Stakes third Sir Reginald. The second dam, Clincher Club (by Polish Patriot), a fair 5f (at 2 yrs) and 7.5f winner, is a half-sister to 9 winners including the dual Listed winner Paradise Isle. (Dr A. Ridha). *"This is the only Kingman I've got but I liked them at the sales and I was delighted to get her. It's a lovely pedigree and I think she was well bought. She's not going to be that sharp but it's a fast pedigree and she's very attractive. She'll be going well from August onwards".*

1302. HOT TEAM ★★★

b.c. Zoffany – Ahd (Elusive Quality). April 1. First foal. €42,000Y. Tattersalls Ireland September. Sackville/Donald. The dam is an unraced half-sister to 3 minor winners. The second dam, Abby Road (by Danehill), won the Listed 5f St Hugh's Stakes at 2 yrs and is a full or half-sister to 5 winners. (Mr L L Lee). *"A very strong, solid, tank of a horse who looks a 2-y-o type. He's not vast but he's certainly big enough and he's one we're getting on with. I would have thought that May over six furlongs would be his starting point. I'd like to aim him for the Tatts Ireland Sales race because it's a race I'd like to win having just been touched off in it once before".*

1303. IRON CLAD ★★

br.c. Dubawi – Heat Haze (Green Desert). April 7. Brother to the very useful dual 7f winner and Group/Graded stakes placed Forge and to the useful 2-y-o 7f winner and Listed-placed Radiator and half-brother to the useful 2-y-o 7f winner and dual 3-y-o Group 3 third Mirage Dancer (by Frankel). The dam,

winner of the Grade 1 Matriarch Stakes and the Grade 1 Beverly D Stakes, is closely related to the Group/Grade 1 winners Banks Hill, Intercontinental, Cacique and Champs Elysees, and the Group 2 winner and high-class sire Dansili. The second dam, Hasili (by Kahyasi), won over 5f at 2 yrs and stayed a mile. (Khalid Abdullah). *"He's not here yet because of a small setback but he'll be here shortly and the reports are that he's absolutely gorgeous. You'd have to assume that he'll be a back-end horse and then have an exciting 3-y-o career".*

1304. KAHINA ★★ ♠

b.f. Camelot – Close Regards (Danehill). April 30. Eighth foal. €70,000Y. Goffs Orby. McKeever/Ferguson/Speers. Half-sister to 5 winners including the Australian Group 1 12f winner Magic Hurricane (by Hurricane Run), the quite useful 7f to 10f winner and Listed-placed Maybe Grace (by Hawk Wing) and the fair 5f (at 2 yrs) and 6f winner Fast In The Wind (by Footstepsinthesand). The dam is an unraced half-sister to 7 winners. The second dam, La Luna (by Lyphard), a winner over 9f at 3 yrs in France, is a sister to the Group 3 Prix Daphnis and Group 3 Prix Thomas Bryon winner Bellypha and a half-sister to the Prix Eugene Adam winner Bellman and the Peruvian Grade 1 winner Run And Deliver. *"I think this filly is quite forward despite being almost a May foal and I'm wondering whether Camelot isn't quite the influence for stamina we thought he might turn out to be".*

1305. NATHLESS ★★★

ch.c. Nathaniel – Dudley Queen (Excellent Art). March 5. Second foal. 40,000Y. Tattersalls October Book 2. Amanda Skiffington/Hugo Palmer. Half-brother to the fair 2017 2-y-o 7.5f winner Poet's Dawn (by Poet's Voice). The dam is an unraced sister to the Listed-placed winner Lucy The Painter and a half-sister to 6 winners including the useful dual Listed 1m winner and Group 3 1m Dahlia Stakes second Harvest Queen. The second dam, Royal Bounty (by Generous), a quite useful 2-y-o 7.5f winner, is a half-sister to 3 minor winners here and abroad. (The Rat Pack Partnership 2017). *"More forward than my Nathaniel fillies, he's very strong and looks very 'Excellent Arty' in that he's muscular. It's not a slow family and he looks the part".*

1306. PERSEPONE ★★★
b.f. Dubawi – Filia Regina (Galileo). March 10.
Second foal. Half-sister to the quite useful
2017 2-y-o 1m winner Best Blue (by Oasis
Dream). The dam, a fair 14f winner, is a sister
to the top-class colt Australia (winner of the
Derby, Irish Derby, etc) and a half-sister to the
Australian Group 3 winner Voodoo Prince.
The second dam, Ouija Board (by Cape Cross),
was a top-class winner of 10 races from 7f (at
2 yrs) to 12f including seven Group/Grade 1
races and is a half-sister to 6 winners. *"She is
absolutely stunning. A filly with quite a quick,
fast ground action that does everything with
an air of class. She isn't likely to be a 2-y-o but
hopefully she will run this year. The family just
gets better and she's something to look forward
to as a 3-y-o".*

1307. RACHEL ZANE (IRE) ★★★
b.f. Sea The Moon – Mark Of An Angel (Mark
Of Esteem). March 20. Fifth foal. 27,500Y.
Tattersalls December. Mark McStay/ Hugo
Palmer. Half-sister to the very useful Group
3 1m Park Express Stakes winner Queen
Blossom (by Jeremy) and a minor winner in
Spain by Duke Of Marmalade. The dam was
placed three times including when third in
the 2-y-o Group 3 7f Silver Flash Stakes and
is a half-sister to 3 minor winners. The second
dam, Dream Time (by Rainbow Quest), placed
once over 12f at 3 yrs, is a half-sister to 4
minor winners. (FOMO Syndicate). *"I love her,
she's going to race in Covert Love's colours
and Rachel Zane is the character that Meghan
Markle played in 'Suits'! She does incredibly
well on fresh air which is always great, she has
a lovely action and a good attitude and I see
her as a seven furlong to a mile filly from July
onwards".*

1308. STARTEGO ★★★
b.c. New Approach – Tafiya (Bahri). May 4.
Sixth foal. Half-brother to the fairly useful
2-y-o 6f and 7f winner Overpowered (by
Choisir) and to the modest 10f winner
Sovereign Power (by Royal Applause). The
dam, a fair 7f (at 2 yrs) to 11f placed maiden,
is a half-sister to 5 winners including the useful
Group 3 Dahlia Stakes winner Tarfah (dam of
the 2,000 Guineas and Derby winner Camelot).
The second dam, Fickle (by Danehill), a fairly
useful 1m and Listed 10f winner, is a half-sister

to 7 winners including the Listed winners
Birdie and Faru. (Al Asayl Bloodstock Ltd). *"I
think I've known all of them out of the mare
and I think this colt is the nicest since the first
foal Overpowered who was very highly thought
of but died early. I can't see why this colt
shouldn't be winning races at two".*

1309. WILLIAM MCKINLEY ★★★
b.c. Exceed And Excel – Pure Song (Singspiel).
April 13. Seventh foal. 40,000Y. Tattersalls
October Book 1. Not sold. Half-brother to the
very smart 10f and 11f winner and Epsom
Derby and King George VI third Romsdal (by
Halling), to the fairly useful Listed-placed 7f
and10f winner Pure Art (by Dutch Art) and
the fair 2-y-o 9.5f winner Wolf Albarari (by
Medicean). The dam, a fair 12f and 14f placed
maiden, is a half-sister to 4 winners including
the smart 7f (at 2 yrs) and Group 3 10.5f Prix
Fille de l'Air winner Goncharova. The second
dam, Pure Grain (by Polish Precedent), won
the Group 1 12f Irish Oaks and the Group 1
12f Yorkshire Oaks and is a half-sister to 8
winners including the dam of the Japanese
Group 1 winner Fine Grain. (W. J. and T. C.
O. Gredley). *"This is a nice colt but he's not
forward and I should think he's going to make
up into a miler towards the end of the year.
He's doing plenty to suggest he'll win a race or
two this year".*

1310. UNNAMED ★★★
b.f. Sepoy – Akhmatova (Cape Cross).
February 10. Third foal. 75,000Y. Tattersalls
October Book 2. Blandford Bloodstock. Half-
sister to the quite useful 2017 6f and 7f placed
2-y-o Left Alone (by Reckless Abandon) and
to the modest 2-y-o 6f winner Walaaa (by
Exceed And Excel). The dam, a quite useful
1m and 10f winner of 4 races, is a half-sister
to 4 winners including the 2-y-o Group 3
Anglesey Stakes third Rudolf Valentino. The
second dam, Maganda (by Sadler's Wells), a
quite useful 10f winner, is a sister to the Listed
winners In The Limelight and On The Nile and
a half-sister to the German and Italian Group 1
winner Kutub. (Sheikh R. D. Al Maktoum).
*"I train the half-sister by Reckless Abandon
who we felt should have won as a 2-y-o last
year. This is a really strong, muscular and
athletic filly".*

1311. UNNAMED ★★★
b.f. Deep Impact – Amanee (Pivotal). January 26. Second foal. Half-sister to the fair 6f and 7f placed maiden Omneeya (by Frankel). The dam, a South African Grade 2 1m winner, is a half-sister to 2 winners. The second dam, Moon Is Up (by Woodman), a Listed 1m winner and Group 3 placed in France, is closely related to the French 2,000 Guineas, the St James's Palace Stakes and Prix du Moulin winner Kingmambo and the smart Group 3 6f winner Miesque's Son and a half-sister to the high-class triple Group 1 winner East of the Moon. (Sheikh M. B. K Al Maktoum). *"It's a bit of a treat to have a Deep Impact because not only is he one of the best stallions in the world but there are so few of them in Europe. I like this filly, she's not what I think of as a Pivotal (the damsire) to look at but she's lovely. She's bred to be good and at this stage she looks the part".*

1312. UNNAMED ★★★ ♠
ch.c. New Approach – Anayid (A P Indy). March 27. Tenth foal. €30,000Y. Goffs Orby. Amanda Skiffington. Half-brother to 6 winners including the very useful 2-y-o Listed 7f winner of 6 races Titus Mills, the fairly useful Irish 2-y-o 7f winner Sniper (both by Dubawi), the quite useful 2-y-o 7f winner Mirabella (by Motivator), the quite useful 7f (at 2 yrs in France) and 9f winner Sand Tiger (by Indian Ridge) and the fair French 10f winner of 4 races Ana Lichious (by Makfi). The dam is an unraced half-sister to 3 winners. The second dam, Aqaarid (by Nashwan), winner of the Group 1 Fillies Mile and the Group 3 7.3f Fred Darling Stakes, was second in the 1,000 Guineas and is a half-sister to 2 winners. *"This colt is gorgeous; he has lovely angles, does everything right and moves beautifully. He's got a pedigree to be a good horse and I just can't understand why he didn't cost a lot more at the sale".* TRAINER'S BARGAIN BUY

1313. UNNAMED ★★★★
ch.f. Slade Power – Beautiful Filly (Oasis Dream). May 7. Fifth foal. 50,000Y. Tattersalls October Book 1. Not sold. Half-sister to the smart Group 2 German 1,000 Guineas winner and Group 3 Nell Gwyn Stakes second Unforgetable Filly (by Sepoy), to the quite useful 6f and 7f winner at 2 and 3 yrs Speedy

Move (by Iffraaj), the quite useful dual 7f winner Raven's Corner by Raven Pass) and the fair 2-y-o 7f winner Wickhambrook (by Dubawi). The dam, a fair 6f and 7f winner at 3 yrs, is a half-sister to one minor winner in the USA. The second dam, Royal Alchemist (by Royal Academy), was placed once in the USA and is a half-sister to 4 winners including the Group 1 Sprint Cup winner Dowsing and the US Grade 1 winner Fire The Groom (dam of the dual Group 1 winning sprinter Stravinsky). (Dr A. Ridha). *"I like this filly a huge amount and of all the first season sires Slade Power is the only one I have multiples of, because I have three. I like them all and other than the fact this filly is a chestnut and her half-sister Unforgetable Filly is a bright bay they are very similar. She's a May foal but she does everything comfortably at this stage and she could easily make a 2-y-o. May foals don't actually have a bad record as 2-y-o's at Royal Ascot".*

1314. UNNAMED ★★★
b.f. Iffraaj – Birdie (Alhaarth). Half-sister to the fairly useful 2-y-o 7f winner and Group 3 Acomb Stakes third Il Paparazzi (by Royal Applause) and to the French 12f winner Salvation (by Montjeu). The dam, a 1m and Listed 11.5f winner, is a half-sister to 7 winners including the French middle-distance winner of 10 races (including four Listed events) Faru and the Listed winner Fickle (herself dam of the Group 3 winner Tarfah). The second dam, Fade (by Persepolis), is an unraced half-sister to Tom Seymour, a winner of five Group 3 events in Italy. *"If everything goes to plan I think she's likely to follow a similar programme to her half-brother Il Paparazzi and aim for the Acomb Stakes at York".*

1315. UNNAMED ★★★
b.f. Lawman – Bright Sapphire (Galileo). March 4. Fourth foal. €100,000Y. Goffs Orby. Amanda Skiffington/H Palmer. Half-sister to the useful 6f (at 2 yrs) to 14f winner and Australian Group 2 placed Wall Of Fire (by Canford Cliffs). The dam ran twice unplaced and is a half-sister to 4 minor winners. The second dam, Jewel In The Sand (by Bluebird), a winner of 4 races including the Group 2 6f Cherry Hinton Stakes and the Listed Albany Stakes, is a half-sister to 4 winners. (Mr A.

HEERAAT (IRE)

Dark Angel (IRE) (gr.2005) *42 BTW*	Acclamation (GB) (1999) *BTW* *46 BTW*	Royal Applause (GB) *50 BTW*	Waajib		
			Flying Melody		
		Princess Athena *1 BTW*	Ahonoora		
			Shopping Wise		
	Midnight Angel (GB) (1994) *2 BTW*	Machiavellian (USA) *71 BTW*	Mr Prospector (USA)		
			Coup de Folie (USA)		
		Night At Sea *1 BTP*	Night Shift (USA)		
			Into Harbour		
Thawrah (IRE) (b.2003) *2 BTW*	Green Desert (USA) (1983) *BTW* *94 BTW*	Danzig (USA) *198 BTW*	Northern Dancer		
			Pas de Nom (USA)		
		Foreign Courier (USA) *2 BTW*	Sir Ivor (USA)		
			Courtly Dee (USA)		
	Arjuzah (IRE) (1990) *BTW* *2 BTW*	**Ahonoora** *43 BTW*	Lorenzaccio		
			Helen Nichols		
		Saving Mercy *2 BTW*	Lord Gayle (USA)		
			Fair Darling		

By **DARK ANGEL** out of a half sister to Gr.1 winning sprinter and Gr.1 sire **MALHUB**

Won at 2, 3 and 4, **TFR 117**

The **fastest winner** of the Hackwood Stakes since 2001

YEARLING AVERAGES
Over **£54,000** at Goffs UK Premier Sale

65,000gns
at Tattersalls October (Book 2) Sale

BUYERS
Willie Browne, Karl Burke, Peter Doyle x 3, Tim Easterby, Jo Hughes, Joseph Murphy, John Quinn, Mick Quinn, Shadwell x 2, etc.

Stud Fee: £5,000 Special Live Foal

Standing at MICKLEY STUD, Ternhill, Market Drayton, Shropshire TF9 3QW
Richard Kent T: 079 73 315722 • E: mickleystud@btconnect.com
www.mickleystud.com or John Walsh Bloodstock T: +353 (0)86 2558945

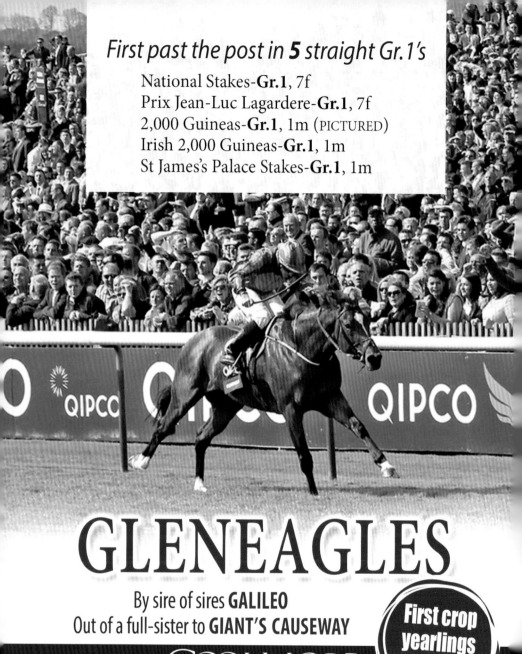

THE RACING POST APP.
HOME TO RACING'S TOP INFORMATION.
HOME TO RACING'S TOP BOOKIES.

Why continuously flit between apps when racing's best information, and top bookies are sat side by side in one app? Better yet, you can remain logged in to all four bookies at once, and simply switch account to bet with the best odds. Home sweet home, as they say.

RACING POST

WHEN YOU BET ON RACING, YOU CAN BET ON RACING POST.

Racing Post backs responsible gambling. 18+ gambleaware.co.uk

Kheir). *"She's a lovely combination of what a Lawman looks like and what her half-brother Wall Of Fire looks like. She has fabulous athleticism and walks like Wall Of Fire did. A very nice filly, I think she'll be well forward enough to win races at two".*

1316. UNNAMED ★★★

b.g. Slade Power – Heart's Desire (Royal Applause). March 24. Tenth foal. 65,000Y. Tattersalls October Book 1. Nick Bradley. Half-brother to 6 winners including the Irish 2-y-o Listed 6f winner Heart Of Fire (by Mujadil), the Irish 1m (at 2 yrs) and 14f winner Knight Eagle (by Night Shift), the 6f (at 2 yrs) to 10f winner and Group 3 Diamond Stakes third Unsinkable (by Verglas) – all fairly useful and the fair 8.5f winner Faddwa (by Arcano). The dam, placed over 7f and 1m, is a half-sister to 6 winners including the French Listed winner Bashful. The second dam, Touch And Love (by Green Desert), a French 2-y-o winner and second in the Group 2 Prix du Gros-Chene, is a half-sister to 8 winners. (Nick Bradley Racing 23). *"A good mover, a good size, strong and attractive. If he goes the right way he could be a nice horse as long as he doesn't get too colty".*

1317. UNNAMED ★★★

b.f. Declaration Of War – Lady Wingshot (Lawman). March 15. Second foal. The dam, a Group 3 7.5f Fairy Bridge Stakes and Listed winner of 4 races, is a half-sister to 8 winners including the 2-y-o Listed 5f Dragon Stakes winner and Group 2 5f Flying Childers Stakes second Bahama Mama. The second dam, Nassma (by Sadler's Wells), a Listed 13.5f winner, is a half-sister to 5 minor winners. *"This filly looks the part, really well-grown and with a lovely way of going. She hasn't been here long but everything points to her being a nice filly".*

1318. UNNAMED ★★★

ch.c. Dawn Approach – Mamonta (Fantastic Light). May 4. Eighth foal. 50,000Y. Tattersalls October Book 1. Hugo Palmer. Half-brother to 4 winners including the very smart 1m (at 2 yrs) and Group 2 Lancashire Oaks and Group 3 Lillie Langtry Stakes winner of 7 races and dual Group 1 second Endless Time, to the fairly useful Listed-placed 10f winner The Sky Is Blazing (both by Sea The Stars) and the fair 10f (at 2 yrs) and 14f winner Marhaba

Malyoon (by Tiger Hill). The dam, placed once over 2m, is a half-sister to 8 winners including the Group 2 12.5f Prix de Royallieu winner and smart broodmare Mouramara. The second dam, Mamoura (by Lomond), won over 10f and 12f in Ireland and is a half-sister to 5 winners. (Mrs C. McStay & Partner). *"A lovely colt that's doing everything we want him to do, developing all the time and despite the fact he's a May foal there's no reason why he shouldn't be a 2-y-o from late summer onwards. I like everything I see".*

1319. UNNAMED ★★

ch.f. Iffraaj – Sloane Square (Teofilo). February 28. Second foal. 70,000Y. Tattersalls October Book 2. Rabbah Bloodstock. The dam is an unraced sister to the Listed Magnolia Stakes winner and Group 3 third Miblish and to the winner and Group 3 third Count John. The second dam, Triton Dance (by Hector Protector), an Irish 2-y-o 5f winner, is a half-sister to 4 winners including the 2-y-o Group 2 6f Cherry Hinton Stakes winner Jewel In The Sand and the German 3-y-o Listed 6f winner Davignon. (Sheikh R. D. Al Maktoum). *"A very big filly but she's nice and I'd be disappointed if she wasn't able to win at two. Having said that I think she'll be a better filly next year".*

1320. UNNAMED ★★★★

b.f. Dark Angel – Vasilia (Dansili). March 12. Seventh foal. Half-sister to the useful 2-y-o 6f winner and Group 2 6f Railway Stakes winner Dream Of Dreams, to the fairly useful 2-y-o 6f winner Candelisa (both by Dawn Approach), the quite useful 5f (at 2 yrs) to 1m winner of 8 races and Group 2 7f Superlative Stakes third Silverheels, the quite useful 7f (at 2 yrs) to 9.5f winner Fiftyshadesfreed (both by Verglas) and the fairly useful 2-y-o 5f winner and Listed-placed Lasilia (by Acclamation). The dam is an unraced half-sister to 7 winners including the Group 1 6f Cheveley Park Stakes and dual Group 2 winner Airwave. The second dam, Kangra Valley (by Indian Ridge), a moderate 2-y-o 5f winner, is a half-sister to 7 minor winners. (Mr V. I. Araci). *"This filly is all class. I don't think she's going to be especially early but I think she'll be a lovely 2-y-o as time goes on and be a lovely 3-y-o as well. Virtually everything the mare has bred has won as a 2-y-o and got some black type".*

AMANDA PERRETT

1321. ABANICA ★★★

b.f. Iffraaj – Abated (Dansili). March 23. First foal. The dam, a fair 6f winner, is a sister to the very smart Group 2 5f Temple Stakes and multiple Group 1 placed Bated Breath and a half-sister to the Group 1 9f Dubai Duty Free winner Cityscape. The second dam, Tantina (by Distant View), a smart winner of 4 races including two Listed events over 7f, was Group 3 placed and is a half-sister to 2 winners. (Khalid Abdullah). *"She's a racy, 2-y-o sort from a family that includes two stallions which is great. A free-moving filly, it won't be long before we get going with her over six/seven furlongs".*

1322. AEGEUS (USA) ★★

b.br.c. First Defence – Supposition (Dansili). February 8. Fourth foal. Half-brother to the Irish Listed 10f and subsequent US Grade 3 13.5f winner Postulation (by Harlan's Holiday). The dam, a useful Irish 2-y-o 7f winner, was third in the Group 1 7f Moyglare Stud Stakes. The second dam, Topicality (by Topsider), won once at 3 yrs and is a sister to the Cherry Hinton and Fred Darling Stakes winner Top Socialite and a half-sister to the US Grade 1 winners Expelled and Exbourne. (Khalid Abdullah). *"He's got a bit of size and scope, he's 15.3 hands now. Very much a second half of the season horse for seven furlongs, he's a big, rangy individual".*

1323. AZETS ★★★★

b.c. Dubawi – Nashmiah (Elusive City). January 10. Fourth foal. 300,000Y. Tattersalls October Book 1. J Connolly / A Perrett/ Peter & Ross Doyle. Half-brother to the French Listed 6.5f winner Fond Words (by Shamardal) and to the fair 7f winner A Legacy Of Love (by Sea The Stars). The dam, a winner of four Listed events at 3 yrs from 7f to 10f and third in the Group 3 Oh So Sharp Stakes, is a half-sister to 6 winners including the useful Listed winners Ighraa and Streets Ahead. The second dam, Frond (by Alzao), a quite useful 2-y-o 7f winner, is a half-sister to 8 winners. (John Connolly & Odile Griffith). *"A compact colt by a great sire, he has an early birthday and he'll be running as soon as the six furlong races start in May".*

1324. BARB'S PRINCE (IRE) ★★★

b.c. Casamento – Bibury (Royal Applause). April 11. Fourth foal. 43,000Y. Tattersalls October Book 2. Amanda Perrett / Peter & Ross Doyle. Half-brother to the very useful 6f (at 2 yrs) and Group 3 Earl Of Sefton Stakes winner Steel Of Madrid (by Lope De Vega). The dam, a fair 7f winner, is a half-sister to 4 winners including the Group 1 Ascot Gold Cup winner Rite Of Passage. The second dam, Dahlia's Krissy (by Kris S), a Listed-placed winner of 5 races in the USA, is a half-sister to 5 winners. (Mrs B. R. James). *"He's got a bit of size and scope and is going to be a second half of the year 2-y-o. I would say he's got enough speed to run over six furlongs but he just wants a bit of time to mature".*

1325. BARRENJOEY ★★★

ch.c. Australia – Heavenly Dawn (Pivotal). April 8. Fourth foal. 45,000Y. Tattersalls October Book 2. Not sold. Half-brother to the quite useful 12f winner Dawn Choir (by Fastnet Rock). The dam, a fairly useful dual 1m winner and Listed-placed, is a sister to the US dual Grade 1 winner Megahertz and to the dual Group 3 Dahlia Stakes winner and triple Group 1 placed Heaven Sent and a half-sister to 2 winners. The second dam, Heavenly Ray (by Rahy), a fairly useful 7f and 1m winner, is a half-sister to 3 winners. (Mr M Quigley & Mr D M James). *"The Australia's were really quite exceptional at the sales and this colt is nice, a bit leggy but does everything right. He just needs a bit of time and I just think from August onwards he'll be ready to go".*

1326. DUTCH STORY ★★★

ch.c. Dutch Art – Shamandar (Exceed And Excel). March 3. Third foal. 55,000Y. Tattersalls October Book 2. Highflyer Bloodstock. Half-brother to the unplaced 2017 2-y-o Salty Sugar (by Oasis Dream). The dam, a fairly useful Listed 6f winner of 3 races, is a half-sister to the Listed winner and Group 3 second Hung Parliament. The second dam, Sensational Mover (by Theatrical), a moderate 12f placed maiden, is a half-sister to 5 winners. (R. Scott). *"This colt's pedigree is 'speed over speed'; the dam won the Dick Poole at Salisbury and was second in the St Hugh's at Newbury. He is a big, strapping horse, nearly 16 hands now and just needs a bit more time to mature. He probably won't need to go that far in terms of distance but he's one for the second half of the year".*

1327. MAYKIR ★★★ ♠

b.c. Mayson – Kiruna (Northern Park). April 30. Eighth living foal. 45,000Y. Tattersalls October Book 2. Amanda Perrett / Peter & Ross Doyle. Half-brother to the quite useful 7f (at 2 yrs) and 1m winner and Listed-placed Serafe (by Byron) and to a minor winner abroad by Numerous. The dam is a placed half-sister to 4 winners including the German Listed 14f winner Kiswahili and the dam of the Group 1 British Champions Fillies/Mares winner Madame Chiang. The second dam, Kiliniski (by Niniski), winner of the Group 3 12f Lingfield Oaks Trial, was second in the Yorkshire Oaks and fourth in the Epsom Oaks and is a half-sister to 5 winners including the dam of the US triple Grade 1 winner Bienamado. (Maykbelieve Partnership). *"Apart from being a fairly late foal he looks well put-together, shows a bit of speed and the dam has proved she can do it. In time he may get a little bit further but he's neat and ready to go when we get the six furlong races".*

1328. MANUCCI (IRE) ★★

b.c. Nathaniel – American Spirit (Rock Of Gibraltar). March 12. Fifth foal. 55,000Y. Tattersalls October Book 2. Amanda Perrett/ Peter & Ross Doyle. Half-brother to the very useful 7f winner of 4 races at 2 and 3 yrs Make It Up (by Halling) and to the fair 9f winner Girl Of The Hour (by Makfi). The dam is an unraced half-sister to 4 winners notably the Racing Post Trophy (at 2 yrs), Derby and Juddmonte International winner Authorized. The second dam, Funsie (by Saumarez), is an unraced half-sister to 9 winners including the Group 3 10.5f Prix Cleopatre winner Brooklyn's Dance (herself the dam of six stakes winners) and the dam of the Group 1 winner Okawango. (John Connolly & Odile Griffith). *"He's got a lovely pedigree that includes plenty of middle-distance Group winners and he just wants time. He's a big, rangy individual and he's a rig – we had to remove one testicle, but apart from that he's a lovely individual for later in the year and he goes really well".*

1329. PASEO ★★★★

b.c. Champs Elysees – Posteritas (Lear Fan). February 7. Brother to the French dual 1m winner Sunflower and half-brother to the Group 1 7f Prix Jean Prat winner Mutual Trust, the useful triple 1m winner Kryptos (both by Cacique), the 9.5f and 15f winner and Group 2 Prix Chaudenay second Pilansberg, the French Listed-placed 1m winner Far Afield (both by Rail Link) and the French 2-y-o Listed 5f placed Pure Joy (by Zamindar). The dam, a fairly useful Listed 10f winner, is a half-sister to 5 winners including the useful 2-y-o dual 7f winner Apex Star. The second dam, Imroz (by Nureyev), a useful 6f (at 2 yrs) and 7f winner, was Listed-placed and is a half-sister to 5 winners. (Khalid Abdullah). *"A lovely horse in every way; as an individual you couldn't better him and the dam has shown she's well capable of producing a nice horse and this is certainly it. He's a February foal and quite mature but he's 16 hands and wants looking after for a bit. A seven furlong 2-y-o to start with – we always try to think of Goodwood but haven't had much luck in the last couple of years!"*

1330. SASH ★★★★

b.c. Oasis Dream – Surcingle (Empire Maker). January 29. First foal. The dam, a fair 2-y-o 1m winner, is a sister to the quite useful dual 10f winner Vital Evidence. The second dam, Promising Lead (by Danehill), a very smart Group 1 10f Pretty Polly Stakes winner, is a half-sister to the very smart Group 3 6f Princess Margaret Stakes and Group 3 7f Oak Tree Stakes winner Visit. (Khalid Abdullah). *"He's quite forward, the dam won as a 2-y-o and he was an early foal. He's 16 hands now, so he's got a bit of size and scope. A really nice individual, we haven't done any fast work with him but he's got a good attitude, a good outlook and has done everything right, so why not?"*

1331. SEEING RED (IRE) ★★

b.f. Sea The Stars – Red Fantasy (High Chaparral). February 29. Fourth foal. 200,000Y. Tattersalls October Book 1. A Perrett / S Conway / Peter & Ross Doyle. Half-sister to the quite useful 2017 2-y-o 7f winner Fabulous Red (by Red Jazz) and to the modest 12f winner Rock 'N Red (by Fastnet Rock). The dam, a useful 10f winner, was second in the Listed Pretty Polly Stakes and is a half-sister to 4 winners including the Irish Listed winner Desert Fantasy. The second dam, Petite Fantasy (by Mansooj), a very useful Irish sprinter, won the Listed Belgrave Stakes, was placed in numerous other Group races in Ireland and is a half-sister to 3 winners. (Mr & Mrs F Cotton, Mr & Mrs P Conway). *"A big filly that needs time, she has lots of energy at the moment but she's one for a bit later in the year. Growing fast, she has a good temperament considering she's out of a High Chaparral mare".*

1332. SPEEDSKATER ★★★
b.f. Olympic Glory – My Love Thomas (Cadeaux Genereux). March 27. Fifth living foal. 30,000Y. Tattersalls October Book 2. A D Spence. Half-sister to the very useful 5f and 6f winner of 5 races and Listed-placed Double Up, to the fairly useful triple 5f winner at 2 and 4 yrs Love On The Rocks (both by Exceed And Excel) and the fair 5f (at 2 yrs) to 1m winner of 4 races Full Support (by Acclamation). The dam, a fair 2-y-o 6f winner, is a half-sister to 10 winners including the Group 1 Haydock Park Sprint Cup winner G Force. The second dam, Flanders (by Common Grounds), a very useful Listed sprint winner of 6 races, was second in the Group 2 Kings Stand Stakes and is a half-sister to 8 winners and to the dam of the dual Group 1 winning sprinter Lethal Force. (Alan Spence). *"She'll be able to shift a bit in time, she was a little bit late coming in but I can see her being a six furlong type for July onwards".*

1333. WEALTH OF WORDS ★★★
b.f. Poet's Voice – Affluent (Oasis Dream). February 9. Fifth foal. Half-sister to the fair 2-y-o 5f to 7f winner of 3 races Aspirant (by Rail Link). The dam, a quite useful dual 5f winner (including at 2 yrs), is closely related to 2 winners including the useful 2-y-o 6f winner and Group 3 7f placed Cantabria and a half-sister to numerous winners including the smart Group 3 7f winner So Beloved, the useful 2-y-o 5f and Listed 6f winner Deportivo and the useful 2-y-o Listed 5f winner Irish Vale. The second dam, Valencia (by Kenmare), placed over 1m at 2 yrs on her only start, is a half-sister to numerous winners including the

dual US Grade 1 winner Wandesta, the Group 2 12f winner De Quest and the smart 10f to 15f winner Turners Hill. (Khalid Abdullah). *"A compact, racy filly, she was an early foal, does nothing wrong and is just cantering away at the minute. The dam won as a 2-y-o and I'd expect to see her in a seven furlong fillies' maiden from mid-season onwards".*

1334. ZUBA ★★★★
b.c. Dubawi – Purr Along (Mount Nelson). January 30. First foal. 210,000Y. Tattersalls October Book 1. J Connolly / A Perrett / Peter & Ross Doyle. The dam won 3 races including the Group 3 7f Prix du Calvados and the Group 3 1m Ridgewood Pearl Stakes and is a half-sister to 5 winners including useful Listed 5f and dual 6f winner Katawi (by Dubawi). The second dam, Purring (by Mountain Cat), a quite useful 7f winner, is a half-sister to the Group 2 1m Falmouth Stakes and Group 3 1m Prix de Sandringham winner Ronda (herself the dam of a Group 3 winner). (John Connolly & Odile Griffith). *"The first foal of a good racemare, he's a lovely horse with size and scope; about 16 hands now, he was an early foal and his knees are mature. I'm quite excited about him. I've never had a Dubawi and this year I have two. One is small and compact whilst the other is rangy and I'm told the smaller Dubawi's are the better ones!"*

JONATHAN PORTMAN
1335. DEMERARA ★★
b.f. Kingman – Caster Sugar (Cozzene). January 28. Fourth foal. Half-sister to the fairly useful 7f (at 2 yrs) and subsequent US 9f winner Barleysugar (by Kyllachy) and to the quite useful 7f, 1m (both at 2 yrs) and 12f winner of 5 races Mukhayyam (by Dark Angel). The dam, a fair 1m to 11f winner of 4 races, is a half-sister to 3 minor winners here and abroad. The second dam, Only Royale (by Caerleon), won 9 races including the Group 1 Yorkshire Oaks (twice) and the Group 2 Jockey Club Stakes and is a half-sister to 5 winners. (Mrs J. Wigan). *"She's still in pre-training but I've seen her and she looks a nice filly that'll take a bit of time. She's by an exciting first-season stallion but she had a setback and hence I won't get her until mid-season".*

1336. EVEN KEEL ★★★
ch.c. Born To Sea – Dew (Whipper). February 13. First foal. 12,000Y. Tattersalls October Book 3. Not sold. The dam ran once unplaced and is a half-sister to 10 winners including the Hong Kong stakes winner Solid Approach. The second dam, Dawn Chorus (by Mukaddamah), is an unraced half-sister to 7 winners. (Berkeley Racing). *"One of the more forward ones although he wouldn't be a five furlong horse, we like him a lot and we know the family because we trained a half-sister to the dam. I see him as a nice six/seven furlong type in due course".*

1337. INVINCIBELLA ★★★
b.f. Kodiac – Sahafh (Rock Hard Ten). February 1. Third foal. 20,000Y. Tattersalls December. Not sold. The dam, a fair maiden, was placed four times over 7f and 1m at 2 and 3 yrs and is a half-sister to 6 winners including the 2-y-o dual 8.5f and minor US stakes winner and Group 2 7f Barbara Fritchie Handicap second Pamona Ball. The second dam, Fireman's Ball (by Hennessy), is an unplaced half-sister to 6 winners including Ozone Friendly (Group 2 Prix Robert Papin). (Hot to Trot Partnership). *"She was an early foal and she's not very big, so she looks like being a sharp 2-y-o. A small filly, she doesn't look impressive physically but she has the most wonderful attitude. She won't let anything get past her and she'll be one of our earlier types".*

1338. MRS WORTHINGTON (IRE) ★★★
b.f. Dark Angel – Mirror Effect (Shamardal). February 25. Second foal. 270,000Y. Tattersalls October Book 1. Howson & Houldsworth. Half-sister to the unplaced 2017 2-y-o Mirror Magic (by Nathaniel). The dam is an unraced half-sister to 2 winners. The second dam, Bella Bella (by Sri Pekan), a quite useful dual 7f winner, is a half-sister to 5 winners including the German Listed winner and Group 3 third Silk Petal and the dam of the Group 2 winners Tashawak and Fairy Queen. (Tony Wechsler & Ann Plummer). *"A nice-looking filly, she's growing rapidly and seems a nice, straightforward filly that shows ability. We like her she's one for the second half of the season".*

1339. PEGGOTTY ★★
ch.f. Assertive – Level Pegging (Common

Grounds). April 6. Tenth foal. Sister to the quite useful 2-y-o 5f and 6f winner Goldcrest and to the fair 6f (at 2 yrs) and 1m winner of 3 races Go For Broke and half-sister to the fair 5f and 6f winner of 6 races Even Bolder and to the fair 2-y-o 6f winner Bold Tie (both by Bold Edge). The dam, unplaced on her only 2 starts at 2 yrs, is a sister to the Listed Scarborough Stakes winner and Group 2 Kings Stand Stakes second Flanders (herself dam of the US Grade 3 winner Louvain) and a half-sister to 6 winners. The second dam, Family At War (by Explodent), won once over 5f at 2 yrs and is a half-sister to 4 winners. (Lady Whent). *"She's been in pre-training, they like her and she's due to arrive here today. It's a reasonably precocious family but I haven't seen her yet so I couldn't comment further".*

1340. SWISS CHEER (FR) ★★★
b.c. Swiss Spirit—Happy Clapper (Royal Applause). May 5. Half-brother to the fair 1m (at 2 yrs), 10f and hurdles winner Jebril (by Astronomer Royal) and to the fair 2-y-o 1m winner Barn Dance (by Country Reel). The dam was unplaced. The second dam, Coir 'A' Ghaill (by Jalmood), was placed second over 6f at 2 yrs. *"We've had the whole family and this is the nicest one the dam has produced. He looks potentially like having a bit more speed than the others and I love him. He's French-bred, so he's qualified for the premiums – and he's still for sale".*

1341. TOYBOX ★★
ch.f. Paco Boy – Play Street (Tobougg). March 5. First foal. £2,500Y. Tattersalls Ireland Ascot. Not sold. The dam, a fair 10f winner of 4 races, is a half-sister to 4 other minor winners. The second dam, Zoena (by Emarati), a modest 5f and 6f winner, is a half-sister to 5 minor winners. (Anthony Boswood & Mrs R Pease). *"A lovely home-bred, I trained the dam and this is a cracking little filly with a great attitude. She's growing a lot at the moment, I love her and she's just a fun 2-y-o who you'd be pleased to have bred".*

1342. UNNAMED ★★★
b.g. Charm Spirit – Arch Of Colours (Monsun). March 27. Third foal. 5,000Y. Tattersalls October Book 2. J Portman. Half-brother to the French 2017 Group 3 7f placed 2-y-o and

2018 3-y-o 7.5f winner Moissson Precoce (by Lawman). The dam, a fair 8.5f winner, is a half-sister to 2 winners and to the unraced dam of the German Group 3 winner and Group 1 Diamond Jubilee Stakes third Signs Of Blessing. The second dam, Sunray Superstar (by Nashwan), a useful 12f winner, is a sister to the Group 1 10f Prix Saint-Alary winner Nadia and a half-sister to 5 winners. *"About a week after I bought him his half-sister was third in a Group 3 in France and recently she broke her maiden – so that's a nice addition to the pedigree. This colt is lovely, we're not rushing him and he'll be one for later on. He was a cheap purchase because he looked quite weak and narrow at the sale and wasn't the obvious speedy type that everyone is looking for. But he's by an exciting new sire and I think he's definitely slipped through the net because he's done well recently and thickened out a bit".* TRAINER'S BARGAIN BUY

1343. UNNAMED ★★
b.f. Medicean – Masque Rose (Oasis Dream). February 13. Third foal. 15,000Y. Tattersalls October Book 3. J Portman. The dam, a dual 1m winner at 3 yrs in France, is a half-sister to 5 winners including the French Listed 7f winner and Group 3 third Nid d'Abeilles. The second dam, Massarossa (by Mr Prospector), is an unplaced full or half-sister to 4 winners and to the unraced dam of the Group 2 winners Silent Honor and Silkwood. (Whitcoombe Park Racing). *"A very nice filly with a lovely action on her; she is a tiny bit hot but if we can contain her I think she'll be a super filly over seven furlongs. She's got a bit of quality about her and I like her".*

KEVIN PRENDERGAST

1344. COCKTAIL TIME (IRE) ★★
b.c. No Nay Never – Barzah (Darshaan). February 17. Eleventh foal. 40,000Y. Tattersalls October Book 2. K Prendergast. Half-brother to 4 winners including the fairly useful 12f to 2m winner of 10 races Arch Villain (by Arch), the quite useful 12f and subsequent Australian winner Thubiaan (by Dynaformer) and the quite useful Listed-placed 1m winner Speculative Bid (by Excellent Art). The dam, a 2-y-o 6f winner, was Listed placed over 11f and is a half-sister to a winner in Japan. The second dam, Lepikha (by El Gran Senor), won

once at 3 yrs and is a half-sister to 5 winners including the dual Group 3 winner and Derby second Glacial Storm. *"A big, strong colt, even though he's by No Nay Never he's going to want at least six furlongs".*

1345. EMRAAN (IRE) ★★
b.c. Invincible Spirit – Wissal (Woodman). April 26. Closely related to the useful Listed 6f winner Ethaara (by Green Desert) and half-brother to 5 winners including the very useful 2-y-o Listed 7f Star Stakes winner and Group 3 7f Prestige Stakes second Mudaaraah (by Cape Cross), the useful dual 7f winner and Group 3 second Muwaary (by Oasis Dream) and the useful 2-y-o Listed 7f winner Sudoor (by Fantastic Light). The dam is an unraced sister to the 2-y-o Group 2 7f Laurent Perrier Champagne Stakes Bahhare and a half-sister to the Group 1 1m St James's Palace Stakes and Group 1 1m Queen Elizabeth II Stakes winner Bahri. The second dam, Wasnah (by Nijinsky), a fairly useful maiden, was placed at up to 10.5f and is a half-sister to the Group winners Dance Bid, Northern Plain and Winglet. (Hamdan Al Maktoum). *"I haven't had him long, he was quite a late foal and he's a backward type we probably won't see out until the autumn".*

1346. MOTASHAKEL (IRE) ★★★
b.c. Olympic Glory – River Test (Beat Hollow). February 26. Fourth foal. £140,000Y. Goffs UK Premier (Doncaster). Shadwell Estate Co. Half-brother to the French 13f and hurdles winner River Frost (by Silver Frost). The dam is an unraced half-sister to 10 winners including the Passing Glance (Group 2 1m Oettingen-Rennen and Group 3 8.5f Diomed Stakes), Hidden Meadow (Group 3 7f Prix de Palais-Royal and European Free Handicap) and the Listed winners Scorned and Kingsclere. The second dam, Spurned (by Robellino), a fairly useful 2-y-o 7f winner, later stayed 10f. (Hamdan Al Maktoum). *"A nice colt, we'll start him off at six or seven furlongs, he's strong and from a good family that Andrew Balding has been successful with".*

1347. MOTAWAAZY ★★★★
b.c. Kingman – Shimah (Storm Cat). February 28. Fifth foal. Half-brother to the fairly useful 2017 2-y-o 1m winner Moghamarah (by Dawn

Approach), to the useful Listed 6f (at 2 yrs), 7f and subsequent UAE sprint winner Mushir (by Oasis Dream) and the fair 1m winner Estikhraaj (by Dansili). The dam, a Listed 6f winner and second in the Group 1 Moyglare Stud Stakes, is a half-sister to 5 winners including the Listed 6f (at 2 yrs) and Group 3 7f Athasi Stakes winner Walayef, the Group 2 6f Diomed Stakes winner Haatef and the Irish dual Listed 6f winner Ulfah. The second dam, Sayedat Alhadh (by Mr Prospector), a US 7f winner, is a sister to the US Grade 2 7f winner Kayrawan and a half-sister to the useful winners Amaniy, Elsaamri and Mathkurh. (Hamdan Al Maktoum). *"We've trained most of the family and this is a big, strong 2-y-o that'll want six furlongs with some ease in the ground. The sire was big and strong, I think he needed the ground to be on the easy side and this colt seems to take after him in that respect".*

1348. MUDLAHHIM (IRE) ★★★

b.c. Tamayuz – So Sweet (Cape Cross). March 30. Fifth foal. 105,000Y. Tattersalls October Book 2. Shadwell Estate Co. Half-brother to the modest 7f seller winner Walking In Rhythm (by Lord Shanakill) and to a minor winner in Italy by Three Valleys. The dam, a fairly useful 2-y-o dual 7f winner, is a sister to the dual Listed winner and Group 3 placed Crosspeace and a half-sister to 4 winners. The second dam, Announcing Peace (by Danehill), is an unplaced full or half-sister to 5 minor winners. (Hamdan Al Maktoum). *"A very nice horse, we like him and he'll want fast ground and probably six furlongs plus".*

1349. MUNTAHEZ (IRE) ★★★

b.c. Camacho – Sonning Rose (Hawk Wing). February 17. Second foal. 110,000Y. Tattersalls October Book 2. Shadwell Estate Co. The dam, a quite useful 2-y-o 6f winner and second in the Listed Chesham Stakes, is a half-sister to 7 winners. The second dam, Shinkoh Rose (by Warning), placed over 9f at 3 yrs in Ireland, is a half-sister to one winner. (Hamdan Al Maktoum). *"Not a speedy horse, he'll want at least six furlongs, but he's a fine, big, strong horse that looks like 2-y-o".*

1350. MUTADARRIB ★★★

b.c. Kodiac – Wonderful Town (Bernstein). January 25. Fourth foal. €500,000Y. Goffs Orby. Shadwell Estate Co. Half-brother to the

fair 12f winner Casablanca (by Cape Blanco) and to the minor US winner of 4 races Moon Over Cuzco (by Malibu Moon). The dam is an unraced half-sister to 5 winners including the 2-y-o Group 3 7f Prix Miesque winner and Group 1 6f Prix Morny second Magic America. The second dam, Shoofha (by Bluebird), is an unplaced sister to the Group 3 and US Grade 3 winner Delilah and a half-sister to 4 winners. (Hamdan Al Maktoum). *"He's very nice but he's a big horse and won't you see him until we get to the seven furlong races, which is quite unusual for Kodiac. He's grown quite a lot since the sales".*

1351. RINTY MAGINTY(IRE) ★★

b.g. Camacho – Peanut Butter (Montjeu). April 16. First foal. €45,000Y. Tattersalls Ireland September. Kevin Prendergast. The dam, placed six times in France at 2 and 3 yrs including over 1m at Saint-Cloud, is a half-sister to 8 winners including the Group 2 5.5f Prix Robert Papin winner Zipping and the Group 3 5f Prix du Bois winner and good broodmare Zelding. The second dam, Zelda (by Caerleon), a French 6.5f winner, is closely related to the dam of the French 1,000 Guineas winner Valentine Waltz and a half-sister to the dual Group 1 winner Last Tycoon and the Group winners Astronef and The Perfect Life. *"A backward sort, I've gelded him and he'll not appear until much later in the season".*

1352. RISAALAAT (IRE) ★★★

b.f. Mukhadram – Naadrah (Shamardal). March 26. Fourth foal. Half-sister to the fairly useful 2017 2-y-o 5f and 6f winner Moonlight Bay and to the quite useful 2-y-o 6f and 7f winner Martini Time (both by Pivotal). The dam, a 2-y-o 10f winner in France and Listed-placed at 3yrs over 10f, is a half-sister to3 winners including the Group 3 Prix du Prince d'Orange second Prince Mag. The second dam, Princess d'Orange (by Anabaa), a Listed-placed winner at 3 yrs in France, is a half-sister to the dam of the Group winners Irish Wells and Sign Of The Wolf. (Hamdan Al Maktoum). *"I had the 2-y-o half-sister last year, we sold her and she went on to win the Birdcatcher Nursery. This is a fine, big, strong filly. We like her but she's going to take time, so I'd say seven furlongs in the second half of the season".*

1353. SAM LANGFORD (IRE) ★★★

ch.c. Footstepsinthesand – The Silver Kebaya (Rock Of Gibraltar). April 19. First foal. €60,000Y. Tattersalls Ireland September. Kevin Prendergast. The dam, a modest maiden, was disqualified after winning once over 1m and is a half-sister to one winner. The second dam, Music House (by Singspiel), a French Listed-placed 12f winner, is a full or half-sister to 5 winners. *"He'll probably run in an auction race he qualifies for at the Curragh at the Guineas meeting. A nice horse that wouldn't want heavy ground, he's a good tempered horse with enough toe to start at six and then work up to a mile later on".*

1354. SCARLET SKIS ★★★

b.f. Kodiac – Red Lady (Dutch Art). March 27. First foal. 55,000Y. Tattersalls October Book 2. K Prendergast. The dam, a quite useful 6f (at 2 yrs) and 5f winner of 3 races, is a half-sister to 6 winners including the Group 3 9f Prix Daphnis and Listed 10.5f winner Lateen Sails and the quite useful 1m winner Mainstay (dam of the Group winners Richard Pankhurst and Crazy Horse), the second dam, Felucca (by Green Desert), a fairly useful 2-y-o 6f winner, is a half-sister to 5 winners including the Group 2 10f Prix Eugene Adam winner Radevore. (Lady O'Reilly). *"She'll start her career in mid-April and might need her first run but we like her a lot and she'll improve with better ground; not a big filly but very active".*

1355. SESTRIERE (IRE) ★★★

b.f. Zebedee – Tatamagouche (Sadler's Wells). March 16. Sixth foal. €33,000Y. Goffs Sportsmans. Kevin Prendergast. Half-sister to 5 winners including the Italian Listed 1m winner Triticum Vulgare (by Frozen Power), the fair 7f winner of 6 races Just Paul (by Clodovil), the fair 7f winner Free One (by Fast Company) and the modest 2-y-o 5.5f winner, from two starts, She Knows It All (by Verglas). The dam, a fair 10f and 12f placed maiden, is a half-sister to 7 winners including the useful Irish Group 3 6f and Group 3 7f winner Ainippe. The second dam, Imitation (by Darshaan), is a unraced half-sister to 4 winners including Darnay (Group 2 Sea World International winner). *"She goes very well and is a nice filly that'll want dry ground and six furlongs. We like her".* TRAINER'S BARGAIN BUY

1356. UNNAMED ★★★

ch.c. Rip Van Winkle – Middle Persia (Dalakhani). March 4. Fifth foal. €22,000Y. Goffs Sportsmans. Kevin Prendergast. Half-brother to the Listed 11.5f Derby Trial winner Kilimanjaro (by High Chaparral), to the fairly useful dual 10f winner Mawaany (by Teofilo) and the quite useful 9f winner of 3 races Maratha (by Cape Cross). The dam, a fair Irish 1m winner, is a half-sister to 8 winners including Nayarra (Group 1 1m Gran Criterium), Gustav Klimt (Group 2 Superlative Stakes) and Wonderfully (Group 3 Silver Flash Stakes). The second dam, Massarra (by Danehill), a Listed 6f winner and second in the Group 2 Prix Robert Papin at 2 yrs, is a sister to the smart sire Kodiac, closely related to the Group 1 6f Haydock Park Sprint Cup winner Invincible Spirit and a half-sister to 8 winners including the Group 3 winners Acts Of Grace and Sadian. (Gareth McCann). *"A very nice horse that goes very well, he has a nice pedigree, being related to a Derby trial winner. He'll want at least seven furlongs".*

SIR MARK PRESCOTT

1357. ALATE (IRE) ★★

b.f. Holy Roman Emperor – Alleviate (Indian Ridge). March 27. Sixth foal. €45,000Y. Goffs Orby. Sir Mark Prescott. Half-sister to the Qatar 3-y-o winner Croara (by Exceed And Excel). The dam, a quite useful 14f and 15f winner of 4 races, is a sister to one winner and a half-sister to 5 winners including the Group 1 Prix Royal Oak and triple Group 2 winner Allegretto. The second dam, Alleluia (by Caerleon), winner of the Group 3 Doncaster Cup, is a half-sister to 7 winners including the Nassau Stakes and Sun Chariot Stakes winner Last Second (dam of the French 2,000 Guineas winner Aussie Rules) and the dams of the Group 1 winners Alborada, Albanova, Yesterday and Quarter Moon. (Mt. Brilliant Farm & Ranch, LLC). *"She looks like the type for July over seven furlongs, maybe a mile. The family has done us very well and I trained the dam, the grandmother and the great grandmother. They all stayed well and this filly will want seven furlongs plus, despite her sire".*

1358. ALBANITA ★★

gr.f. Sea The Moon – Alba Stella (Nashwan).

March 2. Half-sister to numerous winners including the fairly useful multiple 2m winner Moscato, the 7f (at 2 yrs) and 12f winner Hernandoshideaway (both by Hernando), the 14f and 2m winner All My Heart (by Sadler's Wells), the 12f winner All That Rules (by Galileo) – all quite useful, the fair10f to 12f winner of 6 races Aleatricis (by Kingmambo) and the fair 2-y-o 1m winner Albe Back (by Archipenko). The dam, a fairly useful dual 12f winner, is a half-sister to the dual Champion Stakes winner Alborada and the triple German Group 1 winner Albanova. The second dam, Alouette (by Darshaan), a useful 1m (at 2 yrs) and Listed 12f winner, is a half-sister to the dams of the Group 1 winners Quarter Moon, Yesterday, Aussie Rules and Allegretto. (Miss K. Rausing). *"She hasn't arrived here yet but the dam has done me proud; all the family seem to win and most of them stay. The ones I trained didn't win until they were three".*

1359. ALL POINTS WEST ★★★
b.c. Speightstown – Albamara (Galileo). April 13. Second foal. €46,000Y. Goffs Orby. Sir Mark Prescott. The dam, a quite useful 2-y-o 9f winner, was Listed-placed three times and is a half-sister to 5 winners including the stakes winners All At Sea, Algometer and Alwilda. The second dam, Albanova (by Alzao), a triple Group 1 12f winner in Germany, is a sister to the dual Champion Stakes winner Alborada and a half-sister to 7 winners. (Tim Bunting – Osborne House II). *"A thoroughly nice horse in every way, he was turned out in January and he'll be back with us in mid-May. He was a nice horse cantering but it's too early to say anything else about him. I trained the dam who was a good filly, she had a few little problems at three but still got black type".*

1360. ALMA LINDA ★★★
gr.f. Invincible Spirit – Alvarita (Selkirk). February 18. Ninth foal. Half-sister to 6 winners including the useful Irish 1m (at 2 yrs) and Group 3 10f Kilternan Stakes winner Alla Speranza (by Sir Percy), the useful 11f winner and Group 3 second Altesse, the fairly useful 10f to 14f winner of 6 races Alcaeus and the quite useful 12f and 13f winner Albert Bridge (all by Hernando). The dam, a French Listed 10.5f winner, is a full or half-sister 4 winners including the Group 2 10f Prix Greffulhe

second Albion. The second dam, Alborada (by Alzao), won the Champion Stakes (twice), the Nassau Stakes and Pretty Polly Stakes and is a sister to the German triple Group 1 winner Albanova and a half-sister to 7 winners. (Miss K Rausing). *"She's a nice filly and again this is a family we've done well with. This one would be sharper than her siblings; the idea was to use Invincible Spirit to speed things up a bit. The mare was a good old stick as well".*

1361. ANANDITA ★★★
b.f. Showcasing – Joyeaux (Mark Of Esteem). April 16. Fourth foal. 42,000Y. Tattersalls December. Sir Mark Prescott. Half-sister to the fair 2017 7f placed 2-y-o Champs De Reves (by Champs Elysees) and to the fairly useful 6f (at 2 yrs) and 5f winner Dakota Gold (by Equiano). The dam, a modest 5f and 6f winner of 6 races, is a half-sister to 5 winners including the Group 1 Premio Lydia Tesio winner Aoife Alainn and the Italian Listed winner and Group 2 Italian 2,000 Guineas third Adorabile Fong. The second dam, Divine Secret (by Hernando), is an unraced half-sister to 7 minor winners here and abroad. (Lady Fairhaven & The Hon Melanie Broughton). *"Bought for Lady Fairhaven who has had horses with me for forty-eight years, she was bought to be a 2-y-o of sorts and she's ready to start galloping now. I see her being a five/six furlong 2-y-o".*

1362. AUTONOMY ★★
b.c. Dansili – Funsie (Saumarez). January 21. Tenth foal. 75,000Y. Tattersalls October Book 1. Sir Mark Prescott. Half-brother to 4 winners including the Group 1 Epsom Derby, Juddmonte International Stakes and Racing Post Trophy winner Authorized, the quite useful Irish 2-y-o 1m winner Sirgarfieldsobers (both by Montjeu) and the fairly useful 10f and 12f winner Empowered (by Fasliyev). The dam is an unraced half-sister to 9 winners including the Group 3 10.5f Prix Cleopatre winner Brooklyn's Dance (the dam of six stakes winners) and the dam of the Group 1 Grand Criterium winner Okavango. The second dam, Vallee Dansante (by Lyphard), won once in France and is a full or half-sister to 12 winners including Green Dancer (French 2,000 Guineas). (Tim Bunting – Osborne House). *"A full-brother to a Derby winner, he's a very big,*

backward horse that was broken and turned away in January. He won't be back in until June time ".

1363. BATTLE OF PARADISE (USA) ★★★
b.c. Declaration Of War – Garden Of Eden (Curlin). March 9. Second foal. $40,000Y. Keeneland September. Oliver St Lawrence. The dam is an unraced half-sister to several winners including the St Leger winner Millenary, the Group 3 Princess Royal Stakes winner Head In The Clouds and the Derby third Let The Lion Roar. The second dam, Ballerina (by Dancing Brave), a quite useful 2-y-o 7f winner, is a half-sister to the Group 3 12f Princess Royal Stakes winner Dancing Bloom and to the 1,000 Guineas third River Dancer (dam of the Champion Stakes winner Spectrum). (Charles C. Walker – Osborne House III). *"A very big horse, bought at Keeneland where he was absolutely the wrong horse for that sale, being a big horse from a European staying family; he would have brought a lot more money at a sale over here. He's nice enough and one for seven furlongs and a mile".*

1364. BE MY HEART (FR) ★★
b.c. Pastorius – Breezy Hawk (Hawk Wing). March 8. Second foal. €80,000Y. Baden-Baden September. J Brummitt. The dam won two minor races in Germany from 3 to 5 yrs and is a half-sister to 7 winners including the German Group 2 winner Bathyrhon. The second dam, Be My Lady (by Be My Guest), won in Germany at 3 yrs and is a half-sister to 10 winners. (Middleham Park Racing (VII)). *"A seven furlong/mile type 2-y-o, he's always been a very attractive horse and the sire is doing well in Germany but he's an influence for stamina".*

1365. BRASSICA (IRE) ★★★
b.f. Australia – Lasilia (Acclamation). March 9. First foal. €50,000Y. Goffs Orby. Richard Guest. Sir M Prescott. The dam, a fairly useful 2-y-o 5f winner, was Listed-placed twice and is a half-sister to 4 winners including the Group 2 6f Railway Stakes third Dream Of Dreams. The second dam, Vasilia (by Dansili), is an unraced half-sister to 7 winners including the Group 1 6f Cheveley Park Stakes Airwave and the Group 1 Nunthorpe Stakes winner Jwala.

(Denford Stud). *"She'll be a mid-season 2-y-o, she's attractive and from a speedy family. The idea in buying her was that the family was quick and Galileo (the sire of Australia) has done best with speedy mares – or that's the current thought anyway. I would have thought seven furlongs would suit her".*

1366. CHANCER ★★★
b.c. Lope De Vega – Misk (Linamix). April 14. Half-brother to the fair 2-y-o 7f winner Rottingdean (by Oasis Dream) and to the fair 12f winner Gala (by Galileo). The dam, a 10f (at 2 yrs) and 11f winner in France and Listed placed four times, is a half-sister to 3 winners including the French Listed winner and Group 3 placed Mashoor. The second dam, Gontcharova (by Zafonic), won over 1m at 2 yrs in France and was Listed-placed and is a half-sister to 8 winners including the Group winners Roi Normand (US Grade 1 Sunset Handicap), Trampoli and Luth Dancer. (Denford Stud). *"A nice home-bred colt of Prince Faisal's, he's very big, will need time and was turned out earlier this year. He'll be back in the yard in May and he's a nice-moving colt".*

1367. EARLY EDITION (IRE) ★★★
b.f. Dawn Approach – Newsroom (Manduro). February 1. First foal. €35,000Y. Goffs Orby. Axom Ltd. The dam, a minor winner at 3 yrs in France, is a half-sister to 6 winners including the 2-y-o Group 3 Firth Of Clyde third La Presse. The second dam, Journalist (by Night Shift), a useful 2-y-o 6f winner, was second in the Group 3 6f Princess Margaret Stakes and is a half-sister to the Group 2 Flying Childers Stakes winner Sheer Viking. (Axom LXXII). *"She's bred to have a bit of temperament on both sides you might say, but she looks quite sharp and she's a quick learner, so she'll be ready to gallop shortly".*

1368. HEATWAVE ★★★★
b.f. Leroidesanimaux – Here To Eternity (USA) (Stormy Atlantic). March 20. Fourth foal. Half-sister to the useful 2-y-o 7f and French Listed 8.5f winner of 10 races Time Warp and to the quite useful 2-y-o 8.5f winner Glorious Forever (both by Archipenko). The dam, a modest 7f winner, is a half-sister to one winner. The second dam, Heat Of The Night (by Lear Fan), a dual 9f winner here, subsequently won a Listed 1m event in Germany and is a half-sister

to one winner. (Miss K. Rausing). *"A half-sister to a horse who did us so well, Time Warp, who won five off the reel for us including two Listed and was sold very well to Hong Kong where he was even more successful, so everybody has been thrilled. This is a nice filly and will be like Time Warp in as much as he started at six furlongs but wanted seven and a mile to win. I should think she'll be very similar and she's good-topped like him".*

1369. INFALLIBILITY (USA) ★★
gr.c. Oasis Dream – Infamous (Galileo). February 4. First foal. 50,000Y. Tattersalls October Book 1. Not sold. The dam is an unraced daughter of the useful 2-y-o 7f winner and Group 1 Moyglare Stud Stakes second Famous, herself a sister to the multiple Group 1 winning miler and sire Mastercraftsman and closely related to the US Grade 3 winner Genuine Devotion. (Mt. Brilliant Farm & Ranch, LLC). *"Owned by Mr Goodman of Mt Brilliant Farm which is a really successful winner producing stud in America, the horse didn't make his reserve at the sale and they kindly sent him to me. He's a very big, heavy horse but he's not clumsy and you'd expect him out in September".*

1370. MIRABAI ★★
ch.f. Poet's Voice – Classical Flair (Distant Music). February 14. Second foal. Half-sister to the modest 10f winner Lobster Pot (by Dylan Thomas). The dam is an unplaced half-sister to 5 winners including the French Listed 1m winner and Group 1 Prix Morny third Barricade. The second dam, Balleta (by Lyphard), a quite useful 3-y-o 10f winner, also won 3 races in the USA and is a sister to the great 'Arc', 'King George' and 2,000 Guineas winner Dancing Brave and to Jolypha (winner of the Group 1 12f Prix Vermeille and Group 1 10.5f Prix de Diane). (Hot to Trot Racing & Paddy Barrett). *"The first Poet's Voice I've had, she came in a bit late and I haven't done as much with her as the others. She's nice natured, has plenty of size, plenty of bone and looking at her you'd think she'd be one for the latter part of the season".*

1371. MISS CELESTIAL (IRE) ★★★★
b.f. Exceed And Excel – Liber Nauticus (Azamour). March 21. Second foal.180,000Y. Tattersalls October Book 1. Norris/ Huntingdon. Half-sister to Hidden Depths (by Dark Angel), last of 12 on his only start at 2 yrs in 2017. The dam won the Group 3 10.5f Musidora Stakes and is a sister to the winner and Group 3 Musidora Stakes third Serenada and a half-sister to 4 winners including the useful 2-y-o 7f winner and Group 2 Rockfel Stakes second Thetis. The second dam, Serres (by Daylami), is an unraced half-sister to 6 winners including the Breeders' Cup Turf, King George VI and St Leger winner Conduit and the Group 2 Great Voltigeur Stakes winner Hard Top. (John Pearce Racing Ltd). *"The late Mr Pearce left a sum of money to continue racing horses in his name for a while. Lord Huntingdon is the overseer and he bought this horse very well at the Ballymacoll Stud dispersal. It was a very strong sale but if any of them slipped by it was this and one other. I'm sure she'll hold her value even if her trainer made a mess of things! This filly will have a bit of pace and might start at six furlongs before I step her up to seven".*

1372. MON FRERE (IRE) ★★
b.c. Pour Moi – Sistine (Dubai Destination). February 22. Third foal. Half-brother to the fairly useful 2017 2-y-o Listed-placed 7f winner Dark Acclaim (by Dark Angel). The dam, a modest 4-y-o 14f winner, is a half-sister to 4 winners including the useful Group 3 Dahlia Stakes winner Tarfah (herself dam of the dual Derby and 2,000 Guineas winner Camelot. The second dam, Fickle (by Danehill), a fairly useful 1m and Listed 10f winner, is a half-sister to 7 winners including the Listed winners Birdie and Faru. (Elite Racing Club). *"A good-moving horse, he's having a break at present and is due back in May. He's bred to stay really, but the fact I didn't geld him earlier means I think there's a possibility of him doing at least something this year".*

1373. RAMATUELLE ★★★
ch.f. Champs Elysees – Florentia (Medicean). February 27. Fourth foal. Sister to the fairly useful 7f (at 2 yrs) to 10f winner of 5 races Cote D'Azur and half-sister to the fair 2-y-o 6f to 7.f winner of 3 races Flora Medici and the modest 7f to 1m winner of 4 races Anna Medici (both by Sir Percy). The dam, a modest 1m and 10f winner, is a half-sister to 9

winners including the useful 6f and 7f winner of 4 races Flying Officer. The second dam, Area Girl (by Jareer), a fair 2-y-o 5f winner, is a half-sister to 3 minor winners. (Mr N Greig). *"A marvellous family of Neil Greig's, they never stop winning – I don't think there's been a non-winner in the family in two generations. I've been lucky enough to train all of them bar one and there are 10 winners of 39 races out of the second dam. They tend to be useful but rated under 90, they're wonderfully consistent, they all have ability, like to race and are sound. This is a flashy filly – the family mostly tend to come with white eyes and white socks. This filly will want seven furlongs and if she doesn't win she'll be the first one that hasn't".*

1374. ROAD TO PARIS (IRE) ★★★
b.c. Champs Elysees – Alchemilla (Dubai Destination). April 3. Fifth foal. 27,000Y. Tattersalls October Book 2. Sir M Prescott. Half-brother to the very useful Listed 7f Surrey Stakes winner Smuggler's Moon (by Danehill Dancer) and to the fair 7f (at 2 yrs) to 9.5f winner Stardrifter (by Rock Of Gibraltar). The dam is an unraced half-sister to 8 winners including the smart 2-y-o dual Group 2 winner Strategic Prince and the Listed winner and Group 2 placed Yorkshire. The second dam, Ausherra (by Diesis), won the Listed 12f Lingfield Oaks Trial and is a full or half-sister to 9 winners including the Oaks, Irish Oaks and Yorkshire Oaks winner Ramruma. (Jones, Julian, Lee, Royle & Wicks). *"I nice horse with a proper pedigree, he was always going nicely but grew, got turned out and he'll be back in May".*

1375. ROYAL GUILD (IRE) ★★★
b.g. Mastercraftsman – Be My Queen (Sadler's Wells). February 5. Seventh foal. 38,000Y. Tattersalls October Book 2. Sir Mark Prescott. Half-brother to the fairly useful 7f winner Vibe Queen (by Invincible Spirit), to the quite useful 12f winner Batts Rock, the quite useful 2-y-o dual 7f winner Muirsheen Durkin (both by Fastnet Rock) and the minor Italian winner of 6 races from 2 to 5 yrs Relco Nordic (by Raven's Pass). The dam, an Irish Listed-placed 1m winner, is a half-sister to 6 winners including the Group 1 5f Prix de l'Abbaye winner Imperial Beauty. The second dam,

Multimara (by Arctic Tern), placed at 2 yrs in the USA, is a half-sister to 8 winners including the Group 3 May Hill Stakes winner Midnight Air (dam of the US Group 2 winner Midnight Line) and the dam of the Group/Grade 1 winners Together and Jan Vermeer. (Neil Greig – Osborne House). *"I gelded him but didn't turn him out because he was just showing enough to suggest he might run before September, probably over seven furlongs".*

1376. SCHEME ★★
b.f. Pivotal – Between Us (Galileo). February 9. First foal. The dam, a quite useful 11f and 12f winner, is a half-sister to several winners including the Group 3 7f (at 2 yrs) and Group 1 10.5f Prix de Diane winner Confidential Lady. The second dam, Confidante (by Dayjur), a fairly useful 3-y-o dual 7f winner, was Listed-placed and is a half-sister to 6 winners including the US Grade 3 winner Drilling For Oil, the Group 3 7f Solario Stakes winner White Crown and the US Listed winner and Grade 1 second Dr Caton. (Cheveley Park Stud). *"The pedigree has my fingerprints all over it and it's been another very successful family for us. This is a big filly that'll need plenty of time, early on she was looking a bit slovenly, but when she's had a nice break she'll come back all right".*

1377. SHINING SEA (IRE) ★★★
b.f. Sea The Stars – Shamwari Lodge (Hawk Wing). May 3. Fourth foal. 100,000Y. Tattersalls October Book 1. Wentrow Media. Half-sister to the very useful Listed 7f winner of 7 races and Group 3 Diomed Stakes third Oh This Is Us (by Acclamation). The dam, a very useful 6f (including at 2 yrs) and Irish Group 3 1m winner of 6 races, is a half-sister to 5 winners including the Listed Tetrarch Stakes winner Imperial Rome. The second dam, Ripalong (by Revoque), is an unplaced half-sister to 13 winners including the Group 1 6f Haydock Park Sprint Cup and Group 3 5f Palace House Stakes winner Pipalong. (Elite Racing Club). *"Bought by Elite and more expensive than they normally buy, but she was well-bought because about three weeks later the foal made 350k, so the people who bought the foal will be hoping I do well with this! A nice filly and a good mover for seven furlongs in June/July".*

1378. THE GAME IS ON ★★★
b.c. Garswood – Paquerettza (Dr Fong). March 11. Fourth foal. 58,000Y. Tattersalls October Book 2. Sir Mark Prescott. Closely related to the modest 6f winner Lady Atlas (by Dutch Art) and half-brother to the quite useful 2-y-o 6f winner Continental Lady (by Medicean). The dam, a quite useful 1m and 10f winner of 4 races, is a half-sister to the Group 3 2m Sagaro Stakes winner Shipmaster. The second dam, Cover Look (by Fort Wood), won two Group 2 events and was Group 1 placed in South Africa and is a half-sister to 7 winners. (Mr Timothy J. Rooney). "He threw a splint which held him up in the spring but he's been back with the main group now for a couple of weeks and looks alright. He wouldn't run until June or July but he's a big, strong horse".

1379. VOLVANIQUE (IRE) ★★★
b.f. Galileo (IRE)—Pink Symphony (Montjeu). March 23. Third foal. Half-sister to Pink Phantom (by Oasis Dream), unplaced in two starts at 2 yrs in 2017 and to the fair 10f winner African (by Dubawi). The dam, a useful Group 3 12f Give Thanks Stakes winner, is closely related to 2 winners including the Group 3 7f Prestige Stakes (at 2 yrs), Group 3 Nell Gwyn Stakes and US Grade 3 winner and Group/Grade 1 placed Fantasia. The second dam, Blue Symphony (by Darshaan), a fair 10f winner, is a half-sister to one winner. (Mrs F H Hay). "The first horse I've had for the owners, he's by Galileo (I believe he's not a foal share) and out of a useful mare of theirs. She was going nicely in the winter but is having a break at the moment and she'll run in July or August over seven furlongs. The dam won over twelve furlongs but ran respectably over seven as a 2-y-o. Nevertheless this would be a staying type".

1380. YVETTE ★★★
b.f. Le Havre – Macleya (Winged Love). February 26. Half-sister to 3 winners including the quite useful 2017 2-y-o 7f to 1m winner of 4 races Codicil (by Lawman) and the fairly useful Irish 2-y-o 7f winner Saltonstall (by Pivotal). The dam won 7 races including the Group 2 12.5f Prix de Pomone and the Group 3 10f Prix Allez France and is a half-sister to 7 winners including the Group 3 Prix de Barbeville winner Montclair. The second dam,

Minaccia (by Platini), won a Listed event in Germany over 7f at 3 yrs and is a half-sister to 4 winners. (Cheveley Park Stud). "The half-sister Codicil won four on the bounce for us last season and interestingly the total winning distance was less than a length – very unusual! This filly needs more time, she's leggier and taller and will need all of seven furlongs and a mile".

1381. UNNAMED ★★★
b.c. Authorized – Al Jasrah (Shirocco). March 14. First foal. 40,000Y. Tattersalls October Book 3. Sir Mark Prescott. The dam ran once unplaced and is a half-sister to 7 winners including the useful Listed-placed winners Proceed With Care and Dramatic Quest and the dam of the Australian Group 1 winner Hartnell (by Authorized). The second dam, Ultra Finesse (by Rahy), a useful French 8.5f and 10f winner, was second in the Group 2 12f Prix de Malleret and is a half-sister to 6 winners including Suave Dancer (winner of the Prix de l'Arc de Triomphe, the Prix du Jockey Club and the Phoenix Champion Stakes). (Sheikh Juma Dalmook Al Maktoum). "Closely related to Hartnell, he's not over-big and will be a seven furlong 2-y-o".

JOHN QUINN
1382. CAREY STREET (IRE) ★★★
b.c. Bungle Inthejungle – Undulant Way (Hurricane Run). April 29. Fourth foal. €13,000Y. Goffs Sportsmans. Richard Knight/ Sean Quinn. Half-brother to the 2017 7.5f placed 2-y-o, from two starts, Ambient, to the French 1m winner Black Dream (both by Born To Sea) and the quite useful 2-y-o 1m winner Newsman (by Makfi). The dam, a fair 11.5f winner, is a half-sister to 3 winners. The second dam, Arietta's Way (by Darshaan), is an unplaced full or half-sister to 10 winners including the Italian Group 1 winners Court Of Honour and Single Empire. (Mr P G Shorrock). "He ran quite well in the Brocklesby in bad ground and that race is working out well. Considering he was a late foal and just by looking at his pedigree you'd have to say he'll stay further than five furlongs, so he should be able to pick up a race or two this year".

1383. ENCORE MAM'SELLE ★★★
b.f. Dark Angel – Encore View (Oasis Dream).

February 6. Third foal. €40,000Y. Tattersalls Ireland September. Richard Knight/ Sean Quinn. The dam, a moderate 6f fourth placed 2-y-o, is a half-sister to 4 winners including the Listed winners Oh Beautiful and Freedom's Light. The second dam, Aricia (by Nashwan), a fairly useful 3-y-o 7f winner, is a half-sister to 8 winners including the Group 2 5f Kings Stand Stakes winner Cassandra Go (herself the dam of three Group winners including the Irish 1,000 Guineas winner Halfway To Heaven) and the smart Group 3 6f Coventry Stakes winner and Irish 2,000 Guineas second Verglas. (Lowther Racing & Partners). *"It's always nice to have a Dark Angel but they aren't necessarily all early types. This is a nice filly that'll be suited by six and seven furlongs from the middle of the season onwards".*

1384. SIGNORA CABELLO ★★★★
b.f. Camacho – Journalist (Night Shift). January 17. Twelfth foal. 20,000Y. Tattersalls October Book 3. Richard Knight/Sean Quinn. Sister to the quite useful 2-y-o Listed-placed 5f winner Plagiarism and half-sister to 6 winners including the very useful 2-y-o 6f winner and Group 3 Firth Of Clyde Stakes third La Presse (by Gone West), the useful 7f and 1m winner of 4 races Paper Talk, the French winner and dual Listed second Emirates Girl (both by Unbridled's Song) and the quite useful 2-y-o 7f winner Ittasal (by Any Given Saturday). The dam, a useful 2-y-o 6f winner, was second in the Group 3 6f Princess Margaret Stakes and is a half-sister to the useful sprinter Sheer Viking. The second dam, Schlefalora (by Mas Media), won at up to 1m in Sweden and is a half-sister to the 1,000 Guineas winner Las Meninas. (Zen Racing & Partner). *"A filly that we like, she'll be an early 2-y-o for five furlongs and may well have run before your book is published. It's a fast pedigree and the mare has done really well with stallions you wouldn't necessarily think would throw 2-y-o winners".*

1385. THE GREAT STORY ★★★
b.c. Sea The Moon – Lovina (Love The Groom). March 9. Tenth foal. 22,000Y. Tattersalls October Book 1. Abdulla Ahmad Al Shaikh. Half-brother to the Italian Group 3 winners Lohit (by Dutch Art) and Lokaloka (by Pursuit Of Love), to the Italian Listed winner Lasika (by

Pursuit Of Love) and the Italian Listed-placed winner Marziano (by Mark Of Esteem). The dam, a Listed-placed 2-y-o winner in Italy, is a half-sister to 7 minor winners. The second dam, Menem (by Bold Arrangement), won 5 minor races at 2 and 3 yrs in Italy and is a half-sister to 5 winners. (Abdulla Ahmad Al Shaikh). *"Bought by his owner at the Tattersalls Book One sale, he looks like he's bought well because this colt could well start at six furlongs in midsummer before moving up to seven and he's a nice colt".* TRAINER'S BARGAIN BUY

1386. YOURTHEONE ★★★
b.c. Camacho – Cockaleekie (Alphabet Soup). April 19. Fifth foal. €26,000Y. Tattersalls Ireland September. Richard Knight / Sean Quinn. Half-brother to the quite useful 5f (at 2 yrs) and dual 6f winner Dandyleekie (by Dandy Man) and to two minor 3-y-o winners abroad by Art Connoisseur. The dam, unraced, is out of the fairly useful 12f winner Pennygown, herself a half-sister to 11 winners including Invermark (Group 1 Prix du Cadran) and Craigsteel (Group 2 Princess Of Wales's Stakes). (Mrs S Quinn). *"This colt was a fairly late foal but he's keeping up well and I'd say he's one for five/six furlongs on decent ground. A sharp 2-y-o type, we're only waiting for better ground now".*

1387. UNNAMED ★★★
ch.c. Olympic Glory – Alzanti (Arch). March 15. First foal. The dam, a quite useful dual 7f winner (including at 2 yrs), is a half-sister to 7 winners including the dam of the Group 2 Dahlia Stakes winner Bragging. The second dam, Proud Fact (by Known Fact), a French Listed 7f winner, is a sister to one winner and a half-sister to 3 winners including Houseproud (French 1,000 Guineas). *"A colt we recently purchased at the Doncaster breeze up sale, he comes from a very good nursery we've had luck with before. You wouldn't expect an Olympic Glory to be a five furlong specialist but he breezed nicely and I think we can look forward to him starting in early summer and improving as the season goes on".*

1388. UNNAMED ★★★
ch.c. No Nay Never – Challow Hills (Woodman). March 14. Sixth foal. £50,000Y.

Goffs UK Premier (Doncaster). John Quinn. The dam, a modest 1m winner, is a half-sister to 5 winners including the US stakes winner and dual Grade 3 placed Teide. The second dam, Cascassi (by Nijinsky), a fair 10f winner here, also won at 4 yrs in France and is a half-sister to 5 winners including Diminuendo (Epsom, Irish and Yorkshire Oaks winner) and the Oaks second Pricket. (Mr Ross Harmon). *"A big, scopey horse, the dam has yet to have a winner but there are good words being said about first season sire No Nay Never so hopefully this will be her first. He's a big, scopey, quite imposing horse for six/seven furlongs in midsummer".*

1389. UNNAMED ★★

b.f. Nathaniel – Glen Rosie (Mujtahid). February 11. Tenth living foal. 45,000Y. Tattersalls October Book 2. Richard Knight/ Sean Quinn. Sister to the quite useful 12f winner Nathania and half-sister to 5 winners including the useful 2-y-o Listed 7f winner Kings Quay, the fairly useful triple 10f winner Milne Garden (both by Montjeu), the quite useful 7f (at 2 yrs) and 11f winner Vincent's Forever (by Pour Moi) and the quite useful Listed-placed 10f and 11f winner Fastback (by Singspiel). The dam, a 2-y-o 5f winner and second in the Group 3 Fred Darling Stakes, is a half-sister to 5 winners including the Group 3 Irish Derby Trial and triple US stakes winner Artema. The second dam, Silver Echo (by Caerleon), is an unraced sister to the Listed 6f winner Dawn Success and a half-sister to the Group 3 7f Gladness Stakes winner Prince Echo. (Mr D Ward). *"This is a big, scopey filly for seven furlongs and from the midsummer onwards. The sire's stock are more sought after now and this filly is a half-sister to Kings Quay who was a good 2-y-o and was then successful with us. She'll be a better horse next year, but that's what she was bought for".*

1390.UNNAMED ★★★

b.c. Heeraat – Madam Mojito (Smart Strike). March 22. Third foal. £18,000Y. Goffs UK Premier (Doncaster). Sean Quinn. The dam, a quite useful dual 5f winner at 2 yrs, is a half-sister to 3 minor winners. The second dam, Asuncion (by Powerscourt), is an unraced half-sister to 9 winners including the 2-y-o Group 2 and Group 3 winner Enthused. (Dalwhinnie Bloodstock). *"A nice filly for six/seven furlongs, she's a midsummer type 2-y-o, the dam won*

at two and first season sire Heeraat should get plenty of 2-y-o winners".

1391. UNNAMED ★★★★ ♣

b.f. Slade Power – Piccola Sissi (Footstepsinthesand). February 25. First foal. £52,000 2-y-o. Goffs UK Breeze Up (Doncaster). The dam, a minor winner at 4 yrs in Italy, is a half-sister to the Group 1 7f Prix de la Foret and Haydock Park Sprint Cup winner Gordon Lord Byron. The second dam, Boa Estrela (by Intikhab), is an unraced half-sister to 5 winners including the smart Irish Group 3 7f and Group 3 1m winner Cheyenne Star. *"This filly did the fastest breeze at the Doncaster sale the other day, so we were very pleased to get her. Despite the ground being bad there I think she's likely to prefer better ground".*

1392. UNNAMED ★★★

b.c. Zoffany – Queen's Pudding (Royal Applause). March 30. Sixth foal. €20,000Y. Tattersalls Ireland September. Sean Quinn / Richard Knight. Half-brother to the quite useful 2-y-o 6f winner Meringue Pie (by Sakhee's Secret) and to the modest 6f (at 2 yrs) and 1m winner Quoteline Direct (by Sir Percy). The dam, a quite useful 2-y-o 6f winner, is a half-sister to 6 winners including the Group 2 Yorkshire Cup third Defining. The second dam, Gooseberry Pie (by Green Desert), is a placed half-sister to 8 winners including the dual Group winner Rakaposhi King. (The Yorkshire Traders). *"A good-sized, scopey 2-y-o and a good mover, she'll be a six/ seven furlong type. The dam has bred two 2-y-o winners and she was a good 2-y-o herself"*

1393. UNNAMED ★★★

b.f. Heeraat – Skylla (Kyllachy). February 17. Third foal. £58,000 2-y-o. Goffs UK Breeze Up (Doncaster). R Knight/S Quinn. Half-sister to the 2017 modest 2-y-o 6f winner Skyva (by Dick Turpin). The dam, a fairly useful 2-y-o dual 5f winner, was Listed-placed and is a half-sister to 4 minor winners. The second dam, Day Star (by Dayjur), a modest 6f winner, is a half-sister to 6 winners including the French 1,000 Guineas winner Rose Gypsy. *"She did the second fastest breeze at Doncaster breeze up sale, so we're chuffed with her; a proper five furlong 2-y-o, we'll get her out soon".*

1394. UNNAMED ★ ★ ★
b.c. Born To Sea – Start The Music (King's Best). April 4. Seventh foal. €20,000Y. Goffs Sportsmans. Richard Knight/Sean Quinn. Half-brother to the very useful 2-y-o 6f and 6.5f winner and Group 2 6f Sandy Lane Stakes third Mubtasim (by Arcano) and to the fair 7f and 1m winner Stec (by Bushranger). The dam, a minor winner at 3 yrs in France, is a half-sister to 6 winners including the 2-y-o Group 1 Phoenix Stakes second Big Time. The second dam, Beguine (by Green Dancer), is an unplaced half-sister to 8 winners including the champion two-year-old and smart sire Grand Lodge and the Listed winners La Persiana and Papabile. (Mr D Ward). *"A strong colt, he'll be a six furlong 2-y-o around May/June time. The sire was a better 3-y-o but we'd certainly expect this colt to make a 2-y-o".*

KEVIN RYAN

1395. ALOYSIUS LILIUS (IRE)
b.c. Gregorian – Nafa (Shamardal). April 16. First foal. €46,000Y. Goffs Sportsmans. Hillen/ Ryan. The dam, a quite useful 6f winner of 6 races at 3 and 5 yrs, is a half-sister to 4 minor winners. The second dam, Champs Elysees (USA) (by Distant Relative), won 5 races including a Listed stakes at 3 and 4 yrs in the USA and is a half-sister to the Grade 2 San Bernadino Handicap and Group 3 7f Supreme Stakes winner Anshan.

1396. CELEBRITY DANCER (IRE)
ch.c. Excelebration – Dance Hall Girl (Dansili). March 10. Fifth foal. £23,000Y. Goffs UK Premier. Hillen/Ryan. Half-brother to the quite useful 2017 2-y-o 7f winner Highlight Reel, to the very useful 2-y-o Listed 7f winner Tashweeq (both by Big Bad Bob) and the fairly useful Irish 5f (including at 2 yrs) and 6f winner of 4 races Kasbah (by Acclamation). The dam, a quite useful Irish 7f winner, is a half-sister to 3 winners including the Listed winner Solar Deity. The second dam, Dawn Raid (by Docksider), a quite useful Irish 3-y-o 7f winner, is a half-sister to 8 winners including the French and Irish 2,000 Guineas and Richmond Stakes winner Bachir. (Hambleton Racing Ltd XXII).

1397. EMARAATY ANA
b.c. Shamardal – Spirit Of Dubai (Cape Cross).

May 10. Third foal. Brother to the quite useful 2-y-o 6f winner Salamah and half-brother to the quite useful 2-y-o 1m winner Weld Al Emarat (by Dubawi). The dam, a Listed 12f winner, is a half-sister to the Group 3 10f Prix Corrida and Group 3 10.5f Prix de Flore winner Trumbaka and to the French Listed 9f winner of 4 races Arctic Hunt. The second dam, Questina (by Rainbow Quest), won twice at 3 yrs in France and is a half-sister to 6 winners. (A A Al Shaikh).

1398. GLASS SLIPPERS
b.f. Dream Ahead – Night Gypsy (Mind Games). March 25. Half-brother to 6 winners including the useful 2-y-o 6f and Listed 7f winner and Group 3 Oh So Sharp Stakes second Electric Feel (by Firebreak), the fairly useful 2-y-o 6f winner and Listed placed Aunt Nicola, the 5f and 6f winner Mymumsaysimthebest (both by Reel Buddy), dual 7f winner Discression (by Indesatchel) and the 5f winner of 6 races from 3 to 5 yrs Safari Mischief (by Primo Valentino) – all quite useful. The dam, a fair 2-y-o 5f winner, is a sister to the Listed 2-y-o winner On The Brink and a half-sister to 4 winners including the Listed winner and Group 2 placed Eastern Romance. The second dam, Ocean Grove (by Fairy King), a quite useful 2-y-o 6f winner, is a half-sister to 5 winners here and abroad. (Mr T. G. & Mrs M. E. Holdcroft).

1399. HURRICANE SPEED (IRE)
ch.c. Gale Force Ten – Ma Nikitia (Camacho). April 24. Fifth foal. €30,000Y. Goffs Sportsmans. Hillen /Butterworth. Half-brother to the triple 7f winner at 3 and 4 yrs Midnitemudcrabs (by Arcano) and to the moderate 5f (at 2yrs) and 7f winner Zebelini (by Zebedee). The dam is an unraced half-sister to 7 winners including the Listed 6f winner and Irish 1,000 Guineas second Dimenticata and the useful Listed 6f winner Master Fay. The second dam, Non Dimenticar Me (by Don't Forget Me), a modest 5f winner, is a half-sister to 7 winners. (Hambleton Racing Ltd).

1400. INAJUMA (IRE)
ch.f. Iffraaj – Zayn Zen (Singspiel). March 15. Seventh foal. 50,000Y. Tattersalls October Book 1. Rabbah Bloodstock. Half-sister to the

smart Listed 1m winner of 4 races Ennaadd (by King's Best), to the quite useful 10f winner Mezyaad (by Tiger Hill), the fair 5f winner Foolaad (by Exceed And Excel), the fair 1m (at 2 yrs) and 7f winner Hersigh (by Poet's Voice) and the modest dual 6f winner Maakirr (by Street Cry). The dam, a useful 1m Listed winner of 3 races, was Group 3 placed and is a sister to the fairly useful 1m, 10f and UAE winner Zaafran. The second dam, Roshani (by Kris), a fair 1m and 10f winner at 3 yrs, is a half-sister to 8 minor winners here and in the USA. (Mr Sultan Ali).

1401. KALIA ASHA (IRE)
gr.f. Dark Angel – Pivotal Era (Pivotal). April 7. Second foal. 72,000Y. Tattersalls December. Stephen Hillen. The dam is an unraced sister to 3 winners including the smart Group 3 10.5f Prix Penelope winner Humouresque and the smart 4-y-o triple 10f winner and Group 2 placed Mighty and a half-sister to 4 winners including the very smart sprinter Danehurst, winner of the Cornwallis Stakes (at 2 yrs), the Curragh Flying Five, the Prix de Seine-et-Oise and the Premio Umbria. The second dam, Miswaki Belle (by Miswaki), second over 7f on her only start, is closely related to the smart Group 3 6f Cherry Hinton Stakes winner and 1,000 Guineas third Dazzle and a half-sister to 8 winners. (Mr T. A. Rahman).

1402. KATIEJAY
b.f. War Command – Tohaveandtohold (Pivotal). February 23. First foal. 40,000Y. Tattersalls October Book 3. Guy Stephenson. The dam, a moderate 9.5f placed maiden, is a half-sister to 5 winners including the Group 3 placed 2-y-o Rosebride. The second dam, Wedding Party (by Groom Dancer), a quite useful 6f and 7f winner, was Listed-placed and is a half-sister to 4 winners including the Group 2 May Hill Stakes winner Pollenator. (Mr K. Alexander).

1403. LAULLOIR (IRE)
ch.f. More Than Ready – Legs Lawlor (Unbridled). March 13. Sixth foal. €47,000Y. Goffs Sportsmans. Hillen/Ryan. Half-sister to the minor Canadian 12f stakes winner of 4 races Clarinet (by Giant's Causeway) and to a minor US winner by Awesome Again. The dam, a fair Irish 3-y-o 1m winner, is a half-

sister to 8 winners including the US Horse of the Year and champion 2-y-o colt Favorite Trick. The second dam, Evil Elaine (by Medieval Man), was a US stakes winner of 4 races.

1404. MO EMMAD ALI (IRE)
b.c. No Nay Never – Special Assignment (Lemon Drop Kid). May 5. Fourth foal. 100,000Y. Tattersalls December. Stephen Hillen. Half-brother to a minor winner abroad by High Chaparral. The dam is an unraced half-sister to 8 winners including the US triple Grade 2 winner Quest Star. The second dam, Tinaca (by Manila), is an unplaced half-sister to 5 winners including the dual US Grade 2 winner Mariah's Storm (the dam of Giant's Causeway). (Mr Jaber Abdullah).

1405. RATHBONE
b.c. Foxwedge – Frequent (Three Valleys). March 3. Second foal. €87,000Y. Goffs Orby. Hillen/Ryan. The dam is an unraced half-sister to 9 winners including the Group 2 6f Gimcrack Stakes winner Showcasing and the very smart Listed 6f winner Camacho. The second dam, Arabesque (by Zafonic), a useful Listed 6f winner, is a sister to 2 winners and a half-sister to 4 winners including the Australian triple Group 1 winner Foreteller and the Group 2 1m Prix de Sandringham winner Modern Look. (Mrs Angie Bailey).

1406. ROCK PARTY (IRE)
b.f. Society Rock – Bacchanalia (Blues Traveller). February 16. Ninth foal. €24,000Y. Tattersalls Ireland September. Craig Buckingham. Half-brother to the Italian 2-y-o 7f winner Eternity Star (by Baltic King), to the fair 6f (at 2 yrs) and 7f winner of 4 races Bachotheque (by Chineur) and the modest 2-y-o 5f winner of 4 races Granny Peel (by Redback). The dam, a fair 2-y-o 7f winner, is a half-sister to one winner. The second dam, Daffodil Dale (by Cyrano de Bergerac), a modest Irish 2-y-o 5f winner, is a half-sister to 4 winners. (Mr Craig Buckingham).

1407. SENSE OF BELONGING (FR)
ch.c. Dutch Art – Bertie's Best (King's Best). March 15. Third living foal. 40,000Y. Tattersalls December. Hillen/Ryan. The dam, a French Listed-placed 6f (at 2 yrs) and 1m winner, is a half-sister to 2 winners including the Group

3 9f Prix Vanteaux winner Just Little. The second dam, Just Wood (by Highest Honor), won 3 minor races at 3 yrs in France and is a half-sister to the dual Listed winner Katchina Quest. (Mr T. A. Rahman).

1408. SWINGING EDDIE
b.c. Swiss Spirit – Bling Bling (Indian Ridge). February 17. Ninth foal. £38,000Y. Goffs UK Premier (Doncaster). Hillen/Ryan. Half-brother to the fairly useful dual 6f (at 2 yrs) to 10f winner Bling King (by Haafhd), to the quite useful 2-y-o 7f winner Male Model (by Iffraaj), the fair triple 10f winner Go Sakhee (by Sakhee) and the modest 6f winner of 6 races New Rich (by Bahamian Bounty). The dam, a fair fourth over 1m and 10f, is a sister to the very smart dual Listed 5f winner Watching and a half-sister to 4 winners. The second dam, Sweeping (by Indian King), a useful 2-y-o 6f winner, was Listed placed and is a half-sister to 10 winners. (Mr T. A. Rahman).

1409. WILD HOPE
b.c. Kingman – Wild Mimosa (Dynaformer). May 17. Third foal. 35,000Y. Tattersalls October Book 2. Hillen/Ryan. The dam ran once unplaced and is a half-sister to 8 winners including Compton Admiral (Group 1 10f Coral Eclipse Stakes), Summoner (Group 1 1m Queen Elizabeth II Stakes) and the dam of the multiple Group 1 winner The Fugue. The second dam, Sumoto (by Mtoto), a useful 6f (at 2 yrs) and 7f winner, is a half-sister to 5 winners including the dam of the Group/Graded stakes winners Adagio and Arvada. (Hambleton Racing Ltd XXXVII).

1410. YOUSINI
b.c. Siyouni – War Effort (War Front). February 18. First foal. 50,000Y. Tattersalls October Book 2. Middleham Park/Hillen. The dam is an unplaced half-sister to 3 winners. The second dam, Louve Royale (by Peintre Celebre), a US Listed winner and Grade 3 placed, is a half-sister to 8 winners including the Group/Grade 2 winner Loup Breton. (Middleham Park Racing XXI).

1411. UNNAMED
b.f. War Command – Regatta (FR) (Layman). February 13. Second foal. €36,000Y. Arqana Deauville October. Not sold. Half-sister to

the minor French 3-y-o winner Rewa (by Hard Spun). The dam won two Listed events in France over 1m at 2 and 3 yrs and is a half-sister to 6 winners. The second dam, Red Star (by Lure), a minor winner in France, is a half-sister to 5 winners including Punctilious (Group 1 Yorkshire Oaks). (Mr T. A. Rahman).

GEORGE SCOTT

1412. ALBANDERI ★★★★
b.f. Kingman – Hazel Lavery (Excellent Art). April 25. Third foal. €240,000Y. Arqana Deauville August. Al Rabban Racing. Half-sister to the 2017 2-y-o 1m winner, from two starts, The Revenant (by Dubawi). The dam, a 7f (at 2 yrs) and Group 3 12f St Simon Stakes and Listed 10f Aphrodite Stakes winner, is a half-sister to 3 winners including the useful 10f and 12f winner and Group 3 12f second Leo Gali. The second dam, Reprise (by Darshaan), placed fourth once over 10f, is a half-sister to 3 winners. (Al Rabban Racing). *"A gorgeous, big filly with a deep girth. She's only cantering at the moment but she finds everything very easy. We like her a lot and she'll probably start off in a seven furlong maiden in mid-to-late summer. She's a queen!"*

1413. BARDO (IRE) ★★★
b.c. Galileo – Gilt Edge Girl (Monsieur Bond). January 16. Fourth foal. 150,000Y. Tattersalls October Book 2. Tim Gredley. Half-brother to the quite useful dual 1m winner Time's Arrow (by Redoute's Choice). The dam won 5 races including the Group 1 5f Prix de l'Abbaye and Group 3 Ballyogan Stakes and is a half-sister to 7 winners including the Group 2 5f Flying Childers Stakes winner Godfrey Street. The second dam, Tahara (by Caerleon), is an unplaced half-sister to 3 winners and to the unraced dam of the Group 1 Prix Morny winner Arcano. (W J & T C O Gredley & Flaxman Stables). *"A precocious colt that's pleased me and he's going to go into faster work imminently. Being by Galileo I'd very much like him to break his maiden before Ascot and maybe turn up in the Chesham".*

1414. BLUESKY ★★
b.g. Dutch Art – Sea Meets Sky (Dansili). February 11. First foal. £38,000Y. Goffs UK Premier (Doncaster). Elliott & Scott. The dam, a quite useful 10f winner, is a closely related to

the Group 2 10f Prix Guillaume d'Ornano and Group 3 10.5f Rose Of Lancaster Stakes winner Multidimensional. The second Sacred Song (by Diesis), dam won 4 races from 6f (at 2 yrs) to 12f including the Group 3 Princess Royal Stakes and the Group 3 Lancashire Oaks and is a half-sister to the Grade 1 Breeders' Cup Handicap and multiple Grade 2 winner Strut The Stage. (The Rum Babas). *"A strong type of horse that has been a little slow to come to hand. I would very much hope that he'd be ready to make his debut over six furlongs in the summer. A 3-y-o prospect really".*

1415. BYRD (IRE) ★★★

b.c. Kodiac – Precious Gem (Sadler's Wells). April 18. Fifth foal. €75,000Y. Goffs Orby. Elliott & Scott. Half-brother to the very useful 1m to 2m winner of 3 races Flymetothestars (by Sea The Stars). The dam, a Group 3 10f and Listed 11f winner in Ireland, is a half-sister to 2 winners. The second dam, the unraced Ruby (by Danehill), is a sister to Rock Of Gibraltar. (W. J. and T. C. O. Gredley). *"A cool horse, he had a very small setback but I'd hope to have him out this side of Ascot. He should certainly have more speed than his Sea The Stars half-brother and he looks a sound type of horse that should run plenty throughout the year. He's compact, has a good, deep shoulder and he's good-topped".*

1416. CLEM A ★★★

b.c. Helmet – Mondovi (Kyllachy). March 7. Fourth foal. 70,000Y. Tattersalls October Book 2. Tim Gredley. Half-brother to the quite useful 5f winner of 5 races at 2 and 4 yrs Rosina (by Showcasing) and to the fair 6f winner of 4 races Dont Have It Then (by Myboycharlie). The dam, a quite useful winner of 5 races from 5f to 7f here and in Germany, is out of the fair 6f and 7f winner Branston Fizz (by Efisio), herself a half-sister to 11 winners including the Group 2 Sandown Mile winner Desert Deer and the very useful and tough mare Branston Abby, a winner of 24 races at up to 7f including numerous Listed events. (W. J. and T. C. O. Gredley). *"I'm very fond of the sire and this is a very easy-moving colt with speed on both sides of the pedigree, so he should start over six furlongs in the summer and get further in time. I like him".*

1417. CONCIERGE (IRE) ★★★

br.c. Society Rock – Warm Welcome (Motivator). April 20. Fourth foal. £60,000Y. Goffs UK Premier (Doncaster). Elliott & Scott. Half-brother to the fairly useful Listed-placed dual 6f winner at 2 and 3 yrs Danielsflyer (by Dandy Man). The dam is an unraced half-sister to 7 winners including the Listed Give Thanks winner Juliette. The second dam, Arutua (by Riverman), is an unraced half-sister to the Group 2 Prix Greffulhe Stakes winner Along All. (Bartram, Kilburn & Ware). *"A precocious colt physically although he's been a bit slow to catch up mentally. We won't be pushing on with him just yet, but he should be very effective at two and give his owners plenty of fun".*

1418. CRANTOCK BAY ★★★

b.c. Havana Gold – Orton Park (Moss Vale). February 7. Second foal. £50,000Y. Goffs UK Premier (Doncaster). Elliott & Scott. Half-brother to the 2017 7f placed 2-y-o Shawwal (by Harbour Watch). The dam, a fair 2-y-o 5f winner, is a half-sister to 7 winners including the Group 3 Chipchase Stakes winner Knot In Wood. The second dam, Notley Park (by Wolfhound), placed three times over 7f at 3yrs, is a half-sister to 5 winners including the US Grade 3 winner Prince Bobby B and the Listed 5f Scarborough Stakes winner Notley. (Mr K. J. Breen). *"The sire's already had a wonderful start to the year and this chap covers a lot of ground and is a forward-going colt. He still has a degree of filling out to do and therefore I would imagine he'd be ready in early-summer. He's got a great attitude, I do like him and he loves training, so he's got a chance".*

1419. EARTH AND SKY (USA) ★★

b.f. Noble Mission – Youre So Sweet (Storm Cat). March 24. Half-sister to a minor US 2-y-o winner by Smart Strike and a winner in Russia by Dixie Union. The dam is an unraced half-sister to 6 winners including the Derby winner Kris Kin and the French Group 2 10f placed Bravodino. The second dam, Angel In My Heart (by Rainbow Quest), dam won the Group 3 10f Prix de Psyche and was second in the Matriarch Stakes, the Yellow Ribbon Stakes, the Santa Ana Handicap (all Grade 1 events) and the Group 2 Prix de l'Opera.

She is a half-sister to the Group 1 Prix de la Salamandre winner and useful sire Common Grounds. (Flaxman Stables Ireland Ltd). *"A lovely, tall, scopey filly and a very easy mover. She has very similar markings to her dad who I helped train at Warren Place and she's a filly I would very much hope to win a maiden with at the end of the year, but she's a 3-y-o prospect".*

1420. GEORGE GERSHWIN ★★★

b.c. Bated Breath – Sharp Relief (Galileo). March 5. Fourth foal. €80,000Y. Goffs Orby. Elliott & Scott. Half-brother to the fair 2017 7f and 1m placed 2-y-o Sharp Reminder (by Kyllachy) and to the quite useful 10f (at 2 yrs) and 14f winner Calvinist (by Holy Roman Emperor). The dam, a fair 11f and 14f winner, is a half-sister to 3 minor winners. The second dam, Jinsky's Gift (by Cadeaux Genereux), is an unraced half-sister to 8 winners including the triple Listed 7f winner Modeeroch, the Group 1 1m Gran Criterium third Chinese Whisper and the Group 1 6f Cheveley Park Stakes third Danaskaya and the dam of the dual Group 1 winner Belardo. (Chelsea Thoroughbreds Ltd). *"A big horse, the Bated Breath/Galileo cross has worked already and he would be the biggest of my 2-y-o's. He won't be ready until midsummer but he's an easy moving colt with a really nice attitude".*

1421. HEIRESS ★★

b.f. Sir Percy – Sweet Cando (Royal Applause). March 2. Ninth foal. €130,000Y. Goffs Orby. Elliott & Scott. Half-sister to the 9f Hong Kong stakes winner of 6 races Jacobee (by Mark Of Esteem), to the US winner and Grade 2 third Hameildaeme (by Storming Home), the quite useful Irish 2-y-o 1m winner Let Us Fight (by Bushranger), the quite useful 1m winner Glorious Sun (by Medicean) and the minor US winner Candy's Girl (by Bertolini). The dam, a modest 2-y-o 5f winner, is a half-sister to 2 winners. The second dam, Fizzygig (by Efisio), a moderate 7f winner, is a half-sister to 6 winners. (Breen, Elliott & Ware). *"A lovely-moving, gorgeous filly with a great attitude and a great step to her. Although she's strong she's still a bit 'up behind' and therefore I'm in no rush with her. I'd expect to gain a good understanding of her this season before improving significantly at three".*

1422. LAHESSAR ★★★★

b.c. Exceed And Excel – Burlesque Star (Thousand Words). February 29. Second foal. 120,000Y. Tattersalls October Book 1. Al-Rabban Racing. The dam is an unplaced half-sister to 5 winners including the Group 1 Hong Kong Vase winner and Group 2 10.5f York Stakes third Dominant and the smart Group 2 7f Lennox Stakes winner Es Que Love. The second dam, Es Que (by Inchinor), a minor winner at 3 yrs in France, is a half-sister to 4 winners. (Al Rabban Racing). *"A brute of a colt and a nice type of horse, he's tall and leggy but he'll come to hand relatively quickly. He'd be a horse I like, he's tough and I'll give him an opportunity to gallop in mid-May to see if he's up to being an earlier type, but I would imagine he'll be doing most of his racing throughout the middle part of the summer".*

1423. LYNDON B (IRE) ★★★

b.c. Charm Spirit – Kelsey Rose (Most Welcome). January 31. Eleventh foal. €70,000Y. Goffs Orby. Elliott & Scott (private sale). Half-brother to 6 winners including the Group 2 Bet365 Mile and dual Group 3 winner Sovereign Debt, the fairly useful 6f and 7f winner Sorelle Delle Rose (both by Dark Angel), the Group 3 Fred Darling Stakes winner Puff (by Camacho), the quite useful 2-y-o dual 7f winner Marked Card (by Kheleyf) and the fair 2-y-o 6f winner Golden Rosie (by Exceed And Excel). The dam, a fairly useful 2-y-o 5f winner of 3 races, was Listed-placed three times and is a half-sister to 3 winners. The second dam, Duxyana (by Cyrano de Bergerac), is an unraced half-sister to 8 winners. (W. J. and T. C. O. Gredley). *"He's just had a little setback, other than that he was training well and he was never going to be early anyway. I like his pedigree and in particular Sovereign Debt very much and he wouldn't be too dissimilar to him except for his colour. I knew that horse well when I was at Michael Bell's".*

1424. MERGE (IRE) ★★★

b.g. Dandy Man – Interlacing (Oasis Dream). February 25. First foal. £110,000Y. Goffs UK Premier (Doncaster). Orbis Bloodstock. The dam ran twice unplaced and is a half-sister to 4 minor winners. The second dam, Short

Dance (by Hennessy), a very useful 6f, Listed 7f (both at 2 yrs) and Listed 1m winner, is a half-sister to 2 winners. (Orbis Bloodstock).
"A really lovely horse that looks very precocious, I've gelded him purely because he's owned by some Hong Kong guys and they don't worry about that. I'd hope to have him out sometime in May".

1425. MY EXCELSA (IRE) ★★★ ♠
b.f. Exceed And Excel – Emirates Joy (Street Cry). February 27. First foal. £70,0000Y. Goffs UK Premier (Doncaster). Elliott & Scott. The dam, a 7f and 1m placed maiden, is a half-sister to 4 winners including the smart 2-y-o 7f winner and Group 1 Racing Post Trophy second Zip Top. The second dam, Zofzig (by Danzig), a US 2-y-o 6f and 1m winner on her only starts, is a half-sister to the US Grade 1 Acorn Stakes winners Zaftig and Zo Impressive. (Mr A Boyd Rochfort & Mr S Leslie). *"A very straightforward filly, she'll be one of my earlier 2-y-o runners. She's still a bit 'up behind' so I'm letting her strengthen up, but I very much hope that she'll be showing up this season. She looks tough and has a very solid attitude – and that's putting it politely!"*

1426. NARAK ★★★
ch.f. Dubawi – Chachamaidee (Footstepsinthesand). May 29. Third foal. The dam, a winner of 7 races including the Group 1 1m Matron Stakes and Group 2 7f Lennox Stakes, is a sister to the Group 3 7f Oak Tree Stakes winner J Wonder and a half-sister to 3 winners. The second dam, Canterbury Lace (by Danehill), is an unraced sister to the Group 3 Gallinule Stakes winner and Irish Derby second Alexander Of Hales and to the 2-y-o 1m winner and Group 1 1m Criterium International second Chevalier and a half-sister to the 1,000 Guineas winner Virginia Waters. (Mr R A H Evans). *"She's a very late foal and as a result she has some immaturities, so we're giving her time to work through them. She's pleased me in everything she's done and is a very kind, honest type of filly".*

1427. USAIN BOAT ★★★
b.c. Casamento – Emerald Peace (Green Desert). March 29. Twelfth living foal. €23,000Y. Tattersalls Ireland September. Charlie Gordon-Watson. Half-brother to 8

winners including the Listed 6f winner and Group 3 Princess Margaret Stakes second Vital Statistics (by Indian Ridge), the quite useful triple 6f winner (including at 2 yrs) Emerald Lodge (by Green Desert), the quite useful 7f winner Carved Emerald (by Pivotal) and the quite useful Flashheart (by Nayef). The dam, a useful Listed 5f winner of 4 races and second in the Group 2 5f Flying Childers Stakes, is a half-sister to 9 winners. The second dam, Puck's Castle (by Shirley Heights), a fairly useful 2-y-o 1m winner, was Listed-placed and is a half-sister to the champion 2-y-o filly Embassy and the Group 2 Pretty Polly Stakes winner Tarfshi. (Blue Starr Racing). *"I love this horse, he's got a great attitude and he's a lovely, big, strong colt. He has a good mind and everything he's done so far he's found easy, so we're pleased with him at this stage. He hasn't got a particularly precocious pedigree so we'll let him tell us as he goes into faster work".* TRAINER'S BARGAIN BUY

1428. WILLOW BROOK ★★
ch.f. Sepoy – Portland River (Stormy River). January 29. First foal. 8,000Y. Tattersalls October Book 3. A C Elliott. The dam, a minor French dual winner at 3 and 4 yrs, is a half-sister to 6 winners including the Australian Group 1 winner Pornichet. The second dam, Porza (by Septieme Ciel), was placed once at 2 yrs in France and is a half-sister to 2 winners including the Group 1 Prix Maurice de Gheest. (Mr A. Al Mansoori). *"A precocious filly with a great attitude, I hope she'll be able to pick up a novice in her first two starts and then we'll take it from there".*

1429. ZIGELLO (IRE) ★★
b.f. Intello – Zigarra (Halling). January 30. Fifth foal. €200,000Y. Goffs Orby. Orbis Bloodstock. Half-sister to the very useful triple Listed 10f winner and multiple Group 3 placed Battalion (by Authorized). The dam is an unraced half-sister to 7 winners including the US dual Grade 2 winner Silent Name. The second dam, Danzigaway (by Danehill), won the Group 3 Prix Perth and was second in the Group 2 Prix d'Astarte and is a half-sister to 9 winners including French Group winners Gold Away and Blushing Gleam. (Orbis Bloodstock). *"A tall, very pretty filly, she's immature but I would*

very much hope that she'd be up to winning a maiden at the back-end before being put away for the season".

1430. UNNAMED ★★★★
ch.c. Shamardal – Fragrancy (Singspiel). March 13. Half-brother to the useful Listed 1m winner and Group 3 placed Pelerin (by Shamardal), to the fairly useful 6f (at 2 yrs) and 1m winner Masarah (by Cape Cross), the quite useful 7f winner of 4 races Road To Dubai (by Aqlaam) and the quite useful 10f and 12f winner Flower Of Love (by Poet's Voice). The dam, a useful 1m (including at 2 yrs) and 10f winner, was Listed-placed and is a half-sister to 5 winners. The second dam, Zibet (by Kris), a fairly useful 7f winner, is a half-sister to 8 winners including the dam of the dual Group 1 winner Hibaayeb. (M. Al Nabouda). *"He'd be one of my favourite 2-y-o's. A half-brother to Road To Dubai who won four races for us last year, he's very tough, workmanlike and does everything you ask with ease. He's a very nice horse and we're lucky to have him because Shamardal's are hard to get these days. He's still got plenty of developing to do but he'll move into faster work in late April and we'll see how he goes on. He's not big – he's quite fine actually – and he's a cracking horse".*

1431. UNNAMED ★★
gr.f. Foxwedge – Sweet Alabama (Johannesburg). March 13. Second foal. Half-sister to the fairly useful 2017 2-y-o 7f winner Il Primo Sole (by Raven's Pass). The dam, a poor 1m placed maiden, is a half-sister to 5 minor winners. The second dam, Alybgood (by Alydeed), a Listed winner of 5 races in the USA at 2 and 4 yrs, is a half-sister to 10 winners including the German Oaks winner Que Belle. (Biddestone Racing Club). *"A tough filly that always gives 110%, she's a bit immature but I'd hope to see her out in early summer".*

1432. UNNAMED ★★★
b.br.c. Artie Schiller – Sweet Temper (Stormy Atlantic). February 20. Fifth foal. $50,000Y. Keeneland September. Excel Racing. Half-brother to the US Grade 3 9f winner Colonelsdarktemper (by Colonel John), to the 7f (at 2 yrs here) and subsequent US 8.5f winner Sympathy (by Henrythenavigator), the minor US winner of 2 races, at 2 and 3 yrs,

Sweet Citizen (by Proud Citizen) and a minor winner abroad at 2 to 4 yrs by Arch. The dam, a minor dual winner at 2 and 3 yrs in the USA, is a half-sister to 7 winners including the US stakes winners Total Bull and Seattle Pattern. The second dam, Pattern Step (by Nureyev), won the Grade 1 Hollywood Oaks and is a half-sister to the Grade 2 winner Motley. (Excel Racing). *"He's a beautiful, black colt with a great head and finds it all quite easy. He's still a bit weak although I'd expect him to strengthen up relatively quickly and he's one for his owners to look forward to for sure. A nice horse".*

DAVID SIMCOCK
1433. BLAST OFF ★★
b.c. Sea The Moon – Having A Blast (Exchange Rate). February 19. First foal. €140,000Y. Goffs Orby. Orbis Bloodstock. The dam, a minor 3-y-o 1m winner at Chantilly, is a half-sister to 3 minor winners abroad. The second dam, Blasted (by Dynaformer), a minor US 2-y-o winner, is a half-sister to 3 winners including the Canadian Grade 3 winner and Grade 1 placed Breaking Lucky. *"A big horse with lots of size and scope and he's done everything asked of him. He shows a good attitude to his work and he'll be a horse for later in the season".*

1434. CONFECTOR (IRE) ★★★★
ch.c. Mastercraftsman – Uliana (Darshaan). January 9. Twelfth foal. €310,000Y. Goffs Orby. Orbis Bloodstock. Half-brother to 8 winners including the Irish dual Group 3 placed Festival Princess (by Barathea), the useful 2-y-o 7f winner and Group 3 Classic Trial second Intern (by Rip Van Winkle) and the quite useful Irish 2-y-o 1m winner So Amazing (by Galileo). The dam, an Irish 10f winner, is a half-sister to 9 winners including the German Group 1 10f winner Ransom O'War. The second dam, Sombreffe (by Polish Precedent), a fair 7f winner, is closely related to the Group 2 winners Russian Bond and Snaadee and a half-sister to 9 winners including the Group 3 Prix de Conde winner Cristofori. *"He's a fine looking horse and it's surprised me how natural he is. I'm very pleased with him at this stage, he's a good goer and I think he'll make up into a nice horse. We have his half-brother Intern who is consistent and probably better than his mark of 102, but this would be a better-looking, scopier type of horse for seven furlongs and a mile this season".*

1435. DESERT LION ★★★★
b.c. Lope De Vega – Sorella Bella (Clodovil). February 5. First foal. The dam, a fairly useful 2-y-o 7f and Italian Listed 1m winner, was second in the Group 1 Premio Gran Criterium and is a half-sister to 3 winners. The second dam, Anazah (by Diesis), placed fourth once over 12f in Ireland at 4 yrs, is a half-sister to 8 winners including the US Grade 3 winner Rock Lobster. *"A good type of horse, strong and mature. He's a good-actioned horse that's very easy on the eye and very natural. We're just about to do a bit more with him, he doesn't look backward at all and I see him as a seven furlong horse".*

1436. DR JEKYLL (IRE) ★★★
b.c. Scat Daddy – Similu (Danehill Dancer). February 3. First foal. 350,000Y. Tattersalls October Book 1. Stephen Hillen. The dam won once at 3 yrs in the USA and is a half-sister to another minor winner. The second dam, Myth And Magic (by Namid), is an unraced half-sister to 11 winners including the Grade 1 9f Matriarch Stakes, Group 2 1m Sun Chariot Stakes and triple Group 3 winner Dress To Thrill and the dam of the Group 1 Prince Of Wales's Stakes winner Free Eagle. *"A big horse with loads of scope, it's surprised me how quickly he's come to hand. He takes his work very well, does everything asked and is a good-actioned horse that takes everything in his stride".*

1437. PADURA ★★★
b.c. Havana Gold – Indian Story (Indian Ridge). March 15. Fourth foal. £50,000Y. Goffs UK Premier (Doncaster). Orbis Bloodstock. Half-brother to the minor French and Qatar winner Arguia (by Pastoral Pursuits). The dam ran once unplaced and is a half-sister to 5 winners including the Italian Listed winner of 7 races and Group 2 Italian 1,000 Guineas second Love Roi. The second dam, Law Tudor (by Law Society), a minor winner at 3 yrs in Italy, is a half-sister to 5 winners. *"An attractive, good-sized horse, he's training fine and looks like a seven furlong/mile horse. He has a good attitude and gets on with it".*

1438. RANGALI ISLAND (IRE) ★★★
b.c. Camacho – Tender Surprise (Doyen). March 1. First foal. £39,000Y. Goffs UK Premier

(Doncaster). Badger Bloodstock. The dam won 3 races over hurdles and is a half-sister to 2 winners including the 2-y-o Group 2 6f Mill Reef Stakes winner Toocoolforschool. The second dam, Spring Surprise (by Hector Protector), a fair 2-y-o 7f winner, is a half-sister to 10 winners including the useful 6f (at 2 yrs) to 1m and hurdles winner and Listed Heron Stakes second Tucker. *"He came in late but caught up very quickly and has done very well physically since he came into the yard. He looks quite strong now and we've done a lot more with him recently. He's showing up well at the canter, I don't dislike him and he should be starting over six/seven furlongs in midsummer".*

1439. SALTITO ★★★
bl.c. Harbour Watch – Hispanic Dancer (Jeremy). January 8. Second foal. £42,000Y. Goffs UK Premier (Doncaster). Orbis Bloodstock. The dam is an unraced half-sister to 4 winners. The second dam, Hymenee (by Chief's Crown), a minor French 3-y-o winner, is a half-sister to 7 winners including the US Grade 2 winner Globe and the dam of the Group 2 Prix Niel winner Housamix. *"A big horse with a big middle on him, he has a great attitude, is very laid-back and has a good action. He's quite likeable, there's lots of him and is one we're ready to press on with because he's quite mature".*

1440. UPPER SCHOOL ★★
b.f. Oasis Dream – Upper Street (Dansili). January 11. First foal. The dam, a modest 10f winner, is a full or half-sister to 3 winners. The second dam, Islington (by Sadler's Wells), won 6 races including the Group 1 Yorkshire Oaks (twice), the Grade 1 Filly and Mare Turf and the Group 1 Nassau Stakes and is a half-sister to the smart stayer Election Day and the smart 10f performer Greek Dance. *"Not the biggest and she came in quite late but it's a good family and she's a good-actioned filly that wants to get on with it. I should think she's a filly for midsummer, she has a nice way of going and has every chance on pedigree, so we'll see".*

1441. WIXAM (IRE) ★★★
b.c. Camacho – Fork Handles (Doyen). February 25. Second foal. 52,000Y. Tattersalls

October Book 2. Blandford Bloodstock. The dam, a fairly useful 6f (at 2 yrs) and 10f winner, was third in the Group 3 7f Prix du Calvados and is a half-sister to 4 winners. The second dam, Natalie Jay (by Ballacashtal), a fair winner of 5 races from 6f to 1m, is a half-sister to 3 winners including the Listed Sceptre Stakes winner You Know The Rules. *"A big, strong type of horse that has trained very well, he was one of the earliest to train. He's had a break for a few weeks with a slight setback but he's back now and he's certainly strong enough. We'll be looking for six furlong maidens for him around June time. A good type".*

1442. UNNAMED ★★★
ch.f. New Approach – Alasha (Barathea). February 28. Eleventh foal. 70,000Y. Tattersalls October Book 2. Blandford Bloodstock. Half-sister to 5 winners including the smart dual Group 3 7f and dual Listed winner Alanza (by Dubai Destination), the 2-y-o Listed 7f winner Alonsoa (by Raven's Pass) and the quite useful dual 12f winner Alajan (by Alhaarth). The dam, a useful 7f (at 2 yrs) and Listed 1m winner, is a half-sister to 8 winners including the Irish Listed winner Alaiyma. The second dam, Alasana (by Darshaan), won twice in France over 1m and 9f and is a half-sister to the Prix Maurice de Nieuil winner Altayan and the Grand Prix de Vichy winner Altashar. *"Quite a natural filly, not the biggest but with a good action and a good attitude. It's difficult to know where we are trip-wise, but she's not backward and we'll carry on with her because she's making good progress".*

1443. UNNAMED ★★★★
ch.c. Dutch Art – Baileys Jubilee (Bahamian Bounty). March 19. Second foal. 80,000Y. Tattersalls October Book 2. Blandford Bloodstock. The dam won three times over 5f at 2 yrs including a French Listed event, was third in the Group 1 Cheveley Park Stakes and is a half-sister to 2 winners. The second dam, Missisipi Star (by Mujahid), a fairly useful 1m winner, was Listed-placed and is a half-sister to one winner. *"He goes well, he's strong and mature, shows up very well on the canter and has natural speed and a great attitude. There's lots of him, he'll be one of our earlier 2-y-o's and he's a good type of horse. A lovely colt, I see him as a six furlong horse, hopefully starting off in May".*

1444. UNNAMED ★★★★
ch.c. Mastercraftsman – Bunood (Sadler's Wells). April 26. Eighth foal. 110,000Y. Tattersalls October Book 1. Blandford Bloodstock. Half-brother to the 7f (at 2 yrs) and 1m winner and Listed-placed Lanansaak (by Zamindar), to the quite useful 1m winner Estebsaal (by Dansili) and the fair 7f and 1m winner Bakoura (by Green Desert). The dam, a fairly useful 2-y-o 1m winner, was third in the Group 3 12f Princess Royal Stakes and Listed-placed 3 times and is a half-sister to 5 winners. The second dam, Azdihaar (by Mr Prospector), a quite useful dual 7f at 3 yrs, is a half-sister to 5 winners including Shadayid (1,000 Guineas and Prix Marcel Boussac) and the Group 3 winners and sires Dumaani and Fath. *"He's a lovely, big horse that reminds us of a useful horse we have by the same sire, Curbyourenthusiasm. He has a massive stride, a lovely way of going and I really like him. I doubt him being that early but he finds everything very easy and everyone in the yard likes him. I'd say a mile would suit him this year".*

1445. UNNAMED ★★★
ch.c. No Nay Never – Enharmonic (E Dubai). April 4. Second foal. 110,000Y. Tattersalls October Book 1. Blandford Bloodstock. The dam ran once unplaced and is a half-sister to 4 winners including the champion 2-y-o and Group 1 7f Dewhurst Stakes winner Distant Music and the dams of the Group 1 Haydock Sprint Cup winner African Rose and the Group 2 winner Canticum. The second dam, Musicanti (by Nijinsky), a French 14.5f winner, is a half-sister to 9 winners including Vanlandingham, winner of the Washington D.C. International, the Jockey Club Gold Cup and the Suburban Handicap. *"This horse has thrived since he's been in, he's a good type and I liked the stallion as a racehorse. A good-actioned horse that wants to get on with it, he doesn't look backward and we'll push on with him. I'm particularly pleased with how he's progressed since we've had him".*

1446. UNNAMED ★★★
b.c. Intello – Galipette (Green Desert). March 1. Sixth foal. €65,000Y. Arqana Deauville August. Blandford Bloodstock. Half-brother to the fairly useful 7f winner Gymnaste (by

Shamardal), to the French 1m winner Gaetano Donizetti (by Makfi) and the French 5-y-o 7f winner Omy (by Zamindar). The dam, a modest 5f and 6f placed maiden, is closely related to four winners by Oasis Dream including the Group 2 6f Gimcrack Stakes winner Showcasing and a half-sister to four winners including the very smart Listed 6f winner Camacho. The second dam, Arabesque (by Zafonic), a useful Listed 6f winner, is a sister to the useful 5f and 6f winner Threat and a half-sister to the Group 2 1m Prix de Sandringham winner Modern Look. *"A lovely horse, he's very natural for his pedigree and there's a bit of speed on the dam's side which isn't a bad thing with this stallion. He's done very well since he came from the sales, I thought he was a relatively cheap buy and he's matured. He's done everything asked and has a good attitude and a good action".*

1447. UNNAMED ★★★
ch.f. Dawn Approach – Galley (Zamindar). March 13. Sixth living foal. 50,000Y. Tattersalls October Book 2. Blandford Bloodstock. Half-sister to the smart Listed 10f winner of 4 races and Group 3 9f Meld Stakes second Portage (by Teofilo) and to the Italian Listed 10f winner Cape Magic (by Cape Cross). The dam, placed at 3 yrs in France, is closely related to 3 winners by Zafonic and a half-sister to 8 winners including Wharf (Group 3 July Stakes) and the dams of the Prix de l'Arc de Triomphe winner Rail Link and the Group 1 Criterium de Saint-Cloud winner Linda's Lad. The second dam, Dockage (by Riverman), won over 1m at 2 yrs and a Listed 9f event at 3 yrs in France and is a half-sister to 3 winners.
"Not the biggest, she's keen to get on with things and we'll step her up anytime now. A filly with a good, low, flat action but she's quite busy, so it'll be interesting to see how she goes on. She's doing everything asked but I don't see her as a real speedy type".

1448. UNNAMED ★★★
b.c. Charm Spirit – Kite Mark (Mark Of Esteem). February 14. Twelfth foal. 115,000Y. Tattersalls October Book 1. Stephen Hillen. Half-brother to 6 winners including the Group 2 Prix Vicomtesse Vigier and triple Group 3 winner (including at 2 yrs) Kite Wood, the useful 9f winner and Group 2 Great Voltigeur

Stakes third Odeon (both by Galileo), the quite useful 6f (at 2 yrs) and 10f winner Legislation (by Oasis Dream) and the fair 10f and 15f winner Daylami Dreams (by Daylami). The dam ran once unplaced and is a half-sister to the dual Group 2 winner Madame Dubois (dam of the Group 1 winners Indian Haven and Count Dubois) and the dam of the Richmond Stakes winner Daggers Drawn. The second dam, Shadywood (by Habitat), a useful 10f winner and second in the Lancashire Oaks, is a half-sister to 8 winners. *"A lovely big horse that was a bit hot when he arrived, he has a good action and he's one for the second half of the season. The family stay well and he has a likeable way of going".*

1449. UNNAMED ★★★★
b.c. Kodiac – La Chicana (Invincible Spirit). April 1. Fourth foal. 150,000Y. Tattersalls October Book 2. Rabbah Bloodstock. Brother to the quite useful triple 6f winner Fast Enough and half-brother to the 2017 2-y-o 5f and 6f winner Shaheen (by Society Rock) and the smart Group 3 11f and Listed 12f winner and Group 1 placed Desert Encounter (by Halling). The dam, placed once at 3 yrs in France, is a sister to the Group 2 Grand Prix de Deauville winner Allied Powers and a half-sister to 5 winners including the Group 2 Premio Ribot winner Dane Friendly. The second dam, Always Friendly (by High Line), a winner of 3 races including the Group 3 12f Princess Royal Stakes, was second in the Group 1 Prix Royal-Oak and is a half-sister to 5 winners. *"He has a great way of going and a good action. Far more precocious than his brother, he's one I'd love to see out in May or June over six furlongs. Looks the type to get on with".*

1450. UNNAMED ★★★
b.f. Shamardal – Lady Liberty (Shirocco). February 29. First foal. 120,000Y. Tattersalls October Book 1. Not sold. The dam, a German Listed 10f winner, is a half-sister to the very smart 1m (at 2 yrs) and dual Grade 1 12f Northern Dancer Turf Handicap winner Wigmore Hall. The second dam, Love And Laughter (by Theatrical), a fair 2-y-o 7f winner, is a half-sister to 5 winners including the French Listed winner Kissing The Camera. *"She'll need plenty of time, but she's a good-*

looking filly that's done well since the sales. We'll give her all the time she needs, she has a good action and does everything right. A nice type".

1451. UNNAMED ★★★
b.f. Lawman – Leopard Creek (Weldnaas). February 20. Seventh foal. 72,000Y. Tattersalls October Book 2. Rabbah Bloodstock. Half-sister to the 2-y-o Group 3 5f Cornwallis Stakes winner of 4 races Ponty Acclaim (by Acclamation), to the fairly useful dual 2-y-o 5f winner Adham, the modest 7f (at 2 yrs) and 1m winner Killermont Street (both by Dream Ahead) and a winner in Greece by One Cool Cat. The dam, a modest 5f placed 3-y-o, is a sister to the Listed winning sprinter Astonished and a half-sister to 5 winners including the Group 3 Prix du Petit Couvert winner Bishops Court. The second dam, Indigo (by Primo Dominie), a quite useful 2-y-o dual 5f winner, is a half-sister to 5 winners. *"She was a little busy when she came in but she's settled into it well. Certainly big enough, very natural and I see her as being a seven furlong filly come July time".*

1452. UNNAMED ★★★
ch.c. Universal – My Order (Raven's Pass). January 25. Second foal. 21,000Y. Tattersalls October Book 3. David Simcock. The dam is an unraced half-sister to City Style, a very smart winner of 8 races from 6f to 9f at 2 to 7 yrs including the Group 3 Strensall Stakes and Group 1 placed three times in the UAE. The second dam, Brattothecore (by Katahaula County), a dual stakes winner of 4 races at 2 and 3 yrs in the USA, is a half-sister to 5 winners including the Canadian stakes winner and dual Grade 3 placed Sweet Monarch. *"I've got the sister who is quite average, but this is a much nicer type of horse and of all the Universals we've trained for the owner this is the nicest one so far. A good goer, a good actioned horse and strong, he's keen to get on with things and I quite like him".*

1453. UNNAMED ★★★
ch.c. Iffraaj – Ninja Lady (Nayef). March 8. Second foal. €70,000Y. Goffs Orby. David Redvers. The dam ran twice unplaced and is a half-sister to 2 winners including the Group 2 Beresford Stakes second Oklahoma City. The

second dam, Galaxy Highflyer (by Galileo), is an unraced half-sister to 7 winners including the Group 1 winners Opera House, Kayf Tara and Zee Zee Top (dam of the Group 1 winner Izzi Top) and to the dam of the Group 1 Moyglare Stud Stakes winner Necklace. *"A really nice, big horse with loads of size and scope. He's a good goer and really natural and likeable. He's surprised me because he is a big horse but he's filling his frame and I see him as a seven furlong midsummer 2-y-o. I really like him and he's a horse I enjoy watching every day".*

1454. UNNAMED ★★★
br.f. Speightstown – Qushchi (Encosta De Lago). March 1. Second foal. Half-sister to the 2017 2-y-o 1m winner, from two starts, Mrs Sippy (by Blame). The dam, a quite useful 7f (at 2 yrs), 12f and subsequent US Listed 12f winner, is a half-sister to 3 winners. The second dam, La Persiana (by Daylami), a very useful dual Listed 10f winner, is a half-sister to 7 winners including the champion 2-y-o Grand Lodge (Group 1 7f Dewhurst Stakes and Group 1 1m St James's Palace Stakes etc,) and the useful Listed 1m winner Papabile. *"We have the half-sister who is pretty useful but this is a slightly smaller, more precocious filly. She does everything right and is a good-actioned horse like her sister. Very likeable".*

1455. UNNAMED ★★★★
b.f. Rip Van Winkle – Red Avis (Exceed And Excel). February 25. Third foal. €34,000Y. Goffs Orby. Blandford Bloodstock. Closely related to the quite useful 1m winner Whispering Bell (by Galileo) and half-sister to the 2018 French 3-y-o 12f winner Brawler (by Teofilo). The dam, a fair Irish 2-y-o 7f placed maiden, is a half-sister to the 2-y-o Group 3 Albany Stakes winner Newfangled. The second dam, Scarlet Ibis (by Machiavellian), a quite useful French 1m winner, is a half-sister to 4 winners including the US Grade 3 placed Anasheed. *"She goes well. She's very light on her feet and a very natural filly and a good goer. I'm really pleased with her and we'll start moving with her soon".*

1456. UNNAMED ★★★★
b.c. Zoffany – Sanadaat (Green Desert). March 29. Third foal. €42,000Y. Tattersalls

Ireland September. Blandford Bloodstock. Half-brother to the promising 2017 2-y-o 7f winner Fennaan (by Footstepsinthesand). The dam is an unraced half-sister to 2 minor winners. The second dam, Manayer (by Sadler's Wells), is an unraced half-sister to 5 winners including the dam of the Group 1 Phoenix Stakes winner Alfred Nobel. *"A good goer, we bought him a few days before his half-brother won at Newbury. A strong, mature type that shows up well and gets on with it, he's a slightly more precocious type than we usually buy but he's training well and I see him as an early seven furlong horse".*

1457. UNNAMED ★★

b.f. Poet's Voice – Secret Era (Cape Cross). January 25. Second foal. 42,000Y. Tattersalls October Book 3. Rabbah Bloodstock. The dam, a modest 9f winner, is a half-sister to 3 winners including the useful 10f and 11f winner of 7 races Area Fifty One. The second dam, Secret History (by Bahri), won 4 races including the Group 3 Musidora Stakes and is a half-sister to 6 winners. *"She was training well but got a slight injury and missed a bit of time. Back training now, she's one we haven't pushed in any way but she always does everything asked. A nice type with a good action without being flash".*

1458. UNNAMED ★★★

gr.c. Dark Angel – Secret Key (Key Of Luck). May 13. Sixth foal. €200,000Y. Goffs Orby. Stephen Hillen. Brother to the smart 2-y-o Group 3 7f Tyros Stakes winner Exogenesis and half-brother to the moderate Irish 7f winner Secret Path (by Approve). The dam, a modest 7f winner at 4 yrs, is a half-sister to 3 winners. The second dam, Sky Lover (by Ela-Mana-Mou), won once at 2 yrs in Ireland and is a half-sister to 2 winners. *"Not the biggest and he's just starting to change now, putting on weight and growing. He's always gone well but we're aware that he was a late foal so I see him as a six furlong 2-y-o slightly later on".*

1459. UNNAMED ★★★

b.c. Kingman – Starlet (Sea The Stars). February 5. First foal. €140,000Y. Goffs Orby. Blandford Bloodstock. The dam, a fairly useful Irish 12f winner, is a half-sister to 3 winners. The second dam, Treasure The Lady (by Indian

Ridge), won once in Ireland at 2 yrs over 7f and was Listed-placed and is a half-sister to 8 winners including the Derby winner High Chaparral and the Dante Stakes winner Black Bear Island. *"A good type of horse with a good action and a great attitude to his work. He's a good size and it's surprised me how easily he's done things – he just takes everything in his stride. A good-looking colt, I'm very pleased with him and we'll be looking at racing him over seven furlongs and a mile with him later on".*

1460. UNNAMED ★★★★ ♠

b.c. Charm Spirit – Ysper (Orpen). February 6. First foal. The dam, a modest 4-y-o 5f winner, is a sister to the Group 1 6f Cheveley Park Stakes and Group 2 5.5f Prix Robert Papin winner Vorda. The second dam, Velda (by Observatory), was a minor Italian dual 2-y-o 5f winner. *"He's a good goer and arguably as forward as any 2-y-o we've got. Very light on his feet and very natural, he never gets tired which I think is a great trait in a horse. A very likeable horse and I'd say he's above average".*

RICHARD SPENCER

1461. ALFIE SOLOMONS ★★★

b.c. Acclamation – Vastitas (Green Desert). March 25. Second foal. £85,000Y. Goffs UK Premier (Doncaster). Bobby O'Ryan / Rebel Racing. Half-brother to the French dual 2-y-o winner Luck Ahead (by Dream Ahead). The dam, a quite useful Irish dual 7f winner, is a half-sister to the Group 3 Brownstown Stakes winner and Group 1 Prix Marcel Boussac third Queen Catrine. The second dam, Kahira (by King's Best), a fair 2-y-o 7f placed maiden, is a half-sister to the Group 1 6f Haydock Park Sprint Cup winner Tamarisk. (Rebel Racing Premier). *"He's a nice-looking horse, very well put-together and I'd like to think he'll be out by the end of May/early June. He's not just going to be a 2-y-o because he does have scope and he's a good mover that we'll probably start off at six furlongs".*

1462. CALIFORNIA LOVE ★★★

ch.f. Power – La Pantera (Captain Rio). March 6. Third foal. £18,000Y. Goffs UK Silver. Bobby O'Ryan. Half-sister to Pertinace (by Kheleyf), a winner of 4 minor races in Italy from 2 to 4 yrs. The dam, a fair 2-y-o 6f winner, is a half-sister to 2 minor winners. The second dam, Pantita (by Polish Precedent), a fair 1m and 10f placed maiden, is a half-sister to 6 winners abroad. (Mr A. Cunningham). *"It's important that you put this filly in the book because she's the first horse owned by the yard's owner's son, Aidan Cunningham! She would have been running at the end of March but she coughed a couple of times so we backed off her. She goes well and is the bargain buy for this year. If you looked at her you'd think she was a colt, she's an early type, very strong and a good mover"*. TRAINER'S BARGAIN BUY

1463. COBWEB CATCHER ★★
b.c. Swiss Spirit – Sugar Beet (Beat Hollow). April 25. Third foal. 10,000Y. Tattersalls October Book 3. Not sold. The dam, a quite useful 5f and 6f winner of 7 races (including at 2 yrs), was Listed-placed and is a half-sister to 5 winners including the very useful 6f (at 2 yrs), 9f and subsequent Hong Kong winner Zabaglione. The second dam, Satin Bell (by Midyan), a useful 7f winner, is a half-sister to 4 winners including the useful Listed 6f winner Star Tulip and the dam of the dual Group 3 winner Scarlet Runner. (T. H. Chadney). *"We were interested in buying him at the sales and when he didn't make his reserve the owner kindly sent him to us. He's a big horse and shouldn't be going as well as he is doing at this point. For me he's going to be a mid-season 2-y-o, he looks nice and I'm looking forward to running him"*.

1464. COCOCABALA ★★★
b.c. Sir Prancealot – Dream Applause (Royal Applause). April 3. Second foal. £11,000Y. Goffs UK Silver (Doncaster). Bobby O'Ryan / Richard Spencer. Half-brother to the minor 2017 French 2-y-o winner Reboot (by Society Rock). The dam, a fair Irish 6f and 7f winner, is a half-sister to 3 minor winners. The second dam, Rainbow Dream (by Rainbow Quest), is an unraced sister to the Group 3 Jockey Club Cup winner Rainbow High. (Balasuriya, Cook, Cunningham, Gowing, Spencer). *"He's sharp, natural and will probably be our first 2-y-o runner. I'd say we'll start him over five furlongs in mid-April and see where we go from there. He's got an entry in the Supersprint and does everything at home easily"*.

1465. COOKUPASTORM (IRE) ★★★
b.f. Camacho – No Clubs (Red Clubs). April 23. Second foal. €11,000Y. Tattersalls Ireland September. Bobby O'Ryan/Richard Spencer. The dam is an unraced half-sister to 6 winners including the dual Listed 2-y-o 5f winner and Group 2 Railway Stakes second Drayton. The second dam, Exponent (by Exbourne), is an unraced half-sister to 6 minor winners here and abroad. (Balasuriya, Cook, Cunningham, Gowing, Spencer). *"She's just started to work and should hopefully be running by mid-April. She goes nicely and is a very sweet filly with a good temperament and attitude. Looks a 2-y-o"*.

1466. JEAN VALJEAN ★★★
b.c. Bated Breath – Waitingonacloud (In The Wings). February 10. Sixth foal. £30,000Y. Goffs UK Premier (Doncaster). Bobby O'Ryan / Rebel Racing. Half-brother to the fair 12f to 2m and hurdles winner Miss Tiger Lily (by Tiger Hill) and to the modest 11.5f, 2m and hurdles winner Gimme Five (by Champs Elysees). The dam is an unraced half-sister to 5 winners including the Group 1 1m Prix du Moulin, Group 2 Summer Mile and Group 3 7f Jersey Stakes winner Aqlaam. The second dam, Bourbonella (by Rainbow Quest), is an unraced half-sister to 9 winners including the high-class and multiple Group winning stayer Persian Punch and the Group 3 7f Solario Stakes winner Island Magic. (Mr P M Cunningham). *"We'll start him over six furlongs because although his pedigree suggests he wants further he does everything easily, so he'll be out from late April onwards. I like him, he's well-proportioned and has plenty of strength about him. I think he's a nice horse"*.

1467. LOUIS TREIZE (IRE) ★★★★
ch.c. Slade Power – Black Rodded (Bahamian Bounty). February 27. Second foal. £120,000Y. Goffs UK Premier (Doncaster). Bobby O'Ryan / Rebel Racing. The dam, a modest 2-y-o 6f winner, is a sister to the useful 2-y-o Listed 6f winner Queen's Grace and a half-sister to 5 winners. The second dam, Palace Affair (by Pursuit Of Love), a multiple Listed winner from 5f to 7f, is a sister to one winner and a half-sister to 9 winners including Sakhee's Secret (Group 1 6f July Cup). (Rebel Racing Premier). *"I like him a lot, he's a good-moving horse with*

a good temperament and he'll start over six furlongs in May. I'm looking forward to getting him going".

1468. MATERIAL GIRL ★★★

b.f. Pivotal – Apace (Oasis Dream). February 19. Fourth foal. £52,000Y. Goffs UK Premier (Doncaster). Bobby O'Ryan. Half-sister to the fair 5f winner of 3 races at 2 and 3 yrs Curtain Call (by Acclamation) and to the fair 7f winner Rubens Dream (by Dutch Art). The dam, a quite useful 7f (at 2 yrs) and 5f winner, is a sister to the useful Listed 5f winner and Group 3 third Sugar Free and a half-sister to 4 winners including the useful 1m (at 2 yrs) and 9f winner High Twelve. The second dam, Much Faster (Fasliyev), a winner of 4 races including the Group 2 6f Prix Robert Papin and second in the Group 1 Prix Morny, is a half-sister to 5 winners. (Miss L. Cunningham). *"From a Cheveley Park family, she does go nicely, has a good temperament and we'll probably start her off in May over six furlongs".*

1469. NOSTROVIA (IRE) ★★★

b.f. Alhebayeb – Na Zdorovie (Cockney Rebel). March 6. Third foal. £30,000Y. Goffs UK Premier (Doncaster). Bobby O'Ryan / Rebel Racing. Half-sister to the modest French 2-y-o 6.5f winner Mad Rose (by Royal Applause). The dam, a quite useful 2-y-o 7f winner, is a sister to the winner and Group 2 Park Hill Stakes second Groovejet and a half-sister to 7 winners including the useful 2-y-o 7f winner and US triple Grade 2 10f winner Slim Shadey. The second dam, Vino Veritas (by Chief's Crown), placed fourth once over 7f at 2 yrs, is a half-sister to the multiple Hong Kong and Japanese Group 1 winner Bullish Luck. (Bland, Cunningham, Hall, Cliff Stud). *"One that'll be a 2-y-o from the middle to back-end. She's very leggy, still growing and developing and we might aim her to start in July or August, probably over seven furlongs".*

1470. REVICH (IRE) ★★★

b.c. Requinto – Kathleen Rafferty (Marju). April 15. Fifth foal. €34,000Y. Tattersalls Ireland September. Bobby O'Ryan / Richard Spencer. Half-brother to the fair 6f to 9.5f winner City Of Angkor Wat (by Elusive City). The dam is an unraced half-sister to one winner abroad. The second dam, Greek Princess (by Polish Precedent), is an unraced half-sister

to 8 winners. (Middleham Park Racing & Phil Cunningham). *"He goes well and he'll be doing his first bit of work in a couple of weeks. He could be racing in mid-April and he's a nice horse with a good attitude. A very good mover, he's light on his feet and he'll want top of the ground".*

1471. RUMBLE INTHEJUNGLE (IRE) ★★★★

ch.c. Bungle Inthejungle – Guana (Dark Angel). April 18. Third foal. £70,000Y. Goffs UK Premier (Doncaster). Bobby O'Ryan / Rebel Racing. Half-brother to the useful 2017 2-y-o 6f winner and Group 2 Superlative Stakes second Great Prospector (by Elzaam) and to the fair 2-y-o 7f winner Red Guana (by Famous Name). The dam is an unraced half-sister to 3 winners including the dam of the Group 2 Superlative Stakes winner Birchwood. The second dam, Guana Bay (by Cadeaux Genereux), is an unraced full or half-sister to 6 winners including the Group 2 winners Prince Sabo and Millyant, and the dam of the Group 2 Gimcrack Stakes winner Abou Zouz. (Rebel Racing Premier). *"A lovely horse, we haven't done any fast work with him yet but we'll probably run him in late April or early May. He goes nicely, has a very good attitude and a lot of natural ability. Maybe one for Royal Ascot if he proves good enough".*

1472. STALLONE (IRE) ★★★

b.c. Dandy Man – Titian Queen (Tobougg). March 29. Fourth foal. £100,000Y. Goffs UK Premier (Doncaster). Bobby O'Ryan/Rebel Racing. Half-brother to the minor Italian 2-y-o winner Akyra Magic (by Requinto). The dam is an unplaced half-sister to 8 winners including Toylsome (Group 1 7f Prix de la Foret) and Coral Mist (Group 3 Firth Of Clyde Stakes). The second dam, Treasure Trove (by The Minstrel), a modest 5f to 7f placed 2-y-o, is a half-sister to 4 winners including the US Grade 3 winner Ocean Queen and the Queen Mary Stakes, Fred Darling Stakes and subsequent US Grade 2 winner Dance Parade (dam of the St Leger and Ascot Gold Cup winner Leading Light). (Rebel Racing Premier). *"He goes nicely and is probably one to start off in mid-May. I don't know about trip yet because we've done nothing serious with him but he's a strong-looking 2-y-o and hopefully we'll get him going and have some fun with him this year".*

1473. STAY CLASSY (IRE) ★★
ch.f. Camacho – Hollow Green (Beat Hollow). March 24. Third foal. €10,500Y. Tattersalls Ireland September. Bobby O'Ryan/Richard Spencer. Half-sister to the modest 5f and 1m winner at 3 and 4 yrs Limerick Lord (by Lord Shanakill). The dam, a fair 7f (at 2 yrs) to 11.5f winner of 8 races, is a half-sister to 4 winners including the French Listed winner Safe And Sound. The second dam, Three Greens (by Niniski), a winner and 12f Listed-placed in France, is a half-sister to 9 winners including the US 2-y-o Grade 1 8.5f Starlet Stakes winner Creaking Board (herself dam of the US Grade 3 winner Crowd Pleaser) and the Group winners Dakhla Oasis and Dyhim Diamond. (Balasuriya, Cook, Cunningham, Gowing, Spencer). *"She was a cheaply-bought filly and we won't be hanging around with her. She'll be working soon and we'll hopefully have a bit of fun with her this year. She does everything easily and goes nicely. Probably a six furlong type 2-y-o".*

1474. SUSSUDIO ★★
b.f. Compton Place – Glen Molly (Danetime). March 19. Fifth living foal. £11,000Y. Tattersalls Autumn. Richard Spencer. Half-sister to the modest 2017 2-y-o 5f and 6f winner Cuppacoco (by Stimulation) and to the fair French 5.5f to 7f winner of 5 races If I Say So (by Sayif). The dam, a fairly useful 6f (at 2 yrs) and 7f winner, is a half-sister to one winner. The second dam, Sonorous (by Ashkalani), an Irish 1m and 10f winner, was Listed-placed and is a half-sister to 5 winners. (Balasuriya, Cook, Cunningham, Gowing, Spencer). *"She's done well physically since we bought her and she's a nice filly with a good temperament and is light on her feet, so she'll want top of the ground. She's in the Tattersalls sales race at the end of the year. We'll look to start her around May/June time".*

1475. THRILLA IN MANILA ★★★
b.c. Iffraaj – Tesary (Danehill). March 29. Eighth foal. £80,000Y. Goffs UK Premier (Doncaster). Bobby O'Ryan / Rebel Racing. Half-brother to 5 winners including the quite useful 5f (at 2 yrs) and 6f winner of 5 races Englishman (by Royal Applause), to the quite useful 5f (at 2 yrs) and 6f winner Verbeeck (by Dutch Art) and the fair 5f and 6f winner of 4 races

Englishwoman (by Acclamation). The dam, a useful 5f (at 2 yrs) to 7f winner, is a half-sister to 5 winners. The second dam, Baldemara (by Sanglamore), is an unraced half-sister to 5 winners including the Group 1 5.5f Prix Robert Papin winner Balbonella (dam of the top-class sprinter Anabaa, the French 1,000 Guineas winner Always Loyal and the useful sire Key Of Luck). (Rebel Racing Premier). *"From a nice family that's been unlucky not to get a bit more black type, this colt is probably not going to be an early 2-y-o. He's much more likely to start off at six furlongs unless he comes to hand and shows us a bit more speed, so we'll aim him for May/June. He's a big horse that has the scope to be a 3-y-o and I do like him".*

1476. YOU NEVER CAN TELL (IRE) ★★
b.c. Elzaam – Zanida (Mujadil). March 25. Fifth foal. £42,000Y. Goffs UK Premier (Doncaster). Bobby O'Ryan / Rebel Racing. Half-brother to the quite useful 2-y-o 6f and 1m winner Crimson Sunrise (by Holy Roman Emperor), to the fair 9f and 10f winner Storm Ranger (by Bushranger) and the modest 6f and 7f winner Man About Town (by Dandy Man). The dam, a quite useful 2-y-o 5f winner, is a half-sister to 5 winners including the useful sprinter and Listed winner of 6 races Double Quick. The second dam, Haraabah (by Topsider), a useful 5f to 7f winner, is a half-sister to 3 winners. (Mr P. M. Cunningham). *"He goes OK but we'll take our time with him because he won't be early. I do like him but I couldn't tell you his trip, we haven't pushed any buttons yet because his knees are still a bit immature. He'll make a 2-y-o by May though I should think".*

HENRY SPILLER
1477. COMPTON MACKENZIE ★★★
ch.c. Compton Place – Corryvreckan (Night Shift). February 3. Tenth foal. £19,000Y. Goffs UK Premier. Not sold. Brother to the fair 2-y-o 6f and 7f winner Mecado and half-brother to 5 winners including the quite useful 2-y-o 5f winner Leftontheshelf (by Namid), the fair 2-y-o 6f winner Entwined (by Elusive City), the fair dual 6f winner Tanaasub (by Lope De Vega) and the modest Irish 2-y-o 7f winner Dearg (by Intikhab). The dam, a fair Irish 7f and 1m placed maiden, is a half-sister to 9 winners including the very useful Listed sprint winners Bufalino and Maledetto. The second dam,

Croglin Water (by Monsanto), is an unplaced half-sister to the smart sprinter Governor General. (Saville House Racing Club). *"A very sharp, early type that should be running in April. A quintessential early 2-y-o, he's just a little powerhouse and I wouldn't think he'd have much scope. Definitely one for the first half of the season, he's showing plenty and we're quite keen on him".*

1478. DAPHINIA ★★★
b.f. Kuroshio – Phantom Spirit (Invincible Spirit). March 8. Fourth foal. £8,000Y. Tattersalls Ireland Ascot. Not sold. The dam, placed once at 4 yrs, is a half-sister to 5 winners including the Listed-placed Glisten. The second dam, Jackie's Opera (by Indian Ridge), is an unraced half-sister to 5 winners including the French dual Listed winner Arabian King. (The Hightailers). *"A lovely, sharp, early filly with a lot of heart. She'll start at five furlongs but will improve for a step up to six".* This filly was a five furlong winner on her debut at Wolverhampton on the 14th April.

1479. LAST TO BID (FR) ★★
ch.c. Makfi – Last Song (Singspiel). February 1. Second foal. Half-brother to the fair 2017 dual 7f placed 2-y-o Launceston Place (by Le Havre). The dam was placed over 10f in France and is a half-sister to 3 winners. The second dam, Last Rhapsody (by Kris), a 2-y-o 1m winner in France, is a sister to the Group 3 7f Nell Gwyn Stakes winner Lil's Jessy and a half-sister to numerous winners including the smart French 1m Listed winner Lone Bid and the useful 1m and 12f winner and Listed-placed Love Galore. (Mr R. P. A. Spiller). *"A nice, big, backward horse that's cantering away for now. He's very similar to his half-brother whom I rate pretty highly Launceston Place. From the little we've seen of him he might be able to win later on and he'll start off at seven furlongs, but next year will be his time to shine really".*

1480. UNNAMED ★★★
ch.f. Tagula – Lady Kildare (Bachelor Duke). April 10. Second foal. The dam was a fair 5f and 6f winner of 3 races from 26 starts and is a half-sister to 7 winners. The second dam, Teodora (by Fairy King), a 2-y-o winner, is a half-sister to 6 winners. *"She's just arrived to us but she'd already done two little bits of work in Ireland beforehand and she's showing up very*

nicely here too. She'll be ready to run in April and I'm very keen on her. The sire produces solid types and he gets plenty of winners".*

1481. UNNAMED ★★
br.f. Mukhadram – Patuca (Teofilo). February 8. Second foal. 8,000Y. Tattersalls October Book 3. Not sold. Half-sister to Victory Charm (by Campanologist), placed fourth once over 1m at 2 yrs in 2017. The dam, a minor German 3-y-o winner, is a half-sister to 4 winners including the Group 1 Premio Roma and Group 2 Prix Dollar winner Potemkin and the German Listed 1m winner and Group 3 placed Paraisa. The second dam, Praia (by Big Shuffle), a Listed-placed 3-y-o winner in Germany, is a half-sister to 4 winners including the Group 1 Criterium de Saint-Cloud winner Paita. (Saville House Racing Club). *"She's backward but quite nice. It's a very stout German family, Ralph Beckett trained the 2-y-o half-brother last year and he showed bits of form over a mile at the back-end. The dam was favourite for the German Oaks at one stage but I don't think she quite got that far. A nice, big filly, she's a correct individual and was very 'up behind' at the sale so probably looking at her worst – hence the reason she didn't sell. Definitely one for the late summer onwards".*

1482. UNNAMED ★★★
b.f. Lawman – Sensational Samba (Exceed And Excel). May 7. Second foal. 30,000Y. Tattersalls October Book 3. Not sold. The dam is an unraced half-sister to 3 winners including the French Listed winner and Group 3 second Gwaihir. The second dam, Twilight Tango (by Groom Dancer), is an unraced sister to the Group 3 Chester Vase winner Twist And Turn and a half-sister to the Group 3 Gallinule Stakes winner Meath. (Saville House Racing Club). *"She's a really nice filly and would be about the pick of our fillies. Very straightforward, she should be out in May or June, she's sharp with a nice pedigree. A very correct individual, I'm quite keen on her, she'll start at six furlongs and will probably want seven in time".*

1483. UNNAMED ★★
ch.c. Makfi – Soho Rocks (Rock Of Gibraltar). April 4. Second foal. The dam, a minor French winner of 3 races, is half-sister to one

winner. The second dam, Millisecond (by Royal Applause), a fair 5f and 6f winner, is a half-sister to 4 winners and to the unplaced dam of the Group 2 Sun Chariot Stakes winner Kissogram. (Saville House Racing Club). *"He's very similar to the other Makfi we have. A nice, big, backward horse for the second half of the season over seven furlongs and a mile. He's potentially quite nice".*

1484. UNNAMED ★★★
b.c. Paco Boy – Seduct (Intense Focus). April 13. First foal. The dam is an unraced half-sister to several winners including the Group 1 Italian Oaks winner and Group 1 Moyglare Stud Stakes third Menhoubah and the Irish 2-y-o 7f winner and Listed-placed Private Alexander. The second dam, Private Seductress (by Private Account), a stakes-placed winner of 3 races in the USA, is a half-sister to 4 winners including the Group 2 Cherry Hinton Stakes third Ahla Wasahl. (Charles & Fiona Spiller). *"Small but quite racy, she's nice and worth including but she'll have to be a 2-y-o because she wouldn't have the scope to train on".*

FOZZY STACK
1485. ECLIPSE STORM ★★★
ch.c. Dream Ahead – Gentle Breeze (Dubawi). January 25. First foal. The dam, a fair 6f placed 2-y-o, is a half-sister to one winner. The second dam, Laureldean Gale (by Grand Slam), a very smart 2-y-o 6f winner and second in the Group 3 7f Prix du Calvados, is a half-sister to numerous winners including the Group 3 Musidora Stakes winner Secret History. *"He goes nicely, seems quite a mature horse and I'm pleased with what he's done so far, probably a horse that won't get further than seven furlongs in his life".*

1486. NEVEREVERSAYNEVER (IRE) ★★★★
b.f. No Nay Never – Dowager (Groom Dancer). April 18. Tenth foal. €80,000Y. Goffs Orby. C McCormack. Half-sister to the quite useful 2-y-o 5f winner La Cuesta (by Showcasing) and to the Scandinavian 2-y-o 5f winner Sasha Waltz (by Rip Van Winkle). The dam, a useful 2-y-o 6f (Listed) and 7f winner, is a half-sister to 3 winners including the useful 1m (at 2 yrs) and 10f winner Dower House. The second dam, Rose Noble (by Vaguely

Noble), a modest 11.5f winner, is a half-sister to 7 winners including the champion two-year-old Grand Lodge, winner of the St James's Palace Stakes and the Dewhurst Stakes. *"She's a strong girl, has plenty of size, scope and strength about her, she goes nicely, has a speedy pedigree and will start off at six furlongs. It wouldn't surprise me if she got a little bit more than six furlongs and she might even get a mile eventually".*

1487. NICARO (IRE) ★★★
b.c. No Nay Never – Mironica (Excellent Art). April 18. Second foal. Half-brother to the 2017 Irish 2-y-o Listed 5f winner Sirici (by Choisir). The dam, a quite useful Irish 2-y-o 6f winner, is a half-sister to 2 winners. The second dam, Lisfannon (by Bahamian Bounty), placed fourth three times from 5f to 6.5f, is half-sister to 4 winners including the Listed 5f winner of 5 races Dazed And Amazed. *"He looks like being sharp but he has more size and scope than his half-sister last year. A strong horse for five/six furlongs, I could see him setting off in May".*

1488. WARGRAVE (IRE) ★★★★
b.c. Galileo – Scream Blue Murder (Oratorio). March 11. First foal. The dam, an Irish 5f (at 2 yrs) and Listed 6f winner, is a half-sister to 5 winners including the Irish 2-y-o and subsequent South African triple Group 2 winner Gibraltar Blue. The second dam, Holly Blue (by Bluebird), a useful Listed 1m winner, is a half-sister to 6 minor winners. *"He goes nicely, looks sharp and we trained her mother who won over five furlongs. This colt will probably set off over six furlongs in May, he's not over-big, he's mature and one we can crack on with. He's quite like an Oratorio in that he's strongly-built and although he's by Galileo he's certainly not one for middle-distances".*

1489. WOODY CREEK ★★★
b.f. Zoffany – Belle Isle (Pastoral Pursuits). March 3. Second foal. €180,000Y. Goffs Orby. De Burgh Equine. Half-sister to the useful 2017 2-y-o Group 3 5f Cornwallis Stakes winner Abel Handy (by Arcano). The dam is an unplaced half-sister to 2 minor winners. The second dam, Bowness (by Efisio), a quite useful 5f and 6f winner, was third in the Listed 5f Land O'Burns Stakes and is a half-sister

to 3 winners including the Group 2 5f Kings Stand Stakes and Group 3 5f Cornwallis Stakes Dominica. *"A very good-looking filly, she's starting to grow now, moves well but we haven't done a lot with her yet. She looks the part though".*

1490. UNNAMED ★★★★
b.c. Dark Angel – Ashtown Girl (Exceed And Excel). April 3. Fourth foal. €80,000Y. Goffs Orby. De Burgh Equine. Half-brother to the fair 2017 5f and 7f placed 2-y-o Ziarah (by Iffraaj) and to the modest 6f winner Brave Display (by Requinto). The dam is an unraced half-sister to 3 winners including the Group 2 Temple Stakes and Group 3 Cornwallis Stakes winner Hot Streak. The second dam, Ashirah (by Housebuster), is an unraced half-sister to the US dual Grade 3 winner Mustanfar and the dual Listed winner Tadris. *"He looks quite nice and I'd say he'll be quite fast too. One for five/six furlongs in May, he'll make up into a grand 2-y-o as the season progresses. He's a strong 2-y-o and he's got some size about him too".*

1491. UNNAMED ★★
b.f. Zoffany – Dacio (Harlan's Holiday). February 8. First foal. £32,000Y. Goffs UK Premier (Doncaster). Sackville/Donald. The dam, placed at 3 yrs in France, is a half-sister to 3 winners. The second dam, Allegro Lady (by Souvenir Copy), was placed at 2 yrs in the USA and is a half-sister to 8 winners. *"She's a sharp little filly for five/six furlongs, she should be running in May so we'll get her out and see how we go on; the type for nurseries possibly".*

1492. UNNAMED ★★★
b.f. No Nay Never – Falling Rain (Danehill Dancer). February 1. Third living foal. £50,000Y. Goffs UK Premier (Doncaster). C McCormack. The dam is an unraced half-sister to two minor winners out of the minor French 3-y-o winner Neartica (by Sadler's Wells), herself a half-sister to 12 winners including the outstanding filly Goldikova. *"A big, strong filly, she's a very good mover and you'd like her. She'll be out around June time I would say".*

1493. UNNAMED ★★★
b.c. Zoffany – Foolish Act (Sadler's Wells). January 25. Tenth foal. €55,000Y. Goffs Orby. BBA (Ire). De Burgh Equine/C McCormack.

Half-brother to 4 winners including the fairly useful 6f winner and 2-y-o Group 3 6f second True Verdict, the fairly useful Irish 2-y-o 6f winner and Listed-placed Foolish Ambition (both by Danehill Dancer) and the fair 1m and hurdles winner Lone Star (by Sea The Stars). The dam is an unraced full or half-sister to 6 winners including Circle Of Gold (Group 3 Prestige Stakes) and the Listed winner Crystal Crossing (dam of the St Leger winner Rule Of Law). The second dam, Never So Fair (by Never So Bold), is an unplaced half-sister to 10 winners including Amaranda (Queen Mary Stakes) and Favoridge (Nell Gwyn Stakes). *"A sharp horse and a five/six furlong 2-y-o for the first half of the season, we'll set him off in late April/early May".*

1494. UNNAMED ★★★
b.c. Camelot – Israar (Machiavellian). April 22. Seventh foal. €48,000Y. Goffs Orby. De Burgh Equine. Half-brother to the fairly useful 2-y-o 7f winner Contrast (by Dutch Art), to the quite useful Listed-placed 12f winner of 4 races Soul Searcher (by Motivator), the fair 2-y-o 7f winner and UAE Group 2 third Rutland Boy (by Bertolini), the moderate 5f and subsequent Greek winner Exceed Power (by Exceed And Excel) and a winner in Greece by Teofilo. The dam is an unraced half-sister to 5 minor winners. The second dam, El Opera (by Sadler's Wells), a useful dual 7f winner, is a half-sister to 8 winners including the very useful Group 1 6f Phoenix Stakes winner Pharaoh's Delight. *"He's a big, good-moving horse and his 3-y-o half-sister Harvestfortheworld recently broke her maiden for us over a mile. She made her debut as a 2-y-o in October and I'd say this colt will be much the same. A big, raw horse at the moment but he moves very well and has a bit of class about him".*

1495. UNNAMED ★★★
ch.c. Ruler Of The World – Lady Miletrian (Barathea). January 28. Tenth foal. €50,000Y. Goffs Orby. C McCormack. Half-brother to the useful 2-y-o 6f winner and Group 2 Park Stakes third Himalya (by Danehill), to the quite useful 9f winner Approaching Squall (by New Approach), the quite useful 2-y-o 1m winner Perfect Storm (by Excelebration), the quite useful 6f winner Dama'a (by Green

Desert) and a stakes-placed winner in Japan by Footstepsinthesand. The dam, a useful 1m winner, was Listed-placed twice and is a sister to the Listed winning 2-y-o Duty Paid and a half-sister to 3 winners. The second dam, Local Custom (by Be My Native), placed at up to 7f at 2 yrs, is a full or half-sister to 6 winners including Balla Cove (Group 1 Middle Park Stakes). *"A nice-moving colt, he's pretty mature and he'll be out as soon as the seven furlong maidens start".*

1496. UNNAMED ★★★
b f. Holy Roman Emperor – Mango Groove (Unfuwain). February 8. Ninth foal. €36,000Y. Tattersalls Ireland September. David Wachman. Half-sister to the 2-y-o 1m winner and 3-y-o Listed placed Cristal Fashion (by Jeremy) and to the quite useful 10f and hurdles winner Master Of Speed (by Mastercraftsman). The dam is an unplaced half-sister to 5 winners including the Group 1 Racing Post Trophy third Feared In Flight. The second dam, Solar Crystal (Alzao), won the Group 3 1m May Hill Stakes, was third in the Group 1 1m Prix Marcel Boussac and is a half-sister to 6 winners including the Group 1 Fillies' Mile winner Crystal Spirit. *"A big, fine filly, she moves well and she's quite mature; will get six furlongs and a little bit more".* TRAINER'S BARGAIN BUY

1497. UNNAMED ★★
b.f. War Command – Medicean Star (Galileo). April 2. Half-sister to the Irish 2-y-o 1m winner Optimism And Hope (by Holy Roman Emperor), to the fair Irish dual 10f winner Equity Swap (by Strategic Prince) and two minor winners abroad by Aussie Rules and Oratorio. The dam ran once unplaced and is a half-sister to 3 winners. The second dam, Fear And Greed (by Brief Truce), an Irish 2-y-o 6f winner and second in the Group 1 7f Moyglare Stud Stakes, is a half-sister to 4 winners. *"Goes nicely, she's quite big and will take a bit of time, so probably one for the second half of the year over seven furlongs and a mile".*

1498. UNNAMED ★★★
b.f. Holy Roman Emperor – Tarascon (Tirol). May 7. Tenth foal. Sister to the useful 2-y-o Listed 6f winner High Award and half-sister to

4 winners including the French Listed-placed dual 7f winner (including at 2 yrs) Mayano Sophia (by Rock Of Gibraltar), the quite useful 10f winner Estephe (by Sadler's Wells) and the dual 9f Beucaire (by Entrepreneur). The dam, winner of the Group 1 7f Moyglare Stud Stakes at 2 yrs and the Irish 1,000 Guineas, is a half-sister to the Group 2 winner Mister Monet and to the dual Group 1 placed Mala Mala. The second dam, Breyani (by Commanche Run), a useful winner at up to 2m, is a half-sister to 4 winners. *"She moves quite well, she's strong and should be able to start over six furlongs in June. Going off the family she should get further but considering she was a May foal she's not backward either".*

SIR MICHAEL STOUTE
1499. BUTTERFLY KISS (USA)
b.f. Medaglia d'Oro – Laughing Lashes (Mr Greeley). April 20. Fourth foal. $350,000Y. Keeneland September. Cheveley Park Stud. Half-sister to the minor US 4-y-o winner Lime Beach (by Giant's Causeway). The dam, a 2-y-o Group 2 7f Debutante Stakes winner, was placed in the Group 1 Moyglare Stud Stakes and the Irish 1,000 Guineas and is a half-sister to 2 winners. The second dam, Adventure (by Unbridled's Song), won 2 minor races in the USA at 3 yrs and is a half-sister to 7 winners including the Group 1 Racing Post Trophy winner Palace Episode.

1500. CALCULATION
b.c. Dubawi – Estimate (Monsun). February 4. First foal. The dam won 5 races including the Group 1 Ascot Gold Cup and the Group 2 Doncaster Cup and is a half-sister to the Group 1 winners Ebadiyla (Irish Oaks), Edabiya (Moyglare Stud Stakes). The second dam, Ebaziya (by Darshaan), won from 7f (at 2 yrs) to 12f including three Listed races and was third in the Group 2 12f Blandford Stakes. (The Queen).

1501. CLERISY
b.f. Kingman – Exemplify (Dansili). February 7. Third foal. Half-sister to the very smart 2017 2-y-o Group 2 7f Vintage Stakes winner Expert Eye (by Acclamation). The dam, a French 2-y-o 1m winner, is a half-sister to the Group 1 Cheveley Park Stakes, 1,000 Guineas and French 1,000 Guineas winner

Special Duty (by Hennessy). The second dam, Quest To Peak (by Distant View), ran once unplaced and is a sister to Sightseek, winner of 7 Grade 1 events in the USA from 7f to 9f and a half-sister to the US dual Grade 1 winner Tates Creek. (Khalid Abdullah).

1502. DAVYDENKO ♠
ch.c. Intello – Safina (Pivotal).
March 9. Fourth foal. Half-brother to the useful 2-y-o 7f winner, Group 2 1m May Hill Stakes second and dual Group 3 placed Marenko (by Exceed And Excel) and to the quite useful 2-y-o 6f winners Panova (by Invincible Spirit) and Vesnina (by Sea The Stars). The dam, a fairly useful 7f winner, was Listed-placed over 1m and is a half-sister to 2 winners. The second dam, Russian Rhythm (by Kingmambo), won the 1,000 Guineas, Coronation Stakes, Nassau Stakes and Lockinge Stakes and is a half-sister to several winners including the 2-y-o Group 2 1m Royal Lodge Stakes winner Perfectperformance. (Cheveley Park Stud).

1503. DEREVO
b.c. Dansili – Pavlosk (Arch). February 23. First foal. The dam, a useful Listed 1m winner, is a sister to the useful 7f (at 2 yrs) and Listed 9f winner Rostova and a half-sister to the smart Italian Group 3 10f and 12f winner and Group 1 Gran Premio di Milano third Exhibit One. The second dam, Tsar's Pride (by Sadler's Wells), won over 12f in France and was Listed-placed over 10f. (Khalid Abdullah).

1504. EPIC (IRE)
b.c. Australia – Rock Kristal (Fastnet Rock). April 14. First foal. 135,000Y. Tattersalls October Book 1. John & Jake Warren. The dam, a fair 2-y-o 7f winner, is a half-sister to 2 minor winners. The second dam, Pellinore (by Giant's Causeway), a modest fourth over 10f from 3 starts, is a sister to the 2,000 Guineas winner Footstepsinthesand and a half-sister to 4 winners including the Group 1 Phoenix Stakes winner Pedro The Great and the dam of the dual Group 1 winner Power and the Grade 1 E P Taylor winner Curvy.

1505. INVICTUS SPIRIT
b.c. Frankel – Daring Aim (Daylami). February 8. Half-brother to 6 winners including the useful 10f to 12f winner Highland Glen (by Montjeu), the useful 10f and 12f winner Bold Sniper (by New Approach), the fairly useful Listed 13f winner Daphne (by Duke Of Marmalade) and the quite useful 2-y-o 7f winners Queen's Prize (by Dansili) and Fine Sight (by Cape Cross). The dam, a fairly useful 12f winner, is a half-sister to 6 winners including the smart 2-y-o 6f winner and Group 1 12f Oaks second Flight Of Fancy and the dual Listed 7f winner Golden Stream. The second dam, Phantom Gold (by Sadler's Wells), was a very useful winner from 1m (at 2 yrs) to 12f including the Group 2 Ribblesdale Stakes. (The Queen).

1506. KHAFOOQ
b.c. Kodiac – Al Manaal (Echo Of Light). April 5. First foal. 60,000Y. Tattersalls October Book 2. Shadwell Estate Co. The dam, a quite useful 7f and 7.5f winner of 3 races, is a half-sister to one winner. The second dam, Mall Queen (by Sheikh Albadou), won the Listed Prix Yacowlef and is a half-sister to 8 winners including the Listed winner Munnaya (dam of the US Grade 1 winner Alpha).

1507. MUBAKKER (USA)
gr.c. Speightstown – Ready To Act (More Than Ready). January 26. First foal. $500,000Y. Keeneland September. Shadwell Estate Co. The dam won 3 races at 2 and 3 yrs in the USA including the Grade 2 Beaumont Stakes. The second dam, Always Auditioning (by Mizzen Mast), a minor US 3-y-o winner, the US Grade 1 winner Mast Track and to the Group 1 Prix Saint-Alary winner Jemayel.

1508. NANTUCKET (IRE) ♠
b.f. Sea The Stars – Lucy Cavendish (Elusive Quality). April 30. Fourth foal. 125,000Y. Tattersalls October Book 1. John & Jake Warren. Half-sister to the fair 10f and 12f winner Light Of Asia (by Oratorio), to the Italian winner of 6 races at 2 to 4 yrs Caveran (by Hurricane Run) and the fair 2-y-o 7f winner In Her Stride (by Mastercraftsman). The dam is an unraced half-sister to 7 winners including the 2-y-o Group 3 1m Prix des Reservoirs winner and Group 1 Prix Saint-Alary third Summertime Legacy (herself dam of the French Group 1 winners Wavering and Mandaean). The second dam, Zawaahy (by

El Gran Senor), a fairly useful 1m winner, was placed at up to 11.5f and is closely related to the Derby winner Golden Fleece.

1509. OUT OF THIS TIME ♠
b.c. Frankel – This Time (Zafeen). March 11. First foal. €300,000. Arqana Deauville August. Charlie Gordon-Watson. The dam won the 2-y-o Group 3 Prix d'Arenburg and was second in the Group 2 Criterium de Maisons-Laffitte. The second dam, Scalotta (by Winged Love), a German 10f winner of 5 races, is a half-sister to 7 winners.

1510. SOVEREIGN GRANT
b.c. Kingman – Momentary (Nayef). January 16. Second foal. Half-brother to the fairly useful 6f and 7f winner of 3 races Merlin (by Oasis Dream). The dam, a fairly useful Listed 10f winner, is a half-sister to one winner. The second dam, Fleeting Memory (by Danehill), a quite useful 10.2f winner, is a half-sister to a hurdles winner. (The Queen).

1511. VIVIONN
ch.f. Dubawi – Giants Play (Giant's Causeway). February 9. Fourth foal. 500,000Y. Tattersalls October Book 1. Not sold. Sister to the 2017 2-y-o 10f winner Ispolini and half-sister to the useful Listed-placed 9f to 10.5f winner of 4 races Playful Sound (by Street Cry) and the quite useful 2-y-o 10f winner Azam (by Dansili). The dam, a US Grade 2 10f winner, is a half-sister the US Grade 3 12f winner Anjaz and to the Listed 1m winner Tearless. The second dam, Playful Act (by Sadler's Wells), a Group 1 Fillies' Mile, Group 2 Lancashire Oaks and Group 2 May Hill Stakes winner, is a sister to the Group 2 Yorkshire Cup winner Percussionist and the US dual Grade 3 winner Changing Skies and a half-sister to 5 other stakes winners including the dual Group 1 winner Nathaniel and the Group 1 Irish Oaks winner Great Heavens.

1512. WEMYSS WARE (IRE)
b.c. Dubawi – White Moonshine (Dynaformer). February 11. Brother to the minor French 7f winner Dufay. The dam won the Group 1 Fillies' Mile, Group 2 1m May Hill Stakes and Group 3 7f Sweet Solera Stakes and is a half-sister to the Listed 10f winner Albasharah. The second dam is Desert Gold (USA) (by Seeking The Gold).

1513. UNNAMED
b.c. Sea The Stars – Elegant Shadow (Shamardal). February 5. First foal. 1,000,000Y. Tattersalls October Book 1. Kerri Radcliffe. The dam was a minor winner at 3 yrs in Germany. The second dam, Elle Gala (by Galileo), a German Listed winner, is a full or half-sister to 10 winners including the German triple Group 3 winner Elle Shadow.

1514. UNNAMED
b.f. Camelot – Hurricane Emma (Mr Greeley). February 29. Second foal. 130,000Y. Tattersalls October Book 2. David Redvers. Half-sister to the useful 2-y-o Listed 6f Marble Hill Stakes winner and Group 3 6.5f Anglesey Stakes third Brother Bear (by Kodiac). The dam is an unraced half-sister to 6 winners including the Irish 2-y-o Listed 6f Rochestown Stakes winner and Group 3 Superlative Stakes third King Hesperus. The second dam, Victorica (by Exbourne), a stakes winner of 5 races in the USA, was third in the Grade 3 Dogwood Stakes and is a half-sister to 5 winners including the French 2,000 Guineas second and Hollywood Derby third Noble Minstrel.

1515. UNNAMED
b.f. Acclamation – Malaspina (Whipper). March 11. Fifth foal. 350,000Y. Tattersalls October Book 1. Charlie Gordon-Watson. Brother to the 7f (at 2 yrs) and Group 3 Nell Gwyn Stakes winner an 1,000 Guineas third Daban and half-sister to the very useful 1m (at 2 yrs) and Group 3 1m Thoroughbred Stakes winner Thikriyaat (by Azamour) and the fair 14f winner Cahill (by Lawman). The dam, placed four times at 3 yrs in France, is a half-sister to 8 winners including the Group 3 winners Albisola and Johnny Barnes and to the unplaced dam of the Group 1 winners Ectot and Much Improved. The second dam, Mahalia (by Danehill), won the Listed Prix Imprudence and is a half-sister to 7 winners including the French Group 3 winner Muroto and the smart broodmare Zivania (the dam of 5 stakes winners).

1516. UNNAMED
b.c. Acclamation – Missisipi Star (Mujahid). February 3. Fifth foal. 500,000Y. Tattersalls October Book 1. Charlie Gordon-Watson. Half-brother to the French Listed 5f winner and

Group 1 Cheveley Park Stakes third Baileys Jubilee (by Bahamian Bounty) and to the fair 1m winners Election Day (by Invincible Spirit) and Baileys Strider (by Aragorn). The dam, a fairly useful 1m winner, was Listed placed twice and is a half-sister to one winner. The second dam, Kicka (by Shirley Heights), was placed in Italy and is a half-sister to 8 winners.

1517. UNNAMED

b.c. Australia – Sent From Heaven (Footstepsinthesand). April 3. Third foal. 500,000Y. Tattersalls October Book 1. Charlie Gordon-Watson. The dam, winner of the 2-y-o Group 3 7f Prestige Stakes and fourth in the 1,000 Guineas, is a half-sister to 7 winners including the Group 3 Classic Trial winner Above Average. The second dam, Crystal Valkyrie (by Danehill), a fair 10f winner, is a half-sister to 3 minor winners.

JAMES TATE

1518. ACROSS THE SEA ★★★

b.f. Dubawi – Alsindi (Acclamation). January 26. Third foal. Sister to the fairly useful 7f and 1m winner Big Tour. The dam, a useful 2-y-o Group 3 7f Oh So Sharp Stakes winner and UAE Group 3 10f third, is a half-sister to 4 winners, The second dam, Needles And Pins (by Fasliyev), a useful 2-y-o Listed 5.2f winner and second in the Group 3 5.5f Prix d'Arenburg, is a half-sister to 3 winners. (Saeed Manana). *"A home-bred out of a 2-y-o Listed winner, so she's bred to be nice and early. She's had a few niggling issues as a foal and as a yearling so she hasn't quite caught the others up yet. She looks like she should be a 2-y-o but it's too soon to tell you what ability and speed she's got. On looks you'd think she'd be an early 2-y-o but I've had to go slowly with her so far".*

1519. AUTUMN SPLENDOUR (IRE) ★★★★★ ♠

b.c. Dandy Man – Harvest Joy (Daggers Drawn). February 28. Sixth foal. £52,000Y. Goffs UK Premier (Doncaster). Rabbah Bloodstock. Half-brother to the fairly useful 2-y-o 5f to 7f winner and Listed-placed Andysontherun (by Captain Rio), to the quite useful 2-y-o 6f winner Don Sigfredo (by Majestic Missile) and the quite useful 7f winner Philadelphia (by Roderic O'Connor).

The dam, a fairly useful Listed-placed 6f (at 2 yrs) and 10f winner, is a half-sister to 2 winners. The second dam, Windomen (by Forest Wind), is an unraced half-sister to 4 winners including the Italian Group 1 third and smart broodmare Super Bobbina. (Saeed Manana). *"He's definitely a 2-y-o and one of the best we have. A small to medium-sized colt, he's very strong and shows lots of speed so he's one for five and six furlongs".*

1520. DISTANT MIRAGE ★★★★

b.f. Toronado – Oasis Jade (Oasis Dream). February 9. 28,000Y. Tattersalls October Book 3. Rabbah Bloodstock. Half-sister to the quite useful 2017 2-y-o 5f and 6f winner Expecting (by Bated Breath). The dam, a modest 5f placed 2-y-o, is a half-sister to 9 winners including the fairly useful 6f winner of 11 races and Listed-placed Million Percent. The second dam, Royal Jade (by Last Tycoon), a fairly useful 7f winner, is a half-sister to 6 winners including the Group 3 5f King George Stakes winner Averti. (Saeed Manana). *"Big and strong, there's a lot of speed on the dam's side and she looks like she's taken some of that. She goes really nicely and she'd be towards the top of our fillies at the moment".* TRAINER'S BARGAIN BUY

1521. DUPLICITOUS (IRE) ★★★

b.f. Oasis Dream – Eleanora Duse (Azamour). March 30. Fourth foal. 65,000Y. Tattersalls October Book 1. Rabbah Bloodstock. Sister to Capesthorne, last of 8 over 6f on her only start at 2 yrs in 2017. The dam, a smart 1m (at 2 yrs) and Group 2 10f Blandford Stakes winner, was third in the Group 1 Yorkshire Oaks and is a half-sister to 6 winners including the Listed 10f winner and Group 1 12f Irish Oaks second Scottish Stage. The second dam, Drama Class (by Caerleon), a useful 10.2f winner, is a half-sister to the Group 2 10.3f winner Stage Gift. (Saeed Manana). *"She shows plenty of speed, she's small and strong and looks like a 2-y-o. I don't think she'll be a five furlong sprinter, but six and seven furlongs from the middle of the season onwards should be fine for her".*

1522. EVOLUTIONARY (IRE) ★★

b.f. Morpheus – Lilium (Nashwan). January 22. Twelfth foal. 62,000Y. Tattersalls October Book 3. Rabbah Bloodstock. Half-sister to 4 winners including the fair 7f winner Pollination (by Bushranger), the fair 10f and hurdles winner Bolanderi and the minor French dual 3-y-o winner Corn Flower (both by Seeking The Gold). The dam, a very useful Listed 7f (at 2 yrs) and Listed 12f winner, was third in the Group 3 Princess Royal Stakes, and is a half-sister to 6 winners including the 2-y-o Group 1 6f Middle Park Stakes winner Lujain and the Group 3 6f Coventry Stakes second Botanical. The second dam, Satin Flower (by Shadeed), a smart winner of the Group 3 7f Jersey Stakes and second in the Grade 1 9f Queen Elizabeth II Challenge Cup, is a half-sister to 7 winners including the US Grade 1 10f Santa Anita Handicap winner Martial Law. (Saeed Manana). *"She's done nothing but grow all winter and she's now big, long and strong. She's nearly my biggest 2-y-o, including the colts, so we haven't done a lot with her and she's definitely one for the second half of the season if at all".*

1523. FIELDS OF ATHENRY (USA) ★★★
b.br.c. Candy Ride – Purple (Galileo). March 12. Third foal. $95,000Y. Keeneland September Book 1. Not sold. The dam, a fair Irish 8.5f winner, is a half-sister to one winner. The second dam, Necklace (by Darshaan), won the 2-y-o Group 1 Moyglare Stud Stakes and was third in the US Grade 1 Beverly D Stakes. (Saeed Manana). *"Very much bred to be a middle-distance horse, he'll be one for the second half of the season. He's a strong, attractive colt and he goes nicely so I'll be looking forward to him in the second half of the year".*

1524. FUTURISTIC (IRE) ★★★
b.c. Shamardal – Aqlaam Vision (Aqlaam). February 10. First foal. 70,000Y. Tattersalls October Book 1. Blandford Bloodstock. The dam, a fairly useful 2-y-o Listed 7f winner, is a half-sister to 2 minor winners. The second dam, Dream Vision (by Distant View), is an unraced half-sister to 5 winners including the Group 2 Hardwicke Stakes winner and Group 1 third Await The Dawn and the French Listed winner and Group 1 third Putney Bridge. (Saeed Manana). *"A very big, strong horse, I like him but I don't think he'll be out in the early months of the year because of his size".*

1525. HARD TASKMASTER (IRE) ★★★
b.c. Moohaajim – Barracade (Barathea). April 24. Sixth foal. 55,000Y. Tattersalls October Book 2. Rabbah Bloodstock. Half-brother to the fairly useful 2-y-o triple 6f winner and Group 2 Rockfel Stakes second Blockade (by Kheleyf), to the fair 2-y-o 7f winner Kakashan (by Kodiac) and the fair dual 7f winner Black Rider (by Elnadim). The dam, a modest 10f placed 3-y-o in Ireland, is a half-sister to the US stakes winner and triple Grade 2 placed Spider Power. The second dam, America Calling (by Quiet American), a fair 6f winner at 3 yrs, is a half-sister to 8 winners. (Saeed Manana). *"He'll be an early 2-y-o. He's not my fastest but he's in the top few and I can see him running a lot of times this year. He's tough, hardy and likeable".*

1526. IMPLICIT (IRE) ★★★
b.f. Kodiac – Alioonagh (Giant's Causeway). February 29. Second foal. 50,000Y. Tattersalls December. Not sold. The dam is an unplaced sister to the US dual Grade 2 winner Oonagh Maccool and a half-sister to 8 winners including the 1,000 Guineas winner Sleepytime, the Group 1 1m Sussex Stakes winner Ali Royal and the dual Group 1 winner Taipan. The second dam, Alidiva (by Chief Singer), a winner of 3 races from 6f to 1m including a Listed event, is a half-sister to 6 winners including the dual French Group 1 winner Croco Rouge. (Saeed Manana). *"She came in later than most of them and looked quite sleepy over the winter, but she's just started to wake up. It's too soon to say exactly what she's going to be but she's showing signs of being a nice early 2-y-o. A little on the small side but very strong".*

1527. NOBLE LINEAGE (IRE) ★★★
ch.c. Iffraaj – Regal Hawk (Singspiel). March 26. First foal. 42,000Y. Tattersalls October Book 1. Not sold. The dam, a fairly useful Listed-placed 8.5f to 10f winner of 4 races, was Group 3 third in Sweden and is a half-sister to one winner. The second dam, Elegant Hawk (by Generous), a quite useful 9f and 12f winner, is a half-sister to 4 winners. (Saeed Manana). *"A medium-sized colt and not one for the first half of the season, he does go nicely enough so I'd like to think he could be nice a bit later on this season".*

1528. PROMOTE (IRE) ★★★

b.f. Dandy Man – Park Haven (Marju). April 1. Sixth foal. £32,000Y. Goffs UK Premier (Doncaster). Rabbah Bloodstock. Half-sister to the fair dual 1m winner Tadaany (by Acclamation) and the fair 2-y-o 1m winner Quick Bite (by Red back). The dam, placed once at 2 yrs, is a half-sister to 4 winners including the Group 3 Gordon Stakes winner Rebel Soldier. The second dam, En Garde (by Irish River), a quite useful 2-y-o 5.7f winner, is a half-sister to 7 winners including Observatory (Group 1 1m Queen Elizabeth II Stakes and Group 1 9.3f Prix d'Ispahan) and High Praise (Group 2 Prix de Malleret). (Saeed Manana). *"A speedy type and definitely one for early season 2-y-o races, she's a good-sized filly with plenty of spirit about her. Working nicely at the moment, I would have thought she'd be out reasonably early".*

1529. SECOND GENERATION ★★★

b.f. Dawn Approach – El Manati (Iffraaj). March 8. Second foal. 22,000Y. Tattersalls October Book 2. Not sold. The dam, a useful 2-y-o 6f winner, was third in the Group 3 5f Cornwallis Stakes and is a half-sister to 5 minor winners. The second dam, Limit (by Barathea), a modest 2-y-o 7f winner, is a half-sister to 5 winners. (Sheikh Rashid Dalmook Al Maktoum). *"I trained her dam who was very speedy and she got six furlongs but was better over five. I think it's fair to say that the sire Dawn Approach could have had a better first season last year. This filly shows plenty of speed and plenty of early signs, so fingers crossed she'll be a nice early 2-y-o".*

1530. SOCIAL NETWORK (IRE) ★★

ch.f. Australia – Mona Lisa (Giant's Causeway). April 1. Tenth foal. €100,000Y. Goffs Orby. Rabbah Bloodstock. Closely related to the fair Irish 8.5f winner Cabin (by Galileo) and half-sister to the fair 2-y-o 1m winner Manangatang (by Fastnet Rock). The dam, an Irish Listed 12f winner, was third in the Group 1 Coronation Stakes and the Group 1 Irish Oaks and is a half-sister to 6 winners including the Group 2 1m Falmouth Stakes second Croeso Cariad and Photogenic (Irish 2-y-o Listed 7f Debutante Stakes). The second dam, Colorsnap (by Shirley Heights), is an unraced half-sister to the Irish Champion Stakes winner Cezanne and the Irish Oaks winner Colorspin (dam of the Group 1 winners Opera House, Kayf Tara and Zee Zee Top). (Saeed Manana). *"A quality filly but a 3-y-o type bred for middle distances. At the moment she's only cantering because she's up behind, still growing and developing. One for the second half of the year if at all".*

1531. SOUL SEARCHING ★★★

ch.f. Iffraaj – Remember (Selkirk). February 13. First foal. 29,000Y. Tattersalls October Book 2. Not sold. The dam, a fairly useful Listed-placed 6f and 7f winner at 2 and 3 yrs, is a half-sister to 2 winners. The second dam, Forgotten Dreams (by Olden Times), ran unplaced twice and is a half-sister to 4 winners including the Group 1 Italian Oaks and dual Group 2 winner Zomaradah (herself the dam of three stakes winners including Dubawi). (Saeed Manana). *"The dam was Listed-placed at Newmarket over six furlongs for Richard Hannon and this is her first foal. A medium-sized filly, strong and showing lots of speed, she'll be out early over five and six furlongs".*

1532. WAR AND GLORY (IRE) ★★★

b.f. War Command – Foreplay (Lujain). February 11. Seventh foal. £92,000Y. Goffs UK Premier (Doncaster). Blandford Bloodstock. Half-sister to 5 winners including the useful dual 5f winner and Group 3 Molecomb Stakes second Anticipated, the French 2-y-o 5f winner Finisterien (both by Whipper), the quite useful 5f and 6f winner of 5 races Midnight Rider (by Red Ransom) and the fair 5f and 6f winner Random Success (by Shamardal). The dam, a fair 6f (at 2 yrs) and 7f winner, is a half-sister to the smart Listed 9f and Listed 10f winner and Group 1 Prix Jean Prat third Rocamadour and to the Irish 2-y-o 5f winner and Listed-placed Church Cross. The second dam, Watch Me (by Green Desert), a useful 6f winner and third in the Group 3 6f Cork And Orrery Stakes, is a half-sister to 3 winners here and abroad. (Saeed Manana). *"A nice filly, she's bred to be pretty quick and we've liked what we've seen. She's quite tall so we haven't pushed the button entirely yet, but I do like her. I haven't galloped her enough yet to be able to work out her trip".*

1533. ZMHAR (IRE) ★★★★★ ♠
ch.c. Shamardal – Guarantia (Selkirk). March 22. Seventh foal. Half-brother to the quite useful 6f (at 2 yrs) and 7f winner Certified (by Raven's Pass), to the fair 6f winner Surety and the fair 2-y-o 6f winner Daraa (both by Cape Cross). The dam, a fairly useful Listed-placed 7f winner, is a half-sister to 6 winners including the very smart dual Group 3 12f winner Laaheb. The second dam, Maskunah (by Sadler's Wells), is an unraced half-sister to 6 winners including the high-class middle-distance horses and multiple Group 1 winners Warrsan and Luso, the Nell Gwyn Stakes winner Cloud Castle and the Group 2 Gallinule Stakes winner Needle Gun and to the dams of five Group 3 winners. (Saeed Manana). *"He goes really well, he's a good-sized, strong colt that shows a lot of speed and he'd be at the top of our pecking order at the moment".*

1534. UNNAMED ★★★
ch.f. Speightstown – Aerocat (Tale Of The Cat). April 5. Fifth foal. $215,000Y. Keeneland September. Ashland Park. Half-sister to the US Grade 2 1m San Clemente Handicap and Grade 3 Arlington Classic winner Istanford (by Istan) and to the US winner of 5 minor races Tale Of Peace (by Peace Rules). The dam won two minor races in the USA at 3 yrs. The second dam, The Envelopeplease (by Deputy Minister), is an unplaced half-sister to 6 winners. (Sultan Ali). *"Our most expensive 2-y-o, she goes really nicely, shows plenty of speed, is a bit on the small side but looks a 2-y-o. She worked nicely this morning and looks quick".*

1535. UNNAMED ★★★★
b.c. New Approach – Ahla Wasahl (Dubai Destination). April 2. Fifth foal. 100,000Y. Tattersalls October Book 1. Not sold. Brother to the quite useful 1m winner Generalship. The dam, a useful 6f (at 2 yrs) and Listed 1m winner, was third in the Group 2 Cherry Hinton Stakes and is a half-sister to 4 winners including the dam of the Group 1 Italian Oaks winner Menhoubah. The second dam, In Full Cry (by Seattle Slew), a winner at 2 and 3 yrs in the USA, was second in the Grade 2 6f Adirondack Stakes and is a half-sister to 6 winners including the top-class miler Posse. *"A tall, rangy New Approach colt and whilst not a sprinting type he's very nice and we like him a lot".*

1536. UNNAMED ★★
b.f. Camelot – Carioca (Rakti). February 13. Fourth foal. 80,000Y. Tattersalls October Book 1. Rabbah Bloodstock. Half-sister to the very useful triple Listed winner from 5f to 7f and Group 2 7f Vintage Stakes second Tupi (by Tamayuz) and to the quite useful 1m winner Tukhoom (by Acclamation). The dam, a useful Italian Listed 1m winner, is a half-sister to 3 winners including the 5f Windsor Castle Stakes winner and Group 2 6f Mill Reef Stakes second Irony. The second dam, Cidaris (by Persian Bold), ran once unplaced and is a half-sister to 3 winners. (Saif Ali). *"A lovely, big, strong filly that goes nicely but when we've done little bits of work with her she doesn't look like one for five or six furlongs. She's probably one for the second half of the season".*

1537. UNNAMED ★★★
b.f. Lope De Vega – Dazzle Dancer (Montjeu). April 9. Fifth foal. €85,000Y. Goffs Orby. Rabbah Bloodstock. Sister to the useful 10f winner and dual Listed-placed Linguistic. The dam, a fair Irish 4-y-o 12f winner, is a half-sister to 3 winners. The second dam, Another Dancer (by Groom Dancer), won the Group 2 Prix de Malleret and is a half-sister to 6 winners. (Sheikh Juma Dalmook Al Maktoum). *"A little on the small side but she goes nicely and is bred for the 1m to 10f races, so we'll probably not start her until she gets the chance to run over seven furlongs. I like what I've seen so far".*

1538. UNNAMED ★★★
b.f. Kingman – Deveron (Cozzene). April 21. Eighth foal. Half-sister to the fairly useful 2017 dual Listed-placed 2-y-o 5f winner Haddaf (by Dawn Approach), to the very useful Listed 1m winner of 6 races from 2 to 5 yrs Lamar (by Cape Cross), the quite useful 2-y-o 6f and 7f winner Hope Cove, the quite useful 2-y-o 7f winner Dffar (both by Shamardal) and the modest 2-y-o 1m winner Open Letter (by New Approach). The dam, a very useful 2-y-o 7f winner and third in the Group 1 1m Prix Marcel Boussac, is a sister to the Canadian dual Grade 2 winner Windward Islands and a half-sister to 5 winners. The second dam, Cruisie (by Assert), a triple US 3-y-o winner, is a half-sister to 4 stakes winners including the dam of the US Grade 1 winner Capote Belle. (Saif Ali). *"She's home-bred and related to two useful horses I've had, Lamar and Haddaf.*

She had some issues as a yearling so she's a bit behind the others but I like her. She's not over-big, but quite strong and it's too early to say how good she is, but anything out of this dam we like".

1539. UNNAMED ★★★
b.f. New Approach – Excel's Beauty (Exceed And Excel). January 25. First foal. 320,000Y. Tattersalls October Book 1. Rabbah Bloodstock. The dam, a fairly useful Listed-placed 2-y-o 5f winner, is a sister to the Group 3 Molecomb Stakes (at 2 yrs) and Group 3 Dubai International World Trophy winner Cotai Glory. The second dam, Continua (by Elusive Quality), is an unraced sister to the 2-y-o winner and Group 1 Middle Park Stakes third Huntdown and a half-sister to 5 winners. (Sheikh Juma Dalmook Al Maktoum). *"When she came in as a yearling she looked like her mother who was a five furlong 2-y-o, but as time has gone on she looks more like her father. Getting taller and longer, she's growing and looks like one for the second half of the season but she won't be a sprinter".*

1540. UNNAMED ★★★
b.c. New Approach – First City (Diktat). April 29. Third foal. 33,000Y. Tattersalls October Book 3. Not sold. Half-brother to the 2017 2-y-o 8.5f winner from two starts Laieth (by Dubawi). The dam, a smart 6f (at 2 yrs) and UAE Group 2 1m winner, was third in the Group 1 Falmouth Stakes and is a half-sister to 2 winners including the Group 2 Royal Lodge Stakes third Sea Fox. The second dam, City Maiden (by Carson City), is an unraced half-sister to the French Listed winner and Group 3 placed Vernoy and to the dam of the US Grade 1 winner Sheikhzayedroad. *"A home-bred, he's medium-sized and probably a 1m+ 3-y-o type, but he goes nicely".*

1541. UNNAMED ★★★
ch.f. Lemon Drop Kid – Night Song (Oasis Dream). February 18. First foal. 45,000Y. Tattersalls October Book 2. Rabbah Bloodstock. The dam, a fairly useful 2-y-o 7f winner, is a sister to the Group 2 6f Cherry Hinton Stakes winner and Group 1 Cheveley Park Stakes second Misheer and a half-sister to 2 winners. The second dam, All For Laura (by Cadeaux Genereux), a fairly useful 2-y-o 5f winner, is a full or half-sister to 5 minor

winners. (Saeed Manana). *"A nice filly, very strong and medium-sized, there's speed on the dam's side but stamina on the sire's side. She looks like she'll be a mid-season 2-y-o and I don't think she's a sprinter".*

1542. UNNAMED ★★★
ch.c. Exceed And Excel – Wahylah (Shamardal). March 6. Third foal. The dam, a quite useful 2-y-o 6f winner, is a half-sister to 2 winners, The second dam, Neshla (by Singspiel), a poor 11f placed maiden, is a half-sister to 9 winners including the Group 3 7.3f Fred Darling Stakes winner and Group 2 10f Nassau Stakes third Sueboog (herself dam of the Group 1 winner Best Of The Bests) and the Listed winners Sell Out and Marika. (Saeed Manana). *"A big, strong horse that goes quite nicely but he's too big to be running very early. From what we've seen of him we quite like him".*

1543. UNNAMED ★★★
br.f. Cape Cross – Without Precedent (Polish Precedent). February 10. Fifth foal. 40,000Y. Tattersalls December. Rabbah Bloodstock. Half-sister to the quite useful 2-y-o 7f winner Marvel Joy (by Helmet) and to the modest 11.5f winner Mistamel (by Rip Van Winkle). The dam, a French Listed-placed 2-y-o 6f winner, is a half-sister to 3 winners including the German dual Listed winner Stark Danon. The second dam, Sue Generoos (by Spectrum), a Listed-placed dual winner in France, is a half-sister to one winner abroad. *"She's a bit small but very strong and goes quite nicely. I don't think she'll be that early but she's one to put in the book".*

MARK TOMPKINS
1544. ASTROMERRY ★★★
br.f. Farhh – Astrodonna (Carnival Dancer). April 7. Fourth foal. The dam, a fair 9f (at 2 yrs) and 1m winner of 4 races, is a half-sister to 3 winners. The second dam, Mega (by Petardia), is an unplaced half-sister to 7 winners including the Listed winners Bolino Star and Don Fayruz. (Mystic Meg Ltd). *"She's very nice and although the mare has yet to breed a winner they've all run all right and this is the nicest one to date. She's strong, the sire has had a great start to his stud career and this filly is showing all the right signs at present. Six/seven furlongs will suit her from May onwards and she'll get a mile in time".*

1545. FARNE ODYSSEY ★★
b.f. Farhh – Diverting (Nayef). February 9.
Second foal. The dam, a quite useful 1m and
9f winner of 4 races, is a half-sister to one
winner. The second dam, Tawny Way (by Polar
Falcon), was a quite useful 9f to 12f winner of
4 races. (J. A. Reed). *"She's sharp, strong and
looks a 2-y-o type. The 2-y-o last year out of
the dam, Sandwood Bay, always showed me
plenty but never did it on the track, but I'm
more hopeful of this filly".*

1546. ISAAC MURPHY ★★
b.c. Medaglia d'Oro – Marietta (Machiavellian).
March 10. Fifth foal. 20,000Y. Tattersalls
October Book 1. Not sold. Half-brother to the
US 6.5f (at 2 yrs) and 6f winner Consortium,
to the minor French 7f winner Heartlines,
the minor winner abroad Hiawassee (all by
Bernardini) and the minor US 4-y-o winner
Dowager (by A P Indy). The dam won two
Grade 3 stakes in the USA and is a half-
sister to 6 winners including a Listed winner
in France. The second dam, Minister Wife
(by Deputy Minister), won the US Grade 2
Demoiselle Stakes and is a half-sister to 3
winners. (Sarabex). *"He's bred to win anything
because he's got a fantastic pedigree and the
sire had two winners at the Breeders' Cup just
after we bought this colt privately after the
Book 1 sale. He's going to need a bit of time
because he's tall, unfurnished and needs to fill
his big frame out, so he's one for the second
half of the season and especially next year. I
don't think he'll have that many runs this year
but you never know and he has a lot in his
favour if he does".*

1547. MELO PEARL ★★★
ch.f. Paco Boy – Jewelled (Fantastic Light).
April 29. Second foal. The dam, a fair 1m to
12f winner of 7 races, is a half-sister to one
winner. The second dam, Danemere (Danehill),
a fairly useful 2-y-o 6f winner, was Listed-
placed over 1m at 3 yrs and is a half-sister 3
winners. (Mr M. Franklin). *"Quite a nice filly,
she's grown a bit and she's a fairly late foal but
she'll be running from May/June onwards. A
strong filly, she's built like an ox and has the
right attitude so she should be perfectly all
right and six/seven furlongs will suit her".*

1548. PAGEANT MASTER (IRE) ★★★
ch.c. Casamento – Skiphall (Halling). March

18. Tenth foal. €16,000Y. Goffs Sportsmans. M
O'Sullivan. Half-brother to 5 winners including
the Grade 1 10f E P Taylor Stakes and Group
2 10f Prix Jean Romanet winner Folk Opera
(by Singspiel), the quite useful 12f and hurdles
winner Art Trend (by Hawk Wing) and the
quite useful 7f winner One True Love (by Duke
Of Marmalade). The dam, placed 5 times at 3
yrs in France, stayed 10.5f and is a half-sister
to 7 winners including the 2-y-o Listed winner
Innocent Air, the French and US Listed winner
and US Grade 1 placed Skipping and the dam
of the Group 1 2-y-o winner Proportional.
The second dam, Minskip (by The Minstrel),
won once at 2 yrs and is a sister to the US
Grade 2 winner Savinio and a half-sister to the
Italian dual Group 1 winner St Hilarion and the
Group 3 winner Ballet De France (dam of the
dual Group 1 winner Muhtarram). (Dullingham
Park). *"I love him, he's a proper early season
2-y-o. He's strong, goes well, is a half-brother
to a Group 1 winner and shows all the right
signs. He's not big but he's built well and has
the right attitude. I haven't had an early 2-y-o
for a while but he looks like one".*

1549. QUANAH (IRE) ★★★
ch.c. Dandy Man – Boucheron (Galileo).
February 18. Third foal. 28,000Y. Tattersalls
October Book 2. M H Tompkins. Half-brother
to the quite useful 2-y-o 7f and 1m winner
Geneva Convention (by Clodovil). The dam,
a quite useful 12f winner, is a half-sister to
a minor winner. The second dam, Rainbow
Lyrics (by Rainbow Quest), is an unraced half-
sister to 4 winners including the Irish triple
Listed winner Hard To Speak. (Killarney Glen
& Sarabex). *"A very nice horse we bought at
Newmarket, if he had a better pedigree he'd
have made 100K. He could be a proper horse,
he has a great attitude, tries and is a great
mover. He just had a touch of a sore shin in
January so we left him alone and he'll be a
May/June 2-y-o. We love him".* TRAINER'S
BARGAIN BUY

1550. VELVET VISTA ★★
b.f. Sea The Moon – Battery Power (Royal
Applause). April 8. Third foal. Half-sister to
Velvet Vision (by Nathaniel), placed second
over 1m on her debut at 3 yrs in 2018. The
dam, a fair 1m (at 2 yrs) and 12f winner, is a
half-sister to 7 winners including the quite

useful Irish 2-y-o 7f winner Captain Cullen. The second dam, Missouri (by Charnwood Forest), a quite useful 15f winner, is a half-sister to several winners. (Sarabex). *"We train her half-sister Velvet Vision who recently broke her maiden as a 3-y-o at Newcastle over ten furlongs and she's very useful. This is a nice filly that's still developing so I see her as one for the middle of the season onwards. The family just need that bit of time".*

MARCUS TREGONING

1551. ALAMINTA
b.f. Archipenko – Almamia (Hernando). March 29. Seventh foal. Half-sister to the useful 2-y-o 6f winner and Group 3 7f Oh So Sharp Stakes second Alamode (by Sir Percy), to the fair 11f winner Aloha (by With Approval) and the modest dual 2m winner Alternate Route (by New Approach). The dam, a fair 1m and 9f placed maiden, is a half-sister to 4 winners including the Listed winners Algonquin and Alvarita. The second dam, Alborada (by Alzao), won the Group 1 Champion Stakes (twice) and is a sister to the triple German Group 1 winner Albanova. (Miss K Rausing).

1552. MOGHRAM
b.c. Sir Percy – Red Blossom (Silver Hawk). March 24. Tenth foal. 40,000Y. Tattersalls October Book 2. Shadwell Estate Co. Half-brother to 6 winners including the French 2-y-o 7f and 1m winner and Group 1 Criterium de Saint-Cloud second Hannouma (by Anabaa), the fair 12f, 14f and hurdles winner Dominada (by Mastercraftsman) and the fair French 13.5f winner Red Hurricane (by Hurricane Run). The dam, placed once in France, is a half-sister to 6 winners including the 2-y-o Group 3 7f winner and Group 1 placed Governor Brown and the dual Listed winner Hataab. The second dam, Miss Mistletoes (by The Minstrel), won over 7f and 9f in Ireland and is a half-sister to the Irish Group 3 winner Lomond Blossom. (Hamdan Bin Rashid Al Maktoum).

1553. MOHAATHER ♠
b.c. Showcasing – Roodeye (Inchinor). April 26. Ninth foal. 110,000Y. Tattersalls October Book 2. Shadwell Estate Co. Brother to the US Grade 2 and Grade 3 winner Prize Exhibit and to the Hong Kong 6f winner Super Sixteen

and half-brother to 5 winners including the fairly useful 2-y-o 7f and 7.5f winner Harbour Master (by Harbour Watch), the quite useful 5f (at 2 yrs) and 7f winner Roodle (by Xaar) and the fair 2-y-o 6f winner Must Be Me (by Trade Fair). The dam, a useful 5f (at 2 yrs) and 7f winner, was Listed-placed and is a half-sister to 7 winners including the Group 1 Prix Morny second Gallagher. The second dam, Roo (by Rudimentary), a quite useful 2-y-o 5f and 6f winner, is a half-sister to 6 winners including the Group 2 6f Gimcrack Stakes winner Bannister. (Hamdan Bin Rashid Al Maktoum).

1554. SUMMER SKIES
b.f. Leroidesanimaux – Sunset Shore (Oasis Dream). January 15. Second foal. Sister to the quite useful 2017 2-y-o 7f winner Watheer. The dam, a fair 2-y-o 5.5f winner, is a half-sister to 7 winners including the 2-y-o Group 3 1m Prix des Reservoirs winner and Group 2 Park Hill Stakes third Songerie and the useful Listed winners Soft Morning, Souvenance and Sourire. The second dam, Summer Night (by Nashwan), a fairly useful 3-y-o 6f winner, is a half-sister to 7 winners including the Group 3 Prix d'Arenburg winner Starlit Sands. (Miss K. Rausing).

1555. TELL WILLIAM
b.c. Invincible Spirit – Swiss Kiss (Dansili). January 21. First foal. 60,000Y. Tattersalls October Book 2. M Tregoning. The dam, a fair 1m winner, is a half-sister to 8 winners including the Group 3 6f Prix de Meautry and Group 3 5f Prix de Petit Couvert winner Swiss Diva, the 6f (at 2 yrs) and Group 3 5f winner Swiss Spirit, the useful triple Listed 6f winner Swiss Dream and the smart 2-y-o 5f winner and triple Group 2 placed Swiss Franc. The second dam, Swiss Lake (by Indian Ridge), a dual Listed 5f winner (including at 2 yrs), and second in the Group 2 Flying Childers Stakes, is a half-sister to 4 winners. (R. C. C. Villers).

1556. UNNAMED
b.c. Dark Angel – Spirit Of Cuba (Invincible Spirit). January 28. Second foal. €35,000Y. Goffs Orby. Not sold. The dam, a fairly useful Irish dual 10f winner, is a half-sister to 5 winners including the Listed 6f winner of 4 races at 2 and 3 yrs Shanghai Glory and the Listed 7f winner of 4 races Choose Me (dam of

the Group 1 Queen Elizabeth II Stakes winner Persuasive). The second dam, Hecuba (by Hector Protector), a fairly useful 10f winner, is a half-sister to 7 winners including the German Group 2 winner Bad Bertrich Again and the Group 3 Scottish Classic winner Prolix. (Owenstown Stud).

1557. UNNAMED
b.c. Sea The Moon – Summer Night (Nashwan). April 14. Fifteenth foal. 35,000Y. Tattersalls October Book 2. M Tregoning. Half-brother to 10 winners including the 2-y-o Group 3 1m Prix des Reservoirs winner Songerie, the fairly useful 2-y-o 7.2f winner and Group 3 1m Prix des Reservoirs third Souvenance (both by Hernando), the useful Listed 9.5f winner of 3 races Soft Morning (by Pivotal) and the fairly useful 7f (at 2 yrs) and Scandinavian Listed 8.5f winner Sourire (by Domedriver). The dam, a fairly useful 6f winner, is a half-sister to 7 winners including Starlit Sands (Group 3 Prix d'Arenberg). The second dam, Shimmering Sea (by Slip Anchor), a fairly useful Irish 2-y-o 5f and 7f winner and Group 3 third, is a half-sister to the King George VI winner Petoski.

JOE TUITE
1558. ALL BACK TO MINE ★★★★
ch.f. Dutch Art – Exotic Isle (Exceed And Excel). March 29. Second foal. £23,000Y. Goffs UK Premier (Doncaster). Hillen & Tuite (private sale). Half-sister to the 2017 2-y-o 7f winner, from two starts, Qaroun (by Dark Angel). The dam, a fair dual 5f winner (including at 2 yrs), is a half-sister to 3 winners. The second dam, Paradise Isle (by Bahamian Bounty), a useful 5f (at 2 yrs) and 6f winner of 8 races including two Listed events, was third in the Group 3 6f Summer Stakes and is a full or half-sister to 9 winners including the useful broodmare Clincher Club. (Lech Racing Ltd). *"A half-sister to a horse of Sir Michael Stoute's that won its maiden at Newbury last year. She goes nicely and will be running at the end of April/ early May and will possibly be better over six furlongs than five".*

1559. ANGEL MEAD ★★★
b.f. Archipenko – Red Sovereign (Danzig Connection). March 22. Seventh foal. Half-sister to the modest 2017 5f placed 2-y-o

Frostbite (by Lethal Force), to the fair dual 6f winner Red Alert (by Sleeping Indian), the fair dual 5f winner Royal Award (by Cadeaux Genereux) and the quite useful 2-y-o 5f winner Three Crowns (by Three Valleys). The dam, a fair 6f (including at 2 yrs) and 5f winner of 5 races, is a half-sister to 2 winners. The second dam, Ruby Princess (by Mac's Imp), is a placed half-sister to one winner abroad. (David Klein). *"A home-bred, she's a half-sister to a nice little horse I trained called Red Alert. A very nice filly, she'll be a mid-season 2-y-o, she's well-made and a nicer specimen than her brother. We like her a lot but she was late in".*

1560. CHARLOTTE ROUSSE (IRE) ★★
b.f. Showcasing – Tartiflette (Dr Fong). April 8. Second foal. Half-sister to the modest 2018 1m placed 3-y-o Taifbalady (by Dark Angel). The dam, a quite useful 6f (at 2 yrs) and 7f winner of 3 races, is a half-sister to 3 winners including the Group 3 Chipchase takes and Listed winner Aeolus. The second dam, Bright Moll (by Mind Games), a fairly useful 2-y-o 5f and 6f winner, is a half-sister to 7 winners including the Group 2 Mill Reef Stakes second Doctor Brown. (Malcolm Forbes). *"One for the second half of the season, she's a nice filly and a big, strong-looking type".*

1561. GRANDMASTER FLASH ★★★
ch.c. Australia – Kittens (Marju). February 2. Second foal. 52,000Y. Tattersalls October Book 2. Stephen Hillen/J Tuite. The dam, a modest triple 12f winner, is a half-sister to 5 winners including the Group 3 7f Prix du Calvados winner and Group 3 1m Ridgewood Pearl Stakes winner Purr Along and the Listed winner Katawi. The second dam, Purring (by Mountain Cat), a quite useful 7f winner, is a half-sister to the Group 2 Falmouth Stakes and Group 3 1m Prix de Sandringham winner Ronda (herself dam of a dual Grade 3 winner) and to the Listed 2m winner Silver Gilt. (Lech Racing Ltd). *"A beautiful, big horse with a lovely attitude and a lovely way of going; one for the back-end of the season".*

1562. MESSUA (IRE) ★★★
b.f. Bungle Inthejungle – Playful Promises (Elnadim). February 14. Second foal. Half-sister to the fair 5f winner Liquid (by Zoffany). The

dam is an unplaced half-sister to one winner. The second dam, Playful (by Piccolo), a fairly useful 2-y-o dual 5f winner, was Listed-placed and is a half-sister to 5 winners. (Joe Tuite & Cooneed Stud). *"The sire has started the year well with a couple of winners. I trained the dam as a 2-y-o and she was very quick but unfortunately she had an injury and didn't run. The filly shows me plenty of speed and she's one I'd run in the first half of the season over five furlongs".*

1563. SHAFFIRE ★★★
b.f. Clodovil – Wigan Lane (Kheleyf). February 14. Fourth foal. 34,000Y. Tattersalls October Book 3. Hillen & Tuite. Half-sister to the fairly useful 2-y-o dual 5f winner Lathom (by Compton Place) and to the German 2-y-o winner Woomera. The dam, a fair 2-y-o 6f winner, is a half-sister to 2 winners including the useful 5f and 6f winner of 5 races and Group 3 Palace House Stakes second Hoh Hoh Hoh. The second dam, Nesting (by Thatching), is an unplaced full or half-sister to 3 winners and to the dams of the Group 2 winners Tariq and Wi Dud. (Richard Gurr). *"A beautiful filly, she shows me plenty of speed and will be running in April. Very straightforward, I think she'll be an out-and-out five furlong filly".*

1564. SOPHOSC ★★
ch.c. Society Rock – Ichiuma (Mizzen Mast). May 7. First foal. €17,000Y. Goffs Sportsmans. Hillen/Tuite. The dam is an unraced half-sister to 5 winners. The second dam, Trekking (by Gone West), a quite useful 10f winner, is a half-sister to 6 winners including the smart dual Listed 7f winner Tantina (herself dam of the Group winners Bated Breath and Cityscape). (Harefield Racing Club). *"A nice type of horse that goes to work in the morning with a smile on his face – he just loves his work. He can't do enough to please you and he'll be racing by the end of May".*

1565. SYLVIA'S MOTHER ★★★
b.f. Foxwedge – Majestic Song (Royal Applause). February 16. First foal. 20,000Y. Tattersalls October Book 3. Hillen & Tuite. The dam, a fair 6f winner, is a half-sister to 2 winners including the very useful 2-y-o 6f winner and Group 2 6f Mill Reef Stakes third Taayel. The second dam, Sakhee's Song (by

Sakhee), a useful Italian 5f and 6f winner, was Group 3 placed three times. (Jon Beard/Mat Morgan/ Mark Wellbelove). *"A good, strong filly that shows me enough on the gallops to say she'll be racing in mid-May; she looks like a filly with a future as a 2-y-o, shows a bit of speed and I like her attitude".*

1566. THE GREY DANCER ★★★
gr.c. Alhebayeb – Key Girl (Key Of Luck). May 4. Eighth foal. €20,000Y. Goffs Sportsmans. Hillen/Tuite. Half-brother to Apex Predator, unplaced in two starts at 2 yrs in 2017, to the useful 2-y-o 6f and 7f winner and Group 3 Solario Stakes third Music Theory (both by Acclamation) and the moderate 7f winner Turaathy (by Lilbourne Lad). The dam is an unplaced half-sister to 9 winners including the smart Irish 5f and Listed 6f winner Rolo Tomasi and the US and German Group 2 Elegant Ridge. The second dam, Elegant Bloom (by Be My Guest), a quite useful Irish 2-y-o 6f winner, stayed 7f and is a full or half-sister to 12 winners. (Mr & Mrs Bright). *"We gelded him because he was a rig, but he's now in full work. I think he's a very nice horse; he's tall and raw at the moment but I think he'll be out before the end of May, he has a beautiful attitude and a beautiful way of going".*

1567. UNNAMED ★★★
b.g. Bated Breath – Espagnolette (Oasis Dream). February 2. Third foal. The dam is an unraced half-sister to 7 winners including Deportivo (Group 2 Flying Five) and So Beloved (Group 3 Supreme Stakes). The second dam, Valencia (by Kenmare), placed over 1m at 2 yrs on her only start, is a half-sister to 8 winners including the dual US Grade 1 winner Wandesta and the Group 2 12f winner De Quest. (Oakgrove Stud). *"He literally only arrived two days ago but I love what I've seen already. He's a gorgeous horse that looks an out-and-out five furlong sprinter. I've been told there's a 100% record for the Bated Breath – Oasis Dream cross, but of course I don't know how large the sample is. Hopefully he's a late arrival but a surprise package".*

ROGER VARIAN
1568. APPARATE ★★
b.c. Dubawi – Appearance (Galileo). April 9.

Fourth foal. Brother to the quite useful 4-y-o 9.5f and 12f winner Appeared. The dam is an unraced three-parts sister to six winners including the dual Group 3 1m winner Apsis, the Group 2 12.5f Prix de Royallieu winner Dance Routine, the useful French Listed 10f winner and Group 3 10.5f Prix de Flore second Concentric and the Group 3 placed Light Ballet. The second dam, Apogee (by Shirley Heights), won the Group 3 12f Prix de Royaumont and is a half-sister to the Group 2 12f Grand Prix de Chantilly winner Daring Miss. (Sheikh Mohammed Obaid Al Maktoum). *"A horse that will take a bit of time but he's a nice big horse for the future".*

1569. BARDO CONTIGUO (IRE) ★★★
b.c. Lope De Vega – Jillnextdoor (Henrythenavigator). January 25. First foal. €110,000Y. Arqana Deauville August. Roger Varian. The dam, a useful 2-y-o 5f winner, is a half-sister to 4 winners including the useful 7f and 1m winner and Listed-placed Commander Cave. The second dam, Royal Shyness (by Royal Academy), a useful 2-y-o 6f winner, was third in the Group 1 6f Cheveley Park Stakes and subsequently won a Listed stakes race in the USA and is a half-sister to 8 winners. (Sheikh Mohammed Obaid Al Maktoum). *"A nice horse that moves well, he's done well physically recently and should be a fun horse. I'm not sure he's a star but he's a nice type".*

1570. BAYROOT (IRE) ★★★★
b.c. Exceed And Excel – Alwarga (Street Sense). April 1. Second foal. The dam is an unraced half-sister to 7 winners including the dual Group 2 winner Kabool. The second dam, Sheroog (by Shareef Dancer), a fair 1m winner, is a sister to the dam of Dubai Millennium, closely related to the Group/Grade 1 winners Hamas, Northern Aspen and Fort Wood and a half-sister to the Grade 1 winner Timber Country. (Sheikh Ahmed Al Maktoum). *"He's a big horse, so not an early Exceed And Excel, but he carries himself extremely well for a big 2-y-o and I'm sure he'll be winning races later in the year".*

1571. DUBRAVA ★★★
gr.f. Dansili – Rose Diamond (Daylami). April 20. Fourth foal. Half-brother to the quite useful dual 10f and subsequent US Grade

3 10.5f winner Real Smart (by Smart Strike) and to the quite useful 7f winner To Dibba (by Dubawi). The dam, a fairly useful 2-y-o 6f winner, was second in the Group 3 7f Prestige Stakes. The second dam, Tante Rose (by Barathea), a winner of 5 races including the Group 1 Haydock Park Sprint Cup, the Group 4 7f Fred Darling Stakes and Group 3 6f Summer Stakes, is a half-sister to several winners including the Sweet Solera Stakes winner Bay Tree. (Sheikh Mohammed Obaid Al Maktoum). *"I quite like her but she's not going to be doing anything anytime soon. One to make a 2-y-o by the late summer, she has a nice way of moving and she's quite attractive".*

1572. ELAMIRR ★★★
b.c. Exceed And Excel – Ameerat (Mark Of Esteem). February 29. Half-brother to 5 winners including the fairly useful 2-y-o 1m winner and dual Listed-placed Oojooba (by Monsun), the fairly useful 2-y-o 1m winner Sowaylm (by Tobougg), the quite useful 7f winner Kawssaj (by Dubawi) and the quite useful 7f winner Own Boss (by Seeking The Gold). The dam won the 1,000 Guineas and is a full or half-sister to 3 winners including the smart UAE 1m winner of 11 races Walmooh. The second dam, Walimu (by Top Ville), a quite useful winner of 3 races from 1m to 12f, is a half-sister to 6 winners. (Sheikh Ahmed Al Maktoum). *"A nice type of horse that's a little bit feminine and very athletic, he takes the eye at this early stage and I quite like him. This could be a quite a good mating for Ameerat who has been largely disappointing as a broodmare. He has the action of quite a nice horse and I think he's got a future because he's likeable".*

1573. ENOUGH ALREADY ★★★
b.c. Coach House – Funny Enough (Dansili). April 14. Fourth foal. 125,000Y. Tattersalls October Book 2. Roger Varian. Half-brother to the useful 2017 2-y-o 6.5f winner Laugh A Minute (by Mayson), to the fairly useful dual 7f winner Horroob (by Showcasing) and the fair 2-y-o 7f winner Puzzled Look (by Sakhee's Secret). The dam is an unplaced half-sister to 6 winners including the Lingfield Listed winner Oasis Dancer. The second dam, Good Enough (by Mukaddamah), a US 3-y-o winner, was third in the Group 1 Prix Saint-Alary and is a half-sister to 5 winners including the Group 3

Molecomb Stakes winner Classic Ruler. (Sheikh Mohammed Obaid Al Maktoum). *"An athletic horse that goes quite nicely, I'm getting to know the family having trained Horroob and Laugh A Minute out of the mare. They were both quite talented and this horse looks in a similar mould. He'll be a fun horse".*

1574. FABRIANO (GER) ★★★
b.br.c. Sinndar – Four Roses (Darshaan). February 14. Eleventh foal. 300,000Y. Tattersalls October Book 2. Roger Varian. Brother to the Group 2 10f Blandford Stakes and Group 3 Blue Wind Stakes winner Four Sins and half-brother to the quite useful Irish 2-y-o 1m winner Frontier, the modest 2m winner Force Of Destiny (both by Galileo) and 3 minor winners in France and Germany by Sea The Stars, Montjeu and Seattle Dancer. The dam is an unraced half-sister to 10 winners including the Group 3 7f Rockfel Stakes winner Germane and the very useful German 10f winner Fabriano. The second dam, Fraulein Tobin (by J O Tobin), a fair 1m winner, is a half-sister to 6 winners including the very smart 10f performer Running Stag. (Sheikh Mohammed Obaid Al Maktoum). *"A lovely horse, he has the stamp of a nice horse because he's well-made, has plenty of scope and carries himself well on the canters. Probably an autumn 2-y-o for seven furlongs and a mile, he's quite likeable".*

1575. FIFTH POSITION (IRE) ★★
b.c. Dark Angel – Ballet Move (Oasis Dream). February 22. Third foal. 68,000Y. Tattersalls October Book 2. De Burgh Equine. The dam, a French 1m 7f winner, is a half-sister to 2 other minor winners. The second dam, Penchee (by Grand Lodge), a French Listed 11f winner, is a half-sister to 4 winners. (Sheikh Mohammed Obaid Al Maktoum). *"A nice-moving horse but the dam stayed very well and I don't think this will be a fast Dark Angel. He'll want a mile plus in time, but he's OK".*

1576. FLEURSALS ★★★★
b.f. Poet's Voice – Entitlement (Authorized). April 6. Second foal. 32,000Y. Tattersalls October Book 2. J Shack & G Barnard. The dam, a modest 4-y-o 2m winner, is a half-sister to 11 winners including the Group 2 12f Princess Of Wales's Stakes winner Craigsteel

and the Group 1 Prix du Cadran winner and Ascot Gold Cup second Invermark. The second dam, Applecross (by Glint Of Gold), a smart winner of 3 races from 10f to 13.3f and placed in the Park Hill Stakes and the Princess Royal Stakes, is a half-sister to 6 winners including Coigach (Group 3 Park Hill Stakes). (The Happy Go Lucky Partnership). *"I really like her, she's from a successful family and I thought she was cheap, probably because the sire isn't the most commercial (unfortunately he's dead now). This is a really nice filly and I like her a lot. One for July onwards and she would have been my 'Bargain Buy' for the book if she'd been two grand cheaper!"*

1577. FUJAIRA KING (USA) ★★
b.c. Kitten's Joy – Cat On A Tin Roof (Catienus). May 13. Third foal. 220,000Y. Tattersalls October Book 1. Roger Varian. The dam is an unraced sister to the US dual Listed stakes winner and Group 1 Golden Jubilee Stakes second Cannonball and a half-sister to 5 winners. The second dam, No Deadline (by Skywalker), a minor dual winner at 3 yrs in the USA, is a half-sister to 10 winners. (Sheikh Mohammed Obaid Al Maktoum). *"He's going to take a bit of time because he was a late foal, but he's a nice moving horse for the second half of the season".*

1578. GLEEFUL ★★★★
b.f. Pivotal – Merletta (Raven's Pass). January 19. First foal. The dam, a fairly useful 2-y-o 6f winner, is a half-sister to one winner. The second dam, Light Hearted (by Green Desert), a quite useful 6f winner, is a sister to 2 winners including the smart 2-y-o Group 2 6f Mill Reef Stakes winner Byron and a half-sister to 5 winners including the useful 1m and 10.3f winner Gallant Hero and the US Grade 3 placed Gallant. (Cheveley Park Stud). *"I like her a lot, she's a big filly but not weak and she's well-made, has a good action and a good head on her. Shows plenty of promise".*

1579. GOING PLACES ★★
ch.c. Frankel – Khor Sheed ((Dubawi). January 15. Fourth foal. The dam, a Group 3 1m Premio Sergio Cumani, Listed 6f (at 2 yrs) and Listed 7f winner, is a half-sister to 4 winners including the Group 1 Prix d'Ispahan winner Prince Kirk. The second dam, Princess Manila

(by Manila), is an unplaced half-sister to 3 winners including the Group 1 Italian Derby winner Hailsham. (Sheikh Mohammed Obaid Al Maktoum). *"He's quite a nice colt but he's big and a bit immature at the moment. I think he will be a nice horse one day, but that's likely to be later on as a 2-y-o and especially next year".*

1580. GONE SOLO (IRE) ★★

b.c. Kingman – Go Lovely Rose (Pivotal). April 14. Fifth foal. €650,000Y. Goffs Orby. Roger Varian. Half-brother to the French 10.5f and 12f winner and Group 3 Prix Minerve second Game Zone (by Hurricane Run). The dam, a French 1m winner, is a sister to the Group 1 Coronation Stakes and Group 1 Prix Jacques le Marois winner Immortal Verse. The second dam, Side Of Paradise (by Sadler's Wells), a French Listed 1m winner, was second in the Group 3 10.5f Prix Fille de'Air and is a full or half-sister to 10 winners including Last Tycoon (Breeders Cup Mile, Kings Stand Stakes and William Hill Sprint Championship). (Sheikh Mohammed Obaid Al Maktoum). *"I loved him at the sale but then he sort of grew and went out of shape. He's just coming back to himself now but he's going to take a bit of time. I quite like him but I haven't seen enough of him in proper work to form a proper opinion".*

1581. HEALING POWER ★★

b.c. Kodiac – Loch Ma Naire (Galileo). January 30. First foal. 280,000Y. Tattersalls October Book 1. Roger Varian. The dam, a fair 10f winner, is a half-sister to 3 winners including the Group 1 Fillies' Mile and Group 1 Falmouth Stakes winner Simply Perfect. The second dam, Hotelgenie Dot Com (by Selkirk), a 7f winner at 2 yrs, was second in the Group 1 7f Moyglare Stud Stakes and third in the Group 1 Fillies' Mile and is a half-sister to 4 winners including the Moyglare Stud Stakes and the Group 2 6f Lowther Stakes winner Bianca Nera. (Sheikh Mohammed Obaid Al Maktoum). *"A nice looking horse but his knees aren't mature yet so we won't see him out until later on. A medium-sized, solid horse".*

1582. INTUIT ★★★

b.f. Intello – Sindirana (Kalanisi). April 29. Sixth living foal. 75,000Y. Tattersalls October Book 2. Cheveley Park Stud. Half-sister to the French Listed 12f winner of 3 races Sirrin (by Sea The Stars), to the 1m (at 2 yrs) and 10f winner Sindjara (by Include), the Listed-placed 10f winner Doyeni (by Smart Strike), the 9.5f winner Sidra (by Elusive Quality) and the 2-y-o 7f winner Sinaniya (by More Than Ready) – all fairly useful. The dam won over 7f (at 2 yrs) and the Listed 11f Lingfield Oaks Trial and is a half-sister to 5 winners. The second dam, Sinndiya (by Pharly), won over 13f and is a half-sister to the Derby and Arc winner Sinndar. (Cheveley Park Stud). *"A very nice mover, she has plenty of temperament but hopefully that won't hold her back. She's one for the second half of the season and has an eye-catchingly good action".*

1583. INVINCIBLE KNIGHT ★★★

b.c. Invincible Spirit – Nancy O (Pivotal). February 3. First foal. 90,000Y. Tattersalls October Book 2. Andrew Sime. The dam, a Canadian 3-y-o winner, was third in the Grade 2 Natalma Stakes. The second dam, Arravale (by Arch), won the Grade 1 Del Mar Oaks and the Grade 1 E P Taylor Stakes and is a half-sister to 4 winners including the Canadian Listed stakes winner Hollywood Hideaway. (Z. A. Galadari). *"He's a smallish horse with a nice way of going and I think he'll be a summer 2-y-o".*

1584. JALEEL ★★★

b.c. Iffraaj – Precariously Good (Oasis Dream). February 3. First foal. 80,000Y. Tattersalls October Book 2. Hugo Merry. The dam, a moderate dual 5f placed maiden, is a half-sister to 4 winners including the French Listed 9f winner and dual Group 3 placed Rainbow Dancing. The second dam, Danceabout (by Shareef Dancer), won the Group 2 Sun Chariot Stakes and is a half-sister to the dual Group 3 winner Pole Position. (Mr A Al-Abdulrazzaq). *"A solid horse that moves nicely, he'll be a June/July 2-y-o I should think and I quite like him. So far so good".*

1585. KAHALA QUEEN (IRE) ★★★★ ♠

b.f. Shamardal – Whazzis (Desert Prince). February 7. Eighth foal. 525,000Y. Tattersalls October Book 1. Roger Varian. Half-sister to 6 winners including the fairly useful dual 10f winner Valiant (by Galileo), the fairly useful 2-y-o 6f and 7f winner Culturati (by Dubawi), the French 2-y-o 1m winner and 3-y-o

Listed-placed Whim (by Nayef) and the fair 7f winner Feng Shui (by Iffraaj). The dam, an Italian Group 3 1m winner, is a half-sister to 6 winners including Whazzat (Chesham Stakes). The second dam, Wosaita (by Generous), a fair 12.3f placed maiden, is a half-sister to 10 winners including the Group 1 10.5f Prix de Diane winner Rafha (dam of the Haydock Sprint Cup winner Invincible Spirit) and the Group 3 12f Blandford Stakes winner Chiang Mai (dam of the Group 1 Pretty Polly Stakes winner Chinese White). (Sheikh Mohammed Obaid Al Maktoum). *"I like her, she'll be a summer runner over six/seven furlongs I should think. She's quite sharp and I think she's a good prospect".*

1586. KENZOHOPE (FR) ★★★
gr.c. Kendargent – Bedford Hope (Chato). May 11. Seventh foal. Brother to the Group 3 Prix de la Grotte winner Kenhope and to the minor French 2-y-o winner Kenohope. The dam was placed 6 times in France and Germany at 2 and 3 yrs and is a half-sister to 4 winners including the German triple Listed winner from 2 to 4 yrs Bedford Set. The second dam, Bedford Flame (by Doulab), was an unraced half-sister to 6 winners including Bobzao (Group 2 Hardwicke Stakes). *"He's a May foal but he's done well recently and I should think he'll be running in the second half of the season. A nice, attractive horse with a good way of going".*

1587. KHABEERAH ★★★
b.f. Dubawi – Hadaatha (Sea The Stars). February 19. First foal. The dam, a smart Listed 10f winner and Group 1 Prix de l'Opera third, is a half-sister to 3 winners. The second dam, Hathrah (by Linamix), winner of the Listed 1m Masaka Stakes and third in the 1,000 Guineas, is a half-sister to 5 winners including the smart Group 2 12f Premio Ellington winner Ivan Luis and the French/German Listed winners Amathia and Zero Problemo. (Hamdan Al Maktoum). *"A nice filly, we like the dam a lot because we trained Hadaatha to be third in the Prix de l'Opera. Medium-sized, quite well-made, has a good action and should be racing this year from July onwards".*

1588. LEGEND OF DUBAI (IRE) ★★
ch.c. Dubawi – Finsceal Beo (Mr Greeley). May 23. Seventh foal. 650,000Y. Tattersalls

October Book 1. Roger Varian. Half-brother to the promising 2017 Listed 1m fourth La Figlia (by Frankel), to the 2-y-o Group 2 1m Beresford Stakes winner Ol' Man River (by Montjeu), the quite useful Irish 10f winner An Cailin Orga (by Galileo) and the fair 2-y-o 10f winner Too The Stars (by Sea The Stars). The dam, winner of the Prix Marcel Boussac, 1,000 Guineas and Irish 1,000 Guineas, is a half-sister to 6 winners including the German Group 2 1m winner Frozen Power. The second dam, Musical Treat (by Royal Academy), a useful 3-y-o 7f winner and Listed-placed twice, subsequently won four races at 4 yrs in Canada and the USA and is a half-sister to 6 winners. (Sheikh Mohammed Obaid Al Maktoum). *"This horse has a lot of class but he was a very late foal, he's quite immature and to me he looks like a horse to get out in the autumn. He has the look of a 3-y-o to him, but it's a good look".*

1589. LEHOOGG ★★
ch.c. Bated Breath – Button Moon (Compton Place). April 11. Third foal. 85,000Y. Tattersalls October Book 2. Shadwell Estate Co. Half-brother to a minor 2-y-o winner abroad by Champs Elysees. The dam, a quite useful 6f winner, was Listed-placed in Germany and is a half-sister to 8 winners including the very smart 2-y-o Group 2 7f Champagne Stakes winner and Group 1 6f July Cup third Etlaala and to the unplaced dams of the Group 2 winners Battaash and Tasleet. The second dam, Portelet (by Night Shift), a fairly useful 5f winner of 4 races, is a half-sister to 4 winners. (Sheikh Ahmed Al Maktoum). *"He's going to take some time, I quite like him but he's not precocious and is one for the second half of the season".*

1590. LOOK CLOSELY ★★★
b.c. Sea The Stars – Lady Heidi (High Chaparral). March 23. First foal. 150,000Y. Tattersalls October Book 2. Roger Varian. The dam, a 2-y-o Listed 1m winner, is a half-sister to 4 winners. The second dam, Water Feature (by Dansili), is an unraced half-sister to 13 winners including the Group 1 1m Grand Criterium and Group 2 10.4f Dante Stakes winner Tenby and the dual Listed winner and US Grade 2 placed Bristol Channel. (Sheikh Mohammed Obaid Al Maktoum). *"Very light*

on his feet and a nice-moving horse, I like what I've seen of him so far. He's by Sea The Stars and out of a High Chaparral mare which doesn't suggest precocity, but he should be able to run a bit and have some sort of a 2-y-o career later on".

1591. LUFRICIA ★★★★
br.f. Kodiac – Lucrece (Pivotal). March 26. Second foal. €180,000Y. Arqana Deauville August. Roger Varian. The dam won 3 minor races in France at 3 and 4 yrs and is a half-sister to the Group 1 Prix Maurice de Gheest and triple Group 3 winner Signs Of Blessing. The second dam, Sun Bittern (by Seeking The Gold), is an unraced half-sister to 3 minor winners. (Sheikh Mohammed Obaid Al Maktoum). "I like her. She has a sharp look to her, could be a May runner and shows a bit of zip in her work. So I think she's a nice prospect".

1592. MACKAAR (IRE) ★★★★
b.c. Cape Cross – Albemarle (King's Best). February 1. Second foal. 80,000Y. Tattersalls October Book 2. Shadwell Estate Co. The dam is an unplaced half-sister to 2 winners in Japan. The second dam, Adonita (by Singspiel), a French 11f winner, is a half-sister to 8 winners including the Group 3 winner and Group 1 Irish 1,000 Guineas second Anna Salai. (Sheikh Ahmed Al Maktoum). "I like this horse, he goes very well and I think he's got a bright future. One for seven furlongs to a mile this year".

1593. MAWAKIB ★★★
b.c. Havana Gold – Keladora (Crafty Prospector). April 22. Seventh foal. 190,000Y. Tattersalls October Book 2. Shadwell Estate Co. Half-brother to 5 winners including the fair 2017 2-y-o 5f winner Wensley (by Poet's Voice), the fair 12f and 14f winner Kelamita (by Pivotal) and the modest 12f to 14f winner of 3 races Coarse Cut (by Duke Of Marmalade). The dam, a French Listed-placed winner of 3 races, is a half-sister to 4 winners including the Group 1 Prix Marcel Boussac second On Verra. The second dam, Karmifira (by Always Fair), winner of the Listed Prix Finlande and second in the French 1,000 Guineas, is a half-sister to 5 winners including the Listed 1m Prix Coronation winner Kart Star. (Sheikh Ahmed Al Maktoum). "I quite like

him, he's a strong, well-made horse and one of my earlier colts I think. He goes nicely and could be running in May".

1594. MILITARY MOVE ★★★
ch.c. Dubawi – Rainbow Dancing (Rainbow Quest). April 15. Fifth foal. €230,000Y. Goffs Orby. Roger Varian. Half-brother to the fair dual 1m winner Arctic Sea (by Oasis Dream). The dam, a French Listed 9f winner, was second in the Group 3 Prix Fille de l'Air and third in the Group 3 Prix de Flore and is a half-sister to 3 winners. The second dam, Danceabout (by Shareef Dancer), won the Group 2 Sun Chariot Stakes and the Listed 7f Oak Tree Stakes and is a half-sister to 3 winners including the Group 3 6f Prix de Meautry winner Pole Position. (Sheikh Mohammed Obaid Al Maktoum). "A nice, attractive horse with a good way of going, he'll take a bit of time but he's a nice prospect for later in the year".

1595. MONSIEUR NOIR ★★★
b.c. Shamardal – Night Frolic (Night Shift). February 20. Ninth foal. 500,000Y. Tattersalls October Book 1. Roger Varian. Half-brother to the Group 2 Dante Stakes winner Bonfire, to the Group 2 Windsor Forest Stakes winner Joviality, the fair 7.5f to 8.5f and hurdles winner Burns Night (by Selkirk) and the modest 2-y-o 5f winner Chicita Banana (by Danehill Dancer). The dam, a modest 1m winner, is a half-sister to 5 winners including the US Grade 3 Cardinal Handicap winner Miss Caerleona (herself dam of the Group winners Karen's Caper and Miss Coronado). The second dam, Miss d'Ouilly (by Bikala), a Listed 9f winner, is a half-sister to 6 winners including Miss Satamixa (Prix Jacques le Marois). (Sheikh Mohammed Obaid Al Maktoum). "I like him, he has a good, strong, well-made look to him and he should be a summer 2-y-o. He moves along nicely at the moment".

1596. MORAAWED ★★★
b.c. Swiss Spirit – Hot Secret (Sakhee's Secret). February 17. Second foal. £120,000Y. Goffs UK Premier (Doncaster). Shadwell Estate Co. The dam, a fair 2-y-o 5f winner, is a half-sister to 6 winners including Temple Meads (Group 2 Mill Reef Stakes). The second dam, Harryana (by Efisio), was a fair 2-y-o dual 5f winner.

(Hamdan Al Maktoum). *"A solid horse, he should be a 2-y-o and he should be fast".*

1597. MOTAWAJ ★★★
b.c. Dubawi – Tantshi (Invincible Spirit). March 15. Second foal. The dam, fairly useful 6f (at 2 yrs) and Listed 7f winner of 4 races, is a full or half-sister to 6 winners including the very useful 2-y-o Listed 7f winner Toolain. The second dam, Qasirah (by Machiavellian), a useful 2-y-o 6f winner, was third in the Group 3 8.5f Princess Margaret Stakes. (Sheikh Ahmed Al Maktoum). *"A nice, solid, square horse out of a mare that did well for us and it's a family we know well. I see no reason why this guy won't be winning nice races and he should be a 2-y-o for late summer or autumn. He should win this year hopefully".*

1598. MUNAAZIL (IRE) ★★★
br.c. Dubawi – Aljaaziah (Medaglia d'Oro). March 28. First foal. The dam is an unraced half-sister to 3 winners including the 2-y-o 6f winner and Group 1 Fillies' Mile third Firdaws. The second dam, Eswarah (by Unfuwain), won 3 races including the Group 1 Epsom Oaks and is a half-sister to 9 winners including the Group 3 12f Princess Royal Stakes winner Itnab, the very useful 6f winner of 4 races Haafiz and the useful 7f and 1m winner and Irish 1,000 Guineas third Umniyatee. (Hamdan Al Maktoum). *"A nice colt with a lot of class, he'll take a bit of time but he's a handsome horse – easy on the eye. I think the Eswarah line is going to come good again because I have two or three nice juveniles that are closely related to her".*

1599. MUTAMAASIK ★★★
ch.c. Dubawi – Muhawalah (Nayef). March 4. First foal. The dam, a quite useful 1m winner, is a sister to the Group 1 Prix Jean Prat and Group 1 Prix Jacques le Marois winner Tamayuz and a half-sister to 5 winners including the fairly useful French 2-y-o 7f winner and Group 3 Prix Miesque second Nuqoosh. The second dam, Al Ishq (by Nureyev), a 1m winner in France, is a half-sister to the French Derby winner Anabaa Blue. (Hamdan Al Maktoum). *"I like him, he's quite a 'square' colt but he has a good way of going, a good temperament and just a nice outlook. A nice horse to have in the yard, he's*

one for July onwards and Dubawi's definitely get better with age".*

1600. MUTASAAMY (IRE) ★★★★
b.c. Oasis Dream – Eswarah (Unfuwain). March 24. Half-brother to the 2-y-o 6f winner and Group 1 Fillies' Mile third Firdaws (by Mr Greeley), to the quite useful 9f winner Qawaafy (by Street Cry) and the fair 11.5f winner Elraazy (by Dubawi). The dam won 3 races including the Group 1 Epsom Oaks and is a half-sister to 9 winners including the Group 3 12f Princess Royal Stakes winner Itnab, the very useful 6f winner of 4 races Haafiz and the useful 7f and 1m winner and Irish 1,000 Guineas third Umniyatee. The second dam, Midway Lady (by Alleged), won the Prix Marcel Boussac, the 1,000 Guineas and the Oaks and is a half-sister to 5 winners including the very useful 11.8f Listed winner Capias. (Hamdan Al Maktoum). *"I really like this horse, I think he's got masses of class. He'll take a bit of time but I hope he's got a future and he's probably an autumn 2-y-o. To me he looks a middle-distance prospect for next year".*

1601. NAAEELL (IRE) ★★★★
b.c. New Approach – Sajjhaa (King's Best). February 21. Second foal. Brother to Allieyf, unplaced in one start at 2 yrs in 2017. The dam, a UAE dual Group 1 9f and dual Group 2 winner, is a full or half-sister to 3 winners. The second dam, Anaamil (by Darshaan), a quite useful 11f winner, is a half-sister to 3 winners. (Sheikh Ahmed Al Maktoum). *"I love this horse, he really looks the part and I'd say he's a July type 2-y-o. He has a really good outlook and we trained the dam (she won a Group 3 and two Listed races for Michael Jarvis) before she went to Godolphin. She was a lovely filly".*

1602. NABEYLA ★★★
b.br.f. New Approach – Feedyah (Street Cry). March 22. First foal. The dam, a fairly useful 2-y-o 7f and 1m winner and 3-y-o UAE Group 3 9.5f third, is a half-sister to the useful 2017 Listed-placed 2-y-o 7f winner Red Mist. The second dam, Red Dune (by Red Ransom), a useful 7f and 1m winner, was Listed-placed and is a full or half-sister to 4 winners. (Sheikh Ahmed Al Maktoum). *"She's quite a nice filly and people tell me that Street Cry is a good broodmare sire. This is a family that comes*

alive again and she's not a bad type at all. I quite like her and she's make a second half of the season 2-y-o".

1603. NEAROOZ ★★★★
b.f. New Approach – Modeyra (Shamardal). March 17. Third foal. The dam, a useful 1m (at 2 yrs) and Listed 10f winner, is a half-sister to one winner. The second dam, Zahrat Dubai (by Unfuwain), won the Group 1 10f Nassau Stakes and the Group 3 10.4f Musidora Stakes and is a half-sister to 4 winners. (Sheikh Ahmed Al Maktoum). *"I like her, she's got the make-up of a filly for the first half of the season and although she's by the Derby winner New Approach we must remember that he had three Royal Ascot 2-y-o winners in his first crop. I think this filly could run in May and I like her very much at the moment".*

1604. NESPOLA ★★
b.f. New Approach – Nargys (Lawman). March 2. Second foal. Half-sister to the quite useful 2017 7.5f and 1m placed 2-y-o Global Conqueror (by Dubawi). The dam, a useful 6f (at 2 yrs) and Group 3 7f Sceptre Stakes winner, was second in the Group 2 7f Rockfel Stakes, is a full or half-sister to 3 winners. The second dam, Spesialta (by Indian Ridge), a quite useful Irish 7f winner, is a half-sister to 5 winners including the Group 3 Prix du Pin winner Best Dating. (Sheikh Mohammed Obaid Al Maktoum). *"A great big, late maturing filly, not a bad type but she'll take a lot of time".*

1605. PRINCE EIJI ★★★
ch.c. Dubawi – Izzi Top (Pivotal). March 11. Third foal. 2,600,000Y. Tattersalls October Book 1. Roger Varian. Half-brother to the 2017 2-y-o 7f winner, from two starts, Willie John (by Dansili) and to the fairly useful 2-y-o 6f and 7f winner (both his starts) Dreamfield (by Oasis Dream). The dam, a winner of 6 races including the Group 1 Prix Jean Romanet and the Group 1 Pretty Polly Stakes, is a half-sister to 2 winners including Jazzi Top (Group 2 Prix de la Nonette). The second dam, Zee Zee Top (by Zafonic), won the Group 1 10f Prix de l'Opera and is a half-sister to the Group 1 winners Opera House and Kayf Tara and to the unraced dam of the Group 1 winner Necklace. (Sheikh Mohammed Obaid Al Maktoum).

"A jolly nice horse and a lovely mover, he's grown a bit recently which isn't a bad thing and he has a lot of class. He's not too backward so he could be a July/August runner. You'd be hoping he could be a miler next year but being out of that mare there's every chance he could be a middle-distance horse".

1606. SAN DONATO (IRE) ★★★★★
b.c. Lope De Vega – Boston Rocker (Acclamation). February 25. First foal. 500,000Y. Tattersalls October Book 2. Roger Varian. The dam, a fairly useful 2-y-o 5f winner and second in the Group 3 6f Ballyogan Stakes at 3 yrs, is a half-sister to 4 winners. The second dam, Rocking (by Oasis Dream), a quite useful 2-y-o 5f winner, is a half-sister to 10 winners including the very smart Group 2 5f Flying Childers Stakes winner Superstar Leo (herself the dam of two stakes winners) and the dam of the 2-y-o Group 1 winner Rivet. (Sheikh Mohammed Obaid Al Maktoum). *"I love this horse; I think he's really nice. One for June/July and although I don't like comparing horses I see a lot of Belardo in him. He's a lighter type of Lope De Vega, Belardo won on his debut in June and I think this horse is in the same mould. I'm not suggesting he's as good as Belardo but he has the make, shape and brain to be a summer 2-y-o – but with a future".*

1607. SEZIM ★★★
b.c. Dansili – Serres (Daylami). February 28. Half-brother to the useful 2-y-o 7f winner and Group 2 Rockfel Stakes second Thetis, to the fair 10f winner Indelible Ink (both by Invincible Spirit), the Group 3 10.5f Musidora Stakes winner Liber Nauticus, the fairly useful 10f winner and Musidora Stakes third Serenada (both by Azamour) and a minor winner in Australia by Verglas. The dam is an unraced half-sister to 6 winners including the Breeders' Cup Turf, King George VI and St Leger winner Conduit and the Group 2 Great Voltigeur Stakes winner Hard Top. The second dam, Well Head (by Sadler's Wells), is an unraced half-sister to 6 winners including the dual Group 1 winner Spectrum and the dam of the champion filly Petrushka. (Mr Nurlan Bizakov). *"A nice type, he's a well-made colt that'll make 2-y-o by the second half of the summer and he's got a nice outlook. The dam was recently bought by Hesmonds Stud from Ballymacoll".*

1608. SMART NADA (IRE) ★★★
ch.f. Lope De Vega – Solar Event (Galileo).
April 10. Fourth foal. 350,000Y. Tattersalls
October Book 1. Roger Varian. The dam, a
modest 12f placed maiden, is a half-sister to 5
winners including the Group 2 Prix de Malleret
and Listed Cheshire Oaks winner Time On and
the dam of the Group 1 Moyglare Stud Stakes
winner Cursory Glance. The second dam, Time
Away (by Darshaan), won the Group 3 10.4f
Musidora Stakes, was third in the Group 1
Prix de Diane and the Group 1 Nassau Stakes
and is a half-sister to 6 winners including the
Prix de Diane second Time Ahead. (Sheikh
Mohammed Obaid Al Maktoum). "A lovely filly
with a lot of class and from a good family. She's
a nice prospect but a big filly so she'll take a bit
of time".

1609. SPOKESMAN (IRE) ★★★
b.c. Alhebayeb – Xema (Danehill). February
21. Eighth foal. 50,000Y. Tattersalls October
Book 2. Amanda Skiffington. Closely related
to the useful 6f to 1m winner of 8 races from
2 to 5 yrs and UAE Group 2 second Dark
Emerald (by Dark Angel) and half-brother to
the modest 7f winner Beau Duke (by Bachelor
Duke), the moderate 6f winner Jordi Roper (by
Traditionally) and the moderate 1m winner
Ippi N Tombi (by Captain Rio). The dam is an
unraced half-sister to 4 winners. The second
dam, Xaymara (by Xaar), won once at 3 yrs
in France and is a half-sister to 9 winners
including the Grade 1 Washington Lassie
Stakes winner Contredance and the dam of
the 1,000 Guineas winner Wince.
(H Moorhead, C Fahy & J Collins). "An athletic
colt, he's definitely a summer juvenile and I
don't know his level but he'll be winning races.
I don't dislike him".

1610. SUSHI ROLL ★★
ch.f. Iffraaj – Sweet Cecily (Kodiac). March
4. Fourth foal. €130,000Y. Arqana Deauville
August. Roger Varian. Half-sister to the quite
useful 5.5f and 6f winner Sweet Dragon Fly
(by Oasis Dream). The dam won the 2-y-o
Listed 6f Bosra Sham Stakes. The second dam,
Yaqootah (by Gone West), is a fair 5f winner at
3 yrs, is a half-sister to 6 winners including
the dam of the US dual Grade 1 winner
Brody's Cause. (Sheikh Mohammed Obaid
Al Maktoum). "There's not much wrong with

her and she could win this year but she hasn't
improved since the sale as much as I'd hoped".

1611. TAMMOOZ ★★★
b.c. Lawman – La Concorde (Sadler's Wells).
February 13. Fourth foal. 35,000Y. Tattersalls
October Book 2. Shadwell Estate Co. Half-
brother to the fair 2017 7f placed 2-y-o
Briscola (by Redoute's Choice). The dam,
a fair 12f winner, is a half-sister to 2 other
minor winners. The second dam, La Leuze (by
Caerleon), is a placed half-sister to 4 winners
including the multiple Group 1 winner and sire
Montjeu. (Sheikh Ahmed Al Maktoum). "He's
a gorgeous horse and I think he was cheap. I
know he'll take time and horses like him are
losing their commercial appeal to people, but
this is a beautiful horse whose pedigree goes
back to the family of Montjeu. He's one to run
over a mile in the autumn".

1612. TAUTEKE ★★★
b.f. Sea the Stars – Tamarind (Sadler's Wells).
March 15. Sister to the quite useful 10f
winner Tamasha and half-sister to the fairly
useful 2-y-o 8.5f winner and Listed-placed
Tansholpan (by Dansili) and the fair dual 10f
winner Taraz (by Oasis Dream). The dam won
the Group 3 12f Give Thanks Stakes and is a
sister to the smart German Group 2 8.5f and
Italian Group 2 1m winner Crimson Tide and
a half-sister to the US Grade 2 and Group 3
Prix de Sandringham winner Pharatta and the
US stakes Listed stakes winner and Grade 2
placed La Vida Loca. The second dam, Sharata
(by Darshaan), is an unraced half-sister to the
dual Derby winner Shahrastani. (Mr Nurlan
Bizakov). "She's a nice, well-made type and I
like her a lot. She's a filly for the second half of
the season and more of a 3-y-o type really".

1613. THRIVING ★★★
b.f. Kodiac – Najam (Singspiel). April 8. Fifth
foal. 30,000Y. Tattersalls October Book 2. J
Shack & G Barnard. Half-sister to the quite
useful 12f winner Cape Peninsula (by Cape
Cross) and to the fair 9.5f to 12f winner of 4
races Fit The Bill (by Iffraaj). The dam, a fair 12f
winner, is a half-sister to 9 winners including
the very useful 1m to 10f winner and Italian
Derby third Lundy's Lane, the very smart 1m
(at 2 yrs) and dual Group 3 middle-distance
winner Blue Monday and the very useful

Australian stakes winner Rugged Cross. The second dam, Lunda (by Soviet Star), is an unplaced half-sister to 6 winners including the middle-distance Group 1 winners Luso and Warrshan. (J Barnett, J Shack & G Barnard). *"This filly goes along quite nicely and she should be an early 2-y-o – maybe a May runner. She's a nice type and I should imagine she'll want six furlongs to start with".*

1614. TICKLE THE MOON (IRE) ★★★★
b.c. Sea The Moon – Tickle Me Pink (Groom Dancer). February 14. Fifth foal. 525,000Y. Tattersalls October Book 1. Tattersalls October Book 1. Roger Varian. Half-brother to the German Listed 9f winner Tickle Me Blue (by Iffraaj) and to a minor winner abroad by Royal Applause. The dam is an unraced half-sister to 4 winners including the Listed winner and useful broodmare Irresistible. (Sheikh Mohammed Obaid Al Maktoum). *"I love this horse, he has a lot of class and I think he has a bright future. At the sales he was just a nice, solid horse and I think we paid more than we expected but that seems to be the market. I think he's a jolly nice horse and we'll probably see him out in August or September".*

1615. UAE JEWEL ★★
b.c. Dubawi – Gemstone (Galileo). April 2. Fourth foal. 400,000Y. Tattersalls October Book 1. Roger Varian. Half-brother to the quite useful 6.5f (at 2 yrs) and 1m winner Bedrock (by Fastnet Rock). The dam, a useful 2-y-o Listed 1m Silken Glider Stakes winner, was second in the Group 3 Park Express Stakes and is a half-sister to 4 winners. The second dam, Kincob (by Kingmambo), a modest 1m placed 3-y-o, is a half-sister to 7 winners including the Irish 2,000 Guineas winner Bachelor Duke. (Sheikh Mohammed Obaid Al Maktoum). *"A gorgeous horse, he has a big frame and the look of an autumn 2-y-o. He's much more a 3-y-o type, so he's not a horse to do much with this year".*

1616. VOICEOFTHEEMIRATES ★★★
b.c. Showcasing – Makaaseb (Pulpit). May 2. Third foal. €85,000Y. Goffs Orby. Roger Varian / Ahmed Alshakh. The dam, a useful 2-y-o 7f winner and Listed-placed over 10f at 3 yrs, is a half-sister to 5 winners including the US stakes winner Sirpa. The second dam,

Turn And Sparkle (by Danzatore), a minor US winner of 3 races at 2 and 3 yrs, is a half-sister to 7 winners including the US stakes winner and Grade 1 third Turn And Dance. (A. Al Shaikh). *"He's quite a nice horse, very athletic and not an early type but he should be a July/August runner. A colt with a nice way of going".*

1617. YOURTIMEISNOW ★★★
b.f. Charm Spirit – Maid For Winning (Gone West). March 28. Sixth foal. 120,000Y. Tattersalls October Book 1. Roger Varian. Half-sister to the very useful 7f (at 2 yrs) and 1m winner and Group 2 third Hors de Combat, to the useful 6f (at 2 yrs) and 6.5f winner and Group 3 third Stroll Patrol (both by Mount Nelson), the fair dual 6f winner Zumran (by Rock Of Gibraltar) and a minor 2-y-o winner in Germany by Forestry. The dam is an unplaced half-sister to 7 winners including the US Grade 1 9f winner Stroll and the US stakes winner and Grade 1 third Patrol. The second dam, Maid For Walking (by Prince Sabo), a 2-y-o 5f and 6f winner, was second in the Group 3 Princess Margaret Stakes and is a half-sister to 5 winners. (Sheikh Mohammed Obaid Al Maktoum). *"A medium-sized filly with a nice way of going, I don't think she'll be early but she should make a summer 2-y-o. There's not much wrong with her and she should be winning races".*

1618. ZAULA ★★★
gr.f. Dark Angel – Zimira (Invincible Spirit). February 26. Third foal. Half-sister to the triple 1m winner at 2 and 3 yrs Zymyran (by Henrythenavigator). The dam, a quite useful 2-y-o 1m winner, is a half-sister to numerous winners including the Group 2 placed Mathematician, the Irish 2,000 Guineas third Oracle and Areyaam (dam of the Group 2 Champagne Stakes winner Saamidd). The second dam, Zibilene (by Rainbow Quest), a useful 12f winner and Listed-placed over 10f, is a half-sister to 7 winners including the Breeders' Cup Mile, Irish 2,000 Guineas and Queen Anne Stakes winner Barathea and the Fillies Mile and Irish 1,000 Guineas winner Gossamer. (Mr Nurlan Bizakov). *"She's a nice type of filly, I like her and I think she'll be a summer 2-y-o. She has a nice way of going and the dam is a half-sister to Areyaam who has bred us some very nice horses".*

1619. UNNAMED ★★★
ch.c. Mastercraftsman – Cochabamba
(Hurricane Run). February 29. Third foal.
150,000Y. Tattersalls October Book 2. Charlie
Gordon-Watson. Half-sister to the fair 7f
winner Multicultural (by Fastnet Rock). The
dam, a fairly useful 6f (at 2 yrs) and 8.5f
winner and second in the Group 2 Rockfel
Stakes and the Group 3 Prestige Stakes, is a
half-sister to one winner. The second dam,
Bolivia (by Distant View), is an unraced half-
sister to 11 winners including 3 stakes winners.
(Mr P. D. Smith). *"A nice type, he's grown a bit
and done well physically since the sale".*

1620. UNNAMED ★★★★
b.f. Scat Daddy – Entwine (Empire Maker).
April 7. Third foal. $300,000 foal. Fasig-Tipton
Kentucky. Al Shahania Stud. The dam is a
US placed half-sister to 5 winners including
Filimbi (Group 2 Goldikova Stakes winner
and Grade 1 placed four times). The second
dam, Flute (by Seattle Slew), won the Grade
1 Alabama Stakes and the Grade 1 Kentucky
Oaks. (Sheikh Mohammed bin Khalifa Al-
Thani). *"I really like this filly. She could be a
summer 2-y-o, has a nice way of going, strong
and with a bit of class".*

1621. UNNAMED ★★★
b.f. Dabirsim – Glorious Adventure (Galileo).
March 7. First foal. €190,000Y. Goffs Orby.
Blandford Bloodstock. The dam is an unraced
half-sister to one minor winner. The second
dam, a useful 1m winner, was second in the
Group 3 Irish 1,000 Guineas Trial and is a sister
to the top-class miler Rock Of Gibraltar and
to the very useful Irish 2-y-o 6f winner Great
Pyramid and a half-sister to 6 winners. (Sheikh
Juma Dalmook Al Maktoum). *"She's done well
physically recently because I thought she was
quite light following the sale but she's starting
to do well now. I don't think she's an early type
but she should be a July/August 2-y-o".*

1622. UNNAMED ★★★
b.f. Dalakhani – Mid Mon Lady (Danetime).
March 28. Third foal. €42,000Y. Goffs Orby.
Ebonos. The dam, a useful 9f, 10f and 11f
winner of 6 races, was Group 3 placed four
times and is a half-sister to 3 minor winners.
The second dam, Shining Desert (by Green
Desert), a quite useful 2-y-o 5f winner, is a

half-sister to 2 winners including the Listed
winner Wing Collar. (S. Ali). *"I like her, she
moves nicely and should be one for the second
half of the season. I don't think she looks like a
Dalakhani which means I don't think she'll take
too much time. Probably a seven furlong filly in
late summer".*

1623. UNNAMED ★★★
b.c. Mastercraftsman – Nebraas (Green
Desert). February 9. Tenth foal. €230,000Y.
Goffs Orby. China Horse Club. Half-brother
to 6 winners including the Group 3 7.5f
Concorde Stakes and Group 3 Irish 1,000
Guineas Trial winner Yellow Rosebud (by
Jeremy), the fairly useful Listed 6f (at 2 yrs)
and 10f winner and Group 3 third Seeharn,
the quite useful 8.5f winner Aimhirgin Lass
(both by Pivotal), the quite useful 5f winner
at 2 and 3 yrs Megan Lily (by Dragon Pulse)
and the quite useful 6f and 7f winner of
10 races My Kingdom (by King's Best). The
dam is an unraced half-sister to 6 winners
including the Group 1 Golden Jubilee Stakes
winner Malhub. The second dam, Arjuzah (by
Ahonoora), won the Listed 7f Sceptre Stakes
and is a half-sister to 2 winners. (China Horse
Club). *"A nice horse, I like him, he moves along
with a bit of purpose and I think he'll be all
right from mid-season onwards".*

1624. UNNAMED ★★★
ch.f. Mastercraftsman – White Cay (Dalakhani).
March 19. Sixth foal. 40,000Y. Tattersalls
October Book 2. Rabbah Bloodstock. Closely
related to the quite useful 7f to 10f winner
and US Grade 3 second Cay Dancer (by
Danehill Dancer) and half-sister to the quite
useful dual 1m winner Dynamic (by Teofilo)
and the modest 7f winner Cape Cay (by Cape
Cross). The dam, a minor winner of 2 races
at 3 yrs in France, is a half-sister to 7 winners
including the Group 1 1m Coronation Stakes
winner Balisada. The second dam, Balnaha
(by Lomond), a modest 1m winner, is a sister
to Inchmurrin (winner of the Group 2 Child
Stakes and herself dam of the very smart and
tough colt Inchinor) and a half-sister to 6
winners including the Mill Reef Stakes winner
Welney. (Sheikh Juma Dalmook Al Maktoum).
*"I like her, she's a nice type for sure. She's going
to take a little bit of time but she has a real
nice way of going".*

ED VAUGHAN

1625. ATTORNEY GENERAL ★★★★

b.c. Dream Ahead – Avodale (Lawman). March 28. Third foal. Brother to the fairly useful 5.5f (at 2 yrs) and Listed 6f winner of 4 races Visionary. The dam, placed at 2 and 3 yrs in France, is a half-sister to one minor winner. The second dam, Aldovea (by Nashwan), a minor French 3-y-o winner, is a half-sister to 8 winners including the French Listed winner and Group 2 second Bashaayeash. *"A nice colt, he got a touch of sore shins a few weeks ago so I laid off him but he goes very well. His full brother won a Listed race over six furlongs and I should imagine this fella will be at home over six as well. A lovely, big, strong, mature colt and I like him a lot".*

1626. EXMOOR BEAST ★★★

ch.c. Sepoy – Junket (Medicean). April 23. Third foal. 22,000Y. Tattersalls October Book 3. Front Runner Racing/Paul Moroney. Half-brother to the fair 2-y-o 6f winner Mississippi Miss (by Equiano). The dam, a fair 6f winner, is a half-sister to 6 other minor winners. The second dam, Gallivant (by Danehill), a quite useful 2-y-o 6f winner, is a closely related to the smart 2-y-o Group 2 6f Mill Reef Stakes winner Byron and a half-sister to 7 winners. *"He's very high behind at the moment so he has a fair bit of growing to do, but he should make his mark at two. A nice-moving horse with a very good mind, hopefully he'll be quick enough for six furlongs".*

1627. SHADY AFFAIR ★★★★

gr.c. Dark Angel – Capulet Montague (Camacho). March 13. Fourth foal. €350,000Y. Goffs Orby. Form Bloodstock. Brother to the 2017 2-y-o Group 2 7f Rockfel Stakes winner Juliet Capulet and to the fairly useful Irish Listed-placed 2-y-o 6f winner Juliette Fair. The dam, a quite useful 5f and 6f placed maiden in Ireland, won at 3 yrs in Qatar and is a half-sister to 8 winners including the Listed Scarbrough Stakes winner and Group 2 Kings Stand Stakes second Flanders (dam of the Group 1 Haydock Park Sprint Cup winner G Force) and to the dam of the dual Group 1 winning sprinter Lethal Force. The second dam, Family at War (by Explodent), a fair 2-y-o 5f winner, is a half-sister to 4 minor winners

in the USA. *"A big, imposing colt and just four days after he was bought at the sale his full sister won the Rockfel, so although he was expensive he could easily have cost more. The owners were kind enough to send him to me and he's a nice colt for the second half of the season, so we won't be rushing him. He's grown enormously in the time we've had him and he's very correct, big-boned and just a big, strong colt. One to look out for I'd say".*

1628. UNNAMED ★★

b.f. Champs Elysees – Acquainted (Shamardal). March 27. Fourth foal. 34,000Y. Tattersalls October Book 3. Paul Moroney. Half-sister to the fair 10f winner Open The Red (by Lawman) and to a minor winner in Sweden by Poet's Voice. The dam, a fairly useful 12f winner, was second in the Listed Cheshire Oaks and is a half-sister to 4 winners. The second dam, Love Everlasting (by Pursuit Of Love), a Group 3 12f Princess Royal Stakes and triple Listed winner, is a half-sister to 6 winners including the Group 3 10f Scottish Classic winner Baron Ferdinand. *"A lovely, athletic filly that will make her mark towards the back-end of the season. Bought by a very astute judge in Paul Moroney and she'll be at her best next year".*

1629. UNNAMED ★★

ch.c. Poet's Voice – Caldy Dancer (Soviet Star). January 29. Tenth foal. 14,000Y. Tattersalls October Book 3. Not sold. Half-brother to the smart 7f to 9f winner of 7 races and dual Group 3 placed Dance And Dance (by Royal Applause), to the Hong Kong 7f and 1m winner and Group 1 third Rewarding Hero (by Exceed And Excel) and the fair 9f winner On With The Dance (by Byron). The dam, a useful 2-y-o dual 5f winner and second in the Group 3 7f Debutante Stakes, is a half-sister to 4 winners. The second dam, Smile Awhile (by Woodman), ran once unplaced and is a full or half-sister to 3 winners. *"I've trained the whole family and they've been very fragile including Dance And Dance who was arguably unlucky not to win a Grade 1 for me. This colt is in a different mould to the rest of them in that he's a big, raw horse and I'll be taking my time with him. He'll have a run or two at the back end I should imagine and he looks like he wouldn't mind a bit of soft ground".*

1630. UNNAMED ★★★
gr.f. Mastercraftsman – Easy Lover (Pivotal).
February 4. Fourth living foal. 42,000Y.
Tattersalls October Book 2. Paul Moroney.
Half-sister to a 4-y-o 1m winner in Hong Kong
by Shamardal. The dam, a fairly useful 7f and
1m winner, was third in the Listed Radley
Stakes and is a half-sister to 3 winners. The
second dam, Easy To Love (by Diesis), a quite
useful 4-y-o 11.5f winner, is a sister to the
Oaks winner Love Divine (herself dam of the
St Leger winner Sixties Icon) and a half-sister
to 5 winners including the Listed winners
Dark Promise and Floreeda. *"She's a nice type
that isn't over-big so I would imagine she'd
do something as a 2-y-o. The dam was quite
precocious and this is a nice, straightforward
filly for the second half of the season".*

1631. UNNAMED ★★
b.c. Aussie Rules – Gala Rose (Selkirk).
January 14. Second foal. 23,000Y. Tattersalls
October Book 3. Front Runner Racing/Paul
Moroney. The dam is an unplaced half-sister
to 5 winners including the Group 2 Pretty
Poly Stakes winner Hanami. The second dam,
Russian Rose (by Soviet Lad), a quite useful 10f
and 17f winner, is a half-sister to 3 winners.
*"A big horse, he's correct and very light on his
feet but very much a 3-y-o in the making".*

1632. UNNAMED ★★★★
b.c. Dubawi – Giofra (Dansili). January 15.
Second foal. €1,550,000Y. Arqana Deauville
August. Kerri Radcliffe. The dam won 4 races
including the Group 1 Falmouth Stakes and
the Group 2 Prix d'Harcourt and was placed in
numerous other Group 1's and is a half-sister
to 7 winners including and the Listed winners
Gradara, Big Baz and Gomati. The second
dam, Gracefully (by Orpen), won the 2-y-o
Group 3 7f Prestige Stakes and is a sister to
the Listed winner and dual Group 3 placed
Lady Grace and to the winner and 2-y-o
Group 3 third Visionist and a half-sister to 3
winners. *"A lovely colt with a lot of quality as
you would expect from his purchase price, he's
currently in pre-training but he'll be joining us
shortly. I'm delighted to get him, he ticks all the
boxes and will be a late season 2-y-o over a
mile with an eye on next year".*

1633. UNNAMED ★★★★
b.c. Pivotal – Hoodna (Invincible Spirit).
February 5. First foal. £140,000 2-y-o. Goffs
UK Breeze Up. Phoenix Thoroughbreds. The
dam, a useful dual 6f winner at 2 and 3 yrs,
was third in the Listed Bosra Sham Stakes
at 2 yrs. The second dam, Heaven's Cause
(by Giant's Causeway), won the Listed 1m
Prix de la Calonne and is a half-sister to 6
winners. (Phoenix Thoroughbreds). *"A very
nice, well-balanced 2-y-o type, just purchased
at the Doncaster breeze up, he'll have an easy
couple of weeks now and we'll get him out
by the middle-to-end of May. The ground at
Doncaster was horrendous but he skipped
through and clocked a good time".*

1634. UNNAMED ★★★★
ch.c. Ruler Of The World – Independent Girl
(Bachelor Duke). February 27. Second foal.
25,000Y. Tattersalls October Book 2. Paul
Moroney. Half-brother to the quite useful
8.5f winner Perfect Soldier (by Kodiac). The
dam, a fair Irish 7f winner, is a half-sister to
the 2-y-o Group 2 5f Norfolk Stakes winner
Waterloo Bridge and to the 1m (at 2 yrs) and
Group 3 12.5f Prix Minerve winner and Group
1 Prix Saint-Alary third Forces Of Darkness.
The second dam, Miss Childrey (by Dr Fong),
an Irish 2-y-o Listed 6f winner, was third in
the Group 3 Irish 1,000 Guineas Trial and is a
half-sister to 6 winners. *"A lovely horse, there's
plenty of speed in the family and he looks a
quick horse despite being by a Derby winner.
He has a great hip, a mature look and is the
type of horse we could run over six furlongs
and get him ready for the seven furlong races.
If he's good enough he could be ready for the
Chesham".* TRAINER'S BARGAIN BUY

1635. UNNAMED ★★
b.c. Alpha – Palestrina (Medaglia D'Oro).
April 19. First foal. €17,000Y. Tattersalls Ireland
September. Bobby O'Ryan. The dam, a minor
US 4-y-o winner, is a half-sister to 5 winners
including the French Listed winner and Group
2 second Penglai Pavilion. The second dam,
Maiden Tower (by Groom Dancer), winner of
the Group 2 1m Prix de Sandringham, was
second in the French 1,000 Guineas and is a
half-sister to French Listed 7f winner Tokyo
Rose. *"He's rather a weak-looking horse so he's
going to take a bit of time, but he's very nice*

cantering and just needs time to strengthen up. Improving all the time, he doesn't have a typical pedigree for here but he was bought with a view that if he's good enough he could go to Dubai next year and race on the dirt". The sire won the Grade 1 10f Travers Stakes and the Grade 1 9f Woodward Stakes.

1636. UNNAMED ★★★
b.f. Point Of Entry – Sweet Emma Rose (City Zip). March 12. First foal. $110,000Y. Keeneland September. Blandford Bloodstock. The dam won three races in North America at 2 and 3 yrs and was second in the Group 2 5f Queen Mary Stakes. The second dam, Miss Moneypenny (by Deputy Minister), is an unplaced half-sister to 4 winners including a stakes winner in Japan. "She's just arrived here and is just cantering away at the minute. A good-quartered filly that looks the type to start at six furlongs by the end of May".

ED WALKER
1637. BARYSHNIKOV ★★★★
ch.c. Mastercraftsman – Tara Moon (Pivotal). March 17. Eighth foal. 120,000Y. Tattersalls October Book 1. J Brummitt. Half-sister to the Group 3 8.5f Princess Elizabeth Stakes and Group 3 10f Select Stakes winner Lady Gloria (by Diktat), to the fairly useful Listed-placed 1m winner of 5 races Light And Shade (by Aqlaam), the quite useful 7f and 1m winner Sir Mike (by Haafhd), the fair 2-y-o dual 6f winner Tara Celeb (by Excelebration) and the modest 11f and 12f winner Pivotal Silence (by Vita Rosa). The dam is an unraced daughter of the fairly useful 2-y-o 5f winner Tarf (by Diesis), herself a half-sister to 7 winners including Nadwah (Group 2 Queen Mary Stakes). (Mr Bjorn Nielsen & Eastwind Racing Ltd). "I thought he'd be quite precocious but he's grown a lot. I still think he will be a 2-y-o, there's lots of speed on the dam's side, he's exceptionally good-looking, moves very well and I'd like to get a run into him at the end of May if I could. I obviously won't force him and he's now grown enough to have the scope that he didn't once have. I'm pleased with him".

1638. CAME FROM THE DARK (IRE) ★★★
br.c. Dark Angel – Silver Shoon (Fasliyev). March 10. Fourth foal. 480,000Y. Tattersalls

October Book 1. Sackville/Donald. The dam, a fairly useful 7f winner, was second in the Group 3 6f Round Tower Stakes and is a sister to the useful 2-y-o 5f winner and Group 2 5f Flying Childers Stakes second China Eyes and a half-sister to 11 winners including the Group 1 6f Haydock Park Sprint Cup and Group 3 5f Palace House Stakes winner Pipalong. The second dam, Limpopo (by Green Desert), a poor 5f placed 2-y-o, is a half-sister to 8 winners here and abroad. (Mr P. K. Siu). "Very expensive, he's obviously a good-looking colt by an exceptional stallion. The mare hasn't proved it yet, so there's pressure on her now but at this stage this colt is showing up well. He doesn't look mega-early because he's grown a lot but I think he'll be a nice 2-y-o for the second half of the season".

1639. CAP FRANCAIS ★★★
b.c. Frankel – Miss Cap Ferrat (Darshaan). February 19. Half-sister to the Listed 10.4f winner of 4 races Miss Cap Estel (by Hernando), to the quite useful 10f and subsequent Listed 9f winner St Jean Cap Ferrat (by Domedriver) and a hurdles winner by Nayef. The dam is an unplaced half-sister to 8 winners including the Listed winners Miss Corniche and Miss Riviera Golf. The second dam, Miss Beaulieu (by Northfields), was a useful 6f and 10f winner. (John Pearce Racing). "He's a very nice, compact, athletic colt that's bred to be one for the second half of this season and more as a 3-y-o really. He does everything well, has a good mind and with Frankel's amazing statistics he's got to be an exciting sort".

1640. DARK PANTHER ★★★★
b.c. Dandy Man – Surreal (Shamardal). April 25. First foal. €50,000Y. Goffs Orby. Sackville/Donald. The dam, a quite useful Irish dual 7f winner, is a half-sister to 2 minor winners. The second dam, Mayonga (by Dr Fong), a useful Listed 1m winner, is a half-sister to 3 minor winners. (Mr C. U. F. Ma). "Very sharp, he's likely to be one of our first 2-y-o runners, he goes well and I hope to have him out at some point during April. A speedy type, he's one we hope will be good enough to go to Royal Ascot. Small, compact and racy with lots to like about him".

1641. GINISTRELLI ★★★
b.c. Frankel – Guaranda (Acatenango).
March 10. Tenth foal. 475,000Y. Tattersalls
October Book 1. J Brummitt. Closely related
to the smart Group 3 14f Lillie Langtry Stakes
winner Gravitation (by Galileo) and half-sister
to a minor winner abroad by Selkirk. The
dam, a fairly useful 10f and 12.3f winner, was
Listed-placed and is a half-sister to 9 winners
including the multiple Group 1 winner Fame
And Glory. The second dam, Gryada (by
Shirley Heights), a fairly useful 2-y-o 7f and
8.3f winner, was third in the Group 3 1m
Premio Dormello and is a full or half-sister
to 4 winners. (Mr Bjorn Nielsen & Eastwind
Racing Ltd). *"A stunning colt from a very good
staying family, he's exactly what you want
from a racehorse – very athletic but with
size and scope. Not too big, he has a good
temperament and a great pedigree to boot,
so he ticks all the boxes at this stage and has
done nothing wrong to put me off. One for the
Classics next year, hopefully, but there's nothing
to say that he won't have a good last three
months of this season".*

1642. GLOBAL ARMY ★★★
gr.c. Lethal Force – Path Of Peace (Rock Of
Gibraltar). March 6. Fourth foal. 115,000Y.
Tattersalls October Book 2. Sackville/Donald.
Half-brother to Belvoir Bay (by Equiano), a
winner of 6 races at 2 and 3 yrs here and in
the USA including two US Grade 3 stakes over
5f and 1m and to the quite useful 2017 2-y-o
6f and 7f winner Peace Trail (by Kyllachy).
The dam, a fair 1m winner, is a half-sister to 8
winners including Please Sing (Group 2 Cherry
Hinton Stakes) and the Group 1 National
Stakes third Mountain Song. The second dam,
Persian Song (by Persian Bold), is an unplaced
sister to the Solario Stakes winner Bold
Arrangement (placed in seven Group/Grade
1 races including the Kentucky Derby) and a
half-sister to 4 winners. (Dr Johnny Hon & KIR
(HK) Ltd). *"He looks exactly as he's bred to look
– a compact, strong, butty 2-y-o that looks
like a sprinter. He'd be more of a midsummer
2-y-o and should have a good second half of
the season".*

1643. GLORIOUS CHARMER ★★★
b.c. Charm Spirit – Fantacise (Pivotal).

January 27. Second foal. 52,000Y. Tattersalls
October Book 2. Sackville/Donald. Half-
brother to the fair 2017 2-y-o 6f winner
Quayside (by Harbour Watch). The dam, a
quite useful 2-y-o 6f winner, is a half-sister
to 12 winners including the Group 3 Queen
Mary Stakes winners Romantic Myth and
Romantic Liason. The second dam, My First
Romance (by Danehill), ran twice unplaced
and is a half-sister to 6 minor winners here
and abroad. (Kangyu International Racing
(HK) Limited). *"A very nice 2-y-o, one of our
earlier types and a proper 2-y-o sort, he's
strong and showing plenty of speed. I would
have thought he'd be out in May, it's very
much a 2-y-o speedy family and he looks
that way. I would imagine he could have
enough boot to start over five furlongs but his
optimum trip would be over further".*

1644. GLORIOUS GALAXY ★★
b.c. Garswood – Celeste (Green Desert).
March 18. Sixth foal. 55,000Y. Tattersalls
October Book 2. Sackville/Donald. Half-
brother to the useful 2-y-o 6f and 7f winner
Van Der Decken (by Dutch Art), to the fair
7f and subsequent Canadian stakes winner
Endless Light and the fair 7f and 1m winner
Cainhoe Star (both by Pivotal). The dam is
an unraced half-sister to 5 winners including
the US dual Grade 1 winner Megahertz and
the dual Group 3 9f winner and triple Grade
1 placed Heaven Sent. The second dam,
Heavenly Ray (by Rahy), a fairly useful 7f
and 1m winner, is a half-sister to 3 winners.
(Kangyu International Racing (HK) Limited).
*"A very nice horse, he isn't one to have a busy
campaign this year and two or three runs
would be about right for him. He's a big horse
that's grown a lot since we bought him and
he'll be trained this year with one eye fixed on
his 3-y-o career. A big, powerful, athletic and
good-looking horse".*

1645. GLORIOUS LOVER (IRE) ★★★★
b.c. Tamayuz – Love Match (Danehill Dancer).
February 2. Third foal. 100,000Y. Tattersalls
October Book 2. Sackville/Donald. Half-
brother to the fair 2017 2-y-o 6f winner Big
Les (by Big Bad Bob) and to a minor winner
in Italy (including at 2 yrs) by Frozen Power).
The dam, a fair 7f winner, is a half-sister to
2 winners including the US Grade 3 8.5f

placed Perilous Pursuit. The second dam, Name Of Love (by Petardia), a 2-y-o Group 3 7f Rockfel Stakes and Listed 7f Oh So Sharp Stakes winner, is a half-sister to 5 winners. (KIR (HK) Ltd & Dr Johnny Hon). *"He's sharp and showing up well at the moment but he's rangy and has plenty of scope too. He's not overly heavy, very light on his feet and athletic and he'll be a May 2-y-o".*

1646. I'M FREEZING ★★★
b.f. Iffraaj – Morning Frost (Duke Of Marmalade). April 13. Second foal. 150,000Y. Tattersalls October Book 1. J Brummitt. Half-sister to the 2017 French 5f to 6.5f placed 2-y-o Morning Dream (by Dream Ahead). The dam, a French 6f (at 2 yrs) and Listed 6.5f winner, is a half-sister to 4 winners including the Group 3 Ballyogan Stakes winner Penny Pepper. The second dam, Evening Time (by Keltos), a smart Irish dual Listed 6f winner (including at 2 yrs), was Group 3 placed twice and is a half-sister to 4 winners including the Italian dual Listed winner of 11 races Distinctly Dancer. (B. E. Nielsen). *"She looked a real, kick-on 2-y-o when we bought her but she's grown a lot and is going to take a bit more time than we thought. That isn't a bad thing and she's a very racy filly and one for June onwards".*

1647. IMMORAL ★★
b.c. Helmet – Loose Julie (Cape Cross). April 23. Fifth foal. 42,000Y. Tattersalls October Book 2. John & Jake Warren. Half-brother to the useful 5f (at 2 yrs) and 6f winner of 4 races Banaadeer (by Tamayuz), to the fairly useful 7f (at 2 yrs) and 1m winner Storm Ahead (by Iffraaj) and the modest 7f winner Crystalin (by Arcano). The dam is an unraced half-sister to 4 winners including the 2-y-o Listed 6f Silver Flash Stakes winner Desert Sky. The second dam, Badrah (by Private Account), is a placed half-sister to 5 winners including the Group 3 Brigadier Gerard Stakes winner Husyan. (Highclere Thoroughbred Racing – Syon House). *"He's an immature type with lots of scope and so one for the autumn and next year; A big, powerful sort that could make up into a nice 3-y-o type".*

1648. JACK D'OR ★★★
b.c. Raven's Pass – Inchberry (Barathea). April 15. Tenth foal. 15,000Y. Tattersalls October

Book 2. Ed Walker. Half-brother to 4 winners including the very useful 2-y-o dual 7f winner and triple Group 3 placed Measuring Time (by Dubai Destination), the quite useful 7f and 8.5f winner Mutamid (by Medicean) and the modest 14f winner Berry Baby (by Rainbow Quest). The dam, placed seven times including when second in a Listed event over 1m at 2 yrs and fourth in the Oaks, is a half-sister to 4 winners including the Listed 12f winner Inchiri and the dam of the Group 3 winners Malabar and Poet's Word. The second dam, Inchyre (by Shirley Heights), a useful 1m winner, is a half-sister to 7 winners including the triple Group 3 7f winner and sire Inchinor. (Ebury Racing 2). *"Very inexpensive given his pedigree, we took a bit of a punt on him because he was a bit weak and small at the sales but he's done exceptionally well and now looks to be very well bought. He's not going to be early, but from the second half of the season onwards he'll be a nice horse to get out over seven furlongs and go from there. He's grown a lot and is looking potentially a nice horse at that level".*

1649. ON THE STAGE ★★★ ♠
b.f. Swiss Spirit—Spotlight (Dr Fong). April 6. Tenth foal. £20,000Y. Goffs UK Premier. Not sold. Half-sister to the smart dual 6f winner and Group 3 second Projection (by Acclamation), to the fairly useful triple 1m winner Up In Lights (by Makfi) and wo 2-y-o winners in Italy by Paco Boy. The dam, a Listed 1m and subsequent US Grade 2 Lake Placid Handicap winner, is a full or half-sister to 5 winners including the dam of the Group 1 Phoenix Stakes winner Zoffany. The second dam, Dust Dancer (by Suave Dancer), won 4 races including the Group 3 10f Prix de la Nonette and is a half-sister to 6 winners including the Group 3 7.3f Fred Darling Stakes winner Bulaxie (herself dam of the Group 2 winner Claxon). (Lordship Stud). *"A lovely filly, she's a proper 2-y-o, not very big but very athletic and speedy-looking. She should be running in late April or early May and she's a sweet filly".* TRAINER'S BARGAIN BUY.

1650. PADMAVATI ★★★
b.f. New Approach – Padmini (Tiger Hill). February 3. Second foal. Half-sister to the French 9.5f winner Lucie Manette (by

Shamardal). The dam, a 2-y-o 7f winner on her only start, is a half-sister to 4 winners. The second dam, Petrushka (by Unfuwain), a high-class Irish Oaks, Yorkshire Oaks and Prix de l'Opera winner, is a half-sister to 5 winners. *"A very attractive filly with plenty of scope but very light on her feet and therefore I think she'll make a 2-y-o. Her family is slightly more 3-y-o based, but I think she'll be one for seven furlongs in due course. Whatever she does this year will be a bonus but I do think she'll be precocious enough to be a decent 2-y-o".*

1651. QUICKSILVER ★★★ ♠
b.f. Coach House – Poulaine Bleue (Bertolini). April 5. Fourth foal. Eighth foal. 12,000Y. Tattersalls October Book 3. Sackville/Donald. Half-sister to the fairly useful Listed-placed 2-y-o 6f winner Still On Top (by Royal Applause) and to the fair 5f and 6f winner Magical Daze (by Showcasing). The dam is an unplaced half-sister to the useful 1m (at 2 yrs) and US Grade 3 winner Genre. The second dam, Blue Indigo (by Pistolet Bleu), was placed 5 times in France and is a half-sister to 6 winners. (Mr B Greenwood & Mr Hatter). *"An inexpensive filly, she was well-bought and has grown a lot since the sale. I thought she'd be really sharp and early, but she's shot up behind and hasn't come up at the front yet. She's a very likeable sort, great temperament, strong-looking and speedy. I think she'll have a good year and I'd like to line her up for the Tattersalls Book 3 Sales race".*

1652. SUNDAY STAR ★★★
b.f. Kodiac – Northern Star (Montjeu). January 24. First foal. The dam, a quite useful 10f winner, is a half-sister to 2 winners including the very useful 2-y-o 6f winner and Listed second Dorothy B. The second dam, Slow Sand (by Dixieland Band), ran twice unplaced and is a half-sister to 5 winners including the French Group 3 and Listed winner Slow Pace. (Mr D. Ward). *"A lovely filly and a classic Kodiac 2-y-o, she's not the biggest – unsurprising given that she's a first foal. She has a certain amount of that Kodiac/Montjeu twinkle in her eye but she's very athletic and very likeable at this stage. A midsummer type 2-y-o".*

1653. SWINDLER ★★★
b.c. Invincible Spirit – Priceless Jewel (Selkirk).

March 9. Third foal. 105,000Y. Tattersalls October Book 2. Not sold. Half-brother to the quite useful 1m winner Trilliant (by Dansili). The dam, a quite useful 6.5f (at 2 yrs) and 6f winner, is a half-sister to 6 winners including the Group 1 6f Haydock Sprint Cup winner Tante Rose, the 2-y-o Listed 7f winner Bay Tree and the dam of the Group 1 winners Make Believe and Dubawi Heights. The second dam, My Branch (by Distant Relative), won the Listed 6f Firth Of Clyde Stakes (at 2 yrs) and the Listed 7f Sceptre Stakes, was third in the Irish 1,000 Guineas and is a full or half-sister to 7 winners. (B. E. Nielsen). *"I'm getting to know the family quite well now because I trained Trilliant and I have a nice unraced 3-y-o out of the mare. This is a nice horse and more precocious than the first two foals, very athletic and hopefully he'll have more of a 2-y-o career than they had. He still won't be early because he's still an immature sort, but I'd like to think he'd have three or four runs later on this season".*

1654. TRIGGERED ★★★
b.c. Dandy Man – Triggers Broom (Arcano). February 4. First foal. €240,000Y. Goffs Orby. Sackville/Donald. The dam, a poor 2-y-o 6f placed maiden, is a half-sister to 3 winners including the 2-y-o Group 2 7f Vintage Stakes and subsequent Hong Kong dual Group 1 1m winner Xtension. The second dam, Great Joy (by Grand Lodge), won at 3 yrs in Germany and was Listed placed and is a half-sister to 4 winners. (Mr P. K. Siu). *"Very expensive for a Dandy Man, but he's from a good family and he's an exceptionally good-looking and athletic 2-y-o type. I think he'll be out quite soon because he's showing up well at home and he's started doing some faster work. He's one we like".*

1655. TURN TO ROCK ★★★
ch.c. Slade Power – Pivotal's Princess (Pivotal). February 20. Seventh foal. €110,000Y. Goffs Orby. Sackville/Donald. Half-brother to the useful 5f and 6f winner of 7 races Robot Boy (by Shamardal), to the fairly useful Listed-placed 6f (including at 2 yrs) and 7f winner of 7 races Accession (by Acclamation), the quite useful 6f (at 2 yrs) and 1m winner Yorkee Mo Sabee (by Teofilo) and the quite useful 6f winner Three D Alexander (by Aqlaam). The dam, a useful 5f winner of 6 races, was Listed

placed five times and is a half-sister to one winner. The second dam, Art Princess (by Fairy King), is an unplaced half-sister to 10 winners. (Mr P. K. Siu). *"The mare's done well and this is a really good-looking colt that moves very well. He's not going to be super-early, but he'll be one to have a good second half of the season. Very likeable, I thought the Slade Power yearlings looked really nice at the sales and this guy is very racy, athletic-looking and tough".*

1656. UNNAMED ★★

ch.f. Fast Company – Melpomene (Peintre Celebre). April 15. Seventh foal. 6,000Y. Tattersalls October Book 3. Ed Walker Racing. Sister to the fairly useful 2-y-o 5f winner Rogues' Gallery and half-sister to 3 winners including the quite useful 2-y-o dual 5f winner Viscount Loftus (by Clodovil) and the quite useful 10f and 12f winner Triple Dip (by Three Valleys). The dam, a quite useful 12f to 14f winner of 3 races, is a half-sister to 5 winners. The second dam, Lady Joyce (by Galetto), is an unraced half-sister to 8 winners including the US Grade 2 winner Lady Blessington and the French Group 3 winner Lowell. (Kingsdown Racing Club). *"A 2-y-o type, she was very cheap and has grown quite a bit since the sale. We'll be ready to start working her in April, it's a good 2-y-o family and the mare's done well so she's an exciting sort for the level we paid for her".*

1657. UNNAMED ★★★

b.c. Xtension – Park Glen (Tagula). January 26. First foal. £115,000Y. Goffs UK Premier (Doncaster). Sackville/Donald. The dam, a quite useful 2-y-o 5f and 6f winner, is a half-sister to 7 winners including the Group 3 Chipchase Stakes winner Knot In Wood. The second dam, Notley Park (by Wolfhound), placed three times over 7f at 3yrs, is a half-sister to 5 winners including the US Grade 3 winner Prince Bobby B and the Listed 5f Scarborough Stakes winner Notley. (Mr S. F. Hui). *"By the first season sire Xtension who was very good in Hong Kong and runner-up in the Guineas, this colt has grown and done very well since the sales and I'd say he's one for August onwards. A very laid-back colt, he's done everything asked of him and potentially he's a nice horse. He probably won't have an overly busy 2-y-o campaign but he'll certainly be out and about".*

CHRIS WALL

1658. CARLEEN ★★

ch.f. Sepoy – Generous Lady (Generous). April 23. Fifteenth foal. Half-sister to 7 winners including the very smart 7f (at 2 yrs), Group 2 12f King Edward VII Stakes and dual Group 3 12f Cumberland Lodge Stakes winner High Accolade (by Mark Of Esteem), the useful 9f (at 2 yrs) and 13f winner and Listed-placed Oasis Knight (by Oasis Dream) and the quite useful 12f to 2m winner Highland Legacy (by Selkirk). The dam, a middle-distance winner of 4 races in Ireland and Listed-placed, is a half-sister to 6 winners including the Italian Group 2 and Group 3 winner Jape. The second dam, Northern Blossom (by Snow Knight), was a champion 3-y-o filly in Canada and won two Graded stakes events. (Ms A. Fustoq). *"A big filly with a stout pedigree on the dam's side so she's much more of a 3-y-o type than for this year. We've trained a few out of the mare, this filly is the right make and shape but destined to debut much later in the year".*

1659. LUCKY CHARM ★★★

b.f. Charm Spirit – Drift And Dream (Exceed And Excel). February 22. First living foal. The dam, a fair 5f (including at 2 yrs) and 6f winner of 4 races, is a half-sister to numerous winners. The second dam, Sea Drift (by Warning), a fair 7f winner, is a half-sister to 8 winners and to the unraced dam of the Group 1 Middle Park Stakes winner and sire Dark Angel. (Lady Juliet Tadgell). *"She looks like being a 2-y-o and she's got plenty of speed, so I can see her running at five and six furlongs. A nice filly by a first season sire, I trained the mother who won as a 2-y-o and this filly looks forward enough to run in May. She looks a nice sort and I'm happy with the way she's going".*

1660. PURGATORY ★★★★

b.c. Dark Angel – Meet Me Halfway (Exceed And Excel). February 15. First foal. 50,000Y. Tattersalls October Book 2. Not sold. The dam, a quite useful 6f (including at 2 yrs) and 7f winner of 4 races, is a half-sister to 3 winners. The second dam, Pivotal Drive (by Pivotal), is an unraced half-sister to 4 winners including the Listed 1m and 10f winner Sublimity and the UAE Group 3 1m winner Marbush. (Mr Des Thurlby). *"He ought to be a 2-y-o a bit later on over seven furlongs, although we may start him at six. A nice colt, he could just do with strengthening up at the minute, I trained the dam who won at two and this is a nice enough colt by the right sire, so hopefully he's got a future. There's a bit of a devil in him so perhaps the name is the right one for him, but a bit of work and some racing will sort that out. He creates a favourable impression and as this is the dam's first foal I hope he gets her off to a good start".* I spotted immediately what a brilliant piece of naming this was. Well done Mr Thurlby! S.T.

1661. SMART SAMBA ★★★
b.c. Intello – Brazilian Bride (Pivotal). February 4. Eighth foal. 24,000Y. Tattersalls December. Chris Wall. Half-brother to the useful dual Listed 6f winner Rivellino, to the fair Irish 5f winner Brazilian Breeze (both by Invincible Spirit) and the fair 7f winner Blue Bahia (by Big Bad Bob). The dam won the Group 3 6f Swordlestown Stakes at 2 yrs and is a half-sister to 6 winners including the French Listed winner Rio Tigre and the Group 3 7f second Brazilian Star. The second dam, Braziliz (by Kingmambo), placed fourth once over 5f at 2 yrs, is a half-sister to 8 winners including the dam of the Group 1 winners Saffron Walden, Insight and Dolphin Street. (Induna Racing). *"We picked him up very cheaply at the December Sales – I think he'd been destined for Book One but had a little problem and couldn't make it. A nice type, just as you'd expect from the sire he's going to need a bit of time, but he's not desperately backward and the dam's side does have a bit of speed in it. This horse will want a mile plus next year but as a 2-y-o he'll be able to run reasonably well and isn't just one for the back-end of the season; he does have a bit of quality about him".*

1662. SPIRITUALLY ★★★
b.f. Charm Spirit – Lalectra (King Charlemagne). March 23. Eighth foal. 35,000Y. Tattersalls October Book 1. Not sold. Half-sister to the smart Listed 1m winner, Group 1 Racing Post Trophy second and 2,000 Guineas third Van Der Neer (by Dutch Art), to the fairly useful 2-y-o dual 5f winner Showing Character (by Showcasing), the fair 6f (at 2 yrs) and 10f winner Goodwood Treasure (by Bahamian Bounty) and the fair 10f winner Possible Future (by Compton Place). The dam is an unraced half-sister to 9 winners including

the Listed winner Intense Pink and the Group placed Sir Reginald and Henrik. The second dam, Clincher Club (by Polish Patriot), a fair 5f (at 2 yrs) and 7.5f winner, is a half-sister to 9 winners. (Valueracingclub.co.uk). *"We've had quite a few members of this family, most of them aren't particularly big and this filly is the same. A speedy, nippy little thing, she ought to be a 2-y-o, wasn't very well early in the year but she's just starting to do some conditioning work now and going on OK. I'm hopeful that she'll be a five/six furlong filly and if she's going to do anything on the track it'll be this year".*

ARCHIE WATSON

1663. ALICE'S LEGACY (IRE)
b.f. Society Rock – Poetry Aloud (Kheleyf). February 24. Sixth foal. £65,000Y. Goffs UK Premier (Doncaster). Blandford Bloodstock / Archie Watson. Half-sister to the 2-y-o Listed 7f winner Big Viollet (by Haatef). The dam is an unraced half-sister to the Group 2 Sun Chariot Stakes and Group 3 Matron Stakes winner of 4 races Independence (herself dam of the dual Group 1 winner Mount Nelson and the Group 2 winner Monitor Closely). The second dam, Yukon Hope (by Forty Niner), is a fair 6f and 1m placed maiden. (Mr C R Hirst).

1664. ARDEN WARRIOR (IRE)
gr.c. War Command – Glowing Star (Clodovil). March 27. Second foal. 32,000Y. Tattersalls October Book 2. Blandford Bloodstock. The dam is an unplaced half-sister to 3 winners including the Group 2 Ridgewood Pearl Stakes winner and Group 1 Irish 1,000 Guineas third Devonshire and the 2-y-o Listed 5f winner Hurryupharriet. The second dam, Nova Tor (by Trans Island), a fair 5f winner of 6 races at 2 and 3 yrs, is a half-sister to 7 other minor winners. (Jack & Freya Cork).

1665. CLOUD SEEDING (IRE)
ch.f. Gale Force Ten – Indian Angel (Indian Ridge). February 25. Fifth foal. £31,000Y. Goffs UK Silver (Doncaster). Blandford Bloodstock. Half-sister to the quite useful 2017 2-y-o 5f winner Angel Force (by Lethal Force). The dam is an unraced half-sister to 4 winners. The second dam, Lochangel (by Night Shift), a very smart winner of the Group 1 5f Nunthorpe Stakes, is a half-sister to the champion sprinter Lochsong. (Mr A M B Watson).

1666. GALLOVIE
b.f. Kyllachy – Rowan Brae (Haafhd). February 2. Second foal. £30,000Y. Goffs UK Premier (Doncaster). Howson & Houldsworth. The dam, a winner at 2 yrs in France and Listed-placed over 1m at 2 yrs in Germany, is a half-sister to 3 winners. The second dam, Ruse (by Diktat), is a placed half-sister to 9 winners including the very useful Group 3 7f Jersey Stakes winner Ardkinglass. (Marlborough Racing – Gallovie).

1667. ISAAN QUEEN (IRE)
b.f. War Command – Dundel's Spirit (Invincible Spirit). February 6. Second foal. €42,000Y. Tattersalls Ireland September. Blandford Bloodstock. The dam is an unraced half-sister to 9 winners including the US stakes winner and Group 2 6f Coventry Stakes third Luck Money and the 2-y-o Group 3 7f Prix du Calvados winner Charlotte O'Fraise. The second dam, Dundel (by Machiavellian), a quite useful 7f winner, is a half-sister to 6 winners including the French Group 3 6f winner Seltitude. (Mr C. R. Hirst).

1668. JULIUS LIMBANI (IRE) ♠
b.c. Anodin – Kshanti (Diesis). March 20. Third foal. €67,000Y. Baden-Baden September. Blandford Bloodstock. The dam was placed once at 2 yrs in Germany. The second dam, Oreanda (by Stravinsky), placed at 3 yrs in the USA, is a half-sister to the US Grade 3 winner Belleski. (Mr W. J. A. Nash).

1669. NATE THE GREAT
b.c. Nathaniel – Theladyinquestion (Dubawi). February 2. Second foal. 30,000Y. Tattersalls October Book 3. Not sold. The dam, a quite useful 6f (at 2 yrs) and 7f winner, is a half-sister to 3 winners including the smart 2017 2-y-o Group 2 6f Mill Reef Stakes winner James Garfield and the fairly useful 7.5f (at 2 yrs) and 1m winner and dual Listed-placed The Shrew. The second dam, Whazzat (by Daylami), a useful 2-y-o Listed 7f Chesham Stakes winner, is a half-sister to 6 winners including the Listed 1m and Italian Group 3 1m winner Whazzis. (Mildmay Racing & D. H. Caslon).

1670. NINA PETROVNA
ch.f. Havana Gold – Naizak (Medicean). March 1. Fourth foal. £32,000Y. Goffs UK Premier (Doncaster). Howson & Houldsworth / Archie Watson. Half-sister to the quite useful 2-y-o 6.5f winner Mujassam (by Kyllachy), to the fair 2-y-o 6f winner Smart Salute (by Royal Applause) and the modest 2-y-o 6f winner Pop Culture (by Equiano). The dam, placed twice at 3 yrs, is a half-sister to 8 winners including the useful 6f (at 2 yrs) and subsequent Swedish Listed winner Warming Trends. The second dam, Sunny Davis (by Alydar), was a fair 2-y-o 7f winner. (Mr Justin Dowley & Mr Michael Pescod).

1671. SECRET ACE
ch.f. Compton Place – Secret Romance (Sakhee's Secret). January 20. First foal. €36,000Y. Tattersalls Ireland September. Blandford Bloodstock. The dam, a quite useful 2-y-o 6f winner, is a half-sister to 4 winners including the Group 2 Temple Stakes winner Pearl Secret. The second dam, Our Little Secret (by Rossini), a useful Listed 5f winner of 6 races, is a half-sister to 3 winners. (Mr C. Brammer).

1672. SURREY BREEZE (IRE)
b.c. Footstepsinthesand – Breezeway (Grand Lodge). February 6. Fifth foal. €35,000Y. Tattersalls Ireland September. Blandford Bloodstock. Half-brother to the fair dual 10f winner Sark (by Zoffany). The dam, a fair 7f placed 2-y-o, is a half-sister to 10 winners including Emerald Peace, a Listed 5f winner of 4 races and second in the Group 2 5f Flying Childers Stakes. The second dam, Puck's Castle (by Shirley Heights), a fairly useful 2-y-o 1m winner, was Listed-placed and is a half-sister to 6 winners including the champion 2-y-o filly Embassy and the Group 2 Pretty Polly Stakes winner Tarfshi. (Surrey Racing Limited).

DERMOT WELD
1673. ACAPELLA BLU (IRE) ★★★
b.f. Dubawi – Galvaun (Galileo). February 29. First foal. 420,000Y. Tattersalls October Book 1. Moyglare Stud. The dam, a French Listed 10f winner, is a sister to the US dual Grade 1 winner Red Rocks and a half-sister to 5 winners including the Listed winner and Group 2 third Medicinal. The second dam, Pharmacist (by Machiavellian), an Irish 2-y-o Listed 6f winner, is a half-sister to 6 winners. (Moyglare Stud Farm). *"This filly isn't over-big*

and goes nicely but is still a bit immature and I would say she'll be a seven furlong 2-y-o in August or September".

1674. ALEZIA (IRE) ★★★
b.f. Dansili – Alanza (Dubai Destination). February 5. Second foal. The dam, a smart dual Group 3 7f and dual Listed winner, is a half-sister to the Listed winner Alonsoa. The second dam, Alasha (Barathea), a useful 7f (at 2 yrs) and Listed 1m winner, is a half-sister to 7 winners including the Irish Listed winner Alaiyma. (H H Aga Khan). *"A very nice filly with a lot of quality to her, she's one for seven furlongs to a mile in the autumn".*

1675. ALL OUR TOMORROWS (IRE) ★★★
b.f. Kingman – Justlookdontouch (Galileo). March 3. Fourth foal. 1,700,000Y. Tattersalls October Book 1. Moyglare Stud. Half-sister to the promising 2017 2-y-o 7f winner Aim Of Artemis (by Leroidesanimaux), to Abingdon (by Street Cry), a smart winner of three Listed events from 10f to 12f and the quite useful 10f winner Superioritycomplex (by Hard Spun). The dam is an unraced half-sister to 9 winners including the Group 1 winners Islington, Mountain High and Greek Dance. The second dam, Hellenic (by Darshaan), won the Yorkshire Oaks and was second in the St Leger and is a half-sister to numerous winners including the Group 2 Lanson Champagne Vintage Stakes second Golden Wave. (Moyglare Stud Farm). *"She's a fine, big filly, a great mover and will be lovely in September or October over seven furlongs, but she is big and will make into a lovely 3-y-o".*

1676. ANDALEEP (IRE) ★★★
b.c. Siyouni – Oriental Magic (Doyen). February 28. First foal. €180,000Y. Goffs Orby. Shadwell Estate Co. The dam, a German 2-y-o Listed 7.5f winner, is a half-sister to 5 winners including the Group 2 placed Oriental Fox. The second dam, Oriental Pearl (by Big Shuffle), a Listed winner at 3 yrs in Germany, is a half-sister to 10 winners. *"He's had a run, he's sharp and will hopefully go on and win for us in May or June over six furlongs".*

1677. ANYA YLINA (IRE) ★★★
b.f. Oasis Dream – Es Que (Inchinor). May 2.

Half-sister to the very useful 7f (at 2 yrs) and 10f winner, Group 2 10.5f York Stakes third and subsequent Hong Kong Vase winner Dominant (by Cacique), the smart Group 2 7f Lennox Stakes winner Es Que Love (by Clodovil), the French 9f and 10f winner and Group 2 placed Listen In (by Sea The Stars), the very useful 6f (at 2 yrs) to 10f winner Zhui Feng (by Invincible Spirit) and the fair 2-y-o 8.5f winner Stoked (by Fast Company). The dam, a minor winner at 3 yrs in France, is a half-sister to one winner abroad. The second dam, Bellona (by Bering), a Listed 11f winner in France, is a half-sister to 7 winners including the Group 2 Prix de Flore winner In Clover. (Moyglare Stud Farm). *"She's a big, quality filly for the second part of the year over seven furlongs".*

1678. ANYONE SPECIAL (IRE) ★★★
b.f. Invincible Spirit – Just Special (Cadeaux Genereux). March 23. Ninth foal. 65,000Y. Tattersalls October Book 1. Not sold. Half-sister to 6 winners including the quite useful 7f (at 2 yrs), 1m and hurdles winner Jalingo (by Cape Cross), the Group 3 7f Prix Du Pin winner Best Dating (by King's Best), the quite useful Irish 7f winner Spesialta (by Indian Ridge), the fair 1m and hurdles winner Al Qeddaaf (by Alhaarth) and the fair 12f winner Cades Reef (by Dalakhani). The dam, a Listed 7f winner and second in the Group 2 Prix d'Astarte, is a half-sister to the Listed winner Blue Gold. The second dam, Relatively Special (by Alzao), winner of the Group 3 7f Rockfel Stakes and third in the Irish 1,000 Guineas, is a half-sister to 8 winners including the Alnasr Alwasheek (Dante Stakes) and One So Wonderful (Juddmonte International). (Mr J. Higgins). *"A nice, sharp filly that could make her debut at Navan in April over five furlongs, she's speedy and will get six".*

1679. AZWAH ★★★★
b.f. Invincible Spirit – Bethrah (Marju). April 14. Fifth foal. The dam won 3 races at 3 yrs including the Group 1 Irish 1,000 Guineas and the Group 3 1m Irish 1,000 Guineas Trial. The second dam, Reve d'Iman (by Highest Honor), a minor 3-y-o 9f winner in France, is a sister to the Group 1 Prix Saint-Alary winner Reve d'Oscar, the Group 2 Prix Hocquart winner Numide and the Listed French 3-y-o winner

Sir Eric. (Hamdan Al Maktoum). *"A lovely, big filly out of Bethrah who won the Guineas for us. Sheikh Hamdan was here on Sunday looking at her, she's a quality 2-y-o and will be out in midsummer over six/seven furlongs".*

1680. BASHIYR (IRE) ★★★
b.c. Invincible Spirit – Baliyana (Dalakhani). March 7. Half-brother to the Irish 2-y-o 7f winner and Group 3 7f Irish 1,000 Guineas second (her only starts) Balansiya (by Shamardal) and to the fair 9.5f winner Baliyka (by Cape Cross). The dam won the Group 3 Irish 1,000 Guineas Trial and is a half-sister to 5 winners including the very smart Group 2 10f King Edward VII Stakes winner Balakheri. The second dam, Balanka (by Alzao), a French Listed winner and third in the Group 2 9.2f Prix de l'Opera, is a half-sister to 7 winners. (H H Aga Khan). *"A nice colt, he's backward and immature at the moment but he'll be very nice in September and October over seven furlongs and a mile".*

1681. COCO BLANCO (IRE) ★★★
gr.f. Dark Angel – I'm Yours (Invincible Spirit). February 9. First foal. The dam, a useful 7f (at 2 yrs) and Listed 9.5f winner, is a half-sister to the smart Group 3 Irish 2,000 Guineas Trial winner and Group 1 10.5f Tattersalls Rogers Cup second Recharge. The second dam, Rebelline (by Robellino), won the Group 1 10.5f Tattersalls Gold Cup and the Group 2 Pretty Polly Stakes and is a sister to the Group 2 Blandford Stakes winner Quws and a half-sister to 5 winners. (Moyglare Stud Farm). *"She's small, sharp and should be ready to run in May over five and six furlongs".*

1682. COEUR D'OR (IRE) ★★★★
b.f. Dubawi – Irresistible Jewel (Danehill). May 2. Half-sister to the Group 2 12f Ribblesdale Stakes winner and Irish Oaks third Princess Highway (by Street Cry), to the Irish Group 3 7f Gladness Stakes winner and multiple Group 1 placed Mad About You (by Indian Ridge) and Group 1 Irish St Leger and dual Group 3 winner of 9 races Royal Diamond (by King's Best) – all smart. The dam won the Group 2 12f Ribblesdale Stakes and the Group 3 10f Blandford Stakes and is a half-sister to numerous winners including the Listed 12f winner Diamond Trim and the useful Irish

1m winner Legal Jousting. The second dam, In Anticipation (by Sadler's Wells), won over 12f and 14f in Ireland. (Moyglare Stud Farms Ltd). *"Very much a quality colt, he'll hopefully make up into a very nice horse in the second part of the year. I see him running in August/ September over seven furlongs to a mile".*

1683. DAWRY (IRE) ★★★
b.c. Showcasing – May Day Queen (Danetime). April 25. Fifth foal. 125,000Y. Tattersalls October Book 2. Shadwell Estate Co. Half-brother to the fairly useful dual 5f (including at 2 yrs) and 6f winner and Listed-placed Mukhmal (by Bahamian Bounty), to the quite useful 5f and 6f winner of 4 races at 2 and 3 yrs Kingsley Klarion (by Arcano) and the modest 7f winner Abbotsfield (by Sakhee's Secret). The dam, a quite useful 2-y-o 6f winner and Group 3 6f third in Ireland, is a half-sister to 6 winners including the Listed winners Accepted and Asidious Alexander. The second dam, Birthday Present (by Cadeaux Genereux), is an unraced half-sister to 3 winners including the Group 1 Moyglare Stud Stakes third Supposition. (Hamdan Al Maktoum). *"A sharp-looking colt I'd hope to have out around May/June over six furlongs".*

1684. DEE SPRINTER (IRE) ★★★
b.c. Clodovil – Inourthoughts (Desert Style). May 1. Sixth foal. €50,000Y. Goffs Orby. Glyn Davies. Half-brother to the fair 2017 Irish 5f and 6f placed 2-y-o Betsey Trotter (by Camacho), to the quite useful 2-y-o dual 5f winner Tilly Trotter (by Kodiac) and the fair 2-y-o dual 6f winner Focusofourthoughts (by Intense Focus). The dam, a quite useful Irish 2-y-o 5f winner, is a half-sister to 3 winners including the 2-y-o Group 2 Flying Childers Stakes winner Green Door. The second dam, Inourhearts (by Pips Pride), a useful Listed 5f winner of 4 races, is a half-sister to 2 winners. (Mr G. Davies). *"A forward 2-y-o, he'll be ready to run by the end of May over five or six furlongs".*

1685. ELZAS CAPRI (IRE) ★★★
b.c. Elzaam – Bloomsday Babe (Cherokee Run). March 19. Third foal. £36,000Y. Goffs UK Premier (Doncaster). Not sold. Half-brother to the fair 6f winner Doeadeer (by Dandy Man). The dam is an unplaced half-sister to 6

winners including the 2-y-o Listed 5f Round Tower Stakes winner Steaming Home. The second dam, County Fair (by Mr Prospector), is an unplaced half-sister to 10 winners including the Grade 1 Travers Stakes winner Corporate Report and the US Grade 3 winner Drachma. (Mr Y. Zhang). *"A strong, powerful, big colt, I can see him running in July/August over seven furlongs".*

1686. ESTRELLA (IRE) ★★★
b.f. Zoffany – Nightime (Galileo). April 21. Eighth foal. €240,000Y. Goffs Orby. Sonessa Ltd. Half-sister to the 2017 2-y-o Group 3 7f Autumn Stakes winner Ghaiyyath (by Dubawi), to the Grade 1 Man O'War Stakes, Irish Group 3 10f and Group 3 12f winner Zhukova (by Fastnet Rock), to the quite useful 8.5f and 12f winner New Year's Night (by Raven's Pass), the quite useful Irish 10f winner and Listed-placed Sleeping Beauty (by Oasis Dream) and a minor French winner by Raven's Pass. The dam won 2 races at 3 yrs including the Irish 1,000 Guineas and is a half-sister to 7 winners. The second dam, Caumshinaun (by Indian Ridge), won 5 races from 6f to 1m in Ireland at 3 and 4 yrs including a Listed event and is a half-sister to one winner. (Mrs C. C. Regalado Gonzalez). *"She's a sweet filly and out of our Guineas winning mare. She's coming forward nicely and I would like to see her out by July/August over six to seven furlongs".*

1687. JEYYAAD (IRE) ★★★
b.c. Dark Angel – Rhythm And Rhyme (Elnadim). March 28. Second foal. 140,000Y. Tattersalls October Book 2. Shadwell Estate Co. The dam is an unraced half-sister to the smart Dragon Pulse, winner of the 2-y-o Group 2 7f Futurity Stakes and the Group 3 Prix de Fontainebleau and second in the Group 1 7f National Stakes. The dam, a useful 1m winner in Ireland, was third in the Group 3 7f Concorde Stakes and is a half-sister to 3 winners. (Hamdan Al Maktoum). *"He's a lengthy colt and I see him being a six to seven furlong 2-y-o in June/July".*

1688. KISS FOR A JEWEL (IRE) ★★★
b.f. Kingman – Sapphire (Medicean). March 2. Second foal. Closely related to Jewel Maker (by Invincible Spirit), placed second over 7f on her only start at 2 yrs in 2017. The dam,

winner of the Group 2 12f British Champions Fillies' and Mares Stakes and two Group 3 events, is a half-sister to the 1m 10f Prince Of Wales's Stakes winner Free Eagle and the very smart triple Group 2 1m and triple Group 3 winner Custom Cut. The second dam, Polished Gem (by Danehill), an Irish 2-y-o 7f winner, is a sister to the Grade 1 9f Matriarch Stakes and Group 2 1m Sun Chariot Stakes winner Dress To Thrill and a half-sister to 7 winners. (Moyglare Stud Farm). *"A very sweet filly, the dam was a very good racemare for us. This will be a lovely filly in August/September over seven furlongs to a mile. I'm looking forward to her 3-y-o career more than this year".*

1689. MANQOOSH (IRE) ★★
b.c. Dubawi – Qaadira (Mr Greeley). March 17. Third foal. Closely related to the quite useful 2-y-o 1m winner Mujaazy (by New Approach). The dam was a quite useful 10.5f winner. The second dam, Makderah (by Danehill), a US Grade 2 10f winner, is a half-sister to 5 winners including the very useful 2-y-o 6f and 7f winner Oriental Fashion (Hamdan Al Maktoum). *"A very big colt, I see him having a run in September or October over seven furlongs to a mile".*

1690. MARIA CHRISTINA (IRE) ★★★
b.f. Kodiac – Suitably Discreet (Mr Prospector). March 4. Closely related to the Group 3 10f Gallinule Stakes winner and US Grade 3 9f second Speaking Of Which (by Invincible Spirit) and half-sister to 5 winners including the Irish 2-y-o 7f winner and Group 2 1m Beresford Stakes second Capital Exposure, the quite useful Irish 9f and 11f winner Designated Decoy (both by Danzig) and the quite useful 2-y-o 7f winner Lost In Silence (by Holy Roman Emperor). The dam is an unraced half-sister to the Group 2 1m Goffs International Stakes and US Grade 2 Arcadia Handicap winner Century City. The second dam, Alywow (by Alysheba), a champion filly in Canada, won 7 races including the Grade 3 8.5f Nijana Stakes and was second in the Grade 1 Rothmans International and the Grade 1 Flower Bowl Invitational. (Moyglare Stud Farm). *"A big filly, her family take a little bit of time, but she's by Kodiac so I'll be aiming for July/August over seven furlongs".*

1691. MIA MARIA (IRE) ★★
gr.f. Dansili – Majestic Silver (Linamix).
February 13. Fifth foal. Sister to the dual
Group 3 9f and dual Listed winner Carla
Bianca (by Dansili) and half-sister to the 2-y-o
7f winner and Group 2 1m Beresford Stakes
second True Solitaire (by Oasis Dream), the
fairly useful German Listed 7f winner Joailliere
(by Dubawi) and the quite useful 7f and 1m
winner Cascavelle (by Shamardal). The dam
is an unraced half-sister to the Irish Group 3
12f and Group 3 14f winner Profound Beauty
and to the useful 7f to 10f winner Rock Critic.
The second dam, Diamond Trim (by Highest
Honor), a Listed winner of 5 races from 1m
to 12f, is a half-sister to 5 winners including
the Group 2 12f Ribblesdale Stakes winner
Irresistible Jewel. (Moyglare Stud Farm). *"She's
a good-sized filly and the family tend to get
better with age so I'll be looking to get her out
in September or October over seven furlongs".*

1692. MIDNIGHT SUNSHINE (USA) ★★
b.f. Medaglia d'Oro – Princess Highway (Street
Cry). March 20. Second foal. Half-sister to the
promising 2017 2-y-o 7f debut winner Chiara
Luna (by War Front). The dam, winner of the
Group 2 12f Ribblesdale Stakes and third in
the Irish Oaks, is a half-sister to the smart
Irish Group 3 7f Gladness Stakes winner and
multiple Group 1 placed Mad About You and
the smart Group 1 Irish St Leger and dual
Group 3 winner of 9 races Royal Diamond. The
second dam, Irresistible Jewel (by Danehill),
won the Group 2 12f Ribblesdale Stakes and
the Group 3 10f Blandford Stakes and is a
half-sister to numerous winners including
the Listed 12f winner Diamond Trim and
the useful Irish 1m winner Legal Jousting.
(Moyglare Stud Farms Ltd). *"An extremely tall
filly, she's a very good mover and should make
into a lovely 3-y-o. I'd like to give her one
run this year possibly over seven furlongs in
October".*

1693. MUFARREJ ★★★★
ch.c. Dubawi – Rasmeyaa (New Approach).
March 30. Second foal. The dam, a useful 2-y-
o 5f winner, was third in the Group 3 7.5f Fairy
Bridge Stakes and is a half-sister to the smart
6f, 7f winner and Group 3 1m Desmond Stakes
winner Future Generation. The second dam,
Posterity (by Indian Ridge), is an unraced half-

sister to 9 winners including the Group 3 6f
Prix de Meautry winner Do The Honours and
the Listed 7f Chesham Stakes winner Seba.
(Hamdan Al Maktoum). *"A medium-sized colt,
he's a lovely horse for the second part of the
year. I would say he'll be an August/September
2-y-o over seven furlongs".*

1694. MUNEES GEMINI (IRE) ★★★
b.f. Australia – Muneefa (Storm Cat).
April 30. Twelfth foal. €62,000Y. Goffs
Sportsmans. BBA (Ire). Half-sister to 7 winners
including the US Grade 2 9f winner Bauble
Queen, the fair 7f(at 2 yrs) to 12f winner of
4 races Brave Archibald (both by Arch) and
the fair 9.5f, 11f and subsequent minor US
stakes winner Leamington (by Pleasant Tap).
The dam, a fair 6f winner, is a half-sister to
4 winners including the Group 3 Rose Of
Lancaster Stakes winner Fahal. The second
dam, By Land By Sea (by Sauce Boat), won
the Grade 1 Apple Blossom Handicap and the
Grade 1 Milady Handicap and is a half-sister
to 7 winners. (Mr Y. Zhang). *"A medium-sized,
sharp filly that goes well and I'd like to have her
ready to roll in June/July".*

1695. NOSTRA CASA (IRE) ★★
b.c. Dubawi – Utterly Heaven (Danehill).
February 15. Half-brother to 4 winners
including the Group 3 14f winner Forgotten
Rules (by Nayef), the Listed 12f winner
Vintage Nouveau (by Montjeu) and the quite
useful 12f winner Time To Inspire (by Galileo).
The dam, a useful Irish 2-y-o 7f winner and
second in the Group 3 1m Park Express Stakes,
is half-sister to 9 winners including the Group
2 11f Blandford Stakes and US dual Grade
2 winner Lisieux Rose. The second dam,
Epicure's Garden (by Affirmed), a useful Irish
7f (at 2 yrs) to 9f winner, was Group 3 placed
three times and is a sister to the Irish 1,000
Guineas winner Trusted Partner (dam of the
high-class filly Dress To Thrill), to the Group
2 winner Easy To Copy (the dam of 3 stakes
winners) and the US Grade 3 winner Low Key
Affair. (Moyglare Stud Farm). *"A fine, big colt,
most of the dam's progeny are better as they
get older and he'll be starting off at seven
furlongs in October".*

1696. SEARCH FOR A SONG (IRE) ★★★★
ch.f. Galileo – Polished Gem (Danehill).

March 3. Seventh foal. Half-sister to the Group 1 10f Prince Of Wales's Stakes winner Free Eagle (by High Chaparral), to the Group 2 12f British Champions Fillies' and Mares Stakes and dual Group 3 winner Sapphire (by Medicean) and the very smart triple Group 2 1m and triple Group 3 winner Custom Cut (by Notnowcato). The dam, an Irish 2-y-o 7f winner, is a sister to the Grade 1 9f Matriarch Stakes and Group 2 1m Sun Chariot Stakes winner Dress To Thrill and a half-sister to 7 winners. The second dam, Trusted Partner (by Affirmed), won the Irish 1,000 Guineas and is a sister to the useful winners Easy to Copy, Epicure's Garden and Low Key Affair. (Moyglare Stud Farm). *"A very, very nice filly, one of the nicest I have, she'll be running at the end of August/September at the earliest. A beautiful moving filly with potential, it'll be seven furlongs to a mile this year for her".*

1697. SHELIR (IRE) ★★★★
b.c. Dark Angel – Shelina (Dalakhani). April 4. Second foal. The dam, placed once over 7f at 2 yrs, is a sister to the French Group 3 10f and Group 3 15f winner Shemima and a half-sister to 4 winners including the French Listed winners Shemaya and Shemala. The second dam, Shemaka (by Nishapour), won the Group 1 10.5f Prix de Diane, the Group 3 10f Prix de la Nonette and the Group 3 9f Prix de Conde. (H H Aga Khan). *"A nice colt, he'll be out in midsummer over six/seven furlongs and I'd keep an eye out for him".*

1698. TAURAN SHAMAN (IRE) ★★
br.c. Shamardal – Danelissima (Danehill). April 11. Eighth living foal. €100,000Y. Goffs Orby. BBA (Ire). Half-brother to the Irish 10f winner and Group 2 Derrinstown Stud Derby Trial third Fergus McIver (by Sadler's Wells) and to a minor winner in Qatar by Medicean. The dam, winner of the Group 3 12f Noblesse Stakes and third in the Group 2 Lancashire Oaks, is a sister to the Irish 2-y-o 7f winner and Listed placed Daneleta (herself dam of the Group 1 Dewhurst Stakes winner Intense

Focus) and a half-sister to 8 winners. The second dam, Zavaleta (by Kahyasi), a useful dual Listed 7f winner, is a half-sister to 9 winners including the 2-y-o Group 1 1m Gran Criterium winner Sholokov and the dam of the Irish Derby winner Soldier Of Fortune. (Mr Y. Zhang). *"A good, strong colt, you can see that he's one that'll be better in the second half of the year. One for August/September over seven furlongs to a mile".*

1699. THIRD WORLD (IRE) ★★
b.c. Dansili – Sense Of Purpose (Galileo). April 27. Third foal. Half-brother to the fair 2017 8.5f placed 2-y-o Crecerelle (by Redoute's Choice). The dam, a useful Group 3 12f Ballyroan Stakes and Listed 14f winner, is a full or half-sister to 6 winners including the fairly useful 1m winner and Listed-placed Dance Pass. The second dam, Super Gift (by Darshaan), a dual 2-y-o 1m winner and second in the Group 3 C L Weld Park Stakes, is a half-sister to 6 winners. (Moyglare Stud Ltd). *"He's a good sort of colt, but all the family are better as 3-y-o's, so this year I would see him as one for seven furlongs to a mile in October".*

1700. TRANCHEE (IRE) ★★★★
b.c. War Front – Terrific (Galileo). April 6. First foal. The dam, fairly useful 2-y-o and 1m winner, was Listed-placed st 3 yrs and is a half-sister to the 2-y-o Group 1 1m Criterium International winner and Irish Derby third Jan Vermeer and the 2-y-o Group 3 7f Silver Flash Stakes winner, multiple Group 1 placed and subsequent US Grade 1 9f winner Together The second dam, Shadow Song (by Pennekamp) won once at 3 yrs in France and is a half-sister to the Group 3 May Hill Stakes winner Midnight Air (herself dam of the Group 3 and US Grade 2 winner Midnight Line) and to the placed dam of the Group 1 Prix de l'Abbaye winner Imperial Beauty. (Moyglare Stud Farm). *"Very much a quality colt, he's strong and I would like to have him out over seven furlongs in July".*

SIRES REFERENCE

This section deals with those sires represented by three or more two-year-olds in the book. All the top British and Irish sires are represented and you will also see some of the best sires standing in America such as Elusive Quality, Kitten's Joy, More Than Ready, Scat Daddy and War Front. There are plenty of first-season sires to look out for including Alhebayeb, Australia, Charm Spirit, Gale Force Ten, Garswood, Heeraat, Kingman, Mukhadram, No Nay Never, Olympic Glory, Sea The Moon, Slade Power, Toronado and War Command.

ACCLAMATION (2000) Royal Applause – Princess Athena (Ahonoora). *Racing record:* Won 6 times, including Diadem Stakes. Also placed in King's Stand and Nunthorpe. *Stud record:* This is his twelfth crop and his Group winners to date are Dark Angel (G1 Middle Park Stakes), Equiano (G1 King's Stand Stakes), Marsha (Group 1 Prix de l'Abbaye, G1 Nunthorpe Stakes), Expert Eye (G2 Vintage Stakes), Harbour Watch & Saayern (both winners of the G2 Richmond Stakes), Mehmas (Group 2 July Stakes and Group 2 Richmond Stakes), Lidari (Group 2 in Australia), Lilbourne Lad (G2 Railway Stakes), Aclaim (Group 2 Challenge Stakes), Angels Will Fall (G3 Princess Margaret Stakes), Alsindi (G3 Oh So Sharp Stakes), Attendu (dual Group winner), Hitchens (G3 Greenlands Stakes), Ponty Acclaim (G3 Cornwallis Stakes), Queen Catrine (Group 3 Brownstown Stakes), Talwar (G3 Solario Stakes) and Sparkling Power (G3 in Hong Kong). He also has numerous Listed winners to his name. Standing at Rathbarry Stud, Ireland. 2018 *fee:* €40,000.

ALHEBAYEB (2010) Dark Angel – Miss Indigo (Indian Ridge). *Racing record:* Won twice, over 5f on his debut and the Group 2 6f July Stakes, also second in the Group 3 7f Horris Hill Stakes (all at 2 yrs). *Stud record:* Retired to stud in 2015, so these are his first two-year-olds. He is a half-brother to the Listed winning sprinter Humidor. Standing at Yeomanstown Stud in Ireland. 2018 *fee:* €5,000.

ARCHIPENKO (2004) Kingmambo – Bound (Nijinsky). *Racing record:* Won the Group 1 10f Audemars Piguet Queen Elizabeth II Cup at Sha Tin and five other Group races including the Group 2 Summer Mile. *Stud record:* His best winners to date are Madame Chiang (Group 1 British Champions Fillies/Mare Stakes), Time Warp (Group 1 Hong Kong Cup), Forty One (Grade 1 in Argentina), the South African Group 2 winner Kingston Mines, Group 3 winners Algometer and Va Bank, and the Listed winners Lady Penko (also Group 1 third), Algonquin, Medrano and Russian Punch. Died in December 2017. His 2017 *fee* was £10,000.

AUSTRALIA (2011) Galileo – Ouija Board (Cape Cross). *Racing record:* Won 5 races from 7f (at 2 yrs) to 12f including the Derby, Irish Derby and Juddmonte International. *Stud record:* By Galileo out of multiple Group 1 winner Ouija Board. His first crop are now two-year-olds. Standing at Coolmore Stud in Ireland. 2018 *fee:* €35,000.

BATED BREATH (2007) Dansili – Tantina (Distant View). *Racing record:* Winner of 6 races over 5f and 6f from 3 to 5yrs, notably the Group 2 Temple Stakes and placed in five Group 1 events. *Stud record:* This is his third crop of two-year-olds. Sire of 49 winners (to Feb 2018) including Beckford (Group 2 Railway Stakes), the dual Group 2 second Al Johrah and the Group 2 and Group 3 placed Gavota. Standing at Banstead Manor Stud, Newmarket. 2017 *fee:* £10,000.

BATTLE OF MARENGO (2010) Galileo – Anna Karenina (Green Desert). *Racing record:* Five wins including the Group 2 1m Beresford Stakes at 2 yrs and the Group 2 10f Derrinstown Stud Derby Trial at three. *Stud record:* This crop of two-year-olds is his first. Standing at Ballyhane Stud. 2018 *fee:* €4,000.

BIG BAD BOB (2000) Bob Back – Fantasy Girl (Marju). *Racing record:* Won 8 races including a Group 3 10f event in Germany and Listed races at Ascot (1m) and Deauville (10f). *Stud record:*

His first crop appeared on the racecourse in 2010. To date he's had the Irish Group 2 winner Bocca Baciata, the Group 3 winners Berg Bahn, Bible Belt, Brendan Brackan and McCreery, and five Listed winners (Backbench Blues, Bible Black and Bob Le Beau, Cherie Good and Tashweeq). Died in 2016.

BORN TO SEA (2009) Invincible Spirit – Urban Sea (Miswaki). *Racing record:* Won a Listed 2-y-o event in Ireland and was second in the Group 1 Irish Derby, the Group 2 Royal Whip Stakes and the Group 3 Killavullen Stakes. *Stud record:* A half-brother to Galileo and Sea The Stars, his first two-year-olds appeared in 2016. Sire of 29 winners on the Flat (13 2-y-o's) up to Feb 2018. They include Sea Of Grace (Group 3 Flame Of Tara Stakes) and the Listed-placed Born To Be Alive and Star Of Rory. Standing at Gilltown Stud in Ireland. 2018 *fee:* €5,000.

BUNGLE INTHEJUNGLE (2010) Exceed And Excel – Licence To Thrill (Wolfhound). *Racing record:* Won four races over five furlongs as a 2-y-o including the Molecomb Stakes and the Cornwallis Stakes (both Group 3). *Stud record:* His first crop are now two-year-olds. Standing at Rathasker Stud. 2018 *fee:* €5,000.

CACIQUE (2001) Danehill – Hasili (Kahyasi). *Racing record:* Won 18 races from 3 to 5 yrs including the Grade 1 11f Man O'War Stakes, Grade 1 10f Manhattan Handicap and the Grade 2 1m Prix Daniel Wildenstein. *Stud record:* From limited books of mares he has 29 winners to date (eight 2-y-o's) including the Group 1 winners Dominant (Hong Kong Vase), Mutual Trust (Prix Jean Prat) and Slumber (Manhattan Stakes), along with the Group 2 Prix de Chaudenay winner Canticum, the Group 3 Geoffrey Freer Stakes winner Census and the German 2-y-o Group 3 winner Colomano. Retired from stud.

CAMELOT (2009) Montjeu – Tarfah (Kingmambo). *Racing record:* Won 6 races including the Racing Post Trophy, 2,000 Guineas, Derby and Irish Derby (all Group 1 events). *Stud record:* His first crop were two-year-olds in 2017 and there were 9 first crop winners including Fighting Irish (Group 2 Criterium de Maisons-Laffitte). Standing at Coolmore Stud, Ireland. 2018 *fee:* €30,000.

CANFORD CLIFFS (2007) Tagula – Mrs Marsh (Marju). *Racing record:* Won 7 races at 2 to 4 yrs and from 6f to 1m including the Irish 2,000 Guineas, St James's Palace Stakes, Sussex Stakes, Lockinge Stakes and Queen Anne Stakes (all Group 1 events). *Stud record:* His first crop of two-year-olds appeared in 2015 and he's bred 86 winners (44 2-y-o's) of 166 races including the Group 2 Railway Stakes winner Painted Cliffs, the Group 3 winners Al Jazi, Most Beautiful and Princess Asta, the Group 1 Oaks and Irish Oaks third Harlequeen, the dual Group 1 placed Salouen and the French Listed winner Aktoria. Standing at Highland Stud, South Africa.

CAPE CROSS (1994) Green Desert – Park Appeal (Ahonoora). *Racing record:* Won 4 races including the Lockinge Stakes, Queen Anne Stakes and Celebration Mile. *Stud record:* First runners in 2003. Sire of fourteen Group 1 winners including two outstanding colts in Sea The Stars (2,000 Guineas, Derby, Prix de l'Arc de Triomphe, etc) and Golden Horn (Derby, Eclipse Stakes, Irish Champion Stakes and Prix de l'Arc de Triomphe), the top-class filly Ouija Board (7 Group 1 wins including the Oaks & the Breeders' Cup Filly and Mare Turf), Awtaad (Irish 2,000 Guineas), Behkabad (Grand Prix de Paris), Nayarra (Group 1 Gran Criterium), dual German Group 1 winner Guignol, the Hong Kong triple Group 1 winner Able One and the Australasian horses Gaze, I'm Your Man, Kindacross, Mikki Street and Seachange. His Group 2 winners include Cape Dollar, Crystal Capella, Halicarnassus, Hatta Fort, Joviality, Moohaajim, Russian Cross, Sabana Perdida and Treat Gently. Died April 2017.

CASAMENTO (2008) Shamardal – Wedding Gift (Always Fair). *Racing record:* Won four races including the Group 1 Racing Post Trophy, the Group 2 Beresford Stakes (both at 2 yrs) and the Group 3 Prix du Prince d'Orange). *Stud record:* This is his third crop of two-year-olds and to February 2018 he's sired 34 winners (27 of them 2-yo's). Now standing in Sweden. 2018 *fee:* €2,500.

CHAMPS ELYSEES (2003) Danehill – Hasili (Kahyasi). *Racing record:* Won the Canadian International, the Hollywood Turf Cup and the Northern Dancer Turf Stakes (all Grade 1). *Stud record:* With three crops to have raced so far he's the sire of 100 winners (28 2-y-o's) including the Group 1 Ascot Gold Cup winner Trip To Paris, the Group 3 Silver Flash Stakes winner and Group 1 Irish Oaks second Jack Naylor, the Group 3 winner and French 1,000 Guineas third Xcellence and the Listed winners and Group placed Avenue Gabriel, Dai Harraild, Eastern Belle, Lustrous, Petite Jack and Regardez. Standing at Castle Hyde Stud. 2018 *fee:* €6,500.

CHARM SPIRIT (2011) Invincible Spirit – L'Enjoleuse (Montjeu). *Racing record:* Won 6 races over 7f (including at 2 yrs) and 1m including three Group 1 events at 3 yrs (Prix Jean Prat, Prix du Moulin and the Queen Elizabeth II Stakes). *Stud record:* This is his first crop of two-year-olds. Standing at Haras de Bonneval. 2018 *fee:* €20,000.

CITYSCAPE (2006) Selkirk – Tantina (Distant View). *Racing record:* Won 6 races from 2 to 6 yrs including the UAE Group 1 9f Dubai Duty Free and three Group 3 events over 1m. *Stud record:* His first crop of two-year-olds appeared last year and he had 7 winners. Standing at Overbury Stud, Newmarket. 2018 *fee:* £4,500.

CLODOVIL (2001) Danehill – Clodora (Linamix). *Racing record:* Won 5 races including the French 2,000 Guineas. *Stud record:* Since his first crop of two-year-olds in 2007 he's had 96 2-y-o winners (to Feb 2018). His best winners to date are Nahoodh (Group 1 Falmouth Stakes), Moriarty (Group 1 and three Group 2's in Australia), the Group 2 winners Coupe de Ville, Es Que Love, Gregorian, Laugh Out Loud, Shining Emerald and Tuttipaesi, the dual Group 3 winner Beacon Lodge and numerous Listed winners. Standing at Rathasker Stud, Ireland. 2018 *fee:* €7,500.

COACH HOUSE (2011) Oasis Dream – Lesson In Humility (Mujadil). *Racing record:* Won twice over five furlongs as a 2-y-o in Ireland including a Listed event and was Group 2 placed over five and six furlongs. *Stud record:* First crop now two-year-olds. Standing at Bucklands Farm & Stud, Glos. 2018 *fee:* £3,000.

COMPTON PLACE (1994) Indian Ridge – Nosey (Nebbiolo). *Racing record:* Won 3 races, notably the July Cup. *Stud record:* First

runners in 2002. Sire of 11 Group winners, 13 Listed winners and 123 2-y-o winners (to Feb 2018), notably the dual Group 1 Nunthorpe Stakes winner Borderlescott, the Group 2 and multiple Group 3 winner Deacon Blues, the US Grade 2 winner Passified, the Group 2 winners Godfrey Street, Pearl Secret and Prolific, the Group 3 winners Easy Road, Hunter Street, Intrepid Jack, Minal, Pleasure Place, Champion Place and Shifting Power, and numerous useful performers including Angus News, Boogie Street, Compton's Eleven, If Paradise, Judd Street, Hunter Street, Master Of War, Pacific Pride and Pearl Secret. Died in 2015.

DANDY MAN (2003) Mozart – Lady Alexander (Night Shift). *Racing record:* Won 6 races including the Group 3 5f Palace House Stakes and two Listed events. *Stud record:* Has sired 97 winners to date including 63 2-y-o's. His best to date are the Hong Kong Group 1 and dual Group 2 winner Peniaphobia, the Group 3 and Listed winner Extortionist, the triple Group 2 placed Parbold and the 2-y-o Listed Roses Stakes winner Big Time Baby. Standing at Ballyhane Stud. 2018 *fee:* €10,000.

DANSILI (1996) Danehill – Hasili (Kahyasi). *Racing record:* Won 5 races in France and placed in six Group/Grade 1 events including Sussex Stakes and Breeders' Cup Mile. *Stud record:* First runners in 2004. 158 2-y-o winners to Feb 2018. Sire of 20 Group/Grade 1 winners including Rail Link (Arc, Grand Prix de Paris), Harbinger (King George VI), Emulous (Matron Stakes), Fallen For You (Coronation Stakes), Flintshire (Grand Prix de Paris, etc), Foreteller (three in Australia), Giofra (Falmouth Stakes), Miss France (1,000 Guineas), Passage of Time (Criterium de Saint-Cloud), The Fugue (four Group 1's), We Are (Prix de l'Opera), Winsili (Nassau Stakes), Zoffany (Phoenix Stakes), Zambezi Sun (Grand Prix de Paris) and in the USA Dank, Laughing, Price Tag and Proviso. Standing at Banstead Manor Stud, Newmarket. 2018 *fee:* £65,000.

DARK ANGEL (2005) Acclamation – Midnight Angel (Machiavellian). *Racing record:* Won four races at 2 yrs including the Group 1 Middle Park Stakes. *Stud record:* First runners 2011. 157 2-y-o winners to Feb 2018. His best winners to date are Lethal Force (Group 1 July Cup & Group 1 Diamond Jubilee Stakes), Mecca's Angel (Group 1 Nunthorpe Stakes, twice), Harry's Angel (Group 1 July Cup & Group 1 Haydock Sprint Cup), Battaash (Group 1 Prix de l'Abbaye), Persuasive (Group 1 Queen Elizabeth II Stakes), Alhebayeb (Group 2 July Stakes), Ardhoomey (Group 2 Flying Five), Birchwood (Group 2 Superlative Stakes), Estidhkaar (Group 2 Champagne Stakes & Group 2 Superlative Stakes), Sovereign Debt (Group 2 bet 365 Mile), Gutaifan (Group 2 Flying Childers Stakes, Group 2 Champagne Stakes), dual Grade 1 second Fanciful Angel and twelve Group 3 winners including Exogenesis, Heeraat, Lily's Angel, Markaz, Mr Genuine, Nations Alexander, Realtra, Sovereign Debt and Stormfly and fourteen Listed winners. Stands at Yeomanstown Stud, Ireland. 2018 *fee:* €85,000.

DAWN APPROACH (2010) New Approach – Hymn Of The Dawn (Phone Trick).
Racing record: Unbeaten champion 2-y-o, won 8 races from 5f to 1m at 2 and 3 yrs including the National Stakes, Dewhurst Stakes, 2,000 Guineas and St James's Palace Stakes. *Stud record:* His first two-year-olds appeared last year and he had 8 winners including the Group 3 placed Dawn Delivers and Fast Approach (in Japan). Stands at Kildangan Stud, Ireland. 2018 *fee:* €20,000.

DECLARATION OF WAR (2009) War Front – Tempo West (Rahy). *Racing record:* Won 7 races from 2 to 4 yrs and from 7.5f to 10.5f including the Group 1 Queen Anne Stakes and the Group 1 Juddmonte International (both at 4 yrs). *Stud record:* His first two-year-olds appeared last year, there were 8 winners and they included the Group 3 Anglesey Stakes winner and Group 1 third Actress, the Listed St Hugh's Stakes winner Eirene, the US Listed winner Speed Franco and the Group 1 Grand Criterium second Olmedo. Stands at Ashford Stud, Kentucky. 2018 *fee:* $25,000.

DRAGON PULSE (2009) Kyllachy – Poetical (Croco Rouge). *Racing record:* Won the Group 2 7f Futurity Stakes at the Curragh (at 2 yrs) and the Group 3 1m Prix de Fontainebleau. Second in the Group 1 National Stakes. *Stud record:* With just two crops racing he's had 25 2-y-o winners including the Italian Group 3 winner Aethos, the Listed Woodcote Stakes winner Legendary Lunch and the Group 2 Duke Of Cambridge second Magical Fire. Standing at the Irish National Stud. 2018 *fee:* €8,000.

DREAM AHEAD (2008) Diktat – Land Of Dreams (Cadeaux Genereux). *Racing record:* Won five Group 1 races from 6f to 7f, at 2 and 3 yrs (Prix Morny, Middle Park Stakes, July Cup, Haydock Park Sprint Cup and Prix de la Foret). *Stud record:* From three crops racing he's had 27 2-y-o winners. His best horses to date are the Group 1 Prix Jacques le Marois winner Al Wukair, the Group 2 Criterium de Maisons-Laffitte winner Donjuan Triumphant, the Group 3 Anglesey Stakes winner Final Frontier, the winner and multiple Group placed Raucous and the Listed winners Basileus (Italy), Dream Of Dreams, Tisbutadream and Ken's Dream (Australia). Standing at Haras de Grandcamp, France.

DUBAWI (2002) Dubai Millennium – Zomaradah (Deploy). *Racing record:* Won the National Stakes at 2 and the Irish 2,000 Guineas and Prix Jacques le Marois at 3. Third in the Derby. *Stud record:* An exceptional sire responsible for 177 2-y-o winners to date (Feb 2018). He has 35 Group 1 scorers and they include Al Kazeem (three Group 1's), Arabian Queen (Juddmonte International), Dubawi Heights (Gamely Stakes, Yellow Ribbon Stakes), Erupt (Canadian International and Grand Prix de Paris), Happy Archer (two Group 1's in Australia), Hunters Light (three Group 1's in Italy and Dubai), Lucky Nine (Hong Kong Sprint), Makfi (2,000 Guineas, Prix Jacques le Marois), Monterosso & Prince Bishop (both Dubai World Cup winners), New Bay (French Derby), Night Of Thunder (2,000 Guineas and Lockinge Stakes), Poet's Voice (Queen Elizabeth II Stakes), Postponed (four Group 1's including the King George VI), Secret Admirer (two Group 1's in Australia), Sheikhzayedroad (Northern Dancer Turf Stakes), Waldpark (German Derby), Willow Magic (in South Africa) and Wuheida (Breeders' Cup Filly & Mare Turf). Standing at Dalham Hall Stud, Newmarket. 2018 *fee:* £250,000.

DUTCH ART (2004) Medicean – Halland Park Lass (Spectrum). *Racing record:* Won four races at 2 yrs including the Group 1 Prix Morny and the Group 1 Middle Park Stakes. *Stud record:* Leading first crop sire in 2011 and a consistently good sire ever since. His Group winners to date including Slade Power (dual Group 1 6f winner), Garswood (Group 1 Prix Maurice de Gheest), Caspar Netscher (Group 2 Mill Reef Stakes and Group 2 Gimcrack Stakes),

Producer (Group 2 in Turkey and the Group 3 Supreme Stakes), Dutch Connection (Group 2 Lennox Stakes and three Group 3's), Dutch Masterpiece (Group 3 Flying Five), Lady's First (Group 3 Atalanta Stakes) and Zonderland (Group 3 Sovereign Stakes). Standing at Cheveley Park Stud. 2018 *fee:* £15,000.

ELUSIVE QUALITY (1993) Gone West – Touch of Greatness (Hero's Honor). *Racing record:* Won 9 races in USA including Grade 3 events at 7f/1m. *Stud record:* Sire of the Kentucky Derby/Preakness Stakes winner Smarty Jones, Breeders Cup Classic and Queen Elizabeth II Stakes winner Raven's Pass, Prix Morny winner Elusive City, dual Group 1 winner Elusive Kate, Australian multiple Group 1 winner Sepoy, the US Grade 1 winners Quality Road and Maryfield, the Group winning two-year-olds Certify, Elusive Pimpernel and Evasive, numerous US graded stakes winners including Chimichurri, Elusive Diva, Girl Warrior, Omega Code, Royal Michele and True Quality, the Group 2 and triple Group 3 winner Shuruq and the smart dual Listed winner Baharah. Retired from stud.

EPAULETTE (2009) Commands (AUS) – Accessories (Singspiel). *Racing record:* Won 3 races in Australia at 3 and 4 yrs including two Group 1 7f events. *Stud record:* A three-parts brother to the sire Helmet, his first two-year-olds appeared last year. He had a good start with 17 winners but only one Group winner, Meryl (Gr 3 in Australia). Standing at Kildangan Stud, Ireland. 2018 *fee:* €7,000.

EQUIANO (2005) Acclamation – Entente Cordiale (Ela-Mana-Mou). *Racing record:* Won 7 races starting with two wins as a 2-y-o over 7f in Spain, before maturing into a high-class sprinter and twice capturing the Group 1 5f King's Stand Stakes. *Stud record:* From four crops he has sired 114 winners including 62 2-y-o's (to Feb 2018). His best progeny include The Tin Man (Group 1 British Champions Sprint), Medicine Jack (2-y-o Group 2 Railway Stakes), the Group 3 winners Baciama Piccola (in the USA), Belvoir Bay (in the USA), Dark Reckoning, Fly On The Night, Lady Macapa and Strath Burn, and the Listed winners Alicante Dawn, Final Venture, Valliano (in Australia) and Waipu Cove (in Ireland). Standing at Newsells Park Stud. 2018 *fee:* £8,000.

EXCEED AND EXCEL (2000) Danehill – Patrona (Lomond). *Racing record:* Champion sprinter in Australia, won 7 races including the Grade 1 Newmarket H'cap, the Grade 1 Dubai Racing Club Cup and the Grade 2 Todman Stakes. *Stud record:* There are 11 Group 1 winners to his name – Excelebration (Queen Elizabeth II Stakes, Prix du Moulin, Prix Jacques le Marois), Margot Did (Nunthorpe Stakes), Outstrip (Breeders Cup Juvenile Turf), Amber Sky (Group 1 Al Quoz Sprint), Guelphe, Helmet, Earthquake, Flamberge, Overreach, Reward For Effort (all in Australia) and Mr Stunning (Hong Kong). His twenty Group 2 winners include Best Terms, Buratino, Fulbright, Heavy Metal, Infamous Angel and Masamah. Standing at Kildangan Stud, Ireland. 2018 *fee:* €50,000.

EXCELEBRATION (2008) Exceed And Excel – Sun Shower (Indian Ridge). *Racing record:* Won eight races from 6f (at 2 yrs) to 1m including three Group 1 stakes – the Prix du Moulin, Prix Jacques le Marois and Queen Elizabeth II Stakes. *Stud record:* His first two-year-olds appeared on the track in 2016 and to date he has 40 winners to his name, including 21 two-year-olds. They include the Group 1 St James's Palace Stakes winner Barney Roy, Listed winners Speak In Colours and Rebel Assault, Group 1 Middle Park Stakes fourth Hey Jonesy and the Group 3 placed Fulminato (in Germany) and Pellucid. Standing at Coolmore Stud, Ireland. 2018 *fee:* €8,000.

FARHH (2008) Pivotal – Gonbarda (Lando). *Racing record:* Won 5 races from 7f to 10f and from 2 to 5 yrs including the Group 1 Lockinge Stakes and the Group 1 Champion Stakes. *Stud record:* His first crop of two-year-olds appeared last season and he had 6 two-year-old winners including the Group 3 winner Acomb Stakes winner Wells Farhh Go. Standing at Dalham Hall Stud. 2017 *fee:* £10,000.

FAST COMPANY (2005) Danehill Dancer – Sheezalady (Zafonic). *Racing record:* Ran only three times, all at 2 yrs, winning the Group 3 7f Acomb Stakes and finishing second in the Group 1 7f Dewhurst Stakes. *Stud record:* Sired 26 individual winners from his first crop in 2014. His best offspring to date include Jet Setting (Group 1 Irish 1,000 Guineas), Baitha Alga (Group 2 Norfolk Stakes), Devonshire

(Group 3 Ridgewood Pearl Stakes and third in the Group 1 Irish 1,000 Guineas), Penny Pepper (Group 3 Ballyogan Stakes), Chilean Group 1 winner Robert Bruce and seven Listed winners. Standing at Kildangan Stud. 2018 *fee:* €9,000.

FASTNET ROCK (2001) Danehill – Piccadilly Circus (Royal Academy). *Racing record:* Raced in Australia and won two Grade 1's, two Grade 2's and two Grade 3 events over 5f and 6f. *Stud record:* A champion sire in Australia and he's produced over 30 stakes winners in Europe. His 32 Group 1 winners include Atlante, Atlantic Jewel, Diamondsandrubies (Pretty Polly Stakes), Fascinating Rock (Champion Stakes), Foxwedge, Intricately (Moyglare Stud Stakes), Irish Lights, Lone Rock, Mosheen, Nechita, Planet Rock, Qualify (Oaks), Rivet (Racing Post Trophy), Rock 'N' Pop, Rock Classic, Sea Siren, Super Cool, Wanted, Your Song and Zhukova. The majority of them have been in Australasia. Standing at Coolmore Stud, Ireland. 2018 *fee:* €70,000.

FIRST DEFENCE (2004) Unbridled's Song – Honest Lady (Seattle Slew). *Racing record:* Won the Grade 1 7f Forego Handicap and the Grade 3 6f Jaipur Stakes. *Stud record:* With three crops racing he is the sire of the winners of 228 races (to Feb 2017). His best runners have been the US multiple Grade 1 winner and $1.6m earner Close Hatches, Dundonnell (Group 3 Acomb Stakes), Antonoe (US Grade 1 Just A Game Stakes) and Irish Jasper (US Grade 3 Miss Preakness Stakes). Standing in Saudi Arabia.

FOOTSTEPSINTHESAND (2002) Giant's Causeway – Glatisant (Rainbow Quest). *Racing record:* Won all 3 of his starts, notably the 2,000 Guineas. *Stud record:* His best winners include Chachamaidee (Group 1 Matron Stakes), the Italian and Argentine Group 1 winners Infiltrada, Sand Bijou and Shamalgan, Canadian Grade 1 winner Steinbeck, twelve Group 2 winners including Barefoot Lady, Formosina, Giant Sandman, Living The Life, Minakshi and, in Argentina, King Kon, Sagitariana and Sand Puce, plus twelve Group 3 winners. Standing at Coolmore Stud, Ireland. 2018 *fee:* €10,000.

FOXWEDGE (2008) Fastnet Rock – Forest Native (Forest Wildcat). *Racing record:* Won

3 races in Australia including Group 1 and Group 2 events over 6f. *Stud record:* Now back in Australia where his best runners to date include the New Zealand Group 1 winner Volpe Veloce and the Australian Group 1 Foxplay. In England he's sired the triple winner and Group 1 Fillies Mile third Urban Fox, the Listed winner Hertford Dancer and the Group 3 placed winners King Of Spades and Seafront. Standing in Australia.

FRANKEL (2008) Galileo – Kind (Danehill). *Racing record:* A champion at two, three and four years of age, he won all 14 of his races, from 7f to 10.5f, including ten Group 1's. *Stud record:* His first crop were two-year-olds in 2016 and he was the leading European first crop sire by worldwide earnings. His best progeny to date are the Group 1 winners Cracksman (Champion Stakes) and Soul Stirring (in Japan), the Group 2 winners Queen Kindly, Eminent, Finche and Rostropovich along with ten Group 3 winners. Standing at Banstead Manor Stud, Newmarket. 2018 *fee:* £175,000.

FROZEN POWER (2007) Oasis Dream – Musical Treat (Royal Academy). *Racing record:* Won five races from 6f to a mile including the Group 2 German 2,000 Guineas. *Stud record:* With three crops racing he's had 27 individual winners of 62 races, but no stakes winners. Now standing in Italy.

GALE FORCE TEN (2010) Oasis Dream – Ronaldsay (Kirkwall). *Racing record:* Won over 6f (at 2 yrs), the Group 3 7f Jersey Stakes and a Listed 7f event at Dundalk (both as a three-year-old). *Stud record:* His first crop are now two-year-olds. Standing at the Irish National Stud. 2018 *fee:* €5,000.

GALILEO (1998) Sadler's Wells – Urban Sea (Miswaki). *Racing record:* Won 6 races including the Derby, Irish Derby and King George VI and Queen Elizabeth Stakes. *Stud record:* First runners in 2005. A great stallion and sire of numerous Group 1 winners in 2017 alone, including Highland Reel, Churchill, Ulysses, Capri, Winter and Hydrangea. Surely his beat performer to date was the outstanding champion Frankel, but others worthy of note are champion 2-y-o's Teofilo and New Approach (subsequent Derby, Champion Stakes and Irish Champion Stakes winner), Derby, Irish Derby and Juddmonte International winner Australia, the triple Group 1 winner Rip Van Winkle, Sixties Icon (St Leger), triple Group 1 winner Noble Mission, Red Rocks (Breeders' Cup Turf), Allegretto (Prix Royal-Oak), Lush Lashes (three Group 1 wins), Soldier Of Fortune (Irish Derby & Coronation Cup), Nightime (Irish 1000 Guineas), Roderic O'Connor (Criterium International, Irish 2,000 Guineas), Cape Blanco (five Group 1 wins), Nathaniel (King George VI & Queen Elizabeth Stakes), Ruler Of The World (Epsom Derby), Treasure Beach (Irish Derby, Secretariat Stakes), dual Guineas and St James's Palace winner Gleneagles, Golden Lilac (French 1,000 Guineas, Prix d'Ispahan and Prix de Diane), Intello (French Derby), dual Group 1 winning 2-y-o filly Minding, triple Group 1 winner Noble Mission, Was (Oaks), Misty For Me (four Group 1 wins), Maybe (Moyglare Stud Stakes) and Galikova (Prix Vermeille). Standing at Coolmore Stud, Ireland. 2018 *fee:* Private.

GARSWOOD (2010) Dutch Art – Penchant (Kyllachy). *Racing record:* Won 4 races from 2 to 4 yrs and from 5f to 7f, notably the Group 1 Prix Maurice de Gheest and the Group 2 Lennox Stakes. *Stud record:* His first runners appear this year. Standing at Cheveley Park Stud. 2018 *fee:* £4,000.

GIANT'S CAUSEWAY (1997) Storm Cat – Mariah's Storm (Rahy). *Racing record:* Won 9 races, 6 of them Group 1 events, including the Prix de la Salamandre, Juddmonte International and Sussex Stakes. *Stud record:* First runners in 2004. The sire of around 100 Group winners including 31 Group/Grade 1 winners including Shamardal (Dewhurst Stakes, St James's Palace Stakes and Prix du Jockey Club), Footstepsinthesand (2,000 Guineas), Ghanaati (1,000 Guineas and Coronation Stakes), Aragorn & Carpe Diem (dual US Grade 1 winners), Eishin Apollon (Group 1 miler in Japan), Heatseeker (Santa Anita Handicap), Maids Causeway (Coronation Stakes), Intense Focus (Dewhurst Stakes), Eskendereya, First Samurai, My Typhoon, Swift Temper (US Grade 1 winners), Dalkala (Prix de l'Opera) and Rite of Passage (Ascot Gold Cup). Died in 2018.

GREGORIAN (2009) Clodovil – Three Days In May (Cadeaux Genereux). *Racing record:*

Won 6 races from 2 to 5 yrs over 7f and 8.5f including the Group 2 Hungerford Stakes and two Group 3's. Placed in four Group 1 events – the July Cup, St James's Palace Stakes, Queen Anne Stakes and Prix Jean Prat. *Stud record:* His first crop are now two-year-olds. Standing at the National Stud. 2018 *fee:* £4,500.

HARBOUR WATCH (2009) Acclamation – Gorband (Woodman). *Racing record:* Won three races at 2 yrs (all his starts) including the Group 2 6f Richmond Stakes. *Stud record:* His first two-year-olds appeared on the racecourse in 2016. To date he's sired 43 winners including 18 two-year-olds, notably the Group 2 Prix Robert Papin winner Tis Marvellous and the Group 2 Norfolk Stakes second Santry. Retired from stud.

HAVANA GOLD (2010) Teofilo – Jessica's Dream (Desert Style). *Racing record:* Won 5 races at 2 and 3 yrs from 6f to 1m including the Group 1 Prix Jean Prat and the Group 3 Somerville Tattersalls Stakes. *Stud record:* By a champion 2-y-o and out of a multiple 5f Group winner. His first two-year-olds appeared on the racecourse last year and he's had a very good start. Amongst his 18 winners were Havana Grey (Group 3 Molecomb Stakes), Treasuring (Group 3 Molecomb Stakes) and Headway (second in the Group 2 Coventry Stakes). Standing at Tweenhills Farm & Stud. 2018 *fee:* £15,000.

HEERAAT (2009) Dark Angel – Thawrah (Green Desert). *Racing record:* Won 5 races over 5f and 6f and from 2 to 4 yrs including the Group 3 Hackwood Stakes. *Stud record:* His dam is a half-sister to the Group 1 winning sprinter Malhub. His first two-year-olds appear this year. Standing at Mickley Stud. 2018 *fee:* £5,000.

HELMET (2008) Exceed And Excel – Accessories (Singspiel). *Racing record:* Won 6 races in Australia at 3 yrs from 6f to 1m including three Group 1's. *Stud record:* His first two-year-olds appeared in 2016 and he's had an excellent start to his stud career. With 25 2-y-o winners to date (Feb 2018) his best runner to date is the Group 1 Criterium International and Group 1 Prix Jean Prat winner Thunder Snow. He also has the Group 2 Premio Roma winner Anda Muchacho, Listed winners Eqtiraan, Met Spectrum (Italy) and Taamol. In Australia he has the Group 3 winners Archives and Limestone. Standing at Dalham Hall Stud, Newmarket. 2018 *fee:* £12,000.

HENRYTHENAVIGATOR (2005) Kingmambo – Sequoyah (Sadler's Wells). *Racing record:* Won the Sussex Stakes, St James's Palace Stakes, 2000 Guineas and Irish 2,000 Guineas. *Stud record:* With five crops to have raced he's had 3 individual Group 1 winners – George Vancouver (Grade 1 Breeders Cup Juvenile Turf), Pedro The Great (Group 1 Phoenix Stakes) and Sudirman (Group 1 Phoenix Stakes). He also has one Group 3 winner in Australia (Lite'n My Veins) and numerous other stakes winners. Standing at Coolmore Stud. 2018 *fee:* €7,500.

HOLY ROMAN EMPEROR (2004) Danehill – L'On Vite (Secretariat). *Racing record:* Won four races at 2 yrs including the Group 1 7f Prix Jean-Luc Lagardere, the Group 1 6f Waterford Phoenix Stakes and Group 2 6f Railway Stakes. *Stud record:* His best winners so far include Homecoming Queen (1,000 Guineas), Morandi (Group 1 Criterium de Saint Cloud), Hong Kong Group 1 winners Designs On Rome and Beauty Only, New Zealand Group 1 winners Rollout The Carpet and Mongolian Khan, Grade 1 Santa Anita Sprint winner Rich Tapestry, 19 other Group winners including Angelic Light, Banimpire, Charles The Great, Mango Diva, Rich Legacy (all Group 2 winners) and the Group 1 placed Amarillo, Honorius, Ishvana, Leitir Mor, Princess Noor and Sunday Times. Standing at Coolmore Stud, Ireland. 2018 *fee:* €15,000.

IFFRAAJ (2001) Zafonic – Pastorale (Nureyev). *Racing record:* Won 7 races including the Group 2 7f Park Stakes (twice), the Group 2 7f Betfair Cup (Lennox Stakes) and the 6f Wokingham Stakes. *Stud record:* His first runners came in 2010 when he had more winners (38) than any first-crop European sire ever. He now has 22 Group winners and amongst the best are Ribchester (multiple Group 1 winning miler), Chriselliam (Group 1 Fillies' Mile and Grade 1 Breeders Cup Juvenile Fillies), Jungle Cat (Group 1 Al Quoz Sprint), Wootton Bassett (Group 1 Prix Jean-Luc Lagardere), Rizeena (Group 1 Moyglare Stud Stakes and Coronation Stakes), Benvenue (Gran Premio di Milano), the Australasian triple Group 1 winner Turn Me Loose, Hot

Streak (Group 2 Temple Stakes) and the Australasian Group 1 winners Gingernuts and Jon Snow. Standing at Dalham Hall Stud, Newmarket. 2018 *fee:* €40,000.

INTELLO (2010) Galileo – Impressionnante (Danehill). *Racing record:* Won 6 races from 1m to 10.5f at 2 and 3 yrs including the Group 1 French Derby, the Group 3 Prix Messidor and Group 3 Prix du Prince d'Orange. *Stud record:* His first crop of two-year-olds appeared last year and there were 5 winners including the French Listed winner Sonjeu. Standing at Haras du Quesnay. 2018 *fee:* €20,000.

INTIKHAB (1994) Red Ransom – Crafty Example (Crafty Prospector). *Racing record:* 8 wins including the Diomed Stakes and the Queen Anne Stakes. *Stud record:* Sire of 10 Group winners and 14 Listed winners including the outstanding racemare and multiple Group 1 winner Snow Fairy, the Group 1 Lockinge Stakes & Group 1 Matron Stakes winner Red Evie, the Group 1 Criterium de Saint-Cloud winner Paita, the Group 2 Yorkshire Cup winner Glen's Diamond and the Group 3 winners Ascertain, Circus Couture, Hoh Mike, Moon Unit, Tell Dad and Toupie. Died in 2016.

INVINCIBLE SPIRIT (1997) Green Desert – Rafha (Kris). *Racing record:* 7 wins, notably the Group 1 Sprint Cup at 5 yrs. *Stud record:* First runners in 2006. High-class sire of fifteen Group 1 winners namely Charm Spirit (QE II Stakes, Prix Jean Prat & Prix du Moulin), Kingman – four Group 1's including the Sussex Stakes and St James's Palace Stakes), Lawman (French Derby & Prix Jean Prat), Fleeting Spirit (July Cup), Moonlight Cloud (six Group 1's in France), Mayson (July Cup), Hooray & Rosdhu Queen (both Cheveley Park Stakes), National Defense (Prix Jean-Luc Lagardere), Profitable (King's Stand Stakes), Shalaa (Middle Park and Prix Morny), Signs Of Blessing (Prix Maurice de Gheest), Territories (Prix Jean Prat), Vale Of York (Breeders Cup Juvenile) and Yosai (three Group 1 wins in Australia), plus fourteen Group 2 winners – Ajaya, Allied Powers, Cable Bay, Campfire Glow, Captain Marvelous, Conquest, Impassable, Madame Trop Vite, Muthmir, Our Jonathan, Speaking Of Which, Spirit Quartz, Spirit Song and Zebedee. Standing at the Irish National Stud. 2018 *fee:* €120,000.

KINGMAN (2011) Invincible Spirit – Zenda (Zamindar). *Racing record:* Won 7 of his 8 races at 2 and 3 yrs and over 7f and 1m, notably the Irish 2,000 Guineas, St James's Palace Stakes, Sussex Stakes and Prix Jacques le Marois. *Stud record:* His first two-year-olds appear this season. A son of the top-class sire Invincible Spirit and the French 1,000 Guineas winner Zenda, he seems to have had an outstanding first book of mares. Standing at Banstead Manor Stud, Newmarket. 2018 *fee:* £55,000.

KITTEN'S JOY (2001) El Prado – Kitten's First (Lear Fan). *Racing record:* Won 9 races including the Grade 1 10f Secretariat Stakes and the Grade 1 12f Turf Classic. *Stud record:* A leading turf sire in the USA. Sire of 81 stakes winners. His best include Hawkbill (Eclipse Stakes), the Grade 1 Breeders Cup Juvenile Turf winner Oscar Performance and other US Grade 1 winners like Admiral's Kitten, Bobby's Kitten, Big Blue Kitten, Chiropractor, Kitten's Dumplings, Real Solution and Stephanie's Kitten. Standing at Hill 'n' Dale Farm in the USA. 2018 *fee:* $60,000.

KODIAC (2001) Danehill – Rafha (Kris). *Racing record:* Won 4 races here and in the UAE over 6f and 7f including the Datel Trophy and Group 3 placed. *Stud record:* His first runners appeared in 2010 and he's a reliable source of decent class winners with 71 stakes performers (to Feb 2018) They include the champion 2-y-o filly Tiggy Wiggy (Group 1 Cheveley Park Stakes), Group 2 Sandy Lane and Group 2 Hungerford Stakes winner Adaay, Group 2 Flying Childers winner Ardad, Group 2 Lowther Stakes winner Besharah, Group 2 Celebration Mile winner Kodi Bear, Group 2 Norfolk Stakes winner Prince Of Lir and 11 Group 3 winners – Altyn Order, Bear Cheek, Best Solution, Coulsty, Danehill Kodiac, Ellthea, Gifted Master, Jamesie, Koropick, Nebo, Shaden and Spirit Of Xian. Standing at Tally Ho Stud, Ireland. 2017 *fee:* €50,000.

KYLLACHY (1998) Pivotal – Pretty Poppy (Song). *Racing record:* Winner of 6 races including the Group 1 Nunthorpe Stakes at 4 yrs. *Stud record:* First runners in 2006. Sire of the dual Group 1 Nunthorpe Stakes and dual Group 1 King's Stand Stakes winner Sole Power, the Group 1 6f Golden Shaheen winner Krypton Factor, Group 1 Haydock Park Sprint Cup and Group 1 Diamond Jubilee Stakes winner Twilight Son, Hong Kong Group 1 winner Dim Sum, the Group 2 winners Arabian Gleam, Dragon Pulse, Heartache, Penitent, Stepper Point, Supplicant and Tariq and numerous smart performers including Awinnersgame, Befortyfour, Corrybrough, Kachy, Mood Music, Gracia Directa and Noble Hachy. Retired from stud in 2017.

LAWMAN (2004) Invincible Spirit – Laramie (Gulch). *Racing record:* Won four races including the Group 1 Prix du Jockey Club and the Group Prix Jean Prat. *Stud record:* First runners 2011. To date he has five Group 1 winners – Harbour Law (St Leger), Just The Judge (Group 1 Irish 1,000 Guineas, E P Taylor Stakes), Most Improved (Group 1 St James's Palace Stakes), Marcel (Racing Post Trophy) and Law Enforcement (Group 1 Premio Gran Criterium), the Group 2 winners Agnes Stewart (May Hill Stakes) and Libran (in Australia) and the Group 3 winners Forces of Darkness (Prix Minerve), Dicton (Prix de Fontainebleau), Loi (Prix de Conde), Lady Wingshot (Fairy Bridge Stakes), Luminate (Prix de Conde), Nargys (Sceptre Stakes) and US Law (Prix Thomas Bryon). Ballylinch Stud, Ireland. 2017 *fee:* €15,000.

LE HAVRE (2006) Noverre – Marie Rheinberg (Surako). *Racing record:* Won 4 races including the Group 1 10.5f French Derby. *Stud record:* Sire of 3 Group 1 winners from his first 3 crops – French 1,000 Guineas and French Oaks winners Avenir Certain and La Cressonniere and US Grade 1 Shadwell Turf Mile winner Suedois. Also the Group 2 Prix Chaudenay winner Auvray, the 2-y-o Group 3 Prix du Calvados winner Queen Bee, Group 3 Prix Vanteaux winner Zghorta Dance, US Grade 3 winner Rymska and twelve Listed winners including the Group 1 Prix Jean Prat third La Hoguette. Standing at Montfort et Preaux in France. 2018 *fee:* €60,000.

LETHAL FORCE (2009) Dark Angel – Land Army (Desert Style). *Racing record:* Won four races including the Group 1 6f July Cup, the Group 1 6f Diamond Jubilee Stakes and the Group 2 7f Hungerford Stakes. *Stud record:* His first crop of two-year-olds appeared last year and he had 21 winners including the Group 3 placed Mokaatil and Would Be King. Standing at Cheveley Park Stud. 2018 *fee:* £8,000Y.

LILBOURNE LAD (2009) Acclamation – Sogno Verde (Green Desert). *Racing record:* Won 3 races including the Group 2 Railway Stakes. Raced only at 2 yrs. *Stud record:* From three crops he's sired 56 individual winners including 27 two-year-olds, but no stakes winners.

LOPE DE VEGA (2007) Shamardal – Lady Vettori (Vettori). *Racing record:* Won four races from 7f (at 2 yrs) to 11f including the Group 1 French Derby and the Group 1 French 2,000 Guineas. *Stud record:* His first crop were 2-y-o's in 2014. He's built himself a very good reputation and had four Group 1 winners last year alone – Santa Ana Lane (Australia), Vega Magic (Australia), The Right Man (UAE) and Capla Temptress (USA). He has another 14 Group winners to his name – Belardo (Group 1 Dewhurst Stakes), Jemayel (Group 1 Prix Saint-Alary), the Group 2 winners French Fern (in Australia), Hero Look (in Italy) and Very Special (UAE) and the Group/Grade 3 winners Blue De Vega, Burnt Sugar, Candy Store, Navarra King, Ride Like The Wind, Royal Razalma, Soustraction, South Seas and Steel Of Madrid. He also has twelve Listed winners. Standing at Ballylinch Stud, Ireland. 2018 *fee:* €60,000.

MAKFI (2007) Dubawi – Dhelaal (Green Desert). *Racing record:* Won four races, notably the 2,000 Guineas and Prix Jacques le Marois. *Stud record:* His first runners appeared in 2014 and to date (Feb 2018) he has 88 winners to his name including 31 two-year-olds. His best winners to date include the French 2,000 Guineas and Prix de la Foret winner Make Believe, the Australian Group 1 winner Marky Mark, New Zealand Group 2 winner Sofia Rosa, the Group 3 winners Fabricate, Miamara, Mate Story and Noor Al Hawa and several Listed winners including Cornwallville in France. Now standing in Japan.

MASTERCRAFTSMAN (2006) Danehill Dancer – Starlight Dreams (Black Tie Affair). *Racing record:* Won 7 races, notably the Phoenix Stakes, National Stakes, St James's Palace Stakes and Irish 2,000 Guineas (all Group 1 races). *Stud record:* His first two-year-olds appeared in 2013 and he was the leading European first-crop sire with 28 winners. The best of his winners to date are The Grey Gatsby (Group 1 French Derby and Group

1 Irish Champion Stakes), Amazing Maria (Group 1 Falmouth Stakes and Group 1 Prix Rothschild), Kingston Hill (Group 1 Racing Post Trophy and Group 1 St Leger), Off Limita (Grade 1 Matriarch Stakes), Thee Auld Floozie and Valley Girl (Group 1 winners in New Zealand), 6 Group 2 winners including Even Song (Ribblesdale Stakes), the New Zealand Group 2 winners Mime, Sacred Master and Thunder Lady, 16 Group 3 winners including Nakuti, Master Apprentice, Craftsman and Iveagh Gardens. Standing at Coolmore Stud, Ireland. 2018 *fee:* €25,000.

MAXIOS (2008) Monsun – Moonlight's Box (Nureyev). *Racing record:* Won 8 races including the Group 1 9.5f Prix d'Ispahan, the Group 1 1m Prix du Moulin and two Group 3's in France. *Stud record:* A half-brother to the multiple Group 1 winner (including the Prix de l'Arc de Triomphe) Bago. His first runners appeared on the racecourse last season and he had 9 winners including two that were Group 3 placed in Germany. Standing at Gestut Fahrhof. 2018 *fee:* €10,000.

MAYSON (2008) Invincible Spirit – Mayleaf (Pivotal). *Racing record:* Won five races over 5f and 6f, notably the Group 1 July Cup and the Group 3 Abernant Stakes. *Stud record:* His first runners appeared on the racecourse in 2016 and to date he's the sire of 31 2-y-o winners in Britain including the Listed winners Dance Diva, Global Applause (also third in the Group 2 Mill Reef Stakes), Private Matter, Raydiance and Rosie Briar, plus the Group 2 Flying Childers third May Girl and the 2017 £147k Doncaster Weatherbys sales race winner Laugh A Minute. Standing at Cheveley Park Stud, Newmarket. 2018 *fee:* €6,000.

MEDICEAN (1997) Machiavellian – Mystic Goddess (Storm Bird). *Racing record:* 6 wins including the Lockinge Stakes and Eclipse. *Stud record:* His first runners appeared in 2005. Sire of 24 Group winners including ten Group 1 winners – Dutch Art (Prix Morny, Middle Park), Nannina (Fillies' Mile, Coronation Stakes), Capponi, Al Shemali (both Dubai Group 1 winners), Siyouma (Group 1 Sun Chariot Stakes and Group 1 E P Taylor Stakes), Almerita & Neatico (both Group 1 German winners), Chevron (Group 1 Raffles International Cup), Bayrir (Grade 1 Secretariat Stakes) and the Hong Kong Group 1 winner

Mr Medici. His five Group 2 winners are Sapphire (British Champions Fillies and Mares Stakes), Bankable (in the UAE), Manieree (Blandford Stakes), Dimension & Medici Code (both in North America). Retired from stud in 2017.

MORE THAN READY (1997) Southern Halo – Woodman's Girl (Woodman). *Racing record:* Won 7 races in the USA including the Grade 1 7f King's Bishop Stakes and the 2-y-o Grade 2 6f Sanford Stakes. *Stud record:* Sire of 73 Group/Graded stakes winners including 24 Group/Grade 1 winners including Roy H and Rushing Fall (2017 Breeders' Cup winners), Benicio, Buster's Ready, Carry On Cutie, Daredevil, Regally Ready, Room Service, Verrazano (all in North America), Dreamaway, Eagle Way, Entisaar, Gimmethegreenlight, More Joyous, More Than Sacred, Perfectly Ready, Perfect Reflection, Phelan Ready, Prized Icon, Samaready and Sebring (all in Australia/ New Zealand). Standing at WinStar Farm, Kentucky. 2018 *fee:* $75,000.

MORPHEUS (2010) Oasis Dream – Kind (Danehill). *Racing record:* Won 3 races at 3 yrs at around 1m, rated 90, no black-type. *Stud record:* A half-brother to Frankel, this is his first crop. Standing at Tally Ho Stud. 2018 *fee:* €40,000.

MOUNT NELSON (2004) Rock of Gibraltar – Independence (Selkirk). *Racing record:* Won the Group 1 1m Criterium International at 2 yrs and the Group 1 10f Eclipse Stakes. *Stud record:* His first two-year-olds ran in 2012 and in 6 seasons he's had 84 winners on the Flat (22 of them 2-y-o winners). His best runners to date are the Group 1 Qipco Champion Sprint winner Librisa Breeze, Group 2 Royal Lodge Stakes winner Berkshire, Highlands Queen (Group 2 Prix de Pomone), Boscaccio (Group 2 Oppenheim Union-Rennen), the Group 3 Prix du Calvados winner Purr Along, Group 3 Chartwell Stakes winner Emerald Star and 11 Listed winners including the Group 1 placed Elbereth, Mohave Princess and Volume, and the Group 2 placed Holy Moly and Weltmacht. Standing at Boardsmill Stud, Ireland. 2018 *fee:* €5,000.

MUKHADRAM (2009) Shamardal – Magic Tree (Timber Country). *Racing record:* Won 5 races from 1m to 10.5f and from 3 to 5

yrs including the Group 1 Eclipse Stakes, the Group 2 York Stakes and the Group 3 Brigadier Gerard Stakes. *Stud record:* A son of the top-class sire Shamardal, his first runners appear this season. Standing at Nunnery Stud. 2018 *fee:* £7,000.

NATHANIEL (2008) Galileo – Magnificient Style (Silver Hawk). *Racing record:* Won four races notably the Group 1 12f King George VI and Queen Elizabeth Stakes and the Group 1 Eclipse Stakes. *Stud record:* His first two-year-olds appeared on the track in 2016 so he's had two crops racing. To date he's had 37 winners including 11 two-year-olds. The most notable of his winners is the outstanding filly Enable, a winner of five Group 1 events in 2017 including the Oaks, the Arc and the King George VI. He's also had the Group 3 Prix Minerve winner God Given, the Listed winners Chasedown (in Italy), Face The Facts and Natavia, plus the Group 1 German Derby second Enjoy Vijay and the Group 2 Park Hill Stakes second Melodic Motion. Standing at Newsells Park Stud. 2018 *fee:* £20,000.

NEW APPROACH (2005) Galileo – Park Express (Ahonoora). *Racing record:* Won five Group 1 events including the Derby, the Champion Stakes and the Irish Champion Stakes. *Stud record:* His first two-year-olds appeared in 2012. Sire of the champion 2-y-o Dawn Approach (Dewhurst Stakes, National Stakes, 2,000 Guineas, St James's Palace Stakes), Talent (Group 1 Epsom Oaks), Elliptique (German Group 1), May's Dream (Group 1 Australasian Oaks), Sultanina (Group 1 Nassau Stakes), Potemkin (Group 1 Premio Roma), Libertarian (Group 2 Dante Stakes and second in the Derby), Beautiful Romance (Group 2 Middleton Stakes), Strathspey (Group 2 Prix de Malleret), Connecticut (Group 2 in Turkey), Herald The Dawn (Group 2 Futurity Stakes), Messi (Grade 2 Sky Classic Stakes), Nearly Caught (Group 2 Prix Kergorlay), New Predator (two Group 2's in Australia) and 9 Group 3 winners including Masar (Solario Stakes), Cap O'Rushes (Gordon Stakes), Newfangled (Albany Stakes), Veneto (in Germany), Montsegure, Sword Of Light and Gamblin' Guru (all in Australia). Standing at Dalham Hall Stud, Newmarket. 2018 *fee:* £30,000.

NOBLE MISSION (2009) Galileo – Kind (Danehill). *Racing record:* Won 9 races from

1m to 12f and from 3 to 5 yrs including the Tattersalls Gold Cup, the Grand Prix de Saint-Cloud and the Champion Stakes. *Stud record:* A full-brother to Frankel, his first crop are now two-year-olds. Standing at Lane's End Farm, Kentucky. 2018 *fee:* $20,000.

NO NAY NEVER (2011) Scat Daddy – Cat's Eye Witness (Elusive Quality). *Racing record:* Won four of his six starts at 2 and 3 yrs and from 4.5f to 6f including the Group 1 Prix Morny, the Group 2 Norfolk Stakes and also second in the Grade 1 Breeders' Cup Turf Sprint. *Stud record:* His sire Scat Daddy won two Grade 1 events in the USA and has an excellent reputation as a sire of speedy horses. Standing at Coolmore Stud, Ireland. 2018 *fee:* €25,000.

OASIS DREAM (2001) Green Desert – Hope (Dancing Brave). *Racing record:* Won four races including the Middle Park Stakes, July Cup and Nunthorpe Stakes (all Group 1 events). *Stud record:* His first crop of two-year-olds appeared in 2007 and he's built himself a top-class reputation. He has the winners of 25 Group 1 races including Aqlaam (Prix du Moulin), Arcano (Prix Morny), Charming Thought (Middle Park Stakes), Goldream (King's Stand Stakes & Prix de l'Abbaye), Jwala (Nunthorpe Stakes), Lady Jane Digby (in Germany), Midday (six Group/Grade One's including the Nassau Stakes, Prix Vermeille and Breeders Cup Filly & Mare Turf), Muarrab (Golden Shaheen), Muhaarar (July Cup, Commonwealth Cup and British Champions Sprint and Prix Maurice De Gheest), Naaqoos (Prix Jean-Luc Lagardere), Opinion (in Australia), Power (National Stakes & Irish 2,000 Guineas), Prohibit (King's Stand Stakes), Querari (in Italy) and Tuscan Evening (US Gamely Handicap). His Group 2 scorers include Approve, Folega (in Italy), Frozen Power, Misheer, Monitor Closely, Peace At Last, Quiet Oasis (in USA), Showcasing and Sri Putra. Standing at Banstead Manor Stud, Newmarket. 2018 *fee:* £30,000.

OLYMPIC GLORY (2010) Choisir – Acidanthera (Alzao). *Racing record:* Won 8 races from 6f to 1m and from 2 to 4 yrs including four Group 1's (Prix Jean-Luc Lagardere, Queen Elizabeth II Stakes, Lockinge Stakes and Prix de la Foret. *Stud record:* His first crop of foals are two-year-olds this year.

Standing at Haras de Bouquetot. 2018 *fee:* €12,000.

PACO BOY (2005) Desert Style – Tappen Zee (Sandhurst Prince). *Racing record:* Won 10 races from 6f to 1m including the Group 1 Prix de la Foret, Queen Anne Stakes and Lockinge Stakes. *Stud record:* From four crops he has the winners of 208 races (to Feb 2018) including the Group 1 2,000 Guineas and Group 1 St James's Palace Stakes winner Galileo Gold, the Group 2 Flying Childers winner Beacon, Group 2 Joel Stakes winner Beat The Bank, the Group 3 winners Smaih and Rainbow Royal (in Italy) and the Listed winners Lexington Times, Making Trouble (in Germany), Peacock and Stella Di Paco (in New Zealand). Now standing in Turkey.

PASTORAL PURSUITS (2001) Bahamian Bounty – Star (Most Welcome). *Racing record:* Won 6 races including the Group 1 6f July Cup, Group 2 7f Park Stakes and Group 3 6f Sirenia Stakes. *Stud record:* His first crop appeared as 2-y-o's in 2009 and his best winners to date are Pastoral Player (Group 3 John of Gaunt Stakes), Rose Blossom (Group 3 Summer Stakes), Ipompieridiviggiu (Group 3 Premio Primi Passi), the Listed winners Angel's Pursuit, Catalina Bay (in Italy), Lightscameraction, Marine Commando, Perfect Pasture, Rooke (in France), Spiritual Lady, Terra Di Tuffi (in Germany) and Ventura Mist, and the Group 2 placed Louie de Palma and Kibaar. Standing at Norton Grove Stud. 2018 *fee:* £2,000.

PIVOTAL (1993) Polar Falcon – Fearless Revival (Cozzene). *Racing record:* 4 wins including the Nunthorpe Stakes and King's Stand Stakes. *Stud record:* His first runners appeared in 2000. An outstanding sire of 26 Group 1 winners. Among the best of them are African Story (Dubai World Cup), Excellent Art (St James's Palace Stakes), Falco (French 2,000 Guineas), Farhh (Champion Stakes & Lockinge Stakes), Golden Apples (triple US Grade 1 winner), Halfway To Heaven (Irish 1,00 Guineas, Nassau Stakes and Sun Chariot Stakes), Immortal Verse (dual Group 1 winning miler), Kyllachy (Nunthorpe Stakes), Maarek (Prix de l'Abbaye), Regal Parade (Haydock Sprint Cup), Sariska (Oaks and Irish Oaks) and Somnus (Sprint Cup, Prix de la Foret, Prix Maurice de Gheest). Other top performers of his include Brando (Group 1 Prix Maurice de Gheest), Captain Rio (Group 2 Criterium des Maisons-Laffitte), Chorist (Group 1 Pretty Polly Stakes), Izzi Top (Group 1 Prix Jean Romanet and Pretty Polly Stakes), Lightning Spear (Group 2 Celebration Mile), Megahertz (two US Grade 1 events), Peeress (Lockinge Stakes, Sun Chariot Stakes), Pivotal Point (Group 2 Diadem Stakes), Saoire (Irish 1000 Guineas), Silvester Lady (German Oaks), Virtual (Lockinge Stakes) and Siyouni (2-y-o Group 1 Prix Jean-Luc Lagardere). Standing at Cheveley Park Stud, Newmarket. 2018 *fee*: £40,000.

POET'S VOICE (2007) Dubawi – Bright Tiara (Chief's Crown). *Racing record:* Won 4 races over 7f and a mile, and at 2 and 3 yrs, notably the Group 1 Queen Elizabeth II Stakes, the Group 2 Champagne Stakes (at 2 yrs) and the Group 2 Celebration Mile. *Stud record:* His first crop were two-year-olds in 2015 and from three crops he has 87 winners, 50 of them being two-year-olds (to Feb 2018). They include the Group 2 winners Poet's Vanity (in Germany) and Viridine (in Australia), Group 3 Glorious Stakes winner and Champion Stakes second Poet's Word, Group 3 Oh So Sharp Stakes winner Poet's Vanity, the Italian Group 3 winners Mi Raccomando, Posta Diletto and Voice Of Love and five Listed winners. Plenty of winners then, but still waiting for anything better than a Group 3 win in England, Ireland or France. Standing at Dalham Hall Stud in Newmarket. 2018 *fee*: £6,000.

POWER (2009) Oasis Dream – Frappe (Inchinor). *Racing record:* Won 5 races from 5f to 1m including the Group 1 National Stakes, the Group 2 Coventry Stakes (both at 2 yrs) and the Group 1 Irish 2,000 Guineas. *Stud record:* His first crop were two-year-olds in 2016 and from two crops he's had 27 winners including 16 two-year-olds (to Feb 2018). They include four stakes winners in Europe – Peace Envoy (Group 3 Anglesey Stakes), Pleaseletmewin (Group 3 Horris Hill Stakes), Cristal Fizz (Listed Radley Stakes) and Biz Power (Listed winner and Group 3 placed in Italy). He also has the New Zealand Listed winner Gift Of Power. Now at stud in Australia.

RAVEN'S PASS (2005) Elusive Quality – Ascutney (Lord At War). *Racing record:* Won 6 races, notably the Group 1 1m Queen Elizabeth II Stakes and the Grade 1 10f

Breeders Cup Classic. *Stud record:* His first crop of two-year-olds appeared in 2012. To date (Feb 2018) he has 120winners including 60 two-year-olds. There are five Group 2 winners – Richard Pankhurst (Hungerford Stakes), Steeler (Royal Lodge Stakes), Secret Number (Bosphorus Cup and also Group 3 Cumberland Lodge), Swashbuckling (in Australia) and Tower Of London (in Japan). Four Group 3 winners – Malabar (Prestige Stakes & the Thoroughbred Stakes), Kataniya (Prix de Royaumont), Greg Pass (in Italy) and Vis Ravenna (Prix Imprudence), plus 16 Listed winners including the Group placed Aquila Solitaria (in Italy), Elas Ruby, Force, Ibn Malik, Lovely Pass (in the UAE), Rosay and Viscount Barfield. Standing at Kildangan Stud, Ireland. 2018 *fee*: €10,000.

RED JAZZ (2007) Johannesburg – Now That's Jazz (Sword Dance). *Racing record:* Won 5 races including the Group 2 Challenge Stakes, the Listed Free Handicap and the Listed Spring Trophy. Also placed in nine Group races including when third in the Group 1 Queen Elizabeth II Stakes. *Stud record:* His first crop of two-year-olds appeared last season and he had a fairly decent start with 15 winners including the Tattersalls Ireland Sales race winner Snazzy Jazzy, but no stakes winners. Standing at Ballyhane Stud in Ireland. 2018 *fee*: €5,000.

REQUINTO (2009) Dansili – Damson (Entrepreneur). *Racing record:* Only ran at 2 yrs and won four races including the Group 2 5f Flying Childers Stakes and the Group 3 5f Molecomb Stakes. *Stud record:* His first crop appeared in 2016 and to date (Feb 2018) he's had 24 winners including 18 two-year-olds, but only one black-type performer (Broken Stones was third in the Group 2 July Stakes). Standing at Coolmore Stud, Ireland. 2018 *fee*: €5,000.

RIP VAN WINKLE (2006) Galileo – Looking Back (Stravinsky). *Racing record:* Won five races from 7f (at 2 yrs) to 10f including the Sussex Stakes, Queen Elizabeth II Stakes and Juddmonte International (all Group 1 events). *Stud record:* His first 2-y-o's ran in 2014 and to date his best have been Dick Whittington (Group 1 Phoenix Stakes), Creggs Pipes (Group 2 Lanwades Stud Fillies' & Mares Stakes), the New Zealand Group 2 winner Capella, The

Magic Prince (Group 3 Renaissance Stakes) and the New Zealand Group 3 winners Euro Angel, First Impressions, I Am Beautiful and Magic Dancer. Now at stud in Australia.

ROCK OF GIBRALTAR (1999) Danehill – Offshore Boom (Be My Guest). *Racing record:* Won seven Group 1 races including the Dewhurst Stakes, 2,000 Guineas, St James's Palace Stakes and Sussex Stakes. *Stud record:* The sire of over 300 individual winners including 100 two-year-olds. The best of his progeny are the Group/Grade 1 winners Diamondrella (in the USA), Eagle Mountain (in Hong Kong), Mount Nelson (Eclipse and Criterium International), Samitar (Irish 1,000 Guineas and Garden City Stakes), Prince Gibraltar (Criterium de Saint-Cloud), dual Group 1 winning sprinter Society Rock and Varenar (Prix de la Foret). Standing at Coolmore Stud, Ireland. 2018 *fee:* €7,500.

RODERIC O'CONNOR (2008) Galileo – Secret Garden (Danehill). *Racing record:* Won 3 races, notably the Group 1 1m Grand Criterium (at 2 yrs) and the Group 1 Irish 2,000 Guineas. *Stud record:* His first crop were two-year-olds in 2015 and in three crops he's had 40 winners, 21 of them two-year-olds. There are 7 Group winners to his name. They include El Shaklan (Grade 1 in Brazil), Biz Heart (Italian Group 2 Premio Gran Criterium) and Great Page (Group 3 Prix du Calvados). He also has the Listed winners Connect, Haalick, Hikmaa and Narnia Dawn.

SCAT DADDY (2004) Johannesburg – Love Style (Mr Prospector). *Racing record:* Won four Graded Stakes from 6f to 9f and at 2 and 3 yrs notably the Grade 1 Champagne Stakes (at 2 yrs) and the Grade 1 Florida Derby. *Stud record:* His best winners to date include 11 Group 1 winners in South America, plus Caravaggio (Group 1 Phoenix Stakes, Group 1 Commonwealth Cup), Celestine (US Grade 1 Just A Game Stakes), Harmonize (Grade 1 Del Mar Oaks), Lady Aurelia (Group 1 Prix Morny, Group 1 King's Stand Stakes), Mendelssohn (Grade 1 Breeders' Cup Juvenile Turf), No Nay Never (Group 1 Morny and Group 2 Norfolk Stakes), Lady Of Shamrock (US dual Grade 1 winner), Sioux Nation (Group 1 Phoenix Stakes and Nickname (US Grade 1 Beldame Stakes), plus numerous Group/Grade 2 winners including Acapulco (Queen

Mary Stakes), Daddy Long Legs (Royal Lodge Stakes), Seahenge (Champagne Stakes) and in the USA Azar, Conquest Daddyo, Dice Flavor, Handsome Mike, El Kabeir, Frac Daddy and Pretty N Cool. Died in 2015 at Ashford Stud, Kentucky after his fee had been raised to $100,000 from $35,000.

SEA THE MOON (2011) Sea The Stars – Sanwa (Monsun). *Racing record:* Won his only start at 2 yrs in Germany over 1m, then three Group races as a 3-y-o, notably the Group 1 12f German Derby. *Stud record:* By the top-class racehorse and sire, Sea The Stars, his first two-year-olds appear this season. Standing at Lanwades Stud, Newmarket. 2018 *fee:* £15,000.

SEA THE STARS (2006) Cape Cross – Urban Sea (Miswaki). *Racing record:* Outstanding winner of 9 races including the Derby, 2,000 Guineas, Prix de L'Arc de Triomphe, Irish Champion Stakes, Juddmonte International Stakes and Eclipse Stakes. *Stud record:* His first two-year-olds appeared in 2013 and to date he's had eight Group 1 winners. They are Cloth Of Stars (Prix Ganay), Harzand (Derby and Irish Derby), Mekhtaal (Prix d'Ispahan), Sea The Moon (German Derby), Stradivarius (Goodwood Cup), Taghrooda (Oaks and King George VI), Vazira (Prix Saint-Alary) and Zelzal (Prix Jean Prat), along with five Group 2 winners – Across The Stars, Armande, Endless Time, Mutakayyef and Storm The Stars, plus twelve Group 3 and 20 Listed winners. Standing at Gilltown Stud, Ireland. 2018 *fee:* €135,000.

SEPOY (2008) Elusive Quality – Watchful (Danehill). *Racing record:* A champion 2-y-o and 3-y-o in Australia, he won four Group 1 sprints at 2 and 3 yrs. *Stud record:* His first northern hemisphere two-year-olds appeared in 2016 and from two crops and he's had 44 winners (24 of them as two-year-olds) to Feb 2018. They include Alizee (Australian Group 1 winner), Unforgetable Filly (Group 2 German 1,000 Gns), Dabyah (Group 3 Fred Darling winner and Group 1 third), Kilmah (Group 3 Prestige Stakes) and three Listed winners. Standing at Dalham Hall Stud, Ireland. 2018 *fee:* €8,000 (almost half his 2017 fee).

SHAMARDAL (2002) Giant's Causeway – Helsinki (Machiavellian). *Racing record:* Won the Dewhurst Stakes, French 2,000 Guineas, French Derby and St James's Palace Stakes (all Group 1 events). *Stud record:* Sire of 133 two-year-old winners in his first nine crops. He has 18 Group 1 winners including Able Friend (four Group 1's in Hong Kong), Baltic Baroness (Prix Vermeille), Casamento (Racing Post Trophy), Dariyan (Prix Ganay), Lope De Vega (French 2,000 Guineas and French Derby), Lumiere (Cheveley Park Stakes), Mukhadram (Eclipse Stakes), Sagawara (Prix Saint-Alary), Speedy Boarding (Prix Jean Romanet and Prix de l'Opera) and Dunboyne Express (renamed 'Dan Excel' in Hong Kong). His 40 Group 2/ Group 3 winners include the Group 1 placed Alrahma, Blue Point, Fintry, Ihtimal, Lucida, Mukhadram No Evidence Needed and Puissance de Lune (both in Australia), Elle Shadow and Royal Solitaire (both in Germany). Standing at Kildangan Stud, Ireland. 2018 *fee:* Private (was €70,000 in 2015).

SHOWCASING (2007) Oasis Dream – Arabesque (Zafonic). *Racing record:* Won 2 races at 2 yrs including the Group 2 6f Gimcrack Stakes. *Stud record:* He's had an excellent start with a total of 13 Group and 10 Listed winners plus 70 individual two-year-old winners from his first three European crops. They include Quiet Reflection (Group 1 Haydock Park Sprint Cup, Group 1 Commonwealth Cup), Prize Exhibit (two Grade 2's and two Grade 3's in the USA), Showboy (Group 2 in New Zealand), Projected (US Grade 2), Tasleet (Group 2 Duke Of York Stakes), Toocoolforschool (Group 2 Mill Reef Stakes), Xpression (Group 2 in NZ), Cappella Sansevero (Group 3 Round Tower Stakes winner and Group 1 third) and Caorunn (2-y-o Group 3 in New Zealand). Standing at Whitsbury Manor Stud. 2018 *fee:* £35,000.

SIR PERCY (2003) Mark of Esteem – Percy's Lass (Blakeney). *Racing record:* A champion 2-y-o, he won five races notably the Derby and the Dewhurst Stakes. *Stud record:* His first runners appeared in 2011 and he's had 58 two-year-old winners to date (Feb 2018). Sire of 7 Group winners – Sir John Hawkwood (Group 1 in Australia), Wake Forest (Grade 1 Man O'War Stakes), Alyssa (Group 2 Park Hill Stakes), Lady Tiana (Group 2 Lancashire Oaks), Sir Andrew (Group 2 in New Zealand), Alla Speranza (Group 3 Kilternan Stakes), Lady

Pimpernel (US Grade 3) and eleven Listed winners including the Group 2 Royal Lodge Stakes second Nafaqa and the Group 2 Queen Mary Stakes third Newsletter. Standing at Lanwades Stud, Newmarket. 2018 *fee:* £7,000.

SIR PRANCEALOT (2010) Tamayuz – Mona Em (Catrail). *Racing record:* Only ran at 2 yrs and won 3 of his 6 sprint races including the Group 2 Flying Childers Stakes and the Listed National Stakes. Also second in the Group 2 Prix Robert Papin. *Stud record:* His first runners appeared in 2016 and he's had 37 two-year-old winners to date (Feb 2018). His stakes horses are few and far between however and his best runners are Madam Dancealot (Group 3 Dick Poole Stakes) and Sir Dancealot (Listed Rockingham Stakes). Standing in Australia.

SIXTIES ICON (2003) Galileo – Love Divine (Diesis). *Racing record:* Won eight races including the Group 1 St Leger, the Group 2 Jockey Club Cup and four other Group events. *Stud record:* His first runners appeared in 2012 and he's the sire of the winners of 131 races on the Flat from 5f to 14f (to Feb 2018) including 35 individual two-year-olds. His best performers include the South American Grade 1 winners Crazy Icon and Sixties Song, the US Grade 2 Royal Heroine Stakes winner Nancy From Nairobi, Group 3 winners Chilworth Icon, Czabo and Epsom Icon, Listed winners Audacia and Cruck Realta, along with the useful Group 3 placed Harrison and the Listed-placed Effie B and Nakeeta. Standing at Norman Court Stud, Wiltshire. 2018 *fee:* £5,000.

SIYOUNI (2007) Pivotal – Sichilla (Danehill). *Racing record:* Won four races at 2 yrs including the Group 1 7f Prix Jean-Luc Lagardere. Placed in two Group 1 events in France at 3. *Stud record:* With four racing so far he has built himself a very good reputation and his stud fee has soared as a result. His best runners to date are the triple Group 1 winner Ervedya (Coronation Stakes, French 1,000 Guineas, Prix du Moulin), Laurens (Group 1 Fillies' Mile), Volta (Group 2 Prix de Sandringham) and the Group 3 winners Bourree, Finsbury Square, Le Brivido, Sacred Life, Siyoushake, Souvenir Delondres, Spectre and Trixia. Standing at Haras de Bonneval. 2018 *fee:* €75,000.

SLADE POWER (2009) Dutch Art – Girl Power (Key Of Luck). *Racing record:* Won ten sprint races from 2 to 5 yrs notably the Group 1 6f Diamond Jubilee and the Group 1 6f July Cup (both as a five-year-old). *Stud record:* His first two-year-olds appear this season. Standing at Kildangan Stud, Ireland. 2018 *fee:* €15,000.

SOCIETY ROCK (2007) Rock Of Gibraltar – High Society (Key Of Luck). *Racing record:* A winner of 6 races over 6f from 2 to 6 yrs, notably the Group 1 Golden Jubilee Stakes and the Group 1 Haydock Park Sprint Cup. *Stud record:* His first two-year-olds appeared last season and he had an excellent tally of 25 individual winners including Unfortunately (Group 1 Prix Morny), the Group 3 placed Corinthia Knight and Tangled, plus the Listed-placed So Hi Society. Died in 2016, stood at Tally Ho Stud for €6,000.

SO YOU THINK (2006) High Chaparral – Triassic (NZ) (Tights). *Racing record:* Won 14 races in Australia, Ireland and England from 7f to 10.5f including an outstanding ten Group 1's, e.g. the Coral Eclipse Stakes, Prince Of Wales's Stakes, Irish Champion Stakes and the Tattersalls Gold Cup (twice). *Stud record:* His first two-year-olds in the northern hemisphere appeared last season but he had very few winners. He has two Group 1 winners in Australia (Inference and La Bella Diosa) and the New Zealand Group 2 winner Gold Rush – all at 3 yrs. Now standing in Australia.

STYLE VENDOME (2010) Anabaa – Place Vendome (Dr Fong). *Racing record:* Won five races including the Group 1 French 2,000 Guineas, the Group 3 Prix Djebel and two Listed events. *Stud record:* His first crop were 2-y-o's last season and to dae (Feb 2018) he has 9 minor winners in France. Standing Haras de Bouquetot. 2018 *fee:* €5,000.

TEOFILO (2004) Galileo – Speirbhhean (Danehill). *Racing record:* Won 5 races at 2 yrs including the Group 1 Dewhurst Stakes and the Group 1 National Stakes. *Stud record:* His first runners appeared in 2011 and he has 38 Group winners so far, including 14 Group 1 winners – Ajman Princess (Prix Jean Romanet), Parish Hall (Dewhurst Stakes), Havana Gold (Prix Jean Prat), Loch Garman (Criterium International), Pleascach (Irish 1,000 Guineas & Yorkshire Oaks), Quest For More (Prix du

Cadran), Trading Leather (Irish Derby), Happy Clapper, Humidor, Kermadek, Palentino & Sonntag (all in Australia), Special Fighter (Al Maktoum Challenge) and Voleuse De Coeurs (Irish St Leger), plus 8 Group/Grade 2 winners including the US Grade 1 placed Amira's Prince, the Group 1 Sussex Stakes second Arod, the Irish Derby third Light Heavy and Oaks second Tarfasha. Standing at Kildangan Stud, Ireland. 2018 *fee:* €40,000.

TORONADO (2010) High Chaparral – Wana Doo (Grand Slam). *Racing record:* Won 6 races from 6.5f to 1m and from 2 to 4 yrs, notably the Group 1 Sussex Stakes and the Group 1 Queen Anne Stakes. *Stud record:* His first crop are now two-year-olds. Standing at Haras de Bouquetot. 2018 *fee:* €12,000.

WAR COMMAND (2011) War Front – Wandering Star (Red Ransom). *Racing record:* Won four races over 6f and 7f as a two-year-old, notably the Group 1 Dewhurst Stakes, the Group 2 Coventry Stakes and the Group 2 Futurity Stakes. *Stud record:* By the top-class sire War Front, he is a half-brother to the 2-y-o Group 3 winner Naval Officer. His first foals are now two-year-olds. Standing at Coolmore Stud, Ireland. 2018 *fee:* €8,000.

WAR FRONT (2003) Danzig – Starry Dreamer (Rubiano). Race record: Won four races at 3 and 4 yrs including the Grade 2 6f Alfred G Vanderbilt Breeders Cup Handicap at Saratoga. *Stud record:* One of the world's top sires, in his first six crops he has sired sixteen Group 1/Grade 1 winners – Air Force Blue, War Command (both winners of the Group 1 Dewhurst Stakes), Brave Anna (Cheveley Park Stakes), Declaration Of War (Juddmonte International, Queen Anne Stakes), Roly Poly (Falmouth Stakes, Prix Rothschild and Sun Chariot), US Navy Flag (Middle Park Stakes & Dewhurst Stakes), American Patriot, Avenge, Data Link, Hit It A Bomb, Jack Milton, Peace And War, Summer Soiree, The Factor, War Flag (all in the USA) and Lines Of Battle (in Hong Kong). Also, he has eleven Group/Grade 2 winners – Bashart, Cambodia, Departing, On Leave, Pontchatrain, Soldat, Spirit Of Valor, State Of Play, Summer Front, War Dancer and War Decree, plus ten Group 3 winners. Standing at Claiborne Farm, Kentucky. 2018 *fee:* $250,000.

ZEBEDEE (2008) Invincible Spirit – Cozy Maria (Cozzene). *Racing record:* Won 6 races over 5f and 6f as a 2-y-o including the Group 2 Flying Childers Stakes, the Group 3 Molecomb Stakes and the Listed Dragon Stakes. *Stud record:* His first runners appeared in 2014 when he was the champion first season sire with 32 winners. The best of his runners include the dual Group 2 winner Ivawood, the Group 2 Duke Of York Stakes winner and Group 1 Sprint Cup third Magical Memory, group 2 winners Barraquero and Spring Loaded, Italian Listed winner and Group 2 Italian Derby second Dee Dee D'Or and the Group 3 placed Manaafidh and Parsley. Sire of the winners of 272 races to date and 82 individual two-year-old winners (Feb 2018). Now in Australia.

ZOFFANY (2008) Dansili – Tyranny (Machiavellian). *Racing record:* Won 5 races as a 2-y-o including the Group 1 6f Phoenix Stakes and the Group 3 7f Tyros Stakes. *Stud record:* His first crop were two-year-olds in 2015 and with three crops racing he's had a good start with 52 individual two-year-old winners (to Feb 2018). His best performers to date are the Group 1 Gran Premio del Jockey Club winner Ventura Storm, the Group 2 winners Foundation, Illuminate, Knife Edge, Waterloo Bridge and Zodiac Ruler (in South Africa), the Irish Group 3 winners Dolce Straga and Washington DC, and five Listed winners. Standing at Coolmore Stud in Ireland. 2018 *fee:* €25,000.

SIRES INDEX

Coach House	371, 911, 962, 1573, 1651
Compton Place	1474, 1477, 1671
Congrats	396
Dabirsim	48, 339, 1621
Dalakhani	746, 1115, 1622
Dandy Man	441, 483, 491, 550, 570, 749, 803, 810, 827, 880, 915, 918, 954, 1037, 1064, 1070, 1138, 1234, 1241, 1424, 1472, 1519, 1528, 1549, 1640, 1654
Dansili	98, 174, 190, 197, 334, 350, 353, 357, 406, 459, 635, 674, 686, 1009, 1023, 1169, 1296, 1362, 1503, 1571, 1607, 1674, 1691, 1699
Dark Angel	16, 43, 50, 125, 126, 143, 221, 224, 225, 232, 233, 250, 268, 275, 340, 344, 402, 439, 456, 462, 468, 474, 482, 564, 579, 581, 625, 656, 673, 694, 704, 710, 716, 718, 741, 780, 783, 794, 797, 816, 830, 849, 854, 871, 874, 897, 902, 907, 920, 921, 924, 946, 947, 951, 970, 1006, 1020, 1071, 1076, 1088, 1107, 1173, 1202, 1227, 1279, 1320, 1338, 1383, 1401, 1458, 1490, 1556, 1575, 1618, 1627, 1638, 1660, 1681, 1687, 1697
Data Link	513
Dawn Approach	165, 194, 206, 207, 208, 212, 364, 378, 381, 400, 419, 421, 422, 1002, 1318, 1367, 1447, 1529
Declaration Of War	144, 472, 1185, 1259, 1317, 1363
Deep Impact	1311
Delegator	119
Dialed In	392
Discreet Cat	1162
Dragon Pulse	319, 361, 479, 488, 493, 594, 717, 877, 1295
Dream Ahead	19, 542, 543, 562, 576, 1011, 1013, 1251, 1253, 1260, 1398, 1485, 1625
Dubawi	9, 37, 76, 146, 173, 187, 203, 261, 266, 274, 330, 405, 411, 412, 417, 418, 431, 435, 437, 524, 623, 629, 637, 645, 648, 665, 680, 692, 706, 719, 764, 939, 950, 1014, 1026, 1028, 1113, 1219, 1303, 1306, 1323, 1334, 1426, 1500, 1511, 1512, 1518, 1568, 1587, 1588, 1594, 1597, 1598, 1599, 1605, 1615, 1632, 1673, 1682, 1689, 1693, 1695
Dunaden	1153
Dutch Art	36, 130, 191, 230, 286, 293, 520, 536, 580, 586, 587, 744, 986, 988, 1019, 1027, 1052, 1151, 1326, 1407, 1414, 1443, 1558
Elusive City	790
Elusive Quality	252, 501
Elzaam	256, 569, 585, 778, 1069, 1476, 1685
English Channel	218
Epaulette	223, 288, 444, 595, 615
Equiano	365, 379, 497, 533, 973
Es Que Love	308, 1033
Exceed And Excel	6, 31, 148, 150, 175, 176, 217, 272, 354, 399, 425, 481, 720, 726, 891, 938, 945, 1073, 1087, 1102, 1116, 1275, 1309, 1371, 1422, 1425, 1542, 1570, 1572

Excelebration	11, 222, 460, 603, 774, 1396
Exchange Rate	13, 17
Famous Name	600
Farhh	159, 184, 228, 578, 763, 825, 1544, 1545
Fast Company	40, 62, 313, 1238, 1656
First Defence	346, 905, 1291, 1322
Footstepsinthesand	505, 563, 826, 1075, 1146, 1353, 1672
Foxwedge	391, 1405, 1431, 1565
Frankel	44, 57, 74, 97, 115, 177, 331, 336, 352, 470, 643, 646, 652, 688, 721, 776, 855, 1100, 1101, 1237, 1294, 1505, 1509, 1579, 1639, 1641
Gale Force Ten	372, 389, 873, 1223, 1285, 1399, 1665
Galileo	7, 659, 666, 670, 679, 739, 753, 1021, 1056, 1175, 1176, 1179, 1180, 1182, 1189, 1190, 1191, 1192, 1196, 1201, 1209, 1214, 1215, 1216, 1217, 1277, 1379, 1413, 1488, 1696
Garswood	51, 171, 172, 238, 271, 567, 572, 573, 575, 589, 599, 607, 788, 802, 904, 989, 1378, 1644
Giant's Causeway	359, 1059
Gregorian	292, 300, 317, 366, 448, 614, 618, 1297, 1395
Hannouma	528
Harbour Watch	170, 281, 1103, 1121, 1439
Hard Spun	1010
Havana Gold	52, 77, 231, 245, 253, 454, 620, 703, 807, 1041, 1105, 1150, 1418, 1437, 1593, 1670
Heeraat	285, 303, 367, 370, 485, 697, 791, 835, 838, 919, 1390, 1393
Hellvelyn	610, 1127
Helmet	229, 469, 486, 853, 888, 964, 995, 1003, 1155, 1416, 1647
Henrythenavigator	32
Holy Roman Emperor	118, 689, 983, 996, 1240, 1357, 1496, 1498
Iffraaj	10, 15, 45, 79, 81, 136, 152, 188, 189, 282, 356, 436, 478, 480, 538, 596, 660, 682, 730, 766, 771, 818, 881, 912, 1008, 1025, 1060, 1099, 1108, 1225, 1239, 1314, 1319, 1321, 1400, 1453, 1475, 1527, 1531, 1584, 1610, 1646
Intello	54, 278, 438, 503, 1130, 1429, 1446, 1502, 1582, 1661
Intikhab	121, 156
Into Mischief	1174
Invincible Spirit	14, 55, 85, 179, 262, 265, 403, 509, 626, 631, 651, 663, 671, 675, 722, 769, 809, 883, 884, 895, 899, 923, 987, 1007, 1074, 1104, 1188, 1345, 1360, 1555, 1583, 1653, 1678, 1679, 1680
Justin Phillip	385
Kendargent	22, 745, 1080, 1254, 1586
Kingman	28, 42, 60, 68, 107, 116, 234, 257, 335, 349, 351, 409, 502, 593, 622, 628, 639, 644, 653, 655, 661, 664, 668, 676, 693, 713, 890, 1301, 1335, 1347, 1409, 1412, 1459, 1501, 1510, 1538, 1580, 1675, 1688

Kitten's Joy	255, 677, 1577
Kodiac	82, 91, 105, 132, 141, 182, 235, 236, 246, 247, 254, 259, 267, 301, 342, 387, 397, 407, 461, 466, 499, 518, 521, 604, 616, 658, 691, 714, 724, 733, 800, 833, 837, 845, 866, 867, 868, 875, 876, 885, 898, 906, 908, 926, 928, 930, 933, 934, 957, 958, 960, 991, 1036, 1082, 1083, 1086, 1141, 1187, 1298, 1337, 1350, 1354, 1415, 1449, 1506, 1526, 1581, 1591, 1613, 1652, 1690
Kuroshio	283, 606, 922, 1124, 1478
Kyllachy	290, 453, 512, 588, 591, 799, 844, 917, 937, 965, 1045, 1154, 1261, 1666
Lawman	20, 168, 199, 798, 975, 1117, 1315, 1451, 1482, 1611
Le Havre	75, 138, 430, 743, 786, 901, 903, 1380
Lemon Drop Kid	1541
Leroidesanimaux	59, 383, 1029, 1368, 1554
Lethal Force	284, 311, 571, 577, 582, 762, 910, 959, 1049, 1128, 1144, 1642
Lilbourne Lad	1159
Lope De Vega	47, 65, 83, 87, 92, 95, 100, 101, 102, 113, 161, 227, 345, 373, 410, 429, 498, 624, 657, 669, 672, 736, 747, 756, 781, 931, 955, 1017, 1032, 1054, 1257, 1263, 1266, 1366, 1435, 1537, 1569, 1606, 1608
Magician	565, 1181
Makfi	1479, 1483
Mastercraftsman	30, 78, 90, 94, 124, 140, 142, 684, 882, 896, 985, 1112, 1132, 1256, 1375, 1434, 1444, 1619, 1623, 1624, 1630, 1637
Maxios	508, 712
Mayson	244, 544, 568, 584, 943, 1062, 1299, 1327
Medaglia d'Oro	180, 226, 1499, 1546, 1692
Medicean	1343
Mizzen Mast	1077
Monsieur Bond	1097, 1106
Moohaajim	515, 940, 1525
More Than Ready	216, 408, 1403
Morpheus	139, 446, 1522
Mount Nelson	1158
Mukhadram	239, 260, 263, 322, 329, 517, 727, 1352, 1481
Nathaniel	33, 88, 106, 114, 597, 662, 813, 822, 978, 982, 1031, 1156, 1281, 1300, 1305, 1328, 1389, 1669
Nayef	333
New Approach	12, 193, 195, 202, 204, 416, 458, 549, 641, 707, 847, 927, 929, 935, 1149, 1308, 1312, 1442, 1535, 1539, 1540, 1601, 1602, 1603, 1604, 1650
No Nay Never	53, 129, 164, 424, 440, 476, 525, 678, 754, 812, 832, 864, 893, 914, 971, 1095, 1163, 1170, 1177, 1197, 1200, 1207, 1208, 1224, 1229, 1233, 1249, 1262, 1269, 1344, 1388, 1404, 1445, 1486, 1487, 1492
Noble Mission	109, 683, 1419
Norse Dancer	72, 553, 554

Sir Percy	279, 583, 695, 980, 1421, 1552
Sir Prancealot	492, 619, 819, 967, 1035, 1122, 1125, 1247, 1464
Sixties Icon	295, 299, 309, 310, 312, 318, 320, 323, 473, 495
Siyouni	112, 242, 490, 728, 768, 804, 913, 1078, 1410, 1676
Slade Power	8, 163, 240, 321, 489, 504, 507, 514, 557, 698, 748, 843, 856, 861, 961, 1024, 1061, 1111, 1152, 1292, 1313, 1316, 1391, 1467, 1655
So You Think	773, 1242
Society Rock	215, 294, 316, 325, 368, 796, 808, 815, 823, 834, 1084, 1244, 1406, 1417, 1564, 1663
Speightstown	5, 117, 273, 328, 1359, 1454, 1507, 1534
Starspangledbanner	979
Stimulation	93
Sunday Break	23, 792
Super Saver	1280
Swiss Spirit	153, 166, 243, 360, 386, 559, 963, 1091, 1139, 1340, 1408, 1463, 1596, 1649
Tagula	452, 793, 1072, 1480
Tamayuz	27, 393, 558, 632, 729, 740, 842, 1348, 1645
Tapit	636
Teofilo	4, 49, 58, 178, 185, 198, 209, 211, 870, 1039
Tertullian	527
Toronado	162, 192, 220, 523, 556, 601, 836, 894, 993, 1016, 1044, 1093, 1118, 1142, 1286, 1520
Union Rags	1167
Universal	157, 1092, 1094, 1452
Violence	1161
Vocalised	196, 201
War Command	84, 147, 384, 450, 506, 755, 852, 863, 900, 976, 1030, 1131, 1255, 1402, 1411, 1497, 1532, 1664, 1667
War Front	249, 251, 270, 638, 649, 687, 1168, 1184, 1198, 1210, 1700
Whipper	537
Wootton Bassett	21
Xtension	1657
Youmzain	155
Zebedee	186, 296, 541, 608, 787, 831, 848, 860, 944, 1123, 1355
Zoffany	131, 465, 487, 500, 757, 824, 828, 869, 998, 1058, 1079, 1109, 1183, 1231, 1243, 1289, 1302, 1392, 1456, 1489, 1491, 1493, 1686

RACING TRENDS

The following tables focus on those two-year-old races that seem to produce winners that improve the following year as three-year-olds. This type of analysis can enable us to select some of the best of this year's Classic generation.

In the tables, the figure in the third column indicates the number of wins recorded as a three-year-old, with GW signifying a Group race winner at that age.

The horses listed below are the winners of the featured races in 2017. Anyone looking for horses to follow in the Listed and Group race events this season might well want to bear them in mind. I feel that those in bold text are particularly worthy of close scrutiny.

Being There	Kew Gardens
Clemmie	**Laurens**
Dee Ex Bee	Nebo
Elarqam	**Saxon Warrior (2)**
Expert Eye	Threading
Global Giant	**U S Navy Flag**
Gustav Klimt	Verbal Dexterity
Hey Gaman	Wells Farhh Go
Juliet Capulet	**White Mocha**

Lowther Stakes
York, 6 furlongs, August.

2001	Queen's Logic	1 GW
2002	Russian Rhythm	3 GW
2003	Carry On Katie	0
2004	Soar	0
2005	Flashy Wings	0
2006	Silk Blossom	0
2007	Nahoodh	1 GW
2008	Infamous Angel	0
2009	Lady Of The Desert	1 GW
2010	Hooray	1
2011	Best Terms	0
2012	Rosdhu Queen	0
2013	Lucky Kristale	0
2014	Tiggy Wiggy	0

2015	Besharah	0
2016	Queen Kindly	1
2017	Threading	

This race is not the force it was of old and you have to go back to Nahoodh's Falmouth Stakes win in 2008 for the last Group 1 success. Queen Kindly did win a Listed event last year however and was Group 3 placed. Threading is out of a full sister to Dubai Millennium so she's worth a fortune already. She was disappointing in the Cheveley Park Stakes though and on her first 3-y-o start was made favourite for the Nell Gwyn Stakes. Although made favourite she was quite well beaten in the end and has something to prove now.

Dewhurst Stakes
Newmarket, 7 furlongs, October.

2001	Rock Of Gibraltar	5 GW
2002	Tout Seul	0
2003	Milk It Mick	0
2004	Shamardal	3 GW
2005	Sir Percy	1 GW
2006	Teofilo	NR
2007	New Approach	3 GW
2008	Intense Focus	0
2009	Beethoven	1 GW
2010	Frankel	5 GW
2011	Parish Hall	0
2012	Dawn Approach	1 GW
2013	War Command	0
2014	Belardo	0
2015	Air Force Blue	0
2016	Churchill	2 GW
2017	U S Navy Flag	

The Dewhurst Stakes remains our premier race for two-year-old colts. Frankel proved himself an outstanding champion of course and Rock Of Gibraltar was a real star too. Other outstanding colts to win this in the last twenty years are Shamardal, Zafonic, Dr Devious, Grand Lodge, Sir Percy and New Approach. After three sub-standard years (although Belardo did win the Lockinge as a 4-y-o) Churchill won the English and Irish 2,000 Guineas last season. In an unusually long campaign of 11 races U S Navy Flag has the distinction of winning both the Middle Park and the Dewhurst. Quite a feat! He should win more races at the top level.

Zetland Stakes
Newmarket, 10 furlongs, October/
November.

2000	Worthily	0
2001	Alexander Three D	2 GW
2002	Forest Magic	NR
2003	Fun And Games	NR
2004	Ayam Zaman	0
2005	Under The Rainbow	0
2006	Empire Day	NR
2007	Twice Over	2 GW
2008	Heliodor	1
2009	Take It To The Max	0
2010	Indigo Way	NR
2011	Mojave	0
2012	Restraint of Trade	NR
2013	Hartnell	2 GW
2014	Crafty Choice	NR
2015	Glamorous Approach	0
2016	Coronet	1 GW
2017	Kew Gardens	

Previous winners include the St Leger and Coronation Cup winner Silver Patriarch, the good four-year-olds Double Eclipse and Rock Hopper, Bob's Return (also a St Leger hero), the Ascot Gold Cup winner Double Trigger and of course Twice Over who won four Group 1's during his career with Henry Cecil including as a 6-y-o in 2011. Hartnell went on to win a Group 1 in Australia as a 4-y-o. So there's clearly an emphasis on winners of the Zetland improving with age and Coronet improved enough to win the Ribblesdale last season and was Group 1 placed three times. Kew Gardens showed on his return that he needs a trip and he'll win again when stepped up to middle distances.

Cheveley Park Stakes
Newmarket, 6 furlongs, October.

2001	Queen's Logic	1 GW
2002	Airwave	1 GW
2003	Carry On Katie	0
2004	Magical Romance	0

2005	Donna Blini	1
2006	Indian Ink	1 GW
2007	Natagora	2 GW
2008	Serious Attitude	1 GW
2009	Special Duty	2GW
2010	Hooray	1
2011	Lightening Pearl	0
2012	Rosdhu Queen	0
2013	Vorda	0
2014	Tiggy Wiggy	0
2015	Lumiere	1
2016	Brave Anna	0
2017	Clemmie	

A number of these fillies have gone on to further Group race success, but not for a while now. Indian Ink saved her best day for Royal Ascot, Natagora and Special Duty both went on to win the 1,000 Guineas and Serious Attitude returned to sprinting for another Group race success and the following year she won a Grade 1 sprint in Canada. Clemmie won her last 3 races as a 2-y-o and will surely win again this year. That could be over a mile or maybe in the Oaks.

Denford Stud Stakes (registered as
Washington Singer Stakes) Newbury,
7 furlongs, August.

2001	Funfair Wane	1
2002	Muqbil	1 GW
2003	Haafhd	3 GW
2004	Kings Quay	0
2005	Innocent Air	1
2006	Dubai's Touch	2
2007	Sharp Nephew	1
2008	Cry Of Freedom	0
2009	Azmeel	2 GW
2010	Janood	0
2011	Fencing	0
2012	Just The Judge	1 GW
2013	Somewhat	0
2014	Belardo	0
2015	Epsom Icon	1 GW
2016	Escobar	0
2017	Hey Gaman	

This race can often provide us with Group race or Classic pointers and in that regard the '90s winners Lammtarra and Rodrigo De Triano were outstanding and Haafhd won the 2,000 Guineas and the Champion Stakes. Azmeel trained on to win the Sandown Classic Trial and the Dee Stakes, but the race needed a pick-me-up and Just The Judge did that when winning the Irish 1,000 Guineas. A very useful colt, Hey Gaman was second in the Group 2 Champagne Stakes and he should be competitive at that sort of level again this year.

Qatar Vintage Stakes Goodwood, 7 furlongs, July.		
2000	No Excuse Needed	1 GW
2001	Naheef	1 GW
2002	Dublin	1
2003	Lucky Story	0
2004	Shamardal	3 GW
2005	Sir Percy	1 GW
2006	Strategic Prince	0
2007	Rio De La Plata	0
2008	Orizaba	0
2009	Xtension	0
2010	King Torus	2
2011	Chandlery	0
2012	Olympic Glory	2 GW
2013	Toormore	1 GW
2014	Highland Reel	3 GW
2015	Galileo Gold	2 GW
2016	War Decree	1 GW
2017	Expert Eye	

All in all this race is very informative in terms of sorting out future stars, with the classic winners Sir Percy, Shamardal, Don't Forget Me, Dr Devious and Mister Baileys, plus the King George hero Petoski being the standouts of the past twenty-odd years. Olympic Glory won two more Group 1's as a 4-y-o, so he can certainly be added to that list. Highland Reel won Grade 1's in the USA and Hong Kong and last year Galileo Gold did his connections proud in winning the 2,000 Guineas and St James's Palace Stakes. War Decree carried on the good record when winning the Diamond Stakes. Expert Eye flopped in the Dewhurst Stakes but the form of his Vintage Stakes win has been franked a number of times and he should be given the chance to redeem himself. If he comes back to form he should be a force to reckon with.

National Stakes, Curragh, 7f, September.		
2000	Beckett	1
2001	Hawk Wing	1 GW
2002	Refuse To Bend	3 GW

2003	One Cool Cat	1 GW
2004	Dubawi	2 GW
2005	George Washington	2 GW
2006	Teofilo	NR
2007	New Approach	3 GW
2008	Mastercraftsman	3 GW
2009	Kingsfort	1
2010	Pathfork	0
2011	Power	1 GW
2012	Dawn Approach	1 GW
2013	Toormore	1 GW
2014	Gleneagles	2 GW
2015	Air Force Blue	0
2016	Churchill	2 GW
2017	Verbal Dexterity	

As one can see by the list of recent winners, this race is as important as any for figuring out the following year's top performers. For instance New Approach was outstanding when winning the Derby, the Champion Stakes and the Irish Champion, Mastercraftsman and Gleneagles both managed a couple of Group One wins at 3 yrs, and both Power and Dawn Approach notched up Group 1 successes as well. Churchill won both the English and Irish 2,000 Guineas last season. Last year Verbal Dexterity went on to be a disappointing fourth in the Racing Post Trophy, but his trainer Jim Bolger will be keen to win another Group race or two with him this year.

Racing Post Trophy Doncaster, 8 furlongs, October.		
2000	Dilshaan	1 GW
2001	High Chaparral	5 GW
2002	Brian Boru	1 GW
2003	American Post	3 GW
2004	Motivator	2 GW
2005	Palace Episode	0
2006	Authorized	3 GW
2007	Ibn Khaldun	0
2008	Crowded House	0
2009	St Nicholas Abbey	0
2010	Casamento	1 GW
2011	Camelot	3 GW
2012	Kingsbarns	0
2013	Kingston Hill	1 GW
2014	Elm Park	1
2015	Marcel	0
2016	Rivet	0
2017	Saxon Warrior	

Some notable performers have won this race, including the outstanding colt High Chaparral, the Derby heroes Motivator and Authorized (both by Montjeu – also the sire of St Nicholas Abbey) and of course the 2,000 Guineas and Derby hero Camelot. It would be both a surprise and a disappointment if the unbeaten Saxon Warrior didn't train on and win again at the top level.

Haynes, Hanson and Clark Stakes Newbury, 8 furlongs, September.

2000	Nayef	4 GW
2001	Fight Your Corner	1 GW
2002	Saturn	0
2003	Elshadi	0
2004	Merchant	NR
2005	Winged Cupid	NR
2006	Teslin	2
2007	Centennial	2 GW
2008	Taameer	0
2009	Ameer	0
2010	Moriarty	0
2011	Cavaleiro	0
2012	Wentworth	1
2013	Pinzolo	1
2014	Snoano	0
2015	Stormy Antarctic	1 GW
2016	Temple Church	0
2017	White Mocha	

The high-class horses Rainbow Quest, Unfuwain, King's Theatre and Nayef have all won this race and indeed Shergar won it in 1980, but it's been a while since those glory days. Despite being Listed-placed Temple Church failed to win last year. White Mocha should improve and win again this year, probably at Group level.

Somerville Tattersall Stakes Newmarket, 7 furlongs, September/October.

2000	King Charlemagne	3 GW
2001	Where Or When	2 GW
2002	Governor Brown	NR
2003	Milk It Mick	0
2004	Diktatorial	0
2005	Aussie Rules	2 GW
2006	Thousand Words	0
2007	River Proud	1
2008	Ashram	2
2009	Sir Parky	0

2010	Rerouted	0
2011	Crius	0
2012	Havana Gold	1 GW
2013	Miracle Of Medinah	0
2014	Maftool	1 GW
2015	Sanus Per Aquam	0
2016	Larchmont Lad	0
2017	Elarqam	

The Group winners speak for themselves but Milk It Mick also went on to win a Grade 1 in America as a five-year-old. Aussie Rules took the French 2,000 Guineas and also won a Grade 1 event in America. Both River Proud and Ashram won Listed races in their 3-y-o season and Havana Gold took the Prix Jean Prat over a mile. Listed-placed three times last season, but Larchmont Lad failed to get his head in front. Elarqam (by Frankel out of Attraction) will no doubt be aimed at the Classics. He was the most expensive Frankel yearling when he was sold for 1,600,000 Gns. It will be fascinating to see how he shapes up against better opposition.

Rockfel Stakes, 7 furlongs, Newmarket.

2001	Distant Valley	0
2002	Luvah Girl	1 in USA
2003	Cairns	0
2004	Maids Causeway	1 GW
2005	Speciosa	1 GW
2006	Finsceal Beo	2 GW
2007	Kitty Matcham	0
2008	Lahaleeb	2 GW
2009	Music Show	2 GW
2010	Cape Dollar	0
2011	Wading	0
2012	Just The Judge	1 GW
2013	Al Thakhira	1
2014	Lucida	0
2015	Promising Run	1 GW
2016	Spain Burg	0
2017	Juliet Capulet	

Three Newmarket 1,000 Guineas winners have hailed from the winners of this race since 1999 – Lahan, Speciosa and Finsceal Beo. For good measure Maids Causeway won the Coronation Stakes and Hula Angel won the Irish 1,000 Guineas (a race Finsceal Beo also added to her tally). Lahaleeb, Music Show and Just The Judge all went on to record Group 1 success at 3 yrs. After disappointing over a mile at the Breeders' Cup, maybe Juliet Capulet will be campaigned over six/seven furlongs this year. She should win more races.

Beresford Stakes, Curragh, 1m.

2001	Castle Gandolfo	1
2002	Alamshar	3 GW
2003	Azamour	2 GW
2004	Albert Hall	0
2005	Septimus	1 GW
2006	Eagle Mountain	1 GW
2007	Curtain Call	1
2008	Sea The Stars	6 GW
2009	St Nicholas Abbey	0
2010	Casamento	1 GW
2011	David Livingston	0
2012	Battle of Marengo	2 GW
2013	Geoffrey Chaucer	0
2014	Ol' Man River	0
2015	Port Douglas	0
2016	Capri	2 GW
2017	Saxon Warrior	

Aidan O'Brien generally wins this race, but before Capri the previous three were disappointing in their 3-y-o seasons. Capri certainly didn't let the side down though. Not only did he win the Irish Derby, but he stayed strongly enough to win the St Leger as well. Saxon Warrior won all three of his starts last year. He's a son of the top-class Japanese racehorse and sire Deep Impact out of Maybe who was a top-class Ballydoyle 2-y-o that didn't train on. You wouldn't put it beyond Saxon Warrior to win a Classic.

Acomb Stakes, York, 7 furlongs, August.

2001	Comfy	NR
2002	Bourbonnais	0
2003	Rule Of Law	2 GW
2004	Elliots World	1
2005	Palace Episode	0
2006	Big Timer	0
2007	Fast Company	0
2008	ABANDONED	
2009	Elusive Pimpernel	1 GW
2010	Waiter's Dream	NR
2011	Entifaadha	0
2012	Dundonnell	1
2013	Treaty Of Paris	NR
2014	Dutch Connection	1 GW

2015	Recorder	NR
2016	Syphax	0
2017	Wells Farhh Go	

There have been a few disappointing seasons since the victories in the '90s of King's Best (2,000 Guineas) and Bijou d'Inde (St James's Palace Stakes), but Rule Of Law turned things around in 2004 with his St Leger victory and Elusive Pimpernel was successful in the Group 3 Craven Stakes. Dutch Connection won the Group 3 Jersey Stakes and was second in the Group 1 Prix Jean Prat. Wells Farhh Go has a Derby entry and although success there would be highly unlikely he should win more races.

Two-Year-Old Maiden Newbury Lockinge Meeting, 6 furlongs, May.

2000	Patsy's Double	1
2001	Amour Sans Fin	0
2002	Cap Ferrat	2
2003	Grand Reward	1
2004	Iceman	0
2005	Championship Point	1
	To Sender	0
2006	Major Cadeaux	1 GW
2007	Coasting	NR
2008	Instalment	1
	Orizaba	0
2009	Canford Cliffs	3 GW
	Meglio Ancora	0
2010	Memen (Div I)	0
	Strong Suit (Div II)	3 GW
2011	Wise Venture	0
2012	Sir Patrick Moore	0
2013	Championship	1
2014	Adaay	3 GW
2015	Qeyaadah	0
2016	Medieval (Div I)	1
	Cunco (Div II)	1 GW
2017	Nebo	

One of the season's first six furlong 2-y-o maidens, it regularly attracts a high quality field with plenty of winners going on to future success. Richard Hannon trained winners have regularly gone on to Group success and Canford Cliffs in particular is a standout here. Adaay did well too, picking up a couple of Group 2's at Haydock Park and Newbury. Last year Cunco won the Group 3 Sandown Classic Trial and Medieval won a

Class 4 Handicap. Nebo went on to win the Horris Hill later in the season and sandwiched between those wins were respectable places in four Group events. He's a very useful colt that should win again.

7 furlong maiden for colts & geldings at Newmarket's July Meeting.

2001	Dubai Destination	0
2002	Tycoon Hall	0
2003	Josephus	0
2004	Belenus	2 GW
2005	Gin Jockey	0
2006	Kalgoorlie	0
2007	Rio De La Plata	0
2008	Soul City	0
2009	Elusive Pimpernel	1 GW
2010	Native Khan	1 GW
2011	Rougemont	0
2012	Ghurair	0
2013	True Story	1
2014	Lexington Times	1
2015	Manaafidh	NR
2016	Dubai Hero	NR
2017	Being There (Div I) Global Giant (Div II)	

Although the statistics don't look that encouraging it should be noted that Dubai Destination took the Group 1 Queen Anne as a 4-y-o and Rio De La Plata was five before he won a pair of Group Ones in Italy. Being There is by Dubawi out of the French Guineas winner Beauty Parlour so he has the form and pedigree to win more races. Global Giant is by Shamardal out of a Dalakhani mare so he should certainly improve this year.

7 furlong Qatar Stallions Maiden. Glorious Goodwood.

2001	Sweet Band	0
2002	Wahsheeq	0
2003	Psychiatrist	0
2004	Jonquil	0
2005	Opera Cape	0
2006	Kilburn	0
2007	Latin Lad	0
2008	Jukebox Jury	3 GW
2009	Stags Leap	1
2010	Pausanias	1 Listed

2011	Nawwaar	0
2012	Steeler	NR
2013	Snow Trouble	0
2014	Dutch Connection	1 GW
2015	Folkswood	1
2016	Lockheed	0
2017	Dee Ex Bee	

This was once a reliable maiden where numerous quality horses made their debuts in '70s, '80s and early '90s. The quality of winners declined markedly but there have been signs of an upturn recently. Dutch Connection won the Group 3 Jersey Stakes as well as finishing runner-up in the Group 1 Prix Jean Prat. Lockheed failed to win last season but was second in the Group 2 German 2,000 Guineas. Dee Ex Bee has been placed in two Listed races (including once over ten furlongs) and he can win more races this year.

Superlative Stakes Newmarket, 7 furlongs, July.

2001	Redback	1 GW
2002	Surbiton	NR
2003	Kings Point	0
2004	Dubawi	2 GW
2005	Horatio Nelson	0
2006	Halicarnassus	3 GW
2007	Hatta Fort	2 GW (in USA)
2008	Ole Ole	NR
2009	Silver Grecian	0
2010	King Torus	2
2011	Red Duke	0
2012	Olympic Glory	2 GW
2013	Good Old Boy Lukey	NR
2014	Estidhkaar	0
2015	Birchwood	1
2016	Boynton	0
2017	Gustav Klimt	

This race was raised to Group 2 from Group 3 in 2006. There are some very decent winners in this list, notably Dubawi and the more recent Olympic Glory who added two more Group 1's as a 4-y-o. Listed placed last season, Boynton has recently easily won a £60k handicap in Meydan. Gustav Klimt has entries in the Guineas and the Derby (also the Irish versions) but we haven't seen him out since

he won this race due to a small injury. This
well-bred son of Galileo will surely win more
Group races.

Fillies' Mile, Newmarket, 1 mile, October.		
2001	Gossamer	1 GW
2002	Soviet Song	0
2003	Red Bloom	1 GW
2004	Playful Act	1 GW
2005	Nannina	1 GW
2006	Simply Perfect	1 GW
2007	Listen	0
2008	Rainbow View	1 GW
2009	Hibaayeb	2 GW
2010	White Moonstone	NR
2011	Lyric Of Light	0
2012	Certify	NR
2013	Chriselliam	Died
2014	Together Forever	0
2015	Minding	5 GW
2016	Rhododendron	1 GW
2017	Laurens	

After a tricky five years when results didn't pan
out, this race came back with a bang in 2016
with the top-class filly Minding. In previous
years, Nannina, Simply Perfect, Rainbow View
and Hibaayeb all won Group 1's as 3-y-o's.
Soviet Song was a multiple Group 1 winner at
4 and 5 yrs, while Certify didn't run at 3 but
won a Group 2 in Dubai at 4 yrs. The O'Brien
trained Rhododendron was just one of several
very good Ballydoyle 2-y-o fillies last year
and in winning this race she probably forced
herself to the top of the pack. Whether or not
she wins another Group 1 over a mile this year,
she could well do so over further.

HORSE INDEX

DAMS INDEX